Romancing the Southland

The Romantic and Unusual in Southern California

by

Robert Badal

Published by
Douglas A. Campbell/
Romancing the West, Inc.

Published by
DOUGLAS A. CAMPBELL/ROMANCING THE WEST, INC.
A Dacamp Venture
P.O. Box 349
Hollywood, California 90078
(213) 874-6370

First Edition, 1994

LIBRARY OF CONGRESS CATALOGING-IN-PUBLICATION DATA
Badal, Robert, 1955-
Romancing the Southland: the romantic and unusual in Southern California/
by Robert Badal.
Edited by Michael Easterbrook and Carol Stanton.

p.   cm.
Includes Index
ISBN 0-9642332-0-7

1. Los Angeles—history, culture—guide.
2. Southern California—history, culture—guide.
3. Restaurants—guide.
4. Architecture—Southern California.
5. Travel—Southern California
I. Title.

Typesetting, book and cover designs by James P. Allen and Suzanne Matsumiya of
Graphic Touch Design & Printing, San Pedro, California
Front cover map courtesy of California Map & Travel Center, Santa Monica

Printed in the United States of America.

*The author and editors have made every effort to include accurate addresses, phone numbers and hours of operation of each listing as of the printing of this book. We regret any errors or omissions, they are not intentional. If you would like to update your listing please send a card to :
Romancing the West, Inc., P.O. Box 349, Hollywood, CA 90078.*

Contents

Contents

Introduction

*I*n starting off the introduction to a book called *Romancing The Southland: The Romantic and Unusual In Southern California,* I can't help but think of the beginning of Rob Reiner's wonderful film, *The Princess Bride.* In this scene, a grandfather, played by Peter Falk, is visiting his ill grandson. The old man has brought the book of the same title as the movie which he starts to read aloud. The boy has his doubts about the whole thing, now heightened by the story's initial slow pace and the impending love scene between the central couple. He interrupts at this point and asks suspiciously, "Is this a kissing book?"

To his young boy's mind, there could be nothing quite so excruciating as a book solely about two people gazing rapturously into each other's eyes—with little else happening. He is absolutely right when you consider the best romantic comedy movies usually involve two unlikely people who inadvertently fall in love while on an impromptu, but compelling, **adventure** together. For it to be exciting (and interesting), there has to be a lot more than kissing. All sweet and no spice makes for a pretty boring experience. Kids know these things.

This book is an adventure. It is the two words of the subtitle that describe it. It is not just a "kissing book," it is a guide to getting the full richness of experience out of Southern California that those two words together suggest. This book was written to help people enjoy what is romantic and unusual in Southern California. It is a journey through Santa Barbara, Ventura, Los Angeles, Orange, San Bernardino, Riverside, San Diego, and Imperial Counties.

I have lived here my entire life and it is undeniably quite a magical place. The bottom third of the state started with generally warm weather and tremendously varying topography. What has been added is interesting people from all over the world with different ways of doing things, but who all decided this would be a good place to do them.

The soup that is Southern California is a powerful combination of natural, agricultural, urban, ethnic, and Anglo ingredients. Because of Hollywood, its culture has affected the world more pervasively than perhaps any other in the 20th century.

Having Hollywood in its backyard has colored virtually every community in the Southland. It has been a strong influence and its blending into so many aspects of life here is a big reason this is such a unique place. So many things could be "only in Southern California."

The first thing you will notice about this book that makes it different from any other about Southern California is that each chapter represents a month, and that the choice of the places that I talk about in each chapter depend on what is happening that month.

Months are very important in Southern California. The climate can be pretty stable here, so the Southland does not really have the four regular seasons. Seasonal differences are instead expressed in a thousand subtle occurrences throughout the year. Real "seasons" can often be most truly expressed in the Southland by annually occurring natural phenomena such as wildflowers or spring waterfalls.

Each agricultural product also marks a season with a festival in its geographic area during harvest time. It is hard to think of the same place that encompasses Hollywood as also encompassing growing areas for dates, apples, cherries, oranges, carrots, strawberries, bananas, and yes, avocados, but it is true. These harvest festivals can serve as a nice way to introduce impressive and interesting features of the Southland that are there for everyone to enjoy.

In adopting this format of describing a location in terms of time of year, I employed a convention of trying to mention the natural occurrence in the first month of its season, whatever it is. Though sometimes I do not follow this to the letter.

In addition to nature and agriculture, our seasons are expressed in a mosaic of ethnic festivals that are part of the different cultures that together constitute the patchwork that is Southern California. These festivals serve as good introductions to talking about some of the wonderful restaurants and things to do in Southern California's many ethnic communities.

There are also theater and music festivals at certain times of the year that can compliment many weekend destinations by adding something interesting to do at night in areas that are otherwise devoid of night life.

We cannot forget the holiday seasons or milestone dates on the calendar that create states of mind that seem especially suited to certain places and activities. Sometimes historical dates are observed in the Southland with celebrations. Taken in total, the story of each of these commemorations tells the story of Southern California.

Then, of course, there are some annual events in Southern California that are "none of the above."

Some of the things I talk about in a particular month are perfectly fine things to do in months other than the one in which I listed them. I have always felt a good index was helpful, so I have created one that cross references places and events by category and location. The table of contents is also intended to be an outline of topics.

Though most romantic and unusual things in the world are inexpensive anyway, my tastes naturally run to activities that are a bargain. (I do also mention some high roller ventures as well, however.) Whatever the price range, I have tried to pick things that are relatively stable in terms of the chance of them still being around in two or three years.

I have listed a lot of places, but endeavored to avoid things that seemed to be in guide books simply because they are in other guide books, not because of the certain quirky or charming or poignant element that I am looking for. I am particularly fond of the oddities of life and have included such treasures as Charley's World of Lost Art, The World's Largest Champagne Glass, and The Air Conditioning and Refrigeration Museum. There are many things listed here which to my knowledge have never been listed in a book before.

This book covers everything from Chinese miniature teapot shops to gondola rides, from Native American cave paintings to helicopter dinners over Downtown L.A. It takes you to China, Vietnam, Cambodia, Japan, the Philippines, Indonesia, India, Germany, Korea, Persia, Morocco, Italy, France, Spain, Mexico, El Salvador, Cuba, England, Scotland, and Russia—all of which exist in miniature form in the Southland.

I have undertaken to weave the (at times) quite startling history of the region into each story. For a place with such a rich and diverse history, even the people who live here are amazingly uniformed of it. Part of what I am trying to accomplish with this book is to increase awareness of Southern California as a place with a past and a future.

I am particularly aware of the historical and seasonal nature of things because I have been doing seminars for nearly thirteen years on this topic at colleges ranging from San Diego to Santa Barbara. These led into producing tours and outings to many of these places. Our company, Romancing the West, Inc. is now the only one to specialize in weekends of film, theatre and arts festivals throughout the Southland. (If you would like more information on these, see the page telling you where to call or write in the back of the book.)

It is only now after living here all my life and writing and doing tours for several years that I am coming to appreciate just how remarkable a land this is. This appreciation affected my motivation to write this book. In addition to wanting to write a useful guidebook, I wanted to write something enjoyable to read from beginning to end that tells the story of this region and reaffirms its sense of place.

I would like to thank my friend and first editor Carol Stanton, my friend and mentor Douglas Campbell, my friend and attorney David Zeligs, and my mother and late father, without whose romantic and unusual parenting, I wouldn't be who I am. The beautiful design of the book is by Suzanne Matsumiya and James P. Allen of Graphic Touch Designs in San Pedro with final editing by Michael Easterbrook and I thank them for their patience. I would also like to acknowledge Jeff Stafford, Erik Miller, Dennis Rouse, and Janne for their support. Lastly and best of all, I would like to thank my darling Terra for staying with me through thick and thin ...

I hope you all enjoy *Romancing The Southland*. For me, it has been a labor of love for the past four years. During all my hours upon hours of research, I have tried to avoid any errors or omissions, but in an imperfect world, all I can do now is fully accept blame, and hopefully maybe worry about making corrections in an updated version.

Thanks,
Bob Badal

JANUARY

New Year's Day (January 1)

Oshogatsu (January 1)

Elvis Presley's Birthday (January 8)

Richard Nixon's Birthday (January 9)

Palm Springs Film Festival

Holtville Carrot Festival

Robert Burns' Birthday (January 25)

Chapter One
JANUARY

Happy New Year! Like all our months, the name "January" is of Latin origin, having been named by the poetic Romans after the god of doors, "Janus." He was the god who presided over beginnings (entrances) and endings (exits). Usually, he is pictured as having two faces: one looking forward, the other, backward.

This is an appropriate name and symbol for the month that begins our New Year. Of course, it seems a little less poetic when one considers that janus is also the root of the word "janitor" (one who is in charge of the doors in a building).

NEW YEAR'S DAY (JANUARY 1)

In Southern California there are two events that occur on New Year's Day that perfectly represent its past over the last century and its future in the next one.

The embodiment of the romantic mythology of the Southern California of the past is the Pasadena Rose Parade and the football game that follows in the Rose Bowl. This is one of the most famous annual events in America, certainly more famous than the other major symbolic marking of the New Year in the Southland— the one that manifests its future—the ringing of the Korean Friendship Bell.

Tournament of Roses Parade and the Heritage of Pasadena

To most people, the most auspicious event of January 1 in Southern California is Pasadena's:

> **Tournament of Roses Parade**
> **Begins at South Orange Grove Boulevard**
> **and Ellis Street**
> **turns east on Colorado Boulevard**
> **turns north on Sierra Madre Boulevard**
> **ends at Paloma Street**
> **Parade begins 8:05 a.m.**
> **(818) 795-4171 (parking and reserved seats)**

The whole history of this area and its famous annual event is as improbable as the name of the town. Pasadena means "Crown of The Valley" in Chippewa, a language of a Native American tribe that never came within a thousand miles of here. The original residents were the Gabrielinos, who may have been also known as the Hagamognas.

They, of course, were displaced first by the Spanish, who were then displaced by East Coast and North Central Yankees. The latter group poured into Southern California from the late 1870s to the 1930s. This "Anglo-ization" of Southern California was one of the largest internal migrations in American history. In many ways the epicenter of it was Pasadena.

Pasadena was not settled by poor immigrants. On the contrary, in 1874 the "Indiana Colony" bought Rancho San Pasqual (which covered the area from east of the Arroyo Seco all the way to Fair Oaks Avenue in South Pasadena) and set it up as large parcels for sale exclusively to wealthy (and conservative) midwesterners.

It was the West Coast dream of the 19th and early 20th century: to escape bad weather and become a genteel citrus and olive grower in California. The "Indiana Colony" became the San Gabriel Orange Grove Association and incorporated the City of Pasadena in 1886.

Santa Fe and Southern Pacific Railroads added convenient rail lines to the warm climate and pretty scenery, enabling local boosters to turn this farming community into a fashionable winter resort. The wealthy Midwesterners soaked up the idea of being "country aristocracy" and came here in droves. Among these new arrivals were David B. Gamble of Proctor and Gamble and William Wrigley, Jr. (of the gum), who would later buy Santa Catalina Island.

These American equivalents of royalty adopted all of the associated affectations of their new gentility. "The Valley Hunt Club" became fashionable, though they hunted coyotes not foxes. The "Tourney of Roses Parade" was started by them in 1888 largely as a way of showing off the good winter weather to prospective customers of real estate. It was patterned after similar extravaganzas in Ancient Rome. The Roman theme was evident in the events, which included jousts, horse and dog races, and a "tourney of rings" wherein lancers on horseback, riding past at top speed, tried to spear three rings.

The idea of a football game at the end of the whole thing did not come right away. When it was first proposed there was much hue and cry that football was an "East Coast game." Public support for football after the Rose Parade was not helped by the outcome of the first game in 1902 when Stanford lost to Michigan 49-0. No West Coast team would agree to play in the 1903 Bowl, so it was replaced by polo. In 1904, the best selling novel *Ben Hur* by Lew Wallace inspired the next Rose Bowl climax: a Roman style chariot race. This went over very well and was extremely popular. Many felt that the true sport of Southern California had been discovered. The chariot races grew in scope until they were so expensive and dangerous that football was again deemed necessary. It returned in 1916. This time, despite a torrential rain, the West Coast team (Washington) beat the East Coast team (Brown) 14-0 and the Rose Bowl game has been an annual event ever since.

The city and what had become the Tournament Association teamed to build a stadium. The city bought an area called "Devil's Gate" in Arroyo Seco and the Association put up $272,000 to build what was originally a 57,000-seat stadium for its opening game in 1923:

Rose Bowl
1001 Rose Bowl Drive
Pasadena, CA 91103
Football game begins at 1:45 p.m.
(818) 577-3100

U.S.C. won the inaugural game over Penn State 14-3. Incidentally, the winning team had recently changed its name to the Trojans. They were originally known as the "Methodists," then the (even worse) "Wesleyans" until 1920, when a *Los Angeles Times* reporter talked them into the "Trojans." It was probably the single greatest contribution to sports in the history of journalism. After all, could you imagine the "U.S.C. Wesleyans" playing anyone and winning? Luckily, they found a name that stuck early in the century. In fact, the team could have even had a fourth name change in honor of a very popular figure on campus: in the '40s and '50s the team had a uniformed dog for a mascot named "George Tirebiter."

Since its opening, the Rose Bowl has been expanded to where it now seats 104,700. That is big enough for the 1994 World Cup for soccer, which was held here.

Though its once-per-year football game is world famous, the greatest use of the Rose Bowl is as a site for a giant swap meet called **The Rose Bowl Flea Market** that happens the second Sunday of each month from 9 a.m. to 3 p.m. You can find everything there, from absolute junk to some real finds in antiques. Call (818) 588-4411 for information.

But the climax—whether football, polo, or chariot racing—was never the biggest draw. It has always been the parade that the world wanted to see. The very first Rose Parade in 1890 was a procession of wagons, buckboards, and other horse drawn vehicles that had been covered with pink cheese cloth. Local wildflowers and cut flowers from people's gardens were pinned to the pink covering.

The tradition of the elaborate "floats" was started in 1910 by a woman named

Isabella Sturdevant Coleman, who was a student at the early CalTech (called the Throop Polytechnic Institute back then). Though she came in second the first time around, her designs would set the standard for more than a half century. Not only did she do the flowers, she designed motor and chassis combinations and mechanical animation.

The parade got so big that The Hunt Club turned the whole thing over to the city in 1898. The event, which has become the focus of national attention, is the world's largest parade. It has an annual budget of around $2,000,000, yet only has 14 paid staff members. The other 1,500 people who work on the parade are volunteers.

If you would like to volunteer to help build a float, the two largest float builders are:

C.E. Bent and Sons
835 South Raymond Avenue
Pasadena, CA 91105
(818) 793-3174
and:
Festival Artists
120 North Aspen
Azusa, CA 91702
(818) 334-9388

Float construction is not all flowers. There is a considerable amount of preparation, much of which is tedious. This is why the volunteers who work on the floats are rotated and the float builders can end up using more of them than the parade itself. Up to 100 people can end up working on just one float. Sometimes corporate sponsors donate logo T-shirts to give to the volunteers.

The floats are available for viewing after the parade. The **Rose Parade float viewing area** is at the intersection of Sierra Madre and Washington Boulevards, adjacent to Pasadena High School. Viewing times are 1:30 to 4 p.m. after the parade on January 1, and 9 a.m. to 4 p.m. on January 2 and 3.

The parade is an old conservative institution struggling to deal with change in many ways. This has come slowly. For example, despite the fact that the main aspect of the modern parade that people care about (the floats) was invented by a woman, women were barred from executive positions up until 1974.

Reality finally caught up with the parade when they made the mistake of having a descendant of Columbus as Grand Marshal in 1992. Since Native Americans regard Columbus in a highly unfavorable light, the protests were so strong that the controversy made the front page of *The New York Times,* a first in the parade's history. The board compromised by having a Native American, Representative Ben Nighthorse Campbell, as Co-Grand Marshal.

The controversy did not stop there. Even though Pasadena has quite a varied ethnic make up, the Tournament Board was still made up of nine white men up until 1993, when comments grew so strong that they voted to add five new posts and five new members to fill those posts. Four of these new positions were given to minority candidates: two African Americans, an Asian American, and a Latino. Two of the five new members were women. And so, "The" Parade goes on.

The headquarters of the Parade Association is in a nearby mansion:

> **Tournament House**
> **391 South Orange Grove Boulevard**
> **Pasadena, CA 91105**
> **(818) 449-4100**

This was Wrigley's first house in Southern California, built in 1911, eight years prior to his purchase of Santa Catalina Island. The same contractor who designed and built this house, David Renton, would also build Wrigley's house on the island.

A lot of people must have been smacking gum even back then, because this Mission Revival house and its surrounding gardens is certainly splendid. It will give you some idea of what the original Orange Grove Boulevard was like at the turn of the century when it was Orange Grove Avenue and "15 millionaires" lived in elevated style along its then stylish Victorian way.

Interestingly enough, the architecture for which Pasadena is famous did not come from its Victorian mansions—they are all gone—but later from an American arts movement, the Arts and Crafts or Craftsman aesthetic and the homes created here in that style.

There were many furniture makers and architects who enthusiastically embraced it as a true American art form. One of the former, Gustav Stickey, even produced a magazine called *Craftsman* from 1901 to 1916. But the Arts and Crafts Movement had two notable stars, architects Charles and Henry Greene, and their canvas was the residential neighborhoods of Pasadena. Their most famous house is now a museum itself:

> **Gamble House**
> **4 Westmoreland Place**
> **Pasadena, CA 91103**
> **Adults: $4, Seniors: $3, Children: free**
> **Tours every 15 minutes**

Thursday-Sunday 12 to 3 p.m.
Bookstore: Turesday 10 a.m. to 4:30 p.m.
Saturday and Sunday 11 a.m. to 4:30 p.m.
(818) 793-3334

The Gamble House was built for David B. Gamble (of Proctor and Gamble) in 1908 and no expense was spared. This is not to say the exterior is gaudy or elaborate. It is not. The architectural style is that of a Swiss Chalet with English Tudor influences and a nuance of the Japanese aesthetic. The latter is expressed in both the deep overhanging roofs and the incredibly crafted wood details.

The polished teak woodwork in the interior is simply beautiful. The furniture and Tiffany glass are all original and designed by the architects as well. The form is expressive of everything about the mythology of California: it is naturally ventilated by breezes and has all of that porch space, so it is casual but it is also cultured and formal in its stylish detailing.

There are about 60 Greene and Greene houses left, most of them in Pasadena. There is a large group of them on the loop of Arroyo Terrace, just behind Westmoreland Place where the Gamble House is located.

The great architectural statements in Southern California are made by private residences, not commercial architecture. Besides the Greenes, many other famous architects have left their marks on the Southland in some remarkable domiciles.

Frank Lloyd Wright contributed to the residential history of Pasadena when he accepted a commission from Alice Millard and built the original concrete block houses a short distance from the Gamble House:

La Miniatura
645 Prospect Crescent
Pasadena, CA 91103

Built in 1923, this was the first of the great architect's "textile block" constructions. Like the Ennis-Brown House (see June), it resembles a Mayan temple, but La Miniatura is hard to see because it is privately owned and is located in a ravine surrounded by lush vegetation. It is best seen from a gate on Rosemont Avenue. From here, you can see a balcony overlooking a pond and a studio added by son Lloyd Wright. This is a private residence, so show extreme courtesy.

The Arroyo Seco was a river at one time and still is used as a park. The areas on its banks were traditionally the neighborhood of the arts community of the city. It is fitting that besides the nearby artistic statements in domestic architecture, there is a romantic statement of infrastructure:

Colorado Boulevard Bridge

This is undoubtedly the most romantic and beautiful bridge in Southern California. It soars 160-feet above the arroyo and when it opened in 1913, it was the highest concrete bridge in the world. Looking like an ancient Roman aqueduct, it is not fashioned in a straight line, but rather gracefully curved. Though this was done for structural, rather than aesthetic reasons, it became a popular spot for strolling lovers. As a young man, William Holden used to amuse himself by walking on his hands along the railing.

It has also been known as "Suicide Bridge." The Crash of 1929 was so traumatic to many wealthy Pasadenans that they decided that death was preferable to reduced wealth. A total of 79 people are listed as having jumped. In 1937, perhaps somewhat belatedly, a fence was installed and a guard was posted.

The bridge was closed in 1989 for renovation. Five years and $27.4 million later, it reopened on December 13, 1993—80 years to the day after it was first completed.

There are many remnants of Pasadena's heyday as a tony resort. One of its original grand hotels is now an apartment building:

Castle Greene Apartments
99 South Raymond Avenue
or:
50 East Green Street
Pasadena, CA 91105

This remarkable collection of buildings are the remains of the Hotel Green. It was designed by Frederick Roehig and originally built in 1898. It was so well-liked that it not only was usually full, but also was enlarged three times.

For the second expansion, a building on the other side of Raymond Avenue was added that was connected by a "Bridge of Sighs." This no longer exists, but the rest of the place is in pretty good shape and has once again been recently renovated. The public rooms still have some of the original Moorish-style furniture. Tours are conducted by the Pasadena Heritage Foundation. Phone (818) 793-0617 for information.

This area of town was where it was happening because of its proximity to the railroad station. Just up Raymond from here is one of the Southland's prettiest stations:

Santa Fe Railroad Station
222 South Raymond Avenue
Pasadena, CA 91105

Built somewhat later (in 1935), this Spanish Colonial Revival depot with its waving palm trees looks as classically Californian as could be. It is beautifully detailed—particularly in the waiting room which features fantastically colored Batchelder tiles. One of the saddest occurrences at the opening of 1994 was the closing of this station. Its future is currently up in the air.

The remnants of the grandest of all of the early Pasadena hotels still stands as well. The Raymond Hotel was built in 1886 by, appropriately enough, Walter Raymond, and was the first great hotel of Pasadena.

It was quite a grand place at the top of Bacon Hill. It had over 200 rooms, a spectacular grand ballroom, numerous billiard rooms (for the men), several libraries and parlors, a celebrated dining room, and 20 chimneys. Unfortunately, a spark from one of those chimneys caught its roof on fire and it burned down on Easter Sunday, 1895.

It was rebuilt six years later, but Pasadena would not last as a resort destination. The old hotel went into foreclosure in 1931 and was torn down in 1934, the same year its builder died. The one part of the second hotel that was not torn down was the caretaker's cottage and this lovely little relic has been restored and opened as a beautifully romantic restaurant:

The Raymond
1250 South Fair Oaks
Avenue
Pasadena, CA 91105
Tuesday -Sunday
11 a.m. to 11 p.m.; Closed Monday
(818) 441-3136

It is hard to say what is more enjoyable, coming here for dinner, lunch, brunch, or afternoon tea. They have excellent food and service and offer a pleasant eclectic menu of salads, chicken and meat dishes, and homemade soup.

The two outdoor patios are beautifully landscaped and can make for a delightful afternoon. The inside is just as wonderful, however. There are three intimate rooms with varnished pine floors and dark paneled walls. The carved wood wine bar is one of the most splendid in the Southland. On a cold night the fireplace is a welcome sight.

The corner of Fair Oaks and Raymond Hill is made more charming by the presence of a cobblestone wall and Craftsman style hut. The hotel's guests used to wait for the Red Car there from about 1902 until when it was scrapped.

A walk down Fair Oaks from here will help you realize what a rail hub Pasadena really was. Quite near The Raymond is the second of the romantic bridges of Pasadena with another waiting station:

Oaklawn Bridge and
Waiting Station
Oaklawn Avenue at Fair Oaks
Pasadena

This is the world's only Greene and Greene bridge, built in 1906. In some ways it resembles a Post Modern aqueduct with its looping arches. It rises steeply over the railroad tracks and comes down in the beautiful Oaklawn Avenue neighborhood.

The Waiting Station is two massive piles of boulders holding up a redwood and tile roof. There is a little park that surrounds both the station and the bridge on the Fair Oaks side.

The walk over is pleasant because Oaklawn Avenue continues on past several lovely Craftsman homes and ends in the Oaklawn Gates, also designed by Greene and Greene. They resemble the Waiting Station where you started.

When you are walking across the bridge, if you can pause at the top long enough for a train to pass underneath, you will be as close to a moving train as you probably will ever want to be.

Trains certainly played an important part in the history of Pasadena. Not only did they bring people in from the East Coast and into town in L.A., but the most popular attraction in the gay '90s was the **Mount Lowe Scenic Railway**. Between its opening in 1893 and its destruction in 1936, it was experienced by over three million people. It was the brainchild of Professor Thaddeus Sobreski Coulincourt Lowe along with the help of an engineer named David Macpherson and it was quite the attraction. Considered to be an engineering marvel, it combined scenery with the fascination for riding an unusual vehicle. Passengers took a trolley up Rubio Canyon to a plaza where the first hotel was located. It was from here that the famous cable car departed. The "Railway to the Clouds" literally took off for a 3,000-foot "flight" with a 1,300-foot vertical rise up to Echo Mountain.

The attraction at the top of the mountain was called "White City" because of the white buildings of the observatory and two hotels that were illuminated at night with searchlights from the Chicago World's Fair.

The third leg of the trip was a 1,200-foot Disneyland-type ride to a watering hole at the very top first called Ye Alpine Tavern and later Mt. Lowe Tavern. It burned down in 1936.

A great hike in the cool air of January that will take you past the ruins of all of this is the **Sam Merrill Trail**. To get to the trail, go north on Lake Avenue about 3-1/2 miles to the top where it ends at Loma Alta Drive. You can park in the street on Lake.

The trail begins after you pass through the forbidding looking old iron gates and stone pillars of the former Cobb Estate, now public property as part of the Angeles National Forest. You go about 500 feet on blacktop along a chain link fence. The paved road bends left, but the walking trail continues straight. Shortly, you will come to the official start of the Sam Merrill Trail. It is marked by a sign and, more importantly, a drinking fountain on the edge of Las Flores Canyon.

One of the great things about taking this hike in January is that you can appreciate the views, since it is one of the clearest months of the year. Likewise, it is cool. And while the views over your shoulder keep getting better and better along the 2-1/2 miles of fairly steep grade, there is no shade.

At the top, go right about 300 feet and you will be walking along the bed of the Mount Lowe Railway. You will come to all that is left of Echo Mountain: a plaque and some rubble. You will see the old bull wheel for the cables in a heap of cement. What was left of the place was blown up by the Forest Service in 1959. According to the Rails-to-Trails Conservancy this is one of the 12 most historically significant and scenically beautiful former rail lines turned trails in the country.

There is one grand old hotel of Pasadena's past that survives as a hotel:

> **Ritz-Carlton, Huntington Hotel and Cottages**
> **1401 South Oak Knoll Avenue**
> **Pasadena, CA 91109**
> **(818) 568-3160**

If there ever was a genteel, restful, and romantic large old hotel, it is this 383 room property. It has a main building, garden units, and cottages. The original was built in 1906 as the Wentworth. For a while it was the Huntington Sheridan. After being de-

The Ritz-Carlton, Huntington Hotel, Pasadena.

clared "earthquake unsafe" it was torn down and rebuilt in 1990 as a replica of itself.

They certainly did a great job. The entrance is like that of a large estate and the interior is gorgeous. There are two ballroom spaces that remain original. One is the **Georgian Room**, which is done in late 17th century French, complete with Flemish tapestries, stained glass, and Louis XIV chairs.

The **Horseshoe Garden** and general landscaping are wonderful and are perfect for a quiet romantic stroll. You can walk through a Southland landmark that has attracted lovers for generations.

The third great romantic bridge of Pasadena is the **Rustic Bridge**, also called the Picture Bridge. It is a redwood footbridge built on the grounds of the hotel in 1913. The reason it is called the Picture Bridge is because in 1933, triangular oil paintings were placed in each of the gables that capture some of the grandeur of the Golden State. These include the Carmel Mission, Red Rock Canyon, and Torrey Pines. The Poet Laureate at the time, Robert Blanding added verses about each, including one about the bridge itself:

> *Like jewels of many hues set in a band*
> *The Picture Bridge is studded with delights*
> *Of beauty chosen from this blessed land ...*

Very close to here is one of the more famous public gardens of Southern California:

Huntington Library and Botanical Gardens
1151 Oxford Road
San Marino, CA 91108
Tuesday-Friday 1 to 4:30 p.m.

Saturday & Sunday 10:30 a.m. to 4:30 p.m.
(818) 405-2100

Henry Huntington was a railroad tycoon who was the nephew of another railroad tycoon, Collis Huntington—who would battle with General Banning over where the Port of Los Angeles should be (see later this month.) While his uncle may have been the historic loser in the matter of the Port, the younger Huntington ended up leaving one of the most beautiful man-made legacies in all of Southern California.

He purchased the J. de Barth estate, "San Marino," in 1892. Work on the destined-to-be-famous gardens was begun in 1904 by architect William Hertrich and continued by Wilbur David Cook.

Today there are 15 distinctly different specialized gardens arranged around the overall landscape. It seems hard to believe that the place is a third as large as it once was. The gardens occupy 130 acres of the 207-acre estate.

In 1910, Huntington retired to devote his time fully to spending money on art, books, and landscaping—a retirement destined to be envied by millions.

Pasadena's early 20th century cultural tradition continues in the beautifully renovated:

Pasadena Playhouse
37 South El Molino Avenue
Pasadena, CA 91101
Tours: (818) 763-4597
(818) 356-7529

The Pasadena Playhouse Association was founded in 1917 and even though the first theater in California was in Monterey, it is the Pasadena Playhouse that is the official "State Theatre." It is a place of considerable cultural significance for several reasons.

This theatre was the first in the United States to stage all 37 of Shakespeare's plays. William Holden, Gene Hackman, Kim Stanley, and many others have graced its elaborate Spanish Colonial Revival proscenium stage.

Designed by Elmer Grey with an interior by Dwight Gibbs, the building itself is beautiful and romantic, with a lovely fountain courtyard. It was restored in 1986 and contains the 120-seat Balcony Theatre and the 450-seat main stage. It was used extensively in the film version of Alan Ackbourne's play *Noises Off*.

Not too far away is a wonderful bookstore that is part of Pasadena history:

> **Vroman's**
> **695 East Colorado Boulevard**
> **Pasadena, CA 91101**
> **Monday-Thursday 9 a.m. to 9 p.m.**
> **Friday-Saturday 9 a.m. to 10 p.m.**
> **Sunday 10 a.m. to 7 p.m.**
> **(818) 449-5320**

Vroman's has been around since 1894. It was founded by Adam Clark Vroman, who was a famous photographer noted for his non-posed pictures of Indians. Some of his photographs were used in the original edition of Helen Hunt Jackson's *Ramona* (see April).

Since that time, they have become dispersed throughout the U.S. They are on display in the Museum of Natural History in Exposition Park in L.A. (see April) and in the nearby Southwest Museum (see October). Like many great names in Southern California history, Vroman was interested in the cultures of many peoples. His collection of Japanese "netsuke," carved ivory figurines used to hold sashes, is on display in the Metropolitan Museum of Art in New York.

Vroman loved books and education. He even helped finance the second bookstore in Pasadena. That enterprise is now long gone, but his own store continues stronger than ever. Its 20,000-square-foot space is its fourth location and they are going to double that in spring of '95. With more than 100,000 titles, stationery, and even a cappuccino bar, it is quite a store. Community oriented since the days of its founder, Vroman's sponsors about 60 events a month from morning storytelling to book signings with the hottest authors.

There is more about Pasadena in the July, November, and December chapters.

Ringing of Korean Friendship Bell and the Port of Los Angeles

The next century of Southern California is exemplified by a simple ritual on January 1 that goes unnoticed by most of it citizens despite its powerful symbolism. The incarnation of the spirit of the new year in the Southland is the tolling on New Year's Day of the largest Asian bell in existence. Overlooking the entrance to the main gateway to its future, The Port of Los Angeles, it sounds only three times per year:

Korean Friendship Bell
Angels Gate Park
Gaffey Street between 32nd and Shepard Streets
San Pedro
Daily 8 a.m. to 6 p.m., rings at 8 a.m.
(310) 832-9611

This enormous bell hangs in a huge, colorful pagoda that rises majestically on the high bluff that forms **Angels Gate Park**. It is lighted at night and is visible to ships at sea like the Statue of Liberty for the Pacific. The 19-ton Korean Friendship Bell was given to the United States by the Republic of Korea in 1976 to commemorate our national bicentennial.

It is certainly one of the world's most unique symbols. It was patterned after the Bronze Bell of King Songdok, which was made in 771 A.D. The mold was handmade by a group of 20 Korean craftsmen under the direction of a well known sculptor named Kim SeJung. It is beautifully cast with ornaments and flowers. Perhaps its most telling images are the Statue of Liberty and the Rose of Sharon, Korea's national flower, being held aloft by a Korean spirit.

The Korean Friendship Bell differs from Chinese bells in that it is hung near the ground over a hollow chamber and has a sound tube on top. It is struck with a log suspended by chains. It was not built for just show: even the alloy it is made of was formulated to create a clear resonance. When it rings, you know it. Because of its proximity to the ground, it causes a rumbling sensation through the earth not unlike a mild earthquake, which makes it even more appropriate for California.

It is rung only on New Year's Day, July 4th and Korean Liberation Day (August 15). The most poetic irony of this symbol of peace and Pacific cooperation is that the bell's site was formerly the location of the U.S. Army's Coastal Defense Battery and is part of the Fort General Douglas MacArthur reservation. The Korean artisans who built the pagoda lived in the old barracks during its construction.

The surrounding 62-acre park offers a magnificent view of the coastline, which from here looking northwest is all green hills terracing down to jagged rocks and crashing surf. The sunsets this month would inspire anyone to think of the future.

Just below Angel's Gate Park is another wonderful park that forms the tip of the point at the harbor's mouth, **Point Fermin Park**. Though it is immediately adjacent to Angel's Gate Park, it is very different. Where the former has a stark, windswept quality, the 37 acre Point Fermin Park has groves of trees and a look like the grounds of an old estate. The park is centered around a lovely and unique Victorian home and lighthouse.

Lighthouses have a romantic mystique to them. They are symbols of hope, of humanitarian dedication, and of solitude. It is sad that all of the manned ones in the U.S. have been replaced by automation.

Los Angeles Harbor has a beautiful relic of an earlier, more romantic era right here:

Point Fermin Lighthouse
Point Fermin Park
Gaffey Street at Paseo del Mar
San Pedro, CA 90731
(310) 548-7756

This combination four story tower and gingerbread-style residence, built in 1874, is the last remaining wooden lighthouse on the California coast. Its light was originally provided by oil lamps, which were updated to electricity in 1925.

The lighthouse was considered a huge structure in its time and saw active service until 1942. The inside is not open to the public, but you can picnic near it. The view from the walkway that snakes its way around the park's perimeter on the cliffs is exceptional.

Point Fermin Park (and to a lesser extent Angel's Gate Park) can also be good whale watching sites during the season, which began last month (see December.)

Across the parking lot from the lighthouse is a colorful cafe:

> **Walker's Cafe**
> **700 Paseo del Mar**
> **San Pedro, CA 90731**
> **(310) 833-3623**

This little place with its view of the park and the ocean has been here since 1942. Owner Bessie Peterson has cultivated an atmosphere of friendliness, lack of pretence and "all home cooked food." Prices are low and the menu includes sandwiches, great french fries, and even turkey soup.

There are only a handful of closely placed tables and a small counter. The decor is best described as "lived in kitsch." The specific "bikers welcome" policy means that there are obviously friendly people of that persuasion here as well.

Three short blocks inland from here is another inexpensive and informal place to have breakfast, lunch, or dinner:

> **Lighthouse Cafe and Deli**
> **508 West 39th Street**
> **San Pedro, CA 90731**
> **Tuesday-Saturday 7 a.m. to 9 p.m.**
> **Sunday 7 a.m. to 3 p.m.**
> **(310) 548-DELI**

The Lighthouse Deli serves a large menu of seafood and deli fare, but their claim to fame is their cioppino, which has won several awards.

Looking at the houses on the surrounding hills, it seems hard to believe today that San Pedro once seemed so far away from the City of Los Angeles that Mary Smith and her sister, the original lighthouse keepers, quit because they could not stand the seclusion. After all, it was only 20 years previous, in 1854, that Union General Phineas Banning had purchased 2,400 acres of Rancho San Pedro marshlands from Manuel Dominguez for $12,000 and began dredging it out with hand pumps and mud scows.

"New San Pedro," as Banning renamed the place, was often referred to as "Goosetown" or "Banning's Hog Waller." He also renamed the more inland portion Wilmington, after his hometown in Delaware.

Banning made himself rich by initiating stagecoach routes between the pueblo of Los Angeles and this fledgling port in San Pedro. Several of these stage routes would eventually set the original pattern of the L.A. Freeway System (see December).

Ten years after starting work on the harbor and 10 years before he built the lighthouse, the good general built his dream house a little way inland from here on the back end of the harbor in Wilmington:

> **Banning Residence Museum**
> **401 East M Street**
> **Wilmington, CA 90744**
> **(310) 548-7777**

History is always ironic. Here is a fine example of a Southern Gothic Greek Revival-styled mansion, built in 1864, that was the home of a Union abolitionist general whose personal ambitions would in effect create 21st century Southern California. It was built of lumber from the Mendocino coast, marble from Belgium, and colored glass from all over Europe. The restored kitchen is used today to prepare meals made from the original recipes of Katherine Banning. The inside of the house is only open to the public during guided tours. There is a donation requested for these.

The 20-acre park where the house is located, though still lovely, is a pale shadow of what the place looked like in its heyday when languid eucalyptus trees lined the endless driveway that wove though innumerable gardens. The grounds are open daily, but tours are not offered on Fridays or Mondays.

One hundred years later, "Banning's Hog Waller" has become the world's largest man made harbor, handling 3,500 vessels with 66 million tons of cargo annually.

From Point Fermin Park you can see the two mile long breakwater that played a big part in the harbor's development. It provides shelter and has what appears to be the Leaning Tower of Pisa on the end. Actually it is the replacement for the Point Fermin Lighthouse, Angel's Gate, or **Los Angeles Harbor Lighthouse**, originally built in 1903. You are not losing your orientation if you notice a slight lean in this automated, 73-foot tall Romanesque looking tower.

You can go for a very romantic (and dramatic) stroll out along the fence that surrounds this unusual structure from nearby Cabrillo Beach. You will have a view of not only the leaning lighthouse and harbor, but of the brightly colored windsurfers that zoom past. Cabrillo Beach is one of the windsurfing centers of Southern California. The area inside the breakwater is gentle and calm, while the area outside is called "Hurricane Gulch"—for good reason.

Situated behind this calm beach on the inside corner of the breakwater is the wonderful:

Cabrillo Marine Aquarium
3720 Stephen White Drive
San Pedro, CA 90731
(310) 548-7563 (real person)
(310) 548-7562 (recording)

From Point Fermin Park, just go down Stephen White Drive to Cabrillo Beach and you will see the aquarium's pipe framework exterior. The museum building was designed by the quintessential architect of modern L.A., Frank Gehry. It is a series of separate, enclosed pavilions and features 38 aquariums, including a 14-foot long tank for small sharks and a "touch tank." Though not as overwhelming as the Monterey Aquarium, it has a number of fascinating displays and there is a picnic area adjacent to the building.

Next to the aquarium are the most accessible of the Southland's tidepool areas, the **Point Fermin Marine Life Refuge**. Since the best time of year to go to these areas is during minus tide season, which runs November through March, this month would obviously be ideal. If you would like a naturalist guided tour of this beautiful and interesting site given by experts from the aquarium, tidepool tour times are announced on the recording number which are usually on Saturday or Sunday during minus tide.

Participants in the tours meet in the aquarium's auditorium where they view a slide show. Then, they are accompanied by a trained naturalist to the tide pools, where they will find sea anemones, crabs, sea urchins and other local tidepool animals.

For more on tidepools, see November.

The aquarium has also been conducting whale watch trips since 1972 jointly sponsored by the L.A. Chapter of The American Cetacean Society. The 2-1/2 hour trips are led by trained naturalists and leave daily. Call (310) 832-4444 for information.

From the beach here you can also see the West Channel Marina, which is at the entrance to the Los Angeles main channel. In many ways, it is like looking down the aorta of the Southland. San Pedro is a great restaurant town, and the restaurant that most captures the feeling of being in the entrance to Southern California is:

> **22nd Street Landing Seafood Grill and Bar**
> **141 A West 22nd Street**
> **San Pedro, CA 90731**
> **Monday-Thursday 11 a.m. to10 p.m.**
> **Friday-Saturday 11 a.m. to 11 p.m.**
> **Sunday 10:30 a.m. to 9 p.m.**
> **(310) 548-4400**

This second floor restaurant in Cabrillo Marina has arguably the best view in Los Angeles Harbor: a panoramic look out across the water toward the main channel though flanking rows of boats. To the right, the hills of the Palos Verdes Peninsula rise. This is where the sun sets as well, creating a wonderful Mediterranean feeling.

The decor is simple and clean: white walls trimmed in dark wood. The oyster bar has a nice sweeping curve to it. The over 14 fresh kinds of fish daily remind you that you are in the heart of the American fishing industry on the West Coast.

There is a formidable fishing fleet based out of here, and on 22nd Street you are directly adjacent to the **wholesale fish markets**. On Saturday morning from 5 a.m. to 9 a.m., all of these markets sell fish to the public.

Come down early for donuts and coffee at:

> **Canetti's Seafood Grotto**
> **309 East 22nd Street**
> **San Pedro, CA 90731**
> **(310) 831-4036**

This friendly place opens at 6 a.m. Fishermen and longshoremen mingle with early morning walkers to enjoy a chat that would seem more likely in New England than L.A.

If you would like a engaging early morning experience, come down to the harbor for a walk. The cruise ships usually come into port between between 7 a.m. and 8 a.m. and it can be quite a romantic sight on a bright morning.

Located next to the wholesale fish markets a little farther along the main channel is:

> **Ports O' Call Village**
> **Main channel of Los Angeles Harbor**
> **at south end of Harbor Freeway (I-110)**
> **San Pedro**
> **(310) 831-0287**

This is a pleasant, touristy collection of shops and restaurants that, like similar commercial developments in Long Beach, Marina del Rey, and San Diego harbors, is inexplicably a "New England Fishing Village." For coffee and breakfast, it has **Ann's Village Bakery** (opens at 7 a.m.) and **The Belgian Waffle** (opens at 9 a.m.), which sits on the main waterway. The newest restaurants are in **Asian Village.**

While you are in Ports O' Call, if the harbor puts you in the mood to eat some fish, go to Berth 78 for the open air **San Pedro Fish Market, Crusty Crab Seafood,** and **Cafe International.** You can have a live crab or lobster or any number of different varieties of extremely fresh fish cooked before your very eyes, and then sit and feast with a view of the main channel. This area sometimes closes earlier in the evening (6 p.m.-8 p.m.) than the other enclosed restaurants.

As I mentioned earlier, while December 26 is the official first day of whale watching season, January is often the first month that the charter boat companies start offering whale watch boat day trips. In Ports O' Call, whale watch trips are offered by:

> **Los Angeles Harbor Cruises**
> **Ports O' Call Village**
> **San Pedro**
> **(310) 831-0996**

which offers one hour cruises of the inner and outer harbor as well as the whale watching trips, and:

> **Spirit Cruises**
> **Ports O' Call Village**
> **San Pedro**
> **(310) 831-1073**

which offers up to 1-1/2 hour cruises aboard a 90-foot motor yacht, an 85-foot schooner or a 50-foot cruise boat in the harbor in addition to three hour whale watching cruises.

Perched on the hill overlooking Ports O' Call is a U.S. Post Office. The structure is an imposing W.P.A. Moderne building, built in 1935. It contains a magnificent **40-foot mural by Fletcher Martin** portraying mail delivery in heroic fashion.

Until you have spent some time in this area, it is hard to think of L.A. as a fishing city. Many people are surprised to learn how important a fishing industry L.A. has had. It is appropriate that it was largely founded by Mediterranean and Asian peoples.

What would have formerly been called the "Yugoslavian Community" of San Pedro numbers approximately 30,000, making it one of the largest enclaves in the United States. About two thirds are Croatian, with about 50 percent of them coming from one town: Komiza, on the tiny island of Viz. They were instrumental in developing the L.A. fishing industry and they started both the Starkist and Van Kamp seafood companies. The remaining 10,000 are Serbian and have made their own unique contribution to L.A. (see December).

San Pedro and Wilmington are the working port towns of Southern California. They always remind me of Raymond Chandler's detective novels about L.A. in the '30s, even though the "Bay City" he refers to frequently is actually Santa Monica.

In those celebrated detective stories, gambling ships were always anchored off the coast and Marlowe was always driving toward the harbor and ending up at a deserted bungalow with a dead body in it.

A bungalow is any small cottage-like dwelling. While many were built throughout the country from 1900 to 1920 as inexpensive residences for average people, the movement started in California—hence the name "California Bungalow." If you would like to go back in time and stay in a classic California Bungalow of the 1920s, check in at:

The Grand Cottages
809 South Grand Avenue
San Pedro, CA 90731
(310) 548-1240

Located on a residential street are four '20s California Bungalows in the classic courtyard configuration. They all have patios and porches and come complete with period furniture. Three of them have fireplaces. This setting was used very effectively by director Jonathan Demme to create a feeling of the '40s in the movie *Swing Shift* with Goldie Hawn and Kurt Russel.

These cottages are actually part of a little complex that once included one of the major restaurants of San Pedro, **The Grand House**. This restaurant was noteworthy for several reasons: from its superb patio under a natural canopy of a gigantic cypress tree to its interior full of warm woods. Hopefully the space will reopen as a regular restaurant, but for now it is only available for private banquets.

The Grand House also has one of the most romantic tables in any restaurant in the Southland. It is in a private dining room for two that is upstairs and comes complete with its own private balcony.

The same person who owns the Grand Cottages also owns a delightful store close by:

> **The Grand Emporium**
> **323 West 7th Street**
> **San Pedro, CA 90731**
> **Monday-Saturday 10 a.m. to 5:30 p.m.**
> **Closed Sunday**
> **(310) 514-8429**

This is a beautiful old world style shop filled with cards, books, toiletries, gourmet foods, candy, collectibles, jewelry, and garden accessories.

Just to confuse you, San Pedro has another place for lodging, a Best Western, that also is called "Grand." Just go up 7th to Gaffey, turn right and at the corner of 1st Street on your left, you will see the:

> **San Pedro Grand Hotel**
> **111 South Gaffey Street**
> **San Pedro, CA 90731**
> **(310) 514-1414**
> **(310) 831-8262 (FAX)**

This is truly a unique hotel property. It was built in 1986 by an independent contrsactor with no previous hotel experience named John Mavar. On the outside it looks like a large block of Victorian buildings somehow imported from San Francisco. This motif is carried over very successfully into the plush interior. The builder traveled all over Europe in search of antiques and they are everywhere.

The first floor is very inviting, with a small lobby that opens onto the lounge, **Club 111,** which in turn connects to the restaurant of the same name. All are done in dark heavy wood, red patterned carpeting, and brass fixtures. Besides breakfast, lunch, and dinner, the elegant dining room is also the home of the San Pedro Grand Victorian Dinner Theatre.

There are 60 guest rooms, each decorated with antiques. The rooms on the hotel's front side have views of the Vincent Thomas Bridge. The high ceilings, heavy mouldings, and overall Victorian feeling are very unusual in a hotel this moderately priced.

San Pedro is a small town, but it has a tradition of ethnic diversity and great restaurants. Back toward 9th Street is my personal favorite:

Babouch Moroccan Restaurant
810 South Gaffey Street
San Pedro, CA 90731
Tuesday-Saturday 6 to 11 p.m.
(310) 831-0246

This family-owned restaurant has built a steady clientele since 1979. The two gracious brothers that own and run it, Kamal and Youssef Keroles, are quite proud of their three star rating from The California Restaurant Writers.

Though more moderately priced than many of the quality Middle Eastern Restaurants in L.A. proper, the food here is exquisite, the service friendly and attentive, and the decor straight out of the Arabian nights. As is traditional, patrons sit on cushions or low benches and eat from large platters after a handwashing ceremony. This is a perfect place to take someone who is fastidiously neat, as it is also traditional to eat with one's hands without using utensils. They provide a towel to protect your lap.

My favorite dish is the "bastilla," a sweet chicken pastry served piping hot. If you are a vegetarian, they have homemade bread, lentil soup, couscous, and aromatic chopped salads.

This is an entertaining place for a number of reasons besides the food. For one thing, there are belly dancing shows, which occur during the multi-course feast. This is also the only Moroccan restaurant in the Southland to feature dinner theater. It is the home of the most exotic of the long running audience participation murder mystery dinner shows in Southern California, *Murder in Morocco,* and *Shahrazad and the Tales of 1,001 Nights,* a delightful story telling show.

San Pedro is pleasantly situated on rising hills in such a way that wherever you are in town you are near the harbor. There are also many views of one of the Southland's most romantic sights. Until 1963, there was ferryboat service across

the harbor between San Pedro and Terminal Island. A popular local Assemblyman fought to build "the bridge to nowhere" and has now been immortalized by having the closest thing to a large romantic bridge we have in L.A. named after him, **The Vincent Thomas Bridge.**

This is the third largest suspension bridge in the state. It was built tall enough for aircraft to fly under it. Bright green, and swooping over the channel with an almost posed quality, it never seems to be burdened with much traffic. It does, however, add a scenic quality to San Pedro.

The old ferry terminal building with its clock facade has been converted into a delightful collection of fantastic ship models and other memorabilia of the sea:

Los Angeles Maritime Museum
Foot of 6th Street at Berth 84
San Pedro, CA 90731
Tuesday-Sunday
10 a.m. to 5 p.m.
(310) 548-7618

Right next to Ports O' Call is this free (donation requested) little niche of history that contains all manner of maritime gizmos and artifacts. There are models of many of the most famous ships of all time. Even the motorized model from *The Poseidon Adventure*, that went through so much hell in that movie, is now calmly berthed here.

This museum also contains one of the truly great oddities of Southern California. Within its walls is a 19-foot cutaway model of the *S.S. Titanic,* complete in every detail down to little doomed rooms with little doomed people in them.

This model, the centerpiece of the museum since 1980, is one of several major ship models built by Roman Catholic priest Roberto Pirrone. He also has done models of the *Lusitania* and *The Normandy,* but it is this one that is the most visually powerful.

Signor Pirrone is a devoted artist. He began working on his model of *The Titanic* when he was 15; so he has been working on it on and off for over 20 years, struggling to make it more accurate.

For example, when the original ship was discovered in 1985, he updated his creation after looking at photos taken of the wreck. What makes this model so remarkable is that *The Titanic* is probably the most famous passenger ship in history, yet because it sank on its maiden voyage, less information is available about it than almost any other vessel.

The Maritime Museum is right next to **The Los Angeles World Cruise Center**, where cruise ships that go up and down the Mexican Riviera arrive and depart. When they are in port, the public is invited to go on board and have a look. (Remember to get off before the ship leaves.)

There is more about San Pedro in the September and December chapters.

Port of Long Beach and the Queen Mary

The main harbor of the Southland is divided into the Port of Los Angeles on one side of Terminal Island and the Port of Long Beach on the other. Both are really part of one distinct geographic area called the San Pedro Bay. Visiting the Port of Long Beach is a good excuse to cross the bright green, 6,060-foot, welded steel Vincent Thomas Bridge. Whatever direction you came from, you should take a ride over this bridge.

It is a toss up whether it is prettier at night or during the day, but I would go at night. The ride is a little better going from San Pedro to Long Beach, plus it is free this direction (50 cents going the other way). If you are going at night, you'll have to imagine that the bridge is bright green by day, forming a nice contrast to the reddish hue of San Francisco's Golden Gate Bridge (though logically the last color a bridge in Southern California should be is green). By day, you can see all of the cruise ships, but by night, Los Angeles Harbor is a wonderland of lights.

After you cross over the Vincent Thomas Bridge from San Pedro, you will be on Terminal Island. As you drive through the dark and obscure area occupied by the Long Beach Naval Base, it is difficult to imagine that during this century it was once a thriving Japanese fishing village. (See later this month under "Oshogatsu.")

After a somewhat bumpy passage, you will approach a second bridge, the even more arcanely titled **Gerald Desmond Bridge**, which was named after a Long Beach City Councilman. It is this bridge that makes the trip better by night.

From the rutted Navy base road, you cannot see the city of Long Beach at all. It is only when you get to the apex of the Gerald Desmond Bridge that suddenly the miniature skyline of the "new" Long Beach suddenly appears, its lights glittering off the harbor like a tiny Hong Kong. I always imagine I am on a cruise ship entering a harbor by night when I take this drive.

If you would like to extend this metaphor, when you come off the bridge in Downtown Long Beach, make a right onto Queensway Drive. It is hard to miss the:

> **Queen Mary Seaport**
> **1126 Queen's Highway**
> **[Via Queen's Bridge Way or I-710]**
> **Long Beach, CA 90802-6390**
> **(310) 435-3511**

If there was ever a gigantic symbol of the paradox of the Southland, this is it: one of the most recognizable tourist attractions in the world. Built by John Brown and Company in Scotland and launched on September 26, 1934, the ship is 1,019-feet, 6-inches long and weighs 81,237 tons. She is

The Oberservation Bar on the Queen Mary, Long Beach.

powered by four 40,000 horsepower steam turbine engines and gets 12 feet to the gallon. A real statement of the Industrial Age, the *Queen Mary* was built primarily to cross the Atlantic in 4-1/2 days—which is somewhat ironic, since she now just sits in this Pacific port.

The Queen Mary is so identified with the Port of Long Beach that in 1992, despite arguments that the ship could require more money spent on repairs than could ever be recovered, the city council voted to keep the ship rather than sell it to Hong Kong. The main reason cited was that its departure would harm the city's image.

Actually, despite its status as a tourist destination, the *Queen Mary* is a very romantic place. As you walk up to it from the parking lot, it is impossible not to feel a real thrill as the sight of its enormous red funnelled presence looms above the city's skyline behind it.

One of the most fanciful spots to have a drink anywhere in Southern California is the **Observation Bar** on the Promenade Deck above the bow of the ship. Originally the First Class Lounge, it is a nickel-plated, polished wood treasure of Streamline Moderne. There is a mural over the bar that is very Industrial Age looking. By covering the windows so the ocean wouldn't show, the Cohen Brothers used it to represent a posh New York watering hole of the '30s in the movie *Barton Fink*.

Glass doors lead off to some of the seemingly endless teak deck that covers the ship on all levels. The wide windows give a great view of the harbor and the underrated Long Beach skyline.

Besides the city views, all of the interior public rooms are incredibly beautiful. The designers took the Zigzag Moderne (Art Deco) style and blended it into what would become the Streamline Moderne (inspired by locomotives and high speed liners) by deftly using a magnificent combination of hardwood. "The Ship of Beautiful Woods" has no less than 56 different kinds. There is a display in the Picadilly Circus shopping area that lists all of them. The superb woodwork is obvious in **The Royal Salon, The Queen's Salon,** and most spectacularly in **The Grand Salon.**

The Grand Salon was the original first class dining room. It is the most impressive example of how the size of the ship works with the interior architectural design and the richness of these woods to create an aesthetic effect almost unmatched in elegance. Every week they have a beautiful Sunday brunch in this room. There is more on Long Beach in the February, May, July, and December chapters.

OSHOGATSU (JANUARY 1)

In Japan, "Oshogatsu" is the biggest holiday of the year. In medieval times, the celebration lasted for a full week and its dates varied from year to year because it was a holiday tied to the change of seasons like the Chinese New Year (see February). Perhaps because of their success in dealing with the West, the Japanese adapted the holiday to the fixed Western calendar. Regardless of the reason, it is now celebrated on January 1.

It historically begins with a volley of arrows arching through the sky that are shot by traditionally garbed bowmen to ward off evil spirits for the coming year. Happiness rules the occasion: it is considered bad luck to sweep your house on New Year's Day because the gods of good luck, who sneak into your house, are irritated by it. Traditional Japanese music, dancing, and food are sometimes featured for the remainder of the day.

One of these dance traditions is to have two or more male dancers in lion head costumes cavort among the revelers. They playfully bite the heads of children they come upon. It is considered an especially good omen if this happens to your child because it means they will be smart.

The place with the longest modern history of "Oshogatsu" festivities is the centerpiece hotel of Little Tokyo:

New Otani Hotel
120 South Los Angeles Street
Los Angeles, CA 90012
(213) 629-1200

This 440 room hotel was built in 1977 as part of the commitment to a "new" Little Tokyo. The area has a very long Japanese history dating to the golden days of Japanese fishing and farming in the Southland. The hotel added a new restaurant in 1993 called the **Garden Grill.** It is a series of counter tops around several grills. You can order a la carte or from a regular menu. The mood is fun and social, but not as boisterous as a sushi bar.

The Japanese presence in the Southland is old and established. Today there are more Japanese here than anywhere except Japan and Sao Paulo, Brazil.

During the 19th century, the first wave of Asian immigration to Southern California was Chinese. The second wave was Japanese, and these "Issei," or first generation, came to both Los Angeles and San Francisco. The San Francisco earthquake in 1906 diverted some of the flow from that city to the south, so that by 1920, at least 50 percent of the non-white population of Los Angeles was Japanese.

Though they were economic refugees, the Issei were among the more educated arrivals in our nation's history—especially in terms of practical skills. Effective farming and fishing techniques were studied and taught in Japan and they were wildly successful when applied here. During the roaring '20s and '30s approximately 90 percent of the produce consumed in Los Angeles was produced by Japanese farmers. So this celebration has both an international and a local tradition.

The party begins with a ceremony wherein a huge 60 gallon sake barrel, called "Kagami Wari," is broken open on top. This is followed by a toast. The party is held on the flagstone patio of the beautiful Japanese garden on the roof of the south wing of the hotel.

This garden is truly one of the unique sights of L.A. It is a full Japanese garden, complete with waterfalls, meandering streams, and exquisite landscaping that has the appearance of being on ground level, but is high above the city streets, framed by the cityscape beyond.

You can look out on this garden through a glass wall in the hotel's lovely formal Japanese dining room, **A Thousand Cranes**. Besides dinner, they have a sensational Japanese Sunday brunch here.

In addition to the sake toast and the lion men "biting" children, another old Japanese tradition that continues in the modern celebration is that of the Taiko Drummers. Pounding on at least a dozen huge tom-tom like percussion instruments incessantly during the toasting, these drummers send vibrating sound waves through the crowd.

Accompanying this rousing toast and martial music is an equally liberating physical ritual. Pre-boiled rice is placed in a large wooden bowl and smashed into paste with a long cartoon-looking wooden mallet. This rice paste is made into flat round cakes called "mochi." Traditionally they are eaten the week of the holiday celebration.

The hotel regularly offers three great overnight packages that are complete down to including the taxes in the price: The "Touch of Japan," "Japanese Weekend Adventure Package," and the "The Japanese Experience." In the Weekend Adventure, a superior room for two comes with room service: continental breakfast, yukata service (Japanese robes), some sake, and free parking. It is $89 for two and is only available Friday, Saturday, or Sunday nights.

The far more elaborate Japanese Experience consists of a night for two in a garden suite complete with soaking tub and sitting room with "shoji" screens. It also includes parking, sake, saunas and massages as well as dinner in A Thousand Cranes. It is $359 Sunday through Thursday and $379 Friday and Saturday.

The $299 "Touch of Japan" is the same except that you get a regular room instead of a suite. You might want to remember all of this for the end of the year when they have a New Year's Eve version of these packages that includes the festivities on New Year's Day (see December).

If you would like to try some "mochi" from a Japanese sweet shop that has been in L.A. for a long time, stop by:

Fugetsu-Do
315 East 1st Street
Little Tokyo
Los Angeles, CA 90012
Daily 8 a.m.-6 p.m.
(213) 625-8595

This is the original location of this traditional confectionery shop. There is another one in Yaohan Plaza (see December). This little strip of stores along 1st Street is called the "Little Tokyo Historic District" for a reason: Fugetsu-Do was opened by Seiichi Kito in 1903. In the window of the store is a concave wood "Mochi-Usi" (to pound rice in) he brought from Japan in 1905.

Though they have a section of Westernized pastries such as pretty little jam cake rolls, the star here is the mochi. They are traditionally white and green and filled with red beans. They can vary from having a kind of rocky road filling of whole beans to a more whipped and shaped variety that is frosted with powdered roasted soybeans.

Another well established Japanese pastry shop is located in the other area of the Southland with a longtime Japanese history:

Sakura-Ya
16134 South Western Avenue
Gardena, CA 90247
(310) 323-7117

Besides Little Tokyo, another area with a considerable Japanese history is the city of Gardena. After WW II, the city gradually reconstructed its heritage.

This family run shop opened in 1954 and it has a lovable hometown feel to it. The mochi is less sweet here and is made entirely the old fashioned way. They are also noted for their wheat flower cakes called "kuri manju." See the November chapter for more about Japanese Gardena.

It is ironic that the Japanese presence in the Southland in the '80s was treated as a new thing. Besides the Serbs and Croats, the fishing industry of San Pedro had another ethnic group that was a major part of its development, but whose presence was erased with remarkable thoroughness: the Japanese.

The fishing industry of San Pedro was number one in the nation by 1929. The American fish canning industry actually started on Terminal Island, which was previously known as Brighton Beach and before that as Rattlesnake Island.

The latter name came from the snakes carried down the then fairly strong Los Angeles River during the spring, the former from the resort status it had around the turn of the century. It was renamed Terminal Island because of the train station built there to handle the canned fish from the growing industry.

Up until around 1916, Brighton Beach at the southern end of Terminal Island was second only to Coronado Island as a fashionable seaside resort. Unfortunately for its future as a resort, the expanding fish canneries and a harbor dredging project that year shrank the beach.

A big part of that expansion was due to the prowess of Japanese fisherman, who began to buy the homes around Brighton Beach that were formerly the summer dwelling places of wealthy Anglos from the East Coast. By the 1940s, the community had grown into a highly productive Japanese fishing village of about 3,000 people.

It was a place that hummed with activity. There were 18 canneries, trains coming in and out, a lively town hall, and the Japanese Fishermen's Association Hall, where movies were shown. In the early days of silent film, a "benshi" or "movie talker" would read the dialogue in Japanese. The island was very much like a miniature island of Japan, right down to a Shinto Temple.

On the other side of San Pedro, there is a place that bears some faint traces of the harbor's Japanese history. Just beyond Point Fermin going around the Palos Verdes Peninsula is **White Point**. Just south of where Western Avenue connects with Paseo del Mar is a little street called Kay Fiorentino Drive. Take it to the pay parking lot at the end.

The little path from here takes you past the ruins of an old Japanese hotel, called **The White Point Hot Springs Hotel**. It was built by Tamiji Tagami, who was a vegetable farmer from West Los Angeles. The area originally attracted the Japanese because of the abalone that at one time were plentiful all along the Palos Verdes Peninsula. These were completely fished out in short order, but the hot springs remained.

The springs are the result of offshore geothermal vents, which also cause the sulfur smell. Some of them were partially sealed in the 1933 Long Beach quake, but before then, they really cooked. Mr. Tagami obtained relief from his arthritis in the hot bubbling waters and decided to go into business. He and his brother Tojuro borrowed money from merchants in Little Tokyo and approached the owner of the property, Roman Sepulveda, who owned most of what had once been one giant rancho called Rancho de los Palos Verdes.

Sepulveda, like many early Californians of both Mexican and American descent, respected the Issei (first generation Japanese) and leased the land to them. The Tagami brothers set to work and built a resort hotel, complete with a grand ballroom, two restaurants, and a kiddy play area with pool. Sepulveda liked it so much, he added a large salt water swimming pool.

It was a very exotic place. There were colorful tropical birds and chattering monkeys in cages set around the grounds. The casino was aglitter with jewels and high stakes gambling. They even had slot machines.

Fishing was another popular pastime. Though the abalone were long gone, the presence of extensive kelp beds made barge fishing a way to while away the afternoon. But the big attraction was the waters (hot springs).

Many of the Japanese fishermen on Terminal Island patronized the hotel after their labors, but when WW II broke out, the military established military checkpoints for anyone going on or off the island. On February 19, 1942, Executive Order 9066 was signed, authorizing the War Department to round up all Japanese and send them off to the camps)see February). This little paradise was blown away shortly thereafter. The fishermen were considered especially dangerous because it was believed they might be sending messages to submarines lurking off the coast. After the war, the Terminal Islanders were not allowed to return to their former life and adapted to often greatly reduced standards of living as cooks or other such laborers.

Today, there is not a single trace of them on the island—except ironically a flotilla of imported Japanese cars fresh off the boat. There are three operating canneries, none of them Japanese. The remaining Terminal Islanders gather and hold a picnic every June to preserve the memory of their past. There is a movement underway to construct a monument. At present the only memorial is an underwater plaque, 100 yards off shore.

The closest place to here that may have some of the flavor of the old Japanese Terminal Island is:

> **Fukuhime**
> **17905 South Western Avenue**
> **Gardena, CA 90248**
> **Monday-Saturday 11 a.m. to 12 a.m.**
> **(310) 324-7077**

Taking Western Avenue inland from White Point (where the remnants of the Japanese hotel lay) takes you into the heart of Japanese Gardena. This is where the pastry shop Sakura-Ya mentioned above is located. Fukuhime is a small pub that opened in 1986. It is in a nondescript late '50s/early '60s building with a slated roof. Inside you pass through a hanging rope curtain into a very folksy room decorated with all kinds of stuff. There are little blond wooden shingles with Japanese characters describing the individual dishes along with their prices. Objects such as dried octopus hang from the ceiling. Large sake bottles decorate several walls. Indeed, they serve 24 different kinds.

Though there is a sushi bar, Japanese pubs called "izaka-ya" specialize in appetizers. They offer over 50 here.

This is also a good place to celebrate Oshogatsu. The atmosphere is quite lively. There are Japanese beer posters and everyone drinks and socializes quite freely.

There is more on Japanese Southern California in the February, March, August, November, and December chapters.

ELVIS PRESLEY'S BIRTHDAY (JANUARY 8)

This month includes the birthday of the King. Every year there is an annual party to celebrate:

> **Elvis Birthday Party**
> **Club Lingerie**
> **6507 Sunset Boulevard**
> **Hollywood, CA 90028**
> **Begins: 8 p.m., Admission: $15**
> **(213) 466-8557**

Every year since 1985, this long time Hollywood club has held an all night Elvis bash. It features a continuous succession of both local and national bands and singers doing Elvis songs. One year Dwight Yokum was a notable success. Drinks and food are not included and the proceeds go to charity.

1993 was the 25th year of this address as a club. Formerly entitled Soul'd Out, owners Dominick Lucci and Kurt Fischer changed the name and the musical slant, but stayed around and are now among the great survivors in the L.A. club world. Club Lingerie is a simple dark space of two brick walls and a high ceiling that holds 333. It is memorable as the site of a big bar scene with Eddie Murphy and Nick Nolte in the film *48 Hours*. Steven Seagal also looked tough here in *Marked for Death*.

RICHARD NIXON'S BIRTHDAY

There is a kinship between Elvis and the late 37th president, beyond the proximity of their birthdays (Nixon's is the 9th) that can be tangibly expressed by stopping by the gift shop at the:

> **Nixon Library**
> **18001 Yorba Linda Boulevard**
> **Yorba Linda, CA 92686**
> **Monday-Saturday 10 a.m. to 5 p.m.**
> **Sunday 11 a.m. to 5 p.m.**
> **Adults (12-61): $4.95, Seniors (62 and older): $2.95,**
> **Children (8-11): $1, and under 8 free**
> **(714) 993-3393**

The 52,000-square-foot library, with nine acres of pretty grounds surrounding it, is really a series of interactive touch screen computers and videos that tell the story of Nixon's life and time as president. It opened in July of 1990 and is quite presidential looking with its rose garden and a reflecting pool.

The exhibits are certainly interesting for the most part. The Hall of Leaders is a roomful of statues of 10 of Nixon's contemporaries, including Khrushchev, de Gaulle, and Churchill. The most famous aspect of Nixon's career, the tapes used to implicate him in the Watergate scandal, are available—supposedly unedited. My favorite display is the recreation of a circa 1960 living room complete with centerpiece black and white television. On its screen, the Nixon vs. Kennedy debates rage on eternally.

There is a path through the rose garden that leads to the Nixon birthplace. This library was built on the land of his parents and it preserves the simple wood house of his childhood down to much of the original furnishings. If you like it, you can buy a birdhouse that is a replica in the gift shop.

The Nixon Library gift shop sells other unusual items. The most popular souvenir of the library is a postcard of "Tricky Dick" beside the King in his latter days. You can also get the same image on a T-shirt, a watch, note cards, an 8-by-10, or even a poster. It seems Elvis was a guest in the White House in the early '70s. He was there to receive an anti-drug award.

PALM SPRINGS FILM FESTIVAL

One of the newer cultural traditions in the Southland takes place every January in the desert:

> **Palm Springs International Film Festival**
> **The Plaza Theater**
> **P.O. Box 2230**

Palm Springs, CA 92263
128 South Palm Canyon Drive
Palm Springs, CA 92262
Usually the second week of the month
(619) 778-8979 (festival)
(619) 327-0225 (theater)

The original glamour hotel of Palm Springs was called The El Mirador Hotel. After failing during the Great Depression, it re-opened in 1932. The Hollywood connection to Palm Springs began right away.

In the 1930s, the "Amos and Andy" radio show was broadcast from the hotel's tower. The two men, whose real names were Freeman Gosden and Charlie Correl, wrote their material by the pool and then performed it over the air the same evening at 7 p.m.

The hotel's popularity in Hollywood created a pecking order not unlike the "A" lists of today. In 1928, actor Ralph Bellamy and silent film star Charles Farrel got bounced off the hotel's only tennis court so Marlene Dietrich could play. They decided they wanted to build tennis courts for themselves and their friends. So they bought 200 acres of land quite cheaply that eventually became the Palm Springs Racquet Club.

The Palm Springs Film Festival, which began in 1989, has been quite successful and runs for about seven days the second week of the month. At least part of this success is due to the celebrity status of the festival's founder—who also happened to be the mayor of Palm Springs—Sonny Bono, formerly partnered with Cher in the singing duo Sonny and Cher.

This film festival presents fewer films than most others. The Seattle and Vancouver film festivals offer 150 and 192 respectively, while Palm Springs only screened 70 in 1992. This has a lot to do with sound business practices (a smaller festival is more likely to break even) combined with a policy of not offering any "filler" whatsoever. The policy is to strive for only the best major pictures that would otherwise go straight to Cannes.

Artistically, this has given this event some fairly rapid status as a venue. In 1992, only its third year, it offered 30 U.S. premiers, 6 world premiers and 15 official contenders for Best Foreign Language Oscars.

This is also a highly commercial festival in that many directors and producers see it as a jumping off point for their films into the American market. Because of Palm Spring's proximity to Hollywood, success here can be likened by the industry to mean potential mainstream box office success. This is partially due to the fact that the desert resort community is not really arts or film oriented, and in order to survive, the festival must attract industry types who come to try and do business.

Most of the shows are near the center of town, at or near the Mission styled Plaza Theatre. There is a lot to do in Palm Springs and the festival is an especially lovely winter experience because of the wonderful weather this time of year in the California desert. The sky is clear and blue and the mountains nearby frame the landscape.

The classic statement of culture-in-the desert in Southern California is the nearby:

Palm Springs Desert Museum
101 Museum Drive
Palm Springs, CA 92262
10 a.m. to 4 p.m. Tuesday-Sunday
1 to 8 p.m. Friday, closed Monday
(619) 325-7186

Behind the stone facade of this regional art center is a surprising eclectic look at the desert. The museum is a large (75,000-square-foot), cantilevered, split level edifice that is both a natural history and an art and cultural museum. There are two lovely sculpture gardens with fountains shaded by palm trees and a multi-level sculpture court.

This is a very entertaining and informative place with a real variety of exhibits. It has an amazing diorama depicting local animal life by day and night. Button activated lights illuminate such animals as a bobcat, a coyote, or a roadrunner.

There is also a wildflower exhibit and a collection of old black and white photos that successfully de-glamorize the American West. There are over 1,300 artifacts of the Native American tribes of the area, including an extensive collection of baskets by the Cahuilla Indians.

They added a new exhibit in '92 on the Santa Rosa Mountains National Scenic Area, which was established in 1988 by The Bureau of Land Management. It is remarkable just how unique and wonderful some of the natural sights are within this region. There are alluvial fans, fault lines, water carved canyons, and palm oases. The exhibit is designed to show the diverse animal and plant communities found there. Because of the changes in elevations encompassed within the region, the flora range from cactus and creosote on the desert floor to cedar and pine forests at the higher elevations in the mountains.

There are two walking trails that lead off from the museum. They have naturalist-led hikes on Friday and Saturday at 9 a.m. that began for the season in October and continue this month and on through May.

Just on the other side of Tahquitz Canyon Way across from the museum is one of the oldest continuously operating inns in Palm Springs:

> **Casa Cody**
> **175 South Cahuilla Road**
> **Palm Springs, CA 92262**
> **(619) 320-9346**
> **(800) 231-CODY**

The Casa Cody was originally built by Buffalo Bill's niece, Harriet Cody, in 1922. She apparently had good judgement in land, because even though it is moderately priced (from under $100 to about $150), the Casa Cody is located in a much nicer spot than most of the much pricier newer hotels.

This hotel is nearer the base of the San Jacinto Mountains, so as the sun goes down, it is cast in the shade of early evening for a cool restful effect. It is very close to everything in downtown (it is less than a block from the plaza in the center of town), so it has both seclusion and convenience.

There are a total of 17 rooms and suites, all with private bath, TV, and phone. The interiors are Southwestern with pine furniture and patterned rugs on terra cotta floors. There are 10 Santa Fe-styled suites arranged in a horseshoe around a pretty little pool and lawn area.

On the outside, it looks more like an inn in Bermuda than the Old West. The buildings are one story pink cottages with blue trim and French doors that are covered with bougainvillea. Many of them have fireplaces and kitchens and one has a private patio with an extraordinary mountain view. They are all surrounded by lots of trees. There are two pools and an outdoor spa.

Though it is a bit farther away and a bit more expensive than Casa Cody, in many ways the perfect place to stay during the Palm Springs Film Festival is the wonderful:

> **Ingleside Inn**
> **200 West Ramon Road**
> **Palm Springs, CA 92262**
> **(619) 325-0046**
> **(800) 772-6655**

Lodging is an interesting subject in the City of Palm Springs because, despite its fame as a glamorous desert resort, most of the places to stay are small and are more charming than glitzy. The Ingleside Inn epitomizes the best in what Palm Springs offers in hotel rooms.

The Ingleside Inn is a classic Old Hollywood-style Mediterranean hideaway with red tile roofs and lush, yet perfectly manicured landscaping, such as you might expect to find in Whitley Heights (see June).

It has 29 rooms and suites which are all exceptionally well appointed. Almost half of them have fireplaces and some have sunken tubs, but all of them have bathroom spas with whirlpool and steam equipped bathtubs. The drinks and snacks in the refrigerators are included, as is continental breakfast at the door and such extras as fresh fruit, bubble bath, monogrammed matchbooks, and daily newspaper. Prices range from about $100 to $300.

Melvyn's, the restaurant in the inn, is often named as one of the best and most romantic in Palm Springs.

There will be more about Palm Springs in the March, May, and November chapters.

HOLTVILLE CARROT FESTIVAL

As often as the Palm Springs area is visited, there are places not that far from there that receive hardly any tourists. Imperial County to the south is the least visited of the eight counties of Southern California. This month, there is a great reason to go to this obscure place because of the annual:

> **Holtville Carrot Festival**
> **Usually the last week of January**
> **Holtville**
> **(619) 356-2923**

Of all of the agricultural festivals in the Southland, this one has the most authentically non-sophisticated quality to it. It originated in 1946 and still seems like something from the post-war period.

The weeklong series of events take place in different parts of town. These include a carnival and livestock shows, but in addition to the usual county fair stuff, there is a recipe contest at the Civic Center for dishes made with carrots, a fair featuring regular and carrot-themed crafts in Holt Park, and a tractor parade down Fifth Street. The high point of the event is the carrot-peeling contest.

The town of Holtville was founded and named, appropriately enough, by a developer named W.F. Holt in 1908. It is 10 miles east of the town of El Centro and is surrounded by irrigated fields of broccoli, asparagus, cauliflower, wheat, alfalfa, cotton, cantaloupe, watermelon and, of course, carrots—4,000 acres of them to be exact—making Holtville the official "Carrot Capitol of the World."

Though agriculture seems to be everywhere in the Southland, Imperial County would qualify as the true "winter vegetable basket." The feeling here can be like some cross between a rural state in the deep South and Mexico: hot and sticky with old Coca Cola signs, dusty roads, and cafes. Though its total dollar volume of agricultural output is impressive, its residents are the poorest of the eight counties in the Southland, and homes and storefronts are unchanged from the depression era.

Driving around here always makes me think I am in some road movie with Geena Davis. Though it is humid, because of all of the agriculture, it is also quite romantic in its removed way. The towns around here have names like Coyote Wells and Plaster City.

If you look at a map of California, at the bottom center of the state border with Mexico is a town called Mexicali on the Mexican side and Calexico on the California side. They are sister cities and epitomize the closeness of the relationship between the two countries. It may seem improbable now, but at one time, this was quite the resort area.

There is a survivor of that time that can make an unexpected romantic destination:

De Anza Hotel
233 East 4th Street
Calexico, CA 92231
(619) 357-1112

This hotel has a unique history that is related to the connection between Calexico and Mexicali. Prohibition brought a mini boom to Calexico because drinking and gambling were both legal in Mexico. Movie stars and wealthy people would stay in Calexico and drive to casinos across the border in Mexicali to play.

The Mission-styled De Anza, with its red tile roof, was built in 1931 in response to the need for a real showplace for the stars. It quickly became the toast of the town. First off, it was not only air conditioned, but it also had beautiful murals, plush furniture, and stunning gaslight chandeliers.

Its heyday would prove to be short, because when Prohibition came to an end in 1932, the hotel began to gradually deteriorate. It was saved in 1966 by a wealthy Imperial Valley rancher named Harold Johnson, who devoted himself to restoring it.

Because of its desolation, Imperial County seems to have more than its share of bizarre destinations. Continuing east from Calexico along I-8, if you pull off 18 miles west of Winterhaven at the Aldgodones Sand Dunes County Rest Stop between El Centro and Yuma in the bottom corner of the state, you will be able to gaze upon the ghostly **Old Plank Road.** You can see it from Grays Well Road.

Before off road vehicles, the only way of crossing the shifting sands of this area was by way of this seven mile stretch, originally built in 1914 by the State of California as an "auto railroad" of wooden planks bound with cross ties.

It was not the easiest thing to drive on, so when it wore out, it was rebuilt in 1916 into 8-by-12 foot sections held together with steel straps that were moved by a team of mules whenever they were covered by sand. This lasted for ten years until the highway was built. If you would like to see a piece of this steel strap highway, the Auto Club has it on display in its main office in Downtown L.A.

Seven miles southwest of Winterhaven, about 1/2 mile northwest of Andrade is a dirt road that will take you to **Charley's World of Lost Art.** This unique site has been called "a sculpture garden in the middle of nowhere." The artist, Charles Kasling, retired from the U.S. Navy after 20 years of "seeing the world." The sight of this desert scenery inspired memories of all the places he had been, and in 1967, he began recreating them here. There is a little of Asia, Africa, and Europe spread over 2-1/2 acres.

If you really want the feeling of being away from it all, the least visited of the parks in the California State system is reasonably close to here. Just continue east on I-8 until you come to the giant metropolis of Winterhaven. Get off at the Winterhaven/4th Street exit. Make a left on 4th Street, a right on SR24 and a final left on Picacho Road and you will be on your way to:

> **Picacho State Recreation Area**
> **Picacho Road**
> **[25 miles north of Winterhaven]**
> **(619) 767-5311 State Parks Office**
> **(619) 393-3059**

Reasonably close means that if you had a normal road, the drive would be pretty short. But the road into this place is truly undeveloped: 18 miles of winding dirt. Forget a big recreational vehicle. This is a good place to try out your new four wheel drive.

Picacho was a gold mining boom town whose mines began in 1852 and had expanded into hard rock quarrying by 1872. The hamlet grew between 1890 and 1904 to 2,500 people. Mining accidents, poor ore quality, and changes in river transportation (caused by dams) led to long periods of inactivity.

Modern mining techniques led to the mine's reopening in 1984, with predictable damage to the local environment. The dams also covered nearly all traces of the town with water. All that remains is the Picacho Mill. Other historic sites are Hoge Rock and Norton's Landing.

The terrain here is quite varied, from the jagged rocks and gorges of the Chocolate Mountains and 1,975-foot Picacho Peak, to starkly beautiful desert scenery along 50 miles of Colorado River front between Imperial and Parker Dams. There is a total of 7,000 acres of land in the park. There are showers and toilets and 55 campsites.

Boating and fishing are big here. A lot of people come in by boat and there are three boat-in group campsites and three man-made, tule-lined lakes here: Taylor, Adobe, and Island. But because of its remoteness, it is also good for just walking around.

There is wildlife such as beaver and feral burros. This month, there will also be migrating birds. Rare Desert Bighorn Sheep (that are especially threatened by the mining activity) are found inland from the river in the back country. If you would like to learn something about the local environment, there are interpretive exhibits as well.

ROBERT BURNS' BIRTHDAY (JANUARY 25)

On January 25, 1759, Scottish poet Robert Burns was born in Galloway in Ayrshire. January 25 is officially called **Burns' Night** and is celebrated by the Scottish with feasting on the notorious dish "haggis." It has been celebrated in the traditional manner for many years in Los Angeles at a very Scottish place:

>**Tam O'Shanter Inn**
>**2980 Los Feliz Boulevard**
>**Hollywood, CA 90039**
>**Monday-Friday 11 a.m. to 10 p.m.**
>**Saturday 11 a.m. to 11 p.m.**
>**Sunday 4 to 10 p.m.**
>**Sunday Brunch 10:30 a.m. to 2:30 p.m.**
>**(213) 664-0228**

This clubby Scottish style restaurant has been here since 1922, making it one of the city's oldest. It was designed by Savo Stoshitch, who also designed the Five Crowns in Corona Del Mar (see April). Scottish pennants hang from the high ceiling with its heavy beams, and the fireplace is framed by huge chairs that look like they belong in a castle.

The piano bar here is a true L.A. classic. It is a friendly place with a piano player every night. Besides flagons of McAndrews Scottish Ale, they feature freshly fried potato chips.

On Burns' Night, the plaid skirted waitresses will offer you the dreaded entrée, which tastes better than its ingredients sound. Haggis consists of ground-up sheep's lungs, heart, and liver (collectively called "pluck"), beef suet, heavily seasoned and mixed with oatmeal that is cooked in a sheep's stomach (you don't eat the stomach).

It is really a giant sausage. Burns himself referred to it as "the great chieftain o' the pudding race." To anyone from the British Isles "pudding" means "sausage." It tastes sort of like a cross between pate and meat loaf.

If you are inclined to want to try serving it at home, you can get it at:

Cameron's British Foods and Imports
12523C Venice Boulevard
Mar Vista, CA 90066
Thursday-Saturday 10 a.m. to 5 p.m.
(310) 397-8137

In an odd twist, haggis-to-go comes precooked and sealed in plastic from a company in Florida.

FEBRUARY

Chinese New Year

Valentine's Day (February 14)

Whale Watching and Santa Catalina Island

Anniversary of Executive Order 9066 (February 19)

African American History

National Date Festival

Chapter Two

FEBRUARY

Oh, February. What a month for romantics. The month of our only holiday that celebrates passion. It has a natural irony built into it, being the month that contains our only true lover's holiday, Valentine's Day, on the 14th, yet it is named for the Latin "Februarius," or "Feast of Purification" on the 15th.

Personally, I prefer to think of it as "The Valentine month." Perhaps we could change the name to Valentine or Valentino. After all, "Feast of Purification" does have kind of a sadistic, cult-like ring to it.

CHINESE NEW YEAR

February is certainly a Valentine of a month in the Southland for many reasons. The weather is crystal clear and cool, and because of the special relationship Southern California has traditionally had with Asia, we can also enjoy celebrating Chinese New Year.

The Chinese lunar calendar differs from the Western, Gregorian calendar in that the New Year is observed on the second moon after the winter solstice and therefore is on a different date from year to year. There are also 12 year cycles, with each year being named for an animal. This chapter is being written in 1994, The Year of the Dog.

The significance of the Chinese New Year as a holiday is greater because in addition to having the "let's have a party" quality of New Year's as practiced in Western cultures, it also has the warm emotions and family get togethers much like Christmas and Thanksgiving. There is a traditional dinner where relatives gather and gifts are exchanged. Since it also celebrates the birth of spring, it also has elements of the May spring revelries that are customary in Europe and Russia.

In Southern California, there are two weeks of festivities that are observed most publically by two Asian communities: the Chinese, whose name for the New Year holiday is "Xin nian," and the Vietnamese, who refer to it as "Tet." Since most Japanese and Koreans celebrate New Years according to the Western calendar in the Southland, the Xin nian and Tet celebrations are the largest Chinese lunar calendar celebrations.

There are many rituals that are similar between the Chinese and Vietnamese ways of celebrating. These include incense burning, firecrackers, dancing, placing paper gods on the door, eating holiday food, and marching down the streets at night with hand held lanterns. Other traditions include doing good deeds, giving offerings to the spirit of one's ancestors, and paying respect to older family members.

The latter two are especially important in the Buddhist faith, which puts special emphasis on honoring parents and elders. Because the holiday also celebrates the rebirth of nature in the form of spring, homes are spruced up with new paint and decorated with peach blossoms.

The Chinese traditionally begin with a reunion dinner on New Year's Eve to give thanks for the whole year. "Dim sum," delightful little appetizers or finger foods, are the holiday specialties.

The Vietnamese have their big dinner the day after. Children are given money in red envelopes, while adults bring prized fruits such as tangerines along with dried fruits, candies, and pastries. The fruits and food consumed are all symbolic of unity, harmony, and togetherness.

Chinese Southern California

There are various places that offer festivities throughout the two weeks of the celebration. Let's start with a dim sum New Year's Eve dinner in L.A.'s **Chinatown**. The premier location is:

> **Ocean Seafood**
> **747 North Broadway**
> **Los Angeles, CA 90012**
> **Daily 8 a.m. to 10 p.m.**
> **(213) 687-3088**
> also at:
> **1015 South Nougales**
> **Rowland Heights, CA 91748**
> **(818) 912-5460**

The gaudy mirrored staircase that takes you up to this second floor restaurant wraps around the lobby waterfall and wishing well. With its huge crystal chandelier overhead, it is quite spectacular. The bustling, crystal chandeliered dining room is equally impressive.

This place does a fantastic lunch and weekend daytime business because the Cantonese fish dim sum is probably the best in the Southland. Modelled after Hong Kong dim sum restaurants, the little seafood creations and dumplings-you-can't-get-enough-of are served from carts. Grab the first one that goes past.

Ocean Seafood is near the 900 block of Broadway, called **Chinatown Plaza**, which was built in 1938 as the theme buildings for what was actually the second Chinatown in L.A. The architecture is of the "Chu Chin Chow" style, which is like Chinese Rococo with extremely curved roof lines and intricate detailing. L.A.'s Chinatown was developed by a gentleman named Peter Soo Hoo from about 1933 to 1938 and is properly called New Chinatown because the original, much older, one was demolished in 1933 to make way for Union Station.

The Chinese have an long history in Southern California. According to the official Chinese Xinhua News Agency, a monk named Faxian blew off course on a trip to Sri Lanka in 412 A.D. and ended up near L.A. Whether that is true or not, the Chinese were one of the first immigrant labor groups that came to the state.

In 1850, the census for Los Angeles showed a Chinese population of exactly two. Because of the Gold Rush and the need for workers for the Southern Pacific Railroad, their numbers swelled. By 1870, they were the largest foreign group in California, comprising 10 percent of the population. Their labor left its mark on the Southland landscape: between 1874 and 1876 the San Fernando Tunnel was dug, using mainly Chinese laborers.

The original Chinatown was a true ghetto, complete with over 100 opium dens. The mainly male laborers, who had arrived with nothing, pinched pennies and pooled their money. They started laundries and other enterprises and began to slowly climb out of poverty. Because of their industriousness, they were seen as a threat by whites and anti-Chinese sentiment resulted in a series of immigration laws that kept the Chinese population down until 1965.

Since that time—particularly in the late '80s—New Chinatown has grown considerably. While it does not yet have the scope and cultural significance of San Francisco's Chinatown, it has blossomed with new buildings, a myriad of great restaurants and shops, grand and simple, and sights, sounds and smells unlike anywhere else in the Southland. For the two weeks of New Years, it is especially exciting.

Do not go down there if you are afraid of fireworks popping. The young people on the street will throw them around quite freely. This time of year, the orange red paper of exploded firecrackers covers the sidewalks like fallen leaves and the gunpowder smoke billows on street corners like fog.

The **Golden Dragon Parade** is usually scheduled for a Saturday afternoon during the official two weeks. The dragon is the symbol of the power of nature and royalty together. The significance of following the dragon in a procession through streets is that those who do will enjoy good fortune and a bountiful harvest in the coming year.

New Chinatown is made up of main streets, like Broadway and Hill, and little alley ways designed to create the feeling of being in a Chinese city. Parking on Broadway at the far end of the 900 block is not a bad idea. From here you are looking down one of these alleys past another Cantonese restaurant serving a completely different specialty from that region:

Happy Valley Seafood Restaurant
407 Bamboo Lane
Chinatown
Daily 12 p.m. to 3 a.m.
Los Angeles, CA 90012
(213) 617-3662

One of the aspects of Chinatown that gives it a different feel is the live animals squawking at you in the poultry stores and carcasses-in-general hanging about in the food stores and restaurants. A Chinese live fish restaurant will feature dinner still swimming in tanks as decoration, as is the case here.

This is a great classic, no frills, live fish Cantonese restaurant. They have a regular menu of Chinese foods, but the star is the seasonal wall sign of available seafood.

It is a nondescript place, except for the fish tanks, but the food is absolutely sensational. Even though this is a reasonable restaurant, eating freshly cooked live fish from a tank can get quite expensive, depending on what and how much you order. With a group of people, you can get a combination of a fish dish or two and some more traditional Chinese food, and thereby keep the cost down.

There are a lot of stores, but I thought I might mention two. On the next alley going towards downtown L.A. are:

Import Bazaar
486 Gin Ling Way
Chinatown
Los Angeles, CA 90012
Daily 11 a.m. to 8 p.m.
(213) 620-8808
and:
Kwan Yuen Company
437 Gin Ling Way
Chinatown

Los Angeles, CA 90012
Monday-Friday 11 a.m. to 8 p.m.
Saturday & Sunday 11 a.m. to 9 p.m.
(213) 625-3176

Both of these stores have interesting little delights for less than $20 among their many offerings.

Kwan Yuen dates from the building of New Chinatown in the late 1930s. Miraculously, it is still run by the original owners, Dan and Annie Jeng. Kwan Yuen is also a major wholesaler for baskets.

Cross Hill Street and you are in a real antique store district: Chung King Road. It is so well established that there was even a book written about it in the early 1960s: *Moy Moy* by Leo Politi. One of the most interesting of the shops is:

Fongs
939-943 Chung King Road
Chinatown
Los Angeles, CA 90012
Daily 11 a.m. to 8 p.m.
(213) 626-5904

The stories of the shops of Chinatown are almost as exotic as the merchandise they stock. Jim Fong first opened this store in 1952. He is an artist who creates the tiny enameled cloisonne. His store didn't start out specializing in miniatures; it ended up that way because of too many teapots.

Yixing teapots are the world's original. Fashioned in whimsical, almost abstract shapes, or designs taken from nature, they are always colored in various earth tones. They have been made this way since the Ming Dynasty (1368-1644).

They come from an area near Lake Taihu, 100 miles west of Shanghai, and are said to have a special quality that makes for ideal tea brewing. They develop a rich patina with use and are to be rinsed, not washed. They were brought to Europe with the first tea shipments, and the teapot thus became a part of Western culture as well as Eastern.

Mr. Fong had so many of them, he didn't have any more room in his shop so he started carrying the smaller ones. He kept going down in size until he finally ended up having the largest number of miniature teapots for sale in Chinatown. They are 1/2 to 1/4 of an inch perfect, working replicas, many of which were samples made for use by traveling salesmen. This miniaturization has carried over to the rest of the shop. There is tiny furniture and in one corner is an exact miniature of the shop that makes me feel like I am in Edward Albee's play *The Doll House.*

Another long established antique dealer is nearby:

> **Alex Cheung Company**
> **936-938 Chung King Road**
> **Chinatown**
> **Los Angeles, CA 90012**
> **Daily 10:30 a.m. to 6:30 p.m.**
> **(213) 629-4705**

Here they have wonderful antiques that range in price from a few dollars to thousands. I sometimes feel as if some small strange creature with furry ears is going to come popping out from behind one of the cases filled with all manner of old oddities in this delightful shop.

Near here, on Alpine, is the appropriately named **Alpine Park.** In the early morning, a group of Chinese senior citizens work out, doing their Tai Chi exercises in the park. Across from here is the best place to have a Chinese "jook" breakfast (note there is no sign in English):

> **May Flower Restaurant**
> **800 Yale Street**
> **Chinatown**
> **Los Angeles, CA 90012**
> **(213) 626-7113**

Jook is Cantonese rice porridge; at May Flower it is served with fresh ginger. In much the same way as a Western breakfast restaurant might advertise "200 different omelets" that each have a different filling, so it is with Chinese breakfast and lunch spots like this that serve jook. The house special is kidney, liver, chicken, and shrimp. This place will not only delight your palate, it will pleasantly surprise you with its extremely low price.

As Chinese as Chinatown is, 90 percent of L.A's Chinese population resides outside of it. Eight miles southeast of here, in the San Gabriel Valley, is the largest Chinese residential community in the United States. All of the cities around here have respectable Asian populations, but the "Chinese Beverly Hills" is the City of **Monterey Park.** Monterey Park is over 50 percent Asian, more than half of whom are Chinese. There are five daily Chinese language newspapers.

There is normally a Chinese New Year's Parade in Monterey Park:

> **Chinese New Year's Parade**
> **Starts in front of City Hall**

320 West Newmark Street
Monterey Park, CA 91756
Usually the first Saturday of the month at 10 a.m.
(818) 307-1458

The second wave of the Chinese immigration of the 20th century that is evident here was quite different from the first. The Chinese of Monterey Park and its nearby communities in the San Gabriel Valley were often wealthy businessmen from Taiwan.

This is a prosperous community that is a mixture of quiet residential avenues and fashionable main streets. It is quite unlike an inner city designated "ethnic area" like Chinatown. The Asian presence is most apparent on the pulsating commercial boulevards and on the signs at the mini-malls.

These are everywhere and are worth paying attention to, because Monterey Park is the home of over 70 great Chinese restaurants, some of which are as undistinguished on the outside as the mini-malls in which they are located.

The area around Newmark and Garfield probably offers a choice of more quality Chinese food of different regional styles than anywhere in the world. Many of these would be famous and trendy if they were located in Santa Monica or Beverly Hills.

Besides the tremendous variety of regional styles, Chinese restaurants also come in many forms. There are the enormous Hong Kong styled banquet palaces, the formica and plastic live fish "finds," but there are also some beautiful variations in between. The most charming and romantic restaurant I have found in Monterey Park is also very near here:

Lake Spring
219 East Garvey Avenue
Monterey Park, CA 91756
Monday-Friday 11:30 a.m. to 9:30 p.m.
Saturday & Sunday 11:30 a.m. to 10 p.m.
(818) 280-3571

This is a hip, Shanghai-style bistro restaurant. The silk flower arrangements here are accented by indirect lighting and heavily polished dark wood. It is relaxing and subdued—a lover's restaurant. The overall mood is elegantly simple and stylish.

Their specialties are sea cucumber braised with shrimp roe and a memorable pork dish called in English, "a noisette of pork pump."

Vietnamese Southern California

While Chinatown and Monterey Park may be the places for Chinese New Year, the best Tet celebrations are to be found in Orange County's **Little Saigon**.

It is not that difficult to grasp why this area is called such. The Westminster/ Garden Grove area has the largest concentration of Vietnamese outside of Vietnam, estimated to be over 140,000. Though not quite as stylized as Chinatown, it is nonetheless a very Asian place. The shopping centers have varying degrees of Asian architectural detailing, but the stores themselves, the businesses, and most of the people you see on the streets are Vietnamese.

The local junior college is the site of a two day Tet Festival early in the month sponsored by The Union of Vietnamese Student Associations of Southern California since 1981:

> **Tet Festival**
> **Golden West College**
> **15744 Golden West Street**
> **Huntington Beach, CA 92640**
> **Saturday from 10.m. to 11 p.m.**
> **Sunday from 10 a.m. to 8 p.m.**
> **(714) 893-3139**

For a mere $2 entrance fee, this celebration includes over 100 booths with exhibitions, artwork, games, and of course, food. There are carnival rides, firecracker shows and ceremonies, but more interestingly, there are traditional Tet skits and Lion and Dragon dances performed by local high school and college students in the afternoons.

On Bolsa Avenue, the main drag of Little Saigon, there are several shopping centers that make up the heart of the commercial district. The only indoor one is really worth a visit, especially at this time of year:

> **Asian Garden Mall**
> **9200 Bolsa Avenue**
> **Westminster, CA 92683**

On the outside Asian Garden Mall looks like a huge, oriental styled box. The parking lot in back seems to be packed any time of the day or night. Because people are always leaving (they all come down a walkway in the center), cars hover in the lanes waiting in hopes of finding someone getting ready to leave so they can stake out their parking place.

When you enter, either from the beautifully elaborate red pagoda roof topped glass front on Bolsa or the somewhat more understated back doors, the first thing that will strike you is that the place smells absolutely wonderful. There are several restaurants and a truly amazing food court that all contribute to the delicious air.

The next things that will hit you are the sounds and sights of all manner of stores, their wares spilling out onto the hallways. Some are like those in a Western mall, but most are quite different. Vietnamese pop music pulsates from more than one store festooned with sexy posters of Asian pop stars hawking their tapes and CDs. The vitality of the place is a little overpowering, but it makes shopping here fun. You are in the heart of Little Saigon and it feels like it!.

Statue inside the Asian Garden Mall in Westminister.

While some of the stores may look as Californian as those found in premier malls such as South Coast Plaza, the food court here is quite different from those normally found in this kind of structure. It is here that the feeling of being in Vietnam, not California, is the strongest. There are a score of places to eat and even a "sidewalk cafe," called the **Cafe Rendez Vous** that might as well be on a Saigon street. Do not even think of sitting down in this cafe if you are irritated by cigarette smoke. The percentage of young Vietnamese sitting here languidly puffing would make a tobacco industry executive proud.

Vietnamese food is quite delicious and is becoming as popular as Thai food. A great way to start the day in Little Saigon is at the other end of the mall from the food court, at a premier place for a "Good Morning Vietnam" breakfast:

> **Pho 79**
> **Asian Garden Mall**
> **9200 Bolsa Avenue**
> **Westminister, CA 92683**
> **Daily 8 a.m. to 8 p.m.**
> **(714) 893-1883**

In Saigon, noodle places with this name are everywhere. The chain here is not related: they used the name for familiarity's sake. There are also locations in

Chinatown, Alhambra, Long Beach, and San Gabriel. Because there are so many of them, they are a good choice for trying Vietnamese noodles in the Southland.

You can have these noodles in a variety of ways, somewhat like Chinese jook. "Pho dac biet," the basic beef broth with noodles, is easy to enjoy without adjustment and is heavenly. "Nuoc mam," the salty amber fish sauce on the side, used by Vietnamese in the same manner as soy sauce, takes a little getting used to.

The blending of French and Asian cultures in Vietnamese cooking is subtle, but tangible in one way that you will particularly appreciate at breakfast: I have never found a Vietnamese restaurant, no matter how small, that did not serve fantastic dark coffee from a French drip maker.

Walk around the mall for a few hours and then go back to the food court for lunch. There are numerous food stands that sell different Vietnamese dishes, but nearly all serve "banh mi," Vietnamese sandwiches on crisp, hot French bread. You can have both breakfast and lunch here for less than $10.

If anything were to epitomize the blending of Asian and California culture, it is the weekly ritual of a sort of community promenade in this mall every Saturday night. Vietnamese of all ages get somewhat dressed up for a combination of socializing and shopping. You may see some women in the traditional long "aodai" formal dress this month because it is the holiday, but normally, everyone looks fashionably Californian.

If you happen to be lucky enough to be in Little Saigon during this time of year, you are in the right place at the right time. The mall will be especially bustling and festive with families doing their holiday shopping.

There will be a line up of dwarf tangerine and kumquat trees brimming with fruit, along with potted daffodils and beautiful silk Tet murals for sale. Other traditional holiday treats will include sweet rice cakes wrapped in banana leaves, dried pineapple and papaya in gift boxes, and dried watermelon seeds. All are wrapped in bright red cellophane.

Within walking distance, on the six acres behind the nearby Asian Village shopping center is the site of the larger of the two Tet Festivals held annually in this area:

Tet Festival
9191 Bolsa Avenue
Westminster, CA 92683
Admission: $3
Date corresponds to second weekend of Chinese New Year

Normally held at least a week after the Tet celebration at Golden West College, this is a bustling three day celebration complete with lion dances, martial arts shows, a beauty contest, art exhibitions, a talent search, and over 200 booths with food, handcrafts and games. It keeps going until midnight on each of the three days and is certainly a major bargain at $3.

VALENTINE'S DAY (FEBRUARY 14)

On February 14th, lovers celebrate their loved one, single people celebrate the idea of love, and greeting card manufacturers celebrate the fact that they will sell more cards now than during any other holiday season, except Mother's Day and Christmas.

This is quite ironic since the original tradition of the Valentine calls for something "home made," given with mock seriousness, and usually signed with a pseudonym. Quite different from the elaborate (and serious) cards and gifts we buy for our lovers today.

I have always been reassured by the fact that we have a holiday like Valentine's Day when we are supposed to send anonymous, lighthearted messages to those we are in love with. There are so many "serious" holidays.

The original St. Valentine was an Italian priest who lived about 270 A.D., but nobody really thinks of it as being his day. Everybody really knows its is Cupid's day, because the little bare-assed guy with wings and the bow and arrow is suddenly everywhere on the 14th.

Cupid is actually the Roman name for the young Greek god of love, "Eros. " Eros was the son of the Greek gods, "Ares" and "Aphrodite," who are better known by their Roman names, "Mars" and "Venus." Ares is the bloodthirsty god of war, hence an appropriate association with the red planet Mars. Aphrodite/Venus is the goddess of beauty and love.

The Greeks considered Aphrodite to be the most beautiful of the Olympians. This is why the lovely planet most commonly called the "morning star" or "evening star" was named Venus. We get our modern words "aphrodisiac" from Aphrodite and "erotic" from Eros.

That Cupid/Eros is the son of the god of war and the goddess of beauty should come as no surprise to you if you have ever fallen in love. Being shot by an arrow is one of the most appropriate metaphors in the history of the world for this occurrence.

Traditional Valentines, Downtown Los Angeles

To celebrate the holiday of lovers, every year at this time, there is an exhibit of classic and antique Valentines at the closest thing to a "Valentine Museum" in Southern California:

Grier-Musser Museum
403 South Bonnie Brae
Los Angeles, CA 90057
Runs entire month of February
Wednesday-Friday 12 to 4 p.m.
Saturday 11 a.m. to 4 p.m.
Closed Sunday
(213) 413-1814

The Bonnie Brae Historic District is one of two concentrations of Victorians that survive in Los Angeles. This Queen Anne styled circa 1898 home has been painstakingly renovated and converted into a museum by retired physician Dr. Anna Krieger and her two daughters, Nancy and Susan.

It is named after Anna's mother, but it really is more of a tribute to the collector spirit in all of us. Though in its totality, it is a museum of Victorian Los Angeles, the collections on display constantly change and can feature anything from makeup compacts to Academy Award paraphernalia.

They also have regularly rotating exhibitions that commemorate a variety of events and people that include Elvis Presley, the Statehood of Hawaii, and Rosemary Clooney's birthday. Besides these noteworthy collections is this annual event coinciding with Valentine's Day.

I would stop by the Grier-Musser during the day and then drive toward the city for the evening. Besides being marked by such a romantic holiday, February is one of my favorite months for being in certain parts of the Southland because it continues the cool weather with the high visibility of January. It makes for a good time to be in downtown proper.

The L.A. skyline, not great during the hot hazy summer months, can be beautiful this time of year when a clear mountain view is visible in the background. Going from the Grier-Musser Museum to downtown can give a glimmer of memories back to a time when Los Angeles was a smaller place, with fine suburbs close in to the city.

The fact that the weather is best for enjoying the city during the day this time of year perfectly lends itself to celebrating the most classic Southern California Valentine's Day tradition in town:

> **Valentine's Day Tea**
> **Rendevous Court**
> **The Biltmore Los Angeles**
> **506 South Grand Avenue**
> **Los Angeles, CA 90071**
> **Afternoons the week of Valentine's Day**
> **(213) 624-1011**

The Rendezvous Court at the Biltmore is the most ornate, luxurious place to have tea in Southern California. For this occasion, they usually have chamber music providing accompaniment.

They serve heart-shaped finger sandwiches and canapes, and from the Biltmore's famous pastry kitchen, heart shaped cookies and all manner of petit fours, miniature fruit tarts, and chocolate roses. They have a good choice of teas and Champagne—with a long-stemmed rose for each lady on the 14th.

The Biltmore is really a remarkable hotel. It was one of the most expensive buildings ever built in L.A. when back in 1923, a consortium of local businessmen put up $10,000,000 to build "the largest and grandest hotel west of Chicago." It was designed by the New York architectural firm of Shultze and Weaver, who also designed the Waldorf Astoria and the Jonathan Club building.

On the outside, it is rather stolid, but inside it features cathedral ceilings handpainted by Italian artist Giovanni Smeraldi, whose work also graces the White House and the Vatican.

It has been used for the filming of nearly 300 movies and television shows including *Beverly Hills Cop, A Star Is Born,* and ironically, *New York, New York.* The 11 flights of intricate wrought iron back stairs were used to make Jimmy Stewart dizzy in *Vertigo* and the incomparable **Crystal Ballroom** was used as the alien's opulent underground headquarters in John Carpenter's *They Live.* The Crystal Ballroom is where, in 1927, the Academy of Motion Picture Arts and Sciences held its first organizing banquet. It was here that the Oscar was conceived, from some sketches on a tablecloth.

All of the public rooms are worth experiencing, but the **Gallery Bar** has a small room called the **Cognac Room** that would qualify as the most romantic place to have a late night drink in L.A. underneath the spectacular murals executed by A.T. Heinsberger.

While the **Grand Avenue Bar** is not my favorite part of the Biltmore (it is the newest), they have an evening weekday jazz series that really is excellent.

Bernard's is the hotel's fine dining room, and though quite expensive, features classic romantic lighting and elegantly simple decor to go along with world class food and service.

In the basement of the hotel, there is a 1920's Roman-style health club with handpainted tile surrounding a Hearst Castle-like indoor pool. The facility is not only fantastic visually, but has a good selection of modern equipment complimented by the pool, a coed jacuzzi, and steam and sauna. To complete the true William Randolf Hearst effect, they give you togas as well as towels.

Because the Biltmore is primarily a business hotel, there are often very attractive weekend specials. They will give you a free limousine ride to the theater if you are a guest, and the concierge will help you with the tickets. Stay up late Saturday night because weekend check out time is not until 6 p.m.

I particularly recommend staying here overnight and combining it with an evening at the imposing white marble Music Center, which is nearby.

The Music Center of Los Angeles
1st Street and Grand Avenue
Los Angeles, CA 90071
(213) 972-7483 (tours)
(213) 972-7211 (reservations)

The Music Center encompasses the 3,200-seat **Dorothy Chandler Pavilion**, home of the L.A. Philharmonic, the **Mark Taper Forum**, which is an excellent 747-seat showcase for drama (see September), and the 2,100-seat **Ahmanson Theatre**, home for so long to *Phantom of The Opera*. *Phantom* played from May of '89 to August of '93, making it the longest running musical in L.A. history. Soon, the Music Center will also include the Disney Concert Hall designed by Frank Gehry.

The Academy Awards were held at the Dorothy Chandler up until quite recently. With its Grand Hall crystal chandeliers, 17th century tapestries, collages of antique instruments, and flock of more than 500 gold leaf sunbirds over the refreshment stand, it is suitably impressive.

But perhaps the best show at the Music Center is its central fountain. It has 160 computer-controlled synchronized jets arranged in four groups around the sculpture, **Peace On Earth** by Jacques Lipchitz. The water can spray as high as 15 feet.

Back at the Biltmore's entrance, the corner of 5th and Grand forms one of the great city intersections of Southern California. Though you are surrounded by high rises, there is an opening to the sky from a city block-sized space occupied by something else. Right across Grand Avenue from the hotel is the magnificent:

> **Los Angeles Central Library**
> **630 West 5th Street**
> **[Between Grand Avenue and Flower Street]**
> **Los Angeles, CA 90071**
> **(213) 612-3200**

This wonderful building was originally begun in 1922 and finished four years later. It was the masterpiece of famed architect Bertram G. Goodhue. He wanted to express the coming together of past and present as represented by Los Angeles, and a more magnificent manifestation of it is hard to imagine. Its central tower rises to a peak in a beautiful, multi-colored tile pyramid. Roman, Egyptian, and Byzantine themes are expressed in 20th century concrete Beaux Arts.

Because of a major fire, attributed to an arsonist in 1986, this remarkable library hasn't been seen much in recent years. It was reopened in 1993 after a $213.9 million rennovation and expansion. I predict it will become a frequent filming site, because it is simply magnificent.

The newly refurbished Central Library in downtown L.A.

The new eight-story **Tom Bradley Wing** is like the royal chamber of some great alien civilization with its towering columns, large folk art chandeliers, and soaring atrium roof. There is a surprise when you enter it because its height was achieved by opening up four basement floors. So while it is only four stories tall on the outside, it abruptly drops down as soon as you enter. Replacing the West Lawn, which had been destroyed even before the fire, is the **Robert F. Maguire III Gardens**. It is a tranquil oasis where people on benches read in peace under the shade of pretty trees.

The Spanish Steps are across the street from the Central Library.

All libraries are romantic to some degree, and this one perhaps more so than any other. Not only is the building itself splendid, the garden, murals, and close up architectural details are perfect for peering at with someone by your side. Goodhue wanted to inspire and uplift with his design, which incorporated carving "eloquent statements about learning" into the tan stone throughout.

Right across the street from the 5th Street entrance to the library is the most beautiful statement of pedestrian architecture of downtown L.A., **The Spanish Steps**, joining the dead end of Hope Street at 4th down the hill to 5th.

Designed to connect the new and old of the city, it climbs appropriately along the west side of the new signature building of the L.A. skyline, the 73-story **First Interstate Tower,** and a more inviting walk would be hard to imagine. This $12 million dollar, five-story, 103-stair/step edifice is L.A.'s answer to the romantic and celebrated Spanish Steps of Rome. On one side is the gleaming new office tower, on the other, a Mission-styled facade. A stream from a bubbling fountain at the top splashes down the center over some rocks. An escalator carries the less romantic (or less physical.)

The steps switch back and forth lazily with a patio at each tier. Nestled among these patios is a place to eat that adds to the romantic mood:

Il Fornaio
633 West 5th Street, #212
Los Angeles, CA 90071
Monday-Friday 6:30 a.m. to 5 p.m.
Saturday 8 a.m. to 4 p.m.
Sunday 10 a.m. to 3 p.m.
(213) 623-8400

This is one of the most fully realized urban settings in the Western United States: the backdrop surrounding these outdoor tables is dramatic and beautiful, and the various Northern Italian dishes prepared here are perfectly matched to the feeling of being in a great city locale.

Once at the top, you are in the "new" L.A. of super modern buildings. One of the best of these is just a few steps away:

Museum of Contemporary Art
250 South Grand Avenue
Los Angeles, CA 90012
Tuesday-Sunday 11 a.m. to 5 p.m.
Thursday 5 to 8 p.m.
Free admission Thursday night only
(213) 626-6828

Designed by famed Japanese architect Arata Isozaki, the Museum of Contemporary Art is as much a piece of modern art as the older buildings nearby are in their own way classical. Isozki has said, "I have a Western head and a Japanese body," and the same could be said for this fantastic building. It has also been used in numerous films—often as a "building of the future."

The museum has a delectable little sandwich cafe, **Il Panino, The M.O.C.A. Cafe,** that serves some of the best sandwiches you will find. Traditionally museum food is miserable, but that is changing and this little shop was one of the pioneers.

Restaurants with a Downtown Los Angeles View and a Helicopter Ride

Whenever I am interviewed for a Valentine's Day story on what to do in Southern California, the most often asked question is to describe a romantic dining experience for the occasion. This is an interesting question because there are so many ways to dine that could be called romantic and theoretically every restaurant in this book is either romantic or unusual or both.

Often it is the view that makes a restaurant romantic. Night time cityscapes are one image indelibly associated with romance. New York is a favorite site for directors of romantic comedies because of its night time array of lights. Perhaps nothing so epitomizes the image of romantic dining as that of a pair of spellbound lovers clinking their glasses together and enjoying a penthouse view while being served by a tuxedoed waiter with a knowing smile.

Probably the most dramatic Valentine's Day dining experience in Southern California takes advantage of the fact that Downtown Los Angeles has a glittering night time cityscape all its own:

The Tower
TransAmerica Building
1150 South Olive Street
Los Angeles, CA 90015
Monday-Thursday 11:30 a.m. to 9 p.m.
Friday & Saturday 11:30 a.m. to 10 p.m.
Closed Sunday
(213) 746-1554

The 32-story TransAmerica Building, built in 1965, is set apart from the central downtown cluster of skyscrapers only a few blocks away. This means that The Tower restaurant, which as you may have surmised is at the top, heads the list of cityscape view restaurants in Downtown L.A. There is not a table in the place that does not have an unforgettable view.

Though expensive, it is the romance of the Southland all over: at night the Santa Monica and Harbor Freeways are endless flowing rivers of red and white light.

If you wished to check out the view without the tab, the building's observation deck is free and accessible during the day from 10 a.m. to 4 p.m., Monday through Friday.

The only way to make dinner here even more memorable is to make arrangements for a pre-dinner aerial tour from:

Benbow Helicopters
3401 Airport Drive
Torrance, CA 90505
(800) 77-Flying
(310) 325-9565

This is a fine F.A.A. approved flight school that grew into a charter business. They have four small two person choppers and two larger turbine models. Among the various rides you can take, the one I am suggesting here is their **Night Heli Tour.**

A limousine picks you up at your home or hotel in the late afternoon and takes you to the flight center. You can start your evening with a ride up the coast to watch the sunset from the air. Then fly back inland and experience the lights of the city as you have never seen them.

Here is your chance to capture your own *Blade Runner* imagery. The spectacle from the helicopter is of soaring towers of lights surrounded by the endless expanse of the city. The birds can fly between the buildings just like they do in the movies. They set you down right on the roof of the TransAmerica Building.

This is also something you can do by yourself if you like. The small helicopters are only two seater, hence one passenger for $140. The Jet Ranger is $180 per person for one couple, $140 per person for two couples. The price includes the limo pick up and also the return after dinner.

Looking directly down from the Tower, you will see one of the prettiest buildings in L.A.; it was also designed by the architect of California's most famous residence (Hearst Castle):

Herald Examiner Building
1111 South Broadway
Los Angeles, CA 90015

In 1912, when this building was built, there weren't very many female architects, but one of them was in the employ of William Randolph Hearst and his mother Phoebe: Julia Morgan. She was the first woman to graduate from the Ecole des Beaux-Arts in Paris. The Hearsts employed her talents throughout the state, the most spectacular example being Hearst Castle on the Central California coast.

You will see the resemblance in this delightful building, which like several other Mission Revival styled buildings of the period, owes its inspiration to the California Building at the World's Fair in Chicago in 1893.

It has a large central dome with smaller domes topping the corners and the entrance. With its white walls, tile roofs, and arches, it certainly adds a touch of romance to an otherwise drab place. The entrance lobby is a spectacular Baroque fantasy.

Right around the corner from here is a perfect place to end your Valentine's cityscape evening at another one of the great buildings of L.A.:

The Mayan Nightclub
1038 South Hill Street
Los Angeles, CA 90015
Friday & Saturday 9 p.m. to 3 a.m.
(213) 746-4287
(213) 746-4674

This former grand movie palace was executed by one of my favorite architectural firms, Morgan, Walls, and Clements in 1926. Fewer and fewer of the grandiose theaters that inhabited Downtown L.A. are around today. Most of the surviving ones are on Broadway (see June).

The cast concrete sculptured facade by Francisco Comeja is as elaborate as any temple and features seven Mayan warrior priests glaring down as you enter. The inside is a Hollywood version of a pre-Columbian civilization that now houses a dance floor and a bar on two levels.

If you would like another take on a cityscape view, right by the library, across the street from the larger Biltmore, downtown Los Angeles is blessed with a classically romantic small city hotel:

Checkers Hotel
535 Grand Avenue
Los Angeles, CA 90071
(213) 624-0000

Designed by Charles Whittlesey and built in 1927 as the Mayflower Hotel, it was renovated in award winning fashion and reopened as the Checkers in 1989. It is an architectural gem. Outside, its facade is a classy Beaux Arts with elaborate detailing, inside it is an intimate European setting with antiques and objets d'art everywhere.

The Checkers is small: 173 rooms, 15 suites, and two magnificent penthouse suites. There is a pubic sitting room called **The Library** that is the picture of cozy elegance. But for a textbook amorous setting, its hard to top the rooftop pool area with its Manhattan penthouse cityscape view that will summon images of all the romantic movies you have seen since you were a child.

The quality of the food and service added to the delight of the building itself make the Checkers a four diamond hotel. Checkers' restaurant has been featured twice in *Gourmet* magazine and is especially celebrated for their breakfasts. Upon arrival, they provide strawberries and creme fraiche and a fresh orchid in your room, choice of three daily newspapers and 50 movies (with free popcorn), plus all of the other usual amenities of a first class hotel—including butler service.

They have a wonderful "Pre-Theatre Dining" mini package that includes complimentary valet parking, appetizer, entre, a free limo to the Music Center and back, and dessert back in the restaurant for $32.50 plus tax and tip per person.

Of course, there are other city view restaurants in L.A., but perhaps the most dramatic view is not in a restaurant, but from the elevators of:

The Westin Bonaventure
404 South Figueroa
Los Angeles, CA 90071
(213) 624-1000

The Bonaventure is a flower shaped bunch of five bronze coated glass cylinders. The glass elevators fly up from the lobby and race up the outside of the building like missiles. The effect is rather thrilling with the freeway on one side and the tall buildings of Downtown L.A. all around.

This structure was finished in 1976 and features a spectacular atrium lobby with multiple levels and sections that offer a food court, shops, and other amenities. It is visually interesting, but a bit confusing and hard to find your way around. The passageways that fan out from the different areas all end up in exits that lead into other buildings nearby via pedestrian bridges.

A few blocks from here is another incredible structure often used in the movies that may be the most romantic place in Downtown L.A.:

Union Station
Los Angeles and Alameda
Streets
(800) USA-RAIL (Amtrak
information and reservations)
All train stations have a certain romance to them. Departures and arrivals are always emotional and train travel conveys the feeling of traveling over a distance much more directly than flying. That being the case, it is hard to top Union Station as a place of departure for a romantic journey.

This was the last of the great metropolitan train stations built in the U.S. Designed by John and Donald Parkinson, it was built from 1934 to 1939. It is an absolutely remarkable blend of Streamline Moderne architecture (that was itself suggested by the streamlining of the new locomotives) and the Spanish Mission style.

The 400-space parking lot in front of the building gives it a unique grandeur (there are spaces for 120 more underground.) The courtyards and grounds merge in landscaping architecture that suggests the indoor/outdoor quality of the Spanish hacienda.

The interior was director Ridley Scott's choice as the interior of the police station in future L.A. in his film *Blade Runner*. It has patterned marble floors, with wood beamed ceilings over 50 feet overhead. Moorish style archways lead to two patios.

There are 16 tracks running through the station. You could take the "Desert Wind" to Las Vegas or Chicago or the wonderful "Coast Starlight" all the way to Seattle. The most popular is the San Diego to L.A. run. There are trains departing as early as 6:20 a.m. and as late as 9:05 p.m.

Restaurant with a San Diego City View

The restaurant with the most acclaimed San Diego cityscape view is:

>**Mister A's**
>**2500 Fifth Avenue**
>**San Diego, CA 92103**
>**Monday-Friday 11 a.m. to 10 p.m.**
>**Saturday & Sunday 6 to 11 p.m.**
>**(619) 239-1377**

High atop the 12-story Fifth Avenue Financial Center building, the view from here gets the cityscape of San Diego with the harbor beyond. Periodically, jets zooming in for their kamikaze approach to San Diego's Lindberg Field add to the excitement by seeming to pass right by the window. The interior decor is lavish, with lots of art and antiques, though some people think it looks like a bordello. The food is fairly straightforward, rack of lamb and the like.

Close by is the romantic:

>**Britt House**
>**406 Maple Street**
>**San Diego, CA 92103**
>**(619) 234-2926**

Built in 1887, this beautiful Victorian comes as a bit of a surprise in an otherwise unremarkable neighborhood a scant two blocks from the western entrance to Balboa Park. Its fairy tale turret rises four stories above its multi-colored main building with its separate cottage in back. There is a lovely garden separating the two, shaded by a huge camphor tree.

The inside of the main house is just as wonderful as the outside, with 10 rooms, half of which are on a second floor that can be reached by one of the most spectacular staircases you will ever find in a bed and breakfast. It is framed by a two-story stained glass window.

The cottage has its own bathroom with a shower, but guests in the other rooms share four bathrooms. Two of these feature antique tubs, the other two have showers.

Though bed and breakfasts are supposed to be strong on breakfast, the really big event here is afternoon tea from 4 to 6 p.m. in the parlor. Such delicacies as cucumber sandwiches might be followed up with chocolate pecan pie. Rates range from $95 to $110.

This area is a great spot to begin a romantic Valentine's Day stroll over some of the nearby bridges without even going into Balboa Park. I have always particularly loved the:

Quince Street Bridge
Between
3rd and 4th
Avenues
San Diego
This white wood trestle span, as tall as a roller coaster at its highest point in the center, is a wonderful scenic en-  hancement to the canyon it crosses. A full 236-feet long, it looks like a picture from the old Hawaiian countryside looming above the green rambling chasm. It was designed in 1905 by George A. d'Hemecourt and was almost demolished. The local residents who fought for its preservation should all get gold medals.

Two blocks north is another romantic bridge to stroll across:

Spruce Street Footbridge
Between Front and Brant Streets
San Diego

This suspension bridge is even longer than the Quince Street Bridge. A full 375-feet long, the walk across takes you over a canyon filled with trees.

Of course, the most beloved bridge in all of San Diego is the **Cabrillo Bridge**. It is certainly one of my favorites, for though it is designed to take cars into Balboa Park on Laurel Avenue, it is a glorious walking bridge. From the better angle and slower speed of foot travel, you can really appreciate its graceful cantilevered structure, the first in California.

It was designed in 1914 by Thomas B. Hunter to cross a 120-foot canyon for the World's Fair of that year. A scenic giant pond was created at the base that is now

Cabrillo Bridge in San Diego.

occupied by SR 163 (Cabrillo Freeway). The first passenger to ride across was none other than Franklin D. Roosevelt, who was Secretary of the Navy at the time.

El Prado and much of Balboa Park will be described in April when the rose garden is in bloom and June when the Shakespeare Festival is happening. Holiday events will be in December.

Restaurants with an Ocean View, La Jolla, romantic oceanside walk, tidepools, beginning of spring wildflowers

Of course, Southern California is celebrated for romantic restaurants with a view of another kind: that of the ocean. There are obviously many restaurants with views of the coast, but it would be most appropriate to start with one of the most renowned:

> **Top O' The Cove**
> **1216 Prospect Street**
> **La Jolla, CA 92038**
> **Daily 11:30 a.m. to 10 p.m.**
> **(619) 454-7779**

Prospect is one of eight streets that have retained their original names since 1887 when the city of La Jolla was laid out. Its name comes from its orientation: it winds above the cliffs and literally encircles the crown above beautiful La Jolla Cove. In its early days it had little wooden cottages along its length that formed the basis for its original identity as an art colony.

All of these cottages have been torn down, except for one, built in 1893, which survived and was made into this restaurant in 1955. You enter this warm and cozy place, consistently voted "Most Romantic Restaurant In San Diego," under huge Morton bay figs. The view of a sunset over the cove has inspired more than one wedding proposal.

La Jolla could cerainly qualify as a town with an old history of romance in the Southland. Its status as an arts colony was enhanced in 1894 when artist and patron Anna Held Heinrich built a house she called "The Green Dragon," after a story by Beatrice Harraden. Other houses followed and soon many well known artists called the area their home.

The original turn-of-the-century wooden buildings of this artist's colony are still called **Green Dragon**, but now they are a little group of shops overlooking the Pacific that are perfect for Valentine's Day strolling. Since La Jolla means "the jewel," it is appropriate that you stop in a store that is located here:

> **The Collector**
> **1274 Prospect Street**
> **La Jolla, CA 92038**
> **Monday-Saturday 10 a.m. to 5 p.m.**
> **(619) 454-9763**

Beautifully colored gems—some unset, some in exquisite settings—flash in a rainbow of colors from the window displays. This store is known internationally as a source for quality colored stones and even has its own mining interests in Asia and Africa. It features settings by a variety of well known jewelry designers.

The owner, Bill Larson, is quite well known in the gem world. In 1972, he was responsible for the discovery of the Himalaya mine, located in the northeastern part of San Diego County. This was a major find of exceptional quality tourmaline, a beautiful colored stone that comes in an incredible variety of colors. They have an especially large selection of tourmaline stones, jewelry, and even carvings.

Prospect is also the location of one of Southern California's most romantic hotels:

> **Hotel La Valencia**
> **1132 Prospect Street**
> **La Jolla, CA 92038**
> **(619) 454-0771**

Designed in 1926 by William Templeton Johnson, the pink stucco Mediterranean styled La Valencia is the epitome of Southland romance. The hotel's terraced gardens and pool overlook the Pacific, and the main window in the elegant lobby has a showstopping view of the Cove.

Besides being a town with a romantic past, La Jolla is also the place to begin one of my all time favorite long strolls. Walking north from La Jolla, I would start somewhere around La Jolla Shores Beach/Kellogg Park. Walk under the pier and continue to where the rocks are. There are tidepools worth exploring here during low tide or minus tide season which is discussed in the November chapter. Once past the tidepool area, you'll soon see the soaring glory of colorful hang gliders above your head.

For the last two miles, you are rewarded with a truly picturesque sight of the cliffs above. Rising in sculpted majesty, these rocky inclines are the tallest you will find in San Diego County. From here, the next stop is the reserve itself:

Torrey Pines State Reserve
12000 North Torrey Pines Road
Del Mar, CA 92014
(619) 755-2063

The Torrey Pine is one of the world's rarest trees. There are probably only about 6,000 native ones left. They are found only here and on Santa Rosa Island in the Channel Islands (see May). A worthy symbol of the Southland in the same way the cypress is of the Monterey coast, the Torrey Pine has a wispy, almost ethereal beauty to it.

The reserve is about 1,000 acres and because of the tree's extreme rarity, very little is permitted besides walking. If you want to picnic, there are some tables near the entrance. Admission is also limited to only 400 people at a time. When this limit is reached, the park is closed until some folks leave; then a few more people are let in.

These limitations create some unique qualities that make the Torrey Pines Reserve different from other natural spots. Because seeds from the wildflowers are not subject to much disturbance, the cycle of blooming includes more species. There are over 330 different kinds of plants represented here. Beginning this month and continuing though May is a continuously changing wildflower display. There is a great network of trails that are all pretty easy walks: only the length and the scenery vary.

What sets the beach below the park, **Torrey Pines Beach**, apart from almost all other Southern California beaches is the unbroken beauty of the landscape. You can walk along this beach for several miles and not have your tranquility disturbed by the sight of a single condo development, power plant, or street.

There is more about La Jolla in the July and September chapters.

Del Mar

If you continued walking up the coast from Torrey Pines Beach, you will see a power plant at the end of your walk, but it is a scenic, sort of model railroad type of structure with a single smokestack, out of which no smoke pours. This relic of earlier days gives the beach here its name, **Powerplant Beach.** It is a lovely end to a walk along the fairly narrow corridor of sand between the cliff and the endless blue water. Now you have reached the little seaside town of Del Mar. As you reenter civilization, you will see two beachfront restaurants. The second one is an old favorite:

> **Poseidon Restaurant**
> **1670 Coast Boulevard**
> **Del Mar, CA 90214**
> **Monday-Thursday 11 a.m. to 10 p.m.**
> **Friday 11 a.m. to 11 p.m.**
> **Saturday 9 a.m. to 11 p.m.; Sunday 9 a.m. to 10 p.m.**
> **(619) 755-9345**

The restaurant began life about the same time I did in the mid-'50s as The Knight's Room. That interesting choice of a name for a beachfront restaurant was changed by new owners two years later with an equally dubious choice: "The Stuft Shirt." In 1962, it was sold again and this time renamed The Fire Pit, which at least was getting a little more accurate. The restaurant does, in fact, have a big one outside as well as a massive fireplace inside.

The Fire Pit was purchased by its present owner, Tom Ranglas, four years later. He struggled for 10 years, but upon renaming it Poseidon in 1977, business went up nearly 50 percent.

Next door is a relatively inexpensive motel that is one of the few on the entire coast located right on the beach:

> **Del Mar Motel On The Beach**
> **1702 Coast Boulevard**
> **Del Mar, CA 90214**
> **(619) 755-1534**

What a pleasant surprise this cheerful white stucco motel turns out to be, with its sky blue roof and doors and white wooden railings. There are 45 rooms that, while not exactly opulent, are bright and colorful and extremely well maintained. You can get a room on the beach during the winter for as little as $60 plus tax.

Possibly the prettiest collection of shops and restaurants on the coast is a short stroll up the street:

> **Del Mar Plaza**
> **1555 Camino Del Mar**
> **Del Mar, CA 92014**
> **(619) 792-1555**

Somehow this stone and brick structure and its arches look more like a large terrace built into the hill than a commercial structure. With two floors, 33 shops and eight restaurants, it is larger than it seems. The restaurants have either second floor patio eating areas or feature sidewalk ambiance. It says a lot about the place that their glossy brochure even features Stanley, the Del Mar Plaza cat.

Within Del Mar Plaza is a very romantic bookstore where you can linger over coffee:

Esmeralda Bookstore and Coffee House
1555 Camino Del Mar, Suite 310
Del Mar CA 92014
Sunday-Thursday 10 a.m. to 9 p.m.
(later in summer)
Friday & Saturday 10 to 11 p.m.
(619) 755-2707

Dallas native Carole Carden opened this delightful store in 1990. She had a background in publishing and wanted to open a place for quality books. Different employees put their recommendations on the shelves near where the books are and regular customer's watch to see what the staff is reading. They have a good selection of biography, classics, mystery, and contemporary literature. The latter is a particular specialty.

They hold six to eight reading events a month. The setting is particularly suited for it. The coffeehouse has four tables inside and there is a large patio behind the store. On the hill above the plaza is a classic bed and breakfast:

Rock Hause Bed and Breakfast
410 15th Street
Del Mar, CA 92014
(619) 481-3784

Built in 1910 for Henry W. Keller, who was the first president of the South Coast Land Company, this house has a rather amazing history. The dining room was used for Catholic Mass a year after it was erected. By the 1920s, it was a speakeasy and casino. Like many wonderful buildings, somehow it fell upon hard times, but now it has been completely renovated and opened as a bed and breakfast.

It has 10 rooms, four with private baths, six that share one of three. The **Huntsman**, with its own fireplace, is the most expensive at $135 per night. The least expensive is the **Wren's Nest** at $75 for twin beds. Most of the rooms have beautiful ocean views. All come with fresh fruit, muffins, breads, coffee or tea, and orange or other juice. The living room is very hearty and large with its beamed ceiling and fireplace. The enclosed glass veranda overlooking the ocean is one of the great sunset spots on the southern coast. There is more about Del Mar in the July chapter.

Restaurants with an Ocean View in Orange County, and Whale Watching

A somewhat newer take on romantic ocean view restaurants can be had a little ways up the coast from San Diego in Dana Point. One of the best ocean view restaurants on the seaboard is located in a large resort here:

> **Watercolors Restaurant**
> **Dana Point Resort**
> **25135 Park Lantern**
> **Dana Point, CA 92629**
> **(714) 661-5000**
> **(800) 533-9748**

All of the tables here have wonderful views of the resort's lush gardens and the ocean beyond since they are set on several tiered levels in a large semicircle.

The resort is very nice as large, modern resorts go. It is on a bluff overlooking the Pacific. There are 350 oceanside rooms and suites with marble baths. If you like to work out, they have a good health club as well as tennis and ocean sports. It is done in the best Southern California "Fake Cod" and probably intrudes upon the landscape as little as could be expected. The staff is attentive without beig too stuffy.

They often have packages that in the past have included whale watching day trips and slide shows given by naturalists in one of the hotel's conference rooms. Though it is hard to see anything to hearken back to its past, Dana Point has an old California history as an ocean center.

For a while it even looked like the major commercial port of Southern California would be located in **Dana Point Harbor**. A beautiful natural cove surrounded by dramatic cliffs, this harbor was named for Richard Henry Dana, who visited here in 1835 as a crewman aboard the sailing ship *Pilgrim,* and wrote about it in *Two Years Before The Mast.* He called it "the most romantic spot on the California Coast."

At the turn of the 19th century, it was the major port between San Diego and Santa Barbara. Ships would anchor here and trade goods from New England for cowhides that local ranchers tossed from the cliffs.

Obviously, Dana Point Harbor did not become the major commercial port of

Southern California. By the time the San Pedro breakwater was completed in 1910, that area that had formerly been marshlands was well on its way to that distinction. The next deepwater port past L.A. is Port Hueneme, a place many people do not think really exists. It became a Navy town.

Today Dana Point Harbor is surrounded by condos and housing tracts, but there is a wonderful replica of the *Pilgrim* anchored in the harbor that is used as a living laboratory to give kids aged 9 to 13 a taste of what it was like to be a 19th century sailor. It is owned by the nearby:

> **Orange County Marine Institute**
> **24200 Dana Point Harbor Drive**
> **Dana Point, CA 92629**
> **(714) 831-3850**

This is actually an educational facility for children which features its own tide pool and a "whale room." They have a number of participatory educational programs for kids that are excellent as well as a lovely park. This month is also the month of their annual **Festival of the Whales.**

While you're in the area, stop in for some great food and music at:

> **The Old Dana Point Cafe**
> **24720 Del Prado**
> **Dana Point, CA 92629**
> **Sunday-Thursday 11 a.m. to 11 p.m.**
> **Friday & Saturday 11 a.m. to 12 p.m.**
> **(714) 661-6003**

This place has a great, modestly priced menu of some unusual food—including vegetable lasagna, cornish hens, and chicken breasts stuffed with cheese and broccoli. They even have live entertainment nightly. It is the home of some of the best Orange County bands. Plan a day at the Marine Institute and Dana Point Cove area, then come here to finish in the evening. There is more about Dana Point in the December chapter.

Heading north up the coast will take you to another justifiably famous romantic coastal view restaurant in another town with a romantic history:

> **Las Brisas**
> **361 Cliff Drive**
> **Laguna Beach, CA 92651**
> **Daily 8 a.m. to 11 p.m.**
> **Bar open till 2 a.m.**
> **(714) 497-5434**

The outdoor patio here is literally set right above the surf crashing on the rocks below. The sunsets at Las Brisas are exceptional due to a unique lighting effect caused by the sun's angle to the restaurant and the way its light bounces off the water.

If passion overcomes you, there is a romantic place to get a room right next door:

Inn at Laguna Beach
211 Pacific Coast Highway
Laguna Beach, CA 92651
(714) 497-9722
(800) 544-4479

With its high ceilings, terra cotta tile roof, white stucco walls, ocean view walkways, and huge picture windows, the Inn at Laguna Beach is the picture of the Mediterranean hideaway. The architect took full advantage of the bluff top location and situated the building to create a 180 degree view of the Main Beach and coastline.

Over two-thirds of the 70 rooms have ocean views. All have VCRs (there is an extensive library of tapes in the lobby). A continental breakfast is bought to your room every morning. There is a rooftop terrace and a year round heated swimming pool enclosed by a glass wall. Parking is underground

If you have a romantic heart, but a thin wallet to match, you can enjoy the same view as dining patrons for free in the adjacent park:

Heisler Park
Cliff Drive
[Between Aster Street and Diver's Cove]
Laguna Beach

The lawn here is a perfect place to stretch out and gaze at the horizon or sit at the picnic tables. Barbeques are provided. Strolling is exceptional along the clifftop walking trails through the gardens. Some trails lead down to tidepools in a marine refuge. The picture is completed by the bowling greens and shuffleboard courts. At the south end, there is a pretty gazebo where weddings are performed.

Cliff Drive runs along Heisler Park past a succession of little coves and tiny beaches. There are actually 26 separate cove parks that make up the Laguna Beaches. At the north end, go left onto Crescent Bay Drive and you will come to **Crescent Bay Point Park.**

This is a lovely little 3/4 acre park with a curved sitting area. It also has a viewing platform from which Seal Rock, a resting place for many aquatic mammals, is in full view.

Another celebrated ocean view restaurant in Laguna is **The Towers**, located in the Surf and Sand Hotel and described in November. There is more about Laguna in the July chapte as well.

Restaurants with an Ocean View, Long Beach and the South Bay, Whale Watching, and Malibu

Up the coast in L.A. County, there is a restaurant by the water that is especially suited to Valentine's Day:

> **Ragazzi Restaurant**
> **4020 Olympic Plaza**
> **Long Beach, CA 90803**
> **Tuesday-Sunday 11 a.m. to 10 p.m.**
> **(310) 438-3773**

This adorable little Italian restaurant is located right on the beach. The building it is in might throw you—it is in the corner of the Belmont Olympic Pool building. The interior is lit with little white lights.

The people who own Ragazzi also own one of Southern California's unique romantic businesses:

> **Gondola Getaways**
> **Long Beach**
> **(310) 433-9595**

Naples is primarily a residential community that borders on Orange County. Its claim to fame is that it is a man-made island criss-crossed by canals. These canals are made scenic by the lovely homes and gardens that front on them and the gracefully arched bridges that cross them. In December the holiday lights are charming.

There are very few packaged romantic activities that really work. Gondola Getaways is one of them. The gondolas are the real and so are singing gondoliers that propel them. You bring your own wine, but you will find a little basket with some fruit and pasta salad waiting. Going for a gondola ride through the canals, then having dinner at Ragazzi is a very special perfect way to spend an intimate afternoon and evening.

The perfect way to finish the day would be to walk up the beach to the:

> **Beach Terrace Manor Motel**
> **1700 East Ocean Boulevard**
> **Long Beach, CA 90802**
> **(310) 436-8204**

This reasonably priced romantic spot has the most unlikely combination of architecture: Tudor on the street side and Mediterranean in its patios terracing that lead down the hill to the beach. Its Mediterranean side was used in the Brian de Palma film *Body Double*. You can see the cranes of the harbor in the distance from here. There is more about Long Beach in the January, May, July, August, and December chapters.

Though there are ocean view restaurants in the South Bay, the most romantic place for a Valentine's Day meal actually answers another question I am often asked. Very often people will ask me about a "storybook" setting for a wedding or a getaway. If that is the setting you want for Valentine's Day, there is a unique place that in many ways epitomizes what people think of when they think of Valentine's Day:

> **Barnabey's Hotel**
> **3501 Sepulveda Boulevard**
> **Manhattan Beach, CA 90266**
> **(310) 545-8466**
> **(800) 562-5285**

What can you say about this Victorian/Edwardian fantasy in the middle of a yuppie California beach town? Barnabey's is a full service 128 room hotel with the intricate detailing you would expect in a 10 room bed and breakfast. From its dark wood lobby with its ticking clocks in gilt cases and glints of crystal to its fairy tale garden, it is a kind of little girl's dream.

Barnabey's is a sixth generation family-run inn. The rooms feature some impressive antiques. It has an indoor/outdoor pool and several wedding areas that are used regularly. The elegant main dining room serves light Austrian fare and there is a bustling British pub connected to it.

There will be more about Manhattan Beach and the other cities of the South Bay in July.

Most Romantic Oceanside Table in Southern California

There are certainly a number of very nice restaurants with coastal views continuing north from here. L.A.'s Malibu coast, in particular, has a number of them (see March). What some have called the most romantic table on the coast is at:

> **Geoffrey's**
> **27400 Pacific Coast Highway**
> **Malibu, CA 90265**
> **Monday-Thursday 12 to 10 p.m.**

Friday & Saturday 12 to 11 p.m.
Sunday 10:30 a.m. to 10 p.m.
(310) 457-1519

The "Crow's Nest" is a table for two that occupies its very own small deck overlooking the Pacific. Malibu is also discussed in the August chapter.

Restaurants with an Ocean View in Ventura County

Ventura County, with oceanside communities in Port Hueneme, Oxnard, and Ventura has numerous restaurants with a view of the water. Perhaps the most beloved one is the namesake dining room of the:

Pierpont Inn
550 Sanjon Road
Ventura, CA 93001
(805) 653-6144

This splendid bluffside property has had an ocean view restaurant that shares its name since 1928. Though the US 101 freeway was built between it and the beach, the lovely view survives.

Today it is a small 70 room hotel with beautifully landscaped grounds, a pool, and a reputation for warm attentive service. Many of the rooms have ocean views and there are eight suites with balconies and two pretty cottages. The dining room does not offer any culinary adventures, but does a nice job with the basic chicken, fish, and meat dishes. The also make their own desserts.

The Pierpont is very popular, so if you can't get in for Valentine's Day and want essentially the same view, right across the street is the:

Chart House
567 Sanjon Road
Ventura, CA 93101
Monday-Friday 5:30 to 9:30 p.m.
Saturday 5 to 10 p.m.
Sunday 4 to 9:30 p.m.
(805) 643-3725

This '70s contemporary-styled restaurant is part of a small chain of steak and lobster joints that dot the California coast.

But Ventura's most traditionally romantic ocean view spot for Valentine's Day is not a restaurant, it's a bed and breakfast:

La Mer
411 Poli Street

Ventura, CA 93001
(805) 643-3600

In 1890, a Cape Cod style Victorian home was built on a hillside with a commanding view of the town and the ocean. It is now a bed and breakfast and if there were ever a destination that looked the part of what people think of as "the place to be" on Valentine's Day, this is it.

La Mer is a y inviting sight, with its flowers and neat white trim. The five distinctly decorated rooms range in price, but each of them come with private baths. The innkeeper, Gisela Baida, is one of the best around. She offers various special packages that can include carriage rides, massages, or homemade dinners.

There will be more about Ventura in the May, July, and December chapters.

Restaurants with an Ocean View in Santa Barbara

But if Valentines Day is the epitome of romantic holidays, then Santa Barbara is the place to spend it. For money reasons, this city can lay claim to being the most romantic in the Southland. Thus, it is appropriate that the last ocean view restaurant I am mentioning for Valentine's Day dinner is also possibly the best on the coast:

Citronelle
Santa Barbara Inn
901 Cabrillo Boulevard
Santa Barbara, CA 93013
Monday-Friday 12 to 9 p.m.
Saturday 5:30 to 10:30 p.m.
Sunday 10:30 a.m. to 9 p.m.
(805) 963-0111

In 1990, well known Los Angeles restaurateur Michelle Richard opened this wonderful restaurant, located on the third floor of the Santa Barbara Inn. It is a bright octagonally shaped room with windows that virtually open up to a larger-than-life view of the entire idyllic Santa Barbara coastline: the boardwalk with its cyclists, the beach and blue ocean with gliding sailboats, and the mountains above the foothills.

There is a pleasant bar on one side of the room and a patio off another. To top it off, the Pacific rim inspired food and service are superb. If you are looking for an ocean view restaurant where the dining is as good as the view, this is the choice on the coast.

The small hotel it is located in is a pleasant place with 71 rooms with ocean or mountain views. It is the tallest building by the water because a moratorium on buildings over two stories tall went into effect shortly after it was built. The hotel's reservation number is (805) 966-2285.

Looking out over the ocean, one is reminded that Santa Barbara was an early port. It has its own take on whale watching: excursions here usually begin this month when the mother whales are returning north with their calves.

Santa Barbara's Maritime Tradition, Whale Watching, and Santa Cruz Island

The predominant feature of the **Port of Santa Barbara** is:

> **Stearns Wharf**
> **Foot of State Street**
> **Santa Barbara**

As you go down State Street toward the ocean, you will come to the inspiring **Bicentennial Friendship Fountain**. It is a simple circular tank whose dominant feature is a trio of bronze dolphins leaping out of the center. Sculptor James (Bud) Bottoms based his vision on Chumash mythology that dolphins circle the earth as protectors of world peace. From here you go right onto the wharf.

Stearns Wharf gets its name from Mr. John Peck Stearns who built it in 1872, which also gives it the honor of being the oldest operating wharf on the West Coast. It was very active for many years, handling both passengers and cargo, and even has a lurid side to its history: gambling ships used to board passengers here in the 1930s.

You can either drive or walk on the wharf, but by all means walk to the end and look back at the city and imagine what it must have looked like to some 19th century arrival by sea.

In its early days, the Chinese cook used to stand on the "widows walk" on top of the town hotel with a telescope to watch for arriving ships at the wharf. That hotel is still around:

> **The Upham Hotel**
> **1404 De La Vina Street**
> **Santa Barbara, CA 93101**
> **(805) 962-0058**

The Upham, like the wharf, is a great survivor. It matches the historical honors of that pile of wood jutting out into the ocean by being the oldest continuously operating hostelry in the Southland. Architecturally it is kind of Italian meets the Old West, but the overall feeling is of an old seaside resort (through it is a few blocks from the ocean). There is a perfectly manicured acre of lawn with an array of classic white Adirondack chairs.

The Upham's 49 rooms all have private baths, telephones, and TVs, but beyond that, they vary quite a bit. The most expensive room—a Master Suite with its own private garden complete with hammock, a bedroom with a king sized brass bed, and a beautiful living room with a fireplace—is in the main building.

The connecting two-story wing off the main building has 12 guest rooms. There are five rooms done in Ralph Lauren patterns in the carriage house and several garden cottages with private patios or porches. Some of the rooms have four poster beds or such touches as ceiling fans or fireplaces.

The hotel is pleasantly civil, with a continental breakfast buffet, afternoon wine and cheese, and coffee and cookies provided daily for the guests. Prices range from about $100 to about $300 per night.

Though it doesn't receive much in the way of cargo or passengers today, Stearns Wharf is still a busy place. It has several restaurants as well as a place for learning about local marine life:

> **Sea Center**
> **211 Stearns Wharf**
> **Santa Barbara**
> **Daily from 9:30 a.m.**
> **Adults: $1.50, Children (under 17): $1**
> **(805) 962-0885**

Though it is small, this center is highly appropriate for whale watch season because it is limited to native sea creatures. A grey whale skeleton and a life sized model of a mother whale and her calf dominate the setting. Besides a sea bird exhibit and a nice summary of local marine archeology, there are six aquariums containing sea life native to the Santa Barbara Channel and a "touch tank."

Whale watching trips are available from:

> **Sea Landing Aquatic Center** *Condor*
> **Breakwater**
> **Santa Barbara, CA 93109**
> **(805) 963-3564**

The *Condor* is an 88-foot diesel-powered boat with a unique personalized quality to it. This is because it was designed by Captain Benko, its skipper. A real lover of the sea, and particularly the waters around Santa Barbara, it is almost disappointing to learn he is a former salesman for a pharmaceutical company.

But better than a regular whale watch trip is the special day trip offered to **Painted Cave** on Santa Cruz Island in the Channel Islands. At Stearns Wharf, you are in the best position to check out that wonderful island because right next door to the Sea Center is the office of its custodians:

> **The Nature Conservancy**
> **213 Stearns Wharf**
> **Santa Barbara**
> **(805) 962-9111**

Looking at the environmental exhibits here will make you want to go straight to **Santa Cruz Island**, the largest of the eight Channel Islands. It is 22 miles long and varies in width from two to seven miles. To put that into perspective, it is about three times as big as Manhattan Island.

Nine-tenths of it is owned by The Nature Conservancy. It is the largest of the more than 1,000 preserves held by this Earth saving group. An average of about 200 of their volunteers a year come to this desolate place to help keep it in its natural state.

Its condition is not really "untouched by human hands" because the indigenous people of the area, the Chumash, had villages there until being forced off and kept in compounds on the grounds of the Mission Santa Barbara. They had minimal impact on the environment, but those that conquered them were not so benign to the landscape.

In 1882, a huge sheep and cattle ranch was started by a Frenchman named Justinian Caire. This grew into a pretty big early agribusiness, complete with its own winery. It was in turn purchased by an Angelino named Edwin Stanton in 1937. How 90 percent of the island came to be protected by The Nature Conservancy is that Edwin Stanton's son, Dr. Carey Stanton, willed this ranch to them upon his death in 1987.

Though Santa Cruz Island is pristine compared to most of the mainland, there are some marks of human habitation. Some of these are interesting and thought provoking in a ghostly way, like old rusted pieces of machinery such as tractors on the ground. The adobe and brick ranch buildings where you stay when you spend the night have this quality—particularly one special little structure.

In a corner of the compound by itself is the loneliest Catholic chapel in California, **La Capilla de la Santa Cruz** or "The Chapel of the Holy Cross." This 24-seat brick chapel, with its stained glass windows and vaulted ceiling painted to look like the starry night sky, was built in 1891 by Italian craftsmen brought over by Justinian Caire. Mass is only said once per year.

Overall, the island is about as near as you are going to get to paradise this close to a giant metropolis. There are only a handful of people here year round and it receives relatively few visitors. It is a green, mountainous place with a fertile central valley that runs most of its length. White sandy beaches and hidden coves rise to a 2,400-foot peak. Groves of eucalyptus trees add a pungent sweetness to the air when the breeze shifts your way.

It also has the greatest biological diversity of any of the Channel Islands. There are over 600 species of plants, some extremely rare. A great deal of ongoing effort is exerted to preserve these. Of the 10 rare and endangered ones of particular interest, nine are only found here. There is also animal life. Besides the sea birds, there are 140 land bird species. Sea-going mammals, such as sea lions, inhabit the coves.

Perhaps the most adorable of the remaining natural species of Southern California is named after this island. It is *urocyon littoralis santacruzae* or simply the island fox. A cousin of the mainland grey fox, the island variety is a little smaller than a house cat and resembles what a cross between a dog and a cat might look like. They apparently made it to the island about 50,000 years ago and somehow even got to all of the other Channel Islands except for Santa Barbara and Anacapa. Perhaps the small size of the latter two islands was unappealing to this intelligent little mammal.

They were intelligent to make it to a place where there are no natural enemies. This has enabled the normally shy and nocturnal fox to be active during the day, particularly in the morning and early evening. This also means that they are not nearly as afraid of humans as they probably should be. They will sometimes actually follow hikers along trails. Campers on the island comment on backpacks being rummaged through and even waking up to find a little visitor or two curled up at the foot of their sleeping bags.

Even though there are about 1,500 island foxes on Santa Cruz Island, they are officially a California Threatened Species. This is a wonderful bonus to a visitor to the Channel Islands; otherwise, some idiot might think it would be great "sport" to shoot them.

Santa Cruz is about as far off the coast as Catalina, so the boat trips are not very long. However, unless you wanted to look for whales, the colder, rougher seas of February might make you want to fly over for either a day trip or a longer stay. There is an airstrip on the island and you can take either kind of trip with:

Channel Island Aviation
233 Durley Avenue
Camarillo, CA 93010
(805) 987-1301

With two departures each day, one at 9 a.m., then another at 10:30 a.m. (with returns at 3 and 4:30 p.m. respectively), this is one late sleepers can enjoy. For less than $100 you get a roundtrip flight that also includes a scenic pass over Anacapa and Santa Rosa Islands followed by the landing on Santa Cruz Island. A National Park Ranger then accompanies the participants on a five hour trek over some of the 54,000 acres of relatively unspoiled early California land. Bring your own lunch and beverages.

There will be more about the other Channel Islands in the May chapter. There will be more on the City of Santa Barbara in the March, May, August, and December chapters.

WHALE WATCHING AND SANTA CATALINA ISLAND

Catalina is about the same size as Santa Cruz, but the two are completely different. Though a surprising amount of Catalina is preserved, it has been basically developed for tourists with hotels, restaurants, and even a little golf course.

The fact that the whales are giving Southern California a wider berth and are getting harder to see from the mainland gives you the first good reason to go to Catalina Island during the winter. The second is that winter in Catalina, a place somewhat crowded with tourists during the summer, is quite lovely. February is one of the least visited of all months, and though some businesses may not be open until President's Day, it may also be the best time to visit.

You can get to Catalina by boat from virtually all of the coast cities of the Southland. The fastest and most convenient way is to go by:

> **Catalina Express**
> **Berth 95, near World Cruise Center**
> **San Pedro, CA 90731**
> **(Also in Long Beach beside the *Queen Mary*)**
> **(310) 519-1212**

With four trips over and two back daily, beginning at 7 a.m. and ending at 6:30 p.m., you could have a great day trip for not too much more than the $34 (less for children and seniors) round trip fare. Their five high speed, 149 passenger boats cross the 21 miles to Catalina in about an hour. The seating is airline style, with high backed seats. They even bring you drinks. Quite a change from the days when "The Big White Steamship" was like a real 2-1/2 hour cruise complete with live music.

Though it has been developed, they don't call Catalina "the island of romance" for nothing. There is always a certain magic to crossing water to get to an island

and, overall, Catalina has been blissfully slow in being destroyed by developers. Because everything has to be brought over by barge, it costs 50 percent more to build anything here than on the mainland.

Cabrillo claimed Catalina (along with everything else) for Spain in 1540. In 1820, it was granted to California Governor Pio Pico, who sold it in 1846 to a Captain Thomas Robbins, who had a schooner that worked the California coast. The selling price represented one of the truly great early California real estate bargains: a good horse with a silver saddle.

The Bannings bought Catalina Island in 1892 with plans to make it into a "fisherman's paradise." The brothers built a summer home there in 1910. They chose the end of the island where it narrows into a half mile wide isthmus, effectively forming two harbors: Isthmus Cove on the mainland side and Catalina Harbor on the sea side. The town here is called, appropriately enough, **Two Harbors**.

You can take a Catalina Express boat that goes here directly, or take one to Avalon 14 miles to the east and take a ferry or go overland by bus. Catalina is 21 miles long and was originally thought of as two separate islands because the two ends are somewhat mountainous, while the Two Harbors Isthmus in between the smaller western and larger eastern end is so near sea level as to be almost invisible until you are quite near. As a winter romantic getaway spot, this is a hard place to top. Lodgings range from the very low budget to moderately expensive.

If you want the best (and only) hotel in town, the Bannings built a fine, wood sided mountain lodge-styled house on a quiet, secluded hill, with a magnificent view overlooking the two harbors. Now it is a bed and breakfast:

> **The Banning House Lodge**
> **P.O. Box 5044**
> **Two Harbors**
> **Catalina Island, CA 90704**
> **(310) 510-0303**

The breathtaking ocean view here is certainly magnified by the fact this is one of the most accessible and breathtaking spots in Southern California that is not cancerously overdeveloped with tract houses.

Two Harbors has a population of 150, one store, a dive center, one restaurant, a one room schoolhouse, dirt roads, and the feel of a deserted atoll. With its empty crescent-shaped beach and coconut palms, it is quite a romantic and photogenic spot.

It has been used as a "South Seas" location in numerous movies, including *Mu-*

tiny *On The Bounty, The Sea Hawk,* and *The Ten Commandments.* Gregory Peck waded ashore here in *MacArthur.* There are even wrecked ships used in the movies at bottom of Catalina Harbor. One of them, the infamous Chinese junk *Ning Po,* appears like a ghostly apparition at low tide.

The Banning House Lodge was used as a hotel by stars making films here from the '20s to the start of WW II. Dorothy Lamour thought it a bit provincial, but Clark Gable was reputed to be quite fond of it.

The hunting lodge exterior motif carries into the interior which features a brick fireplace and wood paneled walls. This modestly priced B & B ($75 to $110) has 11 guest rooms, all with harbor views and private baths, that are decorated with throw rugs and rustic wood furniture.

If you want to spend less money on lodging, there are accommodations available in Two Harbors that could make this a $100-for-two weekend—including the boat ride over.

Two Harbors Campgrounds is 1/4 mile from town. Located in this campground is one of the great bargains in winter waterfront getaway accommodations in Southern California for those who don't want to camp. From October through April, the **Catalina Camping Cabins** are available for a mere $36 per night. They are used as residences for employees the rest of the year. Each cabin has a heater and a small refrigerator and bunk or double beds. You need to bring your own sleeping bag, towel, and pillow.

When you go "rustic low budget" like this, you have all of the amenities; they just aren't "polished." For example, you can take a hot shower, but you must use a coin-operated facility a few steps from your tent cabin. They have an all-gas open kitchen area that you may also use when you stay here. For reservations to any campsite or cabin call (800) 888-4CAT.

The Two Harbors area of Catalina is quite free of summer tourists in February and very much feels like being in some little hidden village far away from Los Angeles. It is not the most lively place, even in summer when the only restaurant, **Doug's Reef Restaurant & Reef Saloon,** is open. (It is open from President's Day Weekend in February through Thanksgiving weekend, then again for New Year's Eve. (See June and October) They serve dinner at the Lodge during the winter.

There are fire rings on the beach which seem to be even more delightful when they are burning in the cooler air of the relative solitude of February. Because it is very clear this month, it is also a good time to gaze upon the California coast.

It is a deep pleasure to be here at this time of year because the winter seclusion really intensifies the illusion of being in quite primitive country, when in fact, it is only a 10 minute walk from the dock at Isthmus Cove. The outback of Catalina is amazingly untouched. As I mentioned earlier, all roads are dirt roads in Two Harbors, which adds to its allure as a walking place.

An obvious walk is the stroll from the village center at Isthmus Cove to Catalina Harbor on the opposite side of the isthmus. You are only 50 feet above sea level on this 1/2-mile across slip of land. You'll go past a real "little red school house" on the way.

You will also go past one of the great follies of California's past: a military barracks built by Lincoln out of fear that the Confederate sympathizing miners on the island would try to disrupt California gold shipments. They didn't, and the soldiers were gone in a year. It is now a yacht club.

As far as animals on the island are concerned, there is a subspecies of the Channel Island Fox about the size of a house cat, wild boar, and, of course, the famous buffalo.

Fourteen buffalo arrived in 1924 for the filming of the movie version of the Zane Grey Western, *The Vanishing American*. They could not be rounded up when the movie was finished, and have been here ever since. The herd number about 450 now and are picturesque, but not considered safe to approach. Give them a nice wide berth if you come upon them; they are not as docile as they look.

Because I like walking the backcountry here so much, I would take a ferry to Avalon, then go overland to Two Harbors. This way, it makes it seem farther away, but if you are going to do any extended hiking, you need to get a permit at an office in town:

> **Los Angeles County Department of Parks and Recreation**
> **Island Plaza**
> **213 Catalina Street**
> **Avalon, CA 90704**
> **(310) 510-0688**

A trail map comes with the permit. Conveniently, right behind the Information Center is the tour bus terminal. The company whose buses will take you to the outback is:

> **Catalina Safari**
> **Box 5004-SG**
> **Two Harbors, CA 90704**
> **(310) 510-2800**

Catalina Safari offers numerous transportation services as well as tours. There are other companies that offer inland guided tours, but Catalina Safari runs what is in effect, the only shuttle service. Their naturalist guided tours focus on the Two Harbors area and can include tidepools, snorkeling, walking, or van tour excursions.

Another great way to get to Two Harbors for a romantic getaway is to bring your stuff in a backpack and take the bus most of the way, then hike in through the backcountry. Besides the incredible views along the way, it will add to the drama of your arrival.

Take the bus to **Little Harbor**. It is quite a scenic ride: you climb up a beautiful twisting drive past **Black Jack Campground**. This campground, the island's most popular, is unique in that it is at a 1,500-foot elevation and is shaded by eucalyptus and pine trees. It is named after Mount Black Jack, which also gave its name to an old mine that was here. From the right spot, you can get a surprising view of the mainland. Continue on to the aptly named **Airport In The Sky**.

This is one of the most romantic small airports in the Southland. There are beautiful hand painted tiles throughout its little tile roofed mountaintop building. They were made from red clay found on the island until 1938. It is fairly quiet too. In the 1920s and '30s there were two real airlines that flew into here, Wilmington Catalina Airlines, and Western Air Express, both out of Wilmington. Now there are a few shuttle aircraft, but most are private planes.

One of my favorite unknown romantic restaurants is the simple:

Runway Cafe
Airport In The Sky
Catalina Island
(310) 510-2196

This is a breakfast and lunch place whose most exotic culinary concoction is buffalo burgers. The lobby attached to it, however, has a classic stone fireplace and a tile patio with a mountain view that is stunning.

A little further on towards Little Harbor is the Wrigley's **El Rancho Escondito** Arabian horse ranch. They do impromptu shows for the visitors and will allow you to watch the horses working out.

The ride to Little Harbor takes about an hour and ten minutes. It is a very pretty place in and of itself. The campground here is certainly the best on the island. It has a rather lurid pirate history, but what is most interesting about it is that it is smack dab on top of a historic Native American site.

I grew up in Southern California with the image of the Southland of the past as a largely uninhabited desert with a few unhappy Indians scavenging for food here and there, who were "rescued" by the missionaries. Actually, there were quite a lot of them here, healthy and happy, with several distinct oral histories. They were all blown away quite expediently: most of them and their traditions have vanished so rapidly and thoroughly it is remarkable.

The tribe that originally inhabited this campground (and all of Catalina) were the "Gabrielinos." This name, the one in common usage, is not even their own. Many native American people were simply renamed to correspond to the closest mission. Sometimes several related, but somewhat separate groups would be put together under one name, as is the case here.

The Gabrielinos were named after Mission San Gabriel, and dwelled in an area from there to here. They shared a common aspect in their religion, which was a cult based partially around smoking jimsen weed. The ones on Catalina managed to also find a way to eat the Catalina Cherry. The last 30 of them on the island were removed in 1832.

If you are going on to Two Harbors from here, walk up Little Harbor Road as it rises and enters Little Springs Canyon. There are often quite a few buffalo in this area because there are two reservoirs here specifically for them. One of these, Lower Buffalo Reservoir, is where you veer to the left (it's unmarked), to Banning House Road.

Here you enter a canyon populated not by buffalo, but by wild boar. At the top of this canyon suddenly looms one of the most inspiring vistas in the Southland: a panorama that includes one of the best views of the twin harbors as well as both ends of the island. From here, you go down a steep slope and arrive in town.

It is amazing the contrast between the two ends of the island. Where Two Harbors can seem like a trip back in time to uninhabited California, Avalon has innumerable shops, hotels, and condos and looks like a Mediterranean resort. This quality has been enhanced by the fact that several cruise ships now anchor next to the yachts in the horseshoe-shaped harbor.

Avalon was christened in 1888 by the sister of one of its early developers, George Shatto. She named it after the island of blessed souls in Celtic mythology, referred to in Tennyson's *Idylls of the King*. Thus, "Lotus Land" was not the first Tennysonian reference to Southern California.

About one square mile in size, with a year round population of around 3,000, it is certainly a gorgeous town, with the hills rising in the background and the blue bay shimmering. The rows of palms and olive trees in planters along the length of its

ocean front boulevard, Crescent Avenue, are accented by the blaze of flowers surrounding them. The hours are tolled by a bell tower high on a hill overlooking the
bay.

Though they built their home at the other end, the Bannings established Avalon
as a summer resort in 1877—a city of tents and one hotel, the Metropole. The
original hotel is long since gone but there is a new one on the original site:

> **Hotel Metropole**
> **Crescent Avenue at Whitney**
> **P.O. Box 1900**
> **Avalon, CA 90704**
> **(310) 510-1884**

The new Hotel Metropole has 47 rooms, many of them ocean view. Eleven of
them have whirlpool baths, some of them have gas fireplaces and balconies. It has
its own little courtyard of shops, The Metropole Market Place, and Catalina's tiny
beach is directly across the street.

Avalon is full of shops selling T-shirts, post cards, sunscreen, and some out-of-
the-ordinary items. The most romantic and unusual store on the island is quite near
this hotel and features quite a different type of merchandise:

> **R. Franklin Pyke**
> **Bookseller and Artist, Custom Frames**
> **228 Metropole Avenue**
> **Avalon, CA 90704**
> **Tuesday-Sunday 10 a.m. to 5 p.m.**
> **(310) 510-2588**

Ron Pyke had a bookstore in Boulder, Colorado for 12 years, but was raised in
the Southland. This is definitely a store owned by an individual and not a cookie
cutter franchise because it combines a frame shop with a bookstore that has a unique
focus: antiquarian California. If you are interested in the background to some of the
Native American peoples of Southern California or if you'd like to purchase a historic book or map, Ron is the fellow to speak to. Rare Catalina tile and pottery, circa
1927-37, are also featured.

The town really became the center of things after the Bannings sold controlling
interest to William Wrigley, Jr., the chewing gum king, in 1919 for $2,000,000. This
was the same year he bought the Chicago Cubs. Though he planned for Avalon to
develop, he wanted to preserve the rest of the island. He got his wish: his son turned
over most of it in 1972 to the non-profit Catalina Conservancy. Fully 86 percent of
the island is protected.

Take a walk up the canyon and pay your respects to the old boy who made it possible at the:

Wrigley Memorial and Botanical Garden
1400 Avalon Caon Road
Avalon, CA 90704
Daily 8 a.m. to 5 p.m.
Admission: $1

This garden is a little less than 38 acres and was set out by Ralph Roth beginning in 1933. It displays indigenous plants and can be a nice way to learn about what you will see when you hike the backcountry.

The Wrigley Memorial is so large and impressive at the top of the hill you'd swear God must be buried there. Actually, Wrigley's remains aren't even here anymore. They were moved during WW II out of fear that the island would be bombed by the Japanese. It is a 138-foot high, gleaming white structure featuring a grand circular staircase with inserts of brilliant Catalina tile leading to a bell tower. The view of the harbor from the monument is wonderful, though it is kind of funny no one is buried in it.

There is a tram that takes you up to the memorial, but walking is much better. It is only a 1-1/2 miles from the center of town and you go past the delightful nine hole:

Catalina Island Golf Club
1 Country Club Drive
Santa Catalina, CA 90704
(310) 510-0530

The small course has a terrific view of the bay.

Wrigley actually bought the island as a place for the Cubs to practice and their field still remains at the Avalon end. He built his second home in the Southland here in 1921 on a hill overlooking the bay and angled it so he could watch the team playing on the practice field from his study.

The house is a somewhat boring, but stately Colonial style structure. This home is now a bed and breakfast and has the honor of having one of the best views in Southern California:

The Inn on Mount Ada
398 Wrigley Road
Santa Catalina, CA 90704
(310) 510-2030

With a million dollar restoration that included replacing the dark period furniture with a lighter, more summery decor, the feeling here is that of a Greek island villa. The old beveled windows and wood paneling and molding are original.

Since 1985, innkeepers Susie Griffin and Marleen McAdam have run this expensive, but unique four bedroom and two suite inn. Rates run from about $200 to $450 per night in January. In summer, they rise to $300 to $600.

They treat you very well here. Guests have the run of the dining room, living room, and club room, as well as the spectacular terrace and sun porch. There is coffee and juice by your door in the morning and a full breakfast in the dining room. During the day, they provide a light lunch and late afternoon hors d'oeuvres with wine.

Dinner is also included and would properly be called the most elegant and romantic on the island. It is so good that it often requires reservations even farther in advance than needed to stay here. The Inn on Mount Ada is somewhat secluded from the rest of Avalon so they give you a golf cart to tool around in.

Despite all of its amenities, what really is outstanding about the Inn on Mount Ada is the view of both the ocean and the harbor. The harbor really has the look of one you would find in the Mediterranean.

Directly across the bay from the inn is its landmark guardian:

Catalina Casino
1 Casino Way
Avalon, CA 90704
(310) 510-2414

Wrigley commissioned the architectural firm of Webber and Spaulding to create an imposing Casino with a movie theater on the first floor and a grand ballroom on the second. The Catalina Casino was completed in 1928 and presides majestically over the northeast side of Avalon Bay. It is an Art Deco Zigzag Moderne structure with Mediterranean influences of Moorish and Spanish.

Never used for gambling, it remains in use in much the same way it always has. In its heyday, there would have been over 3,000 people on its ballroom dance floor, listening to big bands that were being broadcast by radio across the U.S.A. They still have big band concerts here.

The movie theater, officially called the **Avalon Theater**, has been called the finest Art Deco cinema left in the United States. It was the world's first theater to be acoustically engineered for talking pictures. Samuel Goldwyn and Louis B. Mayer, and Cecil B. DeMille frequently came to Catalina by yacht to preview their latest movies.

It has wonderful, full color Art Deco murals depicting the history of the island. There are animals and some romanticized versions of Indians and Spanish missionaries. The theater's proscenium arch features Venus rising in triumph. Particularly appropriate are one of a bare breasted mermaid over the theater box office and two apparently early steroid-using surfers cresting a wave on the auditorium curtain.

The movie theater is active and features a giant theater organ complete with sound effects such as bird calls and automobile horns.

There is also a small museum in the Casino, called appropriately enough, the **Catalina Museum**. There is more about Catalina in the June and October chapters.

ANNIVERSARY OF EXECUTIVE ORDER 9066 (FEBRUARY 19)

February 19, 1942 was an important date in the history of the Southland. That was the date of the signing of Executive Order 9066, which authorized the rounding up and incarceration of all Japanese on the West Coast. They had until March 30 to surrender themselves for detention.

Two-thirds of those put in camps without being charged with any crime, without trial or due process, were native born American citizens. A large number had second generation businesses. As the ax fell, many struggled to sell assets or somehow salvage part of their lives. Most lost everything—a total of about $400,000,000 in real property and capital was simply gone.

Located in Inyo County, and technically outside the realm of this book, the place where many Japanese Americans were taken is a true Southern California landmark: **Manzanar.**

Though its name means "apple orchard" in Spanish, it was one of 10 quickly made prison camps where the 112,000 persons of Japanese descent were locked up. The internees were first held in temporary holding compounds at racetracks or fairgrounds, such as the Tulare County Fairgrounds. These were called "Assembly Centers." They were then transferred to the semi-permanent camps with their barbed wire and guard towers. Manzanar officially opened on April 25th of 1942 and held 10,000.

One of the ironies about this site, and what increases its significance for Southern California, is that it is in the Owens Valley, in the foothills of the Sierra Nevada Mountains, where Los Angeles gets most of its water. The camp's 600 acres are on the 250,000 acre property owned by the City of Los Angeles Department of Water and Power.

It is located 212 miles north of Los Angeles and can be reached by taking US 395 north. Manzanar is 9.6 miles past Lone Pine.

There is more about Japanese Southern California in January, March, August, November, and December

AFRICAN AMERICAN HISTORY

February is Black History Month (a.k.a. African American History Month). One place to start observance of the month is:

> **California Afro-American Museum**
> **600 State Drive**
> **Los Angeles, CA 90033**
> **Daily 10 a.m. to 5 p.m.**
> **(213) 744-7432**

The museum has a permanent collection of fine arts and historical items pertaining to the African American history and life experiences. There are also changing exhibits consisting of paintings, photographs, films, etc.

It surprises a lot of people to find out how much black history is woven into the history of Los Angeles. There were 22 original Mexican adult settlers who are given credit as being "the city's founders." Ten of them were black: escaped slaves with Spanish surnames (see September).

Two of the original 10 had excellent foresight in real estate and invested in a 4,500 acre ranch called "Rodeo de la Aguas," which means "meeting of the waters." The city of Beverly Hills now occupies the former ranch site, from which Rodeo Drive gets its name.

But the African American who may have left the greatest mark on the face of L.A. was native Angelino **Paul Williams**, a very successful architect who designed many very prominent homes and commercial buildings. His was a remarkable achievement. He was born in 1895 at Santee and 8th in Downtown L.A. His parents (who died when he was four) owned a grocery stand on Olvera Street. When he decided to become an architect while at Polytechnic High School, even his teachers tried to talk him out of it.

Architecture was considered a very genteel profession and the happening place for it at the time (where many of the jobs were) was the very genteel Pasadena. In 1915, at age 20, he managed to get a job working for a prestigious architect, Reginald Johnson (whose office was, in fact, in Pasadena). Then some time later, he was able to enroll in architecture studies at U.S.C.

He began working in the 1920s. After some small projects, his first big house came in 1922 for an old classmate from Cal Poly, businessman Louis Cass. It was a large home in the brand new "Flintridge" development founded by U. S. Senator Frank Flint.

As it turns out, Williams had known the Senator as a boy: he had sold newspapers to the lawmaker in front of the bank where his foster father, Charles Clarkson, worked as a janitor. Since commissions came almost exclusively from social connections in those days, what are called networking skills today were just as important back then. Thus, Williams designed a total of about 40 more homes in the same development.

Perhaps the biggest break for Williams came in 1930. Eccentric auto maker E. L. Cord was the first to really give him a shot. Williams was a bold fellow and drove out to the 10 acre site on North Hillcrest Road and worked all night to produce plans for an understated 30-room, red brick Neo-Colonial that had an 18-car garage. Cord was delighted.

A lot of prospective customers did not know he was black until he got there and Williams ability to schmooze often came into play if they balked when they saw him. Since many white people would have been uncomfortable sitting next to him, he learned to draw upside down, a skill eminently suitable for standing over someone in a chair or on a couch while explaining something to them.

Movie stars also played a big part in his success. Such notable as Lucille Ball and Desi Arnaz, Tyrone Power, Danny Thomas, Cary Grant, and even Frank Sinatra had homes designed by him and recommended him to their friends and connections.

The commercial buildings designed by Williams include:

Saks 5th Avenue Building
9600 Wilshire Boulevard
Beverly Hills, CA 90212

This is an elegant Regency Moderne building, built in 1937, in the heart of the richest shopping area in the Southland.

Three years later, another one of his buildings went up in Beverly Hills:

Litton Industries Building
360 North Crescent Drive
Beverly Hills

People driving around where Burton Way and Rexford Drive meet Crescent often wonder about this building, which looks like the capitol of one of the original 13 colonies. Properly called American Federal Revival, it is a stately columned affair enclosed with an equally impressive gate and west garden.

One of the most prominent buildings in Downtown L.A. is also a Williams:

Los Angeles County Courthouse
Hill and First Streets
[northwest corner]
Los Angeles

This is a very severe '50s Modern marble block of a building with no windows on the east side and a clock on the north face of the raised portion. It was built in 1958 and looks like it was designed to withstand a nuclear attack.

Williams' most famous contribution to the architecture of the Southland was recently honored as an "Historic Monument" and it is located at the airport.

Los Angeles International Airport began as a general flying field in 1925. It became Municipal Airport in 1928, but Clover Field in Santa Monica, and even Burbank and Glendale fields (because of their proximity to Pasadena) were more important. Expansion really began from 1959 to 1962 in a giant project by William Pereira and Associates, and it was during this period that the theme building, which Williams helped design, was built.

The **Los Angeles Airport Theme Building** is one of the most noticeable buildings in L.A. In many ways it is the world's greatest example of "Coffee Shop Modern" architecture. It is the flying saucer suspended atop 135-foot tall swooping spider-like legs that most people think is the control tower. Actually it houses **California Place Restaurant**, a bank, and a free observation deck where you can see nearly all of the planes taking off from 9 to 5 daily. Built in 1961, it perfectly epitomizes the spirit of hope in the future that was so strong under President John F. Kennedy and was manifested in the Los Angeles of the early '60s.

Another development where Williams left his mark in the '50s is west of Crenshaw Boulevard between Washington and Venice Boulevards: **Lafayette Square**, a tree-lined haven of beautiful homes. The humanized Modern style of Williams is well represented by three homes on St. Charles Place.

Near here, between Crenshaw and La Brea, is a landmark of Black culture in L.A.:

Ebony Showcase Theatre
4720 West Washington Boulevard
Los Angeles, CA 90016
(213) 936-1107

Founded by Nick and Edna Stewart in 1949, this theater is miraculously still being run by them. They feature such programs as a Wednesday jazz and blues night with food and no cover and a Champagne Sunday Brunch for only $12.95.

Right around the corner is a great little African restaurant:

Kukatonor African Restaurant
2616 Crenshaw Boulevard
Los Angeles, CA 90016
Daily 4 p.m. to 9 p.m.
(213) 733-3171

Kukatonor is filled with colors, sounds, and smells. It serves Liberian cuisine and the clientele is often Africans, who come dressed in beautifully patterned flowing robes. There are signs on the wall with grinning crocodiles pitching a beer from the Congo called Ngok. Flowers decorate each table.

There are some similarities between the different cuisines of Western Africa. Ethiopian food is centered around "injera," a kind of fermented tortilla that is used to scoop up stewed dishes called "wots." Liberian food uses a sort of paste called "fufu" that is made from crushed cassava root. It is less formed than injera and must actually be shaped by the diner into whatever figure it is going to be used for.

There are vegetable stews to dip it in, spicy peanut chicken to pick up with it, and chiles to hide in it. For dessert, the house special is a super sweet cobbler called "jubilee" made with nuts and fruit with toasted coconut on top.

But perhaps the epicenter of Black History in the Southland is to be found at the:

Dunbar Hotel and Museum
4225 South Central Avenue
Los Angeles, CA 90011

A black dentist and businessman named Dr. John Somerville, who moved to L.A. in the 1920s from the West Indies, had trouble finding a hotel that would allow blacks. In 1928, he build a hotel for African Americans called the Somerville. It was the first hotel to be built just for that purpose in the United States.

The property was purchased in 1933 by Lucius Lomax, who changed its name to The Dunbar in honor of the black poet Paul Lawrence Dunbar. His son, Lucius, Jr., and daughter-in-law, Almena, published the *Los Angeles Tribune* and had an office in the hotel.

The Dunbar was always an important gathering place. In the year it originally opened, it was the host of the National Association for the Advancement of Colored People's first national convention to be held on the West Coast. W.E.B. DuBois, Harvard's first black Ph.D. and the founder of the N.A.A.C.P., was a regular guest.

This was symbolic of the place that Central Avenue had in the history of Black America.

Beginning in the 1920s and peaking in a Golden Era in the '30s and '40s, Central Avenue was a rich artery in the bloodstream of American jazz. Starting where Little Tokyo is now, around San Pedro and First Streets, there was a place called Shep's Playhouse. The main strip was three or four miles long and began around 12th Street. By the time you got to 42nd, where the Dunbar is, the streets would be crowded with all manner of people. Former Mayor Tom Bradley walked this beat as a young policman. Watts was farmland in those days.

Right next door to the Dunbar was the Club Alabam. Founded by drummer and band leader Curtis Mosby in the early '20s, the Club Alabam boasted a huge dance floor, an 80-foot bar, and a spectacular show with a line of dancers just like New York's Cotton Club.

Beginning in the '50s, absolute barriers to African Americans began the slow, painful process of being brought down. A big first step was in 1952. That was the year that Buddy Collette became the first black musician to be hired for a high status regular position in Hollywood. Groucho Marx hired him to do "You Bet You Life," first on radio, then on televsion. In 1955, the white musician's union, Local 47, merged with the black musician's union, Local 767. In 1974, the Dunbar was declared a Los Angeles Historical Cultural Monument.

Though the area has obviously changed greatly, you can still get a taste of the past if you look. The neighborhood around Griffith Avenue near 22nd Street will recall the past with its Victorian homes and neighborhood stores. Near this intersection is a restaurant that has been there since 1950:

> **Reds Cafe**
> **1102 East 22nd Street**
> **Los Angeles, CA 90011**
> **Daily 7:30 a.m. to 4:30 p.m.**
> **(213) 745-9909**

This narrow storefront, with a U-shaped formica counter filling the room, is a pleasant island of the past and present. Besides the regular condiments, there are two kinds of hot sauce and a bottle of pepper vinegar by each place at the counter. A TV in the corner is always on.

The dinners are very large, like you would find on a farm in the rural South: fried chicken, meat and threes, pig's feet, oxtails, collard greens, black eyed peas, pinto beans, cabbage, tranchers of long-braised meat, and sweet potato pie—all served with big glasses of lemonade.

Four blocks west of Central on Broadway is what many consider to be the best barbecue in the Southland:

  Gadberry's Bar B Q
  5833 South Broadway
  Los Angeles, CA 90037
  Sunday-Thursday 11 a.m. to 10 p.m.
  Friday & Saturday 11 a.m. to 1 a.m.
  (213) 751-0753

Set back from the street, Gadberry's is located in a small building with a red and white striped awning. It has take out only. The take out window is set on a wall that could best be described as an unexpected sight. The wall is a life size, three dimensional recreation of a forest scene in green textured plaster. It is detailed with a large brown tree trunk and chirping birds. It is especially odd because the rest of the waiting room is as unadorned as the waiting room at an auto repair shop.

The menu is perfect for people who have trouble making up their minds. Beef ribs, pork ribs, hot links, beans, and potato salad.

There is more on African American Southern California in the September and December chapters.

NATIONAL DATE FESTIVAL

This month also contains one of the strangest agricultural festivals in the entire United States:

  The National Date Festival
  Desert ExpoCentre
  46-350 Arabia Street
  Indio, CA 92202
  February 12 through 24 from 10 a.m. to 10 p.m.
  Camel and Ostrich racing daily at 1 p.m.
  General admission: $5 (free if in Arabian nights costume)
  Seniors (62 and over): $4
  Children (5 to 11): $3, Children (under 5): free
  (619) 863-8236

Southern California has some of the most interesting and beautiful desert ecosystems in the world. Within the expansive Colorado Desert is the **Coachella Valley,** about 2-1/2 hours east on Highway 10 from Los Angeles. This area includes the resort cities of Palm Desert and Palm Springs.

The National Date Festival Camel Races, Indio.

Indio is the oldest and second largest city in the Coachella Valley. Algerian date palms were introduced in 1890 and now the area amazingly produces 95 percent of the dates grown in the United States.

The whole area has a kind of California take on the Middle East, sort of like the old Bob Hope *Road To Morocco*. As a matter of fact, this festival dates from 1946. It features a weird mixture of exhibits of arts and crafts, fine arts and photography with agricultural products and flowers. There are also livestock shows and carnival games such as you would find at a county fair—except at this one it is all with a backdrop of an Arabian Nights theme. There are camel and ostrich races, camel and elephant rides, and a pageant featuring "Queen Scheherazade" and princesses.

The most poetic statement of the fair's blend of Middle America county fair and Middle East kitsch is that the **Arabian Nights Parade** in downtown Indio is followed by the Lion's Club pancake breakfast.

A long established date farm is:

> **Oasis Date Garden**
> **59-111 Highway 111**
> **P.O. Box 757**
> **Thermal, CA 92274**
> **(800) 827-8017**

Owned by Ben Laflin and his wife Pat and managed by Pat's sister, Virginia, this 250 acre oasis was started by Ben's father in 1912. This orchard has a particularly dramatic history to go along with its star product, the Medjhool date.

Ninety-eight percent of the world's dates come from the Middle East where plants of the delicate Medjhool were guarded. During the French war in Algeria, a blight struck the Medjhools. A search was carried out to find unaffected plants. Finally, eleven were discovered in a remote oasis by a plant pathologist named Dr. Walter T. Swingle.

They were spirited to America in 1927 and planted on an Indian Reservation in Southern Nevada. Two died, but the nine that survived produced 72 offshoots that were brought to Indio in 1936. Twenty four of them ended up here. Ben Laflin and his son Ben, Jr. are now recognized as among the world's premier growers of the finicky variety. They planted another 40 acres of them in 1990.

The Medjhool and other dates are offered by mail order and through their large retail store. They also have a picnic area and a petting zoo on weekends.

Indio has lots of motels, but the most romantic place to stay is nearby in La Quinta:

La Quinta Hotel Golf and Tennis Resort
49-499 Eisenhower Drive
La Quinta, CA 92253
(619) 564-4111

Originally opened as a 56 room hostelry in 1926, the La Quinta Hotel was designed by famed architect Gordon Kaufman, who also created the mammoth Times-Mirror Building in Downtown L.A. among other landmarks. This somewhat more modest project cost a mere $150,000 to build.

The further development of this property shows how corrupted the concept of "a judicious use of land" can become. This simple compound of a main hacienda surrounded by a few little blue trimmed, red tile roofed casitas was placed on 1,400 acres in the early 1920s by its owner, San Francisco businessman Walter H. Morgan. In 1988, a $45 million "revamping" added a whopping 584 rooms. Though most of the place is obviously "'80s new," some of the original charm remains.

From the beginning, it was a hideaway for Hollywood. Its geographic location makes it a natural for this: La Quinta is tucked into a "cove" of rocks at the base of the Santa Rosa Mountains and not only feels secluded, it is not bothered by the winds that have caused wind turbines to sprout across the rest of the desert.

Greta Garbo was here, as was Irving Berlin. It is part of the mythology of the place that Irving Berlin was so overwhelmed by the heat here that he wrote "White Christmas" out of nostalgia for winter. Errol Flynn, Dolores Del Rio, Ronald Coleman—the list of its celebrity regulars is dazzling.

Perhaps its most famous filmland connection began in the 1930s when it became the personal *Shangri-La* of Frank Capra. He wrote *It Happened One Night* and *Lady For A Day* here. His personal fantasy became reality in 1939 when he and screen-writer Robert Riskin holed up in a casita to write the script for *Lost Horizon*. Just as many classic movie palaces have been divided into multiple screen auditoriums,

Capra's favorite casita has been divided into three rooms that range from $75 to $220. Your view won't be as good as his was. As he sat on his porch, he would have looked upon a plowed field, a grove of trees, and a broad expanse of sand leading up to the Santa Rosa Mountains.

Though it is still a nice place, it must have been hauntingly beautiful in its early days. The Cahuilla Indians revered it as holy ground. There is believed to be a village and burial ground for 1,000, containing priceless artifacts and clues regarding early California life. In another low blow rendered on the Southland by developers, efforts to slow the destruction of the area failed and the bulldozers had their way again. Developers are supposed to stop digging and report any discoveries.

The mountains are still there, and if you have never seen a desert sunset against this range, you are missing something. The view from La Quinta over the various structures that have been erected is still lovely as the peaks glow a soft pink when the sun is on the horizon.

Tennis is big here, with 30 grass, clay, and hard courts and a famous tournament. There are also 24 swimming pools and 30 jacuzzis. Sunday brunch is a La Quinta tradition.

But for romantic desert settings, the best is the:

Thousand Palms Oasis
Coachella Valley Preserve
P.O. Box 188
Thousand Palms, CA 92276
(619) 343-1234

This is the second largest fan palm oasis in California. It was the movie set in 1924 for *King of Kings,* the most famous of Cecil B. DeMille's silent epic films. Over 40 years later in 1969, it would be used for *Tell Them Willie Boy Is Here,* starring Robert Blake, Katherine Ross, and Robert Redford.

The visitor's center building was originally called "Palm House" and it was the main building of a turn of the century ranch owned by Louis Wilhelm. It could have easily ended up being bulldozed for development along with the rest of the surrounding land, but in 1986, Congress, the U.S. Bureau of Land Management, the U.S. Wildlife Service, the California Department of Fish and Game, and the Nature Conservancy all got together and established a 13,000 acre preserve at a cost of $25,000,000.

This was not done just because it is a beautiful place containing a lot of flora and fauna that is fast disappearing from the area; it was done to protect an endangered species: *Uma inornata,* the Coachella Valley Fringe Toed Lizard.

<u>MARCH</u>

Spring

Persian New Year

Spring Equinox Party

Academy Awards

Santa Barbara Film Festival

Koi Festival (Gardena)

Blessing of the Animals

Blessing of the Cars

Feast of the Annunciation

Chapter Three

MARCH

March was named after Mars, the Roman god of war and agriculture. There is truly some of both in the spring fever we all feel that begins in this month. Spring appears after what passed for winter in the Southland and while we may not be digging our way out of the snow, there is certainly something in the air besides smog. Spring brings a feeling of energy, with the official first day coming on the 21st, which is also the "vernal equinox."

There are four key yearly points in the earth's position during its annual orbit, vis-a-vis its tilt toward or away from the sun: two **solstices**, summer, on June 22, and winter, on December 21, and two **equinoxes**, spring (vernal) on March 21, and fall (autumnal) on September 22.

The earth is exactly in balance on the equinoxes: the equator is directly opposite the sun and night and day are of exactly equal length all over the globe. The earth is on its most extreme tilt on the solstices.

During the winter solstice, it is tilted away from the sun in the northern hemisphere; and during the summer, it is tilted towards it. These dates not only correspond to points in the relative tilt of the earth, they also are the official change of season dates.

The reason I am bringing all of this up is that I have never understood it when people tell me there are no seasons in Southern California. There is a change of season that you can feel if you are sensitive to it.

SPRING
Swallows Come Back to Capistrano

We have a natural signal for the beginning of spring in the Southland that has been celebrated ad nauseam in story and song. Two days before the first day of spring, on March 19, St. Joseph's Day, *petrochelidon pyrrhonota,* cliff swallows, do indeed "return to Capistrano" and build their mud nests in the broken arches of:

> **Mission San Juan Capistrano**
> **Camino Capistrano and Ortega Highway**
> **[two blocks west of SR74, one block off I-5]**
> **San Juan Capistrano, CA 92675**
> **Daily 8:30 a.m. to 5 p.m.**
> **(714) 493-1424 or (714) 248-2048**

So what if the swift-flying birds are showing a preference for freeway over-passes in recent times, a few of them still come here too. This mission is the most graceful and evocatively beautiful ruin in Southern California. Founded in 1776, it became the first center of winemaking in the state until the 1840s. During this time, it prospered and outgrew its original adobe.

In 1796, what would turn out to be a nine year construction project began on a cruciform, 108-by-40 foot cathedral with seven domes and a 120-foot belltower. Six years after its completion on December 8, 1811, immediately following an early morning service, the church bells tolled madly in a prelude to a thunderous earth-quake, which devastated the relatively new cathedral and killed the 42 people in-side.

The sanctuary and the original adobe church, Serra Chapel, which is believed to be the oldest operating in California, survived intact. The lovely gardens and ruins seem to work together in unity to create a mood of absolute tranquility. The mission receives a lot of visitors and a lot of attention is given to keeping it up.

As part of a project to recreate the feel of early mission life, they have brought winemaking back after a hiatus of a century and a half, and have planted 14 authen-tic Spanish "criolla" grape vines. With the corn, tomatoes, squash, and peppers that have been planted together along with roses and other flowers, the place has a real feeling of being alive, despite the vestiges of tanning vats, the jail, kitchen, and padre's sleeping quarters.

With its eery beauty and gruesome past, it is only natural that San Juan Capistrano would also be one of the most haunted of the Southern California mis-sions. The mission's graveyard was investigated by the paranormal research team, Psychic Science Investigators, who taped strange voices there. In addition to the voices in the cemetery, there is a ghostly monk who paces the inside courtyard. His stare is supposed to be lethal, unlike the lack of expression of the headless soldier who walks a lonely watch on the grounds.

The most famous ghost is **Magdalena**. She was a beautiful young woman who had been caught in a secret love affair and she was ordered to do penance by carry-ing a candle around the mission grounds for one day—the day of the great earth-quake.

She also seems to have had the worst timing in history: she happened to be passing through the cathedral when the earthquake hit and she was killed when the building collapsed. Now the sad face of her spirit, lit by candlelight, can be seen in certain windows of the ruins.

If the presence of all of these specters whets your appetite, right across the street from the mission is a place to grab a bite:

Cafe Capistrano
31752 Camino Capistrano
San Juan Capistrano, CA 92675
Daily 7 a.m. to 4 p.m.
(714) 493-0607

Though there are Mexican entrees on the menu here, this place is more like the All-American diner—before they were rediscovered and made into such stylized eateries as Johnny Rockets. The specialty here is hamburgers.

A more appropriate but slightly more expensive choice is a short walk away:

El Adobe De Capistrano Restaurant
31891 Camino Capistrano
San Juan Capistrano, CA 92675
Sunday-Thursday 11 a.m. to 10 p.m.
Friday & Saturday 11 a.m. to 11 p.m.
(714) 493-1163

Though this restaurant is old by restaurant standards, having opened on July 8, 1948, the site itself is even older. The property combines two historic sites: the Miguel Yorba Adobe and the Juzgado (jail and courthouse.) The walls of the cocktail lounge were part of the adobe, built in 1797. The wine cellar was made from the cells of the jailhouse and dates from 1812.

This restaurant celebrates the food of early California. They are open for lunch and dinner and can get extremely busy—particularly around swallow time. Nixon loved this place and came here often, especially while in office.

El Adobe De Capistrano is owned by Richard O'Neill, the scion of an old Orange County family who still holds 40,000-acre Rancho Mission Viejo, the largest operating cattle ranch in Southern California. His grandfather was a silver miner named James Flood who purchased the original 200,000 acres in 1882.

Rancho Mission Viejo is roughly split in two by State Highway 74. While many streets and highways have been celebrated in legend and song (Sunset and Hollywood Boulevards, Route 66, and Pacific Coast Highway are just a few of the Southland's famous drives), in many ways, the real road that tells the story of Southern California is this one that begins on the coast not too far from the mission.

It starts by rising from the ocean coast at a diagonal and winds through Orange County to Lake Elsinor. This first part is called **Ortega Highway** after Sergeant

Jose Francisco Ortega, who was a scout for Portola when he passed through here in 1769. It actually follows an ancient passageway through the Santa Ana Mountains called the Juaneno Indian Trail.

Once out of Orange County, it straightens out and runs past Hemet (see April) to the beautiful mountain area of Idyllwild (see May), and then finishes in spectacular fashion by descending to Palm Desert as the **Palms To Pines Highway** (see later this month.) On its way through Orange County, it passes by some of the most romantic spring places in the whole 742 square mile county.

Looking at the endless tract houses that seem to cover every square inch of the foothills of southern Orange County's coast, it is hard to believe that there is any place left to enjoy springtime near here, but there is. Orange County does have a few places that have managed to be preserved, but only because environmentalists fought for every inch. One of these is:

> **Ronald W. Casper's Wilderness Park**
> **33401 Ortega Highway**
> **San Juan Capistrano, CA 92675**
> **Must be over 18**
> **(714) 831-2174**

This is one of three Orange County regional parks that allows camping. It encompasses 7,596 acres. There are six campsites and six self-guiding nature trails of a total length of about 12 miles. It has had some bad times because of two mountain lion attacks that resulted in big lawsuits and restricted public use. Though this sort of thing rarely happens, it is the inevitable result of too-close development outside of a wilderness area indirectly causing damage to the wilderness area's food chain.

The indigenous residents of this area were the Juaneno Indians. They enjoyed the area's canyons and vistas and most especially its hot springs. The mission's fathers are also said to have enjoyed soaking in these sulphurous waters, which are located 13 miles from the mission, right on the highway.

Continuing along Ortega Highway, you can stop and check out one of the easiest-to-see spring waterfalls. It is just a little over 19 miles east of the I-5 (San Diego Freeway), on the **San Juan Loop Trail**. Watch for the Ortega Oaks Store; the parking lot is directly across from it. At the east end of the lot, you will see the sign announcing the trail.

This trail is certainly most people's idea of a nice easy one hour walk. It is a perfect length (about two miles) with a change in elevation of only about 350 feet. It is also a "loop," meaning you end up where you started. Constructed in the 1970s, along with the connecting Chiquito Trail, it is maintained cooperatively between the U.S. Forest Service and Orange County.

You start going somewhat uphill, looking down at the highway, then veer left and start moving down a gorge. You will hear the sound of the waterfall. A little side trail will take you to a very romantic spot. Right here, in the heart of Orange County, set among the granite rocks as if placed there by a landscape architect, is a tranquil reflecting pool. This is the water that collects to form the falls that cascade nearby.

After pausing at the falls, continue down the switchbacking trail. You'll pass through chaparral and end up in the prettiest remaining oak woodlands in the Santa Ana mountains. This flat terrain is the bed of the San Juan Creek.

The Chiquito Trail turns north from here and cuts across the creek. The San Juan Loop Trail continues to the left and goes through Bear Canyon. You really feel like you are in an ancient oak forest, undestroyed by man. The ground underneath the sprawling canopy is thick with vegetation.

The last leg of the loop, up and out of the gorge, takes you back to the parking lot and follows along a hillside that should be covered with wildflowers this time of year.

Wildflowers

Spring begins early in the Southland in numerous subtle ways, but none is more beautiful than the wildflowers of the desert. The spring wildflower show in Southern California takes place in stages. It starts in the low desert in February and early March and proceeds to the middle and higher deserts in April and on to the meadowlands in the mountains in May.

If you would like to locate some wildflower areas, the first thing to do is call the **Wildflower Information Hot Line** at (818) 768-3533. Updated weekly, this is a 24-hours-a-day recording of the best places to enjoy wildflowers that are within a day's drive of Los Angeles. Such areas as the Anza-Borrego Desert State Park, Joshua Tree National Monument, Antelope Valley, Santa Clarita Woodlands, The Santa Monica Mountains Park, and some others, are covered. The recording is amazingly detailed and helpful. It is a service of the:

> **Theodore Payne Foundation for Wild Flowers**
> **and Native Plants**
> **10459 Tuxford Street**
> **Sun Valley, CA 91352**
> **Tuesday-Sunday 8:30 a.m. to 4:30, closed Monday**
> **(818) 768-1802**

This wonderful organization was founded to advance education, conservation, and promotion of California native plants. Its namesake came here from England in 1893. Quite the famous horticulturist, one of his first projects was the garden of Shakespearian actress Madame Helena Modjeska, who briefly lived in Orange County.

The story goes that one day Payne saw a wild matilija poppy plant in flower. In bloom from the end of April to June in hilly places like Malibu Creek State Park and just above the Ojai Valley, and accented by an orange yellow center and sweet fragrance, the white petals of this flower spread out three to four inches across.

The gardener was struck by the flower's beauty and tried to grow these poppies in his garden. It was with great difficulty that he finally succeeded, which naturally heightened his interest in other native Southern California plants. He opened a nursery on Broadway in Los Angeles and in 1915 staged the first show of California native plants in Exposition Park. From the 1930s to the 1950s, he did the gardens at many famous homes.

Besides the wonderful "flower hill" right behind the Foundation's headquarters—five acres of native flowers that are watered in winter and left dry in summer—there is also a gift shop that sells maps and books.

Early Spring Flowers in the Lower Desert

The California lower desert, the **Colorado Desert**, is truly beautiful this time of year. A good place to get close to the beauty of the dessert is at the largest state park in the 48 states, the 600,000-acre **Anza-Borrego Desert State Park**. To put this into perspective, the park is two-thirds the size of the state of Rhode Island.

Obviously, that is an enormous area, encompassing some very unusual terrain that is the result of both pressure from earthquake faults (such as the San Andreas) and flooding from what was the ancient Gulf of California.

It was named for Juan Autista de Anza, who came through this area in 1774, and for borrego (sheep). This was not to imply any lurid connection between the Spanish explorer and four hoofed mammals, but because the rare desert bighorn lives here.

The park has designated campsites, but it is the only park in the state system where you can also park anywhere along the road. There are about 100 miles of scenic highway that are paved, and about 500 that are dirt.

The lower desert can be a rainbow of colors in early spring. One of the most prominent of the wonderfully odd California desert plants is the spindly **ocotillo**.

Towering to a height of 10 feet and looking like a giant spider, it has brilliant scarlet blossoms that some people think look like lipstick hanging languidly off the tips of its legs.

During this month, the flat, sandy ares of Borrego Valley will be covered with a magic carpet of clumps of tiny reddish-purple blossoms of **sand verbena**, a trailing plant with stems up to three-feet long. Mixed in will be splashes of white blossomed **desert primrose** with their larger paper-thin petals, like Japanese origami. Some of the flowers of the lower desert are so small and so near the ground that they are called "belly flowers," because that is the best position to view them from.

If you want to learn something about the flora, fauna, and geology of the area, one of the most interesting visitor's centers at any park in the state is here:

> **Anza-Borrego Desert Visitor Center**
> **Palm Canyon Drive just west of County Road S22**
> **Borrego Springs, CA 92004**
> **October-May: Daily 9 a.m. to 5 p.m.**
> **June-September: Saturday & Sunday 9 a.m. to 5 p.m.**
> **(619) 767-5311**

Constructed of indigenous desert stone and set into a hillside, this is one building that does not intrude upon the landscape. The roof is covered with local desert soil. The imposing carved front doors always make me feel as if I were entering a temple of some lost civilization once buried beneath the shifting sands.

This feeling is enhanced by the huge bronze door handle renderings of the bighorn sheep native to this area. The visitor's center is surrounded by gardens of local plants and the pond in front contains the nearly extinct pupfish. Every half hour, there is a 24-minute slide show.

From here, I would walk about a mile north to the **Borrego Palm Canyon Campgrounds**. The wide alluvial fan at the entrance to the canyon gets narrower as the sheer rock walls start closing in, finally leaving only enough room for the trail and the stream. It is a nice easy walk of about 1-1/2 miles through some pretty desolate terrain until you come to the first grove of about 200 palm trees.

Just past the palms, suddenly you'll feel moisture in the air from the waterfall crashing on top of some gigantic boulders. This is a popular picnic area for good reason—it is quite lovely. The upper canyon contains more palm groves.

Borrego Palm Canyon is the third largest palm oasis in the state. It fits most people's image of the beautiful desert oasis, hidden away in a stunning v-shaped rocky gorge. When you see it, you'll see why it was selected as the first site for a desert state park back in the 1920s.

Many people who see a palm oasis become enthralled with the graceful tree. Since pulling is a no no while you are in Borrego Springs, you might want to stop by:

Ellis Farms
1325 Borrego Valley Road
P.O. Box 961
Borrego Springs, CA 92004
Daily 7 a.m. to 4 p.m.
(800) 826-3993
(619) 767-5234

This desert specialty nursery features over 300 acres of desert trees, including *Washingtonia robusta* and *filifera fan* palms and date palms. It is the largest palm tree growing facility in Southern California. Owner Joe Ellis has been here in the same location since 1969.

Joe is quite a figure in the palm world. They called him when they needed palm trees for the World Financial Center in New York City—a total of 16, each 45-feet tall. His trees have also been replanted in Tokyo and even as far away as Kuwait.

There is a mystique to palm trees, so much so that they are associated with romantic images to no end. Dedicated to this wonder is the International Palm Society, P.O. Box 368, Lawrence, KS 66044. Membership only costs $10.

The town of **Borrego Springs** is quite small, about 3,000 residents. "Like Palm Springs used to be," is a familiar refrain you'll hear a lot. It is the focal point of the Anza-Borrego Desert for more reasons than just the fact that it is the largest town: all of the highways meet here in a place called Christmas Circle.

For lodging, it has several motels and one celebrated romantic resort:

La Casa Del Zorro Resort Hotel
3845 Yaqui Pass Road
P.O. Box 127
Borrego Springs, CA 92004
(619) 767-5323
(800) 824-1884 (CA)
(800) 325-8274

La Casa Del Zorro started as an adobe ranch house in 1937. They have 77 rooms, suites, and villas at this unpretentious desert retreat. The grounds are beautifully landscaped with groves of willowy tamarisk trees providing shade. The villas have either two or three bedrooms, and some even have private pools.

Though it is a casual place, the hotel has an evening dress code that requires jackets in the **Presidio** restaurant. The **Butterfield** is the breakfast, lunch, and dinner room. Both are decorated with paintings of frontier California.

Borrego Springs even has a Chinese restaurant:

Chinese Panda Cafe
818 Palm Canyon Drive
Borrego Springs, CA 92004
Tuesday-Sunday 11:30 a.m. to 9 p.m.
Closed Monday
(619) 767-3182

Located in genuine WW II-vintage quonset huts, this quality Szechuan and Mandarin style Chinese restaurant is a surprising contrast as you enter its pretty pink interior. The food is good and those of you who are intimidated by Chinese restaurants that serve dishes you may have never heard of will breath a sigh of relief when you see the menu.

The Anza-Borrego Desert has many attractions besides wildflowers. One of them is the:

Agua Caliente Hot Springs
County Road S2
(619) 565-3600

One of several faults that passes through the Anza-Borrego area, the Elsinore Fault, continues about 70 miles northeast to the lake (where there are also hot springs). Mineral heavy, 98-degree fahrenheit water bubbles up to the surface in the upwellings caused by the fault-induced fractures.

Of course, there are hot springs in many parts of the Colorado Desert. It is a vast region which includes both the Anza-Borrego area and the Palm Springs area. Both localities share some of the same remarkable natural history that causes a person to think twice about what a desert really is.

Two years after first coming upon the wide-open space that would later become the Anza-Borrego, Juan de Anza was working his way through the Colorado Desert somewhat northeast of there. He came upon some desert Indians kicking back in a hot springs. Clever Spaniard that he was, he named them the "Agua Caliente" or "hot water Indians."

In 1871, these Indians started the first commercial bathhouse, with two pools separated by a wooden fence. The price for a mineral bath then was 25 cents.

These waters have been celebrated for their curative powers by visitors ever since. The mineral springs here are rich in iron, magnesium, and zinc and are hotter than the one in the Anza-Borrego: they come out of the ground at about 105 degrees.

There are three ways to "take the waters." There is an outdoor pool that is open during daylight hours; a huge indoor jacuzzi with added heat that is open only 9 a.m. to 3 p.m.; and a cold plunge called the "Indian Pool" that never closes.

Over the years, there have been many changes. Building a bridge from the past to the present, an annual festival increases awareness of the indigenous peoples:

> **Agua Caliente Heritage Fiesta**
> **Agua Caliente Indian Reservation**
> **Palm Canyon Drive**
> **[four miles south of Palm Springs]**
> **Fiesta usually last weekend in March**
> **(619) 778-1079**

This festival is a celebration of Native American, Mexican, and Western cultures. It is held in the large parking lot of Palm Canyon by the trading post that sells refreshments and souvenirs. There are arts and crafts, music, and nature walks. The proceeds benefit the Agua Caliente Cultural Museum.

There are only about 265 "hot water Indians" left, but because of their relative isolation, they have actually fared better than most Native Americans. It wasn't until 1850, when American explorers discovered the San Gorgonio Pass, that their existence was really threatened.

The U.S. government, seeking to hasten the development of the transcontinental railroad, split up the land between the Indians and the railroad. It was divided into one mile square sections, with the even numbered sections going to the Indians and the odd numbered going to the railroads. The most famous of these is Section 14, which is downtown Palm Springs.

A full 31,127 acres of the Palm Springs area is reservation, primarily in relatively undisturbed condition. The most wonderful springtime experience in Palm Springs hearkens back to why its original residents liked it here so much, the **Agua Caliente Indian Canyons**. There are five canyons: **Chino, Tahquitz, Palm, Andreas,** and **Murray**. The festival is located at the entrance to the largest of these, Palm Canyon.

It was called "La Palma de la Mano de Dios" by the Spanish conquerors which means "the Hollow of God's Hand." Palm Canyon is a kind of sacred place in the Southland, not just to the indigenous people of the area, but because it contains the largest grove of California's only native palm, the *Washingtonia*.

The stands of these palms are very dramatic and beautiful There are vantage points on the rim or you can hike in to the oasis and Seven Pools. The road that leads up to the rim finishes in a 1/2 mile winding narrow passage that is right out of an *Indiana Jones* movie.

The smaller, Andreas Canyon, is even more like the classic movie oasis: a lush landscape fed by a pretty little stream. Not only are there *Washingtonia* palms, there are Indian caves and giant grinding stones used by the Agua Calientes, as well as some unusual rock formations. There is one large rock called "Gossip Rock," because women used to gather there not only to grind meal, but to discuss the various issues of the tribe.

But the most remarkable rock formations are those in the smallest of the three most accessible canyons, Murray Canyon. It is a little harder to get into, but you will be rewarded with some pleasantly weird mortar holes, caves, and looming rock towers.

Chino Canyon is occupied by the Palm Springs Aerial Tramway and Tahquitz requires a permit to enter.

A wonderful way to experience the canyons is on horseback. The trails are somewhat apart from the footpaths, so the perspective is really different. To get this feel of the Old West, the place to go is:

> **Smoke Tree Stables**
> **2500 Toledo Avenue**
> **Palm Springs, CA 92264**
> **Summer: Daily 8 a.m. to 12 p.m.**
> **Winter: Daily 8 a.m. to 5 p.m.**
> **(619) 327-1372**

For a mere $25 per person per hour, you can take a trip back in time on a four hour luncheon picnic ride into Murray Canyon. When the temperature is right, at that perfect point it can hit in the California desert this time of year, this can be one of the truly great Southern California experiences of springtime.

Besides its natural features, Palm Springs is, of course, a resort city. It is doubtful that the early residents would recognize the spot where the first mineral bath was located:

> **Spa Hotel and Mineral Springs**
> **100 North Indian Canyon Drive**
> **Palm Springs, CA 92262**
> **(619) 325-1461**

The Spa Hotel and Mineral Springs was originally built in 1963 by a leassee of the property. It was purchased by the tribe in 1992 and closed for renovation. After a $9 million face lift , it reopened on December 15, 1993.

The Spa is large (five stories, 230 rooms) in a city of mainly small "hotels" (you can't use the word "motel" here). All of the newer, larger resort properties are farther out of town. Despite the remodel, it still has an early '60s look.

Even if you weren't going to stay here, it still is the place to come to "take the waters." They accommodate every way to heat and soak the human body short of boiling it in oil: there are two outdoor mineral spring water pools with whirlpool jets; a large regular hotel pool; a 100 degree Eucalyptus inhalation room; a 150 degree sauna; and a steamroom. They offer various packages, but the $30 one that includes a 1/2 hour massage is a real deal.

On Palm Spring's namesake street is one of the city's more pleasant little attractions:

Moorten's Botanical Gardens
1701 South Palm Canyon Drive
Palm Springs, CA 92264
Monday-Saturday 9 a.m. to 4:30 p.m.
Sunday 10 a.m. to 4 p.m.
(619) 327-6555

Arranged into regional sections on four acres are more than 2,000 varieties of cactus, succulents, and other desert plants from around the world. There are little desert creatures such as chipmunks and rabbits scurrying around rock displays. The high point of this diverse collection is a real dinosaur footprint.

If you wanted to actually stay in a garden, not too far from here is an absolutely lovely place:

Villa Royale Country Inn
1620 South Indian Trail
Palm Springs, CA 92264
(619) 327-2314

Spread out on 3-1/2 lushly landscaped acres are 31 distinctly different rooms, studios, suites and mini villas. They are arranged around three main courtyards that are surrounded by bougainvillea draped patios framed by pillars, brick paths, fountains, pools, and even streams.

Each room is decorated to evoke a particular country. This includes a room with a Bavarian theme that has a cuckoo clock and beer steins and a room with a Spanish theme that has leather chairs and a heavy antique wooden cupboard. The patios of some of them are also landscaped with flora from the theme country. You can also get rooms with features such as a wood burning fireplace, a spa, a kitchen, and even a private swimming pool.

This is a delightful place to awaken to on a clear desert morning in the spring. Included with your stay is a buffet breakfast of fresh juice, fruit, and home baked muffins. It is served either on the poolside patio or in the romantic sun porch with its tiffany lamps, brick colored floor tiles, and beamed ceiling.

The amenities are very complete and include two swimming pools and jacuzzis, plus complimentary bicycles to borrow (There are miles of very good bike trails in Palm Springs).

Some of the drama in the visual aspects of the place can be explained by the fact that the owner, Chuck Murawski, is a Broadway lighting designer. He has also designed sets and lighting for television shows such as "Gimme a Break," "Maude," and "Different Strokes." Chuck and his partner spent six years in Europe collecting the beautiful antique furnishings for the Inn.

Literally right around the corner from here is a wonderful place to spend a few leisurely hours enjoying a spring day in the Colorado Desert:

> **The Living Desert**
> **47-900 Portola Avenue**
> **Palm Desert, CA 92260**
> **September 1-June 15: Daily 9 a.m. to 5 p.m.**
> **(619) 346-5694**

This delightful preserve is a full 1,000 acres of protected California desert. There are enclosures with lizards, tortoises, hawks, owls, and even bighorn sheep. The walk-through aviary houses desert birds such as doves, quail, roadrunners, and hummingbirds. California dessert flora abounds. Besides the indigenous plants on display in natural settings, plants from foreign lands have been transplanted to recreate the different deserts of the world.

One of the most unusual exhibits is the "Desert at Night" room. In the darkness, you can observe the nocturnal activity of desert animals. This is located inside the Pearl McManus Center, right next to the entrance, along with the small live animal exhibits.

There are more than six miles of well-marked, self-guided trails. The trailheads are arranged so you can choose from several different length walks from the very short to the more involved.

Spring in the San Gabriel Mountain Foothills, Annual Party for the World's Largest Flowering Plant

This month, spring manifests itself in so many phenomenal ways in the Southland. A more obscure destination in March is an annual garden party in **Sierra Madre** given to celebrate the blooming of the official "World's Largest Flowering Plant:"

> **Wisteria Fete**
> **Sierra Madre Wisteria Vine**
> **500 Block North Hermosa Avenue**
> **Sierra Madre**
> **normally second weekend of the month**
> **(818) 793-0189**

In 1894, William and Alice Brugman purchased a one gallon container of wisteria vine from a Monrovia nursery for 75 cents. Little did they realize what they were doing as they planted it on their property. Twenty four years later, it had grown so large that they had a public showing, and 12,000 people showed up.

The town adopted the plant as its own and was soon called "Wisteria City." A drawing of the plant is engraved on the city seal, and even today, the word "wisteria" appears in the names of many Sierra Madre businesses.

Certainly, the people who own the property where the vine grows have had their share of adaptations to make. In 1932, the original house collapsed from the weight of it. The new home has been owned by the same people since 1962, Joseph and Maria Feeney.

Each year, they invite the public to come and view the vine in full flower. The local schools, merchants, and clubs set up booths on a little side street called Kersting Court while a shuttle bus takes people over to the viewing area for $2. The lavender flowers cover over an acre and weigh about 300 tons. A trellis of two inch pipes provides support for the vine.

While you are in Sierra Madre, go a little ways west on Carter Avenue to where it ends at Oak Crest Drive. Turn right up the hill and you will come to one of the more unusual homes in Southern California:

> **Pyramid House**
> **751 Oak Crest Drive**
> **Sierra Madre, CA 91024**

This stunning glass pyramid was built to the same specifications as the Pyramid of Cheops, circa 2680 B.C. Construction began on this one acre site in 1972 and the structure was completed in 1976, during a period when the belief in "pyramid power" was quite pervasive in the Southland. The architect was the late John G. McInney.

Of course, Sierra Madre is also the gateway to **Mount Wilson**. From the Pyramid House, it is only a few blocks over to Baldwin and Mira Monte Avenues, which is the main entrance to the Mount Wilson Trail.

For all of its fame, Mount Wilson is not a very tall mountain at 5,700-foot even compared to other Southern California mountains such as Mt. San Jacinto (10,084-foot) or the tallest in the area, Mt. San Gorgonio (11,499). It is, however, very close to the city and has been a hiking place since 1864, which means there are a lot of easily reached, well-marked trails you can take. The San Gabriel foothills are especially pretty in spring because of the proliferation of waterfalls on the front range.

Just above Sierra Madre lies one of the Southland's most romantic sights during the spring: **Sturtevant Falls**. The falls can be reached from Mount Wilson Observatory by way of the Sturtevant Trail, which meets the Gabrielino Trail and leads to the falls.

Take the Santa Anita Avenue exit off the I-10 and go to where it dead ends at the Chantry Flat parking lot. You will pass through an formidable gate that opens at 6 a.m. and closes at 10 p.m. like clockwork every day. **Chantry Flat** is the main way station and take-off point for hikers and pack trains heading up the face of Mount Wilson.

Don't let the first part of the trail (which begins at the south end of the parking lot) throw you. It starts off at the beginning of the Gabrielino Trail, which is paved. The first 1/2 mile, you will be going down into Big Santa Anita Canyon. After you cross a bridge over Winter Creek, the pavement ends. There are public restrooms here.

From here, you continue along the canyon through a grove of alder trees, past some cabins until after about 1-1/2 miles you enter an oak woodlands similar to what once covered large areas of the mountain foothills. At the crossroads here, go to the right and proceed upstream.

This is a wonderful, invigorating experience—you will even be hopping over boulders. Soon you will see the stirring 50-foot falls and its shimmering pool. It takes about 45 minutes each way to get here from the parking lot; the total distance is about 3-1/2 miles.

The fire of 1993 destroyed the study center for the area, but as of the writing of this book, the County of Los Angeles had committed to rebuilding it:

Eaton Canyon Nature Center
1750 North Altadena Drive
Pasadena, CA 91107
(818) 821-3246

Scheduled to reopen in early 1995, this is where you will learn more about the natural history of the area. They are going to reconstruct the center as it was—except they are going to make it out of fireproof materials. Native plants have already made a comeback. Take Sierra Madre Boulevard west towards Pasadena and turn right on New York Avenue.

This pleasant preserve of indigenous California plants occupies 184 acres. There is a little museum about the flora, fauna, and geology of the area where you can get maps to self guided tours. There is also a Naturalist's Room with live animals.

If you would like a pleasant spring walk of about 1-1/2 miles each way, there is a broad dirt road that heads north from the parking lot to **Eaton Canyon Falls**. John Muir once called these "the finest yet discovered in the San Gabriel Mountains." The water rushes through a natural chute and plunges down about 35 feet.

Spring in the San Gabriel Mountain Foothills, Public Gardens

Southern California has one of the largest gardens in the world that is also "always there" for its residents:

Los Angeles Arboretum
301 North Baldwin Avenue
[Baldwin Avenue exit off I-210, go three blocks south]
Arcadia, CA 91006
(818) 446-8251

The arboretum is large: 127 acres, including a four-acre natural lake. Since two-thirds of the visitors come on weekends, if you can come during the week, you will find plenty of very lovely, very private places to be alone.

The **Lucky Baldwin House**, a 100-year-old white, gingerbread Victorian most familiar as the "Fantasy Island" house, stands in the middle of the **Queen Anne Lawn**. The charming **Victorian Rose Garden** is a storybook recreation of the grounds of an English manor with brick walkways meandering through rows of sweet smelling roses. There is a large area, dominated by fountains, called appropriately enough, the **Bower Pool Fountains**. And the sylvan **Meadow Brook** area features a breathtaking little waterfall. (All of the above mentioned places are also rented out for weddings after the Arboretum closes).

With recurring droughts and the inevitability of a future water shortage in Southern California, one permanent exhibit deserves special attention: the **Henry C. Soto Water Conservation Garden.**

One of the things that will strike you most about this exhibit is the brilliant colors and sheer lushness of it. I was half expecting a rock garden, a few cactus and perhaps some of the nondescript shrubbery that grows along freeways. It is nice to know that you can help conserve water and still have a beautiful garden.

There are several other permanent exhibits that are quite interesting. There are five displays by *Sunset* magazine that illustrate five different ways an average-sized single family home could be landscaped—including for children, low maintenance, and the eclectic in taste (with the most amazing variety of plants you could imagine in a household garden).

Eating is confined to a picnic table area near the parking lot. There is a coffee shop althouh you might want to bring a picnic lunch which you can eat when you arrive, and then walk it off. There is quite a bit to see.

For a romantic day spent walking in peace and quiet, the Arboretum is one of the best places in Southern California. If you have ever thought those scenes in movie love stories, where a couple are feeding ducks on a lake together while a breeze ripples across the surface, are only found in remote out-of-town spots, think in-town for a little midweek peace.

Near here is one of the greatest architectural oddities in lodging that you could find anywhere:

> **Aztec Hotel**
> **311 West Foothill Boulevard**
> **Monrovia, CA 91016**
> **(818) 358-3231**

Looking more like a movie set, this Aztec styled, cast concrete and stucco structure completely startles the eye when you first see it while driving along an otherwise uneventful stretch of Foothill Boulevard. This National Historical Landmark was designed in 1925 by a fairly trendy architect named Robert Stacy-Judd, who considered the pre Columbian Revival style "authentically American."

You can continue the joy of spring in the San Gabriel foothills with dinner at the good old:

El Encanto
100 Old San Gabriel Canyon Road
Azusa, CA 91702
Monday-Thursday 4:30 to 10 p.m.
Friday & Saturday 4:30 to 11 p.m.
Sunday 4 to 9 p.m.
(818) 969-8877

The fare here is certainly not experimental in any way: basic steak and lobster. It is very well prepared, however, and the setting is simply outstanding. Though only three miles north of downtown Azusa, this rustic styled restaurant is truly in wooded seclusion in a canyon.

March is a wonderful month in the foothills of the San Gabriel Mountains. Up San Gabriel Canyon Road is a splendid destination for a March hike:

The Narrows Bridge (The Bridge To Nowhere)
East Fork Road

As you walk up to the Narrows Bridge, you will be rewarded with a sight that looks like a scene out of a disaster movie about the future: a ghostly bridge over a deep rocky chasm with no roads connected to it. This arched concrete structure was built in 1937 as part of a planned scenic highway up the east fork of the San Gabriel Canyon. Spanning 150-feet across, it stands a full 250-feet above the Narrows Gorge, which is the deepest in the Southland.

Farther along the base of the mountains, in the beautiful college town of Claremont, is a truly stunning spring garden:

Rancho Santa Ana Botanic Garden
1500 North College Avenue
Claremont, CA 91711
Daily 8 a.m. to 5 p.m.
(714) 625-8767

From the I-10, take the Indian Hill exit and go north two miles, turn right on Foothill and go three blocks to College Avenue.

Associated with the college complex is this 83-acre garden, whose blooming period actually began in late February. The 50 acres are arranged into plant communities by natural geographic groupings. The garden's biggest claim to fame is that it has the largest collection of native California plants in the world, with more than 1,500 species represented. There is a **Desert Garden** complete with indigenous rocks, a **Woodlands**, and a **Coastal Vegetation Garden**. The **Mesa** section features

California's annual spring bloomers.

The California lilacs *(ceanothus)*, manzanitas, and tree poppies are absolutely dazzling. There is a remarkable nature trail that winds through the entire place that is almost like a microcosm of the wide variety of plant life in the entire state of California.

On your way up Indian Hill you passed a most charming little shopping area:

Claremont Village
Indian Hill Boulevard
between 1st and 4th Streets

Claremont Village got its start in 1887 as a rail depot for shipping citrus. It became known as "Oxford of the Orange Belt" with the advent of the Claremont Colleges: Scripps, Pitzer, Pomona, Harvey Mudd, Claremont McKenna, and Claremont Graduate School. There is a Spanish Colonial Revival train depot that is still in operation and is served by Metrolink.

Walking tours of historic Claremont are given the first Saturday of the month at 10 a.m. by Claremont Heritage. They cost $3, last 1-1/2 hours, and begin at Sumitoma Bank, 102 Yale Avenue, Claremont. Call (909) 621-0848 for information.

Perhaps the most unique garden along the San Gabriel foothills is a privately owned nursery:

Van Ness Water Gardens
2460 North Euclid
Upland, CA 91786-1199
Tuesday-Saturday 9 a.m. to 4 p.m.
(909) 982-2425

You have to climb up into hills to find this special place. They have pond after pond filled with every kind of plant that grows in fresh water.

Wisteria in Orange County

Besides the giant wisteria in Sierra Madre, there is an arbor of wisteria in Orange County that also blooms beautifully this month:

Fullerton Arboretum
Cal State University Fullerton
Yorba Linda Boulevard and Associated Road
Fullerton, CA 92631
Garden hours 8 a.m. to 4:45 p.m.
(714) 773-3579

Of all the public arboretums in the Southland, this one is not the largest at 26 acres, but in some ways it is unique. It has numerous varieties of the ubiquitous palm tree, but it also has a rare fruit orchard. There are connecting ponds and streams, but perhaps its most unusual feature is its cavernous plant bog.

There is a restored 1894 home built by Dr. George C. Clark on the grounds with the original name of **Heritage House** that is only open on Sundays from 2 p.m. to 4 p.m. A couple of big almond trees situated right by here might still be in bloom this month.

The fruit trees also begin to flower this month, but perhaps the most dramatic blooming is the huge arbor of wisteria behind the Heritage House to the east. A beautiful wedding site even without the flowers, in March it is a living canopy of lavender blossoms.

Though Orange County's extensive coastline contains numerous romantic ocean view restaurants, ironically Newport Beach's restaurant usually named "most romantic" was the Wine Cellar in the Hyatt Newporter. It, alas, is now only available for private banquets, but Orange County has another romantic cloister for dinner quite near the Fullerton Arboretum that is called simply:

> **The Cellar**
> **305 Harbor Boulevard**
> **Fullerton, CA 92632**
> **Tuesday-Friday 5:30 to 9 p.m.**
> **Saturday 5:30 to 10 p.m.**
> **(714) 525-5682**

The city of Fullerton's pretty downtown is made more so by the Mediterranean-styled Villa del Sol shopping center, where The Cellar is located. An irony is that the restaurant's Wine Spectator Award winning wine "cellar" is on the top floor, which is street level. There is a newer dining area here for those that would prefer to eat while surrounded by hundreds of bottles of vino.

A flight of stairs takes you down into the original old world interior. Here you are surrounded by huge old wine casks set into the walls, heavy beamed ceilings with crystal chandeliers, and extravagant china and silver. The food is Continental and French of a traditional sort.

Coastal Wildflowers, Northern L.A. County Coast

During the dry times in fall and early winter, the rocky cliffs along the coast from Los Angeles County going north on Pacific Coast Highway (PCH) to San Luis

Obispo seem to be dotted with thick dead sticks between two- and six-feet tall. After the winter rains, beginning around February, the dead sticks have sprouted little bright green filigreed leaves at their tips.

By March, the clusters of leaves have grown into bunches of beautiful, brilliant yellow daisylike flowers, *Coreopsis Gigantea,* sometimes also called yellow sea dahlia. This is one of the most easily accessible rarities in the world. This flower only grows along this stretch and on the Channel Islands, yet you can see them on the cliffs going from Santa Monica to Malibu without even getting out of your car.

The restaurant that captures the beauty and romance of spring on the Malibu coast is:

**Beau Rivage
26025 West Pacific
Coast Highway
Malibu, CA 90265
Monday-Saturday
5 to 11 p.m.
Sunday 11 a.m.
to 11 p.m.
(310) 456-5733**

This large ocean view restaurant describes itself accurately as "Mediterranean" and it is a lovely way to enjoy the intoxicating Malibu environment. If I were to say any restaurant epitomizes the feeling of spring, it is this one. It sits in a nook under some undeveloped hills that at this time of year are glowing with yellow flowers.

The restaurant is also surrounded with explosions of color from purple bougainvillea and other garden flowers. The building itself is an imposing two story reddish beige Mission Revival structure with Moorish influences. It looks like a fairy castle on some faraway shore with heavy columns supporting broad arches and a central tower topped with a dramatic green dome.

It was opened in 1982 by Daniel and Luciana Forge. They have added on to it since then, until now it has several rooms, including a second floor ocean view banquet room and a "cellar." The interior is heavy wood beams with iron fixtures and a hearty stone fireplace. It has big picture windows with a view of the Pacific framed by the gardens outside the windows. There are flowers on each table and the place settings are lovingly elaborate.

The restaurant's reputation matches its decor. The California Restaurant Writers awarded them four stars for their wine list and three for the cuisine and made them "Restaurateurs of the Year" in 1987-88. Robert Balzer bestowed the Holiday Travel Magazine Award upon them and they received the Silver Award from the Southern California Restaurant Writers. It has also been given five stars from the International Restaurant Rating Bureau.

Chef Andreas Kisler prepares homemade pastas, fresh fish and game dishes, and a mixture of cuisine from France, Italy, Greece, Spain, and even Morocco. Herbs and spices grown on the property are used in their preparation. The pastry chef, Genevieve Boyer, has been with the restaurant since its opening.

The restaurant is located on the corner of Coral Canyon Road and PCH. Going up Coral Canyon Road will take you to several different places in the Santa Monica Mountains National Recreation Area for wildflower enhanced spring hikes.

The easiest (and one of the nicest) is **Solstice Canyon Park**, less than 1/4 mile up Coral Canyon from PCH. This area has only been open since 1988. It is 556 acres of creekside picnic areas, trails through woodlands of bay, sycamore, and huge live oaks, and ruins of various buildings. The road leads all the way up to Malibu Creek.

A little farther north on PCH is Encinal Canyon Road. If you would like to visit a truly delightful coastal wildflower place, go up about four miles and you will be looking at the easily distinguished entrance to **Charmlee Regional Park**. The gates open at 8 a.m. and close at sunset.

Opened in 1981, the park has 460 acres of chaparral, sage scrub, oak woodland, and coastal meadow. Because most of it is meadowlands, the wildflower displays are amongst the best in the Southland. There is a Nature Center by the parking lot. They will tell you what is blooming in areas reached by the assortment of walking trails and give you a guide to the Fire Ecology Trail.

There are many species of wildflowers represented. You will see mariposa lilies, California peonies, paintbrush, penstemon, and larkspur. One of the most prominent is *Lupinus longifolius*, a woody species of lupine that grows to about three-feet tall with languid racemes of pretty blue flowers a little under an inch long.

Besides the wildflowers, this is one of the best places to go for views of both the

The Malibu Beach Inn.

mountains and the coast. There is a picnic area and an Ocean Vista point that really is wonderful.

If you wanted to have a delightful spring coastal overnighter, just down PCH is the oceanfront:

Malibu Beach Inn
22878 Pacific Coast Highway
Malibu, CA 90265
(310) 456-6444 or (800) 4MALIBU

Though Malibu has been the target of some of the Southland's most aggressive developers of high end residential property, hotel development has been blissfully slow. This was the first hotel built here since 1952 when it was completed in 1989.

Though it has no antiques or expensive art and is not the most remarkable building on the coast, the Malibu Beach Inn has some qualities that make it one of the best spots for a getaway on the coast.

First of all, practically all of the 47 rooms have sensational ocean views. Though there are some rooms with special features—such as the vaulted ceilings in the third floor rooms—overall, they are remarkable for their consistency. They have tropical decor with a cane wall unit holding a wet bar and refrigerator. Besides TVs, rooms have VCRs, hair dryers, safes, and even gas fireplaces.

The beach access is second to none and the hotel is within walking distance of the **Malibu Pier** and some shops and galleries. There is more about Malibu in the August chapter.

PERSIAN NEW YEAR
Zoroastrian Tradition

The birth of spring is certainly celebrated by many cultures. The vernal equinox on March 21 also marks the re-entry of the sun into Aries. It was revered as such over 2,500 years ago by the astronomy and astrology loving Zoroastrians in what is now Iran as "Nouruz," which rhymes with "Mo' Blues" and literally means "new day."

When Islam began to become the region's dominant religion in the 7th century, many of the Zoroastrians fled to India. These expatriates called themselves "Parsi" from the ancient name of Persia. This small band would later become quite important in history: because their culture was not connected to India's caste system, they would be able to successfully work as intermediaries in all fields between the later arriving (and conquering) British and their Muslim and Hindu antagonists. Today there are about 100,000 of them and they continue to celebrate the holiday as "Navroz."

Back in medieval Iran, the celebration remained a Persian tradition. In most cultures of the world, popular customs of the previously dominant people or religion of a given area often become integrated into the new "true way." The world's most famous example of this happened in Europe, where the continued popularity of the pagan winter solstice celebrations resulted in Christmas being moved to December to coincide with the existing revelry.

Nouruz was so popular that it survived the cultural change to Islam. In fact, like the Puritan's Thanksgiving holiday did in America, it actually began to spread and was celebrated by other peoples within the Muslim world—as far away as Moorish Spain.

And why not, it was and is popular for a reason. It is a great holiday. Most of the world's observances of change of seasons—particularly the end of winter and birth of spring—are pretty happy times. In medieval days, Nouruz went on for a week.

Winter can be cold and long in the area that is now Iran and people were mighty glad it was over. There was a universal party mood and the rituals of Nouruz all reflected the spirit of change and renewal. For example, a week before, those with the means would hurl their old clay dishes out the window and buy new ones. New clothes were also purchased. Just as in Chinese New Year, houses were cleaned and bedecked with flowers in preparation for having guests over for lots of eating and gift giving. Colorfully dyed eggs and special sweets were exchanged.

Bonfires would light up the streets like Las Vegas. Revelers wore masks and played games while performers such as acrobats, jugglers, and story tellers carried on until late in the night. A general mood of mirth called for such lighthearted traditions as dunking figures of authority, such as university professors, in public fountains and collecting "ransoms" from them which was spent on more partying. It was like a giant Medieval Persian spring break.

The second to the last day of the original celebration was called Great Nouruz. On this special day, to symbolically link themselves to the cycle of nature, people got up with the dawn and went to the streams and filled pitchers with water. Common people then doused themselves and everyone else in the streets while the aristocracy retired to the privacy of their homes to do the same.

Today, Nouruz is a two week celebration. The way it is observed is a beautiful series of little ceremonies that continue many of the old traditions. Houses and wardrobes are still spruced up in anticipation of almost uninterrupted socializing. A bowl filled with small planting consisting of sprouted lentil, rye, or wheat (called a "sabzi") is placed in a window a fortnight before the big day.

The last Wednesday before Nouruz is called "Charsambe suri" or "Fire Wednesday." On this day, in an interesting precursor to tanning booths, one is supposed to jump over some kind of a fire for luck while intoning, "My pallor for you, your ruddiness for me."

There is a traditional family gathering on Nouruz Eve at a candlelit dinner table that, in a sense, formally declares the holiday period has begun. These candles are not snuffed out, but are allowed to burn down to the end.

This table is also bedecked with seven elements that begin with the letter "s" in Farsi. These "seven s's" are called "haft-sin." This will include the sprouted sabzi from the window and "sabzi polo," the rice dish which is the staple of most Persian meals. It is saffron seasoned basmati rice with green herbs such as chives or green onion tops, parsley, and cilantro.

Because the holiday represents a transition, omens during this time regarding the upcoming season are seen in everything. The future is imagined as hanging in balance. Anything that suggests good luck is very welcome. The coming of Nouruz on the equinox is looked upon as a special moment in time, whereupon the heavens and Earth will feel the energy of the sun entering Aries. In order to have some gauge of the resulting slight tremor in the Earth, it is traditional to set an egg, an orange, or a green leaf floating in a bowl of water and allow it to settle until completely still. This way you are supposed to be able to detect a slight tremble at the exact moment of the equinox.

At this moment, sensed by the floating orange or not, everyone embraces and kisses and gives hopes for good luck in the coming year. This is also when the kids get to open their presents. Because the next person to cross the front threshold is presumed to determine the fortunes of the household for the coming year, the luckiest member of the family is usually chosen to go outside and walk in through the front door.

What follows is 12 days of eating and socializing, after which the 13th and final day of Nouruz is called "sizde be-dar" which means "13 at the door." This day marks the end of the celebration with a picnic with music. "Ash-e reshteh", a noodle soup with several different kinds of beans, including garbanzos, navy, and red kidney, is the traditional fare. It may also have been consumed during the Nouruz eve dinner.

At 5 p.m., lettuce dipped in vinegar and honey is eaten. The final act of the picnic is to take the cute little bowl of sabzi that has been growing in your window and throw it as far as you can. All in all, a very liberating tradition.

Nouruz, Los Angeles' Iranian Community, Therangeles

You can experience much of the feeling of Nouruz in Los Angeles today, because the sentiment for the holiday is very strong in the Persians of the Southland. For many of them, celebrations back home are a fairly recent memory.

As late as the early '70s, there was very little in the way of an Iranian community in the U.S. With the coming of Khomeini in 1979, an exodus began. Today, there are over 800,000 Iranians living in Southern California—about a fifth of the total in the United States. They are Jews, Christians, Bahais or Muslims, though the latter religion is actually the least common among the community here.

Most of the immigrants here would not feel welcome in a Fundamentalist Muslim country. They are a generally cosmopolitan lot with more than half coming from Teheran. They are also one of the best educated immigrant groups in American history. Fifty percent of them have graduate degrees. Iranians are the third biggest group of foreign students at UCLA.

Though the popular image of the Shaw-era Iranians living here is that of expatriated royalty, quite often they literally were escapees with life and limb—and precious little else. Countless stories of grit and determination that would make Horatio Alger proud abound about Iranians, who were the impetus behind a variety of successful business ventures in L.A.

Of any immigrant group, Iranians (along with Koreans) have the highest percentage of their population that is self-employed. The towing business in the Los Angeles area is dominated by Iranians. The Adray's discount store and the glamorous Rodeo Collection in Beverly Hills were created by Iranians. The Los Angeles Iranian Business Directory is nearly 1,000 pages long.

This means that Nouruz is a fairly major event in Southern California. For this holiday, the most popular entertainer for expatriate Iranians is San Fernando Valley resident Viguen Derderian, who could be called the Frank Sinatra of Farsi. He was the late shah's favorite singer and starred in seven movies. On many Friday and Saturday nights, he can be found singing at the very enjoyable:

> **Cabaret Tehran**
> **12229 Ventura Boulevard**
> **Studio City, CA 91604**
> **Wednesday-Sunday 5 p.m. to 2 a.m.**
> **(818) 985-5800**

Pre-revolutionary cosmopolitan Tehran lives on in this second floor supper club. The dining room is the size of a palace and is as romantic as a fantasy with its rows of stately columns and soaring arches outlined by little white lights. Besides musical entertainment, often they have a comedian who tell jokes in Farsi, and of course, belly dancing. The food here is your basic Persian fare: mainly kabobs.

That shish kabobs are what most people identify as practically the only Persian food they have ever heard of is particularly ironic considering that, up until the modern era, the food of the Persian court was probably the most influential cuisine in history. Many of the names of dishes from India are actually Persian. These include "pilaf", "paneer", "samosas", and "kofta."

Yet even under the Western-influenced shah, Iran did not have that much of a restaurant tradition. In pre-revolutionary Iran many people ate their big meals at home and would merely grab a bite to eat while at the marketplace. Most kabobs in Iran are therefore sold outdoors from carts. This is one reason why there are so many fast food kabob carts of various kinds not only in Southern California, but in London and many other places in the world with large populations of transplanted Iranians.

Besides the plethora of fast food Persian kabob joints in the Southland, there are also some wonderful restaurants. Because of the Persian tradition of "taarrof," which is a kind of courtly politeness, the treatment of patrons is normally exceptional in all Persian restaurants—even if only moderately priced.

There is an L.A. based chain of four Persian restaurants that all use the word

"Shahrezad" in some fashion in their names. They all start with the same basic menu, then add their own individual stylistic additions. There are daily specials which during this time of year will usually include Nouruz dishes

Obviously, beef and other shish kabob is pretty much a standard item in all Persian restaurants. These can also be a variety of different meat or fowl including "barreh" (lamb) and "kofta" (onions and parsley in a ground meat base). There is also "barg" or "chelo kabob," which is thin strips about 1-1/2 inches wide of marinated chicken or beef instead of the regular chunk style.

A grilled tomato and/or onion on top of a particularly large mound of rice will normally accompany a good Persian meal. The latter is a tradition that relates to a Persian proverb that basically says that if you have a lot of rice, you are rich.

The plushest of the four Shahrezad locations is:

Darband/Shahrezad
138 South Beverly Drive
Beverly Hills, CA 90212
Daily 11 a.m. to 11 p.m.
(310) 859-8585

Besides being the most luxurious, this one is more like a Persian cabaret with a full liquor bar and live entertainment. The menu is expanded to include some more pricey specialties such as quail kabob.

There are two somewhat less grand locations without the cabaret extras in the Valley and in Westwood:

Shahrezad
17547 Ventura Boulevard
Encino, CA 91316
Monday-Thursday 10 p.m. to 11 p.m.
Sunday 11 a.m.to 11 p.m.
(818) 906-1616
and:
Shahrezad
1422 Westwood Boulevard
Westwood, CA 90024
Daily 11 a.m. to 9:30 p.m.
(310) 470-3242

The two block long strip of Westwood Boulevard where the restaurant is located is often called "Tehrangeles" for obvious reasons. This is one of two Shahrezad

locations here and has long been a Westwood favorite with its Tehran/Paris/Los
Angeles casual atmosphere. But an especially delightful dining experience can be
had down the street from here at the fourth restaurant in the chain:

Shahrezad Flame Restaurant
1442 Westwood Boulevard
Westwood, CA 90024
Monday -Friday 5 p.m. to 12 a.m.
Saturday & Sunday 11 to 12 a.m.
(310) 470-9131

At Shahrezad Flame, the focus is on the bread, brought to your table right from
the oven. It is called tanur "lavosh" or "tanori" and it is a flat, oval shaped loaf up to
about two-feet long, with little holes in it like matzoh. It is baked in a wood burning
clay oven of the same name. This oven is the grandmother of the Indian tandoori
oven (see August).

This restaurant has a kind of a science fiction meets medieval Iran quality. The
building itself has a very smooth, modern look to it and the oven, located at the front
of the dining room, is a large ball covered with little blue tiles under a giant cylinder-
shaped ventilation hood. A lot of the diners stare at it as if waiting for it to speak
while the baker "feeds it" by slapping pancake-like strips of dough on its inside
walls, sometimes causing a little burst of flame to come out of its mouth.

The bread is hot, chewy and delicious. For a great light lunch, order the bread
with sabzi khordan. Most Persian meals are served with this tray of feta cheese,
herbs, and vegetables that is also called a "panir o sabzi."

If you feel like some holiday sweets, near here is a Persian bakery:

Attari Bakery and Sandwich Shop
1388 Westwood Boulevard
Westwood, CA 90024
Daily 7 a.m. to 2 p.m.
(310) 441-5488

If you would like to try making a few of these wonderful sounding dishes, the
largest market in Teherangeles (and the one with the best window display) is:

Jordan Market
1449 Westwood Boulevard
Westwood, CA 90024
Monday-Saturday 9 a.m. to 9 p.m.
Sunday 10 a.m. to 8 p.m.
(310) 478-1706

The window here is a cornucopia of fresh fruits in a rainbow of colors from massive purple red pomegranates to oranges to deep purple bunches of grapes. This theme is picked up inside by the enormous photographs of luscious cut fruits such as watermelons and cantaloupes hanging from the ceiling.

Jordan Market is named after a similar store chain back in Iran and is the place to go for Iranian specialty foods. There is a Persian pastry department near the register filled with all manner of sugared fancies. There are little flower shaped cookies the size of the head of a thumbtack and even cookies made almost entirely of crushed nuts.

I was raised in a ranch-style house in the Valley with hardwood floors covered with thick rugs. To a rug lover like me, there is no more divine a place than the:

Damoka Persian Rug Center
1424 Westwood Boulevard
Westwood, CA 90024
Daily 10 a.m. to 7 p.m.
(310) 475-7900

Everywhere you look in this plush store there is a carpet more fantastic than the previous. The patterns and colors are dizzying and the scenes depicted on some of the antique rugs cover the range from the victory of God to young maidens in a garden.

There is also a Persian bookstore:

Tassveer Bookstore
1414 Westwood Boulevard
Westwood, CA 90024
Daily 11 a.m. to 8 p.m.
(310) 475-7574

SPRING EQUINOX PARTY

Besides the flowers, as the Persian holiday reminds us, spring is also a celestial event. The stars in the night sky change somewhat from solstice to equinox. This is not something we normally notice or think about. The most appropriate place to celebrate this aspect of spring is at the annual star party at the venerable:

Griffith Observatory and Planetarium
2800 Observatory Road
Los Angeles, CA 90027
Daily 12:30-10 p.m.
(213) 664-1191

Ah, the stars! For all of recorded time, man has turned his gaze skyward in wonder at what was transpiring up there. March is one of the best months to take a journey into the heavens in the Southland.

The telescope on top of the observatory is one of the largest available for public viewing in the state. It is open until 9:45 p.m., Tuesday through Sunday. The Los Angles basin doesn't always have the clearest night sky, but this month it is usually clear enough that you can look through the telescope and see varied colors and myriads of moons circling Jupiter.

The observatory itself is a wonderful Classical Moderne building built in 1935 that commands a magnificent romantic view of the city from its hilltop perch. It was featured in James Dean's signature movie, *Rebel Without A Cause,* and Arnold Schwarzeneggar dropped in from the future in the nude and appropriated some clothes from some young thugs here in *The Terminator.* The lights of Hollywood can be quite lovely from many places on the grounds and around the exterior of the building.

The great ornate bronze doors open into an awe inspiring rotunda with fabulous murals and ceilings by Hugo Balin. In the center of this rotunda is a giant Faucault's Pendulum: a huge plumb line swinging back and forth along with the rotation of the earth.

The **Hall of Science** is quite enjoyable to play around in. It will bring back memories of times when learning was fun. It is free and open Tuesday though Friday from 2 p.m. to 10 p.m., Saturday from 11:30 a.m. to 10 p.m., and Sunday from 12:30 p.m. to 10 p.m.

Planetarium shows are Tuesday through Saturday at 3 p.m. and 7:30 p.m., with an additional 4:30 p.m. show on Saturday and Sunday.

Laserium laser shows, set to music, are at 6 p.m. and 8:45 p.m., with additional shows at 9:45 p.m. Tuesday-Saturday. These shows truly are awesome and have a unique mind clearing effect. They can be a wonderful change of pace in entertainment. For info call (818) 997-3624.

The observatory also features a "Sky Report" recorded message on what is happening in our current sky. The number is (213) 663-8171. There are comets to watch for, shifts in planetary location—it really is amazing how important we think our day-to-day activities are and yet we are a nightly witness to how insignificant they really are.

Also here is an example of one of the monuments resulting from President Franklin Delano Roosevelt's many great programs funded from December 1933 to

June of 1942 through the Department of the Treasury and the Works Progress Administration (W.P.A.). These programs allowed jobless artists to paint murals, sculpt statues, and even design public buildings.

Following the W.P.A. philosophy, that work be provided for as many people as possible, six artists created the six cast stone figures for the glittering white four-story monument to science in front of the observatory. Represented are astronomers Sir William Herschel, Sir Isaac Newton, Johannes Kepler, Nicholas Copernicus, Galileo Galilei, and Hipparchus.

If you would like an even better view of the city than you can espy from the observatory, walk to the north end of the parking lot to the trail signs that point you to **Mount Hollywood.**

This is the most popular hike in Griffith Park. An odd experience comes when you cross over the Mount Hollywood Drive tunnel. If you listen, you can hear car horns and motors seeming to come from the earth underneath your feet. There is a place to rest with drinking fountains under eucalyptus trees called Captain's Roost. The peak is 1,625-feet.

Griffith Park is enormous and there are numerous things to see, but in spring, don't miss one of the most beautiful walks in Southern California that also begins at the observatory, but goes the other way. It meanders down from the observatory into Hollywood:

> **The Ferndell**
> **Fern Dell Drive**
> **[bounded by Black Oak Drive and Red Oak Drive]**

From the observatory, take Lower West Observatory Trail down 1-1/4 miles. You will lose about 500 feet of elevation on the way, following a gentle babbling brook surrounded by ferns under a canopy of trees. At the bottom, you will come upon a grove of redwoods.

Ironically this cool moist beauty is the result of an artificial source: the stream's water is condensation from the air conditioning system at the observatory.

There are some nice views as you descend and picnic tables just before you reach the redwoods at the bottom. There is more about Griffith Park later this month and in the September chapter.

ACADEMY AWARDS

No institution has had a greater role in bringing prosperity and fame to Southern California than Hollywood. It is fitting that the first month of spring is the month of the Academy Awards, Hollywood's biggest celebration.

The Academy Awards have had their share of different venues over the years. The site for the past several years has been the:

> **Shrine Civic Auditorium**
> **665 West Jefferson Boulevard**
> **Los Angeles, CA 90007**
> **(213) 748-5116**

Seating capacity was the main reason for the Oscar's move to the Shrine in 1988. With 6,400 seats, it is almost exactly double the capacity of the Dorothy Chandler Pavilion it replaced. Making a comeback after more than a decade of decline, the Shrine's upsurge is ironic because it was the completion of the Music Center in 1969 that led to its deterioration.

In many ways, it is a more fitting site. Completed in 1926, it was designed by A. M. Edelman, John C. Austin, and G. Albert Lansburgh, the designer of the El Capitan and Pacific (Warner) theaters on Hollywood Boulevard.

It is a fanciful structure, a huge Hollywood version of an Islamic temple with two commanding domes, cupolas, Moorish-style arches supported by columns, and windows that look like giant keyholes. The interior is dominated by an ornate ceiling with a chandelier the size of Manhattan and balcony loggia such as you would expect to see in a royal opera house.

Near there is the Southland's most prestigious film school, which even offers free tours:

> **George Lucas Building**
> **University of Southern California Film School**
> **Jefferson Boulevard, Vermont, Figueroa, and**
> **Exposition Streets near Gate 5**
> **tours Friday at 2 p.m.**
> **(213) 740-2311 (main number)**
> **(213) 740-2335**

This is probably the most well respected and technically advanced film and television school in the world. The building is named after its most famous graduate, George Lucas, whose film *THX 1138* began life as a student film while he was enrolled here. Probably their second most famous alumni is John Singleton.

The tour lasts from 1 to 1-1/2 hours and gives a glimpse of the fabulous technical capacity and post production facilities of this remarkable institution. You even get to see the beautiful Norris Theater, the department's own movie theater.

As I mentioned in the January chapter, the Oscar was conceived in the Biltmore in Downtown L.A., but the first Oscar ceremony was held in 1929 in Hollywood at the:

Radisson Hollywood Roosevelt Hotel
7000 Hollywood Boulevard
Hollywood, CA 90028
(213) 466-7000
(800) 333-3333

Built in 1927 and named after Teddy Roosevelt, this Spanish Revival hotel was renovated in a two year project that began in 1984. The hand-painted ceilings and spectacular lobby will dazzle your eyes. A statue of Charlie Chaplain sitting on a bench greets you as you enter from Hollywood Boulevard. The aptly named **Blossom Room** was the site of the first Academy Awards presentation, which was presided over by Douglas Fairbanks.

The **Cinegrill** was formerly not only a haven for artists and writers such as Dali, Fitzgerald, and Hemingway, but also the favorite romantic rendezvous for Clark Gable and Carole Lombard. It is a truly beautiful Art Deco bar and a major live cabaret spot that generally features jazz torch singers. **Theodore's** is the hotel's expensive dining room and it offers late night suppers.

Overlooking the lobby, the mezzanine level has a small, but quite well done exhibit on the history of Hollywood. Vintage movie cameras are set up around the display among the potted palms like statues of Greek gods. There is an interesting and succinct chronology of the history of Hollywood with accompanying still photographs and text that winds around the walls.

As a place for a romantic overnighter, this is a wonderful choice because the rooms are luxurious and beautiful. There are movie-themed suites, cabana rooms in a tropical garden setting, an olympic-size swimming pool painted by David Hockney, and a Tropicana bar.

The Hollywood Roosevelt Hotel is right across the street from:

Mann's Chinese Theater
6925 Hollywood Boulevard
Hollywood, CA 90028
(213) 464-8111

Regardless of how many tour buses are parked out front, I have always loved the Chinese Theater. It is so perfectly Hollywood. You can almost see the old stars getting out of their limousines for a world premier amid flashbulbs popping nonstop.

One of those stars, Norma Talmadge, accidentally stepped into a square of wet cement that should have been roped off. But that workman's error made history, because owner Sid Grauman saw the possibilities and one of the world's most famous traditions was instantly born. Sid quickly talked Mary Pickford and the ever cooperative Douglas Fairbanks into doing it too—with both their feet and their hands. Many other stars have since left their mark and now people come from all over the world to stroll around the front of the theater to see the signature slabs.

Thankfully, no one has seen fit to "modernize" the theater's exterior with its green roofed pagoda,

Mann's Chinese Theater

30-foot dragon, imported temple bells, and giant Fu dog statues. It opened on May 18, 1927 with Cecil B. De Mille's epic silent film *King of Kings* (with organ accompaniment by Gaylord Carter) in what was billed as "The Most Spectacular Opening Ever Held." Joan Crawford, Mary Pickford, and most of the rest of Hollywood rolled up to open the second of the great movie palaces built on Hollywood Boulevard by Sid Grauman. More movies have premiered here since than at any other theater—including the 1991 *Robin Hood* with Kevin Costner.

The stars along the sidewalks of Hollywood Boulevard, the **Walk of Fame**, were inspired by the worldwide notoriety of the prints at Grauman's Chinese. Hollywood Chamber of Commerce member Harry Sugarman proposed them in 1955 and they were dedicated in 1958. Eight film stars, including Burt Lancaster and Joanne Woodward, were honored in that first ceremony.

Twenty years later, the City of Los Angeles made the walkway a cultural and historic landmark. It is the only such honored landmark in Southern California that you can tread upon. As of the writing of this book there were 1,935 stars that have been dedicated with over 260 blank ones left.

A step or two east from the Chinese is the beautifully rebuilt:

El Capitan Theater
6834 Hollywood Boulevard
Hollywood, CA 90028
(213) 467-7674

This theater was originally designed by the man who from the turn of the century until about 1930 was one of the main theater architects for Southern California, G. Albert Lansburgh. Actually, it began life as a legitimate theater in 1926, opening on May 3rd with *Charlot's Review,*

starring Gertrude Lawrence, Jack Buchanan, and Beatrice Lillie. It was converted to the Paramount movie theater in 1941 with accompanying grotesque "modernization" and reopened with the premier of Orson Wells' *Citizen Kane.*

For all practical purposes, this is now a brand new 1,100-seat, $6,000,000 "Golden Age of Hollywood" style movie palace, reopened in June of 1991 with Disney Studios' *The Rocketeer.* It was developed as a cooperative venture between Pacific Theaters and Walt Disney Productions as a showcase for Disney's new releases.

And what a showcase it is. With its brilliant Las Vegas-style marquee lighting up the front of the building completely, to the gleaming gilded ticket booth, to the baroque gargoyles and detailing that adorn the entrance, this theater beckons the moviegoer in a way that the pathetic 14 screen models of today never could.

Stepping inside, you will see that in many ways it offers the best of both the old movie world and the new. It is incredibly plush and ornate with oversized urns and yellow, purple, and green carpeting lit by spectacular chandeliers. The huge 42-by-20 foot screen is covered with an elaborate three-tiered curtain made of silver tinsel and ornate tassels.

The El Capitan has a full balcony with loge section and is equipped with state-of-the-art Spectral Recording Dolby Stereo sound with THX Lucasfilm presentation. It has a cappuccino bar and there is a light and music show as a prologue that precedes each film. For *Alladin* and *The Lion King,* there was a live musical review to kick off the premier.

This theater is the work of one of Southern California's most romantic and unusual individuals, Joseph Musil. He is an architectural designer specializing in period and atmospheric, lavish and exotic environments. For the El Capitan, he came up with four complete sets of architectural models as the design concept changed; he even designed the sign, stage curtains, and the fixtures. A true theater historian, he also did the art direction and fine tuned the opening sequences. In the June chapter, you will be introduced to another one of his unique theater creations: The **Crest Theater** in Westwood.

Strolling down Hollywood Boulevard today, one experiences a bizarre combination of sensations. The pounding rock and roll from the hard rock stores, the street people, the stars on the sidewalk, and the endless tourists and tourist shops. You can still see the splendid architecture of its glorious past in many of the buildings. One worth noticing is very near you at this point, at the corner of Hollywood and Highland:

> **Max Factor Museum of Beauty**
> **1666-68 Highland Avenue**
> **Hollywood, CA 90028**
> **Monday-Saturday 10 a.m. to 4 p.m.**
> **(213) 463-6668**

This lovely Regency Moderne pink and white marble building is appropriate to mention when talking about theaters because it was designed by another of the great theater designers of Southern California, S. Charles Lee. It was remodeled in 1926 from what was formerly just a warehouse during the period that Max Factor cosmetics were really associated with the glamour of Hollywood. Max was so big, he even got his own star on the Walk of Fame.

The free museum is really worth a look. There are hundreds of autographed photographs of the most famous stars, an extensive collection of cosmetic ads from the '20s through the '50s, as well as some vintage gizmos once thought to be effective at making one "beautiful." My favorites among the miscellaneous artifacts are one of Marlene Dietrich's wigs, Fred Astaire's toupees, and wooden heads of Elizabeth Taylor and Charlton Heston. They also have a cosmetics boutique.

If you can pry yourself out of there and continue along The Walk of Fame, you will come upon the remains of what was the first movie palace of Hollywood Boulevard:

> **Egyptian Theater**
> **6712 Hollywood Boulevard**
> **Hollywood, CA 90028**
> **(213) 467-6167**

Most of the wonderful interior and exterior of this remarkable theater is unrecognizable due to a "remodeling" job that looks like it was done by a demolition crew. Also, the earthquake of 1994 damaged it so badly it may have to be completely rebuilt. Of course, no matter what the cost, it must be done.

Originally built in 1922 by architect Charles Toberman as a tribute to the unveiling of the tomb of Tutankhamen that year, it featured a facade that was a replica of the Temples of Ramses and Karnak along the Nile. The original usherettes were dressed like Cleopatra's handmaidens. Ironically, it opened on July 12, 1922 with *Robin Hood* starring Douglas Fairbanks, Sr. It is sad it was not in any kind of shape to host the premier of the remake.

Though the Egyptian as it was in the early '20s is no more, if you keep going east on Hollywood, you will come upon a true survivor of that era:

Musso and Frank Grill
6667 Hollywood Boulevard
Hollywood, CA 90028
Monday-Saturday 11 a.m. to 11 p.m.
(213) 467-7788

This great restaurant originally opened in 1919 and has changed little. The heavy dark paneling and large beam ceilings are matched by dark wood partitions around the plush red leather booths. Along with the enormous red brick grill behind the counter, the look is of an English men's club. The atmosphere, however, is friendly and spirited. Eating here is like going back in time. Even the waiter's uniforms are unchanged, and the service the men wearing them give is delightful. The menu is huge.

It is hard to say which is better, sitting at the counter and chatting with the wisecracking waiters, such as Manny Felix, or sitting in a cozy booth that Dashiel Hammet and Lillian Hellman may have sat in together. This is the place to go and feel all those ghosts of old Hollywood and imagine the conversations that took place. Have a martini while you are here.

Hudson Street has the honor of having murals on the sides of three out of four buildings on the corners where it meets Hollywood. One of my favorite murals here is a **Tribute to Delores Del Rio**, which is shown on the cover.

On the other side of the boulevard is the store for film and theatre books:

Larry Edmonds Bookshop
6644 Hollywood Boulevard
Hollywood, CA 90028

Monday-Saturday 10 a.m. to 6 p.m.

(213) 463-3273

Opened in 1940, Larry Edmonds claims to have the "world's largest collection of books and memorabilia on cinema and theater." It has screenplays, plays, history, criticism, and whimsy. One wall is floor-to-ceiling shelves of original movie posters.

Continuing along the Boulevard going east, there are lots of tourist places, but within a short stroll is one of Southern California's truly great museums:

Lingerie Museum
Frederick's of Hollywood
6608 Hollywood Boulevard
Hollywood, CA 90028
Monday-Thursday
& Saturday
10 a.m. to 6 p.m.
Sunday 12 p.m. to 5 p.m.
(213) 466-8506

Formerly the Brassiere Museum but now broader in scope, this collection depicts the history of lingerie through illustrious examples from Frederick's past. Also included are famous celebrity's choices in lingerie. It is free and open during regular store hours. The building itself is a gorgeous 1935 Streamline Moderne painted purple that is the most striking building on the Boulevard.

The fourth grand old movie palace of Hollywood Boulevard that has survived is coming up as you continue east:

Pacific (Warner) Theater
6423-45 Hollywood Boulevard
Hollywood, CA 90028
(213) 464-4111

This fantastic theater, long marked by its twin neon towers on the roof, was

The side entrance of the Pacific (Warner) Theater.

designed by the original designer of the El Capitan, G. Albert Lansburgh. While he only designed the theater portion of the El Capitan structure, he designed the whole building here. This is one of his greatest creations, and though the auditorium now has been subdivided into three screens, the spectacular lobby and lounges are still among the most impressive in Southern California. Architecturally it is a combination of Rococo, Renaissance, Moorish, and Art Deco, but somehow it all works.

Walking up a few steps to Cahuenga, to your left, you will see a small building brightly festooned with hand painted signs describing what would seem to be shows at several different theaters:

> **Theatre/Theater**
> **1713 Cahuenga Boulevard**
> **Hollywood, CA 90028**
> **(213) 469-9689**

Theatre/Theater is a wonder. As small as it is, it manages to encompass two complete theaters. The main stage theater in front seats 70, the back theater seats only 25. It was started in 1981 by the husband and wife team of Jeff Murray and Nicolette Chaffey who manage to produce both the best new work, as well as their own, on the small stages.

Theatre/Theater presents a greater variety of shows than any theater in Southern California. On Friday, Saturday, and Sunday there are usually two shows in each of the two spaces. It has been the site of several plays that have ended up being made into movies, such as *Daddy's Dyin', Who's Got The Will?* They seem to have especially good luck with one person shows such as 1989's "Best Performance Art" tour de force by Jackson Hughs in *Our Man in Nirvana,* the brilliant one woman show *Madame Mao's Memories* (now touring the U.S.), and the unforgettable one man musical *Adieu, Jacques...!,* winner of the *L.A. Weekly* "Best Musical" Award.

Also on Cahuenga, but on the other side of Hollywood is a large newsstand with a gem of a small restaurant next door:

> **India Inn**
> **1638 Cahuenga Boulevard**
> **Hollywood, CA 90028**
> **Daily 11:30 a.m. to 10:30 p.m.**
> **(213) 461-3774**

Though this restaurant is not as inexpensive as it used to be, it is still an excellent buy. The decor is charming and romantic, the service polite and attentive, and the food is absolutely delicious. The tandoori lamb is so juicy and flavorful, it seems a shame to have to get full and stop eating it. The Indian naan bread cooked in the tandoori oven seems too good to be called bread (see August).

Down Cahuenga a little further towards Sunset is a well know Thai restaurant:

> **House of Chan Dara**
> **1511 North Caheunga Boulevard**
> **Hollywood, CA 90028**
> **Monday-Friday 11 a.m. to 11 p.m.**
> **Saurday & Sunday 5 to 11 p.m.**
> **(213) 464-8585**

This is one of several locations of one of Southern California's best known (and liked) Thai restaurants. There might be a wait to eat inside this small, lively place for "me krob" and "sate." They are open until 11 p.m. (beer and wine only). There is more on Thai Southern California in the April chapter.

Getting back to our eastward trek down Hollywood Boulevard, it is an interesting pause to stop at Hollywood's most famous corner. It is fun to stand on the corner of Hollywood and Vine and imagine what a famous place it really is. The buildings really don't contribute much to the look of Hollywood today. At the time they were built in the 1920s, however, because they were the maximum height allowable (150 feet), they were obviously the center of town.

As I look at the street signs that spell out those names, I can't help thinking Hollywood's beginning's could never have predicted the Hollywood of today.

In 1887, Harvey Henderson Wilcox, a prohibitionist from Kansas, purchased 120 acres with the intent of setting up a Methodist town. His wife, "Daida," named the place Hollywood after a friend's summer home back East.

By 1909, the town was established. Posters from the city boasted of its many paved streets, warm climate, and lack of saloons. Two years later, however, an event occurred that would change Hollywood forever. In 1911, the first film company,

The Nestor Film Company, was set up among the unsuspecting Methodists.

From that time forward, the town had extraordinary growth, but as the decade wore on, there were increasing conflicts between the Methodist founders and the burgeoning film industry. Editorials were written deploring the influx of those most disreputable of citizens, actors.

The skyline of Hollywood today is dominated by one obvious structure. The building that makes the great architectural statement of Hollywood, just up from the corner of Hollywood and Vine, is the:

> **Capital Records Building**
> **1750 Vine Street**
> **Hollywood, CA 90028**

Designed in 1956 by Welton Becker, this building follows the tradition of making a structure look like the product its company makes: it was designed to look like a stack of 45 r.p.m. records with a needle on top. During the holidays, the needle is converted into a Christmas Tree. The whole building has a freshness to its look that is almost entirely lacking in most office buildings built since.

A fairly recent addition is the **mural** on the parking lot wall featuring Nat King Cole and other musical greats. It is the work of artist Richard Wyatt.

Down the street is a classic L.A. theatre venue in its latest manifestation:

> **James Doolittle Theatre**
> **1615 North Vine Street**
> **Hollywood, CA 90028**
> **(213) 462-6666**

I remember going to this theatre as a child when it was called the Huntington Hartford. It is a moderately large (1,038 seats) venue for drama. For after show chit chat, near here is one of my favorite dives:

> **Frolic Room**
> **6245 Hollywood Boulevard**
> **Hollywood, CA 90028**
> **Monday-Thursday 12 p.m. to 2 a.m.**
> **Friday & Sunday 10 a.m. to 2 a.m.**
> **(213) 462-5890**

There are dives and then there are dives. The Frolic Room is almost legendary among writers and other sordid types as a classic of the genre. The neon sign out front is matched by its vintage WW II-era interior.

Walking just a bit father east, you will come to the last of the movie palaces built on Hollywood Boulevard:

Pantages Theatre
6239 Hollywood Boulevard
Hollywood, CA 90028
(213) 468-1770

Though not as overpowering an exterior as the Chinese, the Pantages has the most spectacular interior of any theater on the boulevard. From 1949 to 1959, it was the site of the Academy Awards. It is a historical monument as well as a legitimate theater now.

And what a theater it is: 2,812 seats, a 70-by-180 foot stage, an enormous lobby, and Baroque woodwork worthy of a cathedral. It was designed by Marcus Priteca and built by the owner of the largest theater chain in the U.S., Alexander Pantages, in 1930. Its opening on June 4 was somewhat dimmed in luster by the fact that he was in prison at the time for raping a 17 year-old-girl, Eunice Pringle, who had come to his office to apply for a job.

Pantages was convicted once, but later acquitted in an appeal that actually changed the rape law in California. Pantages' attorney, Jerry Geisler, persuaded the higher court to perform a rather remarkable display of indifference to fair judicial process. He was able to get testimony admitted as evidence that previously had been considered irrelevant: what amounted to a smear campaign against the rapee's moral character. The higher court decided that essentially because Ms. Pringle was a "bad girl," it was not a rape and Pantages walked.

It is ironic that this man, the "king of theater chains" in the U.S. did not achieve the lasting fame of Sid Grauman. His "ultimate movie palace," never that famous for premiering movies, was converted to a live theater by the Nederlander theater family in 1977.

In addition to this magnificent large theater, they own the building diagonally across the street, a former mortuary, and now the home of one of the best repertory companies in Southern California:

West Coast Ensemble Theatre
6240 Hollywood Boulevard
Hollywood, CA 90028
(213) 871-1052

The first thing you will notice upon entering the lobby of the West Coast Ensemble Theatre is the wall full of awards. This is an ensemble company, with actors that pay dues to belong. They have two theater spaces: a fairly large space for a 99 seat theater in back, and a comfortable little 50 seat amphitheater in front that was the viewing room when the building was a mortuary.

Their work under artistic director Les Hansen is inspired. They have done everything from Neal Simon to alternative staging of new work. Since they have been established for a number of years, they even offer a subscription.

In addition to the Academy Awards, March sees both the L.A. Drama Critic's Circle Awards and the *L.A. Weekly* Awards for theater in Southern California. There is more about Hollywood in the June and November chapters. There is more about small theater in L.A. in the September chapter.

SANTA BARBARA FILM FESTIVAL

March is also the month of Southern California's second major film festival of the year:

> **Santa Barbara Film Festival**
> **1216 State Street, #201**
> **Santa Barbara, CA 93101**
> **first two weeks of March**
> **(805) 689-INFO**

Many of the films are shown at the cultural center on State Street:

> **Arlington Center For the Performing Arts**
> **1317 State Street**
> **Santa Barbara, CA 93101**
> **(805) 963-4408**

Built on the site of the old Arlington Hotel in the 1930s, this structure is, like all of the great buildings of this most romantic of the Southland's cities, a beautiful example of Mission Revival architecture. Designed by Joseph Plunkett, its roof rises to a spire recognizable all over town. The entryway is designed like a courtyard and takes you past beautiful tile into the lobby. Here the ceiling features a colorful mural of a platoon of fiesta dancers. Architectural details such as wrought iron, heavy painted beams, and columns appear throughout. The theater auditorium walls are made to resemble a Spanish Mediterranean town complete with a starry night sky on the curved roof. The Arlington also has a glorious pipe organ that is played every night at 7:30 p.m.

Some of the festival's events are also found in the auditorium at the nearby:

> **Santa Barbara Museum of Art**
> **1130 State Street**
> **Santa Barbara, CA 93101**

Tuesday-Saturday 11 a.m. to 5 p.m.
Thursday until 9 p.m.
Sunday 12 p.m. to 5 p.m.
(805) 963-4364

This rather stately white building with its gracefully arched entrance is the former post office. It became the Museum of Art in 1941. This is an extremely pleasant, not overly large museum that makes for an exceptionally enjoyable afternoon. To describe the collection here as eclectic is somewhat of an understatement. They have everything from Greek, Roman and Egyptian antiquities to French Impressionism and American paintings to vintage dolls and musical instruments. There is an Asian arts section as well.

They have a wide variety of workshops, lectures, films, and performances that are scheduled along with changing exhibits even when the festival isn't happening. They have a great bookstore which boasts Santa Barbara's best selection of art books along with cards and interesting jewelry.

Just across the street from here is one of the Southland's most fanciful bookstores:

Earthling Bookshop and Cafe
1137 State Street
Santa Barbara, CA 93101
Monday-Friday 7:30 a.m. to 12 a.m.
Saturday 9 a.m. to 12 a.m.
Sunday 9 a.m. to 11 p.m.
(805) 965-0926

There is a wonderful old-world grace to the dark wood pillars, fireplace, green carpeting, and indirect sconce lights in this labor of love. Owners Terry and Penny Davies keep over 100,000 volumes in stock and also have created a unique atmosphere. The Earthling is also a cafe and features a huge mural on one wall by Barnaby Conrad of 33 famous authors. They have many activities here that include book signings and readings as well as everything from ethnic dance performances to film and slide shows.

State Street has many delightful restaurants. One that is a real classic Santa Barbara spot that goes perfectly with the festival is:

Aldo's Italian Restaurant
1031 State Street
Santa Barbara, CA 93101

Daily 8 a.m. to 10:30 p.m.
(805) 963-6687

Established in 1986, Aldo's patio is a welcome sight along the busy street. With its red carpeting inside and waiters in white shirts and black bolo ties, it combines elegance with a laid back atmosphere. On Friday night, they have two violinists and on Saturday night, they have a harpist. There is also classical guitar on Saturday and Sunday afternoons.

Santa Barbara has a long artistic tradition. There are many wonderful potters and craft artists who live here. A great way to spend an afternoon and also check out some of their work is to wander around the:

Santa Barbara Arts and Crafts Show
Cabrillo Boulevard (going east 3/4 of a mile,
starting at State Street)
Santa Barbara
Sunday 10 a.m. to dusk
(805) 962-8956

What could be nicer than to stroll along by the ocean looking at beautiful artistic creations? There are photos, sculpture, paintings, all manner of ceramics, and functional art such as wind chimes. Everyone is very friendly—including people's dogs, of which there are many, so watch your step.

Whenever I have brought a tour to Santa Barbara, one of the most popular stops is always the:

Santa Barbara Winery
202 Anacapa Street
Santa Barbara, CA 93101
Daily 10 a.m. to 5 p.m.
(805) 963-3633

Located right near both State Street and the Arts and Crafts Show along Cabrillo, this in-town winery is a pleasant surprise. The smaller streets leading downtown from the beach area have a mixture of small light industrial warehouses, some of which have local craft artist's galleries in them. One of them is this little winery and gift shop.

It was founded by Pierre Lafond in 1962, making it the county's oldest producing winery. The vines were planted in 1972 in the 70 acre Lafond Vineyard in the Santa Ynez Valley.

The Santa Barbara Winery's reputation has steadily improved—particularly since 1981 when winemaker Bruce McGuire took the helm. This is particularly gratifying if you like to give wine as a gift, because the labels here are among the prettiest of the Southland's wineries and they have coasters and the like to match.

Though it is not in the center of Santa Barbara on State Street where most of the festival's activities take place, there is one hotel in Santa Barbara with a genuine movie history:

> **Montecito Inn**
> **1295 Coast Village Road**
> **Santa Barbara, CA 93108**
> **(805) 969-7854**

This inn's opening on February 16, 1928 was more like the world premier of a Hollywood epic. Those present included Lon Chaney, Sr., Carole Lombard, Gilbert Roland, Janet Gaynor, Wallace Berry, Norma Shearer, Warner Baxter, Marion Davies, and Conrad Nagel. This is because Charlie Chaplain and Roscoe "Fatty" Arbuckle built it.

Framed with the white walls and red roof of the Mediterranean style, it has 53 rooms with an original two-story honeymoon suite. It has a heated pool, spa, and exercise equipment.

Spring Hikes in Santa Barbara

Beginning in Montecito and going up into the hills are some of the most pleasant places to walk in the Southland. These are several great paths maintained by a group called The Montecito Trails Foundation. In my early college days, a favorite place to hike was to the ruins of the old Hot Springs Hotel along the appropriately named **Hot Springs Trail.**

It is pretty easy to get to from town. Olive Mill Road crosses Alston Drive and turns into Hot Springs Road. Just three miles above the freeway (US 101), you'll hit Mountain Drive, where you make a left. Start looking for a place to park, because the beginning of the trail is only about 1/4 mile ahead on the right.

This is one of those places where public land skirts very exclusive property. This is especially true at the wooded beginning—which intersects numerous private driveways over the span of about 1/4 mile.

As soon you get past these areas and cross over Hot Springs Creek, you are on an old dirt road that dates from stagecoach days. It continues about a mile to the junction on the left with the more recent road to Cold Springs Canyon. Go right at this junction and you will come to the ruins. The plants remaining from the landscaping add an eerie qualtiy.

KOI FESTIVAL (GARDENA)

Every March since 1974, there has been a unique competition in Gardena: a judge off of rare fish. The Southern California Chapter of "Zen Nippon Airinkai," holds their annual Koi Festival this month.

The koi is a member of the carp family that has been mutated through inbreeding from a grey-green colored mud dweller to a multicolored wonder. Properly viewed from above, they are judged on body shape and pureness of color.

Symbols of longevity, fertility, and determination, they are prized in Japan as a family asset and handed down (they can live from 70 to over 100 years.) The record is 226 years. Once limited to the aristocracy in feudal Japan, they can be purchased here for as little as $7 and as much as $30,000!

If you would like to dress up your garden or just look at these living works of art, stop by:

California Koi Farms
3360 Gird Road
Fallbrook, CA 92028
Call first
(619) 728-1483

TheKoi are grown with traditional Japanese techniques here: culled by hand during their breeding season. Only 20 percent of the offspring are deemed fit to be sold. The owner here, Takemi Adachi, learned the technique from his father, a famous breeder in Yonago, Japan.

Besides being beautiful, koi can be surprisingly affectionate. They will nuzzle your hand as you feed them and they even like to be petted.

BLESSING OF THE ANIMALS

One of the most charming annual events in the Southland takes place every spring in Los Angeles, the **Blessing of The Animals**. It happens in front of the venerable:

Plaza Church
(Church of Our Lady the Queen of the Angels)
El Pueblo de Los Angeles Historic Park and Olvera Street
535 North Main Street
Los Angeles, CA 90012
(213) 625-5045

This is the oldest religious building in the city. The Plaza Church started as a basic adobe built between 1818 and 1922 by Indian laborers and their Franciscan overseers. It was enlarged, then remodeled, then later completely renovated.

On Holy Saturday, the Saturday before Easter, children put pretty ribbons on their pets to be blessed by priests. They are joined by animals brought from the nearby L.A. Zoo. Together they form a line that leads up to the church that looks like the procession of animals waiting to board Noah's Ark.

The City of Los Angeles has several annual events on Olvera Street that I will mention in May, September and December. Olvera Street is a pleasant and interesting visit and has many shops and restaurants, but I thought I would mention the very close:

La Luz del Dia Restaurant
1 West Olvera Street
Los Angeles, CA 90012
Note: their line is busy all day
(213) 628-7495

If seeing all of those animals inspired you to go visit them, you are five minutes away via the I-5 (Santa Ana Freeway) from the:

Los Angeles Zoo
5333 Zoo Drive
Los Angeles, CA 90027
(213) 666-4090 (recorded information)
(213) 666-4650
Daily 10 a.m. to 5 p.m. (closed Christmas)

This is the second largest zoo in the Southland, covering 75 acres. There are over 2,000 animals, including about 80 endangered species. They are assembled according to the continent of origin in individual habitats surrounded by chasms so they do not need bars. These habitats are designed to simulate their natural surroundings.

One of the most beautiful of these is Tiger Falls completed in 1993 at a cost of $275,000. The tigers look especially serene with the wall of water behind them.

BLESSING OF THE CARS

Though they no longer actually "bless" the cars, an L.A. annual rite of spring is the:

Blessing of the Cars
Arroyo Seco Park

5568 Via Marisol
Los Angeles, CA 90042
normally first weekend in March
(213) 485-2437

Originally, a priest stood in (what else?) a drive-through booth and blessed about 200 cars that passed through. Because the City of Los Angeles Cultural Affairs became a sponsor, this is no longer part of this event for the obvious reason that church and state must stay separate.

The important thing about the Blessing of the Cars is that it acknowledges L.A.'s cruising culture. You will have a chance to see flashy painted mini-trucks and cars "hit their switches" and move and gyrate almost like human dancers. Many of the vehicles have been customized to include hydraulic lifts that shift them up or down and even lift a wheel like a performing elephant. Other attractions include student paintings with automotive themes, puppet shows, and bands.

Continuing along the Arroyo (or the 110), one arrives in Pasadena where a tribute to the automobile beckons the weary traveler:

Automobile As Art Museum
Route 66 Restaurant
425 South Fair Oaks Avenue
Pasadena, CA 91105
Tuesday-Sunday 11:30 a.m. to 8 p.m.
(818) 793-8462

This unique restaurant/museum surrounds its diners with possibly the most original setting for eating yet. The soft romantic lighting comes from sconces fashioned like hubcaps. French doors lead into 8,000-square-feet of every imaginable object d'art pertaining to the car. Beneath the high-beamed ceiling are metal sculptures, posters, oil paintings, photos, and even real vintage cars.

FEAST OF THE ANNUNCIATION

There are many celebrations in Southern California for Easter. One of the most memorable is the:

Greek Easter Picnic
St. Sophia's Cathedral
1324 South Normandie Avenue
Los Angeles, CA 90006
(213) 737-2424

Easter is traditionally celebrated in the countryside in Greece and this annual picnic is designed to honor that tradition. There is Greek food, dancing, a Greek band, and rides for children.

Built between 1948 to 1952, St. Sophia's Cathedral has been called one of the most beautiful churches in the world. Though the dome is imposing, being of traditional Byzantine style, its exterior is relatively unadorned.

The interior, however, is magnificent. The aisles are as long as a 15-story building laid on its side and the dome is lined with Byzantine styled mosaics. There are 21 Czechoslovakian crystal chandeliers, beautiful icons and murals, and 12 enormous stained glass windows that depict scenes of the Holy Trinity and the Apostles. The naive literally blazes with gold.

Charles Skouras is largely responsible for this architectural marvel. Thus, movie magnate Alexander Pantages was not the only Greek to leave an edifice that is part of the Southern California landscape.

APRIL

Pegleg Smith Liars Contest

Ramona Pageant

Orange Blossoms in the Southland

High Desert Wildflowers

California Poppy

Public Gardens

Renaissance Pleasure Faire

Buddha's Birthday (April 8)

Shakespeare's Birthday (April 23)

Santa Barbara Vintner's Festival

Dodger Baseball Season

La Fiesta Broadway

Chapter Four

APRIL

April is a beautiful young girl, fresh, and all full of hope. The wonders and joys of spring are in full bloom and our desire for love soars with our hearts. April is lights and songs and dancing in the park, with all the happiest and lightest of thoughts:

A Book of Verses underneath the Bough,
A Jug of Wine, a Loaf of Bread—and Thou

I think Omar Khayyám must have had April in mind when he wrote this verse in the 11th century with its inevitable conclusion that today is much more important than tomorrow. (Of course, taxes are also due this month, which on the 15th can definitely mean today is more important than tomorrow.)

Oh, is spring welcome! "April"—some think it Etruscan in origin, others favor the Greek "Aphro" or "Aphrodite," goddess of desire. Though many historians think otherwise, I opt for the latter linguistic option since it is quite obvious to me that spring fever is a very real thing.

Though spring began last month, April is the first full month of spring. It is the month when we "gain an hour" of daylight. Our energy levels increase, resulting in the restless burst of activity we call "spring cleaning." Our lives seem filled with hope and promise. The very sound of the name "April" conjures up images of sweetness and youth.

This is a delicious month in Southern California, a month of colors and smells and tastes. The wildflower season which began at the lowest elevations in late February really comes into its own in April and there are several annual occurrences that are fundamental to the region's identity.

PEGLEG SMITH LIAR'S CONTEST

There are many things happening in the Southland in April, but there is a series of three events that go beyond just telling a story about the unique historical mystique of Southern California. They are the Ramona Pageant, the San Bernardino National Orange Show, and the:

Pegleg Smith Liar's Contest
Calcite Canyon, 13 miles east of the Pegleg Smith Monument
County Road S22 near Borrego Springs, Anza-Borrego

Desert State Park, first Saturday night of April
(619) 767-5311

There was a real person called Pegleg Smith. His legal name was Thomas Long Smith and he was one of the great characters of the frontier days in the Southland. He became Pegleg after he lost his leg as a young man. It was shattered by an arrow in a fight with some California Indians in 1827.

Two years later, while transporting animal pelts from Southern Utah to the dusty little Mexican Pueblo of Los Angeles, Smith camped on the crest of the most hospitable looking of three buttes in what is now the Anza-Borrego Desert. He found some mysterious looking black pebbles. When he scraped off the black "desert varnish," he uncovered some brilliant gold nuggets.

It didn't seem to mean much to him at the time. He spent the next 20 years horse trading and rustling and achieved his greatest success in the latter occupation. In 1840, he and his sidekick Jim Beckwourth pulled off the historical equivalent of the "Great Train Robbery of Horses."

They got the idea from a Ute Indian named Walkara—an aggressive young chief of a renegade band of Paiutes, Utes, and other splintered tribes who engaged in all kinds of enterprises. These included robbing the Spanish trade caravans, stealing women and children and trading them to Navajos for ponies, and a special kind of equestrian grand larceny.

Smith and Beckwourth got a chance to check out the technique while traveling with the young chief. They let horses out of the corrals of several large California ranchos and herded the resulting 600 steeds through Cajon Pass. Inspired by this, Smith put together a scheme for what might rank as the single largest horse rustle in history.

The San Bernardino Valley area, site of the prototype rustle, was a rich picking grounds. The ranchos were vast and horse stockades were often miles from the main ranch houses. This immense amount of territory would be a factor in the plan.

On a full moon night, they all took their places. Beckwourth led a party of horsemen along the Spanish Trail, through the pass and into the valley. Small parties of Walkara's braves positioned themselves at the corral entrances of several of the largest ranchos. At the signal, the gates were opened all at once and the horses galloped into one gigantic thundering herd of about 5,000, heading toward the pass and out of the valley.

This tactic caught the ranchers completely off guard. Though they responded quickly, a herd that big is almost impossible to stop. They worked like demons, but there was still no way they could recover more than about 2,000 animals.

Perhaps the most comical part of the story is what Walkara was doing while all of this was happening. During the melee, the exhausted rancheros were taking a break at a watering hole. The plucky chief and his closest companions snuck up on the weary men—and stole their horses!

Though undoubtedly this little operation was enormously profitable, Mr. Smith was not one to be prudent with his funds. He came back to L.A. in 1850 and began the final phase of his life in which he made his living by getting people excited about his "lost gold." With a little coaxing in the form of a few rounds of whisky, he would tell the story to interested parties. He even talked some people into financing three successive (unsuccessful) expeditions.

Presumably even "the most superlative liar who ever honored California with his presence" can run out of listeners, so at this point moving out of town became a good idea. He moved to San Francisco where he continued his career as a whiskey-powered storyteller and eventually died in 1866.

Ironically, after his death, interest in finding the mine actually increased until it was almost a fad around the turn of the century. Fortune hunters of varying degrees of expertise poked around over ever increasing areas of the desert.

The Liar's Contest celebrates Smith's yarn-spinning abilities. It is held the first Saturday night of April every year at the site of an old calcite mine, 13 miles east of the **Pegleg Smith Monument.**

The monument isn't going to create any competition for Mt. Rushmore. It is basically a big pile of rocks originally started in 1948 by Hollywood art director Harry Oliver, who had founded the "Pegleg Smith Club" in 1916.

Oliver seemed to have had an affinity for Smith. Besides his film work, he was a pioneer of sorts, having homesteaded a plot of land in the remote Anza-Borrego Desert where he particularly liked to watch people looking for the treasure.

He once said that people "seem to figure it's easier to find a mine someone else has lost than to find one no one ever found, so most of them are huntin' for the mysterious lost ones that's been talked about so much."

His club indeed increased awareness of the lost mine—and resultant would-be prospectors—but by the middle of the 1920s, the craze had abated somewhat. Oliver responded by buying about 200 old looking wooden legs, which he planted in caves all over the Anza-Borrego Desert.

The monument was created to introduce the first "Lost Pegleg Mine Trek." It started as a circle on the ground at Oliver's homestead site with a sign that read: "Let him who seeks Pegleg Smith's gold add 10 rocks to this monument. The bigger the rocks, the better luck you'll have." These "treks" were pretty informal get togethers, complete with a big campfire where stories were exchanged. The annual liar's contest is patterned after these gatherings. Since the art director was born on April 1st, it was also a birthday party.

Some of the winning lies have been quite witty. There was one fable about the discovery of "bullsite" and "bolonium," minerals with unique properties used in government cities such as Washington, D.C. Perhaps the most spectacular example in recent years was "Diablo's Gold," an epic 34-verse musical.

Besides the promotional skills of first Smith and then Oliver, the other reason why the legend of the Lost Pegleg has inspired so many searches is the peculiar quality of the terrain where the mine is said to be located. S22 going toward Salton Sea is called **Erosion Road** for a reason: the landscape it passes through is truly bizarre. This is because geologically, the Anza-Borrego Desert is like a frying pan of dozens of little earthquake faults. The large San Andreas Fault cuts across near the northeastern edge of the park.

Four miles south of S22 by dirt road, a short distance east of the Peg Leg Smith Monument, you will come to **Font's Point**. From here, you will have one of the Southland's most unique vistas: a panorama of tilted sandstone, cut this way and that with gashes and ridges, that looks like the surface of Mars.

This is the **Borrego Badlands,** which are the result of sediment from Lake Cahuilla being broken by faulting action into the weird shapes and folds of layered rock you see today. Since the mid- to late-1900s, would-be prospectors have roamed this strange, desolate outback in search of the "Lost Pegleg."

The Anza-Borrego Desert is full of stories of the Old West. The two county roads, S2 and S22, are both rich in tales from the past. If you head south on S2, you will take in some real Southern California history:

Vallecito Stage Coach Station County Park
County Highway S2, 18 miles south of SR 78

In the mid-1800s, the California Gold Rush created a need for transportation and mail service which the Butterfield Stage Line soon provided. In the peak years of operation from 1858 to 1861, the route went from St. Louis to San Francisco and was somehow covered in less than 24 days! The southern route of the overland mail stopped in 1861 due to the outbreak of the civil war.

This station was built in 1857. It is hard to believe by just looking at it that it was a well-known stop between San Antonio and Los Angeles. The Vallecito Stage

Coach Station is basically an empty box made of sod that was reconstructed. But at one time, for those heading West, it was the first outpost after crossing the desert.

Despite the romantic image of travel by stage coach, it was extremely unpleasant. It was very hot and sticky with a steady stream of flying dust and a jolting ride from hard wheels on desolate dirt roads. They hardly ever stopped, so stations along the Butterfield Trail had special meaning for passengers.

Sometimes people died on the way and were buried at the next station. Sometimes fights erupted that were usually settled with guns or knives. This is why there is so much accumulated lore about these stations, which look so unimpressive today.

There seems to be more ghost stories about this area than any other in the desert. Somewhere around 1858-59, the Butterfield Stage was on its way to Vallecito, when it was held up by four bandits. Two of them were shot and killed, but the leader and one of his men got away with $65,000, which they buried in the desert. They were celebrating at Vallecito when they began a heated exchange. The argument escalated into a fight which they settled like men by shooting each other.

Now the "ghost of the leader's white horse" gallops around the desert, disappearing when you are near the buried cash. The loyal stallion is said to protect his former rider's legacy by disguising the loot's whereabouts.

There are so many tales about stagecoaches and the various calamities that befell them, it is a miracle to me anyone made it to California. Back in the 1860s, a stage passing through the area on its way to San Diego with a strongbox of gold met with particularly bad fortune. First the guard became mysteriously ill and abruptly got off. Then the driver was held up and shot dead by outlaws in the Carrizo Wash. Legend has it that as the driver fell forward he urged his mules on with his dying breath.

The noble steeds responded with a supernatural speed that continues to this day. The "Phantom Stage of Carrizo Wash" now haunts the place: the Southland's own "Flying Dutchman," a ghostly four-mule stage with one driver and no passengers hurtling along now unused trails through the desert night.

But the most famous specter of this little corner of the desert is "White Lady of Vallecito." She was a beautiful young woman who had come cross-country from the East Coast to California on her way to Sacramento to be married. Her fiance had struck it rich in the gold fields.

She was a society girl and did not take well to the rough journey. By the time she got to Vallecito, she was very ill. She died at the station and was buried in her white wedding gown. Now in the evenings, she quietly patrols the Vallecito Station bedecked in her ghostly wedding finery.

RAMONA PAGEANT

The Pegleg story says a lot about the dreams that brought people to the Southland. The horse rustling anecdote is almost a microcosm of Early California history. Basically, the native Californians were beat up first by the mission system, then by the rancheros—and then the Yankees beat up both what was left of the Indians and their ranchero tormentors.

Another annual event that takes place every April that in some ways illustrates this historical point, is one of the most romantic and beautiful rites of spring in Southern California. It is the longest-running continuous theatrical tradition in the Southland and has taken place every year beginning this month since 1923 in an outdoor amphitheater, set in a lovely canyon on the slopes of Mount San Jacinto in Riverside County:

> **Ramona Pageant**
> **Ramona Bowl**
> **27400 Ramona Bowl Road**
> **Hemet, CA 92344**
> **late April through early May**
> **Saturday & Sunday 3:30 p.m.**
> **tickets: $16 to $19**
> **(909) 658-3111 or (800) 645-4465**

This is a truly remarkable experience. With a cast of more than 350, it is a spectacular show based on Helen Hunt Jackson's 1883 love story about a Cahuilla Indian and a half-Mexican girl named Ramona. The title character is said to be a mosaic of numerous women the author had met. She had traveled throughout the state as part of a government study about the terrible conditions confronting Indians who had lived under the mission system.

A little side note to Southern California history is that she was assisted in this by a San Gabriel foothills rancher named Abbot Kinney, who acted as her interpreter. He would later found Venice, California (see July) and be instrumental in preserving the area that would become the Angeles National Forest (see May).

Jackson's novel was controversial in its day because it was one of the first times that a depiction of the harsh treatment of the indigenous people of California had been presented to the public. Some citizens thought that it was better to gloss over this particular aspect of American history, but that didn't interfere with the book's popularity—or the success of this show.

It has music and dancing and authentic Native American rituals. The colors and pageantry are wonderful as is the sound in the good natural acoustics of the canyon. The site is a full 160 acres and they use it fully. There are scenes where horsemen appear on the hill in the background, then come charging down center stage.

There is no pay for the actors, but the roles of Ramona and Alessandro are coveted. Raquel Welch once played Ramona. This is a very famous event and early reservations are advised. They start taking them on January 1 by mail. For an order form, write to the Ramona Pageant Association, P.O Box 755, Hemet, CA 92343.

Of course, as the play so dramatically points out, Southern California had residents long before the arrival of the Spanish and there are a number of unusual remains of earlier Southland peoples. If you go west from Hemet on SR 74 (Ortega Highway) for just over 4-1/2 miles to California Avenue and make a right, you will be in an obscure little park which features one of the great odd sights of Southern California:

Maze Rock County Park
Hemet
Daily during daylight hours
(909) 787-2553

"Petrogeny" is the study of rocks (it comes from the same root as "petroleum"). A "petroglyph" is an inscription or a carving on a rock. The many kids who carved their names on rocks probably did not realize that they were petroglyphers at the time. Petroglyphs are often used as proof of everything from the existence of aliens (where they are aimed heavenward) to the existence of unrecorded early races or events.

This one is about three-square-feet, but it is outside, not in a cave, and is on a huge boulder that is extremely prominent. The name is derived from the shape of the design, which looks like a maze you might find in a *Highlights* magazine in the dentist's office, until you notice that it is four intersecting swastikas.

Since the design does not resemble petroglyphs found among the known native American Tribes, its origin is ascribed to a mysterious "Maze Culture." It has also been attributed obliquely to the Mayans via their ancestors, the "Cascadians," about 15,000 years ago. But then, of course, another group believes it proved it to be a Buddhist symbol left by Chinese explorers who visited America around 500 A.D.

It is mind boggling to most Southern Californians to think of someone being here 15,000 years ago. To most people, our history began somewhere around 1963. But there were several native American tribes with distinct cultures that were getting along fine before the Spanish arrived.

Connected to Hemet is Riverside County's oldest incorporated city, **San Jacinto.** This small town with its pioneer heritage still has its Main Street. One of the outstanding buildings, a state historical monument, is one of the oldest operating hotels in California:

Virginia Lee Hotel
248 East Main Street
San Jacinto, CA 92383
(909) 654-2270

This is the oldest continuously operating hotel in Riverside County, having originally opened as the Lockwood House in 1884. It became the Pioneer Hotel in the '40s and was purchased by the current owner, the real Virginia Lee in 1976. She had always loved the place so much that her friends would say jokingly (and prophetically) as they passed by the Pioneer, "Look there's Virginia's hotel!"

The two-story redwood frontier-style building has had minimal changes in its long history. Two big earthquakes, in 1899 and 1918, leveled much of the rest of the original town, but aside from a few cracks, the hotel is much the same as it has always been.

There is a pretty lawn and garden and a bright place for some java called "Al's Coffee Room." The first floor also features a display of vintage clothing that is used to stage fashion shows from the past, as well as a unique little museum of black history.

Each of the 10 rooms is individually decorated and has an old-fashioned style pull chain toilet along with a sink. Also on the second floor, where the guest rooms are, is a big community bath. There are two rooms available with their own showers.

This is a very reasonable place at $40 per night including continental breakfast. Virginia's husband Al is a former baker and his homemade breads and sweet rolls fill the air with a wonderful aroma in the morning.

From here, Highway 74 can be taken toward the ocean or toward Idyllwild in the

San Jacinto mountains (see May). A great stop on your way up to Idyllwild is the good old:

Lypps Fruit Stand
46208 East Florida (Highway 74)
Hemet, CA 92544

I remember stop-
ping here as a young
man on vacations with
my parents. Lypps has
been here for nearly a
half century—and you
can still get a big bag
of tangerines for $1.
As you drive up, you
come upon a scene
you would expect to
find on a country road:
a rustic house with a

mailbox in front, a display that sells home grown produce, maybe some cactus and various other items, and a road lined with citrus groves.

ORANGE BLOSSOMS IN THE SOUTHLAND
San Bernardino, Riverside, Redlands

An annual event that is perhaps somewhat diminished in stature, but which hear-kens back to the roots of the California citrus industry is the venerable:

National Orange Show
689 South East Street
San Bernardino Chamber of Commerce
P.O. Box 658
San Bernardino, CA 92402
last 10 days of April
(909) 885-7515

This festival originated in 1915 and features county-fair type stuff over two weekends and the weekdays in between. In recent years they have added some animated citrus exhibits to the lineup of 4-H displays and animals, midway and carnival games, military parade, hobby and crafts show, model railroad exhibit, marionette show, Polynesian music and dance competition, and the rodeo. It takes place at a 200-acre multi-purpose facility of the same name that includes a stadium that seats 4,500, a restaurant, and several exhibit halls.

How this show came into being and how the California citrus industry came to be born in many ways picks up the story begun in the accounts of Pegleg Smith and the Ramona Pageant.

The Mission San Gabriel was the starting point for many priests and settlers who fanned out though the middle of Southern California in the early 1800s. On the Feast Day of Saint Bernard of Siena, May 20 of 1810, one of these priests named Father Dumetz performed mass in a little chapel he had built in a fertile valley at the foot of the mountains. The pious father called the region, **San Bernardino**. Little did the father realize his name would someday designate the largest county in the United States.

In 1851, a group of Mormons founded what would become the city of San Bernardino. They purchased the ranch from Don Antonio Maria Lugo and built a fortified compound near where the modern day courthouse sits today, on Arrowhead Avenue.

Their need for lumber went beyond what lumbermen at the time could supply by hand cutting and pit sawing the trees. So they went after it themselves and carved "The Mormon Road" up the west end of the San Bernardino Mountains in a mere two weeks.

In three years, there would be six sawmills grinding up the beautiful giant trees that had stood for centuries in the forest-covered mountains to build a "theocracy in the wilderness." The Mormons sent political emissaries to Sacramento and thus America's largest county was formed.

Things were looking good for the colony. Henry G. Sherwood, the architect of Salt Lake City was even going to design the new super city. Unfortunately, the California Mormons started seeing things their own way and even opposed the official church backed candidates for offices in the new county. In 1857, when it became apparent that the California Colony was starting to become more autonomous, Brigham Young summoned all colonists back.

The area was not to lack settlers, however. In 1870, after comparing different areas, abolitionist John W. North founded **Riverside**, not too far from the Mormon colony. That same year, the U.S. Department of Agriculture brought the navel orange from Bahia, Brazil. Twelve small trees provided buds that were propagated on sweet orange seedlings in a greenhouse in Washington D.C.

In 1872, Luther and Eliza Tibbetts had three orange saplings shipped all the way to Riverside. Two survived the long journey and were planted in 1873. The seedless fruit produced by these trees became legendary for its taste and quality. Buds from the Tibbets' trees suddenly were in big demand.

These would give birth to an inland empire industry that would become a fundamental part of the California mystique. It is estimated that by 1910 the spawn of the two trees covered more than 100,000 acres! One of the two original trees is still alive and is a living monument:

> **Parent Washington Navel Orange Tree**
> **City Park**
> **Southwest corner of Arlington and Magnolia**
> **Riverside**

Situated by a busy intersection, there is something delightfully innocent about this little triangle shaped grove of citrus trees enclosed by a wrought iron fence. Amidst them is "California Historical Landmark Number 20," and it still bears fruit.

Two railroads, the Santa Fe and the Southern Pacific, crossed the United States from the East Coast to Los Angeles by 1873. During the same decade, Cahuilla Indians were being used to build canals and as a labor force.

By the middle of the 1880s, the Riverside/San Bernardino area had a growing navel orange industry with annual sales of $200 million. By this time, Chinese immigrants made up the main labor force. In 1893 the California Fruit Growers Exchange was formed. With the advent of refrigerated cars and mechanical processing techniques, California citrus became available throughout the United States.

The prosperity this created became legendary: orange groves, big houses, and an easy lifestyle—all kissed by the sun (hmmm). This was the California that would lure thousands of Dust Bowl farmers during the Great Depression. In *The Grapes of Wrath*, John Steinbeck's masterpiece about the period, Grandpa Joad imagines California to be a place where oranges grow along every road.

As cars and highways developed, orange-shaped stands offering concocted orange drinks became a California trademark. The first "Giant Orange" stand opened along Highway 99 in Tracy in 1926. Over the next 20 years they sprouted at the rate of about one per year. Freeways spelled the end of these and other elements of roadside culture. Fittingly enough, the last Giant Orange closed in 1973—the year that Interstate 5 was completed.

If you would like to experience a little of this brush stroke of California history, start at the **Parent Washington Navel Orange Tree** and take Magnolia south to Van

Buren Boulevard. Make a left here, and when you get to the corner of Dufferin Avenue, suddenly a vision from the past will greet you: a replica of a Giant Orange roadside stand. This is the official sign for:

California Citrus State Historic Park
1879 Jackson Street
Riverside, CA 92504
(909) 780-6222

This unique, still developing park will eventually have 400 acres of lemon, grapefruit, and of course, orange groves. These are interspaced throughout the hilly terrain, which has a trail, lined with palm trees, that runs through it. The brand new wooden buildings include a visitor's center and gazebo.

Besides being an historical center, it also is a working farm. Proceeds from the sale of the fruit will be used to develop the park. Plans include recreating a 1930's W.P.A. worker camp, a packing house, and a mansion such as the owner of a citrus ranch might have lived in.

Though for many, the dream of getting rich as a citrus grower was to remain a dream, great fortunes were made by others. Of course, another monument of sorts to the gilded industry of the California navel orange is a landmark in downtown Riverside:

Mission Inn
3649 7th Street
Riverside, CA 92501
(909) 784-0300

This is one of the great but odd architectural delights of Southern California. It was built over a 30 year period with no central design. The Mission Inn was simply added on to at the personal whim of its remarkable builder, Frank Miller, who bought the original property in 1880. Will Rogers called it "the most unique hotel in America."

The links of this hotel to the heart of Southern California's traditions are deep. Miller was good friends with Charles Fletcher Lummis, immortalized by his home "Al Alisal," now part of the Southwest Museum (see October). Both men were what would

Riverside's Mission Inn.

now be called "multi-culturalists" in that they appreciated and enjoyed other cultures and their impact on the Southland. Likewise, both were interested in preserving the Mexican and Spanish heritage of Southern California through architecture. Arthur Benton, Lummis' associate, was the architect of the lobby (built in 1902) and the two south wings.

Each wing has its own style. The first one Miller added, the Mission wing (1903), is obviously Mission Revival and has a meditative mood with its adobe walls, stained glass windows, and seemingly endless little niches. It is built in a U-shape around the original property. The Spanish wing has a Moorish feel with its elaborate stained glass skylights, hand-painted tiles, and soaring domed ceilings.

Off the lobby is the **Cloister Music Room,** added in 1910. Also off the lobby is the **Spanish Patio,** constructed in 1914. It contains a marble statue of Pomona, sort of a Roman goddess of fruit trees, and a Spanish gargoyle fountain.

In 1920, Miller purchased an ornate 200-year-old gold-leafed Mexican cedar altar made for the Rayas family in Guanajuato. The inveterate collector, he bought it sight unseen without realizing how big and impressive it really was. When it arrived in Riverside and was set up, Miller was so moved by its magnificence that he pledged to build a fitting home around it. The famous result was the Saint Francis Chapel and Courtyard, built on the second level in 1931.

The last addition to the hotel would be its crown jewel: the International Rotunda. It is a five-story, open-air circular courtyard. This type of fantastic architecture is not particularly space efficient however. The Mission Inn has 320,000-square-feet and takes up a full city block, yet it only has 240 rooms. It recently had a $40,000,000 renovation that included some layout changes: for example, The Presidential Suite has been converted into the **Presidential Lounge.**

There are hotels with impressive lists of luminaries who have stayed there, but none to match the pedigree of the Mission Inn. Presidents Benjamin Harrison, William Howard Taft, and William McKinley gave reality to the name of the "Presidential Suite." Richard Nixon married Pat in the suite itself and Nancy and Ronald Reagan honeymooned here. Humphrey Bogart married his first wife on the property as well.

Jessie Van Brunt was the artist who created much of the stained glass work around the hotel. You can stay in a room that bears her name. It features a curved sitting room illuminated by some of her artwork. This is one of several special rooms, more expensive than the regular ones, that are architecturally or thematically unique.

Perhaps the architecture of the Mission Inn is best explained in the words of its builder, Frank Miller: "Dramatize what you do."

The Mission Inn is located in an old-fashioned downtown outdoor mall. It has shops, museums, and pretty landscaping, and it will make you nostalgic for the days when people gathered in the public places of cities to socialize.

Beginning this month and continuing through August, that feeling returns when the Riverside Downtown Association sponsors a **Main Street Market Night** from 4 p.m. to 8 p.m. with live music, a certified farmer's market, pony rides, and food stands. For information on Downtown activities, stop by the Visitor's Center at 3720 Main or call (909) 715-4636 for a recorded message.

Throughout the year, Riverside's museums are free on Wednesday. An excellent museum is extremely close to the Mission Inn:

> **California Museum of Photography**
> **3824 Main Street**
> **Riverside, CA 92509**
> **Monday & Wednesday-Saturday 11 a.m. to 5 p.m.**
> **Sunday 12 p.m. to 5 p.m., closed Tuesday**

(909) 787-4787, (909) 784-FOTO (24 hour events hot line)

Looking at the relatively new (1990) Post Modern facade of this four-level gem, it is hard to believe it was once a 1930's Kress "five and dime" store. It was remodeled by San Francisco archi-

The California Museum of Photography is the West Coast's largest photography museum.

tect Stanley Saitowitz into one of my favorite interior spaces in the Southland. Its 8,000-square-feet make it the largest photography museum on the West Coast.

The California Museum of Photography designed to be a giant poetic representation of a camera. You enter on the first level through a concave glass wall, much as light enters a camera through the lens. The museum's store and two galleries are in this lobby area. The exhibits include both photos and cameras.

The museum began in 1973, at first only showcasing cameras. The collection, a gift from a local surgeon, came from U.C. Riverside where the 3,000 cameras had been stored on campus in obscurity for years. With the acquisition of photos and negatives, the museum expanded its exhibitions. Now the museum archives hundreds of thousands of negatives along with nearly 20,000 prints by such famous photographers as Ansel Adams.

Continuing along Main Street, you can follow the aroma to:

Birdy Coffeehouse
3527 Main Street
Riverside, CA 92501
(909) 781-6691

This pleasant coffee house has real European flair thanks to owner Inga Vormbrock, a German import. After drinking coffee, my first impulse is to browse in a bookstore:

Universal Book Store
3582 Main Street
Riverside, CA 92501

Monday-Saturday 10 a.m. to 6 p.m
(909) 682-1082

Owner Elizabeth Ferree took over a moribund bookstore and together with manager Steve Giuliani created a true focal point in the mall. There are two well-organized floors packed with books—making it the largest new and used bookstore in Riverside. Steve is very knowledgeable about books, having a masters degree in English literature from nearby U.C. Riverside.

The giant corner where San Bernardino and Riverside Counties come together is connected geographically and historically. Besides San Bernardino and Riverside, another city in this triangle with a related history is **Redlands**. It was started as a planned community by Edward G. Judson and Frank E. Brown. They literally meant "red lands" because they named it after the color of the soil.

It was—and is to a certain extent—a place of orange groves. Despite the ever encroaching tract houses and shopping malls, there is still a place that you can stay and create the illusion that you are back in the days of genteel orange growing society. Partially surrounded by orange groves is one of the most amazing structures in the world for lovers to stay:

Morey Mansion
190 Terracina Boulevard
Redlands, CA 92373
(909) 793-7970

When you first look at this elaborate lavender with gold trim gingerbread structure, it is Victorian. As your eye passes over its exterior features, one notes its Russian Orthodox onion dome, Chinese veranda, French roof on the tower, and three styles of windows, and concludes it is more like *Alice In Wonderland* Victorian. At night it must be seen to be believed: it looks like it belongs in fairyland.

Besides its location and its amazing exterior, its history makes it a truly apt place for lovers to stay, especially in April to celebrate the orange blossoms. In 1882, a woman named Mrs. Sarah Morey started an orange tree nursery to raise the then astronomical sum of $20,000 for the family dream home. Her husband David, who was a retired master shipbuilder and cabinetmaker, built the house in 1890 as a symbol of his love and devotion to her.

The interior lives up to the promise of the exterior. It is a time machine back to the 19th century. The carved golden oak entryway, with its heavy wooden staircase coming down, is set off with

One of the exquisitely furnished rooms in the Morey Mansion.

original wallpaper and antiques. Orange blossoms are featured in the elaborate woodworking that also includes anchors, dragon's tails, and assorted flowers and animals. Other details include Belgian beveled glass and Tiffany-styled leaded windows.

Very little has been "modernized." Even the light switches are old fashioned. The overall feel is of old richness: the drapes are plush velvet. Because so much of the original family home has been preserved, their presence seems to be felt.

For a special event in a classic setting while in Redlands, stop by:

Edwards's Mansion Restaurant
2064 Orange Tree Lane
Redlands CA 92374
(909) 793-2031

This restored Victorian house has been converted to a banquet facility. It is a real throwback to the grand old days with its greenhouse and orange trees.

Since railroads played such a crucial part in the development of the citrus industry in Riverside County, it is not unusual that a festival is held this month:

Rail Festival
Orange Empire Railway Museum
2201 South A Street
Perris, CA 92370

Daily from 9 a.m. to 5 p.m.
Trolleys and trains operate on Saturday & Sunday
and holidays 11 a.m. to 5 p.m.
(909) 657-2605

This is like a small city of trains. The grounds are free, but if you buy an all-day pass, you can ride on an amazing assortment of rail vehicles. The old trolleys are really a trip back in time, as you read the original advertising posters on the walls above the seats. The locomotives and cars are staffed by volunteers in uniform who take their roles as conductors and motormen seriously enough to add real flavor to the experience.

Driving as I do, to and from speaking engagements at so many colleges in the Southland, I know the freeways well. Despite L.A. drivers' reputation for fast driving, they can't hold a candle to the drivers on the inland freeways of Riverside and San Bernardino Counties. Since we are within a fairly short high speed run to Corona, I should also mention April is probably the best month to pay a visit to the:

Glen Ivy Hot Springs
25000 Glen Ivy Road
Corona, CA 91719
Daily to 10 a.m. to 6 p.m.
(909) 277-3529

Glen Ivy, like so many other Southern California institutions, got its start in the 20th century as a hangout for Hollywood celebrities. Like many places, it also fell on hard times and was dilapidated when it was bought in 1977 and refurbished by some farsighted investors.

Now it has 16 massage rooms with a choice of Swedish or Shiatsu massage and a salon that does manicures, pedicures, facials, waxing, hair styling and body treatments such as eucalyptus wraps. The ten acre grounds are lushly landscaped. There are also 15 assorted pools, saunas, and the famous mud.

There is a shallow pool where the reddish glop is brought in from a nearby canyon. The mud bath is free and visitors go through 15 tons of it a year. After coating themselves with it, they lie on chaise lounges and bake in the sun like so much terra cotta statuary. This month, area orange groves perfume the surrounding air.

Orange County

Richard Hall Gilman planted the first orange trees here in the 1870s (they were Valencias). Just as Pasadena was settled by wealthy Easterners wishing to grow citrus in the sun, so it was in this community to the south. When the county officially formed in 1889, "Orange County" was the overwhelmingly popular choice for a name.

In 1940, 65,000 acres of groves enriched Orange County. Ironically, though it was named for the luscious fruit, there is very little here today to show why. The developer's bulldozers have relentlessly cut into that acreage. By 1960, it was down to 30,000. By 1980, it was down to 5,400. In 1993, another 1,000 acres were sawed up, leaving a mere 1,000 acres of the sweet smelling trees. What is left is mostly on the eastern edge of Lake Forest and Irvine. The most obvious survivor is a grove of 5,000 trees spread over 20 acres on Jeffrey Road at the entrance to Irvine Valley College.

One Orange County historian I interviewed (who asked that I not print her name) suggested that the name of the county be changed to "Beige County," in honor of the endless rows of tract houses of that color that have replaced the oranges.

The City of Orange was incorporated appropriately enough in the month of orange blossoms on April 6, 1888. It was founded by two lawyers, named A. B. Chapman and Andrew Glassell, who had received 1,000 acres of land as payment for legal services. They decided on the original 40 acre plot in 1871 and set out a blueprint inspired by William Penn's plans for Philadelphia.

They wanted to call the place "Richland," but that name was already taken. One of the more humorous stories of the Southland is how this somewhat staid and conservative city got its present name: the two attorneys and two other men had a poker game in which the winner got to pick from among the names of the town's biggest crops: orange, olive, lemon, and almond. Needless to say, the winner was orange.

Many of the city's older structures still stand; one of these is:

> **Watson's Drugs**
> **116 E. Chapman Avenue**
> **Orange, CA 92666**
> **(714) 532-6315**

This is Orange County's oldest drugstore and the city's oldest business, having started in 1899. The first owner's son, Kellar Watson, Jr., was the first World Champion Surfer in 1934 and '35. He sold it in '65. After a couple of short-term possessors, the present owner Scott Parker bought it in 1970.

Watson's is a pharmacy, but it is also an old-fashioned '50's-style soda fountain that serves full breakfast and lunch. It is a fun place to eat and is decorated with ceiling fans and antiques on the walls.

The San Fernando Valley

I am not particularly old, but I am old enough to remember the orange groves on the corner opposite the house where I grew up in, and I remember what they smelled like this month. I grew up in the San Fernando Valley, notorious for shopping malls and slowly slurred speech among its young. But at one time, it was a place of Southern California dreams in much the same way Pasadena was, except the Valley was the happening place for Anglos who came later. It had Bing Crosby to sing about it and Bob Hope to buy it.

In the '50s, it attracted my parents from the icy winters of Cleveland to the warm evenings of Encino. It was a town of Hollywood celebrities and expatriate Eastern-ers and Midwesterners. My father could wave to Clark Gable in his Jaguar. I went to John Wayne's daughter Aiessa's birthday party at the Wayne estate in Encino when I was in the first grade. Germaine Jackson was in my Business Law class at Birmingham High School. I used to occasionally give him a ride home until he got his first car, which was a turbo Porsche.

Encino means "oak" in Spanish. One of the most endearing sights in the entire Valley is the:

Oak Tree
Louise Avenue
(no address, just south of Ventura Boulevard)
Encino

Now this is an intelligent approach to development: in order to preserve the tree, Louise Avenue was built around it. When you first approach this incredible tree, you might think it was several trees close together. That is because the branches spread over an area about half the size of a football field. The trunk is nearly nine-feet in diameter.

Encino has grown by leaps and bounds, and now it would be unrecognizable to someone living there when my parents first arrived. There are glitzy stores and high rise office buildings, but like an island amidst it all is a secret little throwback to an earlier era:

Rancho de Los Encinos State Historic Park
16756 Moorpark Street
Encino, CA 91436
Wednesday-Sunday 10 a.m. to 5 p.m.
house tours 1 p.m. to 4 p.m. ($2)
closed Thanksgiving, Christmas, New Year's Day
(818) 784-4849

You used to be able to see this restful little site with its spring-fed lake, duck ponds, and eucalyptus trees more easily from Ventura Boulevard. Built in 1849 by Don Vicente de la Osa, it was a stage stop from 1845 to 1915 and the original nine-room adobe still stands.

Though Rancho El Encino, as it was originally called, reached 4,500 acres and had great herds of cattle and sheep, five acres are all that's left. There is a blacksmith's shop and a spooky looking two-story French country-style house that was designed by Eugene Garnier in 1870. There are also picnic tables (reservations required).

The Valley had a long history of growing things. This was epitomized by the role of the romantically designed:

Mission San Fernando Rey de España
15151 San Fernando Mission Boulevard
Mission Hills, CA 91345
(818) 361-0186

This mission was founded in 1797 by Friar Fermin Lasuen and completed in 1806—though nothing remains of the original structures except the ruins of the dam. The choice of location was based on facilitating the agricultural development of the Valley. Up until the secularization of the missions in the 1830s, most of the produce eaten by Los Angeles residents came through here.

The Mission San Fernando has a history of being destroyed by earthquakes. The first one flattened the place shortly after it was finished. It was rebuilt in 1818.

This mission looks—and is—relatively new. I was living in the Valley in 1971 for the Sylmar/San Fernando earthquake, when what was left of the old buildings were rattled to the point that they had to be razed. The restoration project was suppose to be faithful to the original building. The one it replaced, standing since 1935, was a more romanticized version with considerably more ornamentation.

Today, probably the closest manifestation of the old character of the Valley can be found at the:

Orcutt Ranch Horticulture Center
23600 Roscoe Boulevard
West Hills, CA 91304
Daily 7 a.m. to 5 p.m.
Tours last Sunday of each month 2 to 5 p.m.
(818) 346-7449

The former residence of oil geologist and engineer William Orcutt is a classic 1920s Spanish ranch with a rose garden, nature trails, and 33 giant oak trees, including one that is more than 700 years old. There are 16 acres of orange and grapefruit trees that this month fill the air with a delicious fragrance. There are many flowers around the grounds that bloom at different times of the year, including cashmere bouquets, hibiscus, camellias, and some particularly gorgeous azaleas.

As a teenager in the Valley in the late '60s and early '70s, one of my great adventures was finding natural places to climb around. A popular spot for this was **Chatsworth Park** because of its jumble of rocks. Director D.W. Griffith thought it made a good location to represent Hell for his movie *Home Sweet Home* starring Lillian Gish.

In a niche in the lower part of the southern section of the park is one of the last pioneer cottages:

> **The Homestead Acre**
> **10385 Shadow Oak Drive**
> **Chatsworth, CA 91311**
> **first Sunday of each month 1 to 4 p.m.**
> **(818) 882-5614**

All 230 acres of Chatsworth Park were originally the homestead of Minnie Hill Palmer. This is the original house and with its huge black walnut tree for shade and neat shutters, it is as close to "grandma's house" as you will ever find.

At the north end of the Valley, in Sylmar, is one of the great odd museums of the Southland:

> **San Sylmar: The Merle Norman Classic Beauty Collection**
> **15180 Bledsoe Street**
> **Sylmar, CA 93142**
> **(818) 367-2251**

This six-story building houses an extraordinary collection of antique cars with a smattering of assorted "beautiful things" thrown in. The chairman of the board of Merle Norman, J.B. Nethercutt, is responsible for this eclectic assortment.

There is a free two hour tour that starts in the "Rolls Royce Room," named for the six Phantom series cars (ranging from 1913 to 1979) and other special models of that famous marque.

On the third floor is the most bizarre display: gleaming glass cases loaded with hood ornaments. There are sprinting greyhounds, menacing bulldogs, bare-breasted women, and assorted cherubs, archers, and other mythological creatures.

Ventura County Citrus Groves

Adjacent to the San Fernando Valley is Ventura County and the main route of passage between the two is US 101. For a pleasant diversion and a lovely back country drive, take Highway 126 west from Interstate 5 near Bouquet Canyon. In some ways, this road illustrates the agricultural roots that run through all of Southern California. You will pass from L.A. into Ventura County and through some pretty farm areas.

You will go past the towns of Piru and Buckhorn, and then Fillmore. Fillmore is a town of about 12,000 people with a true rural flavor. It produces walnuts and avocados, but is most noted for citrus. The Fillmore Citrus Association operates the largest packing house in the entire state. It is better known as **Sunkist.**

Practically everywhere in town smells like orange blossoms this month, but to really experience the aroma of citrus blooms, drive three miles west of Filmore on Old Telegraph—which breaks away from 126 in town only to reconnect with it about four miles later. Make a right on 7th and another right on Oak and you will arrive at:

> **Kenny Grove Park**
> **823 North Oak Avenue**
> **Fillmore, CA 93015**

Situated in 15 acres of citrus groves are campsites and playgrounds and even a camp store. This time of year, a pretty stream should be running to complement the perfumed air.

Continuing on 126 from Fillmore, you will come to one of the Southland's most charming small towns, **Santa Paula**. This wonderful spring destination bears two monikers: "Hometown, U.S.A." and the "Citrus Capital of the World."

The former is because the town, located in the exact center of Ventura County, is nearly picture perfect with tree-lined Victorian neighborhoods surrounded by rolling hills, with mountain peaks in the distance. The latter reason is obvious from the groves you pass on your way in.

If you drive straight through town along 126, Telegraph Road splits off again and parallels the highway all the way to Ventura. Just outside the town proper on Telegraph is the remarkable:

> **Faulkner House**
> **14292 West Telegraph Road**
> **Santa Paula, CA 93060**

This is one landmark that is impossible to miss. If there were ever a structure that "dominates the landscape," it is this masterpiece of Queen Anne style, surrounded by avocado and citrus groves.

A full 8,000-square-feet, it was built in 1894 by the Ventura architectural and building firm of Herman Anlauf and Franklin Ward for one of the founding fathers of Ventura County agriculture, George Washington Faulkner. It has a three-story octagonal tower that can be seen for miles and a distinct irregular roof line with projecting gables. The front porch gracefully curves around the east side.

It is still in the Faulkner family in the person of great grandson Allan Ayers. Originally 150 acres, the property today occupies 27 acres. The first Mr. Faulkner planted all sorts of things, including apricots and soft shelled walnuts. Now the two primary crops are pumpkins and Christmas trees. The property is also used for weddings and as a film site.

The growth of agriculture in the Santa Clara Valley was paralleled by the arrival of the railroads. The Southern Pacific Santa Paula Depot was built in 1886. In 1887, the Southern Pacific Milling Company set up a chain of warehouses that followed the rail lines. This grew into a retail poultry, grain, and feed business.

With decreasing railroad traffic, the warehouses were sold off. One of them near the depot was purchased by an entrepreneur named Lou Hengehold in 1954. His sons have carried on the family tradition and it survives today as both a feed store and local museum:

> **The Mill**
> **212 North Mill Street**
> **Santa Paula, CA 93060**
> **Monday-Saturday 8 a.m. to 5 p.m.**
> **(805) 525-2710**

Ranchers still come here for supplies, but the building also has developed into an impromptu museum. There are hundreds of photographs on the walls that tell the history of the area. Some of these are over 100 years old.

Old farm and stable equipage is everywhere. An old stone grinding wheel hangs over the door. There are curios attached to the walls and suspended from the rafters. These include everything from buggy whips and harnesses to antique saddles and a grain grinder. Local brands have been burned into the beams.

If you would like to stay in a house that was built during the boom days of the railroad, take Mill Street south to Santa Paula, turn right and you will see:

> **The White Gables Inn**
> **715 East Santa Paula Street**

Santa Paula, CA 93060

(805) 933-3041

The White Gables was built in the same year as the Faulkner House, 1894. It is a three-story Victorian full of antiques. There are only three rooms, all with private baths. Full breakfast is included.

If there is a real Main Street among all of the streets with that name, it would be the 1890-vintage brick and sandstone one here just two blocks over. It has a real flavor to it: the four-sided town clock has bullet holes on its north face—courtesy of a spontaneous target practice session by a drunken ranch hand with a Winchester 30-30 in the year 1900.

Fittingly enough, there are several antique stores along Main Street. One of them has the world's longest name:

Musselman and Luttrull Antiques and Old Lighting

840 East Main Street

Santa Paula, CA 93060

(805) 525-5406

One door down is the more laconically named:

Antiques 848

848 East Main Street

Santa Paula, CA 93060

Thursday- Saturday 1 to 5 p.m.

(805) 525-5547

A little farther along Main is a corporate-sponsored museum:

Unocal Oil Museum

1001 East Main Street

Santa Paula, CA 93060

Wednesday-Sunday 10 a.m. to 4 p.m.

(805) 933-0076

This stately brick and stone Victorian was built in 1890 and was the original headquarters of Union Oil of California. Beautifully renovated, it traces Santa Paula's history and geology from a petroleum point of view.

A separate building in back houses a giant piece of antique machinery, an operating cabletool drilling rig complete with gears and belts that dates from the early days of oil exploration.

The museum's collection is not all antiques, however. There are video games like "Wildcatter" and screens showing old Union Oil television ads featuring none other than Buster Keaton and Marilyn Monroe. The Unocal offices upstairs have been reconstructed to appear as they did in the 1890s down to the original furniture. Sundays from 11 a.m. to 3 p.m., these are opened for tours.

Though not formally an aircraft museum, the Santa Paula Airport is the roosting point for a flock of antique and one-of-a-kind aircraft owned and piloted by professional pilots who love the old airport:

> **Santa Paula Airport**
> **Santa Maria Street**
> **Santa Paula**

Small airports in agricultural areas often have a nostalgic barn storming quality to them. Santa Paula's airport is a real gem in this respect.

If Santa Paula is an archetype Southern California town, there is a restaurant close to the airport that is an archetype Southern California family restaurant:

> **Familia Diaz Restaurant**
> **10th and Harvard**
> **Santa Paula, CA 93060**
> **Daily 11 a.m. to 9 p.m.**
> **(805) 525-2813**

Growing up in the nearby San Fernando Valley, my favorite family dinner out was to the family-owned Mexican restaurant Fernando's. Familia Diaz reminds me of that restaurant with its decor of serapes, bull fighting posters, and Mexican flags.

It has been here in Santa Paula since 1936 and has a full bar that serves great cold margaritas. The kitchen offers huge plates of traditional Mexican specialties. The best part is, this is a very reasonably priced restaurant.

The inland portion of Ventura County does not get much press, but its backroads are certainly pleasant for motoring. Driving out of Santa Paula on Highway 150, you will encounter the second of the area's bed and breakfasts:

> **Fern Oaks Inn**
> **1025 Ojai Road**
> **Santa Paula, CA 93060**
> **(805) 525-7747**

Built in 1929, this pretty Mission Revival home with the arched entrance nestled amongst oak and citrus trees looks every inch the part of the early California retreat. There is a swimming pool and a rose garden that should be in bloom this month.

There are four individually decorated guest rooms, all with private baths. They are called the Violet, Chinois, Williamsburg, and Casablanca. Lodging includes a full breakfast.

Continuing along Ojai Road (Highway 150) 5-1/2 miles north out of town, you will come to a beautiful park and bird sanctuary, **Steckel Park**. This meandering strip of California Oaks is bordered by the highway along its western edge. Santa Paula Creek, which Highway 150 follows most of the way, runs through it. There are five campsites and hookups.

Continuing along Highway 150, you will enter the wonderful Ojai Valley, which will be covered in detail in the June, August, and October chapters.

HIGH DESERT WILDFLOWERS

The desert wildflower show that began at the lower elevations as early as February starts happening this month in the high desert. With one highly celebrated exception, the higher desert areas are considerably less spectacular for colorful flora than the low desert.

The Colorado Desert, whose wildflower display was discussed in the March chapter, certainly has more varieties of color than either the East Mojave Desert or its neighbor Joshua Tree National Monument. But these areas have their own qualities that make them a wonderful spring trip as well.

Both of these desert areas are what I call "rock places," meaning that their outstanding topographical features are geological, rather than botanical. This is why in some ways they make outstanding late fall or winter trips. If you consult the November chapter under Rock Places, you will find considerably more on both of these remarkable areas. For information about spring wildflowers in Joshua Tree, call (805) 259-7721.

One of the best places to look for wildflowers in the East Mojave Desert this month is in the **Ivanpah Valley**. Take the Nipton Road exit off the I-15 and make a right on Ivanpah Road. The flatlands and hills on the way to the New York Mountains will be covered with desert primrose, blooming Mojave Mound Cactus, and Coreopsis.

Another great wildflower area in the East Mojave is a pleasant drive from the Nipton/Ivanpah Valley area. Just take Morningstar Mine Road southwest from Ivanpah Road to the tiny road stop of Cima (where there is a store if you are hungry or thirsty). Continue on from here along Kelso Cima Road to the **Kelso Depot**.

There is an eerie timelessness to this Mission-style station with its stately rows of arches and cottonwood trees. A fairly imposing two-story structure with a red-tile roof and a broad red-brick platform, it was built in 1924 by Union Pacific. The line between Salt Lake City and the growing little Port of Los Angeles had opened in 1906. Kelso was one of only a handful of places in the desert where water was easily obtainable in sufficient quantities to refill the thirsty boilers of steam locomotives.

This same line carried iron ore from the Vulcan Iron Ore Mine to the Kaiser steel mill in Fontana. When World War II broke out, the demand for steel skyrocketed and Kelso experienced an authentic boom. The town grew to a population of about 2,000 and the future seemed bright.

As it happens, diesel replaced steam, the war ended, the mill shut down in 1947—and the town of Kelso did likewise. The depot was actually scheduled for demolition in 1985. Thankfully, it was spared due to the efforts of a coalition of environmentalists and preservationists. Today Kelso has a population of about 24.

But the real attraction of Kelso is a spectacular natural formation that is also a prime wildflower viewing area: **The Kelso Dunes**. This is one of the largest fields of sand dunes in the U.S. There is a full 45 acres of shifting sands up to 700-feet tall!

Closed to off-road vehicles since 1973, it is amazing how different these dunes are from some of the other dune formations that have not been so fortunate. Where the Imperial Dunes are dead piles of sand, beautiful desert primrose and sand verbena add color this month to the stark beauty of the Kelso Dunes. No less than 100 different kinds of plants live on or near the dunes.

There is more on the East Mojave and Joshua Tree National Monument in the November Chapter.

CALIFORNIA POPPY

There is one particular high desert wildflower that makes up for the generally smaller amount of colorful blooms on elevated terrain: the California Poppy, the "Official State Flower."

Their mystique is in every way consistent with that of the state whose symbol they have come to be. The Spanish conquerors called them "copa de oro," which means cup of gold. It is said that would-be gold miners were often inspired by the sight of them as an omen that they would someday find gold.

Usually starting about the first week of this month is the best time to go to the:

> **Antelope Valley Poppy Reserve**
> **between 150th and 170th on Lancaster Road (this is an**
> **extension of Avenue I)**
> **Daily 9 a.m. to 4 p.m. during the season**
> **(805) 724-1180**

The reserve was set aside in 1976 on one of the rare consistent natural poppy growing sites in the state. The centerpiece of the reserve is the **Pineheiro Visitors Center.** It is a gray cement structure built into a hill in a passive solar design. It is named for the artist and self-taught botanist Jane Pineheiro, whose wildflower paintings adorn the interior walls. They provide free maps to areas where flowers are blooming.

Quite near the Poppy Reserve is a remarkable stop:

> **Exotic Feline Breeding Compound**
> **Mojave-Tropico Road**
> **Rosemond, CA 93560**
> **open every day but Wednesday & holidays 10 a.m. to 4 p.m.**
> **(805) 256-3332**

Though technically not in the territory of this book (it is just over the Kern County line), the Exotic Feline Breeding Compound is just up Highway 14 a few miles to Rosemond Boulevard. You will see signs directing you to the compound.

This sanctuary was opened to the public in 1983. Its purpose is to protect exotic cats, whose existence on Earth is threatened around the world.

The walking tour takes somewhat less than an hour, but gives you a chance to see 12 species of felines up close and personal. Touching is expressly forbidden, however, and you can only take pictures if you are a member. The tour includes a slide show and a lecture and the whole thing is free. The presentations rotate the types of cats featured. Because there are new arrivals and the resident animals have kittens, special shows are given throughout the year.

An amazing geological spectacle near the high desert of the Antelope Valley is also a good place to look for spring wildflowers:

> **Devil's Punchbowl County Natural Area**
> **28000 Punchbowl Road**
> **Pearblossom, CA 93553**
> **(805) 944-2743**

It is awe inspiring to consider that the same L.A. County that encompasses Hollywood Boulevard also contains this magnificent rock formation within its own 1,310-acre park. The Punchbowl is a 300-350-foot deep bowl-shaped chasm formed of a jumble of gigantic beige sandstone monoliths. It was created, appropriately enough, by earthquake faults.

The area is only seven miles up Longview Road (County Road S6) from the town of Pearblossom. Located within Angeles National Forest and operated by the county as a special use area, it is an unusual place to go for a spring walk, not just because of the rock formations, but because the Punchbowl's elevation of 4,000-4,700-feet and relative seclusion make it a good place for high desert and mountain wildflowers.

As you approach, you will see the Nature Center. Many local species are on display here, including both a tiny pocket gopher and its chief predator, the gopher snake. From here there is also a vantage point where you can see two earthquake faults: Piñon and Punchbowl. One mile to the north is the San Andreas Fault. The Punchbowl is the rubble piled up between the three of them.

Just behind the Nature Center is a one mile long loop trail that switches back and forth down the rim to the creek at the bottom of Punchbowl Canyon. It then loops back around up and out of the canyon past some of the most dramatic of the upwardly thrust rock towers.

There is also a shorter (about 1/3 mile) self-guided loop nature trail called the **Piñon Pathway** that stays along the rim and goes through a piñon-juniper forest. Native shrubs and trees are identified by signs along this easy little jaunt.

The whole area seems awfully far from L.A. The trees along the trail to the bottom run from piñon and sugar pines at the top, past manzanita, to the sycamores along the bed of the creek. There are plenty of bird species represented, ranging from several species of quail and hummingbirds to red-tailed hawks. There are mule deer and assorted small mammals and reptiles, but there are also bobcats and even a few black bears.

Seventeen miles east of SR 14 is one of the great places in the California desert:

Antelope Valley Indian Museum
15701 East Avenue M
P.O. Box 1171
Lancaster, CA 95384
second weekend of October to second weekend of June
11 a.m. to 3 p.m.
(805) 942-0662
(805) 946-3055

What a sight this is: a storybook white-walled Swiss chalet with two gabled turrets and seven separate roof elevations built halfway into a natural crescent in the side of a hill of rounded desert boulders, surrounded by Joshua trees. There is a barn and a fence and gate with hand painted decorations on top. A 1/2 mile nature trail off the parking lot displays the fauna and flora of the Mojave desert.

If anything, the inside is more spectacular than the outside. You enter a living room of tremendous proportions. The wooden ceiling is supported by huge beams and rafter and rises to the lofty nave of the pitched roof. Symbolic Native American designs, such as Kachina, festoon the spaces between the rafters, giving the room its name: Kachina Hall. This was the first room completed. It is filled with Native American blankets, old firearms, mounted animal heads, and pottery. For the rest of the rooms, the builder followed the natural cavities of the rocks and added a dining room and a multi-level loft for sleeping alcoves. These tower over the main room like nests of great birds.

A modern, ecologically-minded homebuilder will be impressed, not only with the fact that this 1927 building was built into a hill, thus making the interior temperature more moderate, but that all of the inside is a blend of the indigenous boulders and wood. The floor is uneven rock and there are naturally shaped tree branches for handrails. There are slits and gaps in the stones to encourage air circulation. There is a stone hearth and dining room table and rocks rearranged into shelves to display native pottery and natural objects from the desert. There are log benches with cowhides for covers.

This was the dream house of Howard Arden Edwards, a self-taught artist who made his money decorating movie sets during Hollywood's early days. He fell in love with the desert when visiting the Antelope Valley. He and his wife, Rose, and young son, Arden, homesteaded the surrounding 160 acres and lived in a tent while they built it. The rocky outcropping the house is built into is called Piute Butte.

By all reckoning, they must have been a unique family. They organized Native American pageants in the Piute Buttes; seating, of course, was on boulders. They were not successful at farming, however, and were never able to get a crop going. They left after about 10 years, but Edward's portrait remains on the wall in the living room. He died in 1953 at the age of 69.

The house would have faded into nothing had not Grace Oliver, who was working on her thesis in anthropology, stumbled upon it and bought it from Edwards. For nearly 40 years, she developed it into a private museum of Native American artifacts. By 1977, Mrs. Oliver was unable to continue, but by then it was so obvious that the place had real importance that the state took it over as a park and added 140 acres to it. Mrs. Oliver died in 1985 at the age of 86 and her portrait adorns the living room along with that of Edwards.

Edwards left a remarkable collection of artwork in the house. Besides the brightly colored Indian designs which cover almost every exposed wood surface, there is a handmade chest covered with Native American motifs, a pretty little writing table, and many beautiful Navajo blankets. Edward's paintings, of which there are many, depict a romanticized, yet accurate, view of Native American life.

Upstairs in the California Room are two dozen locked cases that have most of the really valuable things in them. The narrow staircase you climb to get up here squeezes between great boulders.

Mrs. Oliver brought objects from Native American reservations in the southwest and solicited donations from others. There are Nez Perce and Apache baskets and two Atavi baskets from the Peabody Museum that are over 300 years old. More local treasures include Navajo bead necklaces and bracelets that came out of nearby archeological digs. The Mojave area was a trading center for several tribes and the range of the locally derived material is very impressive. There is usually an Indian artist on hand offering traditional and modern work and a gift shop with refreshments.

PUBLIC GARDENS

As people flowed into the Southland, the natural desire to build beautiful gardens in a place where it is nice to be outdoors year-round left a legacy of former estates turned gardens-for-all. The collective green thumbs of peoples frustrated by cold weather throughout the world created some remarkable sights, but perhaps nothing expresses this spirit like the:

>**Annual Garden Show**
>**Descanso Gardens**
>**1418 Descanso Drive**
>**La Cañada-Flintridge, CA 91011**
>**April 1 to 9**
>**9 a.m. to 5 p.m.**
>**(818) 952-4400**

In this 60 acre paradise exists the world's largest camellia garden, with over 100,000 individual plants with no less than 600 varieties from around the world. Its beauty is enhanced by the fact that it is enclosed by 30 acres of California Oak. There are five acres of rose gardens nearby. This is a uniquely Southern California setting in that it may be the only outdoor garden in the world where lilacs, daffodils, flowering fruit trees, tulips, camellias, and roses are all blooming at the same time.

The whole thing is the former property of E. Manchester Boddy, editor of the old *Los Angeles Daily News*. The original plot was 165 acres when purchased by him in

1937. The camellias are a beautiful testament to an ugly event: in 1942, Japanese American nurserymen were sent to relocation camps and their prized camellias and azaleas were available for a song. They flourished under the live oaks and have grown tree-sized themselves. The blossoms are the size of teacup saucers.

In 1953, Los Angeles County bought the gardens. In 1966, the Descanso Guild commissioned Whitney Smith and Wayne Williams to design a Japanese Teahouse to set off the camellias that had been appropriated from the internees. The Teahouse is open 11 a.m. to 4 p.m. Tuesday through Sunday. Surrounding the Teahouse are soothing pools and waterfalls.

One of the most fanciful buildings in the Southland is in the upper reaches of nearby Glendale:

> **Brand Library**
> **1601 West Mountain Avenue**
> **Glendale, CA 91202**
> **Tuesday & Thursday 1 to 9 p.m.**
> **Wednesday 1 to 6 p.m.**
> **Friday & Saturday 1 to 5 p.m.**
> **Closed Sunday & Monday**
> **(818) 548-2051**

This amazing building and grounds was at one time the home of Leslie Brand, a celebrated booster for the City of Glendale who was responsible for the Pacific Electric coming to the city in 1904, the same year this house was finished.

It was originally called "El Miradero" ("Look Out Point"). That name still is over the twin minaret-towered gateway. Designed by Nathaniel Dryden, this is the most dramatically Arabian Nights-styled structure you will find outside of an old Hollywood epic. It is quite spectacular from its entrance between rows of palms to its gleaming white palace-like main building.

At the Columbian Exposition in Chicago in 1893, there was an "East India" Pavilion that was the talk of the Midwest. Like many structures built in California in the early 20th century, El Miradero was built with the idea of "outdoing" something Midwestern. Brand eventually gave it to the city on condition that it be used as a public library and park. Its function has been expanded into that of an arts and cultural center and it boasts an extensive music library.

While thumbing through the music library, you can almost hear the melodies. Nearby, a very choice supper club serves up jazz live:

Jax Jazz Club
339 North Brand Boulevard
Glendale, CA 91203
Daily 11 a.m. to 2 a.m.
(818) 500-1604

Opened in 1981 and still owned by Jeff Williams, this New York-style bar and grill is long and narrow and seats 80. Open for lunch, in the evenings they have jazz seven nights a week. They serve a full menu of very good California cuisine and the kitchen is open until 1 a.m.!

Roses in Bloom, World's Largest Rose Garden

April is the first blooming month for roses. An appropriate place to visit in the Southland would be the **world's largest Rose Garden**, which is in front of:

Natural History Museum of Los Angeles County
Exposition Park
900 Exposition Boulevard
Los Angeles, CA 90007
general admission: $5
Tuesday-Thursday,
Saturday & Sunday 10 a.m. to 5 p.m.
Friday 10 a.m. to 8 p.m.
(213) 744-3414
(213) 744-3466

Within the Natural History Museum is the Ralph M. Parsons Insect Zoo. This museum displays a healthy sense of humor. For example, one exhibit consists of a refrigerator with a cartoon trail of ants running down the front with the message "What's to eat? Look inside!" Opening the door, you will discover their preferred food while a tape plays a kazoo version of "The worms crawl in, the worms crawl out." The director of the Insect Zoo is renowned expert Arthur Evans, whose personal collection numbers between 75,000 and 100,000 specimens.

There is a lot to do and see in Exposition Park in addition to the Rose Garden and The Natural History Museum. The **Afro-American Museum** is described in February. There is also a McDonald's of the future, and the Frank Gehry designed:

California Museum of Science and Industry
700 State Drive
Exposition Park

Los Angeles, CA 90037
Daily 10 a.m. to 5 p.m.
(213) 744-7400

Walking through this museum brings a wonderful, adolescent feeling. It features a plethora of various hands-on science exhibits, some of which are a real kick to play with.

The C.M.S.I. also includes the:

Mitsubishi IMAX Theater
California Museum of Science and Industry
Corner of Figueroa and Exposition Boulevard
Los Angeles, CA 90037
Daily at 8 p.m., Admission: $5
(213) 744-2014 (general information)
(213) 744-2014 (box office)
(213) 480-3232 (Ticketmaster)

The IMAX Theater has a screen as tall as a five-story building and as wide as a seven-story building is tall. The exterior, like the Aerospace Museum, was designed by Frank Gehry, who also designed the Hollywood Library and was selected to design the new Disney Hall of the Music Center.

The Mitsubishi IMAX Theater is one of Southern California's most spectacular experiences. Though the screen is as large as four conventional movie screens, the clarity is astonishing. If you have ever seen those brilliant laser-enhanced still photos, this is similar, except it is gigantic and moving, and set to surround-sound and music.

Balboa Park

San Diego's Balboa Park is one of the finer urban parks in America. Comprising 1,400 acres, it encompasses the world's largest zoo, four separate theatres, 13 individual museums, numerous restaurants and gardens—as well as two golf courses and assorted sports facilities.

It was first established in 1868 when the land was set aside as "City Park." The City of San Diego had a contest to come up with a better name—which wouldn't be hard. The winner chose "Balboa" because of the park's hilltop view of the Pacific. The name change honors Vasco Nunez de Balboa, the first European to see the great blue body of water and the man who named it the "Pacific."

Much of the structure of the park as it is today came about as a result of the

Panama-California International Exposition held here in 1915-16. The opening of the Panama Canal was quite a big deal, but the official celebration was in San Francisco. San Diego wanted their own, so money was raised and the project was begun.

They first hired local architect Irving Gill, then the famous Bertram Goodhue, who would later design the L.A. Central Library, to create the buildings along the main promenade, called El Prado. Some of what was built was temporary, a lot of it remained.

A second big fair called the California-Pacific Exposition, held in 1935, created an excuse to add new attractions. Old buildings and gardens were spiffed up and the Pan American Plaza was added. The U.S. Treasury issued a special half-dollar coin to commemorate the 1935 Exposition that features the image of the dome and spire of the California Tower, part of the original 1915 California Quadrangle.

Along with other construction since and in-between, it is the combined legacy of these two events that has evolved into what the park is today.

Because Balboa Park is so large, it is not really possible to take it all in at one time. Since this is April, I will concentrate on touring the gardens this month. I will also describe the zoo, as it is more pleasant in the cooler air of April. There are plays in the theaters year-round, but the summer Shakespeare begins in June, so I will describe the Shakespeare Festival and the museums in that month.

There are many gardens to see in April, but since the subject was roses, we'll start there:

> **Rose and Desert Garden**
> **south of Zoo Place**
> **on the east side of Park Boulevard**
> **across from Plaza de Balboa**

There are almost 1,850 rose bushes here and the site is quite popular for weddings. There are about 150 species of cactus, succulents, and other desert plants in the plot right next to it. These two contiguous gardens should both be in flower this month.

They overlook **Florida Canyon**, a throwback to what the park looked like when it was virgin land. It is 160 acres of natural terrain. Trails wind through the chaparral and tours are offered by the San Diego Natural History Museum. Call (619) 232-3821.

Across Park Boulevard from the Rose and Desert Gardens is **Plaza de Balboa**, added in 1972. Its centerpiece is The Bea Everson Fountain, whose waters spray 50-60 feet in the air. The surrounding pool is encircled by a flower garden making it a popular picture spot. Because of this, the fountain is equipped with a wind sensing device that turns the water down when it is gusting.

From here, you are looking down the signature avenue of Balboa Park, **El Prado**. This complex of buildings in Balboa Park has mystified visitors who do not know their history but have some knowledge of architecture. The buildings along El Prado are a conglomeration of Spanish and North African styles that were originally built for the 1915 Panama Exposition.

Probably the most recognizable of the original 1915 buildings along El Prado is the spectacular **Botanical Building** (open from 10 a.m. to 4:30 p.m. daily) with its stately rectangle of a Lily Pond extending 257 feet from the structure to the sidewalk lining the street. This month the long reflecting surface of the pond will be brightened by pink, yellow, and blue lilies. If the Botanical Building mirrored on its surface reminds you of an iron Victorian train station, it should—because that is what it is.

What was supposed to be a Santa Fe railroad station was reassembled here instead. More than 12 miles of redwood lathe was used to cover the metal skeleton of the building with a lattice work screen that would allow sunlight in. Originally called "La Laguna," it was designed by Gerald Wellington and Carleton Winslow.

The building is free to enter. It is cavernous inside—the structure is about seven-stories tall, 60-feet wide, and 250-feet long. The effect within is quite wonderful: it is like being in some separate world not affected by the outside. The light filters in between the slats of the redwood and dapples on tree ferns that soar overhead while smaller ferns, orchids, and moss lend a hidden jungle quality. For spring, lilies and tulips add color. There are a total of over 350 different species of plants and signs telling you what they are.

The splashing sound of water flowing in fountains and waterfalls adds to the pleasure of a stroll through here. This is another grand old building that was worth saving when it got run down. It was restored in 1957 and it took no less than 70,000 linear feet of redwood to do the job.

Continuing a little farther down, on the other side of the street, you will come to the central garden of EL Prado, **Alcazar Garden**, which was inspired by the gardens of Alcazar of Seville, an ancient Moorish palace. It was originally called Montezuma Garden, but it was re-done and renamed in 1935. The chief architect, Richard Requa, traveled throughout Spain, Algeria, and Tunisia collecting ideas and came up with a truly romantic setting with walkways and benches that is filled with flowers set off by green, yellow, and turquoise tiles. The design as a whole creates the feeling of a seemingly very old and very far away place. Requa also designed the pleasant:

Spanish Village Art Center
Daily 11 a.m. to 4 p.m.
(619) 232-8120

These little tan cottages with arched doorways and red-tile roofs are arranged around a pretty patio painted in bright colors. They are used as studios by about 40 local artists. You can watch them work or purchase pottery, paintings, jewelry, stained glass, photography, sculpture, and several other art forms here.

Located between Spanish Village and the zoo is the:

Balboa Park Railroad
Saturday & Sunday and holidays 11 a.m. to 5 p.m.
(619) 239-4748

This miniature train ride does not last very long, but its 2,200-foot long track does wind through a lovely eucalyptus grove. Curiously enough, the 48-passenger ride was installed in 1948. It is powered by a one-fifth scale model of a General Motors F-3 diesel engine. Right by the railroad is the:

Balboa Park Carousel
Saturday & Sunday and holidays 12 to 6 p.m. (winter)
Monday-Friday 1 to 5 p.m. (summer)
Saturday & Sunday and holidays 11 a.m. to 5 p.m. (summer)
(619) 239-4748

Built in 1910 by the Herschell-Spillman Company, this merry-go-round in the yellow and brown pavillion was installed here in 1922. It is old-fashioned in every way: you try and catch a ring and hope it is brass and not iron, and the horses have horsehair tails.

In the spirit of the carousel's proximity to the zoo, the menagerie of hand-carved animals you can choose from includes a lion, giraffe, zebra, ostrich, frog, and even a dragon and a unicorn.

Of course, the biggest attraction in this locale of Balboa Park is the world famous:

San Diego Zoo
Daily 9 a.m. to 4 p.m., daily 9 a.m. to 5 p.m. (summer)
(619) 234-3153

How the world's largest zoo ended up in San Diego is another one of those random moments in history. The 1915 exposition had a temporary zoo and just before it was to be torn down in 1916, one Dr. Harry Wegeforth heard the lion's roar and was inspired: San Diego didn't have a permanent zoo, so he'd start one. His fledgling menangerie consisted of cages set up along Park Boulevard.

Today the San Diego Zoo occupies 100 acres of mesas and canyons and has over 3,900 animals from 900 different species. In recent years, there has been a great deal of construction because of the process of replacing outdated animal cages with "Habitats," large compounds designed to be as close as possible to the animal's native environment.

One of the most enjoyable is **Tiger River**, which is a full three acres that recreates a tropical rain forest. Chinese water dragons, Sumatran tigers, and Malayan tapirs frolic through a lush southeast Asian jungle complete with waterfalls in a mist made by a fogging machine. Another popular one is **Sun Bear Forest**, which features extremely playful Malyan sun bears along with lion-tail macaques.

There is quite obviously a lot of walking here. You can take a tour by tram that lasts about 40 minutes. There is also the Skyfari aerial ride, which crosses several different landscapes from east to west and offers a great view of not only the zoo below, but the downtown San Diego skyline rising nearby.

The zoo is also a garden. Do not miss **Fern Canyon**. For something really different, the third Friday of each month the **Orchid House** is made available to those who would like to see it. It is only open from 10 a.m. to 2 p.m.

As far as places to stay, two blocks from the park's western entrance there is the Britt House (described in February), but a couple of blocks farther is the lesser known, but wonderful:

> **Park Manor Suites**
> **525 Spruce Street**
> **San Diego, CA 92103**
> **(619) 291-0999, (619) 291-8844 (FAX)**

This 82-suite hotel was designed in 1926 by Frank P. Allen, who also worked on the buildings of the 1915 Panama Exposition. A splendid old building, it had a $2,000,000 renovation that took three years to complete. Once you enter the Italian Renaissance-style lobby, you will see it is not an ordinary small hotel. The guest rooms are beautifully furnished with Chippendale chests and Louis XIV chairs. The larger suites have kitchens and separate dining areas and beautiful views of the park, the city, and the harbor beyond. To make it an even better place to stay in spring, the Park Manor Suites has its own rose garden.

There is more on Balboa Park in the June and December chapters.

RENAISSANCE PLEASURE FAIRE

Since the 1980s, a very different heritage has also been celebrated in great form in the Southland:

The Renaissance Pleasure Faire
Glen Helen Regional Park
San Bernardino County
third week of April to second week of June
Saturday & Sunday (and Memorial Day)
(800) 52-FAIRE or (800) 523-2473

This faire celebrated its 30 year anniversary in 1992. For years, it was held on privately-owned land in Agoura, but now it seems to be well established here.

The English Renaissance took a different form than the Italian in that it was a combination of a nation coming of age not only culturally, but militarily and economically. The time frame was from the accession of Queen Elizabeth I in 1558, to the defeat of the Spanish Armada in 1588, to the accession of James I upon the death of Elizabeth in 1603, and ends with his death in 1625.

It was a tumultuous time in British history. London had been thought of as a kind of backwoods place both economically and culturally by the continental powers prior to the mid-1500s. By the time of the surprise defeat of the "undefeatable" Spanish Armada in 1588, the English Renaissance had already begun. London was becoming a major center of trade. This is the period that is recreated in "renaissance festivals," the best known to us here in Southern California being this one.

After the defeat of the Armada, English confidence soared and found its expression in the dramatic arts, the high water mark of which was, of course, the writings of Shakespeare from the late 1580s to 1610. Times were good and this is why "renaissance faires" recreating these days are filled with the merriment of period costumes, music, theater, and lots of food.

This one is quite extensive with over 1,500 costumed performers and usually about twice that many participants in costume. Events include jousting, music, dance, and of course, theater. Food is everywhere and the scent of everything from barbecued ribs to sweets fills the air. The crafts are usually very good and there are over 30 games to challenge you. They have an Elizabethan cooking contest, a Shakespearing sonnet competition, a home brewing contest, and a "wench lifting contest."

Because the setting offers a lot more space than they had in their previous location, the faire has gotten progressively more elaborate. The pageantry now begins with an "Opening of The Gates" ceremony with a salute of muskets, a raising of the maypole, and continuous parades leading up to dramas on no less than seven stages. They stage a mock battle with over 100 troops. The large Willow Pond, while not big enough for an Armada, accomodates several ships with cannons firing. The Queen arrives on a flowered barque amid great ceremony.

In nearby Riverside, you can find appropriate attire for the faire at:

> **Dragon Marsh**
> **3737 6th Street**
> **Riverside, CA 92501**
> **Monday-Saturday 11 a.m. to 6 p.m**
> **(909) 276-1116**

Dragon Marsh is located in Riverside's historic downtown mall, described earlier in this month under ORANGE BLOSSOMS. There is a variety of other items from candles to replicas of Celtic leather armor. Other Southland Renaissance fairs are mentioned in August and October chapters.

BUDDHA'S BIRTHDAY (APRIL 8)

Buddhism is the world's fourth largest religion with about 300 million adherents, thousands of whom dwell in Southern California. April is the month of the Buddha's birthday, and this event is honored at more than 30 temples throughout the Southland. These include Japanese, Thai, Korean, and Chinese peoples because the religion spreads from China to Korea to Japan and on to Sri Lanka, Burma, and Thailand. Each country's culture affected it in subtle ways, but they all celebrate the birth of Buddha this month.

The word means "awakened one" or "enlightened one." The person who took this name was Siddhartha Gautama and he was born a crown prince of what is now Nepal on April 8th of 544 B.C. by the Western calendar. It is said that when he was born that sweet rain fell and flowers bloomed.

Though blessed with every advantage himself, he was so disturbed by the sickness and poverty that plagued the common people of his country that when he was 29, he abandoned his throne to wander and contemplate. He attained enlightenment after six years and took the name Buddha. His travels brought him to India where he died at the age of 80.

As part of the ceremonies marking his birth, a statue of a baby Buddha is placed in a altar surrounded by flowers. Participants kneel before this altar, then pour ladles of either sweet wine, scented water, or tea over the image—signifying the sweet rain that fell upon his birth.

The largest celebration of this in the Southland is at the:

Hsi Lai Temple
3456 Glenmark Drive
Hacienda Heights, CA 91745
Self-guided tours daily 9 a.m. to 4 p.m.
(818) 961-9697

Situated majestically on a hill overlooking Hacienda Boulevard is the largest Buddhist temple and monastery complex in the Western Hemisphere. It is a green and gold fantasy of 10 pagoda-style buildings with broad gracefully curved eves and glazed tile roofs. Spread out over 14 acres are a lecture hall, a meditation hall, a library, a school of Chinese culture and arts, living quarters for the 40 nuns and monks, and a spectacular main shrine.

Said to have cost over $25 million, it summons all of the romantic images of China with its gilded opulence. The centerpiece of the main shrine is a massive two-ton, gold-plated chandelier imported from Japan that is surrounded by myriad smaller ones. There are over 10,000 statues of Buddha, including three large gilded ones in the main hall that accommodates 700 worshipers. Services are held on Sundays.

The opening of the monastery in 1988 as the national headquarters of **Fo Kuang Shan**, the main Buddhist organization of Taiwan, was marked by the first meeting of the World Fellowship of Buddhists held outside of Asia. Two Americans were also elected as vice presidents.

They have a variety of educational and cultural programs about Buddhism and Chinese culture that are open to the public, including Chinese calligraphy. There is a great dining hall also open to the public.

From the temple, take Glenmark back down to Hacienda Boulevard and make a right. Go right on Colima Road and you will run into a great place for Taiwanese and other Asian cooking: **Rowland Heights**. A wonderful stop for eating and shopping is the striking:

Hong Kong Plaza
18406 Colima Road
Rowland Heights, CA 91748

The neon signs and green neon accents lining the roof of this palace of gastronomic delights would look right at home in its namesake city. There are several shops and restaurants built around the:

Hong Kong Supermarket
Hong Kong Plaza
Daily 9 a.m. to 10 p.m.
(818) 964-1688

This intricately organized store is a real cultural education just to walk through. In addition to ingredients used in Chinese cooking, Hong Kong Supermarket carries Japanese, Thai, Filipino, and Indonesian products. Besides the usual Western cuts of meat and poultry, you will find goat meat, duck legs, frozen pork blood, and chicken feet. The produce section includes, among its many surprises, some miniature bananas that are very sweet.

The selection of fresh fish, still whole and packed on a bed of ice, is dazzling. They also have an assortment of pre-made fish balls and such delicacies as octopus, squid, and both white and black sea cucumbers. A special treat is that the fish market will fry anything you like for no additional charge.

Before you walk into the supermarket, you will go past five distinct Chinese restaurants. Just to the left of the entrance to Hong Kong Supermarket is:

Yi Mei Deli
Monday-Friday 7 a.m. to 9 p.m.
Saturday & Sunday 7 a.m. to 9:30 p.m.
(818) 854-9246

This is a good place to sample Taiwanese snacks and pastries—some of which are pretty uncommon even in Southern California. For a Chinese version of fast food, try a packet of bamboo leaf stuffed with dried shrimp, mushrooms, pork, and glutinous rice. Another Chinese deli is found inside:

Luk Yue Restaurant
Monday-Friday 11 a.m. to 9:30 p.m.
Saturday & Sunday 9:30 a.m. to 9:30 p.m.
(818) 964-8815

While the other restaurants in Hong Kong Plaza are Taiwanese, this chain restaurant is Cantonese. It is very popular because it offers excellent food at very reasonable prices. Another low priced restaurant is nearby:

Good Time Cafe
Wednesday-Monday 11 a.m. to 9 p.m.
(818) 854-0777

Always busy at lunch and dinner time, the Good Time Cafe serves rice and noodle dishes as well as snacks from Taiwan. For something different, try:

Hainan Chicken Restaurant
Tuesday-Thursday 11 a.m. to 9 p.m.
Friday-Sunday 11 a.m. to 9:30 p.m.
(818) 854-0385

It has been said that the Chinese are the cooks to the world. Many a traveler to an Asian country has thought he or she was eating food of that country, only to discover at some point that everything he or she had been eating had actually been made by Chinese.

Malaysia is an Islamic country, but there are Malaysian Chinese who are not Muslim and it is their cuisine that is represented here. Probably the major difference between the Chinese Malaysian cooking and regular Malaysian cooking is that the Chinese eat pork while the Muslims do not.

Another chicken specialty restaurant is:

The Chicken Garden
Thursday-Tuesday 11 a.m. to 9:30 p.m.
(818) 913-0548

Featured dishes here include chicken with black dates, chicken oil rice, and the house specialty, three cup chicken. Probably the nicest interior of the restaurants here is that of the bustling:

Supreme Dragon
Daily 11 a.m. to 12 a.m.
(818) 810-0396

There is a soft white glow from the lighting here that comes from a rice paper skylight and large picture windows with white curtains. Here they have a little of everything, with an emphasis on northern Chinese snacks.

There is more on Chinese Southern California in the February and September chapters.

THAI NEW YEAR

The middle of April may bring anxiety to many because of the IRS, but in the Thai community of Southern California, April 13 means Thai New Year and the three-day **Festival of Songkram** at the Thai cultural and spiritual center of the Southland:

Wat Thai (Buddhist) Temple
8225 Coldwater Canyon Avenue
North Hollywood, CA 91605
(818) 785-9552

Though there is no formally designated "Little Thailand," there are 500 to 600 Thai-owned businesses and a population of about 150,000 Thais in Hollywood and the mid-Wilshire district of L.A. Despite the fact that it is in the San Fernando Valley, this temple is very important to the community. Built in 1979, at the corner of Roscoe Boulevard and Coldwater Canyon, this ornate and stately structure appears out of nowhere and surprises many visitors—particularly on weekends when it hums with activity.

As you approach, the scent in the air comes from food carts selling noodle soup ("keuay teiw nam") that is commonly eaten with sweet sauce and red peppers and sizzling skewers of barbecued beef ("nue yang"). The front of the temple is guarded by two enormous statues of figures from **The Ramayana**. The Ramayana and **The Mahaburata** are two great spiritual epic poems whose characters abound in everything from the architecture to the dance of Southeast Asia.

The chorus of chanting from inside adds to the feeling that you are not in Kansas anymore and the sight of the temple's resplendent interior with its row of saffron colored buddhist monks on a raised dias against the wall completes the transformation.

As a community center, this place functions not only on a spiritual level, but on a social and cultural one as well. New arrivals to Southern California are offered assistance and classes in classical Thai dance and language are also available to make sure the culture is not lost on their American born children.

As in many Asian cultures, veneration for one's ancestors is part of their religious faith and the festival includes an ancestral blessing by the monks. What is considered part of culture can be very broad indeed and it is ironic that another major part of the festival is Thai boxing, which is so fast and furious as to be almost painful just to watch.

The Thais have been one of the more successful groups to adapt to life here. Most first-generation Thais arrived in the early '70s with some assets and with a good command of English, since it is a compulsory subject in the early grades in Thailand.

Thai restaurants are as ubiquitous as taco stands in the Southland. As many as 350 of them are in the City of L.A. alone. One of the oldest in the Valley is just a few miles from the Wat Thai temple:

Jitland West
11622 Ventura Boulevard
Studio City, CA 91604

Daily 11:30 a.m. to 10 p.m.
(818) 506-9355

This is one of the best Thai restaurants in Southern California. I love Thai food and eat it often, and Jitland West is second to none. While the color scheme features the omnipresent Southern California pastel rose color, Jitland West is more homey and less modern in its decor than many, more trendy restaurants. If you are planning on going here on a Friday or Saturday evening, you must make reservations in advance.

The **Mee Grob** features full sized shrimp rather than the usual cut up bits. Thai food is generally sweet with a variety of sauces. The food and sweet sauces here are so delicious it is almost like having dessert for dinner. The ingredients are extremely fresh and the owner is usually floating around making sure everyone is happy. Have a Singha beer from Thailand with your meal. It is a full malty pilsner and goes well with the sweet tastes.

Over the hill from the Valley, in Hollywood, the selection of Thai restaurants is quite impressive. I mention one of them, Chan Dara, in March. As you travel east on Hollywood Boulevard from the Hollywood Freeway, you will begin to see more signs in the elegant Thai script that looks Asian and Middle Eastern at the same time. The area around the 5000 block of the boulevard used to be known as "Little Armenia" because it was predominantly Armenian-owned businesses. Though there are still quite a lot of them, there is now a mix of Thai and Armenian establishments.

There are several different Thai regional cuisines represented by the restaurants you will pass, but you can try all of them at the centerpiece of Thai Hollywood:

L.A. Food Court at Thailand Plaza
5321 Hollywood Boulevard
Hollywood, CA 90027
Daily 11 a.m. to 4 a.m.
(213) 993-9000

This imposing two-story structure opened in May of 1993. On the first floor is **Silom Supermarket.** On the second floor is the L.A. Food Court.

The L.A. Food Court consists of a large rectangular room with a stage at one end and a bar at the other. Eight Thai counter restaurants line one long side wall. The other wall is a long window that looks out at the Sizzler across the street.

The atmosphere is supplied by the food and the people, because besides the less than awe inspiring view, the room is furnished in a kind of low-maintenance style. The floor is pressed concrete that looks like tile. The tables are formica and the jungle of plants are fake. Some relief is provided by the gold Thai-motif minarets on the wall that divide the eating area from the food counters.

There is a lot of energy in the room. There are numerous televisions suspended from the ceiling and a central big screen. Various bands and singers seem to be playing much of the time, but the biggest draw at the place performs Sunday through Thursday nights. He is Kevin Thongpricha, better known as the **Thai Elvis**.

Thongpricha began as an Elvis impersonator in Bangkok nightclubs in 1964. After appearing on Thai television, he came to L.A. seeking fame and fortune. Now he dons a wide-collared shirt, bell-bottoms, a rhinestone belt buckle, and platform shoes and performs here.

But if there is a real star here, it is the food. Collectively, the restaurants offer more than 400 dishes.

CAMBODIAN NEW YEAR

Another Southeast Asian people celebrate a major holiday around April with the arrival of **Cambodian New Year**.

Long Beach has a neighborhood called **Little Phnom Penh** that is named thusly because it has the second largest population of Cambodians in the U.S. At around 40,000, only Rhode Island, of all places, has more Cambodians.

It is here that you will find a unique exhibition venue that focuses on the cultural arts of Southeast Asia:

> **Arts of Apsara Gallery**
> **United Cambodian Community Center**
> **2338 East Anaheim Street, Suite 105**
> **Monday-Friday 1 to 4 p.m.**
> **Long Beach, CA 90804**
> **(310) 438-3932**

The museum derives its name from Apsara, Cambodia's beautiful dancing goddess. You will see her everywhere in Little Phnom Penh, adorning travel posters and miscellaneous objects d'art. Back home in Cambodia, she is carved in the stone walls of Angkor Wat.

Angkor Wat is the equivalent of the Parthenon of Cambodia. It was the center of 12th-13th century Kmere culture and expansion around the time of the Angkor Revolution.

Apsara is a fitting name, because not only is she an artistic icon, she is thought of as a protector. No immigrant group has ever needed one so much as the Cambodian people who came to Southern California.

Exhibits will rotate, but some featured subjects are photos of Cambodia, hand woven fabric, and masks. The latter are particularly bizarre looking, because they are intended to scare off evil spirits. They are sold for as little as $7 in the gift shop, which also has photos, museum posters, books on Cambodian culture, and small works of art.

Weaving is an important part of Cambodian culture. The museum has a giant 10-by-10 traditional style loom that is a working exhibit. Thanks to an N.E.A. grant, three to five master weavers give 15 hours of classes per week. This will allow expatriate Cambodians to reconnect with their past after having so much of it ripped away.

There are a number of restaurants on Anaheim that serve Cambodian dishes. A good one is:

> **Siem Reap Restaurant**
> **1810-1812 East Anaheim Street**
> **Long Beach, CA 90813**
> **Monday-Friday 9 a.m. to 9 p.m.**
> **Saturday & Sunday 9 a.m. to 10 p.m.**
> **(310) 591-7414**

There are several Vietnamese noodle and sandwich shops along here, as well as more than one Chinese. This high-ceilinged restaurant with its three-tiered chandelier and huge wall hanging of Angkor Wat has a sensibility of both, with some Thai and Southern California thrown in.

A popular lunch dish, "Nam Pa Chuk" with curry, illustrates this. It is a big bowl of vermicelli noodles with stewed chicken in sauce. The sauce has a wonderful spicy curry taste, made more interesting with a hint of coconut flavor. It is served with a plate of sliced long bean, shredded lettuce, bean sprouts, and sliced cucumber.

The menu is enormous and everything is printed in four languages. Divided into sections, there are five porridges, eleven soups, and six "sizzling plate, hot pots," as well as thirty rice, two abalone, nine fish, eighteen shellfish, seven chicken, seven beef, four pork, and seven vegetable dishes. These range from the familiar, like "Kung Pao Chicken" to the unusual, such as "fried crispy pig intestine" and "sour and spicy frog soup." Cambodian dishes are often made with a soft rice noodle. The iced coffee is sweet and delicious.

PASSOVER

Passover is celebrated over an eight day period. It begins at sundown with a ritual meal called a **Seder** that retells the escape of the Israelites from bondage under the Egyptians. This escape is called The Exodus.

The Seder commences with the lighting of two candles. The story from the Haggada of the deliverance of the Israelites from Egypt is read aloud. A platter of symbolic food is laid out. This includes a roasted lamb shank, like the lamb sacrificed on the night before the Exodus. This is followed by bitter herbs, symbolic of the woes suffered by the Israelites during their servitude. A mixture of ground nuts, apples, and wine represents the mortar out of which they were forced to make bricks. Rebirth in a new land is symbolized by parsley.

Set beside the main platter is a pile of unleavened bread or matzo along with a dish of saltwater to dip it in. The matzo represents the hurry in which the Jews left Egypt, the saltwater is their tears.

Passover has special meaning in Southern California since the Jewish presence here has been a particularly important one. This is because the film industry—arguably the aspect of the Southland with the greatest impact both here and elsewhere—was founded largely by European Ashkenazic Jewish immigrants and their descendants. In recent years, they have been joined by Sephardic Jews from Spain and the Mediterranean.

One of the most spectacular buildings in Los Angeles was originally the B'Nai B'rith temple:

> **Wilshire Boulevard Temple**
> **3663 Wilshire Boulevard**
> **Los Angeles, CA 90010**
> **(213) 388-2401**

Built in 1929, this is the oldest, largest Jewish Reform Synagogue in Los Angeles. The 135-foot tall Byzantine dome-topped structure is richly inlaid with marble. The interior is stunning with a sanctuary of black Belgian marble columns, doors of teak, gold altar accoutrements, and bronze chandeliers. There is an exhibit area featuring priceless objects of the Jewish faith, but the high point is a series of murals that depict 3,000 years of Jewish history that were executed by Hugo Balin, who did the murals in the entrance to the Griffith Observatory.

Another monument of sorts to Jewish Southern California is:

> **Canter's Deli**
> **419 North Fairfax Avenue**

Los Angeles, CA 90036
Daily 24 hours
(213) 651-2030

North Fairfax Avenue is the business strip of a traditionally East European Jewish neighborhood. You will see plenty of Hasidic men with their beards and hats, and stores carrying books and items pertaining to the faith.

The neon sign of Canter's is almost as much a classic image of L.A. as the Hollywood sign. The interior, with its funky light fixtures and acoustic ceiling, has not suffered any remodeling since the place opened seemingly centuries ago.

The bar is called the **Kibitz Room Lounge**. After 9:30 p.m. seven days a week, it becomes a music venue, featuring blues, rock, jazz, and cabaret/pop performers.

Also on Fairfax is a kosher restaurant with the flavor of the Middle East:

Grill Express
501 North Fairfax Avenue
Los Angeles, CA 90036
closed Friday night to sunset Saturday night
(213) 665-0649

When you sit down for lunch or dinner here, they immediately bring you a big plate of pickled turnips, cabbage, and cracked olives, "shakshuka" cooked tomatoes, onions, and peppers with fried eggs on top, stuffed braised artichoke hearts, and of course, large plates of kabobs.

Along Pico Boulevard a couple blocks west of Fairfax is another kosher restaurant:

Haifa
8717 West Pico Boulevard
West Los Angeles, CA 90035
closed Friday night and Saturday
Sunday-Thursday 9 a.m. to 10 p.m.
(310) 550-2704
and:
15464 Ventura Boulevard
Sherman Oaks, CA 91403
(818) 995-7325

As I mentioned earlier this month, I grew up in Encino not too far from the Valley location of this restaurant. Most of the kids I went to school with were Jewish and I had more than one occasion to sample "Cholent", the traditional Sabbath meal.

It is a stew made from beans, meat, eggs, and vegetables and is offered at Haifa every Sunday.

Also on Pico is the:

> **Beit Hashoah Museum of Tolerance**
> **9786 West Pico Boulevard**
> **Los Angeles, CA 90035**
> **Monday-Thursday 10 a.m. to 7:30 p.m.**
> **Friday 10 a.m. to 3:30 p.m.**
> **Sunday 10:30 a.m. to 7:30 p.m.**
> **(310) 553-9036**

There are two doors at the entrance, one labeled "Unprejudiced," the other "Prejudiced." Only one opens. It leads into the first section, which is a series of interactive exhibits.

The second section, the focal point of the museum, is the Beit Hashoah or "House of the Holocaust." This is designed to project participants back to the initiation and implementation of Hitler's "Final Solution." It uses clay figures fashioned like a human diorama, accompanied by a taped voice-over.

There is more about Jewish Southern California in the December chapter.

SHAKESPEARE'S BIRTHDAY (APRIL 23)
The Shakespeare Tradition

April 23 is thought of as the probable birthday in Stratford-upon-Avon for Shakespeare because he was baptized on April 26. Interestingly enough, he also died on the same day in the same town 52 years later. His will contained the cryptic award of his "second best bed with the furniture" to his wife, a woman older than himself named Anne Hathaway.

Though born in the country, Shakespeare loved London and exciting city life. He probably would have enjoyed knowing that the closest thing to a shrine to him is very near the most bustling part of the Southland. One of the more pleasant little oddities in Hollywood is the:

> **Shakespeare Bridge**
> **Franklin Avenue over Monon Street**
> **[Between Saint George Street and Myra Avenue]**
> **Hollywood**

What a little architectural bonbon this is. A white, open spandrel arch supported by Gothic arches, it features a pair of elaborate peaked Gothic structures at each end that look like miniature 20-foot tall cathedrals with open centers that seem like they should have statues in them. These are so stylized it would appear this bridge must have been built for some movie. Actually it was one J.C. Wright of the City Engineer's office that designed it in 1926. The inscription on the plaque reads "Shakespeare Bridge 1926 with Gothic arches and turrets in a picturesque useful span serving Franklin Avenue."

Hollywood also has a modest theatre for Shakepeare:

Globe Theatre
1107 North Kings Road
Hollywood, CA 90048
(213) 654-5623

The Globe was created in 1972 by actor Thad Taylor, who had founded the Shakespeare Society of America eight years before. Just to show Southern California has its cultural drivers, the intrepid Mr. Taylor also tried to get a star for William Shakespeare on Hollywood Boulevard in 1978. He didn't succeed because Hollywood prefers the living, so they can appear at the ceremony. Instead, a plaque was placed outside the Globe 13 years later.

If you would like to have a little British food and atmosphere to complement an evening at the Old Globe, try the:

Cat And Fiddle Pub
6530 West Sunset Boulevard
Hollywood, CA 90028
Daily 11:30 to 2 a.m.
(213) 468-3800

This indoor/outdoor spot has a very California-ish garden patio and a very British pub interior. The menu is basically fish and chips with English brews on tap.

It is a true British hangout, complete with Union Jacks and dart boards. Kim and Paula are the proprietors.

Another "bit of England" in the Southland is the:

Ye Olde King's Head
116 Santa Monica Boulevard
Santa Monica, CA 90401
Monday-Friday 11 a.m. to 10 p.m.
Saturday 10 a.m. to 10 p.m.
Sunday bar open to 2 a.m.
(310) 451-1402

Entering here is just like walking into someplace you'd find in London—except that it's a block from the beach. There's noise and high energy, pointed missiles flying through the air along the row of dart boards and English accents all around. The food is basic English: fish and chips, and shepherd's pie. The bar is fully stocked with British brews.

One of the most amusing features of the place is a picture of former President Reagan at the entrance to the men's room. This has led to it being christened "The Reagan Loo."

A much more formal take on bringing England to Southern California is at Orange County's:

The sign outside Ye Olde King's Head in Santa Monica.

Five Crowns
3801 East Coast Highway
Corona del Mar, CA 92625
Sunday 10:30 a.m. to 10 p.m.
Monday-Thursday 5 to 10 p.m.
Friday & Saturday 5 to 11 p.m.
(714) 760-0331

This restaurant has won its share of awards since it opened in 1965. Designed by Savo M. Stoshitch, who also designed the Tam O'Shanter Inn in Los Angeles (see January), it is an elaborate two story restaurant that is somewhat of a replica (though not intended to be exact) of Ye Olde Bell, one of the oldest inns in England. A fine restaurant, they are only open for dinner and Sunday brunch.

If the Five Crowns makes you think of English Country Gardens, there is a perfect place for you in another part of Orange County:

Heard's Country Garden
14391 Edwards Street

Westminster, CA 92683
Tuesday-Saturday 9 a.m. to 5 p.m.
Sunday 12 to 4:30 p.m.
(714) 894-2444

This storybook-like nursery specializes in herbs, old fashioned perennials, and cottage flowers that are not normally carried by the average nursery. Surrounding the ivy-colored cottage are beds of such flowers as Cupid's dart, love-in-a-mist, Jupiter's beard, ladybells, and monkshood. As you walk around, the smell is exquisite. If you would like a cut flower bouquet, you will be treated to a practice they have revived: cutting the flowers right off the plant in front of the customer.

SANTA BARBARA VINTNER'S FESTIVAL

Santa Barbara County has ideal conditions for producing premium grape varieties. There are over 30 wineries in Santa Barbara County and though most harvest festivals are in the fall, out of nowhere in April comes the Santa Barbara Vintner's Festival. It is the biggest wine festival in the Southland and was started in 1983.

The wineries like the April date because it is between harvest crush and the time of bottling. It is held at the:

Flag Is Up Farms
901 East Highway 246
Solvang, CA 93463
either Saturday or Sunday 1 to 4 p.m.
$50 (must be paid for in advance)
contact:
Santa Barbara Vintner's Association
P.O. Box 1558
Santa Ynez, CA 93460
(805) 688-0881

Flag Is Up Farms is a horse ranch. This event spreads out over three fields and stresses both food and wine tasting. Area restaurants and hotels set up little pavilions with samples of their food. The price of admission includes everything.

If you enjoyed your small taste of ranch life, there is a place nearby where you can get the full experience:

The Alisal
1054 Alisal Road
Solvang, CA 93463
(805) 688-6411

The Alisal is probably most people's idea of a romantic guest ranch. Sprawling over a full 10,000 acres, it is not a dusty flat cattle ranch. It has a 90-acre private lake surrounded by rolling hills with huge old oak trees providing shade. April is especially lovely because not only are the hills green, the families with children that fill the place every summer have not arrived yet.

There are 73 rooms in cozy California ranch-style cottages, all with private baths, but no telephones or TVs. There is, however, a wood-burning stove in each room. If you are looking for fou-fou room interiors, this is not the place. The guest rooms are furnished with elegant simplicity.

The Alisal is popular with families for a reason. There is practically every outdoor family activity you never did with your parents. They have fishing, motor, sail, and pedal boating, windsurfing, and horseback riding. Besides the summer camp stuff, there are seven tennis courts and an 18 hole P.G.A. golf course. Most of the activities have an extra charge.

Though it costs about $200 a night to stay here, it does include breakfast and dinner. Jackets are required at dinner for men.

Just down the road from the ranch, seven miles southwest of Solvang on Alisal Road, is an 82-acre park with a beautiful work of nature with a Chumash name:

> **Nojoqui Falls Park**
> **Alisal Road**
> **1-1/2 miles northeast of Highway 101**
> **Daily from 8 a.m. to dusk**

Nojoqui Falls swirls and cascades down 164 feet over a limestone cliff decorated with shimmering green moss. It even has its own folklore: a star-crossed pair of Chumash lovers jumped together from the top. You get to the falls from the parking lot by way of a pretty 1/4 mile trail that meanders along a creek in a little forest of California bay, live oak, and sycamore trees and ends in a cool grotto.

Besides the natural sites, there are picnic areas with barbecues, softball diamonds, horseshoe pits, and volleyball courts.

The wineries of Santa Barbara County are described in the March, June, and October chapters.

DODGER BASEBALL SEASON

Perhaps the most romantic of all professional sports played in America is baseball. It is timeless: games can be fairly short or go on and on into extra innings until someone wins.

If there ever were a sports franchise in the Southland that qualifies as romantic and unsusual, it would be the L.A. Dodgers and their wonderful home turf:

Dodger Stadium
1000 Elysian Park Avenue
Los Angeles, CA 90012
(213) 224-1400

When Walter O'Malley disdained Ebbet's Field in 1957 and moved his team West he was proclaimed a traitor by Brooklyn fans. But the emerging city of L.A. had wanted the team and had offered them the Coliseum until a stadium could be built. The Bums from Brooklyn played there for four years.

Ironically, the location eventually chosen for the field had also been looked at by Walt Disney as a possible place for his amusement park: **Chavez Ravine**. After much wrangling, construction finally began on September 17 of 1959.

Officially opened on April 10 of 1962, 56,000-seat Dodger Stadium is probably the nicest ballpark in baseball because it is a park. The field is grass, not plastic. Designed by Emil Prager, it is open at one end. The idyllic setting makes you feel as if you are in the mountains.

And, there are also no pillars in the stands to block the great view. It was built in a futuristic cantilevered design perfectly in keeping with the motifs of some of the other great structures of the early '60s in Los Angeles, such as the Vincent Thomas Bridge and the L.A. Airport theme building.

Though they are an East Coast transplant, the Dodgers are in every way an L.A. team. In 1994, the first Korean player in the Major Leagues made his debut as a Dodger. Besides the famous "Dodger Dog," the stadium proudly serves sushi, along with the standard peanuts, popcorn and Crackerjacks.

Dodger Stadium is actually a park-within-a-park in that you pass though 575-acre **Elysian Park** in order to get to it. Elysian Park is the second largest park in the county and one of the last undeveloped fragments of the original 17,172 acre land grant out of which El Pueblo de la Reina de Los Angeles grew.

Be sure and check out the **Frank Glass and Grace E. Simons Memorial Sculpture**, a gazebo designed by artist Peter Shire. It is a fanciful grouping of columns and shapes that sits on top of Angel's Point.

If you wanted to have breakfast or lunch before or after a hike through this great city park, there is a surprisingly good place to go:

Police Academy
1880 Academy Road

Los Angeles, CA 90012
6 a.m. to 3 p.m.
(213) 222-9136

They serve huge breakfast and lunch portions in a sylvan setting here. The building interior has a suitably manly feel to it with historic photos of the LAPD going back to the turn-of-the-century.

The private banquet facilities here are some of the most romantic in the city. There is also a gift shop where you can buy souvenirs with the LAPD logo on them.

LA FIESTA BROADWAY

April has a spectacular finale in the form of the gigantic downtown celebration: La Fiesta Broadway on the street of the same name in Downtown L.A.

Besides all the little shops in the area, the real energy of Hispanic Broadway has its epicenter in the myriad stalls of:

Grand Central Market
317 South Broadway
Los Angeles, CA 90013
(213) 624-2378

Entering this mammoth building, extending between Broadway and Hill, is nothing less than like suddenly entering the bazaar of some enclosed miniature Mexican city.

There are all kinds of food served from the individual stands, including many Mexican specialties available either to eat there or take home. The tacos and lamb sandwiches at number 43 are celebrated, as is the juice bar on the Hill Street side featuring 75 kinds. The place is very clean, but do not be surprised by the lack of plastic wrap on poultry, meat, or fish. Also, the fruit and vegetable vendors select your produce for you and brown bag it. There is more about Mexican Southern California in the May, August, September, and December chapters.

MAY

Cinco de Mayo (May 5)

Carnaval, Long Beach

Cuban Debutante Ball

Philippine Heritage Festival and Santacruzan

Late Spring Flowers

Strawberry Festivals

Elephant Seal Mating Season

Mother's Day

Memorial Day Weekend

Festa Do Espirito Santo

Chapter Five
MAY

According to the ancient Greeks, the first beings to come out of Chaos were "Ouranos" ("sky") and "Gaia" ("earth"). The Latin-speaking Roman conquerors liked the Greek way of describing the beginning of the world so much that they took it for their own—they just changed the names to "Uranus" and "Gaea."

Uranus and Gaea gave birth to all sorts of creatures, the most important being the Titans, who of course were very large. The most famous Titans were a couple of guys named "Cronus" and "Atlas".

Cronus was the most powerful son of Uranus and Gaea. He was incited by his mother to drive his father away with a scythe (Freud had a field day with this one). The word cronus was actually not a Greek word and was probably confused with the Greek word "chronos", meaning "time." This is perhaps why we call Chronos the "god of time" and picture him as an old fart in robes carrying a scythe.

Atlas gained immortality by leading an unsuccessful war against the gods. As punishment, he was condemned to support the heavens upon his shoulders. Before he became thusly occupied he took time to have a daughter. Her name was **Maia**. The month of May is named after her. If this is not the most ridiculous and convoluted reason to name a month, I do not know what is.

May is a hard month to pin down. Is the weather sunny or cloudy? Is it spring or early summer? Perhaps this seasonal ambivalence is a reflection of the fact that the astrological sign of the month is Gemini the twins.

The word "May" is defined by Webster as "the early vigorous blooming part of human life" and May Day is a traditional springtime festival. In most of the industrialized nations of the West, it is International Labor Day.

This is a strange time of year, particularly in Southern California. There is a tremendous burst of natural energy when winter ends in the last week of March that builds up until tax time on April 15, then there is a lull that lasts until after summer starts in late June. The month of May has a hush to it almost as if our psyches are burned out from the sudden energy change we have just experienced and need to recharge before summer hits.

May is a month to get ready for summer. Many of the weekend destinations in California actually begin filling up around this time. So while it is nice to have a spontaneous escape for a weekend in July or August, it can be hard to do exactly what you want to do at the last minute during the busy summer months. That is why this is a good month to at least think about some of the things you might want to do this summer that you might not be able to do on the spur of the moment. (See June, July, and August.)

CINCO DE MAYO (MAY 5)

The most well known Mexican holiday in the United States is Cinco De Mayo. Many Americans think it is Mexican Independence Day. Actually, it marks the day of a battle at Puebla in 1862, over 40 years after independence was declared, in which Mexican forces overcame those of Napoleon III. In Southern California, it has become sort of a second New Year's Eve in terms of its tradition as party time, and it is actually a bigger holiday here than in Mexico.

Old Town, San Diego

The grandest Cinco de Mayo celebration is at:

Old Town State Historic Park
Bounded by Wallace, Juan, Twiggs, and Congress Streets
San Diego
(619) 237-6770

Though not a tradition for very long, having begun in 1983, the two-day fiesta here features everything from folklorico, flamenco, and Native American dance troupes to trick ropers and riders. There is music playing on several stages that covers the gamut of marimba, salsa, and of course, mariachi bands. Food is readily available from kiosks around the park, but there are plenty of places to get great Mexican food in Old Town anytime.

That the largest Cinco de Mayo celebration is held here is appropriate because just as the holiday is a Southern California/Mexican hybrid, so is Old Town. It is a 13 acre collection of buildings honored as the center of early San Diego and was designed to recreate the period of about 1822 to 1872. However, its main appeal seems to be that it is a safe, festive place with excellent parking that has a variety of fun restaurants and shops. If you are looking for secluded spots, this is not it: Old Town is the park most often visited in the state system.

This blending of historical restoration with commercial development into a kind of "Mexican Disneyland" is epitomized by:

Bazaar del Mundo
2754 Calhoun Street
San Diego, CA 92110
(619) 296-3161

In 1971, a farsighted interior designer named Diane Powers signed a lease with the state and created one of Old Town's most popular stops. It is a bazaar of four restaurants and 16 specialty shops arranged around a courtyard bursting with color and life. There are big blooming hibiscus everywhere

Bazaar del Mundo in Old Town San Diego.

along with terra cotta pots, bubbling fountains, pink, orange and purple umbrellas and awnings and lots of lush greenery.

There is a pretty gazebo in the middle where Rayna's Spanish Ballet has been performing flamenco dancing for free on Sundays since the place opened. In 1976, the Hispanic Mexican Ballet made appearances three times every Saturday afternoon doing their folklorico ballet.

There are two historic structures within the Bazaar. The first, an 1824 wood and adobe, was the childhood home of Governor Pio Pico:

> **Casa de Pico**
> **2754 Calhoun Street**
> **Old Town**
> **San Diego, CA 92110**
> **Sunday -Thursday 10 a.m. to 9 p.m.**
> **Friday & Saturday 10 a.m. to 9:30 p.m.**
> **(619) 296-3267**

In its heyday, this house was the focal point of early San Diego society with its eight entrances and central courtyard. Its next manifestation was somewhat less grand, when in the 1940s, it became the "Pico Motor Lodge." Now it is a very popular Mexican restaurant with dining in the courtyard and mariachis every night but Monday and Tuesday.

Mariachis also play at the:

> **Casa de Bandini**
> **2754 Calhoun Street**
> **Old Town**
> **San Diego, CA 92110**

Daily 11 a.m. 9:30 p.m.

(619) 297-8211

This building was originally built in 1829 for Old San Diego's richest citizen, a Peruvian named Juan Bandini. Forty years later, it was converted to the "Cosmopolitan Hotel." A second floor was added by an American named Albert Seely.

Seely had started the Seeley and Wright Stage Line, the terminal of which was next door. He had rare foresight, because his stages ran between San Diego and Los Angeles and were extremely successful until the 1890s, when the railroad essentially put him out of business.

Today his hotel is a somewhat fancier restaurant than the Casa de Pico, though it is still definitely casual. The patio here is enclosed and the dining rooms are adorned with colorful tapestries and folk art.

The **Seeley Stables**, located beside the Casa de Bandini, have been converted into a museum of antique farm machines and horse drawn vehicles. The Park Service shows a slide show about the development of transportation in Southern California. It has an admission fee, of $2 for adults, $1 for children, but the pretty white museum in the opposite corner of Old Town to the west is free:

Wells Fargo History Museum

2733 San Diego Ave.

Old Town

San Diego, CA 92110

Daily 10 a.m. to 5 p.m.

(619) 294-5549

Located in the historic Colorado House, a former hotel circa 1851, this little museum is worth a visit just to study its huge wall map of the Old West. But its claim to fame is a beautifully restored Wells Fargo stagecoach built by Abbot-Downing in Concord. Painted in the original colors, it is probably the epitome of romantic images of the Old West.

In keeping with its bank theme, there are antique strong boxes and a gold display featuring U.S. gold coins as well as raw nuggets. There is also a video about the history of Wells Fargo.

Overlooking Old Town on a hill is a very pleasant place to stay:

Best Western Hacienda Hotel-Old Town

4041 Harney Street

San Diego, CA 92110

(619) 298-4707

(800) 888-1991

This Spanish hacienda-styled set of buildings was originally a shopping center. As such, it flopped miserably, but hotel developers were able to convert it into a beautiful 152 unit, all suites hotel. It has brick patios made even more tranquil by the bubbling fountains arranged throughout the grounds. The hilltop location provides beautiful ocean and city lights views. Many of the high ceilinged rooms have wooden balconies and all have microwave ovens, refrigerators, VCRs, and handcrafted Mexican wood furniture.

Old Town has its pluses and minuses. It is very clean and safe, but could hardly be called a true center of Mexican culture. Most of the Mexicans you see here are food service workers of various kinds. Everyone else is either a (mainly Anglo) local San Diegan here for lunch or dinner or a tourist. It has been referred to as "Mexican Disneyland" by more people than this writer.

Little Mexico, Solana Beach

Whenever my family drove to San Diego for a vacation, we always stopped on the way down or on the way back at a place we called "Little Mexico." If you would like a less overpowering way to celebrate Cinco de Mayo, just get off I 5 at Via De La Valle and go west, turn right on Valley Avenue and you will be in the beach town of Solana Beach, which is nestled just north of Del Mar.

Around the turn of the century, this area was basically one big bean field—140 acres to be exact. Eugene Batchelder purchased the land in 1923 and planned a perfect beach town.

The little strip along the 600 block of Valley has several family-run Mexican restaurants that have been there a long time. As a matter of fact, the residential area that surrounds it has been a Mexican American neighborhood for several generations.

Stop by:

> **Tony's Jacal**
> **621 Valley Avenue**
> **Solana Beach, CA 92075**
> **Monday-Thursday 5 p.m. to 9:30 p.m.**
> **Friday & Saturday 5 to 10:30 p.m.**
> **Sunday 3 to 10 p.m.**
> **(619) 755-2274**

This homestyle Mexican restaurant has been serving up salsa since 1946. Another old favorite Mexican restaurant is:

Fidel's
607 Valley Avenue
Solana Beach, CA 92075
Sunday-Thursday 11 a.m. to 9:30 p.m.
Friday & Saturday 11 a.m. to 10:30 p.m.
(619) 755-5292

This rancho-like restaurant has almost a cult following. I have talked to people in the oddest places who have eaten here. There seems to be about a dozen rooms and patios—most of them filled with people. Their famous dish here is "tostada suprema".

Solana Beach is also the home of a great music venue:

Belly Up Tavern
143 South Cedros Avenue
Solana Beach, CA 92075
Daily 5:30 to 11 p.m.
(619) 481-9022

Many very well known artists such as Jimmy Cliff and Leon Redbone have played in this cozy place. Its name comes from its architectural design: it was built to resemble an overturned ship. The ceiling is rounded and the walls are covered with beautiful wood paneling.

There will be more on the Northern San Diego County Coast later this month, in July, and December.

Olvera Street, Los Angeles

Though the big celebration for Cinco de Mayo in L.A is usually at the end of April for the Fiesta Broadway, there is a pretty sizable Cinco de Mayo celebration at its historic center:

El Pueblo de Los Angeles
Olvera Street
845 North Alameda Street
Los Angeles, CA 90012
Cinco de Mayo festival:
normally Saturday & Sunday nearest May 5 from 12 to 9 p.m.
(213) 625-5045
Visitor's Center hours:
Monday-Friday 10 a.m. to 3 p.m.
(213) 628-1274

Besides the regular restaurants along Olvera Street, they set up food booths for this two-day fiesta. There are musical acts and folklorico dancers.

There is more on Olvera Street in the March, September, and December Chapters.

Of course, there is a store in El Monte that specializes in something perfect for Cinco de Mayo:

World of Piñatas
10953 Valley Mall
El Monte, CA 91731
Monday-Saturday 9 a.m. to 5 p.m.
(818) 454-4599

Ed Gonzalez opened a warehouse in 1988 thinking he was going to be a wholesaler of pinatas—which are normally sold through mom-and pop stores in Latino neighborhoods. He started getting requests for custom piñatas for special occasions. Now these unique creations account for 50 percent of his business.

You can any kind of piñata you want. For birthday parties, they are often called upon to make a caricature of the person having the birthday. Sometimes they make giant numbers for anniversaries or company logos for corporate events. For bachelor or bachelorette parties, often the theme calls for a more anatomically accurate (or optimistic) design. Mr. Gonzalez' favorite custom piñata was an eight foot flying saucer, complete with opening doors, for Warner Brothers.

Latin American art forms are gaining recognition throughout the world and one of these that is especially predominant is the Mural.

The Southern California area boasts one of the largest number of murals of any place in the world, which is at least partially attributable to the fact that they can be painted year round due to our climate.

There are over 1,500 murals of all kinds here, some from the W.P.A. period, some earlier, and a lot that have been painted more recently. They are in all places in the Southland to some extent—Laguna, Venice, Hollywood, and Long Beach—but there are some 300 to 400 of them in East L.A. and there is no better way to appreciate the vibrancy of L.A.'s Hispanic community than to gaze upon them. A tour is available from:

Mural Tour of Lincoln Heights, Boyle Heights,
and City Terrace
Mural Conservancy
10556 Almyo Avenue

Los Angeles, CA 90064
(213) 470-8864

Even though Mexico City is famous for its mural art, one of the largest murals in the Western Hemisphere is located right here in Southern California:

Great Wall of Los Angeles
Coldwater Canyon Boulevard
[Between Burbank Boulevard and Oxnard Street]
North Hollywood

This mural occupies the side of a metropolitan wash adjacent to Los Angeles Valley College. It describes the history of the world for the last 100 years from the point of view of ethnic events in Southern California. Each slice of history is depicted on a huge panel like a giant slide show. It is one of the most fantastic sights I have ever seen. The style is bold and colorful and it tells tale after tale in dramatic, visual fashion.

There is a park that runs the length of the mural that is set off from the street in a way that gives you a full view of the mural, but isolates you somewhat from the rest of your surroundings.

If you thought there was no place that is romantic to stay in the Valley, try:

La Maida House and Bungalows
11159 La Maida Street
North Hollywood, CA 991601
(818) 769-3857

North Hollywood may seem like an unlikely place for a Mediterranean villa surrounded by blooming orchids, magnolia trees, and 300 varieties of roses, but here it is. La Maida House has 10 rooms, four in the main house, and six bungalows. The bungalows all have private entrances and some have private gardens and jacuzzis.

In addition to the original Italian woodwork, fountains, and ironwork, La Maida House has stained glass windows created by the inn's hostess Megan Timothy. She is also a gourmet cook and her breakfasts include eggs from chickens who live at the inn. It is also quite reasonable at $70 to $195 per night.

Though it is not exactly a Mexican restaurant, as good a place as any to celebrated Cinco de Mayo is close to here:

Norah's Place
5667 Lankershim Boulevard
North Hollywood, CA 91601
Wednesday & Thursday 5 p.m. to 1 a.m.

Friday & Saturday 11 to 2 a.m.
Sunday 11 a.m. to 11 p.m.
(818) 980-6900

This is a family owned Bolivian/Italian restaurant. The Bolivian food is so different and wonderful I almost insist you try it—especially at about $25 for dinner for two, including an Argentinean cabernet. On Thursday nights and Sunday, they have free tango lessons and on Friday and Saturday nights, they have live entertainment. They are so friendly here that you will be completely charmed.

If, however you would prefer some Mexican musical entertainment of the highest order, an L.A. classic is:

La Fonda
2501 Wilshire Boulevard
Los Angeles, CA 90057
Monday-Thursday 11 to 12 a.m.
Friday & Saturday
11 to 1:30 a.m.
Sunday 5 p.m. to 12 a.m.
(213) 380-5055

What a celebration this hacienda-style restaurant is, with or without Cinco de Mayo. Though it is inexpensive to moderately priced, dinner here is worth a million dollars. The menu may not be very big, but the traditional Mexican food is first rate and the music is simply wonderful—and provided with no cover charge.

The proper name of mariachi music is "ranchera." It is a music of passion and is often about broken hearts, love gone bad, or painful memories.

Though the image of mariachis is that of a strolling group composed mainly of strings with a trumpet or two, the truer sound and picture is what you will find here: a 12-piece orchestra of fine musicians that includes French horns with a full brass section and a harpist, among others. The band is called **Los Camperos** and, deservedly, it is world famous and possibly the best in the U.S.

They have played all over the country—including at Carnegie Hall. Linda Ronstadt, who recorded a ranchera album in 1987 called "Canciones de mi Padre," uses them on tours.

There are three shows nightly—at 6:45, 9, and 11 p.m., with a 12:30 a.m. show on Friday and Saturday nights. The band crowds onto the small stage with a mural of a Mexican plaza behind them. All are beautifully costumed. Besides their musicianship (all of them sing as beautifully as they play their instruments), the band's rapport with the audience, no matter what its ethnic makeup, would make any entertainer jealous. The comic banter is surprisingly funny and they even play a Japanese song, "Sakura," for the large numbers of Japanese tourists that often come to the early show. And as if there were room to spare, sometimes they will be joined by brightly costumed folk dancers.

La Fonda is a very popular place for birthdays and celebrations among Mexicans and Latinos. When a large number of Hispanics are in the audience, the air is filled with the shrill yells (called "guacos"), bird noises and whistles that the emotion of the songs unleashes.

Making ranchera music naturally requires some unique equipment; these special tools of their trade are all available at:

> **La Casa del Musico**
> **1850 East 1st Street**
> **Los Angeles, CA 90033**
> **Monday-Saturday 9 a.m. to 5 p.m.**
> **(213) 262-9425**

Walking into this store and not knowing it was for mariachis, you might be surprised by the predominance of short black jackets (called "chamarras") and colorful superwide bow ties (called "monos"). Of course, the spirited music might be the first hint, if you haven't already perused the shelves of merchandise more closely—like the selection of trumpets and other instruments as well as the huge library of mariachi songbooks (called "cancioneros").

But the piece de resistance of Ruben Ortega's musical mall are the sparkling silver "galas." These are the brilliant accent pieces that the performers attach to the front of their jackets, cuffs, and trousers.

CUBAN DEBUTANTE BALL

The majority of the approximately 120,000 Cubans in the L.A. area came here during the 1960s. May sees their biggest annual event:

> **Debutante Ball**
> **Hollywood Palladium**
> **6215 Sunset Boulevard**

Hollywood, CA 90028
normally third Saturday of May
(213) 962-7600

This pageant official announces the marriageability of the 15-year-old participants. There are usually about 100 of these young ladies.

The Hollywood Palladium originally opened in 1940. Since that time, an incredible assortment of events has taken place within its walls. The bands of Glen Miller and the Dorsey Brothers swung here. I have been to concerts ranging from Sly and the Family Stone to Oingo Boingo. It is quite a place to party. A large central dance floor is overlooked by two curved balconies on either side. They have a full bar and very crowded bathrooms.

Hollywood has several Cuban restaurants. My favorite is:

El Floridita
1253 North Vine Street
Hollywood, CA 90029
Daily 11 a.m. to 10 p.m.
(213) 871-0936

Rose Dosti, formerly of the *L.A. Times,* called this the best Cuban Restaurant in L.A. I agree with her. I have taken many groups to enjoy the hospitality of owner Armando Castro.

It is hard to resist the "Pierna de puerco asada" (pork roast) or chicken a la fricassee, both served with rice, black beans, guazana fruit, and plantains (fried bananas). For dessert, they serve "las tres leches," which is a sort of rum pudding cake that is one of the best desserts in L.A. Homemade sangria is also included. During dinner, they often have a band or Piano Melodico, Cuban piano music accompanied by rhythm.

It is a good sign to see the small ethnic restaurants that add such spice to Hollywood are also making their appearance in Orange County. Another personal favorite Cuban restaurant is:

Felix Continental Cafe
36 Plaza Square
Orange, CA 92666
Monday-Friday 7 a.m. to 9 p.m.
Saturday & Sunday 8 a.m. to 8:30 p.m.
(714) 633-5842

This gem of a Cuban restaurant is colorful and friendly with great food. Dinner for two is less than $25.

PHILIPPINE HERITAGE
FESTIVAL AND SANTACRUZAN

It is one of the many surprises about the Los Angeles area that Filipinos are the largest Asian group, numbering over 400,000.

The Filipinos came after the Japanese and Chinese (who had arrived in the 19th century), but before the Vietnamese (who arrived in the 1970s). They began settling in Southern California in large numbers in the 1920s and '30s. The original immigrants were mainly young single men who went to work as farm workers.

In the mid-1960s, this pattern changed to professionals and members of families who were already established here. To this day, Filipinos are willing to endure the longest waiting list of any ethnic group for immigration status.

The largest annual event put on by the Filipino community is the:

> **Philippine Heritage Festival and Santacruzan**
> **Cerritos Regional Park, 19700 South Bloomfield Avenue**
> **Cerritos, CA 90703**
> **normally last Sunday in May**
> **(310) 924-5144**

This festival displays Philippine culture and provides a sense of pride for the community. It also has a religious purpose—to honor the Virgin—though this is not as central to the purpose here as it is back in the islands. The main part of the Heritage Festival is a parade, the "Santacruzan" being the climax. It is a procession of young women called "sagalos." The name Santacruzan comes from Santa Cruz (the Holy Cross). The women represent different aspects of the Virgin as well as figures surrounding Empress Helena and Constantine, her son, who went in search of the cross.

Beside the parade, there are dance shows featuring the "Timikling" in which a kind of hip hop is performed between two long thick bamboo poles, that are clacked together rhythmically. This adds percussion, but also the risk of smashed ankles or feet. Because of this, it is a dance that takes months to learn.

One of the easiest and most delightful ways to sample a little Philippine culture is to stop by nearby Artesia or one of the the other two locations of:

> **Goldilock's Bake Shop and Restaurant**
> **17522 Pioneer Boulevard**
> **Artesia, CA 90701**
> **Tuesday-Saturday 10 a.m. to 9 p.m.**

Sunday 10 a.m. to 8 p.m.
(310) 860-7786
and:
209 South Vermont
Los Angeles, CA 90004
(213) 382-9303
and:
1559 East Amar Road
[corner of Azusa Avenue]
West Covina, CA 91792
(818) 964-1811

These combination restaurant-bakeries are bright and bustling; glass cases are filled with all kinds of goodies—and the most expensive entree on the menu is $5.95!

Fresh "lumpia", a vegetable crepe with garlic sauce made with carrots, garbanzos, and shredded green peppers, is a favorite. Yet, the most interesting looking dish is "Sago at Gulaman," which reminds me of something Kirk and McCoy might be having at some bar in a far off solar system. It is a goblet filled with a soft brownish-gold fluid with ice, little pieces of tropical fruit, and luminous little balls that look like pearls. They are actually pearls of tapioca. "Pansit palabok" is a pretty golden orange dish made with delicate soft rice noodles in shrimp sauce. "Ube yummy" is a purple custard croissant, made with yams.

Pioneer Boulevard around South Street has an evolving Korean commercial area. As you move toward the 91 Freeway, it changes to "Little India" (see August), and then, near the 91, it is Filipino. The Goldilocks location on Pioneer Boulevard is in a shopping center that also features a market offering Filipino specialties:

Maynila Seafood Market
17516 East Pioneer Boulevard
Daily 7 a.m. 8 p.m.
Artesia, CA 90701
(310) 809-0559

Filipino cooking uses ingredients from both Spanish and Asian cuisine. This small market has a variety of unique foods including *"Bagoong,"* a fermented fish or shrimp paste available in many different varieties.

There are several Filipino concentrations in the Southland. Besides the Cerritos/Norwalk communities, they are the Panorama City/Sun Valley/North Hollywood area of the San Fernando Valley, the cities of West Covina, Walnut, Pomona, Rowland Heights, and Diamond Bar, Glendale/Eagle Rock, Carson/Long Beach, and the area most often called Philippine Town: the Temple/Beverly area of Los Angeles.

One of the most established places to eat in Philippine Town is:

>**Bayanihan Restaurant**
>**2300 Beverly Boulevard**
>**Los Angeles, CA 90057**
>**Daily 5 p.m. to 1 a.m.**
>**(213) 383-8357**

This casual restaurant is a great place to try the most common Philippine dinner, *"adobo."* It is chicken or meat marinated in a concoction of soy sauce, palm vinegar, and garlic that is first braised in the sauce, then fried. The marinade is boiled, then put back on the meat before being served.

They are very friendly here and Tuesday and Wednesday nights they have a live band and dancing.

HOT AIR BALLOON FESTIVAL

The first part of May brings a unique festival:

>**Temecula Balloon and Wine Festival**
>**Lake Skinner**
>**usually first weekend of May, $10**
>contact:
>**Temecula Valley Balloon and Wine Association**
>**27475 Ynez Road, Suite 335**
>**Temecula, CA 92591**
>**(909) 676-6713**

The annual event is a spectacle worth experiencing. More than 60 colorful hot air balloons lifting off simultaneously in the early morning is reason enough, but when you add the wine and music that accompany it, you can see why hotel space can be tough to come by for this weekend happening.

Besides food booths, the Temecula Balloon and Wine Festival has arts and crafts exhibits and a "Kid's Faire." If you want to take a ride in a hot air balloon you must make a reservation in advance.

The Temecula area has a compact wine country and a frontier-style "Old Town" (see October), but it also offers a golf resort of unusual beauty:

Temecula Creek Inn
45501 Rainbow Canyon Road
Temecula, CA 92390
(714) 962-7335

This is the area's pre-mier resort, and the best rea-son to take up golf since Pebble Beach. The long driveway is lined with beau-tiful rose bushes of assorted colors. The landscaping is simply breathtaking and the atmosphere of the whole place is of rustic luxury at its best.

The Sunday brunch here is a serious brunch—not because of sheer size, but because of the quality and real selection. The view from the dining room, which overlooks the golf course, com-pletes the serenity of the setting.

LATE SPRING FLOWERS
Higher Altitudes, Mountain Mining Towns

May is the month to experience spring in the higher elevations of the Southland. As you climb into the mountains, up until about 6,000 feet, you will begin to en-counter the white blossoms of **Flowering Dogwood** with their languid white leaves surrounding clusters of tiny white flowers which form into little half-inch long red fruit.

San Gabriel Mountains

The San Gabriel foothills (described in March) run along the base of the San Gabriel Mountains, which in turn form the northern boundary of the San Gabriel Valley. The lower portions of the mountains are covered with the chaparral you see on most of the Southland's hills. As you climb higher, this is replaced with tall trees. Practically all of the 20-mile long, 60-mile wide San Gabriels are within the 693,000 acres of Angeles National Forest.

The communities at the upper reaches of the foothills enjoy a closeness to the mountains that are but a few minutes away for them. The City of La Canada, for example, is the departure point for **Angeles Crest Highway** (State Route 2), which climbs and curves up into the San Gabriels. This is a most enjoyable late spring drive since you can see the changes in vegetation unfold with the difference in altitude.

The so-called "Gateway to the High Country" is the Charton-Chilao Recreation Area. Stop at the:

Chilao Visitor's Center
Angeles National Forest
County Road S2, mile 50.6
27 miles north of I-210 (Foothill Freeway)
Daily 9 a.m. to 4 p.m.
(818) 796-5541

The store has books you can buy as well as exhibits and free printed information. Three short nature loop trails with interpretive signs also begin right here.

Whether you are hiking, camping, skiing, or just taking a drive on the Angeles Crest Highway, there is only one place to have a good meal and/or a drink:

Newcomb's Ranch Inn
(behind Chilao Visitor's Center)
State Route 2
La Cañada, CA 91011
11 a.m. to 7 p.m. Monday-Thursday
8 a.m. to 8 p.m. Saturday & Sunday
(818) 440-1001

The jovial general manager will welcome you to this rustic mountain restaurant for breakfast, lunch, or dinner. Originally established in 1939, Newcomb's Ranch Inn was part of an old 160 acre ranch. The building is made of wood and solid concrete: the Newcomb family made their money in the latter business. The great granddaughter of the founder, Lynn Newcomb, now owns Mt. Waterman Ski Resort (see November).

It has the mood inside of a roadside diner in the Sierras. There are two huge stone fireplaces and a full bar with a 42-foot long, old saloon-style wooden counter. If it is sunny out, there is an outdoor patio. Newcomb's Ranch Inn even has a resident ghost, "Uncle Louis," who apparently was thirsty when he died: his specter opens beer taps when there is no one around.

San Bernardino Mountains

The San Bernardino Mountains begin at their western end at the 20 mile wide Cajon Pass, which cuts them off from the San Gabriels. Since the San Andreas Fault runs through the pass, it is assumed that the two ranges were once one, but were torn apart by seismic activity. They end on their eastern end in the tallest mountain in Southern California: 11,502-foot Mt. San Gorgonio, also known as "Old Grayback."

This range of mountains has the largest number of lakes in the Southland. The two biggest are Lake Arrowhead and Big Bear Lake.

SR 18, which runs from San Bernardino up to the lake country, is better known as **Rim of the World Drive.** This rambling, 101-mile long scenic route is almost like a continuous movie of alpine scenery. Probably the most impressive view is from **Lakeview Point**, which is at 7,203 feet. The view from this turn out catches a corner of Big Bear Lake, framed by the mountains as the road curves around the cliffs ahead. SR 18 borders the true high country woodlands like a frame of asphalt cut into the mountain rock.

Lake Arrowhead was originally Little Bear Valley. Needless to say, there aren't any bears in it now—unless they are wearing scuba gear. In 1911, a dam created what was first called Little Bear Lake and then changed to its present name in the 1920s.

There is 14 miles of shoreline around the lake. The people who own the houses on it actually own the lake too. That is why most of what is happening here is centered in Lake Arrowhead Village.

The centerpiece of the Village is the red steeple-topped dance pavilion, which also dates from the '20s. This 38-acre village has the most alpine atmosphere of any of the Southland's mountain towns.

If you wanted to stay in a place in Lake Arrowhead with that alpine feel to it, drop in at the:

Eagles Landing
27406 Cedarwood
P.O. Box 1510 (Blue Jay)
Lake Arrowhead, CA 92317
(909) 336-2642

Though this small lakeside inn was recently built, its style could best be described as "Mountain Gothic." It has a fireplace and is decorated with art and antiques. Each of the four guest rooms has its own bath, the suite has its own bar, TV, fireplace and deck overlooking the lake. There are also decks open to all guests that really bring out the beauty of the inn's west shore location. A full breakfast in the dining room is included.

The larger lake of the San Bernardino Mountains is **Big Bear Lake.** At one time, I owned half of a cabin up here and miss driving up and forgetting all of my responsibilities. There is really nothing quite like a mountain lake to inspire a feeling of tranquility.

Perhaps the quintessential romantic lake front lodge is the lovely:

Windy Point Inn
39263 North Shore
Drive
P.O. Box 375
Fawnskin, CA 92333
(909) 866-2746

The Windy Point Inn is located in a beautiful se- cluded spot on the north side of the lake past Fawnskin on the way to Minnelusa. It is on a private point that projects out into the lake, bordered on both sides by sandy beaches. Its original owner, the late David Zimmerman, also designed it and a more successful architec- tural matching of natural beauty and human interest would be hard to find.

There are only four rooms, all with private baths and fireplaces. **The Pines** is a split level mountain suite with a corner fireplace, vaulted ceiling and even a skylit wet bar. It has a sense of playfulness to it with its mix of '50s advertising signs, Wild West antiques and heavy antique furniture. It has its own private deck and outside entrance via a private staircase.

The Cliffs features a sunset view over the lake, its own private entrance, and a wet bar sink. **The Sands** also offers a wet bar sink, but offers a sunrise view and a particularly warm feeling. **The Peaks** is glass on three sides and has a full 180 degree lake view and four skylights. Its corner couch in front of the fireplace would rank as one of the great snuggling spots of Southern California. Rates are $125-$225 and $105-$95 midweek. The innkeepers are Val and Kent Jessler.

Two miles south of SR 18 at the base of Bear Mountain Ski resort is a pleasant mountain surprise:

Moonridge Animal Park
43285 Gold Mine Drive
P.O. Box 8352 (mailing)
Big Bear Lake, CA 92315
Daily 8:30 a.m. to 5 p.m.
May through October
$2 adults $1 children
(909) 866-0183

This free little zoo features animals local to the area. These include such magnificent creatures as black bears, bobcats, timber wolves, and mountain lions.

The park was started in 1959 after a big wildfire orphaned many animals. The Moonridge Animal Park's first and most famous resident was Herman the black bear. Operated by San Bernardino County and the Friends of Moonridge Animal Park, it continues its original purpose and takes care of abandoned, orphaned, or injured wildlife.

San Jacinto Mountains

The granite San Jacinto Mountains rise so abruptly from the desert floor that they look like a movie set's backdrop. In the 1800s, they were savagely mauled by a deforestation similar to what was inflicted upon the San Gabriels and the San Bernardinos. In 1897, President Grover Cleveland established the San Jacinto Timberland Reserve, which in 1930 was merged with the San Bernardino National Forest. Four years later, the Civilian Conservation Corps built an excellent trail system.

On their northern side, the San Jacinto Mountains are separated from the San Bernardinos by the San Gorgonio Pass, which was discovered in 1853. One of the main arteries into the San Jacintos rises from here, State Highway 243, also known as the **Banning Idyllwild Panoramic Highway.** In 1948, this paved road opened in a ribbon cutting ceremony (by actress Jane Powell), complete with music by the local high school marching band. It twists and curves up the mountains, going first through chaparral, then past deciduous trees, then into the pines.

On your way up, stop at **Indian Vista,** a mid-level overlook that offers panoramic views. It is pictured in one of the phos on the cover. The trail to Indian Mountain begins here.

After about a half-hour ascent, you will be in the charming mountain town of **Idyllwild.** This perfect destination was originally called "Strawberry Valley" because of the abundance of wild strawberries that flourished here. In 1901, a group of doctors decided the area would be a great place for a tuberculosis sanitorium. They bought most of the land and changed its name.

Even in the middle of the business district, the streets seem to undulate like mountain roads. The centerpiece of town is a shopping center called **The Fort**. It is appropriately named because it is constructed of logs interlaced at the corners and looks like a western outpost. There are carved wood animal statues all over it—including a bald eagle on the very top. The most prominent carving is the three-dimensional mural that fronts on Highway 243.

These carvings are the creation of Jonathan LaBenne, a former resident who moved to Idaho. His most famous work is the **Idyllwild Tree Monument**, a towering totem pole on Village Center Drive.

Right near the pole is a great little bookstore called:

The Book Shop
54235 Ridgeview Drive
Idyllwild, CA 92549
Daily 9 a.m. to 5 p.m.
(909) 659-4455

Next door is the highest rated restaurant in town:

Gastrognome Restaurant
54381 Ridgeview Drive
Idyllwild, CA 92549
Monday-Friday
11:45 a.m. to 9:30 p.m.
Saturday 5 p.m. to 10 p.m.
Sunday 10 a.m. to 10 p.m.
(909) 659-5055

Across from The Fort is a cute mountain cafe:

Jan's Red Kettle
54220 N. Circle Drive
Idyllwild, CA 92549
Daily 7 a.m. to 3 p.m.
(909) 659-4063

Idyllwild's totem pole.

Yes, there is a real Jan. Her name is Jan Bossand and she has lived in Idyllwild since 1967. In 1977, she opened this warm little place with its knotty pine interior and patio.

From downtown Idyll-wild, go up Fern Valley Road to Humber Park. This is the main entrance point for hikers into the **San Jacinto Wilderness**. You would need a wilderness permit if you were going to venture deeply into the wilderness

Jan's Red Kettle, a rustic mountain cafe in Idyllwild.

area, but there is an easy way to get a taste of it without doing any serious backpacking.

The Ernie Maxwell Scenic Trail is a delightful and easy 2.6-mile stroll with only a 300-foot elevation gain that is most people's idea of a wonderful walk in the forest. It has an unending panoramic view of Strawberry Valley framed by the surrounding mountains, yet does not require a wilderness permit. It was built in 1959 and named after Ernie Maxwell, the founder of the local newspaper, *The Idyllwild Town Crier.*

On the other side of the center of the community on SR 243, near the ranger station, is a large inviting cedar-shingled mountain manor with big picture windows and an appropriate name:

Strawberry Creek Inn
26370 Highway 243
P.O. Box 1818
Idyllwild, CA 92349
(909) 659-3202

Two professional urban planners from San Diego, Jim Goff and Diana Dugan, have created almost an archetypal retreat. The huge living room has plush couches in earth tones that reverberate in the wood floors and paneling. There is a wooden deck with four of the Inn's nine rooms arranged around it in a semi circle.

The rooms all have private baths. Four of them have fireplaces. One of the rooms with a fireplace has handicap access. Each of the rooms has a different decor. There's the **Autumn Room** and **The Oak Tree Room**. If you like Victorian, there is the boudoir-styled **Helen's Room**. The **San Jacinto Room** is a kind of All American mountain lodge and the obligatory **Santa Fe Room** has stucco walls with dark wooden beams across the ceiling. There is even a **Honeymoon Cottage** equipped with a fireplace and a Roman tub.

If you like the "breakfast" part of B & Bs, you'll like it here. They are of the "hearty" variety and can include spinach-zucchini quiche and German French toast served with local sausages. Prices range from about $80 to $120.

Local residents refer to Idyllwild as "The Hill." Looking at it on a map, the roads in form a tripod that meets in the town. One of these is 243 that we came in on. It passes through Idyllwild and continues on to the town of **Mountain Station**, where it forms a "T" intersection with State Highway 74. The latter road comes up from Hemet as the **Idyllwild National Forest Highway** and continues east as the **Palms to Pines Highway**. This road is particularly celebrated—and for good reason. It rises from Palm Desert and offers spectacular views. About 26 miles southeast of Idyllwild is the **Bighorn Sheep Overlook**. This is a newly renovated viewing area with a railed-in deck with built-in benches. It overlooks a jagged canyon with a grove of Cottonwood trees called **Horsethief Canyon** that is a favorite hangout of Bighorn Sheep.

If you wanted to experience the change in elevation of the Palms to Pines High-way—but quicker—take a ride on the famous:

>**Palm Springs Aerial Tram**
>**Valley Station**
>**Tramway Road**
>**located six miles northwest of the City of Palm Springs**
>**Monday-Friday 10 a.m.; Saturday-Sunday 8 a.m.**
>**9 p.m. last car up; 10:45 p.m. last car down**
>**$15.95 adults; $9.95 Children**
>**(619) 325-1391**

In the approximately 14 minutes it takes the two 80-passenger tram cars to climb 2-1/2 miles of cable to the top, participants are treated to a dramatic change in eco-logical zones. The elevation at the start in Chino Canyon is 2,643 feet; when you get off at Mountain Station, you are at 8,516 feet.

At the top is the **Alpine Restaurant**, which opens at 11 a.m. Beginning at 4 p.m., they have a good package deal called the "Ride and Dine" that includes a round trip ride and a meal for $19.95, $12.95 for children. There are no reservations taken for this and tickets go on sale at 2:30 p.m. Mountain Station also has a picnic area, observation deck, and a gift shop.

Besides the tram ride and view, this area offers more than 54 acres of high alti-tude hiking trails that meander through 13,000-acre **Mt. San Jacinto State Wilder-ness Park**.

For a heavenly two mile walk from the Mountain Station, simply take the little paved walkway to the sign for the **Desert View Trail**. It offers not only what its name promises, but views of some of the tallest mountains in the Southland. You can see the lush palm canyons below and the cities of the desert resort areas beyond.

Julian and Cuyamaca Mountains, Mining History, and Wildflowers

To the northeast of San Diego is an unusual mountain range with small (4,000-6,500 feet) peaks and abundant rainfall called the Cuyamaca Mountains. Native Californians came here in the summer as early as 5500 B.C. They called the moun-tains "Ah-ha-Kwe-ah-mac," which means "no rain behind," "rain yonder," "rain above," or "the place where it rains." Regardless of the exact translation, what the name refers to is the fact that these peaks trap about 35 inches of rain per year and allow little to get past them going east toward the Anza Borrego Desert.

Don Augustin Olvera, for whom Olvera Street in L.A. was named (see March, May, September, and December), came into possesion of much of the land in 1845 in a grant from the Mexican government. It was called Rancho Cuyamaca. He sold it in 1869 for $1,000. This would turn out to be one of the stupidist moves in the history of California real estate deals.

Gold was struck in nearby Julian the same year. What would be the biggest mine in the area was found on land that was formerly part of the rancho, right by Lake Cuyamaca, on the day before Washington's Birthday in 1870—one year after Olvera sold it.

By the turn of the century, over 2,000 people were employed in the mines. A total of about $15,000,000 worth of gold was pulled out of the ground before it was all gone.

Today, these mountains are a perfect May destination. A substantial amount of them has been protected by the state and county parks located here.

If you are driving in from the north or west on Highway 78 or 79, a great place to stop is where the roads come together, in the little town of Santa Ysabel. It is here you will find (or rather smell):

> **Dudley's Bakery**
> **30218 Highway 78**
> **Santa Ysabel, CA 92070**
> **Wednesday-Saturday 8 a.m. to 5 p.m.**
> **Sunday 8 a.m. to 4 p.m.**
> **(619) 765-0488**
> **(800) 225-3348**

Dudley's started life in 1963 and expanded numerous times, taking over the space formerly occupied by four other businesses. Today it fills up a big, two story building. The reason for their success is their incredible baked-on-premises breads, of which there are nearly 20 kinds. Cookies, pies, and pastries are also featured. There is also a little gift shop. Coffee and tea are available and tables have been set up at one end if you would to stop here and eat a pastry and refresh yourself.

Continuing on the combined 78/79 highway, at 4,500 feet, you will come to the little jewel of a former mining town called **Julian**. Tourism has now replaced gold, and though there are a lot of visitors, the town still has its charm. On the way in, lilac bushes and clumps of daffodils are all along the road.

Julian got its name from Mike Julian, who along with his cousin Drury Bailey, found the first recorded quartz mine, which they called the Warrior's Rest. Though

Bailey owned most of the land, he thought his cousin's name sounded better for a town.

Located on both Highway 78 and 79 (they continue to overlap as you come from the west), just before you come to Main Street is the:

Julian Pioneer Museum
2811 Washington Street
Julian, CA 92036
Tuesday-Sunday 10 a.m. to 4 p.m. (April-November)
Saturday-Sunday 10 a.m. to 4 p.m. (December-March)
(619) 765-0227

This turn-of-the century building was originally a brewery, then it was a blacksmith's shop, then someone's house. It not only has an interesting history, it has picnic tables and now serves as "Julian's Attic."

Once inside, besides the old mining equipment you would expect, such as gold pans and picks and shovels, the museum displays traces of 19th century household life, such as an old spinning wheel and a washboard and boiler. Other even more personal items include high button shoes and wedding gowns with waists so tiny they must have been for either child-brides or women so heavily corsetted it's amazing they could breath in the mountain air.

There are glass cases containing antique handmade lace. Old photos show you what the early white settlers looked like. There are even some Native American baskets and other remnants of the indigenous people whose land this beautiful area used to be. One group that also apparently did not fare so well in early Julian was its local animal population. There are stuffed corpses of these creatures all over the museum's interior.

Just as you enter the town proper by turning right onto Main Street from Washington is an old fashioned soda fountain:

Julian Drug Store
2134 Main Street and Washington
Julian, CA 92036
(619) 765-0332

This was the first brick building built in Julian. The Julian Drug store was originally established in 1886. You can still order a sparkling sarsaparilla at the vintage marble counter.

Right across the street is a white clapboard building. This month, it is the showcase for the:

Julian Wildflower Festival
Julian Town Hall (Julian Chamber of Commerce)
2129 Main Street
Julian, CA 92036
first week of May
9 a.m. to 5 p.m.
(619) 765-1276 or (619) 765-1466

Each day of this one-week festival, volunteers gather dozens of different local species and put them on display inside. The array is quite dazzling and seems right at home in this old building. Though many of the false front stores along the historic Main Street are replicas, some, like this one, are originals.

The first big quartz mine was called:

The Washington Mine
C Street and Geiter Road
Julian
(619) 765-1020

This strike was discovered the Sunday before Washington's birthday in 1870, hence the name. Though this wasn't the biggest producer, it was the one that started the Julian gold rush. There isn't much left. But, not too far from here, one of the original mines is still operating:

Eagle Mining
North end of C Street
Julian
Tours daily 1 to 3 p.m.
(619) 765-0036

This is actually two mines, the Eagle and the High Peak, that are connected underground. They were registered just a few months after the Washington. To get there, take C Street about six blocks north and you will come to Old Miner's Trail.

The mine site has a working five stamp mill, a replica of a mining blacksmith's shop, and an outdoor collection of antique assay equipment. The 90-minute tour takes you below ground in a 1,000-foot hard rock tunnel and explains mining techniques as well as relating local history. After the tour, you can try panning for gold.

There are only six side streets along Main, so this certainly is a place you will want to walk around to see. If you wanted to stay right in town, you could stay in a real 1897 frontier Victorian hotel located a few hundred yards from the site of the original discovery:

Julian Hotel
2032 Main Street
Julian, CA 92036
(619) 765-0201

Located at the corner of B Street, this brown two-story remnant of the town's heyday in the mining era has the honor of being listed in the National Register of Historic Places. It was built by a freed slave named Albert Robinson and is one of the oldest continuously operating hotels in Southern California.

Quite grand in its day, it was called the "Queen of the Back Country," and was presided over by Mrs. Robinson, who entertained local dignitaries with her hot apple pie and cheese. When Albert died, she ran the place until 1921.

Today you walk through a burgundy colored parlor and have your choice of more recent, 1920s-style rooms or the original nine in the main building on the sunny upper floor. There is an old claw foot bathtub here.

The Cuyamaca's have a tremendous beauty in the trees, of which there are numerous species that thrive because of the rainfall. There are, unfortunately, very few places not privately owned right around the town of Julian. The two parks nearby, however, offer a total of well over 100 miles of hiking trails of varying degrees of difficulty. The closer of the two is:

William Heise County Park
(619) 565-3600

From Julian, take 78/79 west a mile to Pine Hills Road, then go south two miles, turn east on Frisius Road for two more miles.

This is a nice park to walk or camp in because the well maintained campsites, fireplaces, picnic areas, water, bathrooms—and even a playground—are all in one section along a creek bed that makes up about 10 percent of the total area. The remaining 90 percent is beautiful wilderness traversed by about seven miles of easy loop trails. Because of the altitude (4,200), the air is sweet and fresh and there is abundant life all around you.

On the way into the park is a delightful, romantic place to stay if you would rather not camp, but would like to spend your days walking under the trees:

Shadow Mountain Ranch
2771 Frisius Road, Box 791
Julian, CA 92036
(619) 765-0323

This ranch house and cottages is located three miles out of town. It is spread out over eight acres overlooking the mountains and a flower filled meadow. There are six rooms, all but one with a private bath. Each room is themed to go along with its name. **The Enchanted Cottage**, for example, does look like it came out of a fairy tale. It has Bavarian/Swiss detailing and a door with a rounded top. Inside, it is peach and green with a bay windowseat perfect for lovers. There is a wood-burning stove and a TV in each room.

Besides the regular quarters, the most unusual room is a tree house equipped with feather beds. If you are afraid of heights, rest easy: it is only seven steps off the ground.

Another nearby place to stay has an interesting history:

> **Pine Hills Lodge**
> **2960 La Posada Way**
> **Julian, CA 92036**
> **(619) 765-1100**

Surrounded by the oak and pine forest in the fragrant air of 4,500-foot elevation, it is hard to believe that this is the former training gym of heavyweight champion Jack Dempsey. The compound was originally built in 1912 and consists of a wood frame lodge with six guest rooms (all sharing the same bathroom with its clawfoot tub).

Somewhat more private accommodations can be had in one of the 12 individual cabins, which not only have private baths, some of them have their own patios and fireplaces. This is also the site of the **Pine Hills Dinner Theatre** where the show is the main course and dinner is limited to two choices: baby back ribs or baked chicken.

The other area open to the public in these mountains is located about 15 miles south of Julian on Highway 79:

> **Cuyamaca Rancho State Park**
> **12551 Highway 79**
> **Descanso, CA 91916**
> **(619) 765-0755**

At nearly 30,000 acres, this is one of the largest parks in the state system. A full 13,000 acres of it is wilderness.

At the south end of the park, just north of Old Highway 80 is one of the easiest waterfalls to walk to in the Southland. Just turn west off of Highway 79 into the Green Valley Campground. There is a parking lot marked "Day Use" at the south end. A sign will indicate the short easy trail to **Green Valley Falls**.

Coastal Flowers, Encinitas, Leucadia, and Carlsbad

The northern coastal part of San Diego County has always been noted as a flower growing region. Though many of the fields have been turned into tract houses, the tradition survives. There is even a shrine that celebrates the glory of plant life on a spiritual level:

> **Self Realization Fellowship Retreat and Hermitage**
> **215 K. Street**
> **Encinitas, CA 92024**
> **Tuesday through Saturday from 9 a.m. to 5 p.m.**
> **Sunday from 11 a.m. to 5 p.m.**
> **(619) 753-1811**

The Self Realization Fellowship was founded by Paramahansa Yogananda. It is dedicated to the universality of all religions and their relationship to nature. The sight of the golden domes atop peerless white towers is peacefully framed by blue sky and Pacific Ocean background. Built from the very beginning as a religious retreat back in the 1930s, its lush tropical gardens have been beautifully maintained.

The view of the ocean here is certainly heavenly—particularly at sunset. But since the place closes at 5 p.m., you will miss the sundown as the days get longer. There is another Self Realization Fellowship Shrine up in Pacific Palisades on a small lake. (See August.)

Going north up the coast a half dozen blocks, Encinitas has a beach with a very mystical name:

> **Moonlight State Beach**
> **End of B Street near 4th Street**
> **Encinitas**

The attraction here is a big gentle horseshoe of sand inside a large cove at the rim of the sandstone bluffs.

Taking Encinitas Boulevard (S9) inland from Moonlight Beach, you will come to one of the most special of the public gardens in the Southland:

> **Quail Botanical Gardens**
> **230 Quail Gardens Drive**
> **P.O. Box 5**
> **Encinitas, CA 92024**
> **Daily 8 a.m. to 5 p.m.**
> **gift shop open Wednesday, Friday, Saturday &**
> **Sunday 11 a.m. to 3 p.m.**
> **(619) 436-3036 or (619) 753-4432**

Just 1/2 mile east of Interstate 5 by way of Encinitas Boulevard is this delightful 31-acre botanic reserve and bird and wildlife sanctuary. Occupying a niche of hillsides and ravines, it has a magical quality to it like some secret fairy garden. There are rare trees, shrubs, and flowers everywhere, but its two main claims to fame are the largest hibiscus collection on the West Coast and the greatest variety of bamboo plants in the U.S.

There are five self-guided nature walks described on leaflets that you pick up by the guest registration book on your way in. The main one, the **Quail Gardens Nature Trail** begins at the Southwest corner of the parking lot and is a pristine slice of Southern California before the onslaught of developers and their bulldozers.

There are redwood signs along this trail that are numbered to correspond to descriptions on the leaflet. There is a loop trail through a chaparral community and a tranquil pond with plants from other parts of California. There is a very rare Torrey Pine (see February) residing next to this pond and a fair amount of wildlife you can see as well.

Taking Interstate 5 north from Encinitas to Leucadia Boulevard, you will come to one of the best reasons why May is a great month to be on the Northern San Diego coast:

> **Weidner's Begonia Gardens**
> **695 Normandy Road**
> **Leucadia, CA 92024**
> **Daily 9:30 a.m. to 5 p.m.**
> **(619) 436-2194**

Originally opened in 1973 by Evelyn Weidner and her late husband Robert as a retirement project from the nursery business, the business has expanded over the years, and now carry many varieties of flowers, some of which are available beginning on April 1 when the gardens open for the season. But the star begins to shine in May: a solid acre of begonias under a giant screen mesh tent. The novel feature here being that you dig your own.

You walk in past a fantastic display of such erotica as strawberry foretells, hanging red flame carnations, double impatiens, yellow Chinese lantern, and royal purple brunfelsia. The begonia plants are in seemingly endless rows. They provide digging forks and you can either bring your own pots or they will give you cartons. Prices start from less than $5 and go on up depending on the size.

There is a wonderful, homey quality to this place that is heightened by the presence of such farm animals as ducks, chickens, a goat, sheep, a pig, and a pony.

Also in Leucadia is:

Stubb's Fuschia Nursery
737 Orpheus Avenue
Leucadia, CA 92024
Daily 9 a.m. to 5 p.m.
(619) 753-1069

Here they have more than 30,000 brilliantly flowering fuchsia plants in over 300 varieties, some of which have great names like "Swingtime," "Nonpareil", and "Voodoo."

The next city up the coast is **Carlsbad**, which got its name from Karlovy Vary, called Karlsbad in English, a health spa in Bohemia (Czechoslovakia). This was because the town's original claim to fame was its well of mineral water, which was reputed to have similar curative properties. The Spanish conquerors of California had called it the somewhat less complimentary name of Agua Hedonia, which means "stinking water."

A gentleman named John Frazier dug the original well in 1881, the same year the railroad came through, and a resort soon followed. The waters eventually ran out, but the town continued.

The site of the original well is the:

Alt Karlsbad Hanse House
2802-A Carlsbad Boulevard
Carlsbad, CA 92008
(619) 434-7020

Built in 1964, this building is a replica of a Hanseatic house and was designed to look like it was in a village in medieval Germany. It contains a museum and gift shop. There is an underground gallery where you can see the old well. As you might imagine, the gift shop features Hummel figurines, beer steins, and the like.

A few doors down is the town's most prominent place to eat:

Neiman's
2978 Carlsbad Boulevard
Carlsbad, CA 92008
Monday-Thursday 11:30 a.m. to 9 p.m.
Friday & Saturday 11:30 a.m. to 11 p.m.
Sunday 9:3a.m. to 9 p.m.
(619) 729-4131

Formerly called the Twin Inns, it was originally built in 1887 as a mansion for a local land promoter. The building then saw service as a boarding house. For the next 70 years, it was the Twin Inns, an all-you-can-eat chicken restaurant. In the 1980s, it was renovated into its present form.

If you like Victorian architecture, Neiman's is a spectacular example. It has an extensive veranda and a huge dining room. The 30-foot bar surrounded by mirrors is particularly impressive. The cafe/bar is decorated with posters by LeRoy Neiman.

The menu is extensive and includes chicken, seafood, and prime rib. The Sunday buffet brunch always draws a crowd of both locals and tourists.

Just around the corner from here, three blocks inland from the beach is a romantic place to stay:

Pelican Cove Inn
320 Walnut Avenue
Carlsbad, CA 92008
(619) 434-5995

This eight-room bed and breakfast was built in 1982 in a pretty Cape Cod style. The modern construction allows for some nice features harder to find in restored older homes. Each room has a private bath, a feather bed, and a gas fireplace. Some of them have their own spa tubs.

Bed and breakfast purists might quibble with the fact that there is a TV and radio in every room as well. No one can argue with the elaborate continental breakfast with fresh fruit and baked goods served in the parlor, on the veranda, on the sun deck, or in your room. There is also a garden gazebo where weddings are sometimes performed.

STRAWBERRY FESTIVALS

The strawberry is one of the world's more luscious fruits and one that is regularly associated with romance (especially dipped in chocolate). According to the California Strawberry Commission, the Golden State produces 85 percent of the strawberries consumed in the United States. The season runs from January to June, with the peak of the season coming in April. This is why strawberry festivals normally take place in late April or early May. There are two of them in Southern California that take place in early May.

Orange County

Orange County produces approximately 15 percent of the state's crop. That came to 50,000 tons valued at $40 million in 1992. Creating the perfect berry is an ongoing project at the University of California, where a 200 acre research station in east Irvine is devoted to just this.

Every year there is four-day festival in the northern part of the county:

Strawberry Festival
Village Green
12862 Euclid Avenue and Main
Garden Grove, CA 92640
Memorial Day Weekend, Friday through Monday
(714) 638-0981

It is nice to know there are still free events in this world. Besides carnival games and rides, there is entertainment and several talent shows. There is a big assortment of strawberry foods for sale as well as a display featuring the world's largest strawberry shortcake. On Saturday, there is a parade with celebrity grand marshals.

Also in Garden Grove is a great restaurant for vittles before or after the festival:

Belisle's Restaurant
12001 Harbor Boulevard
Garden Grove, CA 92640
(714) 750-6560

This 24-hour original boasts one of the largest and most diverse menus you have ever seen. This bright pink restaurant used to have a midget chef who stood out front and rang a bell to attract customers. Now it needs only its reputation for serving everything from fried rabbit with corn fritters to shoofly pie. There are "graveyard specials" for insomniacs, as well.

Oxnard

The strawberry has its day in Oxnard this month:

California Strawberry Festival
Strawberry Meadows at College Park
3250 South Rose Avenue
Oxnard, CA 93033
Usually the third weekend in May
Saturday & Sunday 10 a.m. to 6:30 p.m.
Adults: $5; Seniors and children: $3

(805) 444-5544
(805) 385-7578

About 25 percent of the strawberries grown in the entire state are harvested in this area. This annual festival has an amazing innocence for being 90 minutes from Hollywood. It has occurred every year since it began in 1984. On this 20-acre site, they have the entertainment, petting zoo, games, and arts and crafts you'd expect at an agricultural fair, but they also have a strawberry shortcake eating contest, a strawberry blonde contest, and food booths selling strawberries in all forms (dipped in chocolate, skewered on kabobs, whipped in daiquiris). The fruit is everywhere: sweet, ripe, and succulent.

Though the name of the City of Oxnard is hardly synonymous with romance, besides strawberries, the city is blessed with a large, fairly new beachfront resort that is far more appealing than most developments of its type:

Mandalay Beach Resort
2101 Mandalay Beach Road
Oxnard, CA 93035
(805) 984-2500

Styled like a giant hacienda in Mission Revival, the Mandalay Beach Resort is named after the beach on which it is situated. The courtyards are especially appealing with flowers and palm trees in terra cotta pots blending perfectly with the architecture and landscaping that includes fountains, streams, and waterfalls. The main courtyard features the largest free-form swimming pool in Southern California.

And as a complete resort, it offers all of the amenities. The main dining room, called **Opus One**, is in a huge atrium complete with full-sized palm trees. All rooms are either two or three bedroom suites with kitchens and two marble baths. You can get one that opens directly onto the beach promenade. Complete breakfast and afternoon cocktails are included.

Oxnard is also blessed with a remarkable public library, the largest in Ventura County:

Oxnard Public Library
251 South A Street
Oxnard, CA 93030
Monday-Thursday 10:30 a.m. to 8 p.m.
Saturday from 9 a.m. to 5:30 p.m.
(805) 385-7500

The San Francisco architectural firm of Whisler and Patri designed this 72,000-square-foot, $13 million Post Modern temple of books as part of the new Oxnard Civic Center. It is a half a city block of red bricks with a huge arched portal and pairs of truncated pillars and magnificent fan windows that fill the place with light. There is a particularly wonderful arched window on the landing at the top of the sweeping central staircase. Under its vaulted Roman ceiling, 300,000 books are awaiting readers.

All in all, the feeling inside is elegant and powerful—and curiously restful. The broad floors are slate; carpeting sets off the long countertops of green marble. There are plenty of intimate cozy niches under big windows, and wooden deck chairs on the upstairs terraces. A touch of whimsy is added by the large mural of colorful tropical birds and the literary quotations on the signs that indicate the various sections. There is also a multi-colored children's space with a purple-carpeted amphitheater for storytelling.

ELEPHANT SEAL MATING SEASON

Beside the strawberry festival in Oxnard, a more momentous natural occurrence happens every May off the coast near it: Elephant Seal Mating Season. If you have never seen a four-ton, 16-foot long bull elephant seal snoozing on the beach, you haven't lived. One way to experience this is to contact:

Island Packers
1867 Spinnaker Drive
Ventura, CA 93001
(805) 642-1393 (reservations)
(805) 642-7688 (information)

The elephant seal was almost extinct 100 years ago due to hunters. They have been making a comeback, however, and inhabit five Channel Islands off the California coast at least part of the year. We visited **Santa Cruz Island** in February with The Nature Conservancy. Island Packers offers boat trips to the other islands as part of their tours of varying length. Besides seeing the big guys, May is a pretty good month in general to go to the Channel Islands because there will still be some spring flowers, but the air is a little warmer.

To view the elephant seals in big groups, the cheapest and simplest trip is a day cruise to the southernmost of the five islands, **Santa Barbara Island**, located west of the northern tip of Santa Catalina Island. You can go to this fairly remote place for about $45 for adults and $30 for children. This little 640-acre island is 46 miles (about three hours) out from Ventura harbor. The elephant seals like to sack out in a row on the small cove beaches and are quite a sight.

Though it has no trees, the island offers a pleasant hike. There are trails to the cliff plateau, with the masses of elephant seals and the more normal-sized sea lions clustered below you. Camping is from Memorial day through Labor Day

The other four islands in the park are lined up in a row at a heading almost due west from the California coast just south of Oxnard. At one time they were all one island that is now referred to as Santarosae.

The closest and most often visited is **Anacapa Island**. It only takes 1-1/2 hours to get there from Ventura. Anacapa is really three unconnected, ribbon-like islands in a five mile long whisp of land with a total area of only about a square mile. Many people take a short trip and just go to East Anacapa, which is well set up for a brief look-see. If you climb stairs for exercise, you will be pleased by the fact that you must climb 153 of them from the landing site to the island's plateau. A nature trail about 1-1/2 miles in length begins near the Visitor's Center.

West Anacapa is completely closed—except for a pretty area for picnicking and snorkling called Frenchy's Cove—because its hills are the main West Coast habitat of an endangered species: the brown pelican.

The next one out is **Santa Cruz Island** (see February), followed by the second largest island in the Channel Islands National Park, **Santa Rosa Island**. This 53,000-acre island was the last of the five to be opened to the public when it became part of the park in 1986. Though its landscape was extensively damaged by first sheep, then cattle grazing, and the introduction of non-native grasses, upper slopes and canyons still contain some native plants. Perhaps the most unique of these are two groves of Torrey Pines overlooking Becher's Bay. Like the larger and closer Santa Cruz Island, Santa Rosa was also occupied by Chumash Indians.

The trip out to Santa Rosa takes about 3-1/2 hours, but has the added bonus of passing pretty close to the coastline of Santa Cruz. One thing you can't see unless you scuba dive is the lush forest of kelp that rings the island.

A little farther out (passage time of about 5-1/2 hours) is the westernmost part of the park, the windswept **San Miguel Island**. If you really want to see elephant (and other) seals and sea lions, this is the place. The extreme western tip of the island, Point Bennett, is the Miami Beach of pinnipeds. In addition to this quality, perhaps because of its distance from shore, San Miguel seems to have the most bizarre history and aura to it of any of the Channel Islands.

You land near the west end of Cuyler Harbor, a nearly perfect cove lined by sand. Less than a mile from this point at the east end of the beach, a steep trail begins. It will take you past the Cabrillo Cross, put up in 1937. Though the common assumption is that Cabrillo died and is buried in a lead coffin on San Miguel, recent historical studies indicate this was probably not the case. It is more likely that this occured on Santa Catalina. Thus, this impressive monument overlooking the harbor commemorates a mistake taken as historical fact.

Just past here are the ruins of a ranch house. Two Americans have claimed the island as their domain and even called themselves "King." The best known of these was Herbert Lester, who arrived with his wife, Elizabeth, in 1930. The Lesters had an unusually good life, becoming celebrities by throwing parties that famous people would attend. In 1942, the U.S. Navy decided to start using San Miguel as a bombing range; they told the royal couple they had to leave. King Lester hiked up the hill overlooking his favorite spot on the island (Harris Point), took out a gun, and shot himself.

Continuing farther on the trail for about three miles, you will come to a unique topographic feature: a caliche "forest," located directly west of the Cabrillo Monument. This strange looking rubble is the calcified skeletons of ancient vegetation. It was formed when calcium carbonate was fused by the acids in the plant's organic componds.

You can take a two-day trip here that also includes a visit to Santa Rosa Island. They are not very expensive ($195 adults, $175 children) and include sleeping accommodations aboard the boat. The boat cruises around the west end beaches of San Miguel reveal elephant seal beach parties of epic proportions.

If you don't care for boats, you can get to the Channel Islands by way of:

Channel Island Aviation
233 Durley Avenue
Camarillo, CA 93010
(805) 987-1301

With two departures each day, one at 9 a.m., then another at 10:30 a.m. (with returns at 3 and 4:30 p.m. respectively), this is one flight late sleepers can enjoy. For $75, you get a roundtrip flight that includes a scenic flight over Anacapa and Santa Rosa Islands followed by a landing on Santa Cruz Island. A National Park Ranger then accompanies the participants on a five hour trek over some of the 54,000 acres of relatively unspoiled early California land. Bring your own lunch and beverages.

MOTHER'S DAY

The second Sunday of May is the day you make up for a year's worth of never calling your mom. Like on Valentine's Day, florists sell lots of color and aroma; greeting card companies sell lots of sentiment; and restaurants sell lots of brunches.

Since guilt is an emotionally destructive thing that is better disposed of no matter what the cost, a high-priced restaurant that is beautiful and elegant is called for. If ever there was a restaurant that qualified to be called the mother of all Southland Mother's Day restaurants, it would be the gorgeous:

> **L'Orangerie**
> **903 North La Cienega Boulevard**
> **Los Angeles, CA 90069**
> **Tuesday-Friday 12 to 11 p.m.**
> **Saturday & Sunday 6:30 to 11 p.m.**
> **(310) 652-9770**

Someone once told me they always took their mother here because the lighting made her look 15 years younger. The regal dining room is reminiscent of a French chateau and it opens onto a courtyard garden. Do not bring mom or anyone else here unless you have plenty of cash or very good credit as L'Orangerie is as expensive as it looks.

Of course, if you really wanted to treat mom to a grand experience, escort her across the street after dinner to this great small theatre with a pretty courtyard:

> **Court Theatre**
> **722 North La Cienega**
> **Los Angeles, CA 90069**
> **(310) 652-4035**

I suppose it depends on what kind of mom you grew up with. Mine being inclined toward theater and film, I couldn't come up with a better combination than the ravishing L'Orangerie, followed by a show here.

MEMORIAL DAY WEEKEND

Memorial Day weekend is the last weekend of May. There always seem to be a lot of festive traditions at this time, almost as if it were an unofficial practice weekend for summer—like the "Pre Season" in the National Football League. There are Memorial Day activities throughout the Southland.

Santa Barbara

Probably the most romantic annual Memorial Day weekend event is the delightful:

"I Madonari"
Street Painting Festival
Mission Santa Barbara
Los Olivos and Laguna Streets
Santa Barbara
three days of Memorial Day weekend
(805) 682-4713

The chalk art festival is simply splendid. About 200 artists go to work on the cement piazza in front of the mission's grand columns. There are small, medium, and large squares and a special "square of honor" at the base of the mission's steps. The latter is usually reserved for a well known artist.

It is both fun and inspiring to see all of the artists, in various positions on the ground, creating their works. Some lay templates down, others work from their own sketches. Sometimes you will see an artist take a famous painting and reproduce it, others will make a giant enlargement of some small illustration they happen to like or even just some everyday object.

The Santa Barbara Mission is a perfect place for this. Called the "Queen of The Missions," it is the most Italian looking of all the missions and would not look out of place in Rome.

It is the only one that has been held by the Franciscans since it was founded on December 4, 1786 by Serra's successor, Father Fermin Lasuen. Serra had died in 1784 at the Mission San Carlos, angry and resentful that he would not see the foundation laid at Santa Barbara. The candle on the altar has never been extinguished since the mission was completed in 1820.

The mission has a self-guided tour that starts at the gift shop. The original kitchen and a Franciscan padre's sleeping room have been restored for your perusal. There is a little chapel and sanctuary that are still being used. The Sacred Garden is full of drought tolerant succulents. This pretty place was actually off limits to women until 1959.

An eery spot to walk through is the mission graveyard, easily noticeable by the skull-and-crossbones at the entrance. One of the books I enjoyed as a child was *Island of The Blue Dolphins*. It was based on the story of a girl referred to as "The Lost Woman of San Nicholas," but whose real name was Juana Maria. Her remains are buried in the cemetery at the Mission Santa Barbara and a plaque on the grave-yard wall makes note of it. Along with the families of the early Spanish conquerors, there are at least 4,000 Indians buried here.

Like the other missions, Santa Barbara was built by unpaid Native Americans. Though the church and grounds are beautiful, its history and the suffering it inflicted are exceptionally ugly. It was the third mission to be founded within Chumash territory. Once one of the biggest, happiest, and most productive of California's indigenous peoples, they would be largely wiped out and their centuries-old culture trashed by the mission system.

They were taught all of the skills of manual labor, but not taught to read and write out of fear that education would make them more difficult to control. They were made to follow a specific daily routine and the consequences of any variation in this dreary schedule were flogging and/or the withholding of food. For the first time, they were taught shame and guilt and unmarried men and women were kept separately. This is not to say that there was no sex. Very soon, young women learned to hide when they saw mission soldiers, as rape was the order of the day.

The death rate was extraordinary. The missionaries, soldiers, and settlers had brought with them a host of diseases. Because the Indians were kept penned up in close quarters and actually had no immunity, they died in droves.

Though Native Americans throughout the state periodically tried to escape or throw off their oppressors, they were no match for the Spanish soldiers. Since the mission system could not survive without free labor, it was absolutely necessary for the padres to suppress these uprisings as quickly and brutally as possible.

So successful were the missionaries at creating a nation of slaves that when the missions were secularized in 1833 and private citizens were awarded land grants of former church territory, this unpaid labor force would still be there to enable the rancheros to live the wonderful lifestyle that had been so romanticized until Helen Hunt Jackson's novel *Ramona* (see April).

Today, there is very little left of the Chumash nation that once numbered in the thousands and covered over 7,000 square miles. There are petroglyphs (see November) and a tiny reservation called the Santa Ynez Chumash Reservation, but other than that, all that remains is a memory.

It is easy to see why the Chumash liked this area so much. Subsequent residents have tended to be wealthy and build large red tile-roofed homes. The hill above Santa Barbara near here looks like one overlooking the Mediterranean and in fact is a community called **The Riviera**. It is a fine place to walk because the roads curve around and the neighborhood is full of parks and little nooks and crannies with views of the city below. It also leads up into the Los Padres National Forest.

On the other side of Laguna Street across from the mission is Mission Historical Park with its green lawns and beautiful rose garden. As it heads up into the hills, Laguna turns into Mission Canyon Road. Continuing this way, there is a stone bridge that spans Mission Creek and takes you to **Rocky Nook Park.** This little gem of a park is filled with huge boulders moved from the creek to add dimension and oak trees to add shade.

Back across Mission Canyon Road, just above the mission, is an excellent choice in a Santa Barbara attraction:

> **Santa Barbara Museum of Natural History**
> **2559 Puesta Del Sol**
> **Santa Barbara, CA 93105**
> **Monday-Saturday 9 a.m. to 5 p.m.**
> **Sunday 10 a.m. to 5 p.m.**
> **(805) 682-4711**

This is a nice place to spend some time before hiking on the extensive trails above the city, since the focus of the biological and geological exhibits here pertains to things local to the area. There are also instructional displays about the marine world of Santa Barbara.

In addition to natural history, the museum examines human history. If you are interested in the culture of the indigenous Chumash, the **Indian Hall** is intended as a kind of introduction. Besides the exhibits applying to local biology and anthropology, the museum has a planetarium with shows on Saturdays and Sundays at 1:30, 3, and 4 p.m. Part of the planetarium is the **E.L. Wiegand Space Lab.** This is a high tech series of interactive computer displays.

Mission Canyon Road continues to climb into the hills, but it does a little zig zag when you get to the stop sign at Foothill Road. Here, you must make a right, then a quick left in order to stay on it. Bear right at the intersection where the road splits and you will come to the:

> **Santa Barbara Botanical Gardens**
> **1212 Mission Canyon Road**
> **Santa Barbara, CA 93105**
> **Daily 8 a.m. to sunset**
> **(805) 682-4726**

The Santa Barbara Botanical Gardens were started in 1926 with 13 acres of native plants. They now occupy 65 acres and include flora from arroyo to chaparral. A more pleasant place to walk than this peaceful setting of over a 1,000 species of indigenous plants would be hard to imagine.

For a short stroll of about a mile, take the trail that skirts the perimeter. For a longer, more in-depth look at the leafy residents, there are 5-1/2 miles of trails and side trails. These take you through a meadow of wildflowers and a cactus garden. There is even a miniature coast redwood forest. Also on the grounds is the dam built for the mission in 1807.

When you were on you way up Mission Canyon, if you had taken the left fork where the road splits just before reaching the Botanical Garden, you would have been on Tunnel Road. By taking it to its end and parking, you will pass a locked gate and some power lines before the pavement turns to dirt: this is **Tunnel Trail**.

From here, the road turns left and passes by bridge over the West Fork of Mission Creek. After walking under some ancient oak trees, you will come to a junction. From here, you can continue up an additional three miles to East Camino Cielo, which means "The Sky Road." If you go a little over a mile west, you will be at **La Cumbre Peak Lookout**, which at 3,981 feet is the highest point near the city.

In this Riviera area near Mission Ridge and San Carlos Roads is a well known romantic retreat:

> **El Encanto Hotel**
> **1900 Lasuen Road**
> **Santa Barbara, CA 93103**
> **(805) 687-5000**
> **(800) 346-7039 (CA)**

The view from the restaurant here is second to none, because not only is it an ocean view, it is framed by the Mediterranean hill of Santa Barbara with its lovely red-tiled skyline. There are 100 rooms spread out in cottages and little villas over 10 acres of beautifully landscaped hillside gardens.

The accommodations here are very private. The bungalows are hidden behind big shrubs and trees and are reached by brick walkways that wind around the property. This has made the El Encanto very popular with celebrities and lovers. For the latter, there are gently swinging yellow love seats throughout the grounds. Most of the cottages and villas have country French decor, wood-burning fireplaces and private verandas.

For a final little surprise in the charming Santa Barbara Riviera, make a left on the first street past the El Encanto onto San Carlos Road. Turn right on Mission Ridge Road and you will see the sign on the left for **Franceschi Park**.

This 14-acre park was originally part of the 40-acre estate of a gentleman who called himself Francesco Franceschi, but whose real name was Dr. Emanual Fenzi. Dr. Fenzi was a horticulturist from Florence who came here in 1893.

The view from here might even be a tiny bit better than that of El Encanto. Bring a picnic lunch and sit at one of the tables flanked by huge restful eucalyptus trees. Relaxing here and gazing at the vista below, you will thank the Florentine horticulturist (and the volunteers who keep it up) for his estate. But perhaps Dr. Fenzi's greatest legacy to Southern California was culinary: he was the man who first brought the zucchini to America.

Long Beach

One of the ironies of Southern California is that the town whose nickname is "Iowa By The Sea" has an annual May revelry patterned after Brazil's Carnival in Rio De Janero:

> **Carnival**
> **Broadway and The Promenade, between First**
> **and Third Streets**
> **Long Beach**
> **Saturday and Sunday 10 a.m. to 10 p.m.**
> **$7.50 in advance, $10 at the door**
> **(310) 436-7794**
> To order tickets in advance, send payment to:
> **Rainbow Promotion**
> **211 Pine Avenue**
> **Long Beach, CA 90802**

This annual event, produced by Kimberly Benoit's Rainbow Pomotions with help from the Downtown Long Beach Business Association, supplies some much needed panache to Downtown Long Beach. Even though it is pretty tame compared to other international Mardi Gras-style street festivals, Carnival does feature some fairly exotic touches.

After the parade on Saturday morning at 10 a.m., the grounds open and the party begins. There are four stages of entertainment, one of which is for children. It features clowns, magic acts, and the like. Carnival rides and games are complimented by vendors selling snacks and Caribbean food.

Carnival is also affiliated with one of the longest established music venues in Long Beach:

Birdland West
105 West Broadway
Long Beach, CA 90802
closed Mondays
(310) 432-2004

This great club is located upstairs in a beautifully restored Art Deco building—a rarity in Long Beach, a city which normally destroys its architectural treasures and puts featureless structures in their place. It is owned by Al Williams, a legend in the jazz world. He used to own a place called the Jazz Safari out by the Queen Mary and was lured to Pine Avenue in Downtown Long Beach during the period when the city was first trying to revitalize the street in the 1980s.

It is a splendid place to spend an evening. The decor is elegant. A soft mauve color is used throughout, including the chairs with their black and teal accents. The main stage is in the corner, with a dance floor to the left. The room holds 240 and they book top jazz acts. The cover varies according to the status of the talent, but it averages about $15.

Santa Monica

If the beat of carnival got in your blood, you won't have to look far to find the Caribbean music that seems to go so naturally with the Southland's mind set. Though reggae is popular and there are numerous venues that offer a "reggae night," up in Santa Monica is Southern California's only true all reggae music club:

Kingston 12
814 Broadway Street
Santa Monica, CA 90401
Wednesday-Sunday 6 p.m. to 2 a.m.
$10 cover
(310) 451-4423

If you like glitzy dance clubs, this is not your place. Kingston 12 is a simple red-brick building with wood trim and a big wooden sign with its name on it located near the corner of Broadway and Lincoln. Inside, it has black walls punctuated by Bob Marley and Jamaican tourist posters.

The attraction here is the live music, starting at 10:30 p.m. on Friday and Saturday nights. The house band, Jah-Maka, has played here since 1986 and some people think they are the best reggae band in the Southland. The Jamaican food is excellent—a rarity in any music venue.

Morongo Indian Reservation

It surprises many people to find out how many Indian reservations there are in Southern California. Most of them are tucked away in places bypassed by main roads. This is not true of one of them that offers a Memorial Day weekend festival:

Memorial Weekend Fiesta
Malki Museum, Morongo Reservation
11581 Potero Road (Tribal Offices)
Banning, CA 920
Memorial Day Weekend from 10 a.m. to dusk
(909) 849-4697
(909) 849-7289 (fiesta Information)

The much maligned name of I-10, "The Christopher Columbus Transcontinental Highway," has a bitter irony to it as it slices through this 32,355-acre reservation at Banning and San Gorgonio Pass. There are signs that direct you to the bingo and to the museum, which the fiesta centers around. Take the Fields Road exit north from I-10 and take the Morongo Road cutoff to the museum.

This is a pleasant reservation with between 300 and 400 residents, practically all of whom are local Cahuilla. Cupenos from Pala and Los Coyotes, Serranos from the north, and even Chemehuevis from the Colorado River territory have also resided on the Morongo Reservation since its designation in 1877.

The adobe museum was built in 1964. It looks even smaller than it is on the wind swept open land with the mountains looking down. The Malki Museum has a collection of baskets, tools, fish-bone hooks, and other artifacts, though its main claim to fame is its work in preserving tradition via its publishing arm, the Malki Museum Press. Its name means "dodging" in Cahuilla and it was called thusly to honor the tradition of Morongo residents keeping Bureau of Indian Affairs (BIA) agents off guard.

The festival or "kewet" was started the same year as the museum as a way of keeping their customs alive and making contact between the Native Americans who live on the reservation and people who might otherwise only see Indians in John Wayne movies. There are often Aztec dancers from Mexico in exotic headdresses, Navajo from Arizona offering fine artwork such as rugs, baskets, and jewelry, and "bird singers" from the local tribe. A pit barbecue dinner can be had for about $6.

Not far from here to the east, looming above Interstate 10, is a giant pair of extinct reptiles:

> **Dinosaur Gardens**
> **5800 Seminole Drive**
> **Cabazon, CA 92230**
> **(909) 849-8309**

These rather startling 40-ton replicas of a 65-foot tall Tyrannosaurs Rex and a 45-foot tall, 150-foot long Brontosaurus each have interior viewing platforms. The Brontosaurus has a museum inside that contains fossils and Indian artifacts.

There is also a store in a dino's belly that sells fossils and minerals as well as science, nature and children's books and educational materials. It also offers jewelry made of unusual minerals.

Continuing on Interstate 10 through the San Gorgonio Pass, you can turn south on SR 111 and go to Palm Springs and the lower Colorado Desert (see March), or go a little farther before turning north on SR 62 to visit the higher desert. Since it is getting a bit warm by May for the lower desert, we will take the high road. After passing a giant forest of wind turbines and the desert hamlet of Painted Hills, get off at Pierson Boulevard and go east to **Desert Hot Springs**.

This pleasant town of about 12,000 people at the northwestern end of the Coachella Valley has an elevation of at least 1,000-feet higher than the other desert resort cities of Palm Springs, Palm Desert, etc. Thus, it is somewhat cooler and its tourist season slightly longer. It derives its name from the underground springs of hot mineral water that occur in several places. Like those in Palm Springs and the Anza-Borrego Desert, these were created by water trapped by earthquake faults.

Just as they did in Palm Springs, native Californians soaked in these waters for centuries before the arrival of the Europeans. It took longer for the springs here to be noted by settlers, however.

In 1913, a unique fellow named Cabot Yerxa homesteaded 160 acres of what would become Desert Hot Springs. After traveling the world, he was attracted to the wide open serenity of the California desert. He had first intended to settle in Palm

Springs, but found its population of 107 at that time to be far too many neighbors.

It was Yerxa who discovered the town's namesake mineral springs. There is not a great deal of above ground water in the desert and the hardy homesteader had to walk seven miles to the railroad water tank and then seven miles back to his house every day. This grew thin after a very short while, so he dug a well. Instead of regular water, he found hot mineral water. Samples were sent to the Mayo Clinic, where its mineral content was broken down. In 1939, the clinic proclaimed that this mineral water was possibly curative.

The first promoter of the water as a tourist attraction was Mr. L.W. Coffee. He pitched a group of wealthy Japanese-American farmers and fishermen who wished to duplicate the success of the White Point Hot Springs Hotel on the Palos Verdes Peninsula (see January). They came out by bus in July of 1941 and the deal looked about ready to go. Unfortunately, four months later the Japanese bombed Pearl Harbor and shortly thereafter Americans of Japanese descent were rounded up and put in prison camps (see February).

Development was slower in the post war period here than in the other desert resort cities. This has given Desert Hot Springs a more laid back feel than its companion cities to the south and southeast.

As you drive in, Pierson Boulevard becomes smaller after Palm Drive and then curves to the right and turns into Miracle Hill Road. At Desert View Avenue, make a left and on the left hand side of the street, you will see Yerxa's former residence:

Cabot's Old Indian Pueblo Museum
67-616 East Desert View Avenue
Desert Hot Springs, CA 92240
July through September:
Saturday & Sunday 10 a.m. to 4 p.m.
October through June:
Wednesday-Monday 10 a.m. to 4 p.m.
(619) 329-7610

The pioneer homesteader built this enormous 35-room Hopi-style pueblo with his own two hands. It is filled with Native American, Eskimo, and early 20th century pioneer artifacts of all sorts. There is a 20-ton Indian monument that was carved out of a 250-year-old sequoia. The courtyard is called The Pueblo Art Gallery and displays arts and crafts, many of which were made by Native Americans.

A few blocks south of East Desert View is a street with a very colorful name: Two Bunch Palms Trail. On this street is a desert resort with an equally colorful history:

Two Bunch Palms
67-425 Two Bunch Palms Trail
Desert Hot Springs, CA 92240
(619) 329-8791

The building and original compound here was built by Al Capone in the 1930s. Scarface took a palm oasis and built a desert stronghold out of stone, complete with hidden escape tunnel and watch turret. There was a lavish casino for his guests. The palm trees, here for generations, saw yet another change in their desert landscape and now preside over the two hot crystal clear mineral baths that made their home famous.

The entrance to this 28-acre retreat is still guarded, but the casino is now a fine restaurant and the grounds have been turned into a first class desert resort with broad lawns, tennis courts, swimming pool, a Koi pond, massage therapists, and a nude sunbathing area.

Continuing north on SR 62, you will climb up and finally cross the county line into San Bernardino County. The first town you will come to is **Morongo Valley**, named for a splinter tribe of Serrano Indians. It is at a higher altitude than Desert Hot Springs at 2,688 feet above sea level and is noteworthy among other things for being the home of the:

Big Morongo Canyon Reserve
East Drive (off SR 62)
1/2 mile southeast of Morongo Valley
Wednesday-Sunday 7:30 a.m. to sunset
closed Monday-Tuesday
mailing address:
P.O. Box 780
Morongo Valley, CA 92256
(619) 363-7190

This six-mile long canyon was designated as a 4,500 acre preserve in 1968. It is managed and protected jointly by the U.S. Bureau of Land Management and the Nature Conservancy and is unusual for many reasons. Big Morongo Creek flows above ground for about three miles before going underground. This creates a canyon oasis that passes between the low and high deserts. Once used as a corridor by native Californians, it is vital to local wildlife and migrating birds.

In contrast to the surrounding desert, the canyon bottom is surprisingly wet. After parking, the interpretive exhibits will lead you to a network of trails. These range from a six-mile long jaunt all the way to the end of the canyon at Indian

Avenue to easy loop trails as short as a 1/4 mile. Many of these pass though places so moist that wooden boardwalks have been constructed.

What is especially delightful about a visit here is the transformation from the arid creosote community of the surrounding terrain and upper slopes of the canyon to the riparian community of willow and cottonwood that follow the creek. The sound of frogs croaking and birds singing is a contrast to the silence or man-made noise of the desert.

There are amphibians and reptiles as well as coyotes, raccoons, foxes, and even the occasional bobcat and bighorn sheep. Because Big Morongo Canyon is near the San Gorgonio Pass (which leads from the desert to the coastal climate zone) wedged between two deserts, the number and different types of noticeable bird species is very large. Many people come here just for that reason.

Yucca Valley

If you keep on going down SR 62 (the Twenty Nine Palms Highway), you will come to the largest city in the area, Yucca Valley, population 27,500. It is at an even higher altitude than Morongo Valley at 3,327 feet.

Yucca Valley has a mining and ranching tradition that dates to when there were gold mines in the valley, and the railroad depot in Banning was a vital link to the outside world. The mines are pretty much gone, but the frontier spirit is reawakened every year with an annual Memorial Day weekend event:

> **Grubstake Days**
> **Twenty Nine Palms Highway**
> **Yucca Valley**
> **three days of Memorial Day weekend**
> Updated information obtained from:
> **Yucca Valley Chamber of Commerce**
> **56020 Santa Fe Trail, Suite B**
> **Yucca Valley, CA 92284**
> **(619) 365-6323**

The name of this "Wild West" party comes from the supplies and money a settler would need to get started. The celebration got its kick-off in 1948 from local ranchers and citizens as a way of remembering and celebrating their roots.

Though mining and ranching are quite destructive activities to the environment, the long hard hours of work involved generally create a very jovial mood when it comes time to relax. This is why ranchers and miners have traditionally let off steam in some pretty wild ways. This heritage of craziness is carried on during Grubstakes Days.

Businesses are decorated like the Old West and locals don period costumes. There is a Grubstakes Parade on Saturday morning at 10 a.m. that features local school bands and antique cars. A carnival opens Friday night and continues until Monday evening. There is also a talent show.

Naturally, a big event is the Grubstakes Rodeo, which is an officially sanctioned event of the Professional Rodeo Association. Besides the usual 10K, 5K, and short 2K runs, there are sporting events of a more fitting kind. There is an arm wrestling championship and a tug of war where the losing team goes straight into a huge mud pit. The highpoint of the athletic contests is the "Bike Throw," which is sort of like a shot put except the projectile is a bicycle. They provide the cycles and the test is to see who can throw one the farthest.

Four miles northwest of Yucca Valley on Pioneertown Road is **Pioneertown**. In 1947, this town was built for a Western movie that was never made, and it became a "ghost town." The area certainly is pretty, with beautiful sunsets outlining the Joshua trees and the mountains like a scene to ride off into. Many did, and soon people began moving into the false front structures built along the broad dirt Main Street and voila, a real town grew out of an imaginary one—albeit one with no frontier history.

It does, however, have the only bowling alley to grace the pages of this book:

> **Pioneer Bowl**
> **53613 Mane Street**
> **Pioneertown, CA 92268**
> **Friday-Monday 10 a.m. to 11 p.m.**
> **(619) 365-3615**

The interior here is one of the Southland's great sights. It is very obviously all original and is in sensational condition. As you enter, the sounds of the jukebox (old rock 'n' roll and country), cold beer bottles clanking, vintage pinball machines ringing, and balls crashing into pins at the end of six heavily varnished lanes fill your ears. The walls are covered with knotty pine paneling along the lower portion, with cartoon caricatures of Hollywood filming in the '40s filling up the middle and upper portions. Most of the characters must have been from films that did not become classics because they are mostly unfamiliar, although there is a reference to Gene Autry and a picture of Roy Rogers throwing out the first ball. It is owned by the congenial Ron Young who has had it since August of 1959.

FESTA DO ESPIRITO SANTO

San Diego's fishing industry has had a unique, multicultural history. In the late 19th century, Chinese anglers plied their trade from junks anchored along Point Loma. They were superseded first by Italian, then Portuguese fishermen, who arrived from the Azores in the 1880s.

Point Loma still has an ample number of Portuguese who fish from here and live in long-standing neighborhoods. Probably the most visible manifestation of this is the annual:

> *"Festa do Espirito Santo"*
> **St. Agnes Roman Catholic Church**
> **1145 Evergreen Street**
> **San Diego, CA 92106**
> **(619) 223-2200**

The date for this celebration of thanksgiving varies a little from year to year because it takes place eight weeks after Easter. The party itself is consistent, however. There are demonstrations of dance and culture and a big feast, but the big event is a gala parade through the charming, well-maintained neighborhood.

If you would like to sample a little bit of San Diego's Portuguese culture, not too far away is the:

> **Virissimo Dough Company**
> **2820 Shelter Island Drive**
> **San Diego, CA 92106**
> **Monday-Friday 7 a.m. to 5 p.m.**
> **Saturday 8 a.m. to 5:30 p.m.**
> **(619) 223-4166**

This combination Portuguese deli and bakery is named after its owner, Jeanne Vrissimo. The deli here offers specialties like marinated top sirloin steak sandwiches called "bifana," pork tamales, sausages called "linguica," and even fresh turkey.

The bakery is the star of the show, however. There are not many places you can get "sonhos," sometimes called Portuguese donuts. They are fried puffs of dough dusted with sugar. Other specialties include Portuguese-style cornbread, french bread and baguettes, and sweetbreads. Unsold bread is used to make delicious bread pudding.

 JUNE

June Weddings

Graduation and Summer Vacation

Summer Movies

South Seas Luau

Father's Day

Gay Pride

Summer Theater and Music Festivals

Lompoc Flower Festival

Chapter Six

JUNE

June, June, June. The last month of spring and its 21st day is the summer solstice, the longest day of the year, and the official first day of summer.

The sixth month of the Gregorian calendar, June was named for the Roman goddess Juno, who was Jupiter's wife. Since she was, among other things, the goddess of marriage, the tradition of getting married this month continues today.

JUNE WEDDINGS

In terms of its roster of famous people who have been married there, the Mission Inn (April) has quite a claim on being the wedding place of the Southland. However, all things considered, probably the most celebrated place to get married in Southern California (or anywhere in the world, really) is the:

> **Wayfarer's Chapel**
> **5755 Palos Verdes Drive South**
> **Rancho Palos Verdes, CA 90274**
> **(310) 377-1650**

It is fitting that Lloyd Wright, son of Frank, designed the signature wedding chapel of the Southland since his famous father designed some of its most noteworthy homes. When I go to the Wayfarer's Chapel, I am always amused by people's reactions to it. There is always some variation of, "Now I know why it is such a famous place to get married."

This remarkable blend of geometry and nature is located on the beautiful Palos Verdes Peninsula on a hill with an ocean view. The glass chapel, with huge wooden supporting ribs made from the trees that surround it and a triangular bell tower made from the smooth, irregular-shaped Palos Verdes stone, is so much a part of its landscape as to almost disappear from the outside.

On the inside, the blue sky above and tall trees and thicket of greenery all around harmonize perfectly with its geometric panels of cut glass.

The picturesque Palos Verdes Peninsula has numerous well-known wedding and/or reception sites. The most famous place to do both is nearby:

> **La Venta Inn**
> **796 Via Del Monte**
> **Palos Verdes Estates, CA 90274**
> **(310) 378-0267**

In 1923, the La Venta Inn invested its reputation in the residential community of Palos Verdes Estates. It was designed by Pierpont Davis with landscape architecture by Olmstead and Olmstead. Though it can't be seen from the street now because of the growth of thick vegetation, originally it appeared as a sparkling white vision of a beautiful Mediterranean church on a 1,000-foot high hill.

It has a courtyard with a romantic fountain. Joe Montana, the famous quarterback for the San Francisco 49ers, was married here.

Of course, Southern California has a legion of places that are romantic and charming enough to be considered honeymoon spots. There are mountain, lake, and oceanside resorts: innumerable locations of real beauty and charm. However, if I had to single out the quintessential honeymoon place in the Southland, it would be a resort that has all of these elements:

> **San Ysidro Ranch**
> **900 San Ysidro Lane**
> **Montecito, CA 93108**
> **(805) 969-5046**

This secluded collection of stone and wood framed buildings has a romantic history that is almost unmatched. The San Ysidro Ranch started out as a citrus and cattle ranch in 1788 that raised food for the Santa Barbara mission.

Its celebrity connection began in 1935 when the property was purchased by actor Ronald Coleman and businessman Alvin Weingand. The photos on the wall of the lodge tell the stories of what happened next. In 1940, Vivian Leigh and Lawrence Olivier were married in the garden during a midnight ceremony; Garson Kanin and Katherine Hepburn were witnesses. The most famous couple of my lifetime, Jackie and John Kennedy, spend the first part of their honeymoon here in 1953.

There are 44 rooms and suites parceled out over 21 cottages on 550 acres. Many have private whirlpool baths. The celebrated **Hillside Cottage** graced by John and Jackie goes for $1,145 a night. It has two stories, two fireplaces, a redwood deck, and a view of the ocean along the coastline. You can rent either of the two floors by themselves. The first floor goes for $450, the second floor for $695. None of the rooms are cheap: they start at $195.

The grounds are stunning, with broad lawn-covered hillsides outlined by marigolds and larkspur and cannas, dotted with gently drooping lemon trees. There are seven-story eucalyptus trees and the kind of giant hedges that are only found on old resort properties.

There has always been a tradition of fine dining in the hotel's premium restaurant, **The Stonehouse**. Downstairs from here is the homespun-styled **Plow and Angel Pub**.

GRADUATION AND SUMMER VACATION

Ah, summer vacation in the Southland! Spring brought forth a feeling of restlessness; summer brings a languid contentment in Southern California, almost as if our true season had arrived.

Going to the beach almost religiously during June, July, and August was a major part of my growing up. Very soon we were old enough to connect the feeling of the warm summer evening air to soft sun-kissed skin and bright sparkling eyes, to nights lit by city lights, to being in love and feeling good all over. We will probably all die of skin cancer.

June is not a month to be serious. It is a month to stay up late going to 10 o'clock movies on Tuesday nights. It is a month to pile in the car and drive to the beach. It is a month to laugh and sing and toast to what is wonderful about living. It is a month to relive summer vacation.

Throughout our childhood, adolescence, and young adult lives, June has always meant the end of the obligation to worry about grades. June is the time of graduation and summer vacation. If ever there was a place symbolic of graduation in Southern California, it would be the storied:

> **Athenaeum (Faculty Club)**
> **California Institute of Technology**
> **1201 East California Boulevard**
> **Pasadena, CA 91106**
> **(818) 356-6228**

The California Institute of Technology has produced 22 Nobel Prize winning scientists, the first being its founder, physicist Robert Milikan, in 1923. Others include Linus Pauling, the late great Richard Feynman, and the most recent winner (in 1992), chemistry professor Rudolph Marcus.

Cal Tech began life as the Throop Polytechnic Institute, the school that produced Elizabeth Sturdevant, the inventor of the Rose Bowl float (see January). Since that time, some of the finest architects in Southland history have contributed to the planning and growth of the structure of the campus, including Myron Hunt and Elmer Grey, Bertram Goodhue, and Gordon Kaufmann.

Slightly hidden behind olive, palm, and eucalyptus trees is the Mediterranean style "Ath," as regulars refer to it. Designed in 1930 by Gordon Kaufman, it has a courtyard with Corinthian columns, a red tile roof, and giant arched windows outlined with wrought iron.

Behind the stately columns at the entrance with its "Members Only" sign is probably the most remarkable faculty dining club in the world. The interior features a formal dining area with chandeliers and a heavy beamed ceiling high overhead. The Hayman Lounge has pictures of alumnus who were Nobel laureates. Antique furniture, brass fixtures, black walnut and burnished oak paneling, and a huge stone fireplace complete the imposing physical presence of The Athenaeum.

But it is its tradition as a medium where ideas are exchanged that makes the Athenaeum truly a remarkable place. Quite the forum for thought, its name comes from Athena, goddess of wisdom. Laureate Marcus, who had previously been at Oxford, thought Cal Tech's round tables superior to the long thin ones in the faculty club at the English university.

The food is excellent and inexpensive. Members do not bring money; they merely sign tabs that are paid at the end of each month. Undergraduates may not join, but often work as waiters.

There are 29 guest rooms that are upstairs from the dining areas. The most expensive and most famous is the **Einstein Suite**, where the eminent man slept for months when working on a project. It has a small living room with a fireplace, a bedroom, and a large porch and goes for about $80 per night.

Though long time manager Able Ramirez recommends a coat and tie, the atmosphere is considerably less formal than the stately surroundings might suggest. The best minds frequently are not splendid dressers and often wear sandals and old shirts instead of suits. Einstein himself kept five identical outfits in a row on a rack and merely reached for the next one when he needed a change. This informality can be felt in the buzz of conversation in the air. Frequently the paper placemats and napkins have been used to advance science by a few light years in the jottings of some inspired calculations over cold poached salmon.

Of course, before the formal change in status after graduation, you need to have a little fun to celebrate. One of the first comedy venues in Southern California is also in Pasadena:

> **The Ice House**
> **24 North Mentor Avenue**
> **Pasadena, CA 91106**
> **Tuesday-Sunday 6 p.m. to 12 a.m.**

Comedy starts at 8 p.m.
(818) 577-1894

I remember my older brother took me here when I started college. Given the academic career that was to follow, it was an appropriate choice. They have several rooms and serve dinner. Many famous comics got their start here, including Robin Williams, Steve Martin, and Lily Tomlin. There is more about Pasadena in the January, November, and December chapters.

SUMMER MOVIES

June always makes me think of the movies. Growing up in the San Fernando Valley, I remember how I looked forward to going to the big theaters "over the hill" to see the new summer releases. It was much more fun than going to some little "neighborhood" theater: eating out early in the evening in Westwood or Hollywood, then waiting eagerly in line at a true "movie palace," and finally entering that cool, magical interior.

The exception to this was when something was playing at the La Reina Theater on Ventura Boulevard. It was built in 1938 and is now, alas, a clothing store. It was designed by the architect Charles Lee. He also designed the Max Factor building in Hollywood (see March), but his fame was as a master of theater architecture.

Though its purpose is somewhat more mundane now, the building is still quite striking and forms the centerpiece to the shops and restaurants of Ventura Boulevard in these environs. Across the street from what was the La Reina Theater is one of the Southland's most intimate jazz clubs:

The Room At Le Cafe
14633 Ventura Boulevard
Sherman Oaks, CA 91401
Music nightly 9 p.m. to 1 a.m.
Cover: usually $6
(818) 986-2662

Opened in 1980 by singer Lois Boileau, this is one of the smallest jazz spots imaginable. Though it officially seats 70, it seems like it was built for less than that. The restaurant downstairs serves very good food, but the club does not allow any food upstairs.

This is easily the most intimate place to sit and listen to jazz in Southern California. The audience is arranged around the musicians and their instruments in a very small, very dark room. The artists tend to be smooth, quality jazz musicians—perfect for the end of an evening out.

Besides the La Reina, Lee designed many theaters throughout Southern California, many of which still show movies, not blue jeans. He designed the incredible streamline Moderne **Academy** in Inglewood in 1939 and the beautiful Art Deco **Fox Wilshire Theater** in 1929. In 1937, he designed the:

> **Bruin Theater**
> **925 Broxton Avenue**
> **Westwood Village**
> **Los Angeles, CA 90024**
> **(310) 208-8998**

The Bruin has a look similar to the La Reina. Its broadly curved facade has the Moderne style and works well on the corner. In my memories, this theater was a big part of the experience of going to **Westwood Village**. To a Valley boy like me, going here was the true way to see a blockbuster summer release.

Westwood Village was master planned in 1928 by Harland Bartholomew for the Janss Investment Company. An art jury was convened to oversee architectural standards and, until the '50s they managed to influence development in a very positive way. Though most of the more recent high rises are somewhat lacking in architectural style, old Westwood Village buildings are Spanish and Spanish-Moorish structures with a great deal of character.

Across the street from the Bruin is one of the great examples of that character:

> **Village Theater**
> **961 Broxton Avenue**
> **Westwood Village**
> **Los Angeles, CA 90024**
> **(310) 208-5576**

The Village was built in 1931 as part of the original master plan of Westwood. Though the skyscrapers have made it a little harder to see, the tower of this theater is a real landmark. Its architecture has that delightful blend of Moderne with Spanish Colonial Revival that you will find on L.A.'s best buildings from this era.

Though the Bruin and Village are wonderful theaters and will take you back to the old Westwood to some extent, the most spectacular movie palace in Westwood is a much newer design:

> **Crest Theater**
> **1262 Westwood Boulevard**
> **Los Angeles, CA 90024**
> **(310) 474-7866**

The Crest started life in 1936 as the "Uclan". It was simply a dull gray box with a movie projector in it. In 1987, Pacific Theaters decided they wanted a Westwood showcase, so they sought out Joe Musil, who would later do the El Capitan (see March).

And what a showcase it is. An Art Deco tower soars above a zigzag green and orange neon marquee. The deep magenta and gold lobby sets off the marble candy counter, behind which a '30s-style mural of a smiling, uniformed counter man and a dancing couple obviously having a good time sets a fun, movie-going mood. It was painted by Bill Anderson, a celebrated Disney artist, whose work you will see in even more dramatic form inside the auditorium.

The auditorium features elaborate three-dimensional Art Deco plaster structures in gold and white along the sides, but the star is the mural that curves around in a 270 degree horseshoe beginning on the back wall and continuing up the side walls to the screen. It was also painted by Bill Anderson, but in a florescent paint made to glow under black light. It depicts a collage of the year 1939. Hollywood starts on the back wall and gradually disappears and leads into Westwood.

Musil's designs always involve embellishing the presentation of the movie by building up the feature. For this reason, the Crest has two curtains. One is a scene of the Pacific Ocean and the California coast. The second is an Art Deco design of leaves and flowers. Before the movie starts, there is an overture of Geshwin themes selected by the designer himself. When the house lights go down, a single shooting star flits across the make-believe sky. The curtains then rise majestically, one at a time.

Everything about the theater is new, down to the plumbing. They removed 350 of the original 850 seats to improve sight lines and comfort. The 35/70 mm projectors and THX and Dolby sound systems are state-of-the-art.

Though Hollywood Boulevard became historically associated with movie premiers with stars and flashbulbs popping, the original street of movie palaces in Southern California was Downtown L.A.'s Broadway. This month, there is a wonderful way you can recapture some of those golden days every Wednesday, courtesy of a unique group:

The Last Remaining Seats
Los Angeles Conservancy
727 West 7th Street, #955
Los Angeles, CA 90017
(213) 623-CITY

The L.A. Conservancy is a extraordinary organization founded in 1978. They were originally responding to the threat to just one building: the Central Library. Since that time, they have expanded to function as the angels of historic architecture in Los Angeles. They have 11 fun and informative walking tours every Saturday morning that take you through landmarks ranging from Union Station to classic movie palaces.

The original grand theaters of Southern California were located along both Broadway and nearby Hill Street. This area has changed much over the years, but the remnants of its glorious past still linger.

"The Last Remaining Seats" was begun in 1987 to increase public recognition and awareness of the area that is now officially called the **Broadway Historic Theater District**. It is a series of Wednesday nights, each of which features a different classic film that is screened in one of the area's theaters. Tickets are available individually or in a series at a reduced rate.

The theaters vary somewhat from year to year based on what condition they are in and what is available. Sometimes they are being used as swap meet sites or churches. The Mayan Theatre that was described in the February Chapter at 1040 South Hill is now a nightclub. One theater that usually still sees use as a theater is down near 9th Street:

> **The Orpheum**
> **842 South Broadway**
> **Los Angeles, CA 90014**
> **(213) 239-0937**

G. Albert Lansburgh, the architect of the El Capitan and the Pacific on Hollywood Boulevard (see March), designed this elegant vaudeville theatre in 1926. It was the last home of the Orpheum vaudeville circuit in L.A. Such luminaries of show business as Edgar Bergen, Sophie Tucker, Nat King Cole, Eddie Cantor, Lena Horne, Will Rogers, Jack Benny, and the Marx Brothers graced its stage.

It features a French theme reminiscent of the Paris Opera. When you pass through its polished brass doors, you enter into a plush interior of silk wall panels and thick brocade drapery framed by marble pilasters. Lighting is provided by massive chandeliers.

Besides the Los Angeles Conservancy, there are two volunteer groups working to preserve this irreplaceable treasure: the Friends of the Orpheum and the Los Angeles Theater Organ Society. The latter group is especially concerned with the Orpheum because it contains the last of the great theater organs remaining on Broadway. Originally installed in 1928 and still in working order is a thirteen-rank, three-manual Wurlitzer organ with both metal and wood pipes that can simulate more than 24,000 orchestral sounds.

Across the street is the finest Art Deco building remaining in Southern California:

Eastern Columbia Building
849 South Broadway
Los Angeles CA 90014

After the peerless black and gold Atlantic Richfield building (designed by Morgan, Wall, and Clements) was razed to make way for the featureless Arco Towers, this green, terra cotta masterpiece became the reining queen of one of L.A's most important architectural styles. Let us hope that a similar lack of concern by some other property owner in the City of Los Angeles does not someday doom it to demolition.

Though it is badly in need of restoration, it is impossible to look at this giant work of art designed by Claude Beelman in 1929 and not say "Wow!" The alien hunter in the movie *Predator II* looked even more bizarre and threatening when he stood atop its highest point and brandished his spear.

Made to suggest a magic city in a tropical paradise, the Eastern Columbia Building's structure is a vertical series of columns outlined in a geometric pattern of gold ornamentation. The building rises to a central square tower with a clock face on each side. Above each clock face, the word "Eastern" is illuminated in huge letters. It originally was the home of two stores called Eastern Outfitting and Columbia.

Years before he put his mark on theaters in Westwood Village and the Valley, Charles Lee designed a noteable theater a little farther down Broadway:

Tower Theater
802 South Broadway
Los Angeles, CA 90014

This great building was built in 1927. This was an important year in theater design, since it was the year when movies made the transition to sound. The 900-seat Tower was the first theater to be designed for talking pictures in Los Angeles. It is currently for rent and its future is in doubt.

Another surviving movie palace is:

Lowe's State
703 South Broadway
Los Angeles, CA 90014
(213) 792-6227

This theater was designed in 1921 by the San Francisco architectural firm of Charles Weeks and William Day, who also did the Mark Hopkins Hotel in that city and the Fox Theater in San Diego, which is now Copely Symphony Hall (see September).

This corner Spanish Renaissance building is the largest brick-clad structure in L.A. It was built for Marcus Lowe, who founded Metro-Goldwyn-Mayer Studio three years later in 1924. For a long time, Lowe's State was the site of M.G.M. premiers.

About this time, you might want to eat before continuing on the tour. A perfect choice to enhance the fantasy mood would be the venerable:

Clifton's Brookdale Cafeteria

648 South Broadway

Los Angeles, CA 90014

Daily 6:45 a.m. to 7 p.m.

(213) 627-1673

After walking over terrazzo roundels of L.A. landmarks that date from the 1930s, you now enter one of the most bizarre restaurant interiors in the city. The large room is built to look like a forest of redwoods. The posts supporting the ceiling are covered with bark.

There are several rooms and six levels with such details as a waterfall and stream, a stuffed deer, a neon crescent moon, and plenty of plastic shrubs. The clientele is "colorful" and the food is definitely cafeteria.

The next movie palace on Broadway, designed by G. Albert Lansburgh, has an appropriate name:

Palace Theater

630 South Broadway

Los Angeles, CA 90014

Built in 1911, this is the oldest surviving Orpheum theater in the world. You can see the French influence in the beautiful interior that was evident in his later Orpheum described above. It is a combination of pale pastel terra cotta decoration and garland-draped columns. Sculptor Domingo Mora created four muses representing Song, Dance, Music, and Drama.

Coming up on the other side of the street is architect Charles Lee's crowning achievement, "The Last Great Movie Palace Built in Downtown L.A.":

Los Angeles Theater

615 South Broadway

Los Angeles, CA 90014
(213) 239-0957

The Los Angeles Theater opened in 1931 with Charlie Chaplin's *City Lights* and had to be closed that same day because of the crowds and limousines. It was designed by the architect to be "a palace that someone could go in for 35 cents."

Often called the most opulent motion picture theater in the country, the Los Angeles features an elaborate French Renaissance exterior leading into a crystal fountain surrounded with marble fish at the head of a grand staircase.

It is the interior of this theater that is most reknowned. The enormous lobby is a feast for the eyes in gold and ivory. Movie-going was an event in the days of this theater's heyday and it featured a restaurant, two glass enclosed "crying rooms" for parents with infants, and a ballroom.

If you descend the wide, carpeted double stairway to the stately wood-paneled ballroom and enter the arched doorway, you will find yourself in one of the best women's bathroom in Southern California. The stalls are as large as individual bathrooms.

Originally, there was a kind of periscope to the projector that relayed the image of the film to a rear projection screen in the lounge like a camera obscura. There are 13 beautifully carved mahogany vanities with mirrors set into Rococo painted walls—all lit by a chandelier fit for the Taj Mahal.

Though Broadway has lots of stores and there is quite a bit of economic activity, many of the old theaters are experiencing the ravages of time. Another treasure that must be preserved is one of the oldest movie palaces in the United States that, alas, is currently being used as a church:

Million Dollar Theater
307 South Broadway
Los Angeles, CA 90013

For this theater, built several years before any of his Hollywood Boulevard theaters in 1917, entrepreneur Sid Grauman gave architects Albert C. Martin and William L. Woollett virtual carte-blanche. They responded by creating a 2,200-seat, florid architectural throwback to 18th century Spanish architect Jose Churriguera. With its numerous gargoyles and elaborate facade featuring Texas steers fashioned into a coat of arms, it appears they succeeded.

On opening night in 1918, Mary Pickford, Charlie Chaplin, and Lillian Gish arrived to see William S. Hart in *The Silent Man*.

Across the street is one of the most magnificent relics of 19th century architec-

The Bradbury Building in downtown Los
Angeles.

ture you could see anywhere:

Bradbury Building
304 South Broadway
Los Angeles, CA 90013

This building is one of only four office buildings in the city with the status of being a National Landmark. Named for a gold miner named Lewis Bradbury, it was built in 1894 for the then enormous cost of $500,000. Architect George H. Wyman was inspired by the ghost of his recently departed brother who came to him in the form of a dangling pencil over a Ouija board and wrote: "Take the Bradbury Building—it will make you famous." He was a $5 per week draftsman at the time.

When the building was completed, it contained a true masterpiece of interior space. The largest plate glass windows in Los Angeles look over a five-story glass-roofed central court with Mexican floor tiles, surrounded by Victorian cast iron grillwork (including 288 radiators). There are open-cased, originally water-powered bird cage elevators from Chicago and Italian and Belgian marble and polished oak balconies and staircases.

The building also contains 50 fireplaces and 215 wash basins. It was art directed into the weird setting for the climax of Ridley Scott's futuristic movie *Blade Runner,* where Harrison Ford is being stalked by the android played by Ruger Haer. Restoration of this wonderful building was completed in 1991 at a cost of over $7,000,000.

Besides old movie palaces, Southern California is also the home of the world's only theater dedicated solely to showing silent films:

Silent Movie
611 North Fairfax
Los Angeles, CA 90036
(213) 653-2389

Opened as the "Old Time Movie" on February 25 of 1942, the price of a ticket was 10¢ for an adult, and 5¢ for under 12. Though this was well past the heyday of silent movies, it was started by two people who never wanted them to die.

John and Dorothy Hampton were married in 1934. Both were film buffs, but John was truly a film devotee. They drove to L.A. in 1940—ironically in search of healthier air for John's asthma—and bought a small lot on Fairfax with the idea of building a movie theater that showed silent films.

Build it they did—complete with 150 unupholstered wooden seats. For 37 years, Dorothy took the tickets and counted the money and John ran the projector. They lived upstairs in a small apartment.

Every good story has its sad parts and the dark side of this one is that the theater closed in 1979 for what was supposed to be a temporary hiatus upon the death of John's mother. This would turn out to be a dark period, because John's health declined during the same time and he had to sell almost half of his priceless collection of films.

After John Hampton passed away in May of 1990, the situation got even worse. Just like in the movies, the brother entered the picture and tried to take over the theater, so he could tear it down and build something more profitable. He sent his son to clean out what was left of his brother's dream, and his offspring responded to his awful scheme with alacrity. Before he could be stopped, he trashed a priceless part of film history.

John had restored many rare prints—sometimes one frame at a time over months and months. His nephew tossed out between 200 to 300 of them, along with original lobby cards, promotional stills, and movie posters. This is one of many events that has convinced me that the relentless urge to clean and throw out old things is a sick one and should be resisted by kind-hearted pack rats the world over.

Fortunately, this story has a happy ending, courtesy of a real life hero, Lawrence Austin. A fellow film buff, he had been a friend of the Hamptons since 1942 and when he found out what was going on, he became progressively more involved. When he told the brother's son to stop throwing out the old films and he refused, the old family friend stepped in. After a legal fight, the father and son were sent back whence they came.

Austin had a few hundred films in his own collection and fortunately Hampton kept the largest part of his collection (about 1,500 films) in a warehouse at another location. With new blood and vigor, the theater reopened on January 18 of 1991 with Cecil B. de Mille's *King of Kings,* which was the film that had originally opened the theater and the one John would have wanted the theater to reopen with had he lived.

Today, Dorothy Hampton lives next door in the King Solomon Home for the Elderly and walks over to greet customers and tear tickets. Sitting in the projection booth is Laurence Austin, a true angel of silent film.

A theater that in my life has always been a big part of the Southland's movie-going experience is the:

Nuart Theater
11272 Santa Monica Boulevard
West Los Angeles, CA 90025
(213) 478-6379

Pleasantly remodeled and featuring a dazzling neon marquee, the Nuart is the major non-commercial film venue in Southern California. They show old films, foreign films, and cult classics. There are always interesting people in line here.

A movie at the Nuart would not be complete without dinner at:

Dem Bones
11619 Santa Monica Boulevard
West Los Angeles, CA 90025
Daily 11 a.m to 11 p.m.
(310) 475-0288

Dem Bones is a funky barbecue joint featuring ribs of various kinds as well as chicken and side dishes. It has achieved legendary status among the art film-goers at the Nuart for its inexpensive tab (less than $30 for two including beer and wine), fun atmosphere, and delicious food.

Drive-in Theaters

One of the most revered romantic traditions of summer in the post-WW II period is a warm evening under the stars with one's lover at the drive-in movie theater. So linked are the images of young lovers entwined together in a car while action plays on a huge outdoor screen that one of the comic-sad 1950's songs in the musical *Grease* laments, "I'm All Alone, At A Drive-In Movie."

The world's first drive-in theater (called a "park-and-watch") opened in Camden, New Jersey in 1933. It only took one year for someone to realize that this was something made for Southern California. A group of investors bought some land at the corner of Pico and Westwood Boulevards and opened the "Drive-In The-atre" with "the world's largest screen." Instead of speakers in the cars, it had giant loudspeakers booming the sound for blocks.

This same group gradually grew into Pacific Theatres. Seeing a good thing, they were the first to develop individual speakers to go in each car. The original was moved to Olympic and Bundy, where it eventually succumbed to rising real estate prices.

With the post war period bringing with it a love of the automobile that manifested itself most strongly in the West, it was natural that with our warm weather there should be a lot of drive-ins built here during the '50s.

They thrived during this period all over the country: 1958 was the peak year with 4,063 screens. But by the '70s, they were not a practical use of space and many closed. In 1981, there were 3,354 drive-in screens. Today only 910 are still operating, 160 of which are in California.

Despite the land they require, they have managed to survive in the Southland and today there are more outdoor movie screens in Southern California than anywhere else in the world. Pacific is the largest chain of drive-in theaters with 33 locations and 71 screens. Though most of these are in outlying areas with lower land prices, their most spectacular Southland drive-in is the:

Pacific's Winnetka 6 Drive-In
20210 Prairie Avenue
Chatsworth, CA 91311
(enter on Winnetka Avenue, one block south of Plummer)
(818) 349-6808

Of the 50 remaining drive-ins in Los Angeles County, this is the king. It was one of the last to be built in the U.S., and with six screens spread over 29 acres, it was also one of the largest ever made when it opened in 1978. Because of the distance to the screen, the projectors must use 4,500 watt bulbs—twice what is used at most walk-in theaters. Sound called "Cine-Fi" is now broadcast over A.M. radio so you can hear through your car's own speakers. Pacific's Winnetka 6 Drive-In is also a bargain at $4.50 for adults, and children under 12 for free.

American Film Institute Festival

Los Angeles may be the film capital of the world, but the city's biggest film festival—which happens this month—is not that well known:

American Film Institute Festival
American Film Institute Campus
2021 North Western
Hollywood, CA 90018
(213) 856-7600 (213) 466-1176

This hillside site was once the campus of Immaculate Heart College. Now A.F.I. and its Center for Advanced Film Studies resides here. There is a small 135-seat theater, the Sony Video Center, and the Louis B. Mayer Library, with the world's largest collection of movie scripts.

The festival began in 1986. Screening sites have ranged from Santa Monica to West Hollywood to Century City to the A.F.I. campus. In 1993, the program stated that the Laemmle Sunset 5 Theatres in West Hollywood would be the festival's new permanent home, but now it looks like they will be screening at:

> **Laemmle Monica I-IV**
> **1332 2nd Street**
> **Santa Monica, CA 90403**
> **(310) 394-9741**

The theater was originally a two-plex, but was made into one medium sized auditorium (about 400 seats) and three smaller ones of 100-odd seats each. The giant lobby is perfect for a film festival mood—people mingling and buzzing. Santa Monica is also a good location for a film festival as far as attracting westside residents, many of whom act like they will get the bends if they go east of Sepulveda Boulevard.

This festival is pretty large: in 1993, there were 120 films from 38 different countries. As far as American films, the focus is on the independent sector. This is a burgeoning part of the creative force in the U.S. To give you an idea how much, consider that in 1992, 100 new directors made their first films. Of these, 20 made critic's "Top Ten" lists.

Santa Monica's 2nd Street, where the theater is located, is near many of the best eating and most interesting shopping areas and sights in Southern California. Third Street Promenade, the Santa Monica Pier, and Main Street are covered in July. If there was ever a restaurant in Santa Monica appropriate to be mentioned with the A.F.I. Festival, it would be the legendary:

> **Michael's**
> **1147 3rd Street**
> **Santa Monica, CA 90403**
> **reservations taken for the following days/times:**
> **Tuesday-Friday 12 p.m. to 2 p.m.**
> **Tuesday-Saturday 6:30 p.m. to 9:30 p.m.**
> **(310) 451-0843**

Michael McCarty opened his bright culinary showcase in 1979 and has continued to impress customers non-stop since then. Though initially most famous for its prices and celebrity clientele, the decor and quality and inventiveness of the food and service have made Michael's a landmark among Southland restaurants.

Though it is still an expensive place to eat, prices at Michael's were actually lowered a few years ago. A cook friend of mine once said that the "California cuisine" here brought respectability to the name. There are simpler dishes, such as grilled salmon, and complex sounding combinations that are made from the freshest possible ingredients.

The setting is as beautifully done as the food. The garden terrace with its flowers and big white umbrellas is beloved by everyone. The dining room features art by Jasper Johns and David Hockney.

SOUTH SEAS LUAU

There are many indicators in Southern California that summer is beginning. School's out, the summer "blockbuster" movies are starting their advertising barrage, and the sun is shining hotter and longer. There has always been an implied connection between the Southland and the tropics. In many ways, Southern California really is a big Pacific Island.

There is no annual rite in June that epitomizes this like the:

> **South Seas Luau**
> **Two Harbors**
> **Catalina Island**
> **normally third Saturday of June**
> **(310) 510-0303**

If you are in a mood to go to Hawaii this summer, there is no need to go that far. The Two Harbors end of Catalina is a good substitute at most times with its South Seas island look (see February), but for this celebration, begun in 1992, it goes Polynesian all the way.

Participants are usually a combination of boaters, campers, and people who happen to be staying in the Banning House Lodge at the time. Everyone dons the traditional floral attire and arrives ready to have a good time. A show starts at 8 p.m. with live music, hula dancers, and a fire eater. The musicians continue to play for a while after the other performers are through.

There is, of course, a big luau dinner for $39.50. It consists of a large buffet of which the centerpiece is the familiar stuffed pig buried in the sand under rocks and hot coals.

The Two Harbors end of Catalina is not only beautiful, but it has its own spirited social center:

Doug's Reef Saloon
P.O. Box 5044
Two Harbors, CA 90704
Daily 6 p.m. to 10 p.m.
(310) 510-0303

Doug's Reef hearkens back to the "tiki room" bars of the '40s and '50s (see July). It reminds me of the old TV show "McHale's Navy," in which Ernest Borgnine's crew were always lounging in hammocks and drinking out of coconut shells. There is a patio and a nautical-style dining room with fish net, woven mats, and lamps made of sea shells.

The food is good and includes prime rib, pork ribs, teriyaki chicken, swordfish steak, and shrimp tempura. Drinking at the bar is enthusiastic, as is the friendly mood. Breakfast and hot coffee are available at the connected snack bar.

Concessionaire Doug Bombard was actually born on Santa Catalina Island. He married his sweetheart, Audry, in 1947. She was from Belmont Shore in Long Beach, where I lived for many years. The restaurant had actually been there for some time, but they officially formed Doug Bombard Enterprises in 1975. Now their son, Randy, helps them run things at the Two Harbor end of the island. A more light hearted family would be hard to imagine.

There are numerous campgrounds on Catalina Island, at both ends, and they start getting more crowded as summer goes on. To the west of Two Harbors, on the smaller western end is **Parson's Landing Campgrounds**, the most remote. It is 6-3/4 miles out of town on an absolutely stunning trail called the West End Trail that takes you through dramatic canyons and around gorgeous, crescent-shaped coves, many of which were used by bootleggers as hide-outs during prohibition. Because there are fewer plant-eating animals at this end, the flora can be more lush.

One of the real draws to the outback of Catalina is that it is rich in life. There is a considerable amount of vegetation, about 10 percent of which is rare. Species include Catalina ironwood, Saint Catherine's Lace, the Catalina Cherry, and a languid flowering buckwheat that can grow up to 10-feet high. The overall landscape of the backcountry is not lushly forested, but rather somewhat stark like a Greek island.

About 1-1/4 miles down the trail, you'll come to **Cherry Cove**, named for the profusion of Catalina Cherry trees, where a small valley meets the ocean. In spring, these shrubbery looking trees will be adorned with spiny clusters of white flowers that by this month have turned into a kind of pseudo cherry that is actually an edible native plant.

About a mile before you get to Parson's Landing is **Emerald Bay**, a suitably named cove that is worth hiking to even if you aren't going all the way to the campground. Not only is it as crystal green as a gemstone, there is a small island at its entrance you can swim to.

Parson's Landing is secluded. You can camp either on the beach or on a bluff overlooking the ocean with no assigned sites—which means there is a chance you might be able to create the illusion that you are really on a deserted island.

Of course, at the other end of the island, **Avalon** (described in detail in February) really begins to come alive this month because of the warmer air and water. Though it is more crowded with tourists than it was in February, it is still a pretty and fun little town.

Around the corner of the bay from the Casino is **Avalon Underwater Park**, which unlike the underwater park in the Channel Islands is a municipal park, the only such one in the State. It varies in depth up to 100 feet and features a dense kelp forest reminiscent of the central tank at the Monterey Aquarium.

Besides the creatures of the sea, there are shipwrecks to explore, a total of seven, including a graceful 70-foot schooner. Perhaps the most foreboding is a 163-foot pleasure boat that sank in the 1930s.

Catalina is an acclaimed place for scuba diving and snorkeling, but there are also glass-bottomed boats if you are not inclined to get wet. During the summer, there are night tours to see flying fish as well.

I mentioned The Inn on Mt. Ada in February, but right above the Casino is another romantic place to stay with a fabulous harbor view:

> **Zane Grey Pueblo Hotel**
> **P.O. Box 216**
> **Avalon, CA 90704**
> **(310) 510-0966**
> **(310) 510-1520**

The harbor bell tower looks over this former home of the famous American Western writer that is now a bed and breakfast inn. Grey was a fisherman and in his own way, a naturalist. In addition to his well known novels of the West, he wrote about fishing and the outdoors with genuine love.

This is a good alternative to The Inn on Mt. Ada because not only is it considerably less expensive, it is completely different in style. Where the Inn on Mt. Ada is like staying in an East Coast mansion-style villa, the Zane Grey is a Hopi Indian-styled pueblo, built in 1926. It has a long hall separating the ocean and mountain view rooms. On either side, the view is terrific. There is a also a swimming pool in a garden.

FATHER'S DAY

Father's Day has a vastly different feel to it compared to Mother's Day. This translates to a different kind of celebration. Where mom usually gets taken to brunch on her day, dad seems to get dinner at home and a gift box with an ugly tie in it. Since we took mom to a pretty feminine place, we need to take dad to a masculine one. Probably the most inspired choice in the Southland for a Father's Day restaurant is:

Engine Company Number 28
644 South Figueroa
Los Angeles, CA 90017
Monday-Friday 11:15 a.m. to 9 p.m.
Saturday & Sunday 5 to 9 p.m.
(213) 624-6996

The 1912 firehouse was remodeled into a restaurant that opened in January, 1989. With its 16-foot high pressed metal ceiling, brick floor, iron grill starcase, and heavy mahogany all around, it is appropriately manly. The firehouse roots have been subtly downplayed—there are no poles coming down from holes in the ceiling. The entrance, however, is flanked by two ceramic dalmatians.

Another "manly" restaurant is found in Orange County:

Trabuco Oaks Steak House
20782 Trabuco Oaks Drive
Trabuco Canyon, CA 92679
Daily 5 to 9 p.m.
(714) 586-0722

Trabuco Oaks has a dirt parking lot, and on the inside it looks like a cave with windows. The place mats are made of denim. There are rough tree trunks holding up a low ceiling. From this ceiling hangs an upside down forest of ugly neckties. It is a tradition here for waiters to cut off ties with a pair of scissors and hang them from the rafters. After all, an atrocious tie is the usual Father's Day gift.

As you might imagine, the food isn't going to win any awards from the American Heart Association. They serve mesquite-grilled meat—and lots of it. The steaks have names like the "Rustler" and the "Ramrod."

But if anyplace in the Southland would qualify as a temple of fatherhood, it would be the inimitable:

San Diego Hardware
840 5th Avenue
San Diego, CA 92101
Monday-Saturday 8:30 a.m. to 5 p.m.
(619) 232-7123

For anyone who ever went with their father to a big family-owned hardware store on a Saturday morning to peer at a seemingly endless selection of wigets, this place will create a sense of awe. Owned by the same people since 1910, San Diego Hardware is a city block filled with over 50,000 separate items. The Swiss Army Knife display is semi-famous and sure to inspire those looking for the appropriate gift.

GAY PRIDE

June is the month of Gay Pride Week throughout the United States. It is not just an arbitrary choice of months, because there was a precipitating event in the gay rights movement that was a galvanizing moment.

As recently as the late '60s, it was illegal in the City of New York for two men to dance together. Gay clubs were frequently raided.

On June 28 of 1969, a club called the Stonewall Inn was raided simply because it was a gay place. It had been a location of repeated police harassment, but for the first time, the patrons resisted. The police barricaded themselves within the club and a full scale riot broke out, involving 200 to 300 people. It is this act of defiance that Gay Pride week celebrates.

There are parades and festivals all throughout the country. They actually begin in April in a nationwide, coordinated effort and continue through May, with the largest ones in New York and West Hollywood coming last in June.

One of the most important people in the Southern California gay rights movement is Morris Kight. During the '50s, when being homosexual was a very misunderstood thing, he worked as an "underground gay liberationist." In the '70s, he was a spokesman in L.A.'s Gay Liberation Front, and was one of the founders of the L.A. Gay Pride Committee. He currently serves on the Los Angeles County Human Relations Commission.

Southern California occupies an important place in gay history because it is the site of the first "gay city," West Hollywood.

West Hollywood was originally a district of L.A. It had a somewhat sordid reputation, and was a traditional location for agents and nightclubs.

A lot of gay clubs began to open in West Hollywood because it was out of the jurisdiction of the LAPD. Its identity as a "gay place" was firmly established by 1985, when it incorporated as a separate city. Today, the city flies the rainbow colored gay flag over its city hall.

The Gay Pride celebration here originated in 1970 and is obviously a large one, attracting 400,000 people in 1993. It usually starts with concerts in West Hollywood Park on a Thursday, with events culminating in a big parade on Sunday. The parade route begins at Crescent Heights and continues up Santa Monica Boulevard (which is the main gay commercial street) for two miles.

My first introduction to L.A.'s gay subculture came in the late '70s. This was the period of the first openly gay performers such as the Village People and Freddy Mercury of the group Queen gaining wide acceptance in the straight world.

My girlfriend at the time liked to go dancing at Studio One, a former warehouse turned nightclub. It was quite a wild place with pounding music and decor that was a mixture of Greek columns and warehouse/techno. The Greek columns are gone and the name has been changed, but the location lives on as:

Axis
652 North La Peer
West Hollywood, CA 90048
(310) 659-0471

The only remaining Greek-themed part of the place is the urinal in the men's bathroom: it is a large Grecian fountain.

There are several other nightspots in the area. One of the hottest gay dance clubs in West Hollywood is:

Rage
8911 Santa Monica Boulevard
West Hollywood, CA 90069
(310) 652-7055

There is a lot more to West Hollywood than clubs, however. One of the first gay-oriented bookstores is just a few doors down:

A Different Light Bookstore
8853 Santa Monica Boulevard
West Hollywood, CA 90069
Daily 10 a.m. to 12 a.m.
(310) 854-6601

Here they have over 14,000 books both by gay writers and on themes pertaining to gays and lesbians, as well as works by artists such as Keith Haring.

Another West Hollywood landmark is the:

Celebration Theatre
7051 Santa Monica Boulevard
West Hollywood, CA 90069
(213) 957-1884

Opened in 1973, the Celebration is the first and biggest arts complex to feature works by gay and lesbian writers and performers. It has a 99-seat main space as well as a smaller venue.

The '90s brought more visibility to lesbians, traditionally more anonymous than gay males. They are more prominent in gay male clubs now, and bars and restaurants that cater to women are more numerous. A West Hollywood classic is:

The Palms
8572 Santa Monica Boulevard
West Hollywood, CA 90069
Daily 12 p.m. to 2 a.m.
(310) 652-6188

Sometimes called the "Cheers of L.A.'s lesbian community," The Palms is a neighborhood bar, not a dance club. Though it is old and dark, the mood inside is very friendly and full of fun.

Not too far away on the same side of the street is a coffeehouse that also has a predominantly female clientele:

Little Frida's
8730 Santa Monica Boulevard
West Hollywood, CA 90069
(310) 652-6495

Besides coffee, they also serve up music and poetry readings.

There are gay communities and establishments in all counties of the Southland. The City of San Diego, for example, has a large homosexual population. One of the city's oldest gay businesses caters to women and is ironically called:

The Flame
3780 Park Boulevard
San Diego, CA 92103
Daily 5 p.m. to 2 a.m.
Friday 4 p.m. to 2 a.m.
(619) 295-4163

This building originally housed a restaurant with a very famous name, The Garden of Allah. The name change came before the orientation change: The Flame was named for the fire that destroyed the first building in 1954. This was a particularly devastating blaze because the original structure was an Egyptian Revival design built in 1946.

The Flame has been the main women's bar in San Diego since 1974 and the crowd is quite eclectic. It has several rooms, including a big dance floor and a cozy video bar.

Perhaps providence has a sense of humor after all. A final irony is that the Gay and Lesbian Center in the San Diego area is on Normal Avenue.

SUMMER THEATER AND MUSIC FESTIVALS
San Diego Shakespeare Festival, Balboa Park

Live theater is a very special kind of diversion from reality because the stage creates a kind of reality of its own. That is why summer theater festivals are such a natural in the Southland. Summer outdoor theater festivals are a tradition, not only in Southern California, but all over the world. What would be properly called the most prestigious of these festivals is held yearly in our second largest city:

> **San Diego Shakespeare Festival**
> **Old Globe, Festival Stage, and Cassius Carter Theaters**
> **Balboa Park, San Diego**
> mailing address:
> **P.O. Box 2171**
> **San Diego, CA 92112-2171**
> **(619) 239-2255 (box office)**

With all of the national focus on the cultural growth of the City of Los Angeles, as well as its Hollywood history, it isn't surprising that San Diego has been consistently under-rated as a cultural center. Many recent national and Broadway hits, such as the forever-running *Forever Plaid* actually originated at the festival.

There are three theatres, all completely different. Though it is sort of Tudor styled on the outside, the 581-seat **Old Globe Theatre** is more like Downtown L.A.'s Mark Taper Forum on the inside than the original Olde Globe in England. It was rebuilt in 1982 at a cost of $6.5 million after a fire that is commemorated by the semi-melted bust of Shakespeare that now adorns the lobby. The thrust stage is supported by a full range of technical special effects.

There is also the 225-seat theatre-in-the round **Cassius Carter Centre Stage.**

The most sylvan setting is the 612-seat, outdoor **Lowell Davies Festival Stage** with a grove of eucalyptus trees and a ravine for a background.

The Old Globe Theater.

I have been going to this theatre festival since I was in my first year of college and have seen some memorable shows, both by Shakespeare and by contemporary writers. There is no better way to cap a summer weekend in San Diego than a great play in Balboa Park.

In the April chapter I described some of the gardens of Balboa Park. For the summer Shakespeare Festival, it is appropriate that I mention the museums. There are 13 separate museums in Balboa Park that together make for a cultural complex second only to the Smithsonian in size.

One of the best values I have encountered anywhere is the **Passport To Balboa Park**, which is a pass that allows you to put together your own combination of museums for one $9 fee. It can be used at any of the following locations: the San Diego Natural History Museum, Museum of Man, the San Diego Aerospace Museum and International Aerospace Museum of Art, the San Diego Automotive Museum, and the Rueben H. Fleet Space Theater and Science Center.

As you drive or walk over the Cabrillo Bridge, the building that passes over El Prado just behind the theatre area and to the side is the California Quadrangle, which was mentioned briefly in the April chapter. Originally started by San Diego architect Irving Gill in more restrained modernist style, it was finished by architect Bertram Goodhue for the 1915 Exhibition in a more elaborate fashion. The New York architect appended the design with Baroque detailing and Beaux Art balconies.

Within the quadrangle is the:

> **Museum of Man**
> **1350 El Prado**
> **San Diego, CA 92101**

Daily 10 a.m. to 4:30 p.m.
(619) 239-2001

After a glamorous beginning in 1915 as reception sites for international dignitaries, the rooms inside this inviting building were then converted into a military hospital during WW II. After that, they sat almost vacant. The whole building was saved from demolition in 1978 by its inclusion (along with the other buildings along El Prado) in the National Register of Historic Places. It had a $2,000,000 renovation in the late '80s.

The Museum of Man has had many incarnations. It started life after the exposition ended as the "San Diego Museum," and was basically an extension of the anthropological and archeological studies done therein. The museum's first director, who was known as "Bull" Hewitt, was able to get a very ambitious research project/ exhibit co-sponsored by the Smithsonian Institute that was called "The Story of Man Through the Ages." The resulting 5,000 piece collection would form the basis for the Museum of Man.

This is a fun and interesting museum. There are objects of various kinds from around the world pertaining to human history. These include fossils, pottery, baskets and one of fewer than 25 casts in existence of what is now accepted as the skeleton of our oldest walking ancestor, Lucy.

The best exhibits tell a story. There is a re-creation of part of a Mayan ruins: the carved pillars of Qiriqua in Guatemala. A display called "Lifecycles and Ceremonies" shows the link between culture and biology. The most recent semi-permanent exhibit, "Life and Death On the Nile," came about as a result of a large bequest of Egyptian artifacts. Every June, usually on the second weekend, the museum holds a two-day Indian Fair devoted to Native American culture.

Balboa Park has three pretty wedding sites. One, the Rose and Desert Garden, was described in April. The second of them is within the California Quadrangle, the Chapel of St. Francis.

Once you have passed through the California Quadrangle, next to the theatres on the east side and set back somewhat from El Prado is the:

San Diego Museum of Art
1450 El Prado
San Diego, CA 92101
Tuesday-Sunday 10 a.m. to 4:30 p.m.
(619) 232-7931

A lot of people get this museum mixed up with The Museum of Contemporary Art, San Diego (see September). To make it even more confusing, it used to be called "The Fine Arts Gallery of San Diego." Whatever it is called, it is a great way to spend an afternoon.

The elaborate entrance is a clue to what's inside. Designed by William Templeton Johnson in an intricate, 16th century Spanish Renaissance style, it has the individual coat of arms of Spain, America, California, and San Diego above the door.

The collection here includes Spanish Baroque and Italian Renaissance paintings, pieces by American masters, Asian art, and special exhibitions—some of which have been quite unusual.

Some of the eclectic changing art shows have included an 1,800-square-foot model of a Frank Lloyd Wright house and an exhibit of illustrations from the late Dr. Seuss, who was, after all, a San Diego resident. There is also a museum store.

Within the museum's enclosed courtyard is the **Sculpture Garden Cafe.** It is only open from 11:30 a.m. to 2 p.m. and is a wonderful setting for lunch. The menu is simple—soups, salads, sandwiches, pastries, beer, wine, and beverages—but tables are set among the sculptures. The statuary is by contemporary artists, such as Francisco Zuniga and Henry Moore.

Parking for the festival can be a problem—particularly when the Starlight Amphitheater also has a show. It is actually better to park closer to the edge of the park up by the lawn bowling area and walk over the Cabrillo Bridge. If you do drive all the way in on El Prado and make a right to where the parking lots are, you will pass the statue of El Cid. Just east of this statue is the lovely building that houses the:

Cafe Del Rey Morrow
1549 El Prado
San Diego CA 92101
Monday-Friday 11 a.m. to 4 p.m.
Saturday 11 a.m. to 4:30 a.m.
Tuesday-Friday 4:30 to 8:30 p.m.
Saturday 5 to 8:30 p.m.
Sunday 4 to 8:30 p.m.
(619) 234-8511

Now this is one way to make the parking easier and also do your pre-theatre dining: park early, before the theatre crowds hit and have dinner here, then simply walk leisurely to the play. This is the third of the nice wedding sites in Balboa Park and, I must say, it is a splendid one. The dining area of the restaurant overlooks the brick terraces and lily pond where the ceremonies are held.

The food is moderately priced and includes popular Mexican specialties and American basics such as hamburgers, steaks, and salads. They also sell box lunches for picnics.

Immediately behind the Cafe Del Rey Morrow is the **Casa del Balboa,** a large building which contains the Museum of San Diego History, the Museum of Photographic Arts, the San Diego Hall of Champions, and possibly the most charming of all the museums:

> **San Diego Model Railway Museum**
> **1649 El Prado**
> **San Diego, CA 92101-1621**
> **Wednesday-Friday 11 a.m. to 4 p.m.**
> **Saturday & Sunday 11 a.m. to 5 p.m.**
> **(619) 696-01**

Located on the lower level of the Casa del Balboa is the "World's Largest Operating Model Railroad Exhibit." For a mere $2, you can experience 22,000-square-feet of operating model trains and miscellaneous railroad equipment. Created as a history of the great railroads of the West, even San Diego's own Santa Fe Station (described in January) is lovingly recreated.

They have a gift shop of "rail-related" art and collectibles, as well as train toys of various kinds, books and videos, and even clothes. If you have been wanting to complete your wardrobe with an ensemble of Osh Kosh B' Gosh coveralls and cap, you have found the right store.

Children under 15 are admitted free at this delightful place of escape, but then, once inside, everyone becomes a child the first moment they catch a glimpse of the trains.

There are two other outdoor performing areas within Balboa Park that are especially apt for summer: the **Starlight Amphitheater** and the **Spreckles Organ Pavilion.** The elegant structure of the latter was given to the City of San Diego on December 31 of 1914 for the original Pan Pacific Exposition. Its centerpiece is one of the world's great concert organs. It was, of course, Adolph and John D. Spreckels who did the giving.

The sugar kings chose the prestigious Austin Organ Company in Hartford, Connecticut to build the instrument itself, and what a set of pipes it is! There are 4,445 of them arranged in 72 ranks controlled by four keyboards. The range of sounds produced runs from the peeping of 1/4-inch mites to the rumble of 32-foot giants.

Perhaps the most perfect place to stay to enjoy the festival and its Balboa Park setting is the gingerbread Britt House (described in February) or the Park Manor Suites (described in April). If you missed eating at Mister A's Restaurant on 5th Avenue (described in February), it is two steps from the Britt House.

Concerts By The Bay, Shelter Island

Besides the Shakespeare Festival, June in San Diego starts the season of another delightful summer tradition in that city:

> **Concerts By The Bay**
> **Humphrey's Half Moon Inn**
> **2303 Shelter Island Drive**
> **San Diego, CA 92106**
> **(619) 224-3411**
> **(800) 542-7400**

This Polynesian-style resort hotel is done in the "tiki style" of the late '50s and early '60s. Humphrey's the restaurant has an adjoining outdoor amphitheater where musical concerts—usually jazz—are held, beginning this month and continuing through the rest of summer. The restaurant also has a great Sunday brunch.

Humphrey's tropical resort setting, on its man-made island surrounded by San Diego Bay, makes for a great weekend if you would like to stay in one place and have something to do that night. There are 182 rooms, most of which have a yacht harbor or bay view. There are 30 suites with kitchens and some of these have balconies overlooking the stage. The whole hotel is Southern California tropics all the way with palm trees, poolside wet bars, and a poolside waterfall cascading on swimmers. Other tiki style buildings are featured in July.

The Hills (of L.A.) Are Alive

Though there is no formal name for it, there is a "hill culture" in Los Angeles. Beginning around Dodger Stadium and heading west, the flatlands of L.A. and Hollywood rise up into several communities that are different from one another, but run in a continuous band all the way to Beverly Hills.

These residential neighborhoods can be very private and quite lush with plants and trees, but have a close commercial area interface. For this reason, they all have a tradition of attracting a lot of creative people who like city living but want some seclusion as well. At the same time, the hills of Hollywood also have a legacy of coming alive during the summer because of the three outdoor summer music and theatre venues that are located here.

Greek Theater Summer Season

Beginning every June since 1930, there has been a tradition of outdoor evening entertainment at the:

> **Greek Theater**
> **2700 North Vermont Avenue**
> **Hollywood, CA 90027**
> **(213) 468-1767**

Though it does not have the architectural majesty of the Hollywood Bowl, the Greek's faux Doric-columned facade is nonetheless impressive amidst the trees. It seats 6,000 and features mainly popular music performers. They sell box dinners, beer, and wine and there are convenient picnic tables.

Another old L.A. monument that is quite near the Greek perches on the hill overlooking Hollywood:

> **Ennis-Brown House**
> **2607 Glendower Avenue**
> **Hollywood, CA 90027**
> **Tours on second Saturday of odd-numbered months**
> **Admission: $19; seniors/students/children: $5**
> **11:30 a.m. and throughout the day until 3:30 p.m.**
> **reservations required; special tours by request**
> **(213) 660-0607**

Adored by some, reviled by others, this is certainly the most imposing of Frank Lloyd Wright's "knit-block" houses in L.A. It has been referred to as a mausoleum, a Mayan Temple, a fortress, and a palace. Built in 1924, the Ennis-Brown House sits on a steep slope buttressed with a retaining wall and was the last of the four cast concrete block structures built by the architect in L.A.

The effect of the design pattern cast in each block, with the blocks then stacked and lined up forming more lines and patterns, still has a futuristic look. The stained glass windows, also designed by Wright, are quite unlike any I have seen anywhere else. Director Ridley Scott used the interior of the Ennis-Brown house as Harrison Ford's apartment in the film *Blade Runner* about 21st century L.A.

The tours are a treat, but are not given very often. In fact, tours are offered during odd numbered months on one day only. I put the Ennis Brown House here in June because it is so much a part of the "hill culture" of L.A. and Hollywood and is impossible to miss on your way to the Greek. Besides the stunning interior, because of its hillside location, the view of Hollywood from the house is also justifiably famous.

The gift shop here (only open during the limited tour hours) sells blocks and tiles in the Ennis-Brown pattern. They also have planter boxes, note cards, and other interesting derivatives.

The district just below the Greek is known as Los Feliz, after Domingo Los Feliz, whose rancho this once was. He was murdered in 1836 by his pretty young wife's secret boyfriend. The homicidal lovers were caught and both lynched a week later.

Today the neighborhood is full of life and the presence of the arts. A little way down Vermont from the Greek, you will come into a great little strip of the street; an area with several wonderful moderately-priced restaurants that seem to have been there forever. Along with these restaurants are good bookstores, a small theatre, a movie theater, and several European delis.

The neighborhood coffeehouse is the:

Onyx Gallery
1804 North Vermont
Los Angeles, CA 90027
(213) 660-5820

The very high ceiling in this small coffeehouse gives one the feeling of being inside a giant shoebox, only with huge paintings on the walls.

If you continue walking in the same direction, a fun little gift shop comes up on your left:

Y Que Trading Post
1770 North Vermont
Los Angeles, CA 90027
Daily 12 to 6 p.m.
(213) 664-0021

From the window displays, you will get a clue that this small store is packed with all kinds of interesting things and has a twist to it that is appropriate for its location. Two doors down is one of the Southland's most unique bookstores:

Amok Bookstore
1764 North Vermont
Los Angeles, CA 90027

Tuesday-Sunday 12 to 7 p.m.
(213) 665-0956
(213) 663-8618 (office)

This remarkable store was started by Stuart Swezey in 1989 and moved here in 1992. It specializes in books no other book dealer carries. They have a catalogue that is almost legendary. You can find books that deal with everything from proving that Jesus was a space alien to detailing how to make explosives out of Drano. Right next to Amok is:

The Dresden Restaurant and Lounge
1760 North Vermont
Los Angeles, CA 90027
Monday-Saturday 10 a.m. to 11:30 p.m.
Sunday 3 to 10 p.m.
(213) 665-4294

In the same location since 1936 and under the same ownership since 1948, The Dresden retains the flair of a bygone era. It has a bar and a dining room, with decor that will carry you back to the good old days: Art Deco floor-to-ceiling swirled black lacquer pillars, soft white circular booths, and attentive waiters in crisp uniforms. Philip Marlowe would be right at home.

The menu is a throwback to the days before restaurants specialized in one type of food, and includes prime rib, fish, pasta, and specials. All dinners come with garlic bread, vegetable, and salad, and are priced from the low to high teens. By all means, order their Blood and Sand cocktail.

Across the street is:

Theatre 1761
1761 North Vermont
Los Angeles, CA 90027
(213) 664-0680

This former camera shop was turned into a theatre in 1985 by artistic director Sal Romeo. The box office and entrance are in the back, off the parking lot.

At the corner where Hollywood meets Vermont is a hill that rises abruptly. On top of it is another Frank Lloyd Wright House that is the gilt-edge of an arts complex:

Hollyhock House
4808 Hollywood Boulevard
Hollywood, CA 90027

Tours Tuesday-Sunday 12, 1, 2, and 3 p.m.
(213) 662-7272

This house, built in the knit block manner, was designed by Wright for Aline Barnsdale, a wealthy oil heiress. The name comes from its hollyhock motif embellishment that runs as a theme throughout the building and even the furniture. It was the owner's favorite flower, so plenty of them were also planted on the grounds.

The Hollyhock House was the first house Frank Lloyd Wright designed in L.A. He worked on it from 1917 to 1920. It seems larger than its 6,000-square-feet because the rooms are built on different levels and almost all of them open onto terraces or courtyards.

The interior is wonderfully idiosyncratic. For example, a stream runs around the big stone fireplace. It is interesting to see how the architect's personal views affected his plans. The music room, with its perfect acoustics, contains wood cabinets for all of the instruments—including the old record player. Wright felt that all objects he didn't design should be kept out of sight. This is why there is no art or ornamentation. The architect explained it simply: "My houses are the art."

The dining room table seats only six and cannot be extended. Wright felt that more than six people at a table was too many to maintain a good conversation. The ceilings are only 6 feet 6 inches tall because he was only five foot six and thought a foot over that would be enough for anyone. By the way, the tours here are much cheaper (about $1.50) than at the Ennis-Brown House. They are also offered a lot more often.

This is because Barnsdale gave the property to the city to be used as an art center, which is why the complex that contains the house is called:

Barnsdale Art Park
4800 Hollywood Boulevard
Hollywood, CA 90027
Daily 12:30 to 5 p.m.
(213) 662-7272

This is a very active place with a nice, medium sized theatre, the **Barnsdale Art Theater,** and two galleries, the Municipal and Junior Art Galleries. They have exhibits as well as classes for children and adults.

One block above Hollywood Boulevard is Franklin Avenue. Going west from Vermont, at the corner of Bronson, there is a short commercial strip that appears suddenly along this pretty tree-lined, but otherwise residential street. Here, there are several sidewalk cafes, a bookstore, and a very comfortable coffeehouse.

For me, the perfect little French restaurant is:

La Poubelle Brasserie des Artists
5907 Franklin Avenue
Hollywood, CA 90028
Dinner 5:30 to 10:30 p.m.
Sunday brunch 1:30 to 3 p.m.
(213) 465-0807

I remember bringing a date here when I was a senior in high school in 1972. Miraculously, the same person owns it: French chef Jacqueline Foster opened this romantic place with the unusual name in 1970.

And quite romantic it is. The inside is fairly dark with warm yellow lighting illuminating antique-framed pictures and miscellaneous objects. Tile and wood predominate. There is an open kitchen and a little counter. The whole room has a mysterious quality to it. If you prefer to dine outside, there are tables out front for warm evenings or brunch.

The menu has an excellent selection of tasty, moderately-priced fare. There are salads, pasta dishes and pizza, but also French specialties, soups, and crepes. It seems as though crepes are not that easy to find these days. Perhaps it is because there are so very many Italian restaurants.

Right next door is a "previously experienced" book and record shop:

Counterpoint Records and Books
5911 Franklin Avenue
Hollywood, CA 90028
Daily 1 to 9 p.m.
(213) 957-7965

Since 1979, this store has offered a good selection of used books, ranging from paperbacks for as little as 25¢ to some pretty rare editions. The used record and tape selection has been augmented with CDs.

One of the things that sets this little strip apart is that it has a particularly active small theatre:

Tamarind Theater
5919 Franklin Avenue
Hollywood, CA 90028
(213) 856-4784

Producers of quality small theatre like this space because it is in a much prettier, more inviting part of Hollywood than most of the other 99-seat theatres. It also has valet parking and a lot of nearby restaurants.

No restaurant row in the Southland would be complete without an Italian place that serves pasta and gourmet pizza:

Prizzi's Piazza
5923 Franklin Avenue
Hollywood, CA 90028
Sunday-Thursday 5:30 to 11 p.m.
Friday & Saturday 5:30 p.m. to 1 p.m.
(213) 467-0168

Now this is a small restaurant. The dining area inside seems like it is about a quarter of the size of La Poubelle's. It has small triangular-shaped tables. Out front, crammed into a small patch of sidewalk, there are an amazing number of tables that always seem to be occupied.

Next door to tiny Prizzi's is a larger restaurant space that is also the neighborhood bar:

Birds
5925 Franklin Avenue
Hollywood, CA 90028
Wednesday-Monday 12 to 11 p.m. (kitchen)
Wednesday-Monday 12 p.m. to 2 a.m. (bar)
closed Tuesday
(213) 465-0175

Birds is the largest restaurant space along this romantic little stretch. It is twice the size of La Poubelle and is divided into a bar half and booths. The food is rotisserie chicken and a mixture of different vegetarian side dishes that also do fine on their own. The bar serves beer and wine and excellent coffee. Sunday brunch ranges from the $6.95 gourmet continental, to the $9.95 "free flowing Champagne," or the $16.95 with full appetizer, entree, and dessert.

This is also one of the most comfortable, unpretentious, and even witty restaurants in Hollywood. On the long exposed brick wall is a large picture of Alfred Hitchcock with the two birds on his shoulders. As you walk back to the bathrooms, the pictures lining the wall include basketball great Larry Bird. A combination of '60s and '70s music plays constantly.

Co-owner Mary Preston is an actress who spent 17 years banging on the door to get her own TV sit-com. During that time, like many actors, she worked in restaurants. Deciding that perhaps the cosmos was trying to tell her something, she borrowed on her credit cards and along with writer Henry Olek opened Birds. It is currently my favorite "hang."

As coffeehouses go, they don't get much more snug than:

Bourgeois Pig Coffeehouse
5931 Franklin Avenue
Hollywood, CA 90028
Tuesday-Thursday 12 p.m. to 2 a.m.
Friday-Saturday 12 p.m. to 3 a.m.
Sunday 12 p.m. to 2 a.m.
(213) 962-6366

This cozy, medium-sized coffeehouse is dark with lighted paintings. The Bourgeois Pig has a somewhat more finished and less seedy quality than most coffeehouses, and even has a separate room in back with a pool table.

For a fitting end to a great little strip, stop by the corner bookstore/newsstand:

The Daily Planet
5931-1/2 Franklin Avenue
Hollywood, CA 90028
Monday-Friday 12 p.m. to 12 a.m.
Saturday & Sunday 9 a.m. to 12 a.m.
(213) 957-0061

As you continue west on Franklin, looming above you ever since Vermont has been a very famous sign. If you turn right up Beachwood Canyon before you get to Cahuenga, you'll have a chance to get close to it.

In 1923, a subdivision built by the Engineering Service Corporation needed a sign. John D. Roche built a 50-foot high, 4,000-bulb edifice proclaiming the name of the subdivision: "Hollywoodland." He later said that he didn't think it would be up for more than a year and a half.

The "land" part is no longer with us, but the remaining 450 feet of it is. **The Hollywood Sign** was deeded by the developer to the Recreation and Parks Department in 1945. In 1978, they spent $250,000 spiffing it up.

Over the years it has been temporarily modified by pranksters to read "Hollyweed," "Go Navy," "Caltech," and the loathsome "Ollywood" in dubious honor to Oliver North.

The Hollywood Sign is located on the lower slope of Mt. Lee, above Beechwood Canyon. The drive up there is closed to the public, but you can drive up to the **Hollywoodland Gates**, built in the same year as the original sign.

It is poetic that these sandstone block structures that look so fanciful as you drive between them on your way up the hill were the entrance to the original Hollywoodland. They remind me of Sleeping Beauty's Castle at Disneyland.

By all means, stop once you are inside the gates. There is a tiny, pleasant little commercial area with a great market, some shops, and, if you are early enough for breakfast or lunch, one of my favorite breakfast stops:

Village Coffee Shop
2695 North Beachwood Drive
Hollywood, CA 90068
Monday-Friday 8 a.m. to 6:30 p.m.
Saturday 8 a.m. to 5 p.m.
(213) 467-5398

The Village started life as a counter in a drug store. It has expanded over the years and now occupies a large room with a high ceiling and a smaller connected room. It is styled like the Old West with heavy wooden booths and wrought iron fixtures.

Continuing up Beachwood, you will come to a place that was important in my childhood:

Hollywood Sunset Ranch
3400 North Beachwood Drive
Hollywood, CA 90068
Daily 9 a.m. to 4 p.m.
(213) 464-9612
(213) 469-5450

It was here that I learned to ride a horse. They are rented by the hour and lessons are available. A traditionally romantic thing to do here is to go on a group moonlight ride on a Friday night through the wilds of Griffith Park and finish at a Mexican restaurant in Burbank for dinner.

Hollywood Bowl Summer Festival

The summer festival at the Hollywood Bowl, with the opening classical concert of the season, is the premier Southern California summer experience:

Hollywood Bowl Summer Festival
Hollywood Bowl
2301 North Highland Avenue
Hollywood, CA 90068
Season usually runs from the end of June through
the middle of September
Tuesday-Sunday evenings
(213) 850-2000

The bowl is old Hollywood, palm trees, and box seats with regular season sub-scribers who bring gourmet dinners and a candelabra. Summer night music concerts have been performed here since 1922, when it was a natural amphitheater. The original shell, designed by Wayfarer's Chapel architect Lloyd Wright in 1924, was first replaced by another by Lloyd Wright in 1928, and then a much inferior cement one by someone else in 1931. Since 1982, it has had one designed by Frank O. Gehry and Associates.

The bowl's charm can be felt in the three 1935 Federal Arts Project statues by George Stanley, representing music, drama, and dance that you will pass on your way in. A graceful concrete figure of a kneeling woman playing a harp crowns a spectacular Art Deco fountain at the entrance off Highland and seems to beckon passing motorists to abandon their destinations and turn in and listen to music in-stead.

Going to the bowl can present its difficulties, however, because the long estab-lished subscribers are so well entrenched in the best box seats. Likewise, the bowl can really be too big for some classical pieces; the outer seats are only OK for the more "booming" performers with a lot of brass, whose sound really carries.

For this reason, if you are not a subscriber, I really recommend actually going down to the box office and finding out what is available for the season on the day they start selling tickets. There are a lot of concerts and sometimes some boxes will still be available. You also might want to ask when they start selling season tickets for next season. If you can sit in one of the box seats or in one of the rows that is a reasonable distance from the stage, an evening of classical music at the bowl is one of the most wonderful evenings you will ever have.

The bowl has a restaurant called **The Patio**. Right next to it is **The Hollywood Bowl Museum**, which has exhibits on the history of the bowl. These include repro-ductions of the original drawings by Lloyd Wright. There are also two listening rooms where you can hear great concerts.

On the other side of Highland from the bowl is a particularly fun and interesting museum with a nice picnic area:

> **Hollywood Studio Museum**
> **2100 North Highland Avenue**
> **Hollywood, CA 90068**
> **Saturday & Sunday 10 a.m. to 4 p.m.**
> **(213) 874-2276**

This big yellow structure was originally a horse barn located at the corner of Vine and Selma. In December of 1913, a fellow named Cecil B. De Mille rented it, horses and all, and set about the business of making movies. The first feature-length western shot in Hollywood, *The Squaw Man,* was made here. The actor's dressing rooms were next to the horse's stalls and the office work and shooting all took place outside the same building.

The holiday arrived in its present location by a roundabout route. It was picked up and trucked to the Paramount Studios lot in 1926 where it sat until the '70s. Then it went to a lot across from Capitol Records. Finally, in 1983 it was brought here and restored by Hollywood Heritage.

They have a little screening room where they show a 20-minute film on the museum and general Hollywood history. There are costumes and antique movie projectors and cameras. Memories of old pirate films will come back when you see the models of Spanish galleons that were used to make them. The most famous artifact is the chariot used in *Ben Hur.* There are picnic tables in the adjoining park.

The Hollywood Studio Museum is at the base of a hill which is covered with unique Mediterranean-style homes built right into the hill. If you walk up Milner Road, just south of the museum, you will be in Whitley Heights, one of the most romantic neighborhoods in the Southland, and where I call home.

Built during the 1920s and '30s by Hobart J. Whitley, the entire community is listed in the National Register of Historic Places for its architecture and what it represents about the history of Hollywood. Gloria Swanson, Rudolph Valentino, and Ethel Barrymore are just three of the stars that have lived here.

The roads are very narrow and twist and turn up and down the steep hillsides. There are stairways that go up between the houses and their fountains, gardens, and courtyards.

There are so many unique architectural statements in the hills around here, it is amazing that the same region of the world that encompasses some of the endlessly repetitive beige "planned communities" of the suburbs also includes this area. Many Europeans say it reminds them of Italy's hills.

If you cross Highland from Milner, walk up Camrose and turn right at High Tower Road, you will see:

> **The High Tower**
> **[elevator at the north end of High Tower Road]**
> **Hollywood**

Like Whitley Heights on the other side of Highland, the model for this community designed by Carl Kay was sunny southern Europe—in this case specifically Bologna, Italy. That city is celebrated for its villas on hills that are reachable by elevators in towers. That is what the High Tower is, an elevator tower. Built in

1920, it looks like an Italianate Washington Monument squeezed between the hills.

The High Tower takes the rider up the hill, or if you do not live here and do not have a key, you can take the stairwalk. This is one of the most magical walks you could ever go on. You will pass under a canopy of trees between gardens and houses with no garages. It is like being in a gigantic treehouse. Just remember, when walking through neighborhoods like this, be extra respectful of people's privacy.

As you approach the cul de sac where the tower is, you will pass between the streets signs for Los Altos Place, which is a walkway that High Tower Road cuts across. The entrance on your left will take you up the hill to Broadview Terrace, past the tower on your right. The house at number 2200 was designed by Lloyd Wright. Make a right at Alta Loma Terrace and come back down the hill. You come out in the parking lot just above Highland-Camrose Park, and walk down the driveway to Highland. A little ways south on Highland, you will pass another landmark of the Hollywood Hills in the striking:

American Legion Headquarters Building
2035 North Highland Avenue
Hollywood, CA 90068

Though this building was built in 1929, for some reason it looks new—not because of its Classical architecture with Beaux Arts influences, however. It is beautiful in the same way as the L.A. Central Library is, and there are no recent buildings that have that kind of appeal. It is the ceramic tile detailing that somehow has kept its luster.

This building is best known for being the site of *Tamara*, the longest running play in Los Angeles history. It ran from 1983 to 1993 and was based on a true story and set in an Italian villa in 1927. Members of the audience followed the characters through the building where the story unfolded; it was a perfect show for the Hollywood Hills.

Walking down Highland from here, you will pass several motels and small hotels and see a large one coming up on your right, the Holiday Inn. For a great view of the Hollywood Hills and the city below it's hard to top:

Windows
Holiday Inn
1755 North Highland Avenue
Hollywood, CA 90028
Monday-Saturday 6 to 11 p.m.
Sunday 11 a.m. to 11 p.m.
(213) 462-7181

This is one of those rooftop revolving restaurants that were symbols of the future in architecture of the '60s and '70s. They have a great Sunday brunch and jazz trio for entainment. It sits on top of a 470-room rectangle of a hotel that is pleasant and businesslike, without being fussy.

If you turn onto Franklin going west, then turn right on Hillcrest Boulevard and right on Glencoe Way, you will come upon the third of the great Frank Lloyd Wright houses of Hollywood:

> **Freeman House**
> **1962 Glencoe Way**
> **Hollywood, CA 90068**
> **(213) 743-4471**

Built in 1924 and now owned by the University of Southern California, this 1924 knit block mixture of Islamic and Mayan architecture above the Methodist Church at Highland and Franklin is quite a sight. Most of the furniture was designed in 1927 by Rudolph Schindler.

If you go back down to Franklin and continue west, on your right you will see The Magic Castle, which will be described in October when I talk about Halloween. At the same place, you will also see a sign directing you to turn right to go to:

> **Yamashiro Restaurant**
> **1999 North Sycamore Avenue**
> **Hollywood, CA 90068**
> **Sunday-Thursday 5:30 to 10 p.m.**
> **Friday & Saturday 5:30 to 11 p.m.**
> **Bar open till 1 a.m.**
> **(213) 466-5125**

It is hard to believe that this stunning Japanese palace and garden was once someone's house, but it was. The building is now a restaurant whose name means, appropriately enough, "castle on a hill." Its original name was the somewhat more prosaic "Bernheimer Bungalow" after the two brothers who built it as a residence in 1913. Adolph and Eugene were importers of oriental art, which in Hollywood qualifies you to live in a house like a medieval castle out of a Kurosawa film.

Being "in the business" so to speak, the Bernheimers spared no expense. A 600-year-old pagoda was imported from Japan and placed beside the small lake where the water from the various waterfalls, moats, and cascades surrounding it ends up. Hundreds of skilled craftsmen were imported from all over Asia to carve the assorted cottages and ceremonial structures that enhance the 12 acres of the estate. It opened as a restaurant in 1960.

The view from here is stunning, particularly at night when the lights are glittering and the haze is less apparent. You can go here for drinks and late supper after an evening at a movie on Hollywood Boulevard and look down at that famous street and wonder.

Highland flows up from Hollywood Boulevard, goes under the freeway and merges with Cahuenga Boulevard on its way into the San Fernando Valley. Along the way on your right is the third outdoor theatre of the Hollywood Hills, the:

> **John Anson Ford Theater**
> **2580 Cahuenga Boulevard**
> **Hollywood, CA 90068**
> **Season usually runs from the end of June through the**
> **middle of September**
> **Saturday & Sunday**
> **(213) 466-1767**

This is kind of a sleeper among theatre venues because it is such a charming surprise, although nowhere near as famous as its two hillside neighbors. Nestled into a tight little canyon, the Ford is narrow with a steep hill rising behind the stage. With its 1,300 seats, it is less than one-tenth as big as the Hollywood Bowl.

Its architectural style reminds me of a child's version of a Gothic castle—like a giant toy fort. Two towers flank the performance area and there are heavy wooden grills and wrought iron chandeliers throughout. The stage and side walls are made from stone set with thick grout; stone walkways terrace up the hill behind the stage. The Ford is yet another surviving treasure of the many W.P.A. projects that brightened up the Southland.

The Ford does an eclectic mixture of smaller productions such as chamber music, dance, and plays. The picnic areas are especially pleasant.

A short drive up Cahuenga, there is a small bridge that crosses the freeway. Once across, signs give you the choice: Woodrow Wilson Drive to the right, Mulholland Drive to the left. Either will do, because Woodrow Wilson will reconnect with Mulholland going north, and either road will give you a chance to see the:

> **Malin House ("Chemosphere")**
> **776 Torreyson Drive**
> **Hollywood, CA 90046**

These hills are full of wonderful houses, but all through my boyhood in the early '60s, this was the best house in the world. Besides the L.A. Airport Theme Building (described in February), there is no building like this one that epitomizes the space age vitality of Los Angeles during that decade. Architect John Lautner took a small hillside lot in 1960 and created a flying saucer on a pedestal. There are great shots of it in director Brain de Palma's film *Body Double*.

Though the Chemosphere is at the end of a private drive, there are places you can get a look at it on Woodrow Wilson Drive between Laurel Canyon and Mulholland and on Torreyson itself, which connects to Mulholland just north of the intersection with Woodrow Wilson.

The road named after the czar of water, Mulholland Drive was a place of romantic legend when I was growing up. Though most of the vacant lots with the great views of the Valley have been developed, it still has a certain mystique to it.

Lake Hollywood, on the other side of the freeway, came about in 1925 during the aggressive waterworks program headed by William Mulholland. The dam is actually quite picturesque with its row of gargoyle heads. It was used for the climax in Brian de Palma's film *Body Double* and its surrounding territory appeared in *Chinatown*. In the film *Earthquake*, the dam was destroyed, flooding the city below.

There are several ways up there, but from here, the easiest is to go back down to Cahuenga and make a left, then make a right on Barham. Make a right on Lake Hollywood Drive and follow it all the way to where you start to see parked cars lining the street. Park and follow the walkers, joggers, and runners on their way around the perimeter.

Will Geer Theatricum Botanicum

The late Will Geer started a Southland summer theatrical tradition that continues in Topanga Canyon:

Will Geer Theatricum Botanicum
1419 North Topanga Canyon Boulevard
Topanga Canyon, CA 90290
(310) 455-3723
(310) 455-2322

Will Geer is probably most famous for his sage presence on the reassuring TV show "The Waltons." The outdoor amphitheater that bears his name is appropriately countrified in setting, but the shows come from Elizabethan England. Mr. Geer's directorial duties are carried on by his wife.

And of course, not too far from here is one of the true classics of romantic dining in Southern California:

Inn Of The Seventh Ray
128 Old Topanga Canyon Road

Topanga, CA 90290
Monday-Friday 11:30 a.m. to 10 p.m.
Saturday 9:30 a.m. to 10 p.m.
Sunday 10:30 a.m. to 10 p.m.
(310) 455-1311

This lovely garden restaurant was designed around an old church. With a meandering creek trickling past, classical music in the air, and herb gardens all around, it epitomizes Topanga and the canyon mystique perfectly. They have vegetarian entrees as well as seafood, poultry, and meat.

If you would like to stay in a place that has some of the feeling of old Topanga, take Topanga Canyon Road down to the beach. Right across the street from the sand, tucked into a niche between some hills is the:

Topanga Ranch Motel
18711 Pacific Coast Highway
Malibu, CA 90265
(310) 456-5486

This cluster of 30-moderately priced little wood cottages arranged around a long circular driveway was built in the 1920s when there was very little of anything out here. They are fairly plain and a little long in the tooth, but are kept up beautifully and have "character." Some of them have kitchens.

Ojai Music Festival

Since 1946, a wonderful tradition has taken place around the first weekend of June:

Ojai Music Festival
Libbey Bowl (within Libbey Park)
normally first weekend of June
P.O. Box 185
Ojai, CA 93023
(805) 646-2094

What a perfect weekend this festival makes—so perfect in fact that it is one of the most popular of my weekend tours. It does not get much better than three days of concerts in one of the Southland's most romantic spots. We normally stay in coastal town of Ventura because it is only 20 minutes away from the festival. It is described in July.

The Ojai Valley is located north and inland of Ventura. The name is a Chumash word meaning "moon" and a more appropriate name would be hard to find. Ojai

Topanga Ranch Motel

Valley is a compact, magical little area with a tradition of attracting artists and those seeking spiritual enlightenment. Interestingly enough, the original name of the town was "Nordhoff," after a journalist named Charles Nordhoff. Residents changed the name during WWI because they thought it sounded too German.

Geographically somewhat isolated, you drive in via one of two roads: SR 33 or SR 150. They form a "Y" within the Ojai Valley in the place where they cross. SR 33 runs from Ventura to Taft and SR 150 goes from Carpenteria to Santa Paula, which I described in April. While the easiest entrance to the valley is up SR 33 from US 101 in Ventura, the remaining two branches of the "Y" offer beautiful mountain views.

The cultural center of Ojai, **Libbey Park** is a lovely place with spreading oaks. It is located across Ojai Avenue (SR 150) from the gracefully arched Arcade, which is the commercial hub of the city. If you notice any similarity between this structure and Alcazar Garden in Balboa Park, it is because they were both designed by Richard Requa. Both the park and the Arcade were built by glass maker Edward Drummond Libbey in 1917, who also built the original Ojai Valley Inn.

The outdoor Libbey Bowl, located in the park is an active performance site. This month, it presents classical music; in August, it will offer the Shakespeare Festival; and in October, it will host the "Bowlful of Blues" festival.

On Saturday and Sunday of the festival from 9 a.m. to 5 p.m., Libbey Park is also the site of **Art in the Park and Ventura County Potter's Guild.** This is one of the best craft and art shows I have ever seen. Some of these artists and potters have won awards for their work.

The artistic and mystical elements of Ojai are expressed in a unique store located one block east of the Arcade:

> **Heart of Light**
> **451 East Ojai Avenue (SR 150)**

Ojai, CA 93023
Sunday-Thursday 10:30 a.m. to 5:30 p.m.
Friday-Saturday 10:30 a.m. to 7 p.m.
(805) 646-3812

Soft music plays and a fountain continuously babbles in the cool interior of Heart of Light. The books, stones, and gifts are all somehow related to healing. They also offer workshops and readings in channeling, tarot, and numerology.

Ojai is full of wonderful artists' studios and galleries. One of the most interesting is the:

HumanArts Gallery
310 East Ojai Avenue
Ojai, CA 93023
Daily 11 a.m. to 5 p.m.
(805) 646-1525

The works of over 160 artists are on display here. These include wood carvings by Bruce Vincent, sculpture by Theodore Gall, and award-winning pottery by Otto and Vivika Heino—who have their own studio in town. Other artists represented are silversmith Caludia Gall, painter and printmaker Christine Brennan, ceramist Leslie Thompson, and of course, Beatrice Woods.

The owners, Stan and Hallie Katz, are artists themselves. Their medium is gems and precious metals, and they have been designing custom jewelry for over 20 years.

Montgomery Street forms the east border of Libbey Park. Here is where you will find the:

Ojai Center for the Arts
113 South Montgomery Street
Ojai, CA 93023
(805) 646-0117

This indoor facility presents shows from a variety of art forms, including painting and sculpture, as well as drama, and dance. They usually schedule a special program to coincide with the festival. Next door to the art center is the:

Ojai Valley Museum
105 South Montgomery Street
Ojai, CA 93023
Wednesday-Monday 1 to 5 p.m.
(805) 646-2290

Located in a historic old firehouse built during the Depression by the W.P.A., this museum tells the history of the area. It includes material from both of the original resident peoples: the Chumash and the Oak Grove Indians.

The Oak Grove Indians were the earlier tribe. They lived here between 5,000 and 9,000 years ago. They gathered seeds and ground them into meal. Some of their grinding stones, called "matates" are on display. The Chumash are represented by artifacts and their signature art form, the pictograph.

The museum's claim to fame came during the '70s when the curator, Robert Browne, found a 7,000-year-old relic in his backyard in Oak View. It was a diorite effigy of a toad, a replica of which is in the museum. The significance of it is that it is one of the earliest works of art ever found in North America. It lead to a large excavation of Browne's back yard that yielded more than 4,000 artifacts.

Besides historical items from indigenous people, the museum contains an odd assortment of other relics such as an old ciderwand wine press and a collection of animal eggs.

Next to the museum is a pottery shop and art gallery:

> **Massarella Pottery and Gallery**
> **105 South Montgomery Street**
> **Ojai, CA 93023**
> **Daily 10 a.m. to 5 p.m.**
> **(805) 646-9453**

If you time it right, you can watch Frank Massarella turning pottery on the potters wheel. His wife Debbie helps with the glazing. Their work is wonderful: plates, mugs, and bowls by Frank Massarella adorn my table.

Long before herbal cooking was fashionable, an Ojai institution has been serving up fantastic cooking seasoned with nature's aromas:

> **The Ranch House**
> **South Lomita (no street address)**
> **P.O. Box 458**
> **Ojai, CA 93024**
> **Wednesday-Friday 6 to 8 p.m.**
> **Saturday 6 p.m. and 8:30 p.m.**
> **Sunday 1 to 4 p.m., 6 to 7:30 p.m.**
> **closed Monday and Tuesday**
> **(805) 646-2360 or (805) 646-4384**

In 1959, former jazz musician Alan Hooker converted this ranch style home into a showplace for his recipes, which are available in cookbooks here as well. Most of the dining takes place outdoors in a beautiful garden surrounded by meandering streams and lush foliage, some of which you will have a chance to eat. This is because the Ranch House has a tradition of growing its own herbs and some vegetables.

Freshness is a part of their motif here. In addition to the freshly picked herbs, they also feature homemade breads and desserts. Entrees include fresh fish, chicken, meat, and a variety of vegetarian dishes. The ambiance matches the quality of the food. The service is very attentive and there is usually live music, such as a flute player.

Another outdoor Ojai attraction goes perfectly with good food and good music:

Bart's Books
302 West Matilija Street
Ojai, CA 93023
Tuesday-Sunday 10 a.m. to 5:30 p.m.
(805) 646-3755

This wonderful used bookstore has the feeling of being in Europe with its oak-shaded patio enclosed by numerous roofed bookstalls. They follow a practice of placing the cheapest books on open shelves facing the street. After hours, customers pick out the books they want and then put the money into a slot there for that purpose. There is also an enclosed bookstore portion that features rare books.

Driving east on SR 150 up the hill, you will come to a very famous **Vista Point**. Watch for the stone bench on the right. The view from here is the same one Ronald Coleman had of Shangri-La in the movie *Lost Horizon*. Continuing on SR 150, about one mile beyond the top of Dennison Grade, you will find a pink mailbox on the left. This is the landmark for the:

Beatrice Woods Studio
Ojai-Santa Paula Road
(SR-150)
Upper Ojai
Daily 11 a.m. to 5 p.m.
(805) 646-3381

Of all of the places we have visited on my tours, the one that everyone seems to like the most is the stop here. Beatrice Woods is so often described by her age—over 100 years—that you might get the impression that it is the most remarkable thing about her. Actually, her ceramic art is delightful and has a whimsical quality to it. It is also quite bawdy in its humor. The pretty location of her studio at the end of a private drive seems to show it off especially well.

Though her showcase is worth a visit whether you have a chance to speak to her or not, it is a real treat if you can. Ms. Woods has been all over the world and has known some of the legends of the art world. It is very interesting to hear what literally all of the experience in the world has produced in terms of personal belief. She feels that education for the young should be a top priority, and is a passionate foe of censorship of any kind, for any reason. When asked what she attributes her longevity to, she will reply, "I eat chocolate every day and prefer the company of young men."

Ojai has always been a spiritual place. A lovely spot open to the public and devoted to spiritual reflection is the:

> **Krotona Institute and School of Theosophy**
> **46 Krotona Hill**
> **Ojai, CA 93023**
> **Monday-Saturday from 10 a.m. to 4 p.m.**
> **Sunday 1 p.m. to 4 p.m.**
> **(805) 646-1139**

Located off Highway 33 near the "Y" at Hermosa Road is this peaceful 118-acre estate with its rose gardens and lily ponds. There are lots of trees and the whole place is on a rising hillside that offers wonderful views of the mountains and the valley.

Inside the main building are the library and various rooms where classes are offered. The library is most people's fantasy of a dream reading room. A wooden ladder extends to the upper reaches of the bookshelves. It has a vaulted ceiling with heavy wooden beams and a chandelier. A towering window lets in light and a woodland vista.

There are separate buildings that are dormitories for students and a bookstore. The library and bookstore both feature books on philosophy and the religions of the world.

Theosophy has an old history: it was named for an intellectual settlement founded by Pythagoras in Sicily around the year 500. It does not have a dogma, but rather seeks the truth as expressed in all religions. The list of people who have embraced its quest is quite impressive; among its followers were William Butler Yeats and Thomas Edison. The Southern California branch originally started in

Hollywood, but moved here in 1926.

There is more about Ojai in the August and October chapters.

Pacific Coast Performing Arts Theaterfest

The next summer theater festival farther up the coast in the Southland, and the last major one that begins in June, is the:

Pacific Coast Performing Arts Theaterfest
Festival Theater
410 2nd Street
Solvang, CA 93463
and:
Severson and Marion Theaters
Marion Performing Arts Center
Allan Hancock College
800 South College Drive
Santa Maria, CA 93454
(800) 221-9469 or (805) 922-8313
(800) 549-PCPA (tickets)

The PCPA Theaterfest has grown considerably since 1964, when it started as a theater training program for Allan Hancock College in Santa Maria. It now features seven plays and musicals at two theaters. During the summer, they rotate the shows back and forth. The indoor Marion Theater has shows throughout the year. The outdoor Festival Theater in Solvang opens its season in June and runs through September. The theaters are small: the bigger of the two, indoor Santa Maria Theater, seats 500, the outdoor Solvang theater seats 780.

Whether you go to Santa Maria or Solvang, the Theatrefest rounds out a trip to both of these small towns. Neither place has any nightlife whatsoever and having a play to go see makes a stay in either locality seem much more complete.

I do weekend trips to both places, and, I must say, though it is very much for tourists, **Solvang** is probably more fun for a short getaway. It is a "Danish Village" and is a great town to walk in, full of the distinct air of what a "Danish-land" at Disneyland might be like. At night it is all lit up with tiny white lights. If you like the idea of a place with cute little stores filled with crystal and Danish memorabilia and enough bakeries to fatten up a city the size of Los Angeles, you will be in nirvana in Solvang.

One of the obligatory stops is:

The Danish Inn
1547 Mission Drive
Solvang, CA 93463
Daily 11 a.m. to 9 p.m.
(805) 688-4813

The smorgasbord for lunch and dinner are superb and the desserts are outstanding. For breakfast, all of the locals meet at:

Paula's Pancake House
1531 Mission Drive
Solvang, CA 93463
6 a.m. to 3 p.m.
(805) 688-2867

Non-dietary breakfast is served all day here from 6 a.m. On weekends and during the summer, there can be a wait if you get here much past 8 a.m. This is because they have regular pancakes, Danish pancakes, waffles of all kinds, egg dishes, extra thick bacon, and yes, Danish pastries that just seem like the right thing to eat in this environment.

The outdoor theatre in Solvang is an absolute joy. There are many places to stay and the town is so compact, everything is within walking distance. When it starts getting near to curtain time, it is a very pleasant experience to walk toward the theatre and see other people out in the sweet evening air all headed the same way along the streets of this fairy tale town.

As far as places to stay, we have used several of the better motels and they are all remarkably similar in pricing and quality.

Just on the outskirts of town is the beautiful:

Old Mission Santa Ines
1760 Mission Drive
Solvang, CA 93463
(805) 688-4815

The graceful architecture of the mission is quite a contrast to the Danish motif of the town. Of course, unlike Solvang, it was not built for tourists. Constructed in 1804 on a rise that overlooks a spectacular vista, it still conjures up a feeling of what this area was like 100 years ago. Besides the view and the general area around the mission, there is also an old graveyard, a lovely garden, and an ornate altar of gilt, green, and red.

Two minutes down the road, down a long drive through beautiful vineyards, is a delightful stop:

The Gainey Vineyard
3950 East Highway 246
Santa Ynez, CA 93460
Daily 10 a.m. to 5 p.m.
(805) 688-0558

The Gainey Vineyard is quite new, having been built in 1986. It is literally a wealthy family's "pet" winery, creating only 18,000 cases per year of excellent wine, which is sold only at the vineyard itself. And what a lovely place it is. The building is an immaculate white Spanish-styled structure with a tiled tasting room and gift shop.

After a tasting, a picnic on the tables out in the vineyard is like a little bit of heaven. The low rolling hills covered with grape plants surround you. Gliders from the nearby airport soundlessly add a flash of silver elegance to the brilliant blue sky.

The Santa Ynez Valley is just about the perfect place to spend some time moseying around and checking out little towns and wineries. Just north of Solvang, three miles east of US 101 is the hamlet of **Los Olivos**. It has a historic tavern (see November) and a winery that has its own unusual festival this month:

> **Bouillabaisse Festival**
> **Brander Vineyards**
> **2401 Refugio Road**
> **Los Olivos, CA 93441**
> **Daily 10 a. to 5 p.m.**
> **(805) 688-2455**

Brander has a French leaning. Not only do they sponsor this annual festival, they had a big Bastille Day luncheon once with heavyweight French chefs that even Julia Child went to. The pink chateau surrounded by flower beds completes the Gallic mood.

If you visit Brander Vineyards and need a place to stay overnight, I recommend the beautiful:

> **Los Olivos Grand Hotel**
> **2860 Grand Avenue**
> **Los Olivos, CA 93441**
> **(805) 688-7788**

Though this little gem of a hotel is quite expensive, it is one of the most luxurious small hotels in Southern California. There are 21 plush rooms, all with gas fireplaces.

Santa Maria, where Allan Hancock College is located, is somewhat less picturesque than Solvang, but it does have less of a tourist atmosphere. Though it is also located in a valley, the area around it is flat farmland.

The most well known place to stay is the:

> **Santa Maria Inn**
> **801 South Broadway**
> **Santa Maria, CA 93454**
> **(805) 928-7777**

The inn has 170 rooms, a lobby with an Old English style walnut ceiling, marble floors, and is furnished with antiques.

Twelve miles southeast of Santa Maria is a great Southland winery stop:

> **Byron Vineyard and Winery**
> **5230 Tepusquet Road**
> **Santa Maria, CA 93454**
> **Daily 10 a.m. to 4 p.m.**
> **(805) 937-7288**

Winemaker Byron "Ken" Brown had his first vintage in 1984. Since then the winery has expanded, most dramatically in 1989. That year they bought the oldest commercial vineyard in Santa Barbara County, the Nielson Vineyard. Pinot Noir and Chardonnay are featured, but the Sauvignon Blanc and Cabernet Sauvignon are also noteworthy.

The landscaped picnic area is pretty enough, and cellar and tasting room are warm and friendly in knotty pine. There is more about the wine country of Santa Barbara County in the April, October, and November chapters.

LOMPOC FLOWER FESTIVAL

A festival that happens the last full weekend of June in **Lompoc** epitomizes the season:

> **Lompoc Flower Festival**
> **Lompoc Valley Chamber of Commerce**
> **111 South I Street**
> **Lompoc, CA 93436**
> **usually the last weekend of June**

(805) 735-8511 (festival office)
(805) 736-4567 (Chamber of Commerce)

One of the most amazing statistics of all about the Southland is that half of the world's flower seeds come from this small area of Santa Barbara County. Nearly 20 kinds of flowers are grown, seeded, and shipped annually. The town is surrounded by about 1,000 acres of flower fields, which in May and June are absolutely dazzling to the eye. The Chamber offers a map and self-guided tour that tells what flowers are growing where. Guided bus tours are also offered.

For the festival, they have a floral parade with locally made floats, an arts and crafts show, food booths, music, and (what else) a flower show. The festival, at first, was just for the two days but now includes several weekdays.

If you would like to do your own flower field driving tour, just take North H Street to Ocean Avenue, which is also Highway 246. Go west on 246. Beside the highway and along some of the side roads for the next 19 miles you will be treated to sweet smelling fields of petunias, zinnias, asters, marigolds, larkspur, and sweet peas.

The beaches of Northern Santa Barbara County are noteworthy for their wild beauty and windswept quality. A particularly enjoyable beach experience can be found quite near Lompoc. Take Highway 246 toward Vandenberg Air Force Base about eight miles, then turn right on Ocean Park Road. This is the "Ocean Park/ Coastal Access" exit. After an uninspiring drive of about a mile, you will come to the parking lot of **Ocean Beach County Park.**

Vandenberg Air Force Base takes up a full 35 miles of Southern California coastline. This county park is for public use, but is located within the base. It offers you a chance to walk on some small versions of the sand dunes that mark the central coast. There is also a picnic area.

Lompoc is also the home of the most completely renovated of the missions:

La Purisima Mission State Historic Park
2295 Purisima Road
Lompoc, CA 93436
(805) 733-3713

This is one of two missions operated by the State of California instead of the Catholic Church. It was the eleventh mission in the system and was founded in 1787. An earthquake flattened it in 1815 and its cleric, Fray Mariano Payeras, died eight years later in 1823.

In 1934, the Mexican government sold the property. Abandoned and falling apart, it was rescued and became one of the most successful of the many restoration projects of the Civilian Conservation Corps in the 1930s. The mission and surrounding buildings have been returned to their original state, using 18th century tools and building techniques.

Visiting here is a very interesting experience. You can walk on the dirt floor between the skinny cots of the "cuartel," which housed the soldiers. Cattle hides hang on drying racks not too far from the tallow vats where candles and soap were made. The shops of the candlemaker, potter, carpenter, and weavers are filled with fascinating tools and accouterments.

This mission has experienced some particularly bizarre happenings. When the C.C.C. workers were rebuilding the floor of the church, they found tiny skeletons under the tiles. They were the remains of infants who died of smallpox. When the church tomb of Fray Mariano Payeras was opened, it was discovered that his body had been cut in half at the waist and that the lower half was missing! It turned up in a crypt at the Mission Santa Barbara. No one knows why this was done.

Like at the Mission San Juan Capistrano, psychics and ghost hunters have identified plenty of spooks. These include a phantom gardener with his hoe, and a ghost in the kitchen of a nobleman, named Don Vicente, who was murdered there in the 1820s. There are also "cold spots" in the church over the infants' tombs. There is a museum near the entrance with some Chumash artifacts and displays that relate some of the mission's history.

South of Lompoc by about five miles is Jalama Road, one of my favorite short drives. It runs 15 miles through picture postcard valleys and jagged canyons.

There are many wonderful backroads in the central and upper parts of Santa Barbara County. One of the most whimsical places to spend the night is located in a tiny town right in the middle between Lompoc, Solvang, and Santa Maria:

> **Union Hotel**
> **362 Bell Street**
> **Los Alamos, CA 93440**
> **(805) 344-2744**

The hotel is the restored version of an 1880 lodging for Wells-Fargo stagecoach passengers. The original burned down in 1886, reopened 15 years later as the Los Alamos, and was purchased by the present owner in 1972.

To call what he has done a restoration would be putting it mildly. With only an 1884 photo of the original, no effort was spared to recreate an authentic frontier look. Twelve 50- to 100-year-old barns were disassembled and their wood and fixtures were used throughout the exterior and interior.

The "Victorian Mansion" is a pretty yellow Queen Anne originally built in Nipoma, California (40 miles north) in 1864. It was discovered abandoned in 1981, cut in five pieces, and rebuilt next to the Union Hotel. The clock tower was only one of many major hand-crafted additions—which explains why the project was not complete until April of 1989!

JULY

Fourth of July Fireworks (July 4)

Summer Seaside Tradition

Summer Music Festivals

The Tropics in Southern California

Lotus Festival

Cocteau's Birthday (July 5)

*Laguna Beach Pageant of the Masters
and Sawdust Festival*

Racing Season in Del Mar

Raymond Chandler Writing Contest

Old Miner's Days

Betty Boop Festival

Chapter Seven

JULY

One of the perks that came with the job of being emperor of Rome was that, not only would everyone do exactly what you said, they would also name very important things to commemorate the most basic elements of your life.

Julius Caesar, for example, was born in the seventh month of the year 44 B.C., so they named the month of July after him. Julius was in good company since the Romans liked to name months after only the really big people—gods usually.

July is the first month that really feels like summer At night we toss and turn, and finally get out of bed, turn on the lights, and go out in the hot summer air. It's amazing how different the arrival of the "real" summer heat can make us feel about almost everything.

The relentless heat can turn city streets that seemed so light and airy to walk during the day in spring into hot, sooty, concrete hell in summer. The bright heat compels us to start romances and torments us to end them. But most of all, it seems to make us acutely aware of our surroundings, as if because they are more blindingly illuminated, we are seeing their faults for the first time. This is probably why we get the urge to just leave during the summer. We do most of our moving or traveling during the summer months that extend into September.

FOURTH OF JULY FIREWORKS (JULY 4)

While June 21st is the "official" first day of summer, summer doesn't really start happening in the Southland until July. June can be a muggy halfway, but July is really summer. The 4th of July is the unofficial kickoff celebration that gets things rolling. After all, it is the only holiday we celebrate with big fireworks displays.

Fireworks on Independence Day in Southern California, like most places in America, are omnipresent, but the Southland used to have a tradition of pyrotechnic displays at almost all of the piers along the coast. This tradition has largely given way to having "street fairs" of arts and crafts. The reason cited is usually that a "bad element" was attracted to the pier shows.

Most summer public firework shows now are being held at stadiums or places that charge an admission fee. The most spectacular of these is at the Rose Bowl (see January) in Pasadena at 9 p.m. This is one of the largest fireworks celebrations in the entire county.

Pasadena is pretty hot during the summer. Cooling down starts at the soda fountain, a classic American rite of summer. The quintessential example is the:

Fair Oaks Pharmacy
1526 Mission Street
South Pasadena, CA 91030
Monday-Thursday 9 a.m. to 9 p.m.
Friday-Saturday 9 a.m. to 10 p.m.
Sunday 12 to 9 p.m.
(818) 799-1414

Its chrome bar stools with the red leather seats, brass rail, and marble counter may bring back pleasant memories from either your own life or countless images in films like *It's A Wonderful Life*.

The location has a long history as a pharmacy/soda fountain dating to 1915. After numerous remodel jobs, the flavor (literally) of the original was recreated in 1990 by owners Michael and Meredith Miller. The look is heightened by working antique accouterments such as old-fashioned syrup dispensers, bubble gum machines, and an orange juice squeezer.

Soda jerks serve banana splits, ice cream sodas, and sundaes, as well as cherry-lime rickeys and egg creams. Besides the old time treats, such modern libations as cappuccino are offered.

The 4th of July makes me think of innocent Americana—of old Coca Cola signs, of baseball, and all manner of straw hat summer pastimes and playthings. Pasadena is home to a colorful specialty store that features one of those traditional playthings:

Chuck's Antiques and Marble Memorabilia
23 North Altadena Drive
Pasadena, CA 91107
Tuesday-Saturday 12 to 6 p.m.
closed Sunday & Monday
(818) 564-9582

Owner Chuck Porter began collecting only a fairly short time ago, in 1984. He opened this remarkable shop in 1988 and it is now the home of half a million marbles.

There is a rainbow of them from ruby knucklers for 5 cents to $50 Depression-era globes that glow under light. There are very rare sulfides: crystal with magical clay figurines of whimsical creatures imbedded inside. They were made by a few East German families in the early 1800s.

SUMMER SEASIDE TRADITION

Though firework displays off the end of piers may be pretty much a thing of the past, the tradition of 4th of July weekend as a big time to hit the beach still continues. The seaside always has been a place of summertime relaxation and renewal.

Piers and oceanside playgrounds have always been part of the American culture of summer fun. It is no coincidence that there is a unspoken tradition that new or rebuilt piers tend to open in big ceremonies on the 4th of July. Also, prior to the advent of amusement or theme parks like Disneyland, people flocked to beach towns with piers where all kinds of oceanside diversions were available.

Coronado

If there ever was a town that could be said to still have that "old seaside" feeling, it would be Coronado. Sometimes referred to as "Coronado Island," it is actually part of the tip of the peninsula that encloses San Diego Bay from the south. It derives its name from a group of islands off Baja, California called Los Coronados and was incorporated in 1890.

While the history and physical presence of the Mission Inn hotel in Riverside is inextricably linked to that city (see April), the history and landscape of Coronado is completely dominated by the stately presence of the:

Hotel Del Coronado
1500 Orange Avenue
Coronado, CA 92118
(619) 435-6611

While San Diego was being settled in the late 19th century, Coronado was thought of as an island where men would go by boat to hunt jackrabbits and quail. One day, two men who enjoyed such a pastime, H.L. Story and Elisha S. Babcock, Jr., mused that it would also be a good place for a resort hotel so spectacular that even wealthy people accustomed to the marvels of Chicago or New York City would be impressed.

They did what one or two other people would end up doing in California: they put together a group of investors and bought some land. The cost in 1885 for 4,100 acres—virtually the entire peninsula—was $110,000. They broke some of it into lots, which in less than two years, they sold for about $2,000,000. The plan was to use the money from the sale of the lots to build the hotel.

In March of 1887, work started on the Hotel Del Coronado. Workmen worked round the clock assisted by a new invention: the electric light. The architects,

James, Watson and Merritt Reid, were given nothing but a description of the dream hotel as Babcock pictured it in his head. Incredibly, they never drew up a complete architectural plan, but instead created drawings of "the vision" and made the details up as they went along!

It formally opened just eleven months later, in February of 1888, at a total cost of $1,000,000 for the building and all the furnishings. Since 1963, close to one hundred times that amount has been spent lovingly restoring it.

Fortune is not always kind to visionaries and the two old hunting pals were flattened by an economic downturn. In 1900, John D. Spreckles, who would later put up the money for the organ pavilion in Balboa Park (see June), stepped in and took over. The "Son of Sugar" turned the former hunting spot into a glamorous resort destination. Babcock was reduced to being just another employee.

They still came to hunt, but Spreckles was smart and knew what it would take to make the place really take off. South of the hotel, along the section known as the Silver Strand, he built an outdoor resort complex, first called Camp Coronado, then referred to as "Tent City." It resembled a giant summer camp for all ages and consisted of a vast assortment of furnished white and red-striped tents with wood floors. Attractions included music concerts and an indoor saltwater plunge.

Tent City was a big hit, and for most of the next three decades, Coronado was the most fashionable resort in America. The Depression hit hard and the hotel had its ups and downs (mostly downs) for the next few decades until 1963, when well-known developer and financier Larry Lawrence took over. This was perhaps the brightest moment in the landmark's history. Not only has he both restored and maintained the Del with great care, he developed it as a viable business as well by increasing its attractiveness as a meeting site.

Today, the Del is a classically romantic place for a getaway. It is a sprawling, five-story fairy castle of white wood siding and over two million red shingles that cover its peaks and towers. With 33 acres of lushly landscaped beachfront land, it is the largest beach resort on the Pacific coast in North America.

It has a 19th century quality throughout. The lobby is a heavily polished, two-story fortress of Illinois oak illuminated by a massive chandelier. An iron bird cage elevator is still in use. A thickly carpeted hallway leads to stairs that go down to shops and The History Gallery, which tell the hotel's wonderful story.

As impressive as the lobby is, the most spectacular part of the interior is the Crown Room. Its dome is one of the largest unsupported ceilings on the continent. The beautiful sugar pine beams and paneling that form the cover to this amazing room are an imposing 33 feet above. They were put together without nails, using only small wooden dowels. This majestic 66-by-156 foot hall was where in 1970, the late President Richard Nixon met with Mexican President Gustavo Ordaz. Sunday brunch is justifiably famous and includes a harpist.

The original main wooden building is built around a large garden courtyard with a gazebo in the center. There are palm trees here that were planted in 1888 by San Diego's most famous gardener, Kate Sessions. It is a popular wedding site, not only because it is a gorgeous setting with excellent banquet facilities a few steps away, but because the Del has a romantic soul you can feel.

The ocean side of the hotel is where the pool and tennis courts are located. If you play tennis, the courts are superb. They always make me feel like I am on some tropical island under British rule. The outside area is like a cross between Hawaii and Brighton Beach. There is also a fully equipped gym and a game room full of electronic entertainment.

No hotel has had a more dramatic or illustrious history. In April of 1891, Benjamin Harrison was the first of 13 U.S. Presidents who have stayed here. Frank Baum, the author of the *Wizard of Oz*, came to the Del many times after the turn of the century to write. It is said he drew inspiration for the Land of Oz from its fanciful architecture. He eventually moved to Coronado and designed the crown-shaped chandeliers in the Crown Room.

Edward, Prince of Wales came in 1920. It is said that he first laid eyes on Coronado housewife Wallis Warfield Simpson in the hotel's ballroom. He became King Edward V, only to abdicate in 1936 for the most famous (and romantic) reason in history: "the woman I love," who was, of course, the fetching Ms. Simpson. Her former residence has been restored and now adorns the northwestern end of the hotel grounds.

Many films and TV shows have been shot at the Del, the most famous example being *Some Like it Hot*, the Marilyn Monroe comic classic directed by Billy Wilder. It was filmed here in 1958.

There are 700 rooms, 399 of which are in the main building. The other 301 are in a much newer tower just to the south. The best rooms can be expensive, but it is worth it to get an ocean front room. The distinction is made price-wise between ocean "view" and ocean "front." Sometimes the former appellation is applied somewhat optimistically, so I would pay the extra money and avoid disappointment. All of the old rooms are very Victorian and because many have been updated with the addition of a bathroom (there were only 75 with them originally), the shapes and sizes vary greatly.

The Del being a giant sandcastle of sorts, it is quite fitting that the largest sand castle building competition in America is held just south of the peninsula on the South Bay:

Sand Castle Days
Imperial Beach
normally second weekend of July
Saturday & Sunday
(619) 424-6663

Who does not recall going to the beach and building sand castles at least once when they were little? I remember digging and packing the wet, bubbly sand into architectural masterpieces with my dad at Santa Monica Beach as a high point of childhood summers. Besides nostalgia for our lost innocence, perhaps it is the ephemeral nature of sand castles that gives them their romantic mystique: "building sandcastles" is even a phrase in common speech to describe the activities of someone who dreams of something unreachable.

The Imperial Beach Sand Castle Days is the Olympics of sand castle making competitions. As a matter of fact, it is also called the U.S. Open Sandcastle Contest. Up to 400,000 people come to see hundreds of sand sculptors scooping, wetting, and packing the sand into some pretty amazing forms.

When the sandcastle competition is not going on, the 1,500-foot wooden **Imperial Beach Municipal Pier** is the dominant physical feature of broad, sandy Imperial Beach. When Imperial County was growing in the early 20th century, many people from there flocked to this beach to escape the incredible heat during the summer. So many in fact, that what started as a nickname became the name of the southwestern-most city in the U.S.

Palm Avenue runs due west from Interstate 5 as Highway 75 and either continues straight as Palm Avenue into Imperial Beach or curves north into Coronado as Highway 75 (now Silver Strand Boulevard). Not as many people enter Coronado via its southern end; most take the two mile long San Diego-Coronado Bridge built in 1969.

Before the bridge, there was ferry service, which made a big comeback in recent years when the bridge was paid off by the tolls. They rebuilt the old Coronado-to-San Diego ferry dock in 1987 as:

The Old Ferry Landing
1201 1st Street
Coronado, CA 92118
(619) 435-8895

This Victorian/California-styled center has red roofs like the Del. It features 25 shops, fast food, and bike and roller skate rentals. A terrific bike path runs from here down along the Silver Strand. There is also a restaurant with perhaps the best view of San Diego Bay and the city skyline:

> **Peohe's**
> **1201 1st Street**
> **Coronado, CA 92118**
> **Monday-Thursday 11 a.m. to 10 p.m.**
> **Friday & Saturday 11 a.m. to 11 p.m.**
> **Sunday 10:30 a.m. to 11 p.m.**
> **(619) 437-4474**

Opened in January of 1989 by the Chart House restaurant group, this place is quite different from the motif of those well-known eateries. Peohe's definitely has a Hawaiian theme, with waterfalls, tropical plants, and pretty little bridges. The friendly general manager, long time Chart House employee Roger Boomer, loves welcoming guests to the "island on the island," as the restaurant is nicknamed. The kitchen specializes in fresh Hawaiian fish like ono and ahi, but it also serves such non-island dishes as prime rib.

Besides being a place to eat and shop, the ferry boats arrive every hour and depart every half hour from here all day until 10:30 p.m. The ride takes 15 minutes. The service is provided by:

> **Cruise San Diego**
> **1050 North Harbor Drive**
> **San Diego, CA 92101**
> **(619) 234-4111**

This same company also offers the San Diego Harbor Excursion. For a ride that goes very well with the theme of Coronado, go south on Harbor from the ferry dock on the San Diego side at the corner of Harbor Drive and Broadway until you see the signs for **Seaport Village**.

Built on the site of the original San Diego-to-Coronado Ferry landing, Seaport Village is a "created" tradition, rather than an expression of what was already there. It is similar in some ways to its cousin of the same name in Long Beach (to be described later). The San Diego version is much larger and has less of the inexplicable New England-style fishing village theme that seems to fascinate Southland developers of seaside multiple-use shopping centers so much (the style is also found in Oxnard and Marina del Rey). Seaport Village features a 45-foot tall reproduction of a lighthouse in Everett, Washington called the Mukiltea Lighthouse.

Street entertainers such as jugglers and mimes mingle with the crowds. There is a grassy park that meanders out into the bay and some 75 shops, and several restaurants, the most architecturally unique being:

San Diego Pier Cafe
885 West Harbor
San Diego, CA 92101
Sunday-Thursday 7 a.m. 9 p.m.
Friday & Saturday 7 a.m. to 10 p.m.
(619) 239-3968

They serve breakfast, lunch, and dinner at this casual place that juts out over the water on its own little pier at the west end of Seaport Village. But the most endearing thing about Seaport Village, and what secured its place in this book, is that it contains a lovely relic of the past, the handcarved:

Broadway Flying Horses Carousel
Seaport Village
849 West Harbor Drive
San Diego, CA 92101
(619) 234-6133

If there were ever a San Diego Harbor attraction that belonged across the bay in Coronado, this is it. The "Golden Age" of carousels was the 45 year period between 1880 and 1925. During this time, over 6,000 were built, including this one built in 1890 by the master, Charles Looff. His work will be described more fully under Long Beach in this same section.

There is more about Coronado in the December Chapter.

San Diego on the Beach

If you are from the East Coast and your idea of how to spend the summer came from trips to the seashore in New Jersey, you'll feel right at home in:

Belmont Park
3126 Mission Boulevard
(between San Fernando and Ventura Place)
San Diego, CA 92109
Sunday-Thursday 10 a.m. to 8 p.m. (summer)
Friday & Saturday 11 a.m. to 10 p.m. (summer)
Sunday-Thursday 11 a.m. to 7 p.m. (winter)
Friday & Saturday 11 a.m. to 9 p.m. (winter)
(619) 488-0668

Having established Coronado's tent city in 1925, John D. Spreckels built a classic seaside amusement complex with a roller rink complete with organ, roller coaster, arcades, salt water plunge, and a dance casino. It rode high during WWII, when sailors whose ships were in port at the Navy base needed a place to take their girlfriends, but suffered when theme parks blossomed in the '60s. The city closed it in 1976.

After much ado between preservationists and city historians against the condo-building real estate developers, a restoration project was begun. The roller coaster survived and has been beautifully reborn:

> **The Giant Dipper**
> **Monday-Thursday 11 a.m. to 10 p.m.**
> **Friday & Saturday 11 a.m. to 11 p.m.**
> **Sunday 11 a.m. to 10 p.m.**

Originally designed by Frank Prior and Frederick Church and reopened on July 4, 1990 after restoration, The Giant Dipper had a big 65th birthday party. A National Historic Landmark, it looks like a birthday party by itself just sitting there with its half mile long pink and mint green wooden frame glistening in the summer sun. It is at night, however, that this magnificent relic really shines, because all of its dips and curves are lined with twinkling white lights. Though it is old, it is safe: the entire length of the tracks and 33 percent of the frame were replaced in the restoration.

Belmont Park was rebuilt is stages. Two years before the coaster reopened, an unlikely restoration project was completed:

> **The Plunge**
> **3115 Ocean Front Walk**
> **Mission Beach, CA 92109**
> **(619) 488-3110**

The Plunge is no less than a 175-foot long indoor salt water swimming pool originally built in 1925. Like the architect of the Santa Fe train station, the architect here, Lincoln Rogers, was inspired by the buildings of the 1915 Panama Pacific Exposition in Balboa Park, and he created a Spanish Renaissance palace. In 1988, it reopened as part of an upscale fitness club.

A few blocks north on Mission Boulevard is a shrine to California's signature summer diversion:

> **California Surf Museum**
> **Promenade Shopping Center**
> **4150 Mission Boulevard**

Pacific Beach, CA 92109
(619) 630-9313
(619) 942-9549

Surfing has a long history. Chronicles indicate that Hawaiians were doing it as early as 400 A.D. One of the oddest bits of surfing trivia is that the word "cowabunga" came from the old "Howdy Doody Show" of the 1950s. Early California surfboards were quite daunting in their appearance. Twelve feet of wood with no fins, they looked more like logs than today's high tech models.

The 400-foot fishing pier in Mission Bay, called **Crystal Pier** was originally built in 1925 as "Pickering's Pleasure Pier." The main feature of the original Crystal Pier was a dance hall with a bouncy cork dance floor called The Crystal Ballroom. It was to last for less than a year because marine borers attacked the untreated wood pilings, and it was condemned.

A project was started to rebuild and widen it which was completed in 1935. This pier was to last almost 50 years until it was wrecked in the storms of 1982. It was rebuilt and reopened in 1987. The pier closes at sunset to allow quiet and privacy for the guests of the:

Crystal Pier Motel
4500 Ocean Boulevard
San Diego, CA 92109
(619) 483-6983

There are places to stay that front on the ocean, but this is the only motel in Southern California that is above the ocean. There are 26 cottages perched on the pier, 20 of which are original. Motel guests are allowed to drive their cars onto the pier and park in front of their rooms.

There are many other places to stay in San Diego. My favorite is still the:

Pacific Terrace Inn
610 Diamond Street
San Diego, CA 92109
(619) 581-3500 or (800) 367-6467

When my girlfriend and I go to San Diego to see the Shakespeare Festival (see June), this is where we usually stay. It is a beautiful little hotel right on the beach at the top end of Pacific Beach just below La Jolla. Most of the rooms front the water to at least some degree and the way the hotel's pool area, building architecture, and location work together is a triumph of good taste.

Oceanside

Oceanside has a 1,942-foot long pier that is second in the Southland only to the Ventura Pier in length. First built in the 1890s, the **Oceanside Pier** was partially destroyed in the big storm of 1982 and rebuilt in 1987. Though it is a fishing pier, not an amusement pier, they do have a tram for 25 cents that runs from Monday through Thursday from 11 a.m. to 10 p.m., Friday from 11 a.m. to 11 p.m., Saturday 8 a.m. to 11 p.m., and Sunday 9 a.m. to 10 p.m. There is a snack shop and, on the very end of the pier, a restaurant:

> **Fisherman's Restaurant and Bar**
> **1 Oceanside Pier**
> **Oceanside, CA 92054**
> **(619) 722-2314**

There is an oyster bar upstairs and a great ocean view at this moderately priced, mesquite-broiled seafood place. The decor is heavy wood with glass all around. It opens early and offers breakfast and lunch, as well as dinner and a full bar.

Or if you prefer something even more informal, right by the pier is a grassy strip of a park that is perfect for picnicking. Oceanside has three miles of white sand beach with no rocks and the area around the pier is the best. The sand slopes gently down into the water and it is quite clean.

Just inland from the pier, at the corner of 3rd and Pacific is the:

> **California Surf Museum**
> **308 North Pacific Street**
> **Oceanside, CA 92054**
> **Monday-Friday 12 to 4 p.m.**
> **Saturday-Sunday 11 a.m. to 5 p.m.**
> **(619) 721-6876**

This is the second of the surf museums you'll find going up the California coast. Though they have a few giant old surfboards that are too big to relocate, twice a year most of the displays are changed. Each of the different exhibitions illustrates a separate aspect of surfing—from history to surfboard construction techniques. There is a gift shop with books, jewelry, art, and, yes, T-shirts.

North of the pier by the harbor is a wonderful place for lunch or dinner:

> **Rockin' Baja Lobster Bar and Grill**
> **264 South Harbor Drive**
> **Oceanside, CA 92054**
> **11 a.m. to 10 p.m. (later on weekends)**
> **(619) 754-2252**

This pretty white place with a blue trim accent sits right on the harbor by the Oceanside lighthouse. There is more about Oceanside in the December chapter.

Newport-Balboa

Lower Newport Bay is almost completely enclosed by the Balboa Peninsula that curves in a 2-1/2 mile long southeastern hook toward Corona del Mar. From Pacific Coast Highway, Highway 55 starts as Newport Boulevard, then turns into Balboa Boulevard and runs along this strand.

At 20th Street, you pass wooden the **Newport Pier**, built in 1944. Stop here and you can sample the wares of the last remaining dory fishing fleet in Southern California. They have been setting out and returning at around 7 a.m. since 1891. Scales are set up and the day's catch is then offered for sale on wooden planks.

Continuing down Balboa, you could go all the way to the end to **Jetty View Park** with its great views. Right by here is the infamous surfing spot known as "The Wedge" with its eight-foot tall waves. If you are not in the mood for surfing or contemplating views, a few streets back, you crossed Main Street, the epicenter of activity in Balboa.

Main Street ends in the **Balboa Pier**, where Glenn Martin launched his seaplane when he flew to Catalina in 1912 in the first water-to-water flight. At the tip of the pier is:

> **Ruby's Diner**
> **1 Balboa Pier**
> **Balboa, CA 92661**
> **Daily 7 a.m. to 10 p.m.**
> **(714) 675-7829**

Opened in December of 1982, this would be the first of what is now a chain of 17 casual eating spots with curved lines and red booths. It is a "'40s" (not '50s) style diner—the main difference being that the waiters and waitresses do not attempt to be cute by acting rude. Actually, Ruby's has good omelettes, hamburgers, fries and malts—and this one certainly wins the prize for location and view.

For entertainment, nearby is the:

> **Studio Cafe**
> **100 Main Street**
> **Balboa, CA 92661**
> **Monday-Thursday 11:30 a.m. to 1 a.m.**
> **Friday 11:30 a.m. to 1:30 a.m.**

Saturday 10 a.m. to 1:30 a.m. , Sunday 10 a.m. to 1 a.m.
(714) 675-7760

The food is standard California cuisine, but the music can be jazz, rock, blues, or reggae. The melodies start every night of the week from 9 p.m. until closing and on weekend afternoons from 2 until 4 p.m.

Turning toward the bay side of the strand, you will come upon the landmark structure of the area:

Balboa Pavilion
400 Main Street
Balboa, CA 92661
(714) 673-5245

The Balboa Pavilion was built in 1905 by Henry Huntington, who also left us his gardens in Pasadena (see January). It is especially pretty on warm summer nights when its Victorian cupola is outlined in twinkling white lights. Originally the terminal of the Pacific Electric Trolley Car Company (Red Car), which brought summer visitors from Downtown Los Angeles in about an hour, it is now the site of a restaurant, as well as functioning as the sign up point for boat cruises of the harbor and to Catalina. The latter are offered by Catalina Passenger Service, (714) 673-5245, aboard the largest passenger carrying catamaran in the U.S., the *Catalina Flyer*.

Summer vacation used to mean going down to seaside amusement parks or piers and strolling, riding on Ferris wheels, eating ice cream, and playing games in the warm ocean air. In the environs of the Pavilion is a place of eternal summer vacation, **The Balboa Fun Zone,** where all of these things still happen daily.

It has everything you might expect: cotton candy, skee ball, carnival and video games, bumper cars, and a four-story tall Ferris wheel that offers a great view of the harbor. This is also where you take the **Balboa Ferry** to Balboa Island.

These small (three-car capacity, plus pedestrians) barges have been chugging back and forth since 1919 and represent one of the few remaining operational ferryboat services in the state. Though they only cross 1,000-feet of water, the ride has a fun, foreign kind of ambiance. Don't ride in your car—it is much better to park and go over on foot. The feeling of the sea air on your skin and the blue water all around and the boats going past with their white sails is rejuvenating.

Balboa Island is one of eight residential islands within Newport Harbor. It forms the end of Jamboree Road, which turns into Marine Avenue, the island's little commercial strip. One of the most romantic restaurants in Orange County has been located here since 1963:

Amelia's on Balboa Island
311 Marine Avenue
Balboa Island
Daily 11:30 a.m. to 11 p.m.
(714) 673-6580

Behind the wrought iron scroll work adorning the entrance is the perfect cute little Italian restaurant for lunch or dinner followed by a nice stroll. Another reason to park near the Balboa Pier and take the ferry over is that Balboa Island, like most Southland well-to-do oceanside communities, is highly congested and parking is limited, to say the least. Parking tickets are given out with a zeal unmatched by almost any other place in Southern California, except Belmont Shore in Long Beach.

There is no shortage of charming (usually expensive) places to stay in the Newport area. You could stay at the Doryman's Inn up by Newport Pier (see December), or the Balboa Inn right across the street from the Studio Cafe, but for summer, I especially like the:

Portofino Inn
2306 West Oceanfront
Newport Beach, CA 92663
(714) 673-7030

Located just north of Balboa Pier, the Portofino Inn is hardly secluded from the crowds that hit Newport Beach during the summer. Yet somehow it is much sexier during the summer because it is so very Southern California on the outside. It could almost be a mock up of what people probably imagine the "Hotel California" of the song to look like, with its palm trees, tile roof, and neon glowing on the water.

Inside, however, it is plush Country French with Mediterranean influences like a small, luxurious European hotel. There are 17 rooms and suites, all on the second floor, all furnished with antiques, beautiful private baths, and draperies and pillows done in rich fabrics. One great non-bed and breakfast feature you'll appreciate this month is that all of the rooms have refrigerators.

Rooms vary as to view and price (from about $175 to about $275). There are also three suites with fireplaces (not much good this month), dual spa tubs, and best of all, private ocean view decks.

Huntington Beach

A celebrated beach town in Southern California surfing lore is Huntington

Beach. A big part of that mythology is **Huntington Beach Pier** which began life before the city was incorporated.

Originally a 1,000-foot wooden structure built in 1904, the same year the town's namesake bought the Red Car, it was destroyed in 1912, and replaced in 1914 by a 1,350-foot concrete pier—the first in the U.S. In 1930, they added a cafe and 500 more feet. Hammered by waves, it has been rebuilt twice—in 1940 and 1985—only to be nearly totalled in the great storm of 1988.

A coalition of government, local business, and citizens got together and raised $11.7 million. With it, they built a whole new pier, 1,856-foot long, styled after the 1940 W.P.A. design with a diamond shaped head

Huntington Beach is large and encompasses Bolsa Chica State Beach, Huntington City Beach, and Huntington State Beach. The pier area has always been the premium surfing spot. The north end and near the south edge of the pier are considered "off limits" to non locals or beginners.

Perhaps the most graceful image in the whole city is at the corner of Pacific Coast Highway and Huntington. It is a dynamic statue of a surfer navigating a dramatic curling wave called **"The Ultimate Challenge"** that was created by artist Edmund Shumpert. Originally built at City Hall, where it was supposed to be placed, because a conservative City Administrator thought it "too wild," it sat in its crate and finally was located here in 1973.

Sitting at the foot of the pier is a 1924 building with a restaurant inside:

> **Maxwell's**
> **317 Pacific Coast Highway**
> **Huntington Beach, CA 92648**
> **Sunday-Wednesday 8 a.m. to 10 p.m.**
> **Thursday-Saturday 8 a.m. to 11 p.m.**
> **(714) 536-2555**

With its Art Deco styling inside, Maxwell's looks quite unlike the other restaurants in the area. The specialty is seafood, but many other dishes are available for breakfast, lunch, or dinner.

Two blocks from the beach is the third surf museum on the coast:

> **Huntington Beach International Surfing Museum**
> **411 Olive Avenue**
> **Huntington Beach, CA 92648**
> **Wednesday-Sunday 12 to 5 p.m.**
> **(714) 960-3483**

Everywhere in this small museum there are surfboards of every length. The old longboards are so big they look scary compared to contemporary designs. This is also the site of the second great work of surfing art in Huntington Beach: a magnificent bust of the man who first brought surfing to California from Hawaii in the 1920s, **Duke Kahanamoka**. Formerly on the pier, the sculpture was moved here in '88. If you get sufficiently inspired you can buy a dictionary of surfing terms and slang called the *Surfin' ary*, written by Trevor Cralle.

Growing up, I saw a very different Huntington Beach than what I see today. I remember when the area around the pier was funky and somewhat uninhibited— when a very casual music venue called "The Golden Bear" offered top rock performers and we would drive from the San Fernando Valley down to Huntington to party. Some of that old feeling is captured in Kem Nunn's novel *Tapping The Source*, which is a modern day hard-boiled school story about coming to the coast in search of one's dreams.

Practically all of the older, seedier places of my youth are gone, having been replaced by more upscale businesses or condos. One of these new businesses is appropriate for summer fun:

Huntington Beach Brewing Company
201 Main Street
Huntington Beach, CA 92648
Sunday-Thursday 11:30 a.m. to 11 p.m.
Friday & Saturday 11:30 a.m. to 2 a.m.
(714) 960-5343

This is the second of Orange County's brew pubs on the coast. It is a large (5,800-square-foot), festive place with an outdoor patio. The huge bar area gives you a good look at the gleaming tanks of the beer brewing equipment.

Seal Beach

Seal Beach is one of Southern California's most charming places. I lived here for some of my checkered college years. Located just south of Long Beach, it is geographically isolated by natural features: a Naval Weapons Station to the south and east, and a marina to the north. This has prevented it from merging with surrounding communities and losing its true small town identity.

The town began life in 1850 as "Anaheim Landing." It came to be known as Seal Beach because of the large population of (you guessed it) seals, who enjoyed living here until the arrival of mankind.

Like all small towns, Seal Beach has its main street, called appropriately enough, "Main Street," which runs perpendicular to the ocean and PCH and ends at the **Seal Beach Pier.** Walking to the end of the pier you will pass all the patient, dedicated pier fishermen whose lines dangle hopefully in the frothy surf. At the end, you will come to another **Ruby's Diner** (see under Newport-Balboa).

Main Street has several bars and places to eat. If you are in a mood for fish, fresh is the word at this Seal Beach restaurant:

Walt's Wharf
201 Main Street
Seal Beach, CA 90740
Daily 11 a.m. to 11 p.m.
(310) 598-4433

As you enter the nautical interior with its exposed wood, your nose will tell you that the specialty is mesquite broiled food. They usually have at least a dozen different kinds of fresh fish here daily. You will also notice the clear wine case with its excellent collection of California wines.

Main Street is also the location of the place I have been going for 15 years to get my framing done:

Main Street Art and Framing Company
220 Main Street
Seal Beach, CA 90740
Monday-Saturday 10 a.m. to 5 p.m.
(310) 430-4054

Joe Kalmick opened his print and frame shop in 1978 and has been cheerfully greeting customers ever since. What he does professionally is offer an amazing selection of frame styles and a very personalized approach. Either he or one of his staff will offer several different alternatives and discuss them with you.

The walls of my home are covered with examples of his work.

Across the street is a small, but endearing used bookstore:

Bookstore on Main Street
213 Main Street
Seal Beach, CA 90740
Daily 10 a.m. to 9 p.m.
closed Wednesday
(310) 598-1818

You are not imagining it if you hear some soft jazz as you walk up Main. It is coming from Bookstore on Main Street. Owner Nathan Cohen opened this shop in 1982. A book collector who retired from the Merchant Marines, he stocks mostly out-of-print or hard to find books. There are not a lot of periodicals, but the selection of financial newspapers is quite impressive.

Seal Beach is an unpretentious town and does not have the rich-and-famous quality of Newport Beach. It is neither as cutesy as some "romantic" places or as overdeveloped as Huntington Beach.. To fully capture the small town by the sea feeling of old Seal Beach, spend the night at the:

Seal Beach Inn and Gardens
212 5th Street
Seal Beach, CA 90740
(310) 493-2416

The Seal Beach Inn, built in 1924, is extremely pretty on the outside. Surrounded by flowers, it is very inviting and an easy walk to either the beach or Main Street.

Truly an inn and not a bed and breakfast, there are 23 rooms, all with private bath, some with kitchens. There are 14 suites. If you are a film lover, they have a room with a bed from the John Barrymore estate. Some suites have jacuzzis and fireplaces.

Outside, there is a small landscaped pool area with a 17th century fountain and a library. Paths like you would find in an English country garden connect the different buildings.

Innkeeper Marjorie Bettenhauser-Schmaehl provides rich hospitality in the form of a full breakfast. This includes juices and coffee, and all manner of breads and muffins, Belgian waffles, and several quiches. In the afternoon, wine and cheese is served to guests in the library. Don't miss their chocolate chip cookies baked fresh daily.

Long Beach

Though it does not have much to outwardly show it today, Long Beach has an old history as a seaside city with a resort atmosphere. Between Chestnut and Pine on Ocean Boulevard, where towering office buildings and hotels line the street, back in 1902 there used to be a "Walk of a Thousand Lights," complete with a saltwater plunge.

This recreation area kept adding attractions and grew into the largest amusement park west of the Mississippi: The Pike. In 1930, they constructed the "Cyclone

Racer." It was fully one mile long and the "World's Fastest Double Track Roller Coaster." I rode this coaster more than once as a boy. Besides the fact that it was a great ride, I loved the notion that I could ride over the same wood frame that the monster from one of my favorite movies, *The Beast From 20,000 Fathoms,* had attacked and torn up (to me) rather convincingly.

Like Belmont Park in San Diego, attendance at the Pike was greatly boosted by a nearby Navy base. For a long time, it really was a hot place to go; it had all kinds of weird attractions, like the "Flaming Man" (who I never saw) who several times a day would slide down a cable into the sea like an Icarian sacrifice to the summer sun.

Several places throughout this book I have referred to **Charles Looff**, the master maker of carousels. Long Beach played a large part in his history. In 1911, already a famous woodcarver, he arrived in the city from Rhode Island and bought into The Pike. He built a big house with a dome rising in the center that contained his living quarters, workshop, and the first hand-carved carousel in Long Beach.

Though best known for his carousels, Looff also created a midway game in 1941 called "Lite-A-Line." In this contest, the object is to roll heavy little balls, which then fall into holes, lighting a display, and (hopefully) completing a line before anyone else in the room—just as in bingo.

Unfortunately, as it did elsewhere, the growth of Disneyland and other inland theme parks doomed the Pike. The Cyclone Racer was torn down in 1972, and after most of the Navy left in 1974, the end was sealed. The Pike closed in 1979.

As of the writing of this book, most of the land formerly occupied by the Pike is asphalt or dirt parking lot. There is supposed to be a tunnel under Ocean Avenue lined with early California tile with heavy chandeliers still intact that used to connect Pine Avenue to the seaside amusements, but it was sealed off by the developers of a giant condominium tower that now looms over the area. Strangely enough, Looff's building still stands:

> **Looff's Amusements**
> **300 The Pike**
> **Long Beach, CA 90802**
> **Daily 11:30 a.m. to 2 a.m.**
> **(310) 436-2978**

Though Looff's Building looks a little forlorn surrounded by acres of mostly empty asphalt parking places, the Lite-A-Line game goes on. You enter a room filled with people seated in rows staring intently at their individual polished wood alleys with the line of lighted score patterns on the wall behind. Rolling techniques vary, but all are trying to do the same thing: hit the holes that will make a line. It costs 50 cents to play and if you win, you get $10. Every hour they have a $25 bonus game.

Another legacy of Charles Looff is to be found across Shoreline Drive from Looff's in:

Shoreline Village
Shoreline Village Drive at the foot of Pine Street
Long Beach

This is yet another in the continuing series of fake New England-style fishing villages built to somehow boost Southern California tourism. Long Beach has (or had) a history of its own that could have been preserved or expressed somehow in its development, but as a city, it seems bent on trying to be uninteresting in its construction projects.

However, Shoreline Village is the home of one of 10 surviving carousels built by Charles Looff. The irony is that this monument to a glorious past was actually not indigenous to the area at all. It was built in 1906 in Riverside, Rhode Island, five years before he arrived in Long Beach. The carousel's original location was Luna Park in Seattle.

It survived a fire in 1913 which destroyed nearly everything else and then went to San Francisco's Playland where it remained until 1973. After that, it was bought by a Marianne Stevens of Roswell, New Mexico and put into storage. The carousel ended up in Long Beach, where it was named a California Historic Point of Interest on May 13 of 1984.

The 62 carousel animals were all hand-carved of wood and include horses, leaping camels, giraffes, and rams. There are also four chariots. The whole thing weighs over 35,000 pounds and is decorated with Austrian crystal jewels.

While you are in Shoreline Village, its hard not to notice the most striking of the buildings:

Parker's Lighthouse
435 Shoreline Village Drive
Long Beach, CA 90802
Monday-Friday 11 a.m. to 3 p.m.
Saturday-Sunday 11 a.m. to 2 p.m.
Sunday-Thursday 5 to 10:30 p.m.
Friday & Saturday 5 to 11 p.m.
bar open until 1 a.m.
(310) 432-6500

Long Beach does not have a lighthouse on land, but it does have a restaurant that looks like one. This landmark multi-story building was made to look like a giant Cape Cod lighthouse. The main dining room serves wood fired seafood.

The bar on the top floor is by far the best room., with its circular view of the harbor and Queen Mary. With its vaulted ceiling, like a giant Gothic tepee, it is quite a dramatic setting.

After hitting bike trails all over Southern California, I am convinced that one of the best is the **Shoreline Village to Long Beach Peninsula Trail**.

Long Beach got its name for an obvious reason. The beach runs from Shoreline Drive along the cliffs into Belmont Shore and all the way to the end of the peninsula that encloses Los Alamitos Bay. There is a bike trail that starts in Shoreline Village and curves around through the marina then runs the length of this beach.

The Bike trail passes the Beach Terrace Manor Motel (see February) and goes past the foot of **Belmont Pier**, a 1,300-foot hammerhead-shaped cement fishing pier. Behind the pier is a hill on which is perched the most romantic brew pub in the Southland:

> **Belmont Brewing Company**
> **25 39th Place**
> **[at the Belmont Pier]**
> **Long Beach, CA 90803**
> **Monday-Friday 11:30 a.m. to 10 p.m.**
> **Saturday & Sunday 9 a.m. to 11 p.m.**
> **(310) 433-3891**

This is the only brewed-on-premises beer restaurant located right by the ocean in California and it is as light and sunny as a summer's day. Owner David Lott has created a beautiful setting. The restaurant has two floors and a huge outdoor patio with a fire pit. The tasting room with it row of huge stainless steel tanks is on the top floor. There are views of the ocean from almost anywhere in the building.

The beer is excellent and the way they do the tasting is really cute. For $2.50, they serve you a palette of five large shot glasses, each filled with a different variety of frothy, fresh beer. These include Top Sail (amber), Black and Tan (light and porter), Penny Fogger (amber and porter), J.C. Marathon (light and dry), and the dubiously-named Long Beach Crude (porter). They are all brewed in a custom-built, seven barrel system that can make up to 4,000 gallons a month.

The food is good and inexpensive; so even if you are not a beer drinker, it is worth going. They take pride in making meals better than what you would expect from a brew pub. Besides excellent hamburgers, they feature BBQ chicken pizza and Angus Coulotte Steak. Breakfast is served on weekends and includes huevos rancheros, shrimp frittata, and eggs Benedict. It is particularly splendid on a July morning.

This area can be a good buy for an overnighter. Right across the bay from Parker's Lighthouse, next to the *Queen Mary* (described in January) is the:

> **Travelodge Hotel Resort and Marina**
> **700 Queensway Drive**
> **Long Beach, CA 90802**
> **(310) 435-7676**

In many ways, this is a sleeper among hotel properties. Its well-manicured, landscaped grounds create a park-like setting right on the water. Because it is on a finger of land that encloses the harbor, the view takes in the city skyline over the slowly lapping sea. At night, the reflection of the city lights make it seem just like Hong Kong.

Because its clientele is mostly business people, the Travelodge offers an attractive weekend rate on its 197 rooms. This is usually around $69—which is very cheap for an ocean-front hotel as nice as this one. The rooms have balconies and some have better views than others, so ask what is available when you arrive. If you are hopelessly in love and decide to get married while you are here, they have an absolutely lovely little arched wedding gazebo on the grounds that is one of the best deals I have encountered. There is more about Long Beach in the January, February, May, August, and December chapters.

Redondo, Hermosa, and Manhattan Beach

The beach cities that are usually referred to collectively as the "South Bay" are Redondo Beach, Hermosa Beach, and Manhattan Beach. The name comes from the fact that collectively they make up the southern curve of the Santa Monica Bay.

Though Huntington Beach calls itself "Surf City," surfing in Southern California actually originated in the area from Redondo Beach to Malibu. Henry Huntington, whose family owned most of Santa Monica, wanted to stimulate Southland tourism. In 1907, he brought a celebrated Hawaiian surfer named George Freeth to Redondo and held exhibitions. Freeth became known as "The Man Who Can Walk On Water." By 1920, L.A. County had six boards.

The wearing of wetsuits also began in Redondo. They had been developed by the Navy during WWII, but were considered so bizarre looking as to be suspect.

This was changed by a brilliant marketing ploy in the 1960s. During the winter surfing season, the Dive and Surf Shop offered several suits for free to the top locals. The sight of these hot doggers in full rubber regalia, and their testimonials as to the warmth they provided, banished the wet suit stigma forever.

Redondo Beach has an interesting profile to the sea. At the south end, Redondo State Beach is an endless curving ribbon of white sand with a hillside behind covered with the ubiquitous ice plant. The word "redondo" means "round." The Palos Verdes Peninsula rising to the south imbues a Mediterranean look.

At the north end, it is almost one continuously enclosed harbor called King Harbor. Beginning at the foot of Torrance Boulevard, the area includes two privately owned piers, a Fisherman's Wharf, an amusement zone, a heated salt-water wading lagoon, tennis courts I used to play on, and a luxury hotel:

> **The Portofino Hotel and Yacht Club**
> **260 Portofino Way**
> **Redondo Beach, CA 90277-2092**
> **(310) 379-8481**
> **(800) 835-8668**

This small and private hotel is set on its very own little peninsula. Inside it has a three-story lobby and lounge with big lattice windows and French doors that look out on the water. Each of the 170 guest rooms has a balcony and is equipped with a mini bar. They also have suites with their own jacuzzis.

Redondo Beach butts up against Hermosa Beach. The street that forms the boundary is descriptively called "Herondo Street." Hermosa has more of a funky beach town atmosphere. **The Strand,** the cement boardwalk that runs along the beach, is arguably the best body show in the Southland. The 1,320-foot concrete **Hermosa Pier** was never an amusement place, it has always been just for walking and fishing.

Hermosa Beach's Pier Avenue, which descends down a hill and ends in the pier, is lined with shops and places to eat—particularly between the intersection of Hermosa Avenue and the boardwalk. Right here is a landmark Southland place to dine and listen to music:

> **The Lighthouse Cafe**
> **30 Pier Avenue**
> **Hermosa Beach, CA 90254**
> **Monday-Saturday 6 p.m. to 2 a.m.**
> **Sunday 9 a.m. to 2 a.m.**
> **(310) 372-6911**

With its brick facade and brick-walled interior, there is nothing pretentious about The Lighthouse. It is just one big room that seats about 160. The ceiling is exposed beams that crisscross and support a curved roof like an airplane hanger.

Though this was originally a jazz venue, it is now a showcase for all kinds of music. You can even dance. Jazz is featured on Sunday from 9 a.m. to 2 p.m. They serve a full breakfast menu at this time that includes a "Build-Your-Own" Bloody Mary Bar.

Just up the hill a few steps is one of the Southland's great independent bookstores:

Either/Or Bookstore
124 Pier Avenue
Hermosa Beach, CA 90254
Daily 10 a.m. to 11 p.m.
(310) 374-2060

Originally opened in 1966, the Either/Or occupies five connected side-by-side storefronts that terrace up the curve of the street and overlook the intersection like the literary conscience of the hedonists roller blading below. With over 70,000 books and a selection to please the most esoteric bibliophile, this is a true booklover's store. The huge picture windows provide a brightly lit Eden for hours of browsing. A snoozing black cat in the sun adds an ambiance no other decoration could provide.

Connected to Hermosa Beach, the next town going up the coast is **Manhattan Beach.** In the late 1950s, when surfing was beginning to go beyond being just a pastime and becoming a lifestyle, a group of local young men who surfed together during the day began writing and recording surf songs together at night. Thus, The Beach Boys made their cultural contribution to the mythology of the Southland.

Like Hermosa, Manhattan has a basic fishing pier, though the **Manhattan Pier** is somewhat shorter at 900-feet long. Manhattan does not have the funky feel of Hermosa and has been called "Yuppie Beach" by some Hermosa residents. Its convenience to the L.A. Airport is not lost on many business people, and the homes are very nice. Just a little ways up is the sister brew pub to the Huntington Beach Brewing Company:

Manhattan Beach Brewing Company
124 Manhattan Beach Boulevard
Manhattan Beach, CA 90266
Sunday-Thursday 11:30 a.m. to 12 a.m.

Friday & Saturday 11:30 a.m. to 1 a.m.
(310) 798-2744

This 2,600-square-foot brew pub offers about four brewed-on-premises beers. It offers a similar menu and taste in drink to the Huntington Beach Beer Company because they are both owned by the same people.

Venice

In 1880, a well-to-do tobacco producer named Abbot Kinney came to San Francisco as the last stop on a round-the-world voyage. Forced to wait before he could return by train to the East Coast due to snowstorms in the Sierras, he decided instead to go south.

Because he suffered from asthma, Kinney was always interested in health resorts. He ended up at the Sierra Madre Villa Hotel in the San Gabriel Mountains, where his asthma improved so much he decided to move nearby. The result was a house on a hill called "Kinneloa."

He had an education in biology and horticulture and planted citrus trees. He also started a library and funded a college. When Helen Hunt Jackson was gathering information for what would turn out to be the novel *Ramona,* he rode with her as an interpreter (see April).

Summers are hot in the foothills of the San Gabriels, so he built a summer house by the beach in Santa Monica. California has experienced numerous land price boom/bust cycles and 1887 was a year of a big upsurge in prices. Kinney tried to develop the area that is now Pacific Palisades, but the boom ended and his original project with it. His next enterprise was a larger development on the beach that began in what is now the Ocean Park area. There originally was a pier at what is now Pier Avenue.

The death of his original partner and conflicts with his heirs caused a breakup of the company, the assets of which were divided in a very scientific way: they flipped a coin. Kinney won the coin toss and for reasons of his own chose the undeveloped, marshy part of the property, south of Ocean Park.

He chose the undeveloped part because he wanted to do something different. Instead of a regular beach town, he wanted to create a "Venice In America," a city as a majestic cultural center designed after the famous Italian original. In 1904, he hired the architectural firm of Norman Marsh and Associates to lay out canals and lagoons. A spectacular three-day opening gala commenced on July 4 of 1905.

Some of the high minded ideals of the founder got lost along the way. The proximity to the beach invited amusements, not culture. Instead of the university he had in mind, a casino was built in 1907. The pier attracted hawkers, not scholars. A roller coaster called "The Race To The Clouds" was added in 1912.

Things got worse after Kinney died in 1920. Oil was discovered and the resultant drilling rigs blighted the landscape. In 1925, residents voted for annexation by the City of L.A. Soon after, in 1929, the process of filling the canals began, as the roads were widened. The pleasure pier was demolished in 1946. This did not lead to increased property values: in the 1950s, Venice was nicknamed "the slum by the sea."

Ironically, the decline of Venice up into the 1960s also created a place today more like the one its founder envisioned. The low rents and wide open mind set made the area a mecca for artists. Jim Morrison of The Doors lived here. Though the '80s produced considerable gentrification, Venice is still a place for free spirits.

The best examples of the original architecture that have survived are on Windward Avenue between Speedway and Pacific Avenue and the Venice Center building. The Grand Lagoon of the original Venice brought ducks to these environs from 1905 to 1929. Orson Wells used this locality to represent Tijuana in *Touch of Evil*. With buildings with rows of archways supported by columns, it has the romantic flair. Located in the old Hotel St. Mark's is a thriving jazz club:

> **St. Mark's**
> **23 Windward Avenue**
> **Los Angeles, CA 90066**
> **Tuesday-Sunday 6 p.m. to 2 a.m.**
> **closed Monday**
> **(310) 452-2222**

Though it is old-style on the outside, on the inside St. Mark's has a trendy and modern look of smooth, elegant marble. They even have closed-circuit TV monitors for the seats with bad views of the stage. The food is fairly expensive, but extremely good for a supper club. They even boast "the freshest seafood on the beach."

From here, if you walk over a few steps, you will be standing on one of Southern California's most interesting tourist attractions, the world famous **Venice Beach Boardwalk**.

Though local boosters in other Southland beach towns have taken to hiring mimes and other street entertainers to add color to their gentrified surroundings, there is no other beach scene like the year-round street fair that is the Venice Beach

Boardwalk. There are merchants selling everything from jeans to sunglasses for dogs. Music comes from dancing roller skaters, impromptu jam sessions, and of course, the one and only Harry Perry, the singing, Stratocaster electric guitar-playing roller skater in his familiar turban. He sells cassettes  of his music if you would like to add something original to your collection. Other performers juggle chain saws, yodel upside down, and perform feats of magic.

South of Windward Circle, around 18th Avenue, you will come upon the bulging endomorphs of Muscle Beach. Formerly called "The Pit," this outdoor gym has become an official asset of the city and has been spruced up, much to the chagrin of the regulars. The baby blue color of the outdoor railing seems just too nice. More women are using it, however.

If you get hungry along the way, stop in at the bustling:

Sidewalk Cafe
1401 Ocean Front Walk
Venice, CA 90291
Monday-Thursday & Sunday 8 a.m. to 12 a.m.
Saturday 8 a.m. to 1 a.m.
(310) 392-4687

Though there are many other great places to eat along here, for most people, the funky indoor/outdoor Sidewalk Cafe is the epitome of dining in Venice. They serve breakfast, lunch and dinner and showcase local bands at night. Carrie Nation would have been appalled by the early morning drinkers who line up at the bar at 8 a.m.

Besides the Boardwalk, Venice has so many nooks and crannies, stimulating little galleries and other expressions of human creativity, it is fun to stay right in town and really take the time to explore. Amazingly, there is an "urban bed and breakfast" here, just a stroll off the ocean front walk at its south end:

Venice Beach House
15 30th Avenue

Venice, CA 90291
(310) 823-1966

This bed and breakfast occupies a real California bungalow, built in 1911 while Abbot Kinney was still alive. You can really feel the history when you enter the living room, which is paneled in dark wood and has a heavy beam ceiling and big fireplace. There is a dining room and a veranda; an expanded continental breakfast and afternoon snacks are available in both settings.

It has nine rooms, five of which have private baths. Two of the rooms are suites: one has a fireplace, the other, a private hot tub. They are all furnished with patterned wallpaper, antiques, and period artwork.

Many artists live in Venice and there are several arts groups that offer shows to the public. The old Mission Revival-style city hall is now a unique cultural center:

Beyond Baroque Literary Arts Center
681 Venice Boulevard
Los Angeles, CA 90015
(310) 822-3006

They have all kinds of activities. These include concerts and lectures. Poetry readings are a regular feature. Right next door, the former police and fire station is now the:

Social and Public Art Resource Center
685 Venice Boulevard
Los Angeles, CA 90015
(310) 822-9560

This is a very beautiful building, built in the early '30s, that expresses an Art Deco sensibility on a very solid looking Moderne concrete structure. Over the main entrance, with its lettering proclaiming "Venice Police Station, Division 14," is an Egyptian-style bas-relief of a scene from the royal court.

On the inside, the cell blocks have been converted into an art gallery. Besides the cutting-edge art on display here in their gallery, S.P.A.R.C sponsors lectures and mural art projects and tours all over the city. They are best known for creating the mural "The Great Wall of Los Angeles" in the San Fernando Valley (see May). The store sells folk art.

One of the things that makes Venice an arts center is the presence of a collective sense of humor. This is present in the very existence of the Boardwalk, in many of the murals and businesses, and most prominently in the wittily named:

Museum of Jurassic Technology
9341 Venice Boulevard

Los Angeles, CA 90034
Thursday 2 to 8 p.m.
Friday-Sunday 12 to 6 p.m.
(310) 836-6131

The title of this delightfully odd little museum is a giveaway to its whimsical nature: there was no technology during the Jurassic period. It contains exhibits of seemingly random categories of natural history and human endeavor. Each has a taped voice-over that purports to explain it.

The natural history includes a diorama of a Cameroon rain forest where the vines are covered with ants that emit a stinking spray and an exhibit about a kind of *Buckaroo Banzai* bat called the Deprong Mori that flies through solid matter using a radar beam. There is a display devoted to a woman who grew a horn from her head, featuring the appendage itself.

Human achievement is represented in a history exhibit honoring a philosopher and memory researcher named Geoffrey Sonnabend whose life work is summed up in the quote "forgetting is the inevitable outcome of experience." The closest thing to a "technology" display is the "Nanotechnology" exhibit. The word refers to ultra tiny machines that are so small they can only be seen under extreme magnification.

If you wish to write someone and thank them for providing the world with such a completely executed example of a gigantic wink of the eye, the Museum of Jurassic Technology was founded by a special-effects designer and urban entomologist named David Wilson and he can be reached in care of the museum. Donations are also welcome.

At the corner of Rose and Main is an eating place with perhaps the signature work of art of Venice:

North Beach Bar and Grill
111 Rose Avenue
Venice, CA 90291
Monday-Friday 11 a.m. to 11 p.m.
Saturday & Sunday 10 a.m. to 11 p.m.
(310) 399-3900

Jonathan Borofsky's 30-foot statue of a ballerina, one leg daintily lifted, toe pointing, would not cause the blue noses to get upset were it not for the extra large white hands and head of a bearded clown with a red nose and hat that complete the image.

The interior of North Beach Bar and Grill is not quite so unusual with its rattan bar and blue terra cotta pots. It is a good place to eat and serves a full menu of "California cuisine": plenty of chicken dishes, steaks, and pasta.

Nearby on Main Street, Venice is also the home of one of the most unusual buildings you have ever seen:

Chiat/Day/Mojo
340 Main Street
Venice, CA 90281
(310) 314-5000

Built in 1991, the entrance to the offices of this world-renowned advertising firm is a giant pair of binoculars more than three stories tall. The building itself was designed by Frank Gehry and Associates and the binoculars are by the German artists Coosje van Bruggen and Claes Oldenburg. But of all of the public art in Venice, the most romantic is located at:

Venice High School
13000 Venice Boulevard
Los Angeles, CA 90066
(310) 306-7981

Though it is now protected from vandals by a fence, in front of Venice High School, there is a statue of a former student who went on to become "the Queen of the Movies:" Myrna Loy, now dead since December of 1993 at the ripe old age of 88. She was best known for playing the witty and sexy Nora Charles in six *Thin Man* movies co-starring William Powell that she made from 1936 to 1947. An interesting side note to her movie history is that an earlier film of hers, *Manhattan Melodrama,* was the film John Dillinger had just seen in the Biograph Theatre in Chicago when the F.B.I. ambushed him outside.

Santa Monica

Venice and Santa Monica are contiguous and, though the former is part of L.A., the latter is a very separate city. The two are similar in more ways than their proximity, however. As you are driving north on Main from Windward in Venice, just one block past Rose, it can be hard to tell that you are now in Santa Monica.

Two blocks past "the border," turn right on Pier Avenue to arrive at an establishment that for many years a friend of mine insisted was really in Venice:

The Novel Cafe
212 Pier Avenue

Santa Monica, CA 90405
(310) 396-8566

The Novel Cafe is a combination bookstore and coffeehouse, and in many ways offers the best of both. Books are arranged on shelves surrounding the tables, chairs and couches of the first floor.

The second floor, overlooking the first, has tables and chairs but no couches. The bustling atmosphere here is quite delightful, with patrons reading to themselves and each other, actors reading scripts, and the smell of coffee, cinnamon, nutmeg, and allspice mingling with a slightly musty book smell. Try the yogi tea with steamed milk.

The Novel Cafe features new and used literature, rare books, coffee, and fine foods. They also buy books. If you have been wanting to find a social way to read, come here and do it until midnight.

On the next street inland from Main, within easy walking distance from here, is a small theater that would make for a perfect evening to go with the Novel Cafe:

Powerhouse Theatre
3116 Second Street
Santa Monica, CA 90405
(310) 392-6529

This pretty little Mission Revival building was the former powerhouse for the trolley that ran up and down Main Street around the turn of the century. The Powerhouse has just about the maximum number of seats it can have and still qualify as a "99 seat (or under) theatre" for Equity purposes (see September). Inside, it is relatively unadorned and the seating is more steeply elevated than in most small theatres, so it is a particularly good venue for avant garde dance. Outside, it has a simple enclosed garden area that is good for a nice break at intermission on a hot night.

Main Street Santa Monica is quite fashionable and has numerous boutiques and galleries. It is also the site of one of Wolfgang Puck's most beloved restaurants:

Chinois on Main
2709 Main Street
Santa Monica, CA 90405
Wednesday-Friday 11:30 a.m. to 2 p.m.
Monday-Saturday 6 to 10:30 p.m., Sunday 5:30 to 10 p.m.
(310) 392-9025

Opened in the early 1980s that seems an eternity ago in the restaurant business, Chinois is a great survivor. One former chef, Kazuto Matsusaka, went on in 1992 to open his own restaurant, Zenzero. Amazingly, with all the time and staff changes, Chinois still has it.

The interior by Barbara Lazaroff, Puck's partner and wife, is a mixture of textures and shiny lacquered surfaces. The tables are like art showcases for the food: black place mats made of bamboo grace turquoise table tops held up by splayed metal bases.

But it is the food that is the real star. The name of the restaurant is reflected in the cuisine, which is Chinese/French. Specialty dishes include grilled whole fresh fish, Peking duck, and Mongolian lamb with tofu and spring onions.

Besides Wolfgang Puck, another of the Southland's famous chefs has a restaurant on Main Street as well:

> **Rockenwagner**
> **2435 Main Street**
> **Santa Monica, CA 90405**
> **Monday-Saturday 11:30 a.m. to 10:30 p.m.**
> **Sunday 9:30 a.m. to 10 p.m.**
> **(310) 399-6504**

Hans Rockenwagner now has three restaurants in the L.A. area; this was his second. Its interior is a unique art form in itself that goes well with the structure-equals-art motif of its exterior. At night, the tiny lights suspended over each table from the ceiling create a magical effect. Lunch, dinner, or Sunday brunch are outstanding. The bakery here is especially noteworthy.

Rockenwagner is located at the back end of an architecturally unique mini mall called **Edgemar**. It was designed by Frank Gehry for writer/developer Abby Sher in 1989 and features a collection of different shaped buildings arranged around a central court.

Within Edgemar, on one side of Rockenwagner, is the:

> **Santa Monica Museum of Art**
> **2437 Main Street**
> **Santa Monica, CA 90405**
> **Wednesday, Thursday & Sunday 11 a.m. to 6 p.m.**
> **Friday & Saturday 11 a.m. to 10 p.m.**
> **(310) 399-0433**

This former egg-processing plant with its industrial/minimalist interior offers showings of contemporary, innovative cutting-edge artists.

Of course, if the heat of July calls for some ice cream, you can get that at Edgemar too:

Ben and Jerry's Ice Cream
2441 Main Street
Santa Monica, CA 90405
Sunday-Thursday 12 to 11 p.m.
Friday & Saturday 12 p.m. to 12 a.m.
(310) 450-0691

The mural of the contented black and white cows that wraps around the south corner of the front and center building of Edgemar should alert you that dairy products are to be found within.

Main Street is not all trendy restaurants, however. A pleasant hangout is:

Tavern On Main
1907 Main Street
Santa Monica, CA 90405
Daily 12 p.m. to 2 a.m.
(310) 392-2772

This bustling, very popular spot would be a good enough choice for before or after theatre food and drink. Opened in 1988, Tavern on Main has a warm, friendly, green-hued interior that is like an Irish bar in San Francisco might look like. The food is good and includes their signature Black Bean Soup and round waffle fries, plus burgers and other American bar standards. The most popular beer is Sierra Nevada on tap, an obscure California brew from Chico.

Besides going by street, it is also possible to walk the Venice Boardwalk and pass into Santa Monica. If you go this way, you will arrive at a delightful historic pier: **Santa Monica Pier**.

Originally, two parallel piers were built here between 1909 and 1921 by the City of Santa Monica Engineering Department. The surviving one was almost demolished in

Ben and Jerry's on Main Street in Santa Monica.

1973 and ravaged by storms in 1982-83, but the good citizens of Santa Monica came to the rescue and the restoration/enhancement project continues today.

The Santa Monica Pier is the only true amusement pier remaining in Southern California. There are restaurants, shooting galleries, video parlors, skee ball and other midway games. A **Bike Trail** runs south from the pier for 19 miles, all the way

to Torrance. When it is dark outside, the white lights strung along the pier's edge add a romantic quality on warm nights that evokes memories and images of summer love.

My favorite (and most people's) part of the pier is the carousel. Not only did I spend quite a bit of time in my high school years near this landmark, but one of my favorite movies, *The Sting*, was filmed here. Finished in 1921, it has a 1900 Wurlitzer organ and 56 prancing horses. For information call (310) 458-8900.

The beaches near here are very popular. On the south side of the pier are volley-ball sand courts where I used to watch Wilt Chamberlain play. There are gymnastic rings and bars as well. Santa Monica has an old tradition of beach sports: the surf-board fin was invented here in 1935 by a gentleman named Tom Blake.

The north side is a very Mediterranean-looking place. If you look up from its wide stretch of beach, you can see the crumbling cliffs of "The Palisades." There is a narrow strip of a park along these cliffs, **Palisades Park**, that was originally laid out in 1912. It runs along Ocean Avenue from where Colorado Boulevard ends at the pier up to Adelaide Drive.

The view from Palisades Park of the pier, the white beach, the blue Pacific, and the curve of the road going north around Santa Monica Bay is extremely pretty,

particularly at sunset. At night, when the lights of the highway and the pier outline the dark waters of the ocean, it is even more romantic.

If you walk from Colorado going north on Ocean Avenue, you will come upon a **Camera Obscura**, sort of a giant simple camera body where astonishing shadow re-

flections of the outside world are projected on the curved walls in a room upstairs from 10 a.m. to 4 p.m.

Continuing on, you will come upon poetically designed Palisades Park Gates, marking the official entrance to the park. Poetic because these are Craftsman styled fieldstone gateways decorated with California tiles. They were designed by a Pasadena architect, a con-

The carousel at Santa Monica Pier.

temporary of Greene and Greene named Ernest Batchelder, who gained great fame for the tiles that bear his name.

There is a certain magic to this area because it is the edge of an urban carpet that stretches along Wilshire Boulevard all the way to downtown L.A. Besides Palisades Park, it is home to several very romantic places.

Across Ocean Avenue from the park is a very charming hotel:

Shangri-La Hotel
1301 Ocean Avenue
Santa Monica, CA 90401
(310) 394-2791

If you like Streamlined Moderne architecture, you will love this gracefully curved, eight-story 1939 jewel designed by William E. Foster. It was the sight of Randy Newman's *I Love L.A.* video.

Completely unpretentious, it has a wonderful view of the ocean over Palisades Park, particularly on the upper floors. The 55 rooms are done in Art Deco pink and gray with frosted glass accents and lacquered and laminated period furniture. Most of the rooms have ocean views, some have sun decks and kitchens. There is no pool, but there is a large sun deck open to all guests where they serve continental breakfast and afternoon tea.

Art Deco Shangri La in Santa Monica.

Santa Monica has a great reputation as a restaurant town. As I mentioned, several famous chefs ply their culinary artistry in some pretty fancy (and expensive) eateries here. One of my favorite obscure Santa Monica restaurants is:

Skorpios II Restaurant
109 Santa Monica Boulevard
Santa Monica, CA 90401
Sunday-Thursday 11 a.m. to 10 p.m.
Friday & Saturday 11 a.m. to 11 p.m.
(310) 393-9020

Just a few steps inland from Ocean Boulevard on Santa Monica Boulevard is this little Greek restaurant with its high rounded ceiling. Originally opened in 1982, Skorpios II still has the same romantic ambiance it always had. On a warm summer night, as the ceiling fans slowly turn overhead, the candle-lit room comes alive with the sweet strains of a mandolin or guitar (Thursday-Sunday nights). A stroll down to the pier would complete the mood of the evening.

If you did not feel like going to the pier before or after dinner, but instead wanted to shop and be entertained, from Skorpios just turn inland, because you are also right by **3rd Street Promenade.**

While Santa Monica's beachfront walk may not have the buzz of unusual artistic activities like the Venice Beach Boardwalk, 3rd Street Promenade, a three block open-air mall that runs from Wilshire Boulevard south to Broadway, has it all.

Formerly the moribund outdoor Santa Monica Mall, it was remodeled and re-energized into a shopping, dining, and entertainment pedestrian zone with something for everyone. There are street entertainers ranging from classical string quartets to people playing the ukulele while seated upside down. Food ranges from

A topiary dinosaur fountain aids whimsy to the 3rd Street Promenade.

places where you can get something interesting and delicious for $2 to the best in fine dining. A multi-screen cinema offers 4,900 movie seats. There is more about Santa Monica in the December chapter.

Ventura

The big storm of 1986 partially demolished and closed the wooden **Ventura Pier**, celebrated as the longest on the California coast. Originally built in 1872, it was never an amusement park type pier, but was always a favorite of lovers and fishermen because of it length. After much wrangling, $3.5 million, and seven years time, it reopened Saturday, October 2 of 1993.

They had a nice big party with a ribbon cutting ceremony, live bands, and even a cannon salute from a boat. After all, they had extended it to 1,958-foot, replaced 17 percent of the pilings, and re-done the whole pier deck. At the pier's end is a sculpture called **Wavespout**. It is a six-foot circular fountain that creates an effect like a blow hole and jets a 10-foot spray of seawater in the air.

Ventura is another seaside town in Southern California with an on-again off-again tradition of fireworks from its pier. As of the writing of this book it was "off again." Partially because of the desire to de-emphasize fireworks, the City of Ventura has their **Old Adobe Day Festival** coincide with 4th of July weekend. They have adopted the tradition of a parade and Street Fair complete with nine stages offering entertainment from 10:30 a.m. to 5 p.m. Call (805) 654-7830 for more information.

Ventura is a good weekend destination for most Southern Californians. It offers not only beautiful beaches, but unexpected charm. The drive is not prohibitively long (about 65 miles from Los Angeles) and US 101 (Ventura Freeway) is a classic "escape route" for Southern Californians.

Located on Main Street is the:

Mission San Buenaventura
225 East Main Street
Ventura, CA 93001
(805) 643-4318

Founded in 1782 along with Santa Barbara, this was the last mission overseen personally by Father Junipero Serra, and the fourth in Chumash territory. Its lands originally stretched all the way to Simi Valley.

The whitewash and red tile Mission San Buenaventura was finished in 1809. The church building was damaged by an earthquake in 1812 and repaired in 1815. It is still used for services. The pretty garden with its pine trees and tile fountain has an antique water pump and olive press.

The contempt the church expressed toward the traditions of the indigenous peoples of California in some ways is epitomized by the fact that the mission's school was built smack on top of the Chumash burial ground, containing the remains of 4,000 of their ancestors.

Next to the mission is the:

Albinger Archaeological Museum
113 East Main Street
Ventura, CA 93001
(805) 648-5823

This museum encompasses an archaeological dig into the foundation of an earlier mission church discovered in 1974. It contains thousands of local artifacts and traces 3,500 years of local history. If you go into the mission gift shop, you can purchase a self-guided tour of the mission for 50 cents. Across the street you will find the:

Ventura County Museum of History & Art
100 East Main Street
Ventura, CA 93001
Tuesday-Sunday 10 a.m. to 5 p.m.
(805) 653-0323

This adobe-style museum is set in grassy Mission Park and is surrounded by a collection of antique farming and oil drilling equipment. It has three galleries devoted to the history of Ventura County, one to folk and fine art, and one that features miniature figures of famous people crafted by Ojai artist George Stuart.

Right behind the museum is a historic place to stay:

Clocktower Inn
181 East Santa Clara
Ventura, CA 93001
(805) 652-0141

The Clocktower Inn is a former fire station built in the 1940s. It has 50 rooms, some of which have nice views of Mission Park from their balconies.

Along Main Street there are numerous thrift and antique shops, so you can really fill up a day just strolling around browsing. Garden Street intersects Main Street a couple of blocks west of the mission. Here is an appropriate place for lunch before or after a museum or mission visit:

Desert Rose Cantina
26 South Garden Street
Ventura, CA 93001
(805) 652-0338

The Desert Rose features a Southwestern Indian style of Mexican food. Many dishes have blue corn tortillas and they serve black beans instead of the more common refried pinto beans.

If you are inspired by all of this history enough to want to celebrate it in your home, drive East on Thompson Road a little ways to the:

Old California Store
1528 East Thompson Boulevard
Ventura, CA 93001
Friday-Sunday 11 a.m. to 5 p.m.
(805) 643-4217

Don Shorts started this unique furniture store in 1989 as a tribute to the romantic view of Early California that prevailed in the 1920s and '30s. It features Monterey-style furniture such as you would find on a rancho. This includes tile-topped tables and gorgeous tile murals, as well as chairs, paintings, and miscellaneous object d'art.

Though Ventura is strong on historical museums, it is a conservative place that does not offer many venues for emerging artists. Ironically, the best place for this may be:

Franky's Place
456 East Main Street
Ventura, CA 93001
Monday-Friday 7 a.m. to 3 p.m.

Saturday & Sunday 7 a.m. to 4 p.m.
(805) 648-6282

The red brick interior walls of this friendly restaurant are decorated with sketches and paintings. The cashier's booth is flanked by shelves displaying glazed ceramic bowls, vases, and other functional art. Brilliant splashes of color are provided by neon sculptures of a blue dolphin, a purple coyote, and a yellow moon. A little display stand with a sculpture of clay or bronze sits at each table.

This gallery motif is explained by the restaurant's history. It was opened in 1983 by a sculptress named Francis Jansen. She was a booster of her boyfriend's work (he was also a sculptor) and displayed it throughout. A waitress who worked there named Kris Pustina bought the place in '87 and now owns it along with her husband Bill Haldane.

They extended the artistic tradition of its founder, but now feature art produced by local talent that is rotated every six weeks. They have also added a solid commitment to quality and customer service that keeps the place pretty busy at all times. Many of the waiters have been here since the days of the original owner.

A chalkboard announces the specials of the day. The food is pretty enlightened in that there are a lot of salads, the sandwiches are made with pita bread, and chicken and turkey replace beef or pork in most dishes.

What makes Ventura perfect for a short romantic getaway is that its historical museums and sites, antique shops, and restaurants are all within easy walking distance of each other.

Right near Franky's Place is a beautifully remodeled hotel:

Bella Maggiore Inn
67 California Street
Ventura, CA 93001
(805) 652-0277
$75 and up (double occupancy)

This hotel was originally built in 1926 and has a grand total of 19 rooms. It is sort of a cross between a hotel and a bed and breakfast in that breakfast and an afternoon snack, served in the lovely lobby, are included. There is more about the city of Ventura in the December chapter.

SMALLER SUMMER MUSIC FESTIVALS

Though most of the larger theatre or music festivals in Southern California began in June, many of the smaller ones begin this month.

Irvine Meadows

The summer classical music experience that is very much like the Hollywood Bowl Summer Festival, but somewhat more accessible, is the:

Irvine Meadows Summer Series
Irvine Meadows Amphitheater
8808 Irvine Center Drive
Irvine, CA 92718
(714) 855-8096

Irvine Meadows Amphitheater seats 10,418 in reserved seats, 4,582 on the lawn (the Bowl seats 20,000) and has large picnic grounds, good parking, and better auto access than the original. The Meadows' picnic grounds open at 6 p.m. and food and wine are welcome in all parts of the amphitheater for the five concerts of the Pacific Symphony Orchestra. Food (including box dinners) and wine and beer are available in the concessions circle.

Subscriptions can include preferred parking, optional dinner service, and post-concert receptions with guest artists. Single tickets for reserved seats are available as is non-reserved seating on the lawn. In order to make the concerts affordable to all and to promote family attendance, the orchestra has priced a percentage of the tickets inexpensively.

The Pacific Symphony's outdoor concerts are especially great because if you decide to go at a fairly late date and end up with last minute tickets, you will not suffer as much with bad seats as you would at the Hollywood Bowl. Have a picnic on the lawn and enjoy the surroundings.

Redlands

Surprisingly, the best summer music festival may be:

Redlands Bowl Summer Music Festival
Smiley Park, Eureka and Grant Street
Redlands
mailing address:
P.O. Box 466
Redlands, CA 92373
Weekends in July & August
(909) 793-7316 or (909) 335-6828 Ext. 11302

In 1924, Redlands resident Grace Mullen was inspired by the brand new Hollywood Bowl to spearhead an inland summer music festival. The Redlands Bowl is a 4,500-seat (though it can hold about 6,000 including those sitting on the grass) concrete-sloped amphitheater. Admission is free, though they do pass the hat.

Redlands is about 70 miles east of L.A. on I-10 and about six miles east of San Bernardino. Though it does not have the overwhelming crowds of the Hollywood Bowl, it is very popular and fills up. Plan your excursion well. Remember it is very hot in Redlands in the summer. For a romantic place to stay, try the Morey Mansion (see April).

Beverly Hills

On Saturday, May 15, 1993, the record for longest line of Rolls Royce automobiles on a public highway was set in Beverly Hills, with 125 of the stately vehicles forming a chain. There was one accident. The previous record of a mere 114 was set in Hong Kong in 1991.

It is stories like this that secure Beverly Hills' reputation as a home to the rich and famous, but actually what the people who live here like the most about it is that it is a village. Everything is close and people are friendly. You may get some attitude in the designer boutiques, but for the most part, if you can pay, you are OK.

The city has excellent services and sponsors some great events. The Department of Parks and Recreation has a long-standing tradition of offering summer music in a beautiful setting:

> **Beverly Hills Summer Concerts**
> **Doheny Mansion**
> **Graystone Park**
> **905 Loma Vista Drive**
> **Beverly Hills, CA 90210**
> **Weekends, July & August 4:30 p.m., September 3:30 p.m.**
> **(310) 550-4654**

The City of Beverly Hills Department of Parks and Recreation has sponsored these outdoor concerts in the garden here since 1973. For $20, you can hear the Beverly Hills Symphony and enjoy a reception. Opera singers are a little less at $15.

The Doheny mansion, built by oilman Edward Doheny in 1928, has 55 rooms and a hillside setting above Sunset Boulevard. It seats 400 for the concerts. You may tour the grounds, but will not be allowed inside the house.

It took three years to complete Gordon Kaufmann's Tudor/Jacobean design of this beautiful gray limestone mansion, but when it was finished in 1928 it was

46,054-square-feet, had 55 rooms and walls three-feet thick. The original estate was 415 acres, most of which was purchased by a developer named Paul Trousdale, who subdivided it into the high rent district known as the Trousdale Estates. The 18-1/2 acres that are left feature the original landscape design of Paul Thiene and are nothing short of magnificent.

Doheny built it for his only son, Edward L., Jr., who was always known as Ned. Ned and his wife and five kids moved in, but five months later he was dead. His body was found with that of his male secretary in the master bedroom. There are two stories: that the secretary shot Doheny, Jr. because he denied him a raise, then shot himself, or that Doheny was gay and was afraid people would find out so he ended it all. The latter, more lurid story seems to be the one believed by the press at the time.

The mansion was vacant for years and finally the City of Beverly Hills bought it in 1965.

This is one of the most frequently used buildings in film and television. About 30 features are shot here every year, even though it costs about $9,000 per day to do so. Recently *The Witches of Eastwick, The Golden Child, Ghostbusters II, The Bodyguard,* and *Indecent Proposal* were adorned with its stately presence, as were the TV shows "MacGyver," "General Hospital," and "Murder, She Wrote."

Another beautiful estate fairly near here is open to the public:

Virginia Robinson Gardens
1008 Elden Way
Beverly Hills, CA 90210
(310) 276-4823

This six-acre estate surrounds the oldest home in Beverly Hills, a Mediterranean Revival built in 1911. The gardens vary in design and influence, but the king palm trees everywhere give it a California feel.

There are certainly many lovely restaurants in Beverly Hills, but there are two that seem to go best with a summer garden. The first one that comes to mind is:

Il Cielo Restaurant
9018 Burton Way
Beverly Hills, CA 90211
Monday-Saturday 11 a.m. to 11 p.m.
(310) 276-9990

A friend visiting from Europe recently told me that there were more "Northern Italian" restaurants in Southern California than in Northern Italy and many of them seem to be located on the west side of L.A. Though it does offer Northern Italian food, Il Cielo breaks the mold by also offering seafood country dishes and cuisine from Tuscani and the coastal regions.

Il Cielo has had the same owner since 1986, Pasquale Vericella, and he has built the restaurant's reputation steadily. Both chefs and all of the waiters are from Italy. Some of the specialties are really excellent, most notably the "brunzino." This is sea bass which is first grilled, then baked and then filleted at the table. It is served with a natural sauce with herbs grown on the premises. They are also celebrated for their excellent "risotto primavera" and oven-baked whole snapper.

What is remarkable about the achievement here in the kitchen is that this was such a beautiful restaurant space, it could have become one of those places that has mediocre food, but people still take their dates to for the ambiance. In terms of the latter, this has to be one of the most romantic restaurants in the Southland. There is an indoor fireplace that during the winter flickers its light seductively on the walls washed in gold earth tones and tile floors and across the backsides of the cherubs frolicking across the azure trompe l'oeil sky ceiling.

It is the two charming patios that make this summer dining experience that it is. With its little white lights and pretty windows overhead it is awfully close to the vision most people have of the romantic patio garden restaurant. On weekends, they have strolling violinists that complete the picture.

The other Beverly Hills restaurant I think of when I think of gardens is a garden:

> **Bistro Garden**
> **176 North Canon Drive**
> **Beverly Hills, CA 90210**
> **Monday-Saturday 11:30 a.m. to 11 p.m.**
> **(310) 550-3900**

Within walking distance of steel and glass office buildings and the most exclusive stores in the Southland is this casually elegant indoor/outdoor eatery. A small dark wood bar and old world ambiance pervades on the inside. On a nice day, however, everyone wants to sit on the patio with its big white umbrellas. The service is prompt and very courteous. I have it on the recommendation of a noted authority on the subject that the shrimp cocktail here is one of the best in L.A.

THE TROPICS IN SOUTHERN CALIFORNIA

This month marks the opening of the season at Southern California's only banana plantation:

Seaside Banana Gardens
Pacific Coast Highway
La Conchita (between Ventura and Carpenteria)
Daily 9 a.m. to 5:30 p.m.
(805) 643-4061
mailing address:
6823 Santa Barbara Avenue
Ventura, CA 93001

Doug Richardson liked the idea of edible landscaping. So when people told him you couldn't grow bananas in Southern California, he naturally had to prove them wrong. He obviously succeeded and opened Seaside Banana Gardens in 1984. It is 12-1/2 acres of lush plants and broad lawns.

Most people are surprised about how many types of bananas there are. Besides the familiar yellow and the big green plantain, there are tiny little blue ones and plump red ones. There are 58 different varieties in various levels of availability here. To stop at the Seaside Banana Gardens, just look for the little jungle that suddenly appears on the inland side of Pacific Coast Highway. I have brought several tours here and everyone loves the place.

Right near the Banana Gardens is a very romantic place to eat and spend the night:

Cliff House Inn
6602 West Pacific Coast Highway
Mussel Shoals, CA 93001
(800) 892-5433 or (805) 652-1381

The Cliff House is appropriately named because it overlooks the ocean. It was voted "most romantic place to stay" in Ventura County by readers of a local newspaper. The same poll also named the Inn's restaurant, **The Shoals**, as having "the best seafood in Ventura County." It also serves pasta dishes and steak.

There are 24 rooms, all ocean view. There is a pretty ocean view poolside area where a continental breakfast of coffee, tea, orange juice, fresh fruit, and breads and cakes is served.

As I said in June when I mentioned Humphrey's Half Moon Inn, there has always been a mythical connection between Southern California and the tropics. That connection has expressed itself in a plethora of kitsch architectural statements of the post WWII period that could be summed up as the "tiki style." A big part of the reason was that soldiers returning from the Pacific Theater had often spent their shore leave on Hawaii and other Pacific Islands where the bars naturally had the "tiki look."

During the '70s and '80s, many of these places were torn down, but there are some survivors. The real San Diego classic of this genre is the:

Bali Hai Restaurant
2230 Shelter Island Drive
Shelter Island
San Diego, CA 92106
Monday-Friday 11:30 a.m. to 10 p.m.
Saturday 5 to 10 p.m
Sunday 10 a.m. to 9:30 p.m.
(619) 222-1181

Bali Hai opened in 1953. The name was suggested by a then popular Hawaiian-style song in which the singer croons, "Here, I am, your special island" after which the other-worldly sounding chorus repeatedly moans the refrain "Bali Hai!" In the Navy town of San Diego, the restaurant nicknamed "Hawaii on the mainland" started by pleasing sailors and hung on to please tourists and residents as well.

The decor is tiki-wonderland. The lobby features an outrigger canoe flying through the air. Palm trees, thatch, and a great view of the water and the city round out the picture.

Where else can you get tropical drinks like the "Aloha Kiss," which comes with a flower lei? In my collection of glasses, I have a little ceramic "Mr. Bali Hai" complete with two sipping-straw holes in the lid. The menu is large and includes the unmodestly named "Chicken of the Gods," which is breast meat cut in strips, cooked in batter, and served with sauce. There is a luau-style buffet Monday through Friday and a Sunday brunch.

Up the coast in Orange County, the beach town of San Clemente has a delightful bed and breakfast with a tropical theme:

Casa Tropicana
610 Avenida Victoria
San Clemente, CA 92672
(714) 492-1234

This is one of the Southland's newest inns, opening in 1990. It is a very inviting looking three-story white Mediterranean-styled building with red-tiled roofs and terraces on all floors. There is a wide green lawn and palm trees between it and the beach.

If staying at the Casa Tropicana gives you an urge to transplant the tropics to your home, nearby Dana Point is the home of:

Palms of The World Nursery
34167 Pacific Coast Highway
Dana Point, CA 92629
Monday-Friday 9:30 a.m. to 5 p.m.
(714) 240-1134

This rainforest in Orange County carries over 400 different varieties of the languid tree. Like Joe Ellis out at Ellis Farms in Borrego Springs (see March), owner Lynn Muir is a member of the International Palm Society. An architect by profession, he started Palms of The World because he always loved the look of the trees. Though there is only one indigenous Southland palm, the "Washingtonia," over 200 different kinds are now found here. Their presence is one way the tiki look will literally always be a part of the landscape of Southern California.

There are traces of the tiki culture throughout Southern California. Another take on this style of architecture is found in the San Fernando Valley in a place that is not just a restaurant, but an entire apartment complex:

Horace Heidt Estates
14155 Magnolia Boulevard
Sherman Oaks, CA 91423
(818) 995-6827

Like Bing Crosby, Bob Hope, and countless other entertainers, big-band leader Horace Heidt thought the San Fernando Valley was a pretty great area and bought a nine acre grapefruit orchard located there in 1940. He wanted to make a fantasy setting where his band could live and practice. Big band concerts still happen on holidays in the **Aloha Room** clubhouse.

As a little boy, I remember pressing my face against the glass of the car's side window as we drove through Horace Heidt Estates, completely enthralled by the concept of a residential community where each section was patterned after a distinctly different locality. Cartoon-ish looking street signs indicate "Palm Springs" or "Hawaii." The latter section features a waterfall shaped like a volcano lit with red lights, called the "Mauna Loa."

There are statues set all over the grounds, along with pools and fountains and a golf course. Like many other locales in Southern California with unusual architecture, many well-known performers have lived here. These include Tom Scott, Bob Cummings, Dick Van Patten, and Ed Begley, Jr.

If you would like to hear some music in a tiki setting, the place to go is:

Jack's Sugar Shack
8751 West Pico Boulevard
Los Angeles, CA 90015
Daily 3 p.m. to 2 a.m
(310) 271-7887

Originally built in 1945, this restaurant space has been many different establishments such as Chinese restaurants or Caribbean night clubs. Though Jack's is a chain, they couldn't have picked a less corporate-seeming location.

Once inside, you will find a palm-thatched roof over the horseshoe-shaped bar, bamboo trim, steel drums, and a waterfall. They serve 32 kinds of beer. The north wall of the bar is so packed with taps, it looks like some kind of war machine. There is a large outdoor patio as well.

The stage is right by the bar and the music is mostly blues with some rockabilly. You can also entertain yourself playing pool or pinball. The food consists of salads and sandwiches with a few California specialties like Cajun shrimp pasta.

But if there was truly a shrine in Southern California to the tiki restaurant, it is:

Bahooka Restaurant
4501 North Rosemead Boulevard
Rosemead, CA 91770
Sunday-Thursday 12 to 9 p.m.
Friday & Saturday 12 to 10:30 p.m.
(818) 285-1241

Family-owned Bahooka used to be in West Covina, but they moved here in 1967. It is definitely a place that the crew of a Pacific-based naval vessel might have gone for some R and R. Manager Stacy Fliegel has been joking with customers since 1984 and it is the mood of friendly goofiness that pervades this establishment that adds to the appeal of the full blown tiki setting.

There are palm trees, rusted nautical odds-and-ends, old street signs, hanging lifeboats, and more tropical fish tanks than you will see anywhere but in a pet shop. They frame each booth and make drunks nervous inside the glass topped bar. Have one of their famous mai tais or maybe a zombie. Their ribs and onion rings have a loyal following.

LOTUS FESTIVAL

Besides representing the fantasy of the tropics in America, Southern California is often called "lotus land." It is particularly appropriate in the languid heat of the second weekend of July that we have a flower festival to celebrate:

> **Lotus Festival**
> **Los Angeles Department of Recreation and Parks**
> **Echo Park Lake**
> **1632 Bellevue Avenue**
> **Los Angeles, CA 90026**
> **usually second weekend of July**
> **(213) 485-5555**

This is a true Asian Pacific cultural celebration and has food, dance, games, and crafts from many of the peoples of the Pacific Islands as well as Asia spread out over the park's 29 acres. Some rare and exotic flora is usually also on display as well, but the highlight is the **Dragon Boat Race** on the lake.

The festival gets its inspiration from a mass of enormously pink flowered lotus plants that occupy the northwest corner of the lake. These are said to be one of the legacies of Aimee Semple McPherson's nearby 1920s Angelus Temple, a legendary chapter in the city's history. One of her missionaries brought lotus seeds back from Asia, threw them in the lake, and the rest is history.

There is a magical feeling here that seems to fuse the energy of old L.A. with the new. In 1894, the City of Los Angeles spent nearly $6,000 to dredge the 15-acre lake making it the largest artificial lake in any county park. Remarkable as it may seem, with all of the changes across the country, it still is.

It has 300-foot illuminated fountains and park recreation facilities such as tennis courts, a picnic area, and fishing. With its old boathouse where paddle boats are still rented, a bright red Asian-motif bridge to the tiny island, and waving palm trees, it evokes the past of L.A. of Chandler and Chinatown. But today it has become a multicultural meeting ground for Filipinos, Salvadorians, Vietnamese, Nicaraguans, and just about everybody else. The late artist Carlos Almaraz captured the hot summer feeling of the lake in his celebrated painting.

The area surrounding Echo Park Lake has always attracted a unique assortment of people. Maria Rasputin, daughter of the "Mad Monk" Gregori, settled here in 1916 after the death of her father that year.

Another local character presided over a temple by the lake:

Angelus Temple
1100 Glendale Boulevard
Los Angeles, CA 90026
Monday-Friday 9 a.m. to 5 p.m.
(213) 484-1100

This imposing white-domed classical edifice was patterned by architect A.F. Leicht in 1925 after the Mormon Tabernacle in Salt Lake City. During the Roaring '20s and Depression '30s, Aimee Semple McPherson made this huge circular structure hop as she preached her Foursquare Gospel.

Just over the hill in Pasadena is a museum that celebrates the roots of the peoples that bring us the lotus festival:

Pacific Asia Museum
46 North Los Robles Avenue
Pasadena, CA 91101
Wednesdayay 10 a.m. to 5 p.m.
(818) 449-2742

This beautiful Chinese palace was designed in 1924 by Marston, Van Pelt and Maybury as a combination shop and home for a dealer in Oriental art and books on Asia named Grace Nicholson. Sometime after her demise it first became the Pasadena Museum of Art and in the late '70s, the Pacific Asia Museum.

A lovely Chinese garden was added to the central court in 1979 so that now it ranks as one of the truly delightful smaller museums of Southern California.

COCTEAU'S BIRTHDAY (JULY 5, 1889)

The first part of July brings the birthday of a famous 20th century French artist, Jean Cocteau. The largest collection of his works outside France is contained in:

The Severin Wunderman Foundation
Jean Cocteau Museum
3 Mason
Irvine, CA 92718
Daily 10 a.m. to 4:30 p.m.
(714) 472-1138

Jean Cocteau has been called "the man who invented the 20th century." He was a writer, actor, artist, and stage designer. His contemporaries included Erté, Picasso, Chagall, and Dali. This museum is the only one in America devoted entirely to Cocteau's work and has been the subject of numerous editorials in French newspa-

pers about the "crime" of such a collection being located in Orange County and not Paris.

Though the location in an industrial park in Orange County is odd, this is one of the most interesting museums in Southern California. Since Cocteau expressed himself in so many ways, the collection here includes a lot of different kinds of stuff. There are letters, films, manuscripts and books, drawings, pastels, paintings, tapestries, lithographs, ceramics, sculpture, and theatre masks. Under the capable hand of the witty and affable Tony Clark, the museum director, a variety of programs are offered to the public. These include lecture tours, catalogues, and festivals.

A perfect place for lunch or dinner before or after a visit to the Cocteau Museum is the:

Cafe Fleuri
Le Meridian Newport Beach
4500 MacArthur Boulevard
Newport Beach, CA 92660
Monday-Friday 6:30 a.m. to 10 p.m.
Saturday & Sunday 7 a.m. to 10 p.m.
(714) 476-2001

Le Meridian Hotel in Newport Beach overall has the finest cuisine in Orange County. The formal dining room, **Antoine**, seems to win every award or restaurant writer's poll when it comes to the question of "the best" in the area. I actually prefer the Cafe Fleuri, the hotel's "coffee shop." It is a bright room with a high ceiling that has a wall of glass overlooking a lushly land-scaped patio.

The wedding gazebo located in the garden of Le Meridian Newport Beach.

Though its grounds are compact, this hotel has 435 rooms. It is very urbane and businesslike: the lobby and public areas are all hard shiny surfaces with art strategically displayed. One of its surprises is an enclosed grassy garden with a white wedding gazebo at the far end. It is like some secret hidden place amidst the marble.

LAGUNA BEACH PAGEANT OF THE MASTERS AND SAWDUST FESTIVAL

Art is the trademark of Laguna and beginning in 1932 the city had its first Summer Festival of The Arts. The next year they added what has grown to be one of Southern California's most famous summer events:

Pageant of The Masters
Irvine Bowl Park
650 Laguna Canyon Road
Laguna Beach, CA 92651
Nightly at 8:30 p.m.
July 1-August 31
(714) 494-1145

The Pageant of The Masters is a series of staged live reproductions of famous works of art. The official name of this art form is "tableau vivant" and the effect is wonderful. With music provided by a 27-piece band and set in the beautiful six-acre Irvine Bowl Park, this is a treat for the whole family. The accompanying Festival of The Arts in the same park runs from 10 a.m. to 11:30 p.m.

Practically across the street is the companion summer arts festival of Laguna:

Sawdust Festival
935 Laguna Canyon Road
Laguna Beach, CA 92651
Sunday-Thursday 10 a.m. to 10 p.m.
Friday & Saturday 10 a.m. to 11 p.m.
(714) 494-3030

This outdoor celebration originated in 1966. It was started by freelance artists who were omitted from the more structured and bureaucratic Festival.

The Sawdust Festival is much more lighthearted and festive. It gets its name from the sawdust covering the paths that wind around literally hundreds of arts and craft displays. Clowns, mimes, and strolling musicians add to the cheerful atmosphere.

There is a beautiful dining site by a waterfall in a 2-1/2 acre eucalyptus grove full of light and music. Though it started humbly enough, now there are more than 200 internationally-recognized and local artists showing pottery, sculpture, paintings, jewelry, glasswork, leatherwork, handmade musical instruments, and prints.

Success has brought irony: in recent years there has been more criticism from local artists that this alternative arts festival has grown too "commercial." One of the critics of the Sawdust Festival has a unique artist's compound that you can visit:

Dr. Neon Laboratories Inc.
2825 Laguna Canyon Road
Laguna Beach, CA 92651
call for invitation
(714) 494-4020

Dr. Neon is Alexander Evans and he is an extraordinary fellow. A former stand-up comic who appeared at the Comedy Store on Sunset (see August), he was roommates with the late Sam Kinneson, with whom he shares a gleefully abrasive sense of humor. He was building a pretty good reputation as a jewelry maker (whose work was available at the Sawdust Festival) when he was struck by what he considered to be the blandness of the setting. He thought, "What this place needs is a neon sign." Thus a career was born.

His artistic medium is sealed glass tubing filled with a mixture of gases. Add electricity and you have a glow of vivid color in an incredible variety of shapes. Some of his pieces are in one color, others have a rainbow of them. He sells tropical fish and parrots for $100, palms and cacti for $200-$300, and even a giant Ferrari sign for $850. The piece de resistance is an eight-foot dragon in four colors for $6,500. Ironically, his most popular items are custom motorcycle parts that light up.

Dr. Neon-land is a 20 acre estate with showrooms filled with neon art. The place is well set up and even offers cappuccino. Everyone is welcome, but they request that you call first and "receive an invitation."

Dr. Neon also makes custom signs. He says one of his favorite signs adorns Divine Pasta on Montana in Santa Monica. A Dr. Neon sign also announces Dr. Neon's restaurant:

Taco Loco
640 South Coast Highway
Laguna Beach, CA 92651
Daily 11 to 2 a.m.
(714) 497-1635

Yes, this restaurant is owned by the good Doctor. You'll get a clue once inside. Anytime they make a new neon piece and bits of extra tubing are left over, something gets put in this 400-square-foot jumble of color with seating for 25. In addition to the stunning visuals, the food is great and the fish tacos are named "Best In Orange County" regularly, by popular vote. Specialties include swordfish, lobster, and calamari tacos and tofu burgers. No fried food is served.

Another Dr. Neon sign adorns the front of Orange County's most famous bookstore:

> **Fahrenheit 451**
> **540 South Coast Highway**
> **Laguna Beach, CA 92651**
> **Daily 10 to 12 a.m.**
> **(714) 494-5151**

This classic independently-owned bookstore is just a few steps from Taco Loco. It is also a coffeehouse and performance space.

Laguna Beach has been a traditional summer destination for Southern Californians for a long time. With the growth in Orange County, some of the magic that was part of Laguna when it seemed so far away is gone. Where once there were artists living in bungalows worth $30,000 at the most, now there are corporate executives who commute in one form or another from their $500,000 and up houses. Much remains of the old spirit of Laguna, however, in the ghosts that inhabit a classic Southern California romantic destination:

> **Hotel Laguna**
> **425 South Coast Highway**
> **Laguna Beach, CA 92651**
> **(714) 494-1151**

During Hollywood's heyday in the '30s and '40s, many of the most famous stars sought refuge in this charming old hotel. Humphrey Bogart and Lauren Bacall, Errol Flynn, Greta Garbo, and many others were regulars. Harrison Ford, who was originally discovered at the Laguna Beach Playhouse in the early '60s, was a regular in the lounge.

Practically across the street from the hotel is the:

> **Laguna Art Museum**
> **307 Cliff Drive [Corner of PCH]**
> **Laguna Beach, CA 92651**
> **Tuesday-Sunday 11 a.m. to 5 p.m.**
> **(714) 494-6531**

In here you will find an excellent showing of local and regional artist's works on display. The featured collection is of contemporary and historic California paintings. This museum also has a section for children.

A restaurant that reflects the artistic roots of Laguna is:

> **Dizz's As Is Restaurant**
> **2794 South Coast Highway**
> **Laguna Beach, CA 92651**
> **Tuesday-Sunday 5:30 to 10 p.m.**
> **(714) 494-5250**

There is something very reassuring about this extremely informal, yet excellent dinner restaurant. There are no reservations: seating is strictly first come first served. The interior is a mishmash of unmatched objects right down to the plates and silverware. The food is eclectic, but anything but a mishmash. It is inexpensive, but very well prepared and ranges from grilled spiced chicken to international cuisine. There is more about Laguna Beach in the November chapter.

RACING SEASON IN DEL MAR

To me, the perfect signal that summer has really started is the bell at the start of the horse racing season at the place "where the turf meets the surf:"

> **Del Mar Thoroughbred Club**
> **Via De La Valle**
> **Del Mar**
> mailing address:
> **P.O. Box 700**
> **Del Mar, CA 92014-0700**
> **nine races daily—first race 2 p.m., last race 6 p.m.**
> **mid-July to mid-September**
> **(619) 755-1141**

When San Diego decided to hold their first county fair in the summer of 1936, Del Mar was picked to be the place. They built the track a year later in '37 to generate income to cover the cost of staging the fair every year. The Turf Club became a big hangout for Hollywood celebrities like Desi Arnaz, Bing Crosby, Pat O'Brien, and Jimmy Durante.

This is a very successful track. Del Mar had the number one daily average attendance of any track in the U.S.A. in 1992 at 35,384 and the highest daily average handle at $7,699,295 per day. In 1993, they beat both figures and set a North American record for highest average daily handle at a cool $8,122,609 per day.

They attribute their success to a combination of the popularity of the area as a summer destination and the quality of the racing: some of best horses in the world come here. In order to handle the volume, the original grandstands were leveled and, from 1992 to 1994, an $80,000,000 construction project created completely new grandstands, architecturally similar to the original.

On the site of the old Hotel Del Mar is the lovely:

L'Auberge Del Mar Resort and Spa
1540 Camino del Mar
Del Mar, CA 92014
(619) 259-1515

Decorated in marble and stone and red oak with photographs of Hollywood celebrities who frequented the place in its heyday in the '20s, '30s, and '40s, the lobby is designed to recreate the days when a hotel's foyer was a locus of social activities. A stone fireplace from the original hotel provides a warm background for the daily afternoon teas, dinner, and dancing.

There are 123 guest rooms, though they are so private the place seems smaller than that. They have outdoor dining on the terrace of the **Tourlas** restaurant next to waterfalls and a stream. Weddings are often held on the pretty bridge that crosses over this stream. High tea is offered on Friday and Saturday and a big Sunday brunch finishes the week. They also have very complete sports, exercise, and spa facilities, including a top level tennis clinic.

The former garage of the original Hotel Del Mar is now a restaurant:

Jake's Del Mar
1660 Coast Boulevard
Del Mar, CA 92014
Monday-Friday 11:15 a.m. to 9:30 p.m.
Saturday 5 to 9:30 p.m.
Sunday 10 a.m. to 9:30 p.m.
(619) 755-2002

The wooden interior here reminds me of an old yacht. Jake's is right on the sand next to the Poseidon Restaurant described in February. The food is very good steak-and-lobster and the Sunday brunch is very popular.

RAYMOND CHANDLER WRITING CONTEST

One of the most well-known and well-liked writers waxing on the landscape of Southern California was Raymond Chandler. A former oil executive whose short stories had been published in the *Black Mask* and other pulp magazines, he achieved fame in 1939 with the publication of his first novel, *The Big Sleep*.

He went on to write *Farewell My Lovely The High Window, The Lady In The Lake, The Little Sister, The Long Goodbye*, and *Playback*.

Though he is, of course, an L.A. writer, Chandler spent his final days in La Jolla from 1949 until his death in 1959. It is the town of "Esmerelda" in the novel *Playback*. Every year, they hold a writing contest here to commemorate this:

International Imitation Raymond Chandler Contest
write to:
Friends of the La Jolla Library
1257 Virginia Way
La Jolla, CA 92037

"My first impulse was to get out in the street at high noon and shout four letter words," was the author's first take on quiet, staid La Jolla. He moved here for the sake of his ailing wife, whose passing broke his heart. After that, he slowly drank himself to death.

What could be a more appropriate way to observe the Raymond Chandler writing contest than a visit to one of Southern California's most endearing bookstores:

John Cole's Books
780 Prospect Street
La Jolla, CA 92038
Monday-Saturday 9:30 a.m. to 5:30 p.m.
(619) 454-4766

This delightful La Jolla landmark is housed in a setting that could make a reader out of anyone. This 1904 seaside cottage was purchased by Ellen Browning Scripps who commissioned famed architect Irving Gill to remodel it. Scripp's sister Virginia loved purple and was responsible for the building's most striking exterior feature: a 60-foot long wisteria trellis that defines the entry.

The cottage welcomed many famous guests entertained by the Scripps, then was used as a church, private school, then finally purchased by the Cole family in 1966 and converted to its present capacity.

In many ways, this is what all bookstores should be: a true literary haven. It feels like what it is, both a store and a cottage, and one goes from room to room for separate specialties. Besides books, there are pottery and crafts on display along with cards and other interesting little objects. There are special ocean view rooms for children with books and toys. There is even a lovely patio where tea is served.

Perhaps the ultimate tribute to the magic of John Cole's Book shop is that the late Ted Geisel, better known as Dr. Seuss, was reputed to be quite fond of it.

The main location of San Diego's museum of up-to-date art is right by here:

Museum of Contemporary Art, San Diego
700 Prospect Street
La Jolla, CA 92037
Tuesday10 a.m. to 5 p.m.
Wednesday 10 a.m. to 9 p.m.
(619) 454-3541

It surprises many people to discover that this building was originally a private residence designed in 1915 for Ell Browning Scripps. It became an arts center in 41. Famed architect Irving Gill designed this original modern villa, along with several other La Jolla structures still standing, such as the La Jolla Women's Club, the La Jolla Recreation Center, and the Bishop's school.

This branch of the museum will be closed until 1996 for renovation. Architect Robert Venturi is bringing back Gill elements, but will add his own signature touch. Venturi designed the new wing to the National Gallery in London, the first American architect to be so honored. The Downtown San Diego Annex will remain open during the construction (see September).

La Jolla has lots of romantic places to stay, such as the La Valencia Inn (see February). Another historic spot for lodging is:

The Bed and Breakfast Inn at La Jolla
7753 Draper Avenue
La Jolla, CA 92037
(714) 456-2066

This was home to John Philip Sousa, the "March King," composer of martial music. There are 16 rooms, all except for one with private baths. The appropriately named Pacific View room has the best view. There is more about La Jolla in the February and November chapter.

OLD MINER'S DAYS

During the month of July, the mining tradition of the San Bernardino Mountains is celebrated in various locations throughout Big Bear Lake. Events include burro races and gold panning exhibitions. For information, call (909) 866-4608.

Between Big Bear and Baldwin Lake, off North Shore Drive (Highway 38) is an appropriate place to stay for Old Miner's Days:

Gold Mountain Manor
1117 Anita

P.O Box 2027
Big Bear City, CA 92314
(909) 585-6997

From its log walls to its inviting porch, the Gold Mountain Manor is every inch the romantic hideaway. It was once part of a large, fashionable mountain resort. In addition to Old Miner's Days, July is opening month for public tours of a unique observatory:

Big Bear Solar Observatory
40386 North Shore Drive
Big Bear, CA 92314-9672
Saturday 4 to 6 p.m. (July-Labor Day)
(909) 866-5791

Opened in 1969 by Cal Tech, this is the world's foremost facility for observing and studying our sun. Built on a point that juts out into the center of the lake, the location makes for ideal climatic conditions for this delicate task. The air here is steady and void of currents of heat that normally rise when the sun warms the ground. The wind also flows smoothly across the lake's flat surface.

These factors, plus the area's average of 300 clear days per year, reduce the amount of distortion on the videotape and film made by the observatory's three telescopes. Visitors climb three flights of stairs and, though you cannot look through the telescopes, you can see close-ups of the sun on computer monitors. There is more about 8ig Bear Lake in the May and November chapters.

BETTY BOOP FESTIVAL

One of the world's best known cartoon characters is Betty Boop. With her enormous saucer shaped eyes, short tight skirt, and little squeak of a voice, the Boopster has always stood for sexiness in an engaging, innocent way.

Betty was created during one of the worst years of the Depression (1930) by a contract artist for the family-owned Fleischer Studio named Myron (Grim) Natwick. She was immediately popular and she made the Fleischers wealthy and enabled their studio to survive a time when small film companies were going out of business right and left. They sold the rights to King Feature Syndicate, who continue to make tons of money to this day licensing the irresistible dark-eyed lass with the heart of gold.

None of this success ever found its way to Mr. Natwick, who died in 1991 at the ripe old age of 100. Though Betty Boop is one of the most famous cartoon characters in history, her creator died in obscurity. He lived in a small one bedroom apartment in Santa Monica, provided by a longtime fan. Other than this thin line of support, he was completely destitute.

Every year since 1985, Betty's fans have thrown a party in her name in Montebello:

> **Betty Boop Festival**
> **Heavenly Choice**
> **872 West Beverly Boulevard**
> **Montebello, CA 90640**
> **normally second or third Saturday of July**
> **10 a.m. to 2 p.m.**
> **(213) 728-2728 or (213) 888-0446**

This delightful gift shop is the site of this annual event, which draws hundreds of hard core Boop fans from all over the country. There is a Collector's Swap Meet, where "Boop-a-belia" of every imaginable description is traded. There is even an appraiser on hand to evaluate pre-1975 Boop items, which are considered antiques. Competitions include "Baby Boop" look-a-like, "Betty Boop Tattoo," and "Wearer of the most Boop-a-belia" contests.

The whole thing is the brainchild of the store's owner, Denise Hapogian. She sponsors the event, along with the Official Betty Boop Fan Club, and the City of Montebello Parks and Recreation. Ms. Hapogian is obviously quite the fan: her large collection of Betty Boop merchandise on display in the store is testimony to this "Boop-A-Mania."

An interesting cultural side note to this event is that the Boopster has a very large following in the Hispanic community of Southern California. This is partially attributable to the fact that very old American cartoons were dubbed in Spanish and have been shown in Mexico for many years.

This manifests itself very charmingly in the Baby Boop contest, which draws about 30 little girls up to five-years-old. Quite often you will get a chance to see a beautiful little Mexican girl dressed up like Betty Boop and singing an old American song from the '30s—in Spanish.

AUGUST

Dog Days of Summer

City Walks

Anniversary of the
Death of Marilyn Monroe (August 5)

Anniversary of the
Death of Will Rogers (August 14)

Nisei Week

Los Angeles Festival

Old Spanish Days in Santa Barbara

Indian Independence Day (August 15)

Ojai Shakespeare Festival

Long Beach Renaissance Art Festival

Basque Picnic and Festival, Chino

Summer Corn

Chapter Eight

AUGUST

The word "august" means "of majestic dignity or grandeur: marked by stateliness or magnificence." It seems hard to believe, but there was a real person from whose name this lofty word sprang. He was the first "official" emperor of Rome: the majestic, stately, and magnificent Augustus, who was born 58 years after last month's namesake, Julius Caesar. There is no modern derivative word for Julius except for his month—unless you count the Orange Julius beverage franchise.

When I think of August in Southern California, I think of so many things: heat, the home stretch of summer vacation, the endless nights. What I am going to be doing in the fall. I also think of Caesar Augustus because it was during this month that I first happened to read Robert Grave's historical novel *I, Claudius*, which was later made into an English TV series shown on PBS (public television) here.

THE DOG DAYS OF SUMMER
The Southland as a Modern Day Rome

If you haven't read *I, Claudius*, or even if you have, it is a great book to read in August on a beach in Southern California. Los Angeles in particular is so much like Rome. This connection became forever a part of my vision of the Southland when once, while reading it lying on the beach surrounded by oiled bodies, I looked up and beheld the:

J. Paul Getty Museum
17985 Pacific Coast Highway
Malibu, CA 90265
Tuesday-Sunday 10 a.m. to 5 p.m.
(parking reservation required)
(310)458-2003

There is nothing that makes quite as poetic a statement of summer in Malibu as this intricate replica of a Roman villa, the Villa of the Papyri, perched majestically on a hill overlooking the Pacific. The original was buried in the eruption of Vesuvius in 79 A.D. and was not excavated until the 18th century. The copy has a colonnaded walkway, mosaics, frescoes, and Mediterranean landscaping. The panoramic view is a broad stroke of blue: blue waters, blue skies.

The ground floor has a noted collection of Roman and Greek antiquities. Upstairs is a collection of European paintings from the Renaissance to Impressionism. Even non-art snobs are impressed by the period rooms filled with ornate European furniture.

The Getty has a reputation for two very important things in the arena of world class museums: the deepest pockets and the most advanced restoration laboratory. These are apparent in several remarkable examples.

Van Gogh's *Irises,* sold for about $10 in the artist's own lifetime, now hangs here in multi-million dollar splendor.

The museum's collection of approximately 400 Old Master drawings is noted as being one of the most superb in the world. That reputation was strengthened in 1993 when the Getty purchased a Michelangelo drawing called *The Holy Family With the Infant Baptist on the Rest on the Flight Into Egypt* for $6.27 million. This was the highest price ever paid at auction for a drawing by one of the Old Masters. While it is only 11-by-15-3/8 inches, it is said to be finest example of Michelangelo's drawing in the U.S. outside of New York.

But the most spectacular showcase of the Getty's financial and technical muscle was the unveiling at the beginning of 1994 of Titian's restored *Venus and Adonis,* an authentic masterpiece that had previously been hidden in obscurity. The London auction price in December of 1991 to a partnership of art dealers was $13.47 million. What they turned it over to the Getty for four months later is unknown.

This is a painting that looks impressive even to someone with no art education. It is pretty large—5-by-6-1/2 feet—and it is filled with color and action and drama. Titian is noted for being an artist whose pieces "tell a story" and the tale here is a particularly interesting one.

Venus is shown in full blown big bare-butted Italian Renaissance style trying to restrain the handsome Adonis from going off to hunt. The story is that he is destined to be gored by a wild boar and that she has been using sex to keep him from setting out for several days. But at this point, he is determined; he has his dogs on leash in one hand and a spear in the other. The mountains are in the distance, and through the clouds the sun is beaming forth in golden splendor.

Venus and Adonis was in pretty bad shape when the Getty got it. It had been poorly restored and stuck on a high wall in the home of the second Earl of Normanton in England. Now, previously hidden details and colors leap forth from the canvas. The Getty's conservation lab worked on it for over two years, cleaning it in four carefully controlled stages. This is an example of why this facility is now said to be the best in the world.

The irony is that the creator of all of this, oil billionaire J. Paul Getty, never set foot in the place. It opened in 1974 and its benefactor would die two years later in England without ever gazing across the Pacific from its exalted promenades.

A little farther up SR 1 (Pacific Coast Highway) is another relic of the goodwill of a wealthy person that may be more culturally significant to the Southland, though it lacks the art collection of the Getty:

> **Adamson House and Malibu Lagoon Museum**
> **23200 Pacific Coast Highway**
> **Malibu, CA 90265**
> **Wednesday-Saturday 11 a.m. to 3 p.m.**
> **(310) 456-8432**

This was the home of Rhoda Rindge Adamson, who was the daughter of

Fredrick Hastings Rindge and May Knight Rindge. The Rindges had come out from the East Coast in 1887 and bought the Topanga-Malibu-Sequit Rancho from the heirs of its owner, Jose Tapia. Tapia had controlled the land since 1805 under the Malibu Spanish Land Grant.

These first generation Yankee owners left their mark. May Knight Rindge was the founder of the Malibu Potteries in 1926. She started operations 1/2 mile east of the Malibu Pier on her beach property.

The products of Ms. Rindge's enterprise were the Malibu Tiles, elaborately patterned glazed ceramic works of art made to set off the Mission and Mediterranean style of architecture that is so much a part of the Southland landscape. To make them, imported clays were mixed with buff and red clays dug locally in Malibu Canyon. Business ceased in 1932. Ms. Rindge died in 1962 and left the house and remaining property to the State.

Completed in 1929, the two-story house is one of the few domiciles designed by Stiles Clements of Morgan, Walls, and Clements, one of the major commercial ar-

Details of tilework at the Adamson House show examples of Malibu tiles from the '20s and '30s.

chitectural firms of the 1920s. The El Capitan Theater building (with theater interior by G. Albert Lansburgh) in Hollywood (see March) and the Mayan Theater Building in Downtown L.A. (see February) are two of the more spectacular surviving examples.

The Adamson House sits right on the beach, where it is best viewed from. When you look at it from that view, with the blue sky behind it, it is just about the prettiest picture of a classic Spanish Colonial Revival house you could imagine. The brightly colored Malibu tiles are used to accent everything from fountains to windows and they are truly beautiful.

The Malibu Lagoon Museum, located next to the house, has Chumash artifacts and details the history of Malibu from 1542 to the present. This is via a smattering of old maps, rare photographs, and documents. They have tours periodically with historical stories about the area and about the Rindge and Adamson families.

The "royal family of Malibu" had a reputation for being somewhat lordly and pretentious. The gift shop sells a book by Frederick Hastings Ringe that he wrote in 1898 called *Happy Days In Southern California*. When you consider its author was writing while sitting in the middle of a 17,000-acre ranch on some of the best land in the Western world, it is easy to see how he came up with that title.

The Rindges did everything possible to keep people out of Malibu. They fought lawsuits (all the way to the Supreme Court), built their own railroad, and even blew things up with dynamite. Perhaps it is this history of determined privacy that caused Malibu to develop into the exclusive community it is today.

Though there are homes being built on seemingly every square foot of ground on the once-beautiful hills, the prices are so high that only the very wealthy can afford to live here. The Hollywood connection began in 1926 when silent movie star Anna Nillson moved into a beach house in the Malibu Beach Colony, which is reached by turning up a sliver of a street called Webb Way just west of the Adamson House.

This same corner is the location of a pretty little shopping center called the **Malibu Colony Plaza.** This structure is smaller than it looks because it only has the one row of shops that parallels Pacific Coast Highway. Built in 1991, it is done in a Mission Revival style and has little patios with some sculptures where you can sit. It also has a Hughes Market with the cleanest floor I have ever seen.

It is in this understated group of stores that perhaps the ultimate contemporary statement of modern Malibu can be found. A mythical temple of sorts to the culture is:

> **Granita Restaurant**
> **23725 West Malibu Road**
> **Malibu, CA 90265**
> **Wednesday-Sunday 11:30 a.m. to 2:30 p.m.**
> **Monday-Tuesday 5:30 to 10:30 p.m.**
> **(310) 456-0488**

On the outside, this restaurant looks like a shimmering green structure that was submerged under the ocean and resurfaced in Malibu. Many people consider this the best of Wolfgang Puck's California restaurants. Its name comes from a granular-textured Italian sorbet and, from start to finish, it is a wonderful dining experience.

The imagery of the exterior is continued in the fantasy decor of the interior—the finishing touches of Puck's wife, Barbara Lazaroff. It is a dreamscape of Atlantis. Each of the columns was hand formed in the shape of multi-colored amoeba spiraling up to the ceiling. The open kitchen is framed by what appear to be the swaying tentacles of a sea anemone. The bar is a cozy hideaway with glass Art Deco lamps hanging languidly overhead.

No detail has been overlooked in the place. The windows are etched or splashes of color. Each table is topped with a hand-blown olive oil bottle and fanciful candy striped glass stoppers.

The menu is a combination of popular items from Chinois on Main and Spago: grilled chicken with garlic, chopped vegetable salad, and of course, pizza cooked in a wood burning oven. The latter is available in such varieties as spicy shrimp, grilled vegetable, lamb sausage, and smoked sturgeon.

Hot in the City

Many a steamy movie plot has been inspired by the heat of August. The same sweltering air, that makes people stay up late and do crazy things, inspired one man to create a museum in honor of a 20th century technological answer to that swelter:

Air Conditioning and Refrigeration Industry Museum
[in the Training Center]
2220 South Hill Street
Los Angeles, CA 90042
call for appointment
(213) 747-0291

Air conditioning was invented in 1902 in Brooklyn by 25-year-old Willis Carrier, a giant step for mankind that was actually ranked once by *Life* magazine as one of the "100 most important developments that shaped America."

This museum was founded in 1979 by H.J. (Hy) Jarvis, brother of Howard Jarvis, the godfather of the tax revolt movement and author of California's Proposition 13. How he came to create this unique tribute evolved from experience at the helm of his own refrigeration equipment manufacturing company.

Though not intended as a tourist attraction, it is nevertheless open to the public. Located in the brick Training Center for the union, it really is a museum, with books recounting the history of refrigeration from early man's search for naturally cool caves to the Grecian-dug pits lined with snow to keep things cold.

Los Angeles, it turns out, is a very important place in air conditioner lore. In 1914, the California Limited out of Union Station became the first air-conditioned train and, in 1921, Sid Grauman opened the world's first air-conditioned theater, The Metropolitan.

Besides the opportunity for deeper study, there are lots of artifacts, such as an old-fashioned icebox and an exhibit of the large tongs used to carry the frozen blocks. You will learn that the ice making machine was originally invented in 1851 in Florida by a doctor to ice down patients suffering from fever or malaria.

There is a turn-of-the-century kerosene-powered fan with a placard that reads, "The Granddaddy of All Air Conditioning Equipment," but the showstopper of the collection is a bright green 1927 system from the Huntington Library. It is fittingly grand and looks like the engine room of the *Titanic*.

CITY WALKS
Melrose Avenue

Hot August nights make me think of strolling in the city. One of the original theatre districts of Los Angeles was along Melrose Avenue. It is here that you will feel at home in the evening swelter. There is no other street with the look of Melrose: nearly all of the store fronts are artistically and imaginatively built out. Some of the signs are more interesting looking than sculpture. Sexy people wander about looking in windows and at each other.

A Melrose bookstore that contributed to the growth of the "New Age" movement is:

> **The Bodhi Tree Bookstore**
> **8585 Melrose Avenue**
> **West Hollywood, CA 90069**
> **Daily 11 a.m. to 11 p.m. (new books)**
> **Daily 11 a.m. to 7 p.m. (used books)**
> **(310) 659-1733**

This was one of the first stores to specialize in books on such topics as astrology, spiritual growth, holistic healing, Western and Eastern philosophy, and women's issues. It was started by two former Douglas Aircraft engineers named Stan Madson and Phil Thompson in July of 1970.

They opened with about 2,000 titles, but bought the building next door in 1975 and created a used book division. In 1982, they added 2,000-square-feet and have grown to where they now carry 30,000 different book titles. In 1994, The Bodhi Tree Bookstore was named "Business of the Year" by the West Hollywood Chamber of Commerce.

There are lots of shops, boutiques, restaurants, and stage productions on Melrose. A real classic L.A. small theatre is a ways up the street:

> **Matrix Theatre**
> **7657 Melrose**
> **Los Angeles, CA 90046**
> **(213) 852-1445**

This 99-seat space is a landmark. Joe Stern, the Artistic Director, is somewhat of a legend. His resident company, Actors For Themselves, won a total of 19 L.A. Drama Critic's Circle Awards between 1975 and 1989. He took a hiatus from the theatre in 1989 to produce the television show "Law and Order" for four years, then successfully returned in 1993. His version of *The Tavern* was the hottest ticket in town for most of that year.

Among Melrose restaurants, everybody loves:

Tommy Tang's
7473 Melrose Avenue
Los Angeles, CA 90046
Daily 11:30 a.m. to 11 p.m.
(213) 651-1810

I remember when this Thai-and-sushi restaurant opened in 1983. It was so trendy you couldn't even get near the place. But today, it is actually much better. Since the food was always great, now that the atmosphere has been softened by time, it seems much friendlier and more low key. A lot of their customers have been coming for years and even bring their kids now.

The trademark here has always been quality ingredients and an interesting twist on traditional dishes. Thai food includes Tommy's legendary duck and "mee krob." The sushi is still among the best in town. Try the "Spicy Tuna Roll."

A couple of doors down is a wonderful success story and a wonderful restaurant:

Caffe Luna
7463 Melrose Avenue
Los Angeles, CA 90046
Sunday-Thursday 9 to 2 a.m.
Friday & Saturday 9 to 5 a.m.
(213) 655-8647

I remember trying Caffe Luna several years ago right after they had opened. The decor of the little 30-seat charmer consisted of white tile floors contrasted with thickly-textured red walls and ceiling, and assorted art everywhere. The effect was almost like being in a painting. To top it off, each table was covered with a sheet of white butcher block paper with a set of crayons to draw with. The bathrooms were decorated with some of the artwork left behind by some of the more talented patrons.

The food was even more delightful than the setting. It featured a menu designed by Laura Franke, former pastry chef at Emillio's that consisted of robust Italian dishes prepared in unusual ways. The owner, the beautiful and charming Corinne Lorain, personally insured that everyone had a wonderful meal.

Her imagination and hard work have paid off, because Caffe Luna put some tables out front on the sidewalk first, then doubled in size by knocking the wall out. They added a landscaped patio in the back along with some little white lights and a silver moon sculpture.

It always seems to be busy and the lively open kitchen adds to the vibrancy. Also, Caffe Luna gets 10 points from me for staying open so late. The menu has also grown considerably and includes a full roster of Italian specialties.

Their "focaccia" bread forms the basis for various "panini" (sandwiches on focaccia). Caffe Luna's focaccia bread, made with a caramel-base and baked with rosemary, is exquisite. Single serving flat pieces of focaccia are offered with a variety of fresh toppings, sprinkled with plenty of herbs and served appealingly on wooden platters.

If you love salads, this is your place. The salad menu is quite extensive and includes such specialties as Waldorf, made with marinated chicken, apples, walnuts, and radicchio, and Caprise salad, made with roma tomatoes, buffalo mozzarella, calamata olives, and basil. All of the chopped salads are made to order—a feature quite unusual in a moderately-priced restaurant such as this. The desserts are a fitting end to the rest of the high-quality food. I recommend the espresso ricotta cheesecake with chocolate espresso sauce. For a dinner paired with a savvy and stimulating show, you could not do better.

Another Melrose Theatre is across the street:

Zephyr Theater
7456 Melrose Avenue
Los Angeles, CA 90046
(213) 466-1767

The courtyard entrance area to this 99-seat playhouse is very pleasant and is used sometimes for pre-theatre brunch. Built in 1953 and originally called the "Horseshoe Stage," it got its name from the design of the auditorium. Probably the most famous show produced here in recent years was the multiple-award-winning *Berlin To Broadway* with Kurt Weill.

On the same side of the street are three classic Melrose stores in close proximity. The first is:

Maya
7452 Melrose Avenue
Los Angeles, CA 90046
Monday-Thursday 11 a.m. to 9 p.m.
Friday & Saturday 11 a.m. to 10 p.m.
Sunday 11 a.m. to 7 p.m.
(213) 655-2708

Called "The Greatest Earring Show On Earth," Maya features a wall covered with thousands of them. Prices range from a few dollars for novelty earrings to hundreds for some designer styles. They also have a great selection of masks and folk art.

Another unusual store is:

> **Wacko**
> **7416 Melrose Avenue**
> **Los Angeles, CA 90046**
> **Monday-Thursday 11 a.m. to 9 p.m.**
> **Friday & Saturday 11 a.m. to 12 p.m.**
> **Sunday 12 to 7:30 p.m.**
> **(213) 651-3811**

This unique store is aptly named. Entering is half the fun: you go down a long corridor with bright-colored mural art on one side and a row of eight side-by-side funhouse mirrors on the other. The stock is an eclectic mixture of cards, weird toys, magic tricks and gags. The latter includes such classics as the farting pillow and the fake dog turd.

A Melrose veteran is the:

> **Soap Plant**
> **7400 Melrose Ave**
> **Los Angeles, CA 90046**
> **Monday-Thursday 10 a.m. to 10 p.m.**
> **Friday & Saturday 10 to 12 a.m.**
> **Sunday 11 a.m. to 8 p.m.**
> **(213) 651-5587**

The Soap Plant's assortment of odd cards, books, little do-dads, and, yes, soap, is legendary. Stop in for some fun.

Melrose Avenue is also the site of the resident theatre for one of the oldest and longest established comedy groups in Southern California:

> **Groundlings Theatre**
> **7307 Melrose Avenue**
> **Los Angeles, CA 90046**
> **(213) 934-9700**

The Groundlings got their start in 1976 and present both improvisation and meticulously staged comic theatre. The latter tend to be satirical in nature and have included such shows as *Just Like The Pom Pom Girls*. The stage is only set Friday through Sunday nights, but if you get inspired, they have comedy workshops.

One of the major intersections that Melrose crosses is at La Brea—an interesting street in its own right. Right near this intersection is an institution among hot dog stands:

Pink's Famous Chili Dogs
711 North La Brea Avenue
Los Angeles, CA 90036
Daily 10 a.m. to 2 p.m.
(213) 931-4223

There's always a crowd standing on the sidewalk under the white neon lights in front of Pink's. They are waiting for the greatest chili dogs in the world—perfect food for a hot August night. The title is not just another colorful name but instead a namesake: after Paul L. Pink who opened the stand in 1939.

On the other side of Melrose on La Brea is a wonderful, original dining experience:

Louis XIV
606 North La Brea Avenue
Los Angeles, CA 90036
Monday-Saturday 6 p.m. to 12 a.m.
(213) 934-5102

I love the contrast between Pink's and this spot—like yin and yang of the Melrose/La Brea corner. Where Pink's is a bright-white open space, Louis XIV is dark space under awnings. Its Art Deco lamps hang along the facade.

This is another little restaurant that grew. The once tiny French bistro took over the Firenze Kitchen next door and, after some remodeling created a very interesting and mysterious restaurant interior. What makes it so stimulating is that the space is broken up into small rooms and it is dimly lit by the candles on each table. Two staircases lead to the upstairs area with its exposed wooden beam ceiling. There is a separate little bar where you could sit and talk for hours.

Not only is the French food delicious, it is of a more hearty variety than is found in "designer" French restaurants. The truly hospitable waiters and charming decor all combine to create a mood wonderfully conducive to romance.

Continuing west on Melrose, you will come to one of the most acclaimed restaurants in the Southland:

Citrus
6703 Melrose Avenue
Hollywood, CA 90038
Monday-Saturday 12 to 11 p.m.

Sunday 6:30 to 11 p.m.

(213) 857-0034

Michel Richard came to Los Angeles in 1977. He has since established several restaurants (Citronelle in Santa Barbara described in February being the most recent). Citrus was the restaurant that really established him as one of Southern California's best loved cooks. Unlike the stereotype prima donna chef, Richard is genuinely gracious.

Citrus is white and bright with gray and black wicker chairs. The main dining area is romantic under umbrellas and the kitchen is on display behind a glass wall. As you enter, to the right is the **Bistro at Citrus**, an informal restaurant-within-a-restaurant. It features a gracefully curved counter and a decor that is playful and fun. The walls are covered with an assortment of different kinds of menus. In the bistro the prices are generally lower than in the regular restaurant.

From here, Melrose continues east and you will come to Highland. Just north of Melrose on this street is a great coffeehouse/performance venue:

Highland Grounds

742 North Highland Avenue

Los Angeles, CA 90036

Monday-Saturday 9 to 12:30 a.m.

Sunday 10 to 12:30 a.m.

(213) 466-1507

With its colorful mural wrapping around the front, Highland Grounds lights up the street. Inside is a room with a high ceiling and a balcony reachable by a staircase. There is a curved blue bar with a green counter. Outside there is a pretty enclosed patio with large palm trees. A large trompe l'oeil mural depicts a cracked and crumbling opening in the wall with the mountains, palm trees, and blue sky showing through.

The coffee and food are excellent. The muffins are baked on the premises and come in several delicious varieties including blueberry, apple, and raisin bran.

The ceiling has a black metal framework that winds its way all around the perimeter. From this framework are suspended various theatre lights. A performance area is visible from anywhere in the interior. An eclectic assortment of readings and musical acts are featured by owner Richard Brenner.

A little ways up El Centro from Melrose is a theater with one of the best locations for before or after theater dinner or strolling:

Cast-At-The-Circle and Cast Theaters
804 El Centro Avenue
Hollywood, CA 90038
(213) 462-0265

This complex of two little theatres (99 and 65 seats respectively) has an old history as a performance space. Charles Chaplin once directed here. It was not doing so well in the early '70s when a $100,000 per year financial public relations man named Ted Schmitt quit his job, divorced his wife, and left his straight life in the suburbs of Orange County to take over the Cast in 1975.

The ebullient Mr. Schmitt energized the moribund theatre and for over a decade served as producer and artistic director. He attracted top quality guest shows to rent the theatre and also put together in-house productions. His death from AIDS was a great loss to theatre in the Southland. There is now a special Drama-Logue award for theatre that bears his name.

Just east of El Centro on Melrose, right across from KCAL Channel 9, is a very special L.A. Mexican restaurant:

Lucy's El Adobe Cafe
5536 Melrose Avenue
Los Angeles, CA 90038
Monday-Saturday 11:30 a.m. to 11:30 p.m.
(213) 462-9421

A picture of former California Governor Jerry Brown has hung in the window here since 1974. More pictures of him surround the register up front. This is because Lucy's was the kick-off point for his Presidential bid that year. The owner's daughter Patricia, the family bookworm, worked on the campaign. Assistant Manager Jane Nunez was originally a campaign worker and ended up staying on at the restaurant. This is a good illustration of the blending of food, intellectual debate, and loving spirit that have characterized Lucy's El Adobe Cafe since it was opene in 1964 by Frank and Lucy Casado. Most of the employees have worked here for 19 or 20 years

Though they have grown with the addition of two rooms, the original space has a palatable warmth and energy you can feel the moment you walk in. It is a small, fairly dark room with eleven booths and a red tile floor. One wall is completely covered with 8-by-10 glossies of the various famous people who come in regularly.

If you sit in the front booth, you can be with Demi Moore, Lyle Lovett, Ricardo Montalbam, Bernadette Peters, Cher, Connie Chung, and CNN correspondent

Charles Jaco, who is pictured standing next to a live bomb stuck in the ground in Kuwait. An original signed Peanut's cartoon cell shows Snoopy in his signature position on his doghouse addressing Linus; the caption reads "L'Ermitage? How gauche. Take me to Lucy's El Adobe." Often, the collection of celebrities is changed or taken down when the frames fall and break. One that was removed recently is that of Joseph Campbell. Lucy wondered if anyone would know who he was. "I miss him," she sighs.

When you ask her about her large circle of friends, she will say that more than once. A lit-up model of the starship *Enterprise* hangs by the register. "Star Trek started the same year as we did," Lucy explained. "What a man, what a visionary. I miss him."

The Casados had been married for 42 years when Frank died in 1990. Well-loved by his patrons, Frank was given a part in a movie made by the late John Candy: *Who Is Harry Crumb?* And a lot of musicians Lucy fed in the '60s and '70s when they were poor, such as the Eagle's Don Henley, have come back now that they have made it.

Singer/songwriter Jimmy Webb, who wrote the song "Adios" for Lucy, sent a piano with a plaque on it bearing the inscription, "In Loving Memory of Frank." It now sits in one of the newer rooms. The first Christmas after Frank's death, she received some unexpected company: Phil Collins and his wife and family came by so she wouldn't be lonely.

Perhaps the most original musical tribute came after none other than the Dahli Lama stopped by for a visit along with 30 Tibetan monks. They mentioned Lucy's El Adobe in one of their recorded chants.

The restaurant's tradition of being a gathering place for important events and announcements continues today. In 1994, the press conference for the opening of Louis Valdez' *Bandido* at the Mark Taper Forum was held here. A continuing series open to the public sets aside one Wednesday evening per month for talks with newspeople; it is called "Drinking With the Enemy."

The great landmark of Melrose Avenue is the wrought iron gate that marks the entrance of:

Paramount Studios
5555 Melrose Avenue
Hollywood, CA 90038
Tours offered Monday-Friday
(213) 468-5575

Of the old studios that started during the silent era, Paramount is the only one that stayed in Hollywood proper. The Spanish Renaissance-style gate, with "Paramount Pictures" gracefully written out in script above it, looks as much the movie set as those found within. The most famous image of it was emblazoned on the big screen in 1950 when Erich von Stroheim drove Gloria Swanson through it in the movie *Sunset Boulevard*.

Some of the biggest names in the history of film have come through these gates. Bob Hope and Bing Crosby, Dorothy Lamour, Marlene Dietrich, Gary Cooper—and even Rudolph Valentino—all worked for Paramount. The familiar mountain in the Paramount logo is said to be Sugarloaf Peak, visible from Paramount Ranch in Calabasas (see October).

Larchmont Boulevard

Just a heartbeat east of where El Centro hits Melrose is another unique walking street of Los Angeles, Larchmont Boulevard. It is ironic that it runs perpendicular to Melrose because the two are such a contrast to one another. Where Melrose features wild and unusual architecture, Larchmont resembles an old-fashioned downtown outdoor mall on the East Coast. It should: in the early 1920s, it was named for the hamlet of Larchmont, New York. Traveling south from Melrose, the section called "The Village" starts at Beverly and ends at 1st Street.

The village section of Larchmont Boulevard comes out of nowhere. Pretty trees shade the sidewalks and, except for a Pay Less drugstore and a Starbuck's Coffee, most of the stores and food vendors are individually owned and uniquely charming.

Every great city street should have a newsstand. Larchmont Boulevard has one called appropriately enough:

> **The Stand**
> **226 Larchmont Boulevard**
> **Los Angeles, CA 90004**
> **Sunday-Thursday 7:30 a.m. to 9 p.m.**
> **Friday & Saturday 7:30 a.m. to 10 p.m.**
> **(213) 962-9626**

Owner Kim Christensen stocks over 300 different publications. Do not be frightened by the plump pit bull curled up on his bed. His name is Boner T. McGinty and he is quite friendly.

Many of these mom-and-pop businesses are threatened by the ubiquitous chains. Also, the gentrification of the area has led to a proliferation of expensive little Italian restaurants employing wanna-be actors. An exception to this is a real Larchmont restaurant original called:

> **The Gingham Garden**
> **123 Larchmont Village**
> **Los Angeles, CA 90004**
> **Monday-Saturday 7:30 a.m. to 4 p.m.**
> **(213) 461-1677**

The decor could best be described as "Pseudo-Nautical Duck Modern." There are yellow plastic ducks in rows along the wall. The owners, Nate and Beverly Blitzer, previously owned a gingham gift shop whose inventory formed the basis for the interior here when it opened in 1981.

The breakfast menu looks like a child's writing assignment. The printing has been placed between wide lines separated by broken lines: the capital letters fill the wide lines, the small letters fit inside broken lines. For lunch, they have a big selection of salads and sandwiches, the most popular of the latter is the tuna with raisin.

Sunset Boulevard

The most exciting street in Southern California at night is the stretch of Sunset Boulevard that runs from Doheny Drive to Crescent Heights. This forms the northern border of West Hollywood and connects Beverly Hills to Hollywood. It is almost as if the glamour of the latter two and the night club tradition of the former all come together here as well.

During my early college years, I was the doorman/bouncer at Pat Collin's Celebrity Club at the top end of this strip. This was the supper club of the entertainer known as the "Hip Hypnotist." It is long gone and I find it somewhat depressing to note that I cannot tell which of the businesses there now is the former night spot. It is either the copy place or the beauty supply store.

The ignominious end of my former place of employ notwithstanding, there is a tradition of clubs and night spots in this locale that continues today.

At the top of the strip is the side-by-side combination of the:

> **Rainbow Bar and Grill**
> **9015 Sunset Boulevard**
> **West Hollywood, CA 90069**
> **Daily 6 p.m. to 2 a.m.**
> **(310) 278-4232**
> and:

The Roxie Theatre
9009 Sunset Boulevard
West Hollywood, CA 90069
(310) 278-9457

In 1964, Mario Maglieri moved to L.A. from Chicago to help his buddy Elmer Valentine with his Sunset Strip club, the Whisky-A-Go-Go. Eight years later, they opened these two places and they are still going strong.

The Rainbow is a two-level restaurant and bar. What is particularly noteworthy about the club is that despite being such a famous place with such a glittering history, it is very warm and friendly.

You'll walk past a little patio before entering the very dark interior. The tiny foyer has a fish tank with a giant collage of snapshots of various rock stars and interesting people. You'll meet Tony Vescio, the dapper and friendly manager, who has been with the Rainbow since 1974.

The atmosphere is glamorous and Old World at the same time. Overhead is a two-story vaulted beam ceiling. Heavy dark wood and lighter inlaid wood over the stone fireplace are set off by the red leatherette booths lit by candlelight. Rock 'n' roll pahenalia is displayed much the same way tapestries or suits of armor might be in a medieval castle.

Along one wall, there are signed cymbals from famous drummers and on the other wall by the tables, there are gold records from bands like Poison. A row of second floor level alcoves display a medley of instruments—including signed electric guitars—like a diorama about Sunset Strip musical life. The food is a mixture of Italian and California specialties.

The Roxie is a major venue for bands. It holds 400-500 with standing room. There is no assigned seating, so if you want to sit at a table and eat, you'd better get there early. Outside, there always seems to be line of people in black waiting to get in. If it weren't for all the bare skin, an unknowing passerby might think it was a funeral for some recently deceased rock star.

A couple of doors down on the same side of the street is a special coffee shop:

Duke's Coffee Shop
8909 Sunset Boulevard
West Hollywood, CA 90069
Monday-Friday 7:30 a.m. to 8:30 p.m.
Saturday & Sunday 8 a.m. to 3:30 p.m
(310) 652-9411

Formerly at 8585 Santa Monica Boulevard, Duke's used to be part of the legend-ary/notorious Tropicana Motel, a hangout of wanna-be rock musicians. When that place of lodging and late night carousing was bulldozed in 1987, the coffee shop moved here. The old signs, nail holes and all, now hang on the wall above the counter.

The tropical theme is barely there, but the 8-by-10 photos and autographs along the wall in front of the counter leave no doubt as to who comes in. Besides musi-cians, Sharon Stone, Harrison Ford, Terri Garr, John Kennedy, Jr., and countless others all smile down on you as you drink your morning coffee.

The breakfasts are great. Many restaurants these days get their blintzes pre-made. Here they are big homemade masterpieces. The menu on the wall includes such specialties as "matzo brie."

Of course, the legendary club that survives on Sunset is the:

> **Whisky-A-Go-Go**
> **8901 Sunset Boulevard**
> **West Hollywood, CA 90069**
> **(310) 652-4205**

The Whisky's purple exterior and script sign are as much a part of rock 'n' roll as the electric guitar. It became known as the place to record albums after Johnny Rivers made a string of hits here. The Doors played here dozens of times in 1966. Other groups included The Byrds, The Animals, The Who, The Young Rascals, and Cream. It seats 450 and serves food continuously.

Farther down the strip, across from the sprawling main building of Tower Records is one of the best bookstores in the L.A. area:

> **Book Soup**
> **8818 Sunset Boulevard**
> **West Hollywood, CA 90069**
> **Daily 9 a.m. to 12**
> **(310) 659-3110**

Glen Goldman opened the original Book Soup a few doors west in 1974. They moved here in 1987, knocked out the wall and doubled in size for Christmas of 1989. Now they carry over 70,000 titles and are particularly strong in art, architec-ture, and film. Maurice Sendack, Ray Bradbury, and Clive Barker all say it is their favorite bookstore.

In April of '94, along the outside east wall, they opened a marvelous newsstand. Illuminated by a string of white lights at night, it looks particularly appealing when you are driving west and see it tucked into the bend in the road. This newsstand completed a little "Book Soup Complex," because it shares a patio with the restaurant they opened next door in January of 1994:

Book Soup Bistro
8800 Sunset Boulevard
West Hollywood, CA 90069
Monday-Friday 11:30 a.m. to 10:30 p.m.
Saturday & Sunday 9:30 a.m. to 11 p.m.
(310) 657-1072

Located in the modern brick Carloco office building, the interior of Book Soup Bistro has the warm yellow/orange glow of fine wood. The centerpiece is the curved rosewood-colored bar with 14 bar-stool height chairs of dark wood. Dark wood tables and chairs are set off by the blond wood of the paneling and the wine case that forms one wall. The hanging dark orange lighting fixtures put a soft light on the mood. Even though there are no books on display, the feeling is like being in a very civilized library.

The semi-exposed kitchen offers a moderately-priced mix of esoteric foods such as Tuscan bread soup, or a very hearty Caesar salad, or liguini with smoked chicken. You can sit inside at a table, out on the patio beside the newsstand—on display like some giant three-dimensional mural—or at the bar. The latter is a very nice blending of the mood of a regular bar and a coffee bar.

Perched on a hill on the other side of the street is the Southland's most famous restaurant of the last 20 years:

Spago
1114 Horn Avenue
West Hollywood, CA 90069
Daily 6 to 11 p.m.
(310) 652-4025

Besides making Wolfgang Puck a household word, the food here helped define California cuisine. I remember the stir over Spago's pizza with duck sausage cooked in a wood flame oven. The smell of it as it comes out of the kitchen is one of the great smells in life.

For such a famous place, it has a simple decor enlivened by explosions of color from a huge floral bouquet. Big windows look out at the lights and people of Sunset Boulevard snaking past below.

As you continue east on Sunset, the road rises and curves and suddenly the strip starts looking more like Beverly Hills than Hollywood, as expensive boutiques and sidewalk cafes line both sides of the street. This area is called **Sunset Plaza** and it was originally built during the 1930s. There are more sidewalk restaurants here than I have ever seen anywhere else, and the view of the Ferraris and beautiful people certainly is stimulating. A good place to go for some pasta salad is:

> **Pasta Etcetera**
> **8650 Sunset Boulevard**
> **West Hollywood, CA 90069**
> **Daily 8:30 a.m. to 10:30 p.m.**
> **(310) 854-0094**

Fresh pasta was a rare commodity when Lenore Breslauer started Pasta Etcetera in the late '70s. A great informal restaurant with about 20 small tables, it also supplies many of the finer restaurants in the area with pasta that is certainly terrific. A lot of people get take-out here as well. They always have a variety of pasta dishes ready to go as well as the uncooked stuff.

The sidewalk cafe style of the place and posh Sunset Plaza location make it a good place to have lunch or dinner and people watch. This is a lovely spot to take a stroll after eating. The parking lot in back, which is on a hill overlooking L.A. and Hollywood, has the most romantic view of any lot in the city and is a great place to snuggle. Also, Pasta Etcetera, for all its glamorous surroundings, is quite inexpensive.

Very nearby is one of the nicest small theaters in Southern California:

> **Tiffany Theater**
> **8532 Sunset Boulevard**
> **West Hollywood, CA 90069**
> **(213) 652-6165**

This theater is a rental so it is impossible to predict the quality of the shows, however, it is the most expensive small theater there is to rent, so whatever show you see here will probably at least have nice sets. There are two cool and comfortable 99-seat spaces.

I have had some wonderful experiences here. On our second date, my darling and I saw John Godber's *Bouncers* at the Tiffany. I chatted briefly with the (at that time) up-and-coming actor Tim Robbins after his Actor's Gang production of *Carnage*. For more on the Actor's Gang, see September.

On the sidewalk in front of building number 8524, next to the Tiffany, is a plaque proclaiming it to be the site of the Warner Brothers' television series "77 Sunset

Strip," which ran from October 19, 1958 to February 7, 1964.

Right next to the Hyatt is the most famous name in a comedy club anywhere in the whole world:

The Comedy Store
8433 Sunset Boulevard
West Hollywood, CA 90069
Daily 8 p.m. to 2 a.m.
(213) 656-6225

Originally opened in 1972 in the site formerly occupied by Ciro's, The Comedy Store is second only to the Ice House in Pasadena in longevity in the Southland among ha-ha houses. The enlarged signatures on the marque over the entrance tells the story: Pauly Shore, Arsenio Hall, Eddie Murphy, George Carlin, Louis Anderson, and Bud Cort are just a sampling of the names of those who have graced the stage here.

Across the street is the newest and most spectacular hot spot on the strip:

House of Blues
8430 Sunset Boulevard
West Hollywood, CA 90069
Daily 11:30 a.m. to 2 a.m.
(213) 650-0247

"On a mission from God" was the phrase repeated throughout the Dan Ackroyd and John Belushi comedy/musical classic *The Blues Brothers* as the two siblings in their suits, dark glasses, and hats hustled to put together their comeback benefit concert and raise money for the orphanage. That refrain is repeated here, along with various other sayings on the fliers, menus and on the walls. Dan Ackroyd is, in fact, one of the owners of this amazing club, as is Steve Tyler from Aerosmith.

"Be nice or leave" is another one of those slogans that is written on the outside of the corrugated metal exterior of this three-story structure built into the hillside. The logo on the tower is of a human heart with a belt of thorns wrapped around it. At night, the whole places glows eerily as the blue/white lights shine on it.

The interior is even more dramatic, with bayou gear and voodoo masks. The whole thing reminds me of the "Pirates of the Caribbean" ride at Disneyland. The main dining room has an A-frame ceiling with large plaster cameos of blues greats under blue lights. The menu features "international peasant fare" (Cajun). Video screens tell the stories of the artists that are performing. There are six bars, and the one in the main dining room splits open when a show starts, allowing the dining patrons to overlook the main stage. The room downstairs has no seats and holds 250 to 300.

Across the street and down the road a bit, the freedom of the American highway is celebrated at a shrine to American motorcycles:

Thunder Roadhouse
8363 Sunset Boulevard
Los Angeles, CA 90069
Daily 9 a.m. to 2 a.m.
(213) 650-6011

This complex includes a restaurant, a clothing and artifact store, and a showroom filled with classic American motorcycles. The seats at the counter are Harley saddles. The menu is American food with specialties such as "American Thunder Pie" (brownies with coffee ice cream).

The House of Blues uses numerous references to *The Blues Brothers* movie starring club co-owner Dan Ackroyd and the late John Belushi. It is ironic that you can stand in front of the club, look up from Sunset Boulevard going east, and see the place Belushi spent his last night:

Chateau Marmont
8221 Sunset Boulevard
Hollywood, CA 90046
(213) 656-1010

Many people, who have only heard the lurid tale of how the former "Saturday Night Live" star died, are surprised when they see—or more accurately—hear the place. It is very quiet; the building and grounds are timelessly serene. The Norman castle-styled Chateau Marmont seems like an old Hollywood Hills estate.

Throughout its history, it has attracted privacy-conscious celebrities such as Greta Garbo. Indeed, in the description of the accommodations it is always mentioned whether or not a room or cottage has its own private entrance. The Chateau offers rooms, suites, cottages, and two bedroom, two bath hillside bungalows complete with fireplace, kitchen, private garden, and "private street entrance and carport."

Across the street from the Chateau Marmont, there suddenly looms a statue of Bullwinkle holding up Rocky. The building behind was the offices of Jay Ward Productions, creators of the legendary moose and squirrel. Around the corner is the:

Dudley Do-Right Emporium
8200 Sunset Boulevard

Hollywood, CA 90046
Tuesday, Thursday & Saturday only
11 a.m. to 4:30 p.m.
(213) 656-6550

From the moment you enter this whimsical store, you immediately begin to smile. It is just one of those places. Opened in 1971, the emporium is the official outlet for merchandise featuring characters of Jay Ward Productions. These include Bullwinkle and Rocky, George of the Jungle, Mr. Peabody, Boris and Natasha, and a host of others. They have T-shirts with the different characters as well as Dudley Do-Right's slogan, "You knew the job was dangerous when you took it."

Mrs. Jay Ward and her daughter and staff create a friendly, family atmosphere. Newspaper clippings with comments about Rocky and Bullwinkle, including an endorsement from Kareem Abdul-Jabbar, adorn the walls. You can even get such esoterica as storyboards from the shows.

Across the street is a one of the many places where I wasted my youth:

Coconut Teaszer
8117 Sunset Boulevard
Hollywood, CA 90046
Daily 6 p.m. to 2 a.m.
(213) 654-4887

This bright purple structure has had so many new bands play here that it is sometimes visited by record company executives looking for diamonds-in-the-rough. Around 8 p.m. each night, several different groups usually begin playing in the main room with its sawdust on the floor. On the side, there is a room for dancing where recorded music is played. Because it is right on the corner where Laurel Canyon dumps out from the Valley, it is a prime destination for disaffected youth from that oven-like place in the summer.

Diagonally across the intersection is a big, round new building that is the home of the:

Laemmle's Sunset 5 Theatres
8000 West Sunset Boulevard
Hollywood, CA 90046
(213) 848-3500

The imposing yellow Post Modern edifice that houses these theaters opened in August of 1992. It seems to suggest both Classical and California themes with its stately courtyard surrounded by the sweep of two floors of stores, arched windows, and faux tiles. These theaters, the nicest art showcases in Southern California, are the newest in the Laemmle chain of art theaters. The Sunset 5 has three 160-seat, one 220-seat, and one 280-seat auditoriums.

Manager Roger Christensen cuts a welcoming figure in his black tuxedo with his friendly manner and knowledge and love of films. He has worked for the theater chain since 1982 and speaks affectionately of the late founder, Max Laemmle.

Karl Laemmle was the founder of Universal Studios. His cousin Sigmond was Max Laemmle's father. Movies were in Max's blood, because he went into the exhibition end of the business in the 1940s. Defying conventional wisdom, he decided to feature foreign language films at the Los Feliz Theater (not a Laemmle now). Since that time Laemmle Theatres have grown to become the only chain to have this policy.

Other locations include the Monica 4-Plex (the site of the A.F.I. Festival in June), the Music Hall in Beverly Hills, the Colorado and Esquire Theatres in Pasadena, the Grande 4-Plex in Downtown L.A., the Town and Country 3-Plex in Encino, and the Royal in West L.A. His son, Bob, and grandson, Greg, carry on the family tradition from the company offices above the latter theater.

In the same building is the:

> **Virgin Megastore**
> **8000 West Sunset Boulevard**
> **Hollywood, CA 90046**
> **Sunday-Thursday 9 a.m. to 12 a.m.**
> **Friday & Saturday 9 a.m. to 1 a.m.**
> **(213) 650-8666**

This large, two-level store has a DJ spinning tunes during evening hours, video, and a separate room for classical recordings. Besides listening stations for CDs, it features a computer with a touch screen to help you locate music. When you find what you are looking for, it prints out a slip with the information.

The former occupant of this corner was the legendary **Schwab's Drugs**, which was both a drugstore and a coffee shop with fountain service. Its post war "modern" interior would have been considered "retro" today: the booths were of gold vinyl with fake marble formica tables and the chandelier looked like a crashing satellite. It probably would not get much interest from today's young trend-conscious actors.

But in its day, it was the place where all Hollywood seemed to go. Deals were made, future stars were discovered, and hearts were broken. Songwriter Harold Arlen staggered drunk out of the nearby Garden of Allah and sat on the stoop of Schwab's. He looked up and in his drunken haze saw a rainbow in the Hollywood Hills above Crescent Heights and wrote the song, "Somewhere Over The Rainbow."

ANNIVERSARY OF THE DEATH OF MARILYN MONROE (AUGUST 5)

There are two dates in August that commemorate the (at the time) unexpected demise of two individuals who left lasting marks on Southern California. The first is that of Marilyn Monroe on August 5. Her sudden death from an overdose was a shock to millions. How could someone so young, so vibrant just be gone?

Since her passing, her mystique has grown. Every year, many people still pay their respect to her at:

> **Westwood Memorial Park**
> **1218 Glendon Avenue**
> **Los Angeles, CA 90024**
> **(310) 474-1579**

The image of Marilyn Monroe is one of the most enduring in the world. It adorns more memorabilia on sale in tourist shops along Hollywood Boulevard than any other female star. Probably the most famous of these came in 1955 in *The Seven Year Itch* when a sudden blast of air from the subway grating blew her skirt up over her head. Later it would be revealed that this was an accident caused by the wind machine operator's miscalculation. This most famous on-camera blunder was not left on the cutting room floor and became one of filmdom's most celebrated moments.

Though now we say that she obviously "had something," success did not come right away. She made the rounds of studios and finally with the patronage of Joseph Scheck, chairman of the board of 20th Century Fox, she got her "big break" in films.

She was found dead in her Brentwood house by her housekeeper in 1962. There was an empty bottle of sedatives by her bed. Speculation has ranged from murder by the mob to murder by the FBI.

Over the years, the crypt's facade has been kissed by so many women wearing a full mouth of lipstick that it has become stained. It also bears the scars from the time when some young men from a nearby fraternity tried to pry it open.

At her funeral, they played "Somewhere Over The Rainbow."

ANNIVERSARY OF THE DEATH OF WILL ROGERS (AUGUST 14)

Will Rogers was one of the most beloved entertainers in history. An American humorist in the tradition of Mark Twain (but without Twain's acerbic side), Rogers not only wrote and gave live performances, he had the benefit of radio to bring his warm, folksy wit to millions.

His death in a plane crash in 1935 (that also killed Wiley Post) was more than just the death of another performer. People felt as if their best friend had died. The man who was most famous for saying "I never met a man I didn't like" would no longer be around to poke fun at life's foibles. I recall as a boy in the mid-1960s when an older man told me he was still sad about it.

Rogers left a large physical legacy to the Southland:

> **Will Rogers Park**
> **1501 Will Rogers State Park Road**
> **Pacific Palisades, CA 90272**
> **Daily 8:30 a.m. to 6 p.m. (park)**
> **Daily 10:30 a.m. to 4:30 p.m. (house)**
> **(310) 454-8212**

Besides his popularity, the humorist achieved considerable financial success. He bought a 187-acre plot of land overlooking the ocean and, in 1924, he built a big ranch house on it. After his death, his wife lived on the property for nine years, then in 1944 gave it to the State of California. It is now a park and museum dedicated to Rogers' life.

The house is great. It is filled with memorabilia collected by Rogers from around the world. The Visitor's Center shows a 10-minute film that tells his story and the store sells books and photos.

The grounds are obviously extensive and include numerous picnic tables, some of which overlook the polo field. Rogers was a devoted player and it was he that gave the famous restaurant in the Beverly Hills Hotel its name: The Polo Lounge. He built a 300-by-100 yard polo field on his estate where matches are still played, usually on Saturday at 2 p.m. or Sunday at 10 a.m.

There are horse trails that meander into the hills behind the ranch. Some of these are used as hiking paths. Just west of the ranger station by the tennis courts is Will Rogers' Trail, a one mile path that will take you to **Will Rogers' Inspiration Point.** Though the rise is only about 300 feet, the views of the bay and the city are wonderful.

If you would like to meditate or take a stroll in a jewel-like setting, on the other side of Sunset Boulevard, closer to Pacific Coast Highway, is the:

> **Self Realization Fellowship Lake Shrine**
> **17190 Sunset Boulevard**

Pacific Palisades, CA 90272
(310) 454-4114

This is the sister to the Self Realization Fellowship Retreat and Hermitage on the coast in Encinitas (see May). The 10-acre site nestled in a ravine was a former movie set that was purchased by Paramahansa Yogananda in 1950. It is a picture-perfect little lake with a walking trail that goes all the way around.

This walking trail is like a miniature journey through life. The trail takes you down through a sunken garden, past threatening cactus, over little bridges, and to restful little glades. The biggest clearing is the lawn enclosed by the Golden Lotus Archway. A sarcophagus holds some of the ashes of Mahatma Gandhi.

Perhaps the most picturesque sight is that of a wooden replica of a Dutch windmill that is the chapel for the Fellowship. It is covered with vines and projects out into the middle of the lake where it is surrounded by water on three sides.

Where Temescal Canyon meets Pacific Coast Highway, you can have a hearty breakfast or lunch at:

Patrick's Roadhouse
106 Entrada Drive
Santa Monica, CA 90402
Monday 8 a.m. to 2 p.m.
Tuesday-Friday 8 a.m. to 3 p.m.
Saturday & Sunday 9 a.m. to 4 p.m.
(310) 459-4544

With its bright green exterior, white lettered sign, and shamrock decorated awnings, Patrick's Roadhouse is hard to miss from Pacific Coast Highway (SR 1). Be prepared to wait a bit for breakfast in particular, because the place is quite fashionable and popular.

NISEI WEEK

California, of all of the states, has had a unique relationship with the Japanese. We had our differences during World War II: Santa Barbara was shelled by a zealous Japanese submarine commander and the forced internment of Japanese Americans living in the Golden State is a black spot in American history (see February). Yet, there has always been a link between us as if we realized inevitably we would have to work together as Pacific neighbors.

There are a lot of things about the Japanese that seem made for Southern Californians to like. First of all, they make the best cars in the world, which is reason enough to get our attention. Sushi bars fit our informal, breezy lifestyle just as naturally as Mexican cantinas.

The Japanese seem equally fascinated by Southern California. The Japanese Disneyland in Tokyo Harbor is beloved like a national treasure. Golf, a game many people moved here just to play, is similarly revered. Some of our greatest buildings, including the Biltmore in downtown L.A., are Japanese-owned. We also have earthquakes, just like back home.

Around August 7 through 14 is the time of Nisei Week, which celebrates Japanese American life. For this, the place to be in Southern California is Little Tokyo in downtown L.A. There are parades, floats, exhibits, bands, cultural events, and a carnival, as well as some very exciting judo, karate, and sword tournaments.

Little Tokyo

Little Tokyo is enclosed by Los Angeles, Alameda, 1st, and 3rd Streets. It is the hub of Southern California's Japanese cultural and economic community and encompasses four shopping centers, containing over 100 restaurants and shops.

This is the closest thing in Southern California to being in Japan. As you walk about, it can have a strong resemblance: many of the shopkeepers begin their morning by washing their windows, and practically all of the restaurants, including the pizza parlor, have colorful plastic food displays in their windows.

The festival is centered around the:

**Japanese American
Cultural and Commu-
nity Center
244 South San Pedro
Los Angeles, CA 90012
Monday-Friday
9 a.m. to 6 p.m.
Saturday & Sunday 9 a.m. to 5 p.m.**

(213) 628-2725
(213) 687-7193 (Nisei office)

The Cultural and Community center, the flanking Japan American Theater, and the broad expanse of Noguchi Plaza on which it fronts, is striking in a rather stark way. One side of the plaza is graced by a row of purple-blossomed jacaranda trees which line up below the soaring L.A. skyline in the background. It is one of the more stunning sights in the city.

One of the most remarkable sculptures in Southern California is the centerpiece of the plaza. The enormous stone sculpture, "To Issei," by the late artist Isamu Noguchi, is dedicated to the first generation of Japanese immigrants. Like its surroundings, it is rather plain but powerful.

It is directly across from the gracefully curved:

Japan American Theater
244 South San Pedro
Los Angeles, CA 90012
(213) 680-3700

A variety of shows from both Japanese and American cultures are staged in this 1982 auditorium designed by George Shinno of Kajima Associates. American productions, ranging from dance to chamber music, are presented. Japanese performing arts include Grand Kabuki, Bugaku, and Noh dramas, as well as Bunraku puppet theater.

Behind the theater, just beyond Noguchi Plaza, is an absolutely lovely Japanese garden:

James Irvine Garden:
Seiryu-en
(Garden of the
Clear Stream)
244 South San Pedro
Los Angeles, CA 90012
(213) 680-3700

Designed by Dr. Takeo Uesugi in 1981, this triangle-

shaped garden of beauty and tranquility, with its soft sounds of rushing water, won the National Landscape Award from the National Association of Nurserymen. This was presented by no less a personage than Nancy Reagan, while she was First Lady at the White House. Tucked into its little niche among the tall buildings, it is one of the most romantic strolling gardens anywhere in Southern California and makes for a meditative experience not to miss.

A grant from the James Irvine Foundation accounts for the American namesake. Vegetation and construction were also provided free of charge by Southern California Gardener's Federation and both the California Associations of Landscape Contractors and Nurserymen.

The Japanese name refers to its 170-foot stream, which symbolizes the consecutive generations of Japanese Americans. The crashing of the water in the little waterfall by the wooden bridge announces the rough arrival of the Issei. The twists and turns of the cataracts represents the Nisei with their initial success in farming and fishing, followed by the horror of the internment period. The stream's third stage, when it settles down and flows quietly into a pond, represents the future where we all live in peace and harmony.

On the final weekend of Nisei Week, there is a Japanese Street Fair with vendors displaying goods and "ondo" dancers in kimonos under the direction of noted dance scholar Yuko Miyatake. This event is directed by Wesley Saiki, whose father has been involved with Nisei Week since Sam Yorty was mayor of Los Angeles. It is held in an area at a diagonal from the J.A.C.C.C., within the confines of another design by George Shimo:

> **Weller Court**
> **123 South Weller Street**
> **(also called Astronaut Ellison S. Onizuka Street)**
> **Los Angeles, CA 90012**

As you walk up this interestingly angled, but somewhat business-like mall, first you will pass the **Friendship Knot** sculpture which makes an eloquent visual statement about the relationship between Japan and America.

The second sculpture you will come upon is the **Astronaut Ellison S. Onizuka Memorial**, dedicated to the Japanese American astronaut who perished in the *Challenger* explosion. It is a likeness of him in front of a replica of *Challenger* space shuttle.

If you continue on inside the three-level Modernist-styled open court, with plants and a glass elevator, you will end up in:

> **Nanban-Tei of Tokyo**
> **123 South Weller Street**
> **Los Angeles, CA 90012**

Monday-Friday 6 to 9:30 p.m.
Saturday & Sunday 5:30 to 9 p.m.
(213) 620-8744

This second floor restaurant, part of a chain with two locations in Tokyo, has my favorite name of any restaurant in Southern California. "Nanban-Tei" means "the Restaurant of the Southern Barbarians." Though this name is perfect for a restaurant in Los Angeles, it has its roots in the history of Japanese cooking.

Most people are familiar with Japanese "yakitori," barbecued marinated chicken on a stick. But there are other types of Japanese dishes cooked on sticks that are lumped under the general category of "kushi-yaki." Interestingly enough, it is a borrowed cooking style.

During the 17th century when the Japanese were encountering Dutch traders who came up from the East Indies to the port of Nagasaki, they also were introduced to food cooked on skewers laid out on a grill. Nanban-Tei specializes in various kinds of "kushi-yaki." This includes vegetables, stuffed mushrooms, and giant clams.

Besides the towering edifices of the new Little Tokyo, there are businesses that are small and traditional. One of the more traditional Japanese experiences can be found near here at:

Tawa's Shiatsu Spa
362 East First Street
Los Angeles, CA 90012
Monday-Saturday 1 to 10 p.m.
Sunday 1 to 9 p.m.
(213) 680-9141

This is a very traditional "sento" Japanese bath and health spa. It is for men only and is probably the only one of its kind in the Southland.

Being clean, physically and spiritually, is part of Japanese culture and Shinto religion. The purpose of many Shinto ceremonies is purification. This offers some insight into the workings of the sento.

Tawa's is a relatively unadorned little storefront with little more than a counter in the front room. You take off your shoes here and put them in a rack. Pay $15 and head for the dressing room.

Once undressed, you grab a bucket and a small plastic bench and scrub yourself down. It is considered extremely rude to get into a soaking tub without thoroughly cleaning off first. The water in the hot soak is very hot—around 110 degrees—and there are ledges built into the side of the tub to sit on. Soak up to your neck, but do not dunk your head.

Though the number of public bathhouses in Japan has diminished in recent years due to a big increase in home baths, they still serve a social, as well as spiritual purpose. You will be sharing a tub with other men and conversation is considered part of the experience.

Across the street is a real celebration of Japanese Americana:

Japanese American National Museum
369 East First Street
Los Angeles, CA 90012
Tuesday-Sunday 10 a.m. to 5 p.m.
Friday 11 a.m. to 8 p.m.
closed Monday
(213) 625-0414

This is the largest repository of Japanese American artifacts and documents in the world. The Japanese American National Museum contains art works, family photo albums, personal belongings, and tools used by early Japanese farmers. There is a section where you can learn "origami," and a little screening area where you can watch the 15-minute film *Through Our Own Eyes*.

For the museum, the internment presents both a unique problem and opportunity for study since much of the experience has been undocumented. Issei and Nisei who went through it lost so much, but when the war was over, for the most part they silently just rebuilt their lives. Many Sansei (third generation) and Yonsei (fourth generation) never heard their grandparents talk about their experience and are only learning about it now.

As constant reminders, the great lessons of history are invaluable. No doubt, a sense of the past and present gives perspective to the future, which somehow seems easier to sort out in a relaxed atmosphere, like this chain of pubs:

Yoro No Taki
432 East 2nd Street
Los Angeles, CA 90012
Daily 5 p.m. to 2 a.m.
(213) 626-6055
and:
2062 Sawtelle Boulevard
West Los Angeles, CA 90025
(310) 444-9676

There are over 3,000 of these in Japan. They are sort of like a cross between a Japanese "Denny's" and a Japanese country inn where a lot of sake is consumed.

The style of eating here is called "ippin-ryori" and it reminds some people of what going to a Chinese "dim sum" restaurant is like (see February)—with some partying added. It is roughly like ordering a series of appetizers while drinking in a friendly bar.

Some of these are quite like American appetizers such as fried chicken wings. Others, like "yakitori," are easy to sample and enjoy, even if you are not adventuresome in your dining. Whatever eating a succession of small dishes is called, it is a style suited to conversation and a festive mood.

Japanese Gardens of the Southland

Isamu Noguchi, the creator of the central plaza and sculpture of Little Tokyo, is also responsible for a 1.6 acre oasis of minimalist beauty in the middle of the steel cubes of Orange County's office buildings:

> **California Scenario**
> **116 Anton Boulevard**
> **[Near corner of Avenue of The Arts and Anton]**
> **Costa Mesa**
> **Daily from 8 a.m. to 12 a.m.**

Noguchi was a native Californian and if there was ever an artistic statement that perfectly expressed the blend of Japanese and California culture, it is this contemporary rendition of a traditional Japanese garden. Flanked by the perfectly blank white walls of a parking structure and reflected off the sides of shimmering glass high rises, the landscape design is meant to symbolize the varied aspects of California.

It incorporates six components of the environment in California, composed of Water Use, The Desert Land, Water Source, Land Use, Energy Fountain, and The Forest Walk. The paving and structures are done in sandstone; there are indigenous rocks, trees, cacti, and that most precious thing, water.

Directly north of here in Anaheim is the largest Japanese restaurant in Southern California:

> **Dohyo Sumo Steak and Polynesian Bar**
> **3500 West Orangewood Avenue**
> **Orange, CA 92668**
> **Monday-Thursday 11:30 a.m. to 10 p.m.**
> **Friday 11:30 a.m. to 10:30 p.m.**

Saturday 5 to 10:30 p.m.
Sunday 4:30 to 10 p.m.
(714) 634-1305

At 9,000-square-feet, this is a large place with huge wooden beams throughout the interior. It is owned by Tom Urata, and either he or General Manager John Kennedy will be there to greet you as you come in.

Though designed to appeal to families and tourists, it does have a built-in bizarre humor that I find appealing. The name means "sumo wrestling ring" and this theme is evident in the lobby. Towering above is a 15-foot tall, hand-carved ceramic statue of a very serious-looking sumo wrestler that was imported from Japan. Naked from the waist up, he wears an elaborate skirt from the waist down. The big guy, Sumoyama, got his name in a contest.

It really is two restaurants: a main tatami room and a Polynesian bar. The latter is a Hawaiian-style setting featuring Chinese dim sum, some Thai dishes, and tropical drinks. Karioki is offered every night. The main room has 20 teppan tables, making it one of the largest of its kind. There are numerous pictures and paintings of sumo wrestlers everywhere.

The Japanese presence in Southern California has been such a long and important one; it should come as no surprise that there are expressions of that culture in many different places in the Southland. A beautiful Japanese Garden is located in a somewhat undignified site:

Japanese Garden
Donald C. Tillman Water Reclamation Plant
6100 Woodley Avenue
Van Nuys, CA 91406
(818) 989-8166

This lovely 6-1/2 acre garden is located on top of a sewage treatment plant and is operated by the City of Los Angeles Bureau of Sanitation. It was designed by the late Dr. Koichi Kawana, and one of the two brochures put out by the city features interesting text and illustrations by him.

Its larger scale is modeled after huge stroll gardens on feudal estates in 18th and 19th century Japan called "chisenk-kaiyushiki," which literally means "wet garden with promenade."

Actually, part of it is a dry garden, "karesansui." This is the area of gravel and stone as you enter from the parking lot. This gives way to more lush landscaping and more architectural details, such as stone Japanese lanterns. The centerpiece is the "shoin" or teahouse.

If you go north on Woodley from here and hang a right, on the left hand side of the street, you'll see:

Kyushu Ramen
15355 Sherman Way
Van Nuys, CA 91406
Wednesday-Monday 11:30 a.m. to 11:45 p.m.
closed Tuesday
(818) 786-6005

In addition to the big bowls of steaming, flavorful ramen, this popular noodle joint also serves such specialties as cold ramen with chicken breast meat.

Another noted Southland Japanese garden that began as something else underwent a somewhat less drastic transformation:

Hannah Center Japanese Garden
University of California, Los Angeles
405 Hillgard Avenue
Los Angeles, CA 90024
[Located off Bellagio Road, west of Stone Canyon Road]
Tuesday 10 a.m. to 1 p.m., Wednesday 12 to 3 p.m.
(reservations necessary)
(310) 825-4574

In some ways this wonderful two acre hillside Japanese garden has the most poetically Southern California history of all. It began life in 1923 as a Spanish garden and was metamorphized from 1959 to 1961 by designer Nagao Sakurai into its present form. It was given to UCLA in 1965.

It takes about 30 minutes to slowly drench yourself in the details that make this garden a work of art. The black foot stones that lead to the arched main gate were individually split by hand to create a symmetrical fan pattern. A total of 400 tons of boulders and rock were brought from Japan. This includes a 400,000-year-old "jade rock" near the entrance that reveals its beautiful color only after it is wet.

There is a stream that feeds a sunken bath and a stone bath house. A teahouse sits calmly at the foot of the hill.

Another Japanese garden is located at the California State University in Long Beach:

The Earl Burns Miller Japanese Garden
Earl Warren Way
California State University Long Beach

1250 Bellflower Boulevard
Daily 9 a.m. to 5 p.m.
(sometimes closed on weekends for weddings)
Long Beach, CA 90840
(310) 985-8885

At 1-1/3 acres, this garden is small, but appealing. There is a zen rock garden, a koi pond, a pretty footbridge, and the whisper of little waterfalls. It is quite popular as a wedding site and is free to visit and easy to find.

The garden does not have a formal address. You just turn into CSULB via Atherton Street and then turn onto Earl Warren Way. The sign and garden gates are on the right about two blocks up.

Other Japanese gardens are found within the Huntington Gardens (see January), Descanso Gardens (see April), and Balboa Park (see April and June.)

Little Tokyo West

If all of this talk about Japanese Gardens has got you thinking of starting one, you might venture to Sawtelle Boulevard between Santa Monica and Olympic Boulevards in L.A. Though not as well-known as Little Tokyo, this is a long-standing Japanese neighborhood as well.

Just before WWII, when this area was considered pretty far away from the city, it was a suburb mainly populated by Japanese gardeners—with an accompanying large number of Japanese nurseries.

Though there are nowhere near as many today, there are still several Japanese nurseries here. One of the most unique is:

Yamaguchi Bonsai Nursery
1905 Sawtelle Boulevard
West Los Angeles, CA 90025
Monday-Saturday 7 a.m. to 5 p.m.
Sunday 8:30 a.m. to 4 p.m.
(310) 473-5444

I once met a man who collected swords and bonsai miniature trees, and it was he who first took me here on his way to a military antique dealer in Culver City. I had not realized there were so many types of bonsai or that some of them were over 100 years old.

There are aficionados who have whole little forests of them. This can present a problem as some of these small wonders are both extremely valuable and somewhat fragile. This nursery accommodates the collector in many ways. For example, if you are a customer and you are going to travel, you can leave you bonsai here. They will give it the best of care in your absence.

Heading toward Olympic, you will encounter another, less specialized nursery:

Hashimoto Nursery
1935 Sawtelle Boulevard
West Los Angeles, CA 90025
Monday-Saturday 6:30 a.m. to 4:30 p.m.
Sunday 7:30 a.m. to 4:30 p.m.
(310) 473-6232

This blooming oasis has been here since 1929. In a supreme testimony to the health benefits of gardening, Mr. Hashimoto was 91 at the time of this writing and still active, though his son Joe runs the place. They used to grow only fuschia's here until 1984. Now they offer a little of everything. On the same side of the street as Hashimoto Nursery is a place that offers other forms of human care:

Golden Cabinet
2019 Sawtelle Boulevard
West Los Angeles, CA 90025
Monday-Saturday 9 a.m. to 6 p.m.
(310) 575-1955

A popular place for shiatsu massage, Golden Cabinet also does acupuncture. There is a little cafe of sorts where herbal elixirs are featured. These have great names that describe their effects in poetic terms like "Albert Einstein" or the lovely sounding "Sweetheart's Dance."

If you are in the mood to buy something Japanese in a unique store, I suggest:

Satsuma Imports
2029 Sawtelle Boulevard
West Los Angeles, CA 90025
Monday-Saturday 10 a.m. to 6 p.m., closed Sunday
(310) 473-3946

Satsuma Imports has had the same owners since 1955. They have many beautiful Japanese and Asian gifts and personal items like "ukata" robes and beautiful china vases. Behind the store, they have a tiny Japanese garden.

Though the internment destroyed much of Japanese Southern California, as you continue down Sawtelle, you will come up on a business that was there before—and came back after:

Safe and Save
2030 Sawtelle Boulevard
West Los Angeles, CA 90025
(310) 479-3810

This survivor has been here since 1932. It is a small family-run grocery store that stocks several different kinds of seaweeds, vegetables, noodles, and impeccable fresh cut fish and meat.

As you approach Olympic, with its flood of cars and tall buildings, the flavor of old Japanese Southern California is hard to detect. By the time you get to the corner of Sawtelle and Olympic, it would seem to be all gone. Here is found an imposing marble and steel urban fortress called the Olympic Collection. If you go up the escalator, you will come to a glass-front restaurant called:

Mishima
11301 Olympic Boulevard, Suite 210
West Los Angeles, CA 90064
Tuesday-Sunday 11:30 a.m. to 9 p.m.
(310) 473-5297

Mishima is an chancy moniker for a restaurant considering it is the name of a celebrated Japanese novelist who committed suicide. Whatever it is called, it is an outstanding restaurant that is urbane and old-fashioned at the same time.

A zen rock garden in the window is a forecast of the minimalist decor inside. The interior is all clean lines with a big square table in the middle.

In Southern California you can get three kinds of Japanese noodles: "ramen," which is usually served in a big bowl with vegetables and/or meat (see November), and the more stylish "udon" and "soba."

White, slightly firm udon noodles are about as thick as a pencil. Thin, chewey soba noodles are made from buckwheat flour, which makes them a lot tricker to prepare. They are a specialty here.

Most flour readily sticks to itself when wet because it has a high gluten content. Buckwheat has a low gluten content, so there is a whole art to making great soba that takes three years to perfect. Soba noodles have an almost mystical place in Japanese history because when Buddhist monks went on retreats, they carried only a sack of ground buckwheat and a pot to cook it in. This is one reason soba purists have the traditional "seiro soba," which is served cold in a flat lacquer box on a little mat made of bamboo called a "zaru."

The specialty of the house at Mishima is "tanuki soba" or "tanuki udon" served with a light soy broth with little crunchy pieces of fried tempura batter. The restaurant started with a fairly simple menu, but in recent years has added more "otsumami" (small side dishes). There is more about Japanese Southern California in the January, February, March, November, and December chapters.

LOS ANGELES FESTIVAL

The Los Angeles Festival began as The Olympic Arts Festival in 1984, and continued on its own three years later. It now happens every three years around the end of August and first part of September. A true international theater festival, the purpose is to show a variety of theater forms and cultural expressions in an explosion of diversity.

Though one of the most extraordinary events in the world, it has not been without its detractors. The first festival was criticized as being too European. It did, however, showcase some of the avant garde in L.A. dance and theater and brought some attention to some great artists from around the world. For example, Le Cirque du Soleil, now practically a household word, was introduced to America at this festival and Peter Brook's nine-hour epic, *The Mahabharata*, stands as one of the greatest achievements in the history of the dramatic arts.

In addition to the bigger ticket events, there were literally hundreds of art exhibits, poetry readings, dance and drama performances, and performance art shows. Many were held in unusual venues or outdoors.

Arts communities are spread out all over the Los Angeles area. For a while it looked like the focus was going to be in the industrial part of Downtown L.A. A number of the first festival events were held down here—including the big tent of Le Cirque. Though the neighborhood has not evolved as some had hoped, it still is the loft/studio arts district of the Southland. This, of course, means there are some funky cafes down here. One of the pioneer dive/performance venues is still around:

Al's Bar and National Theater
305 South Hewett
Los Angeles, CA 90013
(213) 687-3558

A saloon called Al's Bar, named for a truck driver, was opened in 1969 by a gentleman named Alfonso Vasquez. He sold his place to an artist named Marc Kreisel in 1979 for $4,000.

Kreisel wanted to help create a sense of community for the artists who live and work in the downtown loft district. He wanted to establish a place where they could get together and socialize.

Al's is a dark, relatively unadorned space with a bare stage. The assortment of shows you can see here is eclectic to say the least. If you are from New York and are nostalgic for the kind of bizarre entertainment you might find in some of the joints in SoHo, you need look no farther than Al's.

For a quick bite to eat, a great loft district spot is:

Cafe Vignes
923 East 3rd Street
Los Angeles, CA 90013
Monday-Friday 10:30 a.m. to 6 p.m.
(213) 687-9709

Cafe Vignes is the archetype industrial-style arty coffee shop. The open kitchen sits under a pyramid of metal covered wood. Exposed ventilation ducts, white walls, and old brick surround you as you sit on bentwood chairs at a wooden table. The menu is simple and includes salads, pastas, and quiches.

Near here is one of the great signature buildings of Los Angeles:

Coca Cola Building
1334 South Central
Avenue
Los Angeles, CA
90021

Suddenly on Central, there is an ocean liner steaming along: five office buildings with streamlined corners, portholes, hatch covers, and a flying bridge bearing the company logo. The Streamline Moderne-style of architecture was suggested by the streamlining of cars, planes, and trains, so naturally an ocean liner of the same period (1936 and 1937) would make for a perfect whimsical extension. It is complete down to nautical railings, shipdoors and fake rivets. There are two giant Coke bottle statues set into coves in the corners.

It was originally even more nautical in motif all the way down to the interior. The architect, Robert V. Derrah, explained his design: "What therefore, could more aptly express the bottling method of the Coca-Cola Company than a ship motif?"

One long-time Downtown L.A. arts institution recently re-opened in Hollywood:

Los Angeles Contemporary Exhibitions (L.A.C.E.)
6522 Hollywood Boulevard
Hollywood, CA 90028
(213) 957-1777

L.A.C.E. is one of a very tiny group of about 30 artist-run multimedia spaces in the entire United States (which makes you wonder why they are perceived as such a threat to society by right-wing, pro-censorship groups). It was started in 1976 by a largely Chicano artist collective, but never limited itself to that perspective. Karen Finley and Rachel Rosenthal are just two of the performance artists who graced the stage of the old industrial location.

Besides not limiting the perspective of its subject matter, L.A.C.E. never limited itself to media. Besides performance art, dance, and drama, painting and video exhibitions, books, and even a notorious annual Valentine's Day event are part of the L.A.C.E. artistic potpourri.

The new location opened on June 10 of 1994 with a gala that included performance art star John Fleck. It offers a real chance for you to experience creative expression without commercial considerations.

For the second L.A. Festival, the focus was changed by artistic director Peter Sellers to feature only artists from the Pacific Rim: the U.S., Canada, Latin America, and Asia. Sellers himself directed the gargantuan John Adams opera *Nixon In China*.

This festival featured a cornucopia of unusual art and performance that makes it unique in the history of American theatre. Stage performances went beyond European-style drama or drama and included other forms, previously only experienced by Americans traveling in Asia or Latin America. In that respect, it was far more important than the first one. It was daring and exciting and wholly appropriate for Los Angeles.

One of the major cultural accomplishment of the second festival was achieved just before the death of Sultan Hamangkubawana IX of Java in October of 1988. The Sultan agreed to send his sacred "gamelan" and a complete retinue of Court Performers from The Yogyakarta Palace of Java to the United States.

The chance to see the foremost practitioners of one of the most refined and exquisite performing traditions in Asia was a wonderful opportunity at the '89 Festival. These wholly unique performances represented not only the first time a Javanese court ensemble appeared in the U.S., but also the first time this range of repertoire has been seen outside of Indonesia. It was such a major event that the Sultan accompanied the performers to America.

If you would like to experience a little of Indonesian culture, go for lunch or dinner at:

Agung Indonesian Restaurant
3909 Beverly Boulevard
Los Angeles, CA 90004
Monday-Saturday 12 to 9 p.m., closed Sunday
(213) 660-2113

Agung is a small family-owned restaurant in a simple concrete block building. Inside, it is decorated with posters from Indonesia and batik-dyed fabrics. The palm tree decorated menu features some really delicious and unusual dishes such as Indonesian "bakmi" noodles.

Southeast Asian cooking features some combinations that might seem surprising to Americans used to European-style cooking. One of these is "gado gado," which is a lettuce salad featuring peanut butter with chilies and shrimp chips. On of the most delightful surprises is iced, malted coffee whipped up with avocado.

For the year 1993, the Los Angeles Festival took yet another theme: "Home, Place, and Memory." This time African, African American, Middle Eastern, and Middle Eastern American artists were featured. Many of the events were in the Vision Complex in Leimert Park, which is described in December. There is an annual festival that will give you some of the flavor of this every August:

African Marketplace and Cultural Faire
Rancho Cienega Park
5001 Rodeo Road
Los Angeles, CA 90016
normally last two weekends of August
(213) 294-6788 or (213) 485-6793

The African Marketplace and Cultural Faire started in 1986 with one stage and 10 booths and grew to five stages and 300 booths in 1992. Vendors offer African-style clothes and American, African, and Caribbean food such as Jamaican jerk chicken and roast goat from Trinidad. There is a children's area with face painting, storytelling, and puppets.

OLD SPANISH DAYS IN SANTA BARBARA

During the first weekend of August, Santa Barbara has its largest festival of the year: the Old Spanish Days, Santa Barbara celebration. This five-day jubilee, celebrated every year since the early 1940s, honors the city's Spanish and Mexican heritage.

Since the city's founding, **Plaza de la Guerra**, between State and Anacapa on the street of the same name, has been the site for important gatherings. This is where the first city council met in 1850. During the fiesta, it is transformed into a mercado with booths, banners, and several stages where bands are playing.

Across the street is an archetype structure that really represents the ideal of Santa Barbara city planning:

El Paseo
Casa de la Guerra
15 East de la Guerra Street
Santa Barbara, CA 93101

The Spanish word "paseo" means "walk" and specifically refers to pedestrian byways between buildings. Santa Barbara has a system of them, and the delightful effect of going along a narrow walkway then suddenly coming into a hidden courtyard with a fountain is one of the things that make Santa Barbara such a romantic city.

That is precisely what walking into this charming and historic structure is like. There are several outdoor cafes as well as a shop located in a historic house, the Casa de la Guerra, which was built in 1827 by the commandant of the presidio, Don Jose de la Guerra, as a wedding present for his young wife. It is also a museum and has antique photos of the de la Guerra family.

This is one of those rare places where history and romance come together. In 1835, this was the location of the wedding celebration of the youngest daughter of the family. Richard Henry Dana had arrived in Santa Barbara in January after 150 days at sea and was there to record the party, called the "grand fandango" in his book *Two Years Before The Mast* (see February).

An early Santa Barbara adobe survives, not as a dead piece of history, but as a unique bookstore:

Randall House Bookstore
850 Laguna Street
Santa Barbara, CA 93101
Monday-Friday 9:30 a.m. to 5:30 p.m.

Saturday 10 a.m. to 2 p.m. , closed Sundays
(805) 963-1909

This unusual business occupies a section of a historic structure built in 1825 as the Gonzalez Adobe, whose owner would later become mayor. It is beautifully original and well preserved . The floors are of brick, with vaulted beam ceilings overhead. The detailing is extreme, with a fireplace in practically every room and a heavy kitchen sink of pure copper.

The bookstore gets its name from its owner, Ron Randall, and it is one of the great antiquarian bookstores of Santa Barbara for which the city is noted.

Santa Barbara is a center for early California research. You can do a little of your own at the nearby:

Santa Barbara Historical Museum
136 East de la Guerra Street
Santa Barbara, CA 93101
10 a.m. to 5 p.m. Tuesday-Saturday
12 p.m. to 5 p.m. Sunday
Guided tours Wednesday, Saturday & Sunday 1:30 p.m
(805) 966-1601

This lovely Mission Revival-style structure contains a collection that tells the story of Santa Barbara's Spanish, Mexican, and American past. The building has large rooms filled with furniture, costumes, art and crafts, and documents. Edward Deakin's 21 paintings of the California Missions all hang here. There is also a well known research library specializing in Santa Barbara history.

Besides its collection, the museum is a pleasant place to visit just because of its architecture. There is a tranquil, shaded courtyard at the back, and though the floor tiles are from Mexico, the bricks used to make the main structure were composed from the adobe soil on which it sits.

In the Old Spanish Days Parade, there are several antique carriages, a horse-driven, still bright red, steam-pumping fire engine, and a sinister looking horse-drawn black hearse, complete with coffin. These are among the dozens of extraordinary old vehicles on display in the:

Old Spanish Days Carriage Museum
129 Castillo Street
Santa Barbara, CA 93101
Sunday 2 to 4 p.m.
(805) 962-2353 or (805) 569-2077

This unique museum has a collection of 85 carriages of various kinds arranged in rows. The museum building is really a barn with an adobe front on it. It has very much the frontier California feel to it, with an entire long interior wall devoted to a huge collection of saddles. Many of these are the silver-decorated kind, including one owned by Will Rogers. There is also a semi-famous frieze by cowboy artist Edward Borein.

Besides the above mentioned hardware, they also have a covered army wagon, a 350-year-old Spanish festival wine cart, and assorted carriages and buggies of every size and description.

A free map and walking tour of historic Santa Barbara called **Red Tile Tour** is available from the:

> **Visitor's Center**
> **One Santa Barbara Street**
> **Santa Barbara, CA 93101**
> **Daily 9 a.m. to 5 p.m.**
> **(805) 965-3021**

Located across the street from the beach, this little office has information about what to see and do in the city.

Of the Mission Revival-style of buildings, none are more stunning than the:

> **Santa Barbara County Courthouse**
> **1100 Anacapa Street**
> **Santa Barbara, CA 93101**
> **(805) 962-6464**

Built in 1929 by architect William Mooser and his son as the centerpiece of the newly rebuilt, earthquake safe Santa Barbara, this could be the prettiest municipal building in the state. A horseshoe shaped palace, it has considerable Moorish influence due to the fact that Mooser, Jr. had studied that style in Spain. Its 90-foot tower is the architectural landmark of the city and is also a good place to get a sweeping view of Santa Barbara.

Walking inside the entrance tower you will be treated to a ceiling that is a replica of a synagogue in Toledo, Spain that was built in the 1400s. Throughout the interior, there is a wonderful assortment of art. There are beautiful tiles, carvings and murals. Santa Barbara's history is delineated in large murals by Dan Sayre Groesbeck. Within the Law Library are big maps of Santa Barbara County and early California—including one that depicts the future state as an island.

If you wanted to celebrate the architecture of the city in your choice of lodging, the most beautiful large Mission Revival hotel, possibly in the entire country, is on the beach a little way to the south in Montecito:

Four Seasons Biltmore
1260 Channel Drive
Montecito, CA 93108
(805) 969-2261

This has been a Santa Barbara landmark since 1927. In 1988, when the Four Seasons hotel group acquired the property, they spent $20,000,000 restoring it to its original splendor. With its high-arched windows and vaulted wood beam ceilings, the Biltmore is the epitome of Southern California romantic architecture. It has 234 rooms, some in the main building, some in cottages scattered around the grounds. There are 20 acres of lush gardens.

Rooms are large and somewhat expensive—from $290 to $360—though they often have off season, mid-week specials. You have your choice of an ocean or garden view setting. One of the few "Romance packages" for couples I recommend is the two-night, three-day combination they have here. It includes dinner for two in **La Marina**, the hotel's beautiful dining room and champagne upon arrival. The package is $625 on weekends, $525 during the week. As I have said before and will probably say many times again, Southern California's resort weekend destinations are cheaper and better midweek.

The Hispanic tradition of Santa Barbara continues vibrantly at the unpretentious:

La Super-Rica Taqueria
622 Milpas Street
Santa Barbara, CA 93103
Daily 11 a.m. to 9 p.m.
(805) 963-4940

Here is where the best Mexican food in Santa Barbara is to be found. The menu is a blackboard where nothing costs more than $6. Dining is only on the patio under its canvas roof among a jungle of potted plants.

The soft tacos with homemade tortillas and salsa have been praised by such food lofties as Julia Child. Of course, the beef tacos are made with sliced N.Y. steak instead of hamburger.

Santa Barbara Arrival by Train

Probably the most romantic train station to pull up to is the classic Mission Revival:

Southern Pacific Depot
Santa Barbara Train Station
[between Chapala and State Streets]
just south of US 101
(805) 963-1015

This pretty little station with its graceful arches on the platform has been in continuous operation since 1905. It is certainly a nice place to depart from, but it is an even more romantic station to arrive at. The ocean is a stone's throw away and with the palm trees in the background, the words "Santa Barbara" over the platform's central arch look mighty inviting as the train pulls up.

The "Coast Starlight" and the "San Diegan" stop here. This means you could arrive on the former from as far up the western coast of the U.S. as Seattle. The "San Diegan" runs north from that city with 14 stops in between. Virtually every community in the Southland has an Amtrak station near it.

If you would like to stay in a smaller Mission Revival-style hotel, two blocks from the train station is one of the most charming little hotels anywhere:

Villa Rosa
15 Chapala Street
Santa Barbara, CA 93101
(805) 966-0851

Built in the 1930s as an apartment house, this 18-room hotel is a real gem of the period. There is extensive detailing throughout: the windows and doorways are particularly appealing. There is a courtyard with a pool and spa.

What may be the largest tree of its kind in the Northern Hemisphere is also near the train station:

Moreton Bay Fig Tree
Chapala and Montecito Streets
Santa Barbara

This enormous tree, a member of the rubber family, began as a seedling brought from Moreton Bay in Australia in 1876. It is now over 70-feet tall and provides over 21,000-square-feet of shade for Santa Barbara's homeless. Its above ground roots extend over a half a city block and its trunk circumference is nearly 40 feet.

INDIAN INDEPENDENCE DAY (AUGUST 15)

August 15 is a milestone date for two of the Southland's many communities, Korea and India. For immigrants and their offspring from the latter country it is the anniversary of their Independence from the British Empire in 1947. A perfect place to celebrate would be:

Little India
Pioneer Boulevard
[Between 91 Freeway and South Street]
Artesia

Artesia is a small (1.6 square miles) city originally know as Dairy Valley whose ethnic origins were largely Dutch and Portuguese. It is surrounded on three sides by Cerritos, a larger, more affluent city with a considerable Asian population.

Though not as numerous as some other Asian peoples in the U.S., changes in the immigration laws between the U.S. and India in the 1960s led to an increase in Indian immigration. In the '60s and early '70s, southern Indians such as Tamilians, Kannadegas, and Telugu-speaking people began arriving in greater numbers. Indians who are able to immigrate tend to be affluent, well-educated, and status-conscious people such as physicians and engineers, or offspring of wealthy families here as students.

In the late '70s, merchants from Gujarati, which is in Western India, along with the relatives of the earlier wave swelled their numbers. During this period, responding to the difficulty Asian Indians had in finding the spices, lentils, and seeds used in Indian cooking, a Mr. Lahoti opened an Indian grocery store out of his garage in Artesia.

Now, there are about 70,000 Indians living in L.A. and Orange County. Though their residences are not really concentrated in one specific area, many of them live in Cerritos. Mr. Lahoti's store is long gone, but its legacy is Pioneer Boulevard.

A little less than 10 percent of the businesses in Artesia are Indian owned, but the majority of them, over 50, are on Pioneer Boulevard. This makes this area one of the three largest concentrations of Indian stores and restaurants in the U.S., the other two being Jackson Heights in Queens and Devon Street in Chicago.

At the southern end of where the Indian strip begins is a delightful little restaurant:

Jay Bharat Restaurant
18701 Pioneer Boulevard
Artesia, CA 90701

Daily 11 a.m. to 8 p.m.
(310) 924-3310

With its pink linoleum floor and simple blond wood tables and chairs, there is nothing pretentious about Jay Bharat. Other than the wooden framed tapestries depicting scenes from Indian mythology, the main decor is the glass case filled with goodies and a menu on the wall behind it.

India is a vast land with several distinct regional cuisines. Jay Bharat features Western Indian vegetarian cuisine from the Gujarat region. This includes a huge array of snack foods grouped collectively under the poetic little name of "chat."

Probably the most popular is "samosa," a triangle-shaped pastry about the size of a child's fist. It is filled with spiced potato and peas and served with sweet chutney.

"Methai" are sweets that are usually also offered by chat shops.

"Burfi," made from simmered milk combined with a variety of other stuff, has the consistency of fudge. There are many different kinds. Two pretty ones are mushy cookies about the size of fat half dollars. One is made from cashews and pistachios and has a bright red, green, and yellow design. Another has swirls of green and is made with pistachios.

There are several dishes based upon a lentil and rice flour crepe. One of my favorites is "Mesure Masala Dhosa," which is filled with onions, tomatoes, coconut, potatoes, chutney, spices, and masala. It is served with "sambar," a hot lentil puree that is sort of like a tiny bowl of soup.

A few doors down is a unique store:

Sari Boutique
18619 S. Pioneer Boulevard
Artesia, CA 90701
Tuesday-Saturday 11 a.m. to 8 p.m.
closed Monday
(310) 860-1076

This establishment, like several others on the street, sells Indian clothing. The namesake item being the "sari," the fabric wrap worn by Indian women. By tradition, they cannot be less than six yards long. You would think that there would not be that much to shopping for a garment so proscribed in its design, but the colors and fabric variations are dazzling. There are racks designated by price and they go from less than $20 to hundreds.

"Salwar kameez" are a combination of a long shirt and baggy or straight legged pants that are also a traditional outfit for women. Like saris, they come in a rainbow of colors. The scarf that goes with it is called a "dupatta." The selection of bangles—matched sets of glass bracelets is big—as it is in most of the shops along here. The word "bangles" came from the Hindi word "bangri."

Indian fabrics are beautiful and come in many different types. "Chaner choli" is embroidered, art quality material that runs in the $300 to $500 range. The gold embroidery is called "tela."

They also have men's clothes, including embroidered Nehru suits and beautiful headpieces.

If you would like to look at some Indian jewelry to set off your new clothes, perhaps the most beautifully wrought gold I have ever seen for sale is found at an imposing store across the street:

Bhindi Jewelers
18508 Pioneer Boulevard
Artesia, CA 90701
Tuesday-Sunday 11 a.m.
to 7:30 p.m.
closed Monday
(310) 402-8755
(310) 865-6586 (FAX)

The twin columns flanking the heavy glass front door give some preparation for the grandeur within, but not quite. Once inside, everywhere you look is gold—elaborately wrought into rings, bracelets, and necklaces.

The jewelry here all has a distinctly different look to it. This is partially because Indian women go more for the artistry of the gold design than for just having the metal as a setting for an impressive stone.

The other reason is because it is all 22 carat, not the more common 14 carat. Indians, like Middle Easterners, prefer the purer gold over the 14 carat (which is really an alloy) even though it is softer.

The Bhindi's have been jewelers since 1929 and are the largest manufacturers and retailers of 22 carat jewelry in America. They also have stores in San Francisco and in the Jackson Heights area of Queens.

Continuing north on the same side of the street, you will find a unique shop:

India Food and Gifts
17820 Pioneer Boulevard
Artesia, CA 90701
Tuesday-Sunday 11 a.m. to 8 p.m.
closed Monday
(310) 865-3678

This is kind of an Indian "general store." There are aisles of foodstuffs and the counter offers a variety of sweets. Stick on "bindi" (the spot worn in the middle of the forehead to denote marital status) are available in everything from velvet to sparkling versions in a variety of colors. The aroma of spices, incense, and ayurvedic medications fills the air.

Idols of various kinds sit placidly on shelves. You can get a comic book version of the Mahabharata or a sticker of "Laxmi" the goddess of money.

Except for the interior of the Bhindis' jewelry store, Little India is not picturesque in the same way as Chinatown. The most spectacular manifestation of the Indian presence in Southern California is up near Malibu:

Sree Venkateswara Temple
1600 Las Virgenes Canyon Road
Calabasas, CA 91302
(no phone)

Driving up the canyon road, the Sree Venkatewara Temple appears like a dream. The towers are fantastically carved and the cupolas are tipped with gold. It is the largest Hindu Temple in the Western Hemisphere in the elaborate "Chola" style.

This type of temple was named after the Chola Dynasty, the period in Indian history from 900 to 100 A.D. which was the zenith of Indian temple building. It was built according to specifications that date from 900-year-old Hindu writings known as the "Shastra." Most of the craftsmen that built it were Tamali Silpis from Southern India. Each of these workers underwent a seven year apprenticeship before being allowed to work on the temple.

The compound is as imposing close up as it is from a distance. The grounds cover 4-1/2 acres. There are nine domed towers, where a carved statue representing each one of the nine deities of Hinduism are displayed. These are dressed and bedecked daily by temple priests. Gatherings occur in the central meditation hall and the general use auditorium.

Carvings are everywhere you look: the brick and mortar walls are festooned with flowers and lotus blossoms, lions, elephants, dragons and idols and demons.

The most complex of the Hindu gods is the creator of the world, "Shiva." He is alternately feared and honored because he is both the destroyer and restorer. This contradictory nature is sometimes expressed in alternating epicurianism and aestheticism and even further in androgyny. Shiva is sometimes depicted as a combination of himself and his female consort in one body. All of these qualities make him an ideal god for the Southland.

A terrific Indian restaurant is over the hill in the Valley:

Anarkali Restaurant
22721 Ventura Boulevard
Woodland Hills, CA 91364
Daily 11:30 a.m. to 10 p.m.
(818) 224-3929
also at:
7013 Melrose Avenue
Los Angeles, CA 90038
(213) 934-6488

They serve a variety of traditional dishes here including tandoori, samosas, and a kind of an oversized Indian onion ring called "bhajees." The decor is done in sexy maroons and reds and features comfortable booths that look like ocean waves.

OJAI SHAKESPEARE FESTIVAL

The last summer Shakespeare Festival to make its annual appearance in the Southland is this month in Ojai:

Ojai Shakespeare Festival
Libbey Park
mailing address:
P.O. Box 575
Ojai, CA 92023
Saturday & Sunday 1 p.m. (first two weeks)
Thursday-Sunday 7:30 p.m. (second two weeks)
(805) 646-9455

Founded in 1982, the Ojai Shakespeare Festival has been under the artistic direction of USC professor Paul Backer since 1989. They started with just one show for a two week run and have grown in theatrical reputation and popularity until now they do two plays spread over a whole month. These consist of a major evening production in Libbey Bowl (where the Music Festival is held, see June) and a comedy done on the lawn as a matinee.

Entry to the festival area begins one hour before showtime, so you can bring a blanket and a picnic lunch or dinner. There is a pre-show to entertain you that features the Measure For Measure Renaissance Minstrels, who present madrigal singing in other locations on a year-round basis.

If Shakespeare puts you in the mood for a spot of tea or a bit of England, Ojai's original tea room is very near Libbey Park:

Plaza Pantry
221 East Matilija Street
Ojai, CA 92023
Monday-Saturday 9 a.m. to 4 p.m.
Sunday 9:30 a.m. to 4:30 p.m.
(805) 646-6325

The Plaza Pantry is both an English tea room and coffeehouse. They serve breakfast, lunch and snacks. Included are homemade steak & kidney pie, cornish pastries, and quiches.

Next door to the Plaza Pantry is:

Serendipity Toys
221 East Matilija Street
Ojai, CA 93023
Daily 10 a.m. to 5:30 p.m.
(805) 646-2585

Owned by Joe and Lilly Barthelemy, this shop specializes in unique and quality toys and collectibles from around the world.

Another place to go in Ojai for an English touch is:

Tottenham Court
242 East Ojai Avenue
Ojai, CA 93023
Monday-Friday 10 a.m. to 5:30 p.m.
Saturday & Sunday 9:30 a.m. to 6 p.m.
Daily 11 a.m to 4 p.m. (tea room)
(805) 646-2339

Located in the Arcade, the ambiance here is quite British. The Tea Room features windows framing trompe l'oeil paintings of landmarks in London such as Big

Ben, Buckingham Palace, and St. Paul's Cathedral.

They are open for breakfast, lunch, and tea and feature such specialties as scones with preserves and Devon cream. If you are not a tea drinker, they carry an impressive selection of English beers.

Tottenham Court was the recipient of a unique distinction in 1993. Fortnum and Mason, the eleven floor London tea shop, awarded them the "Tea Service Excelsis" a huge, 24 cup porcelain tea cup that commemorates the best in tea service. This was the first time in their history (dating from 1707) that an American establishment was so honored. Owners Andy and Mel Bloom display the giant cup in their window. It bears the logo of Fortnum, and Mason: their landmark clock on Picadilly.

East of Libbey Park on Ojai Avenue is an 1887 farmhouse that has been converted into a bed and breakfast:

> **Theodore Woolsey House**
> **1484 East Ojai Avenue**
> **Ojai, CA 93023**
> **(805) 646-9779**

The Theodore Woolsey House occupies much more land than most B&Bs: seven oak-shaded acres. The private feeling all this land gives is enhanced by the fact that it is surrounded by a Chinese stone wall. With its long rose-lined driveway, rose-covered trellis, tree-shaded veranda, and clapboard walls, the Theodore Woolsey House has a quiet country air about it.

There are seven rooms. Three have full private baths, two of them with antique clawfoot tubs, two with fireplaces, three with balconies, and four with mountain views. There is also a 50-foot swimming pool for the guest's use. Ana Cross is the gracious innkeeper. There is more about Ojai in the June, October, and December chapters.

LONG BEACH RENAISSANCE ARTS FESTIVAL

Speaking of Shakespeare, if you'd like to meet him, you'll have a chance at the:

> **Long Beach Renaissance Arts Festival**
> **Rainbow Lagoon, Shoreline Aquatic Park**
> **Long Beach**
> **Saturday & Sunday 10 a.m. to 7 p.m.**
> **Weekend before Labor Day**
> **Admission: $8**
> **(310) 437-0751**

The Traveler's Aid Society, a group that helps the homeless, started this festival in 1985 to raise money for their efforts. This is a true arts festival with costumed performers, handmade craft art, and, yes, lots of delicious outdoor food.

The setting is lovely—at a man-made lagoon in a pretty park next to the marina. One of the drawbacks to the big Renaissance Faire in San Bernardino County is the inland heat. Not so here.

In addition to the jugglers, musicians, and dancers of the period, you will also be able to meet Sir Frances Drake, Catherine de Medici, and yes, William Shakespeare.

If the faire stirs fantasies of an Elizabethan shopping spree, Long Beach is also the home of the:

House Negra-Khan
aka Frank Lieberman
3129 East 63rd Street
Long Beach, CA 90805
(310) 422-8140

Frank Lieberman makes chain mail jewelry and armor. He was taught by a gentleman named Sir Hugh the Undecided, who he met in 1972 through the Society for Creative Anachronisms. An aerospace quality control manager since 1966 who was born in nearby Signal Hill, Lieberman took to the art and began showing his work at renaissance fairs throughout the country.

His most popular jewelry pieces are the "hand flowers" he makes that twine around one finger and wrap up over the wrist. They are studded with jewels and sell for $20 to $50. He also does headpieces and hair jewelry that sell for $100 to $600. Two of his most spectacular creations are a spiderweb cape made with over 1,200 inches of silver chain and a $19,000 headpiece made of gold.

Some celebrities have taken a fancy to Frank's unique work. Cher has one of his belts. For the opening night party of the movie *Star Trek V*, Gene Roddenbery's wife, Majel Barrett (better known as Nurse Chapel), had five headpieces made for their children.

You can see some of his work in film. Patrick Stewart wore a piece by House Negra-Kahn in *Robin Hood: Men In Tights*. Other movies using his unique creations include *The Sword and Sorcerer, House II*, and *Something Wicked This Way Comes*. Once Frank even appeared on screen himself: in the first scene of the movie *Dragonfight*, he stabs someone in an alley fight and runs away.

Not too far away in the South Bay is an appropriate store to mention:

The Dragon's Breath
95 Del Amo Fashion Center

Hawthorne Boulevard at Del Amo
Torrance, CA 90503
Monday-Friday 10 a.m. to 9:30 p.m.
Saturday 11 a.m. to 7:30 p.m.
Sunday 12 to 6 p.m.
(310) 371-2599

Like Dragon Marsh in Riverside (see April), this is a store that specializes in the world of the English Renaissance. "A World of Fantasy" is their subtitle. They have beautiful fantasy stationery and cards, a good selection of incense and oils, costumes, hand crafted pewter and pottery—but they also feature several different artisans whose specialties are custom swords and knives, chain mail armor, crystal balls, and magic wands.

BASQUE PICNIC AND FESTIVAL, CHINO

Since 1967, a lesser known Southland community has been holding a wonderful summer event open to all:

Chino Basque Club Annual Picnic and Festival
Chino Junior Fairgrounds, Central and Edison Avenues
and indoors at:
Brinderson Hall, Junior Fairgrounds
5410 Edison Avenue
Chino, CA 91710
normally last Sunday of August
(909) 628-5282 (Hall)
(909) 628-9014
(909) 628-6500

Though a lot of Americans don't even know what a Basque is, they are the oldest surviving culture in Western Europe. The word apparently came from Roman historians who referred to one of their tribes as "Vascones." Their language is called "Euskara." Though they are a distinct people, they do not have their own state. About three million Basques live in their homeland, which is the high country of the Western Pyrenees mountains that divide Spain and France.

Explorers by nature, they were active in the colonization of South America. The City of Buenos Aires, Argentina was founded by Juan de Garay and sheep were introduced to that country by Miguel de Urrutia, both Basques.

Though improving conditions back home have slowed immigration, many

Basques found their way to California because of the greater economic opportunity. Because they are sheep herders used to a rugged landscape, most settled in Kern County in the foothills of the Sierras and in Bakersfield. Probably the most famous (or infamous) Basque in Southern California history is Miguel Leonis, whose story is told in the October chapter.

A smaller, but still considerable number came to the Chino Valley. Now there are several hundred families here, and every year since 1967 they have held this big shindig that is open to the public. The Basques wear traditional Basque folk costumes: the men dress in all white with red sashes and berets, the women wear white blouses and colored scarves with red skirts with black aprons.

It opens with a Basque mass in the fairground's Brinderson Hall. This is followed by a steak barbecue, then the fanfare of a Basque marching band called a "klika" leads into the dancing. Traditional Basque costumes are worn. The grand finale is a lamb barbecue dinner.

As you might gather from the picnic, Basque eating is not a lightweight affair. A Basque landmark in Southern California for a hearty meal at other times of the year is:

Centro Basco Restaurant
13432 South Central Avenue
Chino, CA 91710
Tuesday-Friday 11 a.m. to 2 p.m.
Tuesday-Saturday 5 to 9:30 p.m.
Sunday 4 to 9 p.m.
(909) 628-9014

This restaurant was opened in 1970 by the Berterretche family. Mother and father Monique and Pierre, cook and daughter, Bernadette, acts as hostess and tends the full bar.

There are two ways you can have dinner. The regular menu in the Zazpiat Bat Room is full of wonderful choices like lamb and "poulet basque." The french fries come out crisp and sizzling from the kitchen. This room with its red booths is referred to as the "American side."

The other option is every Friday, Saturday, and Sunday night at 7 p.m. At these times, there is an all-you-can-eat family style Basque feast for $11 per person which is served on a long communal table. In order to partake, you must get there early and ask to sit at the Basque family table.

A dinner bell rings at 7 p.m. sharp to announce the beginning of the food—

which is a mystery until it is actually served. It includes a soup, a stew, a salad, two hearty entrees and both red and white house wines. The table is like a cornucopia of heaping plates and rounds of cheese and fresh peasant bread. The Basque feast is also available for Sunday brunch at 12:30 p.m.

SUMMER CORN

When I was growing up in the San Fernando Valley, a big part of the warm evenings of August was getting freshly picked corn from local farm stands and having it as part of a barbecue. Destruction of farm land by the tract house monster has reduced their number, but there are still a few "suburban farms" left. One of them is in the Valley:

Cicero Farms—on the grounds of Pierce College
[corner of Victory Boulevard and De Soto Street]
Woodland Hills
Daily 9:30 a.m. to 6 p.m.
(818) 346-6338

But the piece de resistance among suburban farms has their annual festival this month in Norwalk:

Corn Festival—Paddison Farm
11951 Imperial Highway
Norwalk, CA 90652
first Sunday in August
(310) 863-4567

This low priced ($3) little festival celebrates the three varieties of corn grown on this unique property. It features all kinds of country-inspired activities. They add baby farm animals to the peacocks that normally cruise around the grounds. You can participate in corn shucking, listen to storytelling or bluegrass music, and clog and country western dance. There is craft and folk art, a demonstration of cornhusk doll making, and even a frog-leaping contest. The best part is that you get to see the buildings and grounds of a real family-owned farm that somehow survived as a city grew all around it.

It was back in 1879 when a Welsh immigrant named Scatlebury first plowed this plot. In those days, southeast Los Angeles was a farming and ranching area. The new arrival designed and built a two-story Victorian farmhouse with clapboard siding, four barns, chicken coops, and a blacksmith's shop. Miraculously, his great grandson, Bob, still owns it.

The years have taken their toll on the once large spread. Interstate 5 (the Santa Ana Freeway) sliced through a cornfield, the eastern 20 acres became a Montgomery Wards, and periodic sales to developers whittled the farm down from 300 acres to six.

Today, income to support the property's upkeep comes from renting it out as a location for everything from weddings to corporate events. Listed on the National Register of Historic Places, Paddison Farm also is a frequent film and television site for such shows as "The Wonder Years." This also includes commercials: Frank and Ed sat on the broad wooden porch and discussed the merits of Bartles and James wine coolers.

SEPTEMBER

Birthday of Los Angeles (September 4)

Mexican Independence Day (September 16)

Cabrillo Festival, San Diego (September 28)

Sixth Street Festival, San Pedro

*Fall Theatre, Music, and Dance Seasons
in the Southland*

Watts Towers Day of the Drum and Simon Rodia

Music and Arts Festival

Route 66 Rendezvous

Gene Autry's Birthday

Fall Harvest

Chapter Nine

SEPTEMBER

September is an odd name for the ninth month of the year, since its literal meaning is "seventh month." September was the seventh month in the Julian calendar that dates back to 44 B.C. Rome. The Gregorian calendar we use today was a "revision" to the Julian calendar introduced in 1582 and adopted in England and her colonies (meaning us) in 1752. All of the months from now until the end of the year are similarly poorly named.

Early September feels just like August. Though Labor Day weekend is the unofficial "end of summer" holiday, summer doesn't officially end until the autumnal equinox on the 22nd. That "fall feeling" in Southern California doesn't hit until around the very end of October, if then. There can be a kind of frenzy in all of us when we realize that summer is almost over and once again we have been too busy to enjoy it.

It isn't just that summer is hot and fall is cooler and, in New England, the leaves change color. There is a definite change in our feelings. Summer is a languid time. Fall is the season of the harvest and an energized time of accomplishment. September is the transition month that encompasses both.

There have been many beautiful song lyrics written about September: Many of us grew up listening to the words, "See you in Sept-em-ber, or lose you to a summer love" and later learned what they meant. Or the passionate softness of "September Song": "Oh the days dwindle down, to a precious few. Sept-em-ber, Nov-em-ber. And these few precious days I'll spend with you; these precious days I'll spend with you."

Perhaps we are all so busy now that we don't actually have any time to get ready for a particular season until it's nearly over. I always end up finding September to be the best month of summer for doing things.

BIRTHDAY OF LOS ANGELES (SEPTEMBER 4)

September is an important month in Southern California. In addition to the seasonal change, there are several milestone dates in our history. The first of these on the calendar is the Birthday of Los Angeles on September 4.

In 1781, the Spanish throne chartered the Anza Expedition of settlers to grow food and work the land for the presidios at Santa Barbara and San Diego on farms situated in between these two settlements. Thus, the Spaniards consolidated their control over the territory and made the existing settlements less dependent upon shipments from the older colonies. The expedition came overland from Sinola and Alamos, in Sonora, Mexico to the:

Mission San Gabriel Archangel
537 West Mission Drive
San Gabriel, CA 91776
(818) 282-5191

This mission was founded in September of 1771 by Fathers Angel Somera and Pedro Cambon and was moved to its present site in 1776. Its design, with its narrow windows, vaulted roof, and capped buttresses, was copied from the Cathedral of Cordoba, which was formerly a mosque. Pedro Antonio Cruzado, who designed and built the church, was born in Cordoba, at Alcarazegos. It is architecturally interesting because the facade is a side wall and the main entrance is on the side.

The original structure was built of brick, mortar, and cut stone from 1791 to 1805. Like many old buildings in the Southland, it has been damaged by earthquakes—this one in 1803 and 1812. The barrel vault ceiling went in the first tremblor and was replaced by a timber one the next year. In 1912, the church tower on the facade collapsed, rendering the mission temporarily sans bell. In 1828, a "campanario," or bell tower wall, with three rows of arched openings was added that created the classic look associated with missions. The mission was again damaged by an earthquake in 1987.

The mission was constructed entirely by Native American workers. As I mentioned in January, there were originally four tribes that ranged from here to Catalina. They were all grouped under the heading "Gabrielinos" who endured some ugly moments throughout the history of the mission.

A Spanish rifleman raped the young wife of a chief, and his tribe retaliated by attacking the mission while pursuing the perpetrator. They did not fare very well. The mission was built like a fort and, just as Columbus and Cortez had discovered, bows and arrows were no match for Spanish soldiers protected by their leather armor and armed with muskets. Many Indians were killed, including the chief.

Now, the grounds are a tranquil place. They are covered with cactus gardens and grape arbors. This area was an early winemaking region and the mission was famed for its vineyards, once the largest in California. Next to the mission is the cemetery. It is the oldest in Los Angeles and there are over 6,000 Indians buried here.

The mission was a waystation of sorts at a crossroads of major trails. After crossing the desert to the south, the Anza Expedition settlers must have been happy to see it.

Soon after arriving at the mission, part of the Anza Expedition—44 civilians from 11 families, along with four soldiers—set out in the warm sun. There were exactly 22 adults and 22 children. The **Pobladores Plaque** in the Plaza at Olvera Street lists all of the founders by name, age, and race. Perhaps the most poignant statement about Los Angeles is the mixture of people who created it.

On September 5, 1781, they found a perfect spot nine miles west of Mission San Gabriel on a large river at the Native American village of Yang Na. They gave their new town a very long name: El Pueblo de Nuestra Senora la Reina de Los Angeles de Porciuncula (the Town of Our Lady the Queen of the Angels of Poriuncula).

The actual location of Yang Na ironically seems to be very near where City Hall is today. It was one of about 25 to 30 villages throughout the area that is now L.A. County and probably consisted of between 2,000 and 3,000 people. Most of them died of diseases brought by their conquerors and within 50 years after the arrival of the settlers, there was only a handful of them left in a tiny ghetto at the corner of Alameda and Commercial Street.

The settlers fared somewhat better. Olvera Street still has a remnant of the first settlement—a fragment of the original irrigation ditch used to channel precious water from the Los Angeles River. Built in 1783, it was called "La Zanja Madre" (the mother ditch). The oldest surviving dwelling in Los Angeles is nearby:

> **Avila Adobe**
> **10 Olvera Street**
> **Los Angeles, CA 90012**
> **Tuesday-Friday 10 a.m. to 4 p.m.**
> **Saturday & Sunday 10 a.m. to 3:30 p.m.**
> **(213) 628-7164**

Built around 1818, this was the home of Don Francisco Avila, who was mayor of the little pueblo. Though partially reconstructed and concrete reinforced for earthquake safety in 1971, part of the original two-foot thick walls are still intact. It is a classic one-story Mexican design, the typical wealthy colonial family home. There are seven rooms arranged in a double row: one row facing the front patio, the other facing the garden patio in back.

The inside is furnished as it would have been, with the father's office containing ledger books and cowhides for trading; there is a master bedroom, and a children's bedroom, complete with clothes, dolls, a wooden cradle, a chamber pot, and a kinky bed made out of cowhide. There is an indoor kitchen (which is where the wooden bathtub is located) but most of the cooking was done in the outdoor kitchen on the patio. Ironically, the tile roof, so much associated with Southland architecture, was undoubtedly a much later addition.

The **Visitor's Center** in the nearby Sepulveda House has exhibits that show you what the original rooms looked like, as well as a little screening room where a free 18-minute film about early Los Angeles is shown. There is a lot of history to be experienced on Olvera Street, and it helps to understand the destiny of L.A. as the regional capital of Southern California.

Los Angeles was officially named the capital of Alta California by the Congress of Mexico on May 23rd of 1835, though the physical seat of government was not moved from Monterey until 1845. The last Mexican governor of California was Pio Pico and his term of office was to prove a short one. American troops invaded shortly thereafter, and in 1847, L.A. became the last pueblo in Mexican California to surrender to the United States. California became a state in 1850.

This duality of being both an American city and a conquered Mexican capital is expressed artistically in the mural **"Tropical America"** by David Alfara Siqueiros on the second floor of the Italian Hall. There is more on Olvera Street in the March, May, and December chapters.

Besides the founding of the city, another important historical occurrence happened very near here at another stately relic of old Los Angeles:

Philippe's, The Original French Dip
1001 North Alameda Street
Los Angeles, CA 90012
Daily 6 a.m. to 10 p.m.
(213) 628-3781

According to legend, one of the auspicious events of the year 1908 was the invention of the French dip sandwich in this venerable L.A. institution. Change has come slowly to this place of linoleum-topped tables and sawdust covered floors. It was a major moment in the city's history when, during the 1980s, the price of a cup of coffee was raised from 5 cents to 10 cents.

Today, Angelinos can be proud of their city's government building:

Los Angeles City Hall
200 North Spring Street
Los Angeles, CA 90012
(213) 485-2121

This it the original "landmark building" of the Southland. Built in 1926, its 27 stories made it the tallest structure in the land. It has gradually been dwarfed by new steel and glass and postmodern towers ever since the 13-story limit on building height in L.A. was lifted in 1957. Now it peeps out of a forest of much taller giants like an Art Deco guided missile, while the First Interstate Tower rises above, bearing an uncanny resemblance to a giant spark plug with a cupcake stuck on top.

When this intriguing edifice was built in 1928 its design was referred to as "Italian Classic." It is certainly something beyond that. Famous during the early days of television as the Daily Planet Building on the TV show "Superman," it cost $9,000,000 to build back then, and architectural critics say it would cost 100 times that to replace it today.

The 900,000-square-foot building's eclectic architectural style includes some details so perfect it is almost poetic. At the north and south entrance on the walls between the second and third floor, near the mayor's office in the vestibule connected to the rotunda, and in the City Council Chambers are true examples of Southern California art: beautiful, enormous panels made of original tiles of the Malibu Potteries (see August).

Original tile work from Malibu Pottery adorns the walls of City Hall.

Perhaps the prettiest moment in the building's history came on January 11 of 1949. On that day, real snow fell from the sky and lightly dusted downtown L.A. with sparkling white flakes.

Right by City Hall is a large stand that was my first exposure to multi-culturalism:

Kosher Burrito
110 East 1st Street
Los Angeles, CA 90012
Daily 7 a.m. to 4 p.m.
(213) 626-0998

At one time in the distant past, I had a clerk job in Downtown L.A. and commuted daily from the Valley. One of my co-workers took me to the Kosher Burrito, which has been here since 1946. I recall my amazement that there could be such a thing as a kosher burrito (it is made with pastrami) and even greater amazement that it was run by Asians! (It does not seem to be any more.) Only in Los Angeles.

MEXICAN INDEPENDENCE DAY (SEPTEMBER 16)

The second milestone date in September is Mexican Independence Day. The middle of the month, on September 15, the Southland is host to the largest celebration of this moment in history outside of Mexico City.

Mexico's fight for independence from Spain is said to have started on the night of September 15 of 1810. Father Miguel Hidalgo, Juan de Aldama, and Captain Ignacio Allende had been planning a revolt from Hidalgo's parish village of Dolores. Donna Josefa Dominguez learned that the colonial government had found them out and sent Ignacio Perez to warn them.

The next morning, September 16, Father Hidalgo rang the church's bells and summoned his parishioners to the town square where he delivered a fiery call to arms. This event has come to be known as **El Grito de Dolores**.

Though six months later, Allende, Aldama, and Hidalgo and their peasant forces were defeated near Guadalajara and the three men were executed, they had started a brushfire that was not to be easily extinguished. Two days after El Grito, on September 18, Chile declared its independence as well. Other Latin American counties eventually followed suit. This is why the holiday is also celebrated in Southern California by all Central American peoples.

Los Angeles has been called the capital of the Third World for a reason. Besides being the second largest Mexican city in the world, it is also the second largest Guatemalan and Salvadorian city as well, so it is quite understandable why Mexican Independence Day is such a big event here.

There are usually several days of activities in different parts of Southern California and, of course, a big parade:

> **Mexican Independence Day Parade**
> **East Los Angeles**
> **second Sunday of September at 1 p.m.**
> **(213) 948-5411**

This parade, a tradition since 1948, is the largest manifestation of the general celebration. The East L.A. Parade always features a star, such as boxer Oscar De La Hoya, as Grand Marshal. He will be accompanied by traditional feathered "Xipetotec" dancers, marching bands, equestrian groups, politicians, and beautifully painted low-rider cars and mini-trucks. Though it does not have the elaborate corporate-sponsored floats, there are about three times as many entries as the Rose Parade.

It begins at Lorna and 1st Street and goes east on 1st to Gage Avenue. The procession then turns north on Gage to Cesar E. Chavez Avenue. From there, it goes east on Cesar E. Chavez to Mednik Avenue, turns south on Mednick and finishes up back at 1st Street.

There is normally a festival the day of the parade:

> **Fiestas Patrias Festival**
> **Belvedere County Park**

4914 Cesar E. Chavez Avenue
East Los Angeles, CA 90022

Food booths fill the air with the aroma of delicious Mexican food, while children scream with delight from carnival rides. There is also folklorico dancing and a boxing exhibition as well as a stage for bands.

Just up 1st Street is an old Mexican institution where you can listen to some music, grab a bite to eat, and have a good time shopping:

El Mercado
3425 East 1st Street
East Los Angeles, CA 90063
Daily 10 a.m. to 8 p.m.
(213) 268-3451

There are all kinds of things you can buy here from the individual merchants on the main floor and basement. The mezzanine has several restaurants where you order cafeteria-style and sit and listen to the mariachis—who play all day long.

Of course, if you want handmade tortillas, the place to go is:

La Azteca Tortilleria
4538 Cesar E. Chavez Avenue
East Los Angeles, CA 90022
Monday-Friday 8 a.m. to 5 p.m.
Saturday & Sunday 8 a.m. to 3:30 p.m.
(213) 262-5977

Since 1978, they have started pounding tortillas here every morning at 4:30 a.m., but they don't just make a big batch and then stop for the day. In order to make sure they have the very freshest tortillas available, they make several smaller lots throughout the day. They will sell almost 2,000 corn and flour tortillas from the time they open until closing time.

They also serve food made from their tortillas, on a limited scale. These include burritos, quesadillas, and huevos rancheros. To say they taste better with the fresh, handmade tortillas is somewhat of an understatement.

Heading west on Cesar E. Chavez Avenue, you will come upon a very special East L.A. Mexican restaurant:

La Parilla
2126 Cesar E. Chavez Avenue
East Los Angeles, CA 90033
Daily 8 a.m. to 11:30 p.m.
(213) 262-3434

Over the decorative wrought iron framing of the entrance to this cheerful place is a painting of what appears to be a dark stone bowl full of food on three legs. The caption reads "Made right at your table." This is the "molcajete Azteca," the specialty of the house here at La Parilla. It is brought to the table and the sizzling smell of steak, chicken, salsa, green peppers, and cactus fills the air.

The featured style of Mexican cuisine here is charcoal-grilled marinated meats. These include cooked-at-the-table versions like the "molcajete Azteca" and the "parrillada al brasero," which comes on a grill, as well as pork coated with chile paste, chorizo, chicken, and beef filets.

Plaza de la Raza, Lincoln Park

Ironically, the park that is central to the Hispanic community does not have anything for Mexican Independence Day, but is a nice place to visit in the month of September:

Lincoln Park
3501 Valley Boulevard
[North Mission Road at Valley Boulevard]
East Los Angeles, CA 90031
(213) 237-1726

This 46-acre park was annexed by the City of Los Angeles in 1874, making it one of the city's oldest. It has some huge trees that have stood since the park's beginning. There are over 300 varieties of trees here.

For about the first half century of its existence, "East Lake Park" (as it was known) was famous for its alligator and ostrich farms and pretty man-made lake. The alligators and ostriches are gone, but the lake is still there, complete with ducks. The park has barbecues, picnic tables, a pool, and sports fields. Reflecting the ethnic heritage of the community, the children's playground features structures and figures with an Aztec theme. The park's entrance is one block east of the intersection of Valley Boulevard and Mission Road.

Fronting on the lake is:

Plaza de la Raza
Lincoln Park
3540 North Mission Road
East Los Angeles, CA 90031
(213) 223-2475

Plaza de La Raza means "place of the people." An Aztec Pyramid rises majestically in this center for dance, drama, and music of Hispanic origin.

East L.A. and Boyle Heights are places of great food from south of the border. Perhaps the classic Southern California Mexican restaurant is the venerable:

> **El Tepeyac Cafe**
> **812 North Evergreen Avenue**
> **Boyle Heights, CA 90033**
> **Sunday-Thursday 6 a.m. to 9:45 p.m.**
> **Friday & Saturday 6 a.m. to 11 p.m.**
> **closed Tuesday**
> **(213) 268-1960**

Aficionados come from all over the Southland to munch on El Tepeyac's tacos, steak picado, huevos con chorizo, and other traditional Mexican dishes—all offered in enormous-sized portions. The real stars, however, are the burritos, which are as big as Gucci purses filled with beans and meat. There is a side patio, a take-out window, and a small dining room that seems to always be full.

An interesting side note to El Grito can be had by taking a trip to Whittier and visiting the:

> **Sleeping Mexican Museum**
> **Little Old Bookshop**
> **6546 South Greenleaf Avenue**
> **Whittier, CA 90601**
> **Daily 10 a.m. to 10 p.m.**
> **(310) 698-1934**

A common stereotypical image of Mexicans is the depiction of a male figure in a huge sombrero with his head drooping forward. Clothed in peasant garb, this figure in its many manifestations is usually seated on the ground with his knees drawn up, his head laying atop his folded arms. There is usually a cactus or some other object for him to lean on.

These figures can also have derogatory additions, such as liquor bottles clutched in hand. According to Chuck Philip Jinenez, owner of the Little Old Bookshop, the original connotation of these folk figures was to show the peasant's attachment to the land, as symbolized by the cactus. A negative stereotype of Mexicans caused the figures to take on a new meaning. This led to cheap copies made in other countries—usually the ones with the liquor bottle in hand.

Jimenez has assembled a collection of over 60 of the figurines, and they are on display in a glass case in his bookstore. A true authority on the subject, he spent 20 years researching his large soft-cover book, *Sleeping Mexican Phenomenon*. It is for sale in his store—which is one of the Southland's better used bookstores. Originally opened down the street in 1976, the Little Old Bookshop carries about 115,000 titles. These books can vary in price, from good used books for as little as $1 to rarities for $1,000.

A unique park in San Diego has a history that makes it appropriate for Mexican Independence Day:

> **Chicano Park**
> **under San Diego-Coronado Bridge**
> **near corner of Crosby Street and Logan Avenue**
> **San Diego**

When the San Diego-Coronado bridge was being built in 1969, construction cut right through the Hispanic neighborhood of Logan Heights. As if to add insult to injury, the city also planned to put a Highway Patrol Station under the bridge—despite the fact that residents wanted (and needed) a park.

When the time came to start building the station, construction workers were greeted by angry locals at the site, who had formed a human chain around the area. Others were already digging holes for planting trees and putting up scaffolding around the concrete pillars of the bridge for artists to begin painting murals.

The city thereupon changed their minds about the C.H.P. station. Trees were planted and murals now embody the spirit of Chicano Park, which was officially born on April 22 of 1970. One of the murals celebrates this day as "La Tierra Mia." Since that day, numerous other murals have been added underneath the swooping concrete of the geometrically lined-up supports.

Subjects include Che Guevara, Frida Kahlo, and Quetzalcoatl, the Aztec plumed serpent of knowledge. The whole effect is one of the more startling juxtapositions of urban art and form in the Southland. There are lawns, picnic tables, and children's playground equipment.

For a picnic in Chicano Park, the ideal place to get take-out would be:

> **El Indio Shop**
> **3695 India Street**
> **San Diego, CA 92103**
> **Daily 7 a.m. to 9 p.m.**
> **(619) 299-0333**

Originally opened in 1940 as a little tortilla shop by Ralph Pesquera, Sr. and three female tortilla makers, the Indio Shop has grown into one of the most popular restaurants in San Diego County. Now Ralph, Jr. carries on the family tradition and El Indio's 100 employees can churn out 72,000 tortillas per day! They have every kind of Mexican food you can make with tortillas—even fruit burritos. Since corn tortillas are their specialty, the chips and salsa here may be the Southland's best.

The former take-out stand now has a Southwestern-style indoor dining area with booths. There are some picnic tables across the street if you can't wait until you get to Chicano Park.

CABRILLO FESTIVAL, SAN DIEGO (SEPTEMBER 28)

The third commemorative date in September that helps define Southern California is September 28, celebrated as the Cabrillo Festival. The reason there are so many things named Cabrillo in the Southland is that the gentleman who claimed California for Spain in 1542 was Juan Rodriguez Cabrillo.

His expedition left Navidad, Mexico on June 27 of 1542 to look for a passage to China and generally chart the coast of New Spain. He landed at what is now Ballast Point on Point Loma in San Diego on September 28 and is thus credited with "discovering" Alta California. His original name for San Diego was "San Miguel."

They re-enact the landing every year in September during this festival. This is an interesting annual shebang that opens with Native American, Mexican, Spanish, and even Portuguese folklorico dancers in brilliantly colored costumes. Flags are formally presented and a military band does a little concert during the two hour cermony. The old boy finally comes ashore and claims the place for the King of Spain. Humphrey's Half Moon Inn (described in June) is directly opposite the point of debarkation and site of the big event.

On Sunday, a wreath is placed on the statue of Cabrillo at the:

Cabrillo National Monument Park
Point Loma, San Diego
Daily 9 a.m. to 5:15 p.m.
Admission: $3 per vehicle or $1 per person
(619) 557-5450

Aside from the competition from Huntington's Santa Monica interests vying to be the Port of Los Angeles, that San Pedro would then go on to become the most important trading harbor on the West Coast would have seemed even more unlikely to anyone with sense in those early days. San Diego would have seemed to be a much more natural choice as the main port of Southern California, rather than the secondary one.

If you look at **San Diego Harbor** on a map, it looks like the jawline of a buck-toothed person with a severe overbite. The overbite portion of the jaw ends in Point Loma.

From Point Loma, the view of the bay and the city is fantastic. It is one of the most dramatic bay views in the world because Point Loma is 400 feet above sea level. There is a whale watching station here with a glassed in observatory. There are also whale exhibits and a film on whales in an auditorium. You might think about coming here during the season (end of December through early April).

Nearby is the restored **Point Loma Lighthouse**, which was a beacon for the harbor from 1855 to 1891. This lovely Cape Cod-styled home with its towering light is the oldest of the Southland's lighthouses. It is also the only one open to the public. The inside features period furniture and decorations, but the most poignant image in it is a deck of cards laid out on the living room table for that quintessential game among lighthouse keepers: solitaire.

Like its counterpart at the entrance to **Los Angeles Harbor**, this area is a good peninsula from which to not only gaze for passing whales, but poke around in tidepools. During minus tide season (November through March) they have tidepool tours (call for recorded information). Point Loma also offers one of the more romantic short walks you can take in Southern California: a pathway with a beautiful view all around, the mile long **Bayside Trail**, which winds through the chaparral and near intriguing tidepools.

The tidepools here are very popular. To park near them and avoid the park fees, take the right hand turnoff before the park's entrance. There is a long dirt path from the parking lot to the tidepools, which have signs describing the life forms found there. Like the Cabrillo Aquarium at the entrance to Los Angeles' Harbor, Cabrillo National Monument Park also sponsors slide shows with guided nature walks.

Also like the Port of Los Angeles, the Port of San Diego is graced with a **Bell of Friendship**, this one is from San Diego's Japanese sister city Yokohama, Japan. Though smaller than the Korean Bell of Friendship that adorns Los Angeles Harbor, it is nevertheless quite impressive (being 2-1/2 tons of solid bronze). It was placed on Shelter Island facing the Main Channel in 1960 as a symbol of unity between the two cities.

Unlike the original San Pedro marshlands, San Diego Harbor has always been a beautiful deep water port, and it is surprising the Spanish took so long to come back after Cabrillo. They finally sent an expedition over 100 years later led by Gaspar de Portola and accompanied by Father Junipero Serra to establish the missions and presidios (military posts). There is more on San Diego Harbor in the November and December chapters.

The first settlement came in 1769 in what is referred to today as San Diego's "Old Town" (see May). Father Serra's famous 21 missions that would span the length of the state started near here. But as fate would have it, El Pueblo de la Reina de Los Angeles, founded in 1781, became the commercial leader of the region.

World War II saw the Pacific Fleet move in and thus San Diego become a Navy town, rather than a commercial port. Though San Diego has grown into the nation's sixth largest city, the Navy still contributes 20 percent of the city's economy. This may change, as the city's proximity to Mexico is an advantage in dealing with that country's growing three-way trade between the U.S. and Asia.

Perhaps the best view of the harbor can be had from the appropriately named:

Harbor Hill Guest House
2330 Albatross Street
San Diego, CA 92101
(619) 233-0638

The area where this 1920's home was built was referred to as "Banker's Hill" because of the concentration of wealth there. Money tends to go to high ground, and homes here command a spectacular view of the harbor.

The Harbor Hill Guest House has three levels, each with its own entrance. This allows them to rent both individual rooms, or entire floors. There are seven suites, all with private baths. The best two rooms in terms of view are the appropriately named **Harborview** and **Sunset Rooms.** The entire main floor can be rented on a monthly basis as the "**Banker's Hill Suite.**"

Just as Los Angeles Harbor has its maritime museum, so does its counterpart to the south:

The Maritime Museum of San Diego
1306 North Harbor Drive
San Diego, CA 92101
Daily 9 a.m. to 8 p.m. (winter)
Daily 9 a.m. to 9 p.m. (summer)
(619) 234-9153

Though it does not have the great models like the one in L.A., what is unique about this museum is that it has three real ships. They are the *Star of India,* a beautiful 1863 iron windjammer, the *Medea,* a 1904 English steam yacht, and the *Berkeley,* an 1898 propeller-driven San Francisco Ferryboat.

The most interesting is the *Star of India.* Launched at the Isle of Man in 1863, it is the oldest merchant vessel afloat and went around the world over 20 times when it was active. The main deck features an eerily detailed Captain's Cabin and first class passenger cabins.

The scattered toys and an old rocking horse indicate the presence of children on some voyage long ago. Dusty old uniforms hang in the Captain's closet. The sardine can-like crew's quarters make you realize the old movies didn't quite tell the whole story of the romance of early sea voyages. There is also a museum on board with old photos and miscellaneous sea memorabilia.

Overlooking the *Star of India* is the classic San Diego harbor restaurant:

Anthony's Star of the Sea Room
1360 North Harbor Drive
San Diego, CA 92101
Daily 5:30 to 10:30 p.m.
(619) 232-7408

This is the expensive, coat-and-tie restaurant of the three Anthony's that are side-by-side here. The other two, **Anthony's Fish Grotto** (619) 232-5103, and **Anthony's Harborside** (619) 232-6358 are more casual and reasonably priced, but do not have quite the same view. The Star of the Sea room is positioned quite dramatically over the water.

This is a serious restaurant. Not only do the huge picture windows provide romantic harbor views, the scalloped booths and formal full-backed chairs add an air of sensual luxury. This is accented by the hand-wrought copper serving plates and copper chandeliers overhead.

The food is celebrated not only for its freshness, but for its gourmet preparation. Chef Catherine Ghio comes from a fish market owning family and her creations are noteworthy. Her inch thick abalone steak and Cioppino a la Catherine are justifiably famous. Other specialties include petrale sole stuffed with lobster and a special cut loin of swordfish.

Right off Harbor drive, on B Street is the most convenient way to get to Catalina by boat from San Diego:

Seajet Cruise Lines
B Street Cruise Ship Terminal
San Diego
(800) 622-2538

This company boasts computer-stabilized ships, but trips from San Diego to Catalina are offered less frequently than from companies in San Pedro/Long Beach and can even be unavailable in the month of January. Call for the latest information.

Much of what makes San Diego such a romantic city, besides its natural beauty as a port city, is some of the beautiful Spanish and Moorish architecture that was a legacy of the 1915 Pan Pacific Exposition in Balboa Park (see April and June). Outside of the buildings in the park, the outstanding example of this is near the harbor:

Santa Fe Depot
1050 Kettner Boulevard
San Diego, CA 92101
(800) 872-7245
(619) 239-9021 (recording)

Traveling by train is romantic the world over because you get to see and share the passing views, eat, sleep, read, converse—all with the continuous movement of the train going on and on. Traveling by train is quite romantic in England because the Victorian train stations link you with the past of the place instantly.

Despite its identification with the automobile, train travel played an important part of the development of many of the Southland's cities. We are blessed with a fine collection of train stations that reflect our past architecturally. This one is the perfect place to start.

This is the beginning of the line. The "San Diegan" and the "Coast Starlight" travel up the coast from here and reach all the way to Washington State. There are many coast views that are only visible from this route, so sit on the left side on the ride up. A short trip within the Southland can be made more romantic by booking passage by train.

It is very exciting to arrive or depart from here. This lovely Spanish colonial was designed in 1915 for the exposition by John R. Blakewell to replace the existing one. It features a sparkling dome of blue, yellow, and white glazed tile that is the counterpart to the California Quadrangle, which is the building next to what is now the Old Globe Theatre in Balboa Park.

Santa Fe Station was beautifully refurbished in 1983 and is now one of the most appealing stations in the Amtrak system. The benches of polished wood, the brightly tiled wainscoting, and the beams overhead all contribute to a fresh clean look that seems old and new at the same time.

If you want the extraordinary feeling set by the Santa Fe Train Station to linger, stay downtown at the:

Horton Grand Hotel
311 Island Avenue
San Diego, CA 92101
(800) 999-1886

San Diego has its **"Gaslamp Quarter"** that hearkens back to its more colorful past as a port city. This hotel, originally built in 1886 hearkens back to this period with its cozy Victorian style. It is a nationally registered historic site and everyone from Wyatt Earp to the King of Hawaii has stayed here. The original rate was 50 cents per night. It is somewhat more expensive now, but the rooms are also considerably nicer. They have fireplaces in rooms and suites.

Attached to the Horton main building by 20-foot long bridges is the **Chinese Regal Hotel** wing. This building is a re-creation of two turn-of-the century Chinese brothels that were in the "Stingaree" waterfront district. There are 24 huge 600-square-foot, two-room suites, all of which have bay views. Each of the rooms in the hotel is decorated with period antiques, queen-sized platform beds, and hand-carved armoires.

The brothel theme continues in the naming of the hotel's restaurant located just off the lobby: it is called **Ida Baily's** after a local turn-of-the-century madame. Even if you are not staying here I suggest stopping by for a drink at the bar. With its filigreed brass chandeliers, towering gold framed mirrors, and classic brothel style paintings of buxom nudes frolicking in meadows, this is the Victorian Age at its lusty best.

Something right here that is not very Victorian is nonetheless quite a popular stop:

Horton Plaza
Bounded by Broadway, G Street,
1st Avenue, and 4th Avenue
San Diego
(619) 238-1396

The Horton Grand Hotel was actually moved to make way for this unique mall. Horton Plaza is a three level structure that houses four department stores, about 140 specialty stores, theaters, and a variety of restaurants. It is a shopping adventure. There is an adjacent parking structure. Be sure to note which stores surround the door you entered from the parking lot to the plaza. It is easy to lose your car if you are not a regular shopper here.

San Diego has one of the more wonderful downtowns for an evening out. It is small, has fresh air, and romance in its restored old theatres, the queen of which is:

Copley Symphony Hall
1245 7th Avenue
San Diego, CA 92101
(619) 699-4200
(619) 699-4205 (tickets)

This absolutely magnificent 2,225-seat Spanish Rococo hybrid was designed in 1929 by Weeks and Day as the Fox Theater and restored in 1985 with heavy backing from the owner of the *San Diego Union* and *Evening Tribune*, Helen Copley.

As a movie palace, this one was second to none. It opened in the year of the stock market crash, 1929, with *They Had To See Paris* starring Will Rogers. On hand were stars of the old film world such as Buster Keaton, but also Jackie Coogan and the young George Jessel. The 12-foot wide chandelier held eight chorus girls. For a long time, all of Walt Disney's films premiered here, at his personal request. Despite the fact that it was built in the talkie era, it had a 26,000 pipe organ.

The restoration, as with many other old San Diego landmarks, has been very thorough, making this one of the most enjoyable places in the Southland to hear a classical concert (October through May) or opera, which begins this month.

A downtown restaurant that is suitably dramatic to go with Copely Symphony Hall is just a few steps away:

La Gran Tapa
611 B Street
San Diego, CA 92101
Monday-Thursday 11:30 a.m. to 10 p.m.
Friday & Saturday 11:30 a.m. to 2: a.m.
Sunday 11:30 a.m. to 10 p.m.
(619) 234-8272

"Tapas" are a Spanish pub food that, like its equivalents in the cuisines of other cultures, consists of a series of small appetizers that are perfect for a festive night out. These can be everything from stuffed olives with anchovies, tiny pieces of bread with ham, and grilled shrimp, to little turnovers called "empanadillas." This kind of food goes well with soup, and their garlic soup has a big fan club.

The decor here is very elegant with thick carpets and brass and heavy wood paneling. The restaurateur responsible for La Gran Tapa is former bullfighter Paul Dobson, whose namesake establishment will be described later in the month.

The hotel with the most illustrious history in Downtown San Diego is two blocks away:

U.S. Grant Hotel
326 Broadway
San Diego, CA 92101
(619) 232-3121

The hotel was officially opened by President Ulysses S. Grant in a dedication ceremony on October 15 of 1910. It was built by his son, Ulysses, Jr., on the site of the Horton House, the city's original grand hotel. Guests have included President Harry S. Truman, Charles Lindbergh, and Albert Einstein. There is an "Old Boy" tradition here that still survives to some extent: for much of this century, a sign in the hotel's formal dining room, the Grant Grill, said (not jokingly), "Gentlemen only until 3 o'clock." Incredibly enough, this tradition continued until 1969.

The U.S. Grant has beautiful crystal chandeliers, wingback Queen Anne chairs, and a timeless elegance no new hotel could have, no matter how expensive. The 400 rooms have marble baths and there are suites with fireplaces.

Just a few doors down is the most prominent building on the street:

First Interstate Bank
540 Broadway
San Diego, CA 92101
(619) 557-2260

My first thought was "They don't build 'em like this anymore" when I saw this building, designed in 1927 by William Templeton Johnson. The revolving door that forms the main entrance will make you feel like you are on your way to perform a major financial transaction even if you are just buying a few traveler's checks.

The magnificent painted ceiling and marble floors lend a grandeur to the former main office of the San Diego Trust and Savings Bank. On the first floor is a unique **Museum of Banking** that tells the history of that bank, the building, and various employees. There is more about Downtown San Diego later this month.

SIXTH STREET FESTIVAL, SAN PEDRO

Of the numbered streets that run perpendicular to Harbor Boulevard and feed down into it, the most interesting is the one that runs directly into the L.A. Maritime Museum: 6th Street. Many of the restaurants and stores here feature stylish facades and interiors such as you would find in a seaside metropolis such as San Francisco or Baltimore. The feeling here is much the same. It doesn't hurt that the street rises steeply from the harbor so you are looking down a hill at the channel water from most places on it.

There is a great selection of moderately-priced restaurants of various kinds. A sensational ethnic restaurant is:

Papadakis Taverna
301 West 6th Street
San Pedro, CA 90731
(310) 548-1186

Former University of Southern California (USC) linebacker John Papadakis has created a restaurant that is best described as "The Greekest of The Greek." Waiters, cooks, and their wives sing, dance, and smash dishes exuberantly every night. This is a good place to take someone who is an uptight, upwardly mobile sort. Perhaps a few flying plates whizzing past their head will help them loosen up.

One of the most romantic is the pretty:

Sixth Street Bistro
354 West 6th Street
San Pedro, CA 90731
(310) 521-8818

Restaurateur George Mousalli has brought an appealing style to San Pedro with this French morsel. With its mural adorning one wall and exposed brick along the other there is a cozy, artsy feel to this great little restaurant. The recent patio addition offers outdoor dining.

Coffeehouses are plentiful in Southern California, but one of my favorites is right here:

Sacred Grounds Coffee House
399 West 6th Street
San Pedro, CA 90731
(310) 514-0800

Owners Chris and Jeanette Roth have opened a fairly large art gallery/coffeehouse that is a very good setting for readings and showings.

Though it is short, 6th Street has an appealing mix of businesses. There is a great bookstore that was originally established in 1909:

Williams' Book Store
443 West 6th Street
San Pedro, CA 90731
(310) 832-3631

There is a tavern and several antique stores and interesting shops as well as a great sushi bar/Japanese restaurant:

Senfuku
380 West 6th Street
San Pedro, CA 90731
(310) 832-5585

This is one of the more enjoyable sushi bars in the Southland—not because of any bizarre decor or culinary creations—but because it is a pleasant, comfortable place without pretense; the sushi is excellent, and everyone is very friendly without being obnoxious.

The room is square, as is the centrally located sushi bar, which is right there as you walk in. Tokyo-trained master chef Yoshi Kikuchi is one of the best. There is more about San Pedro in the January and December chapters.

FALL THEATRE, MUSIC, AND DANCE SEASONS IN THE SOUTHLAND

September is a traditional month when theatre companies come alive after their summer hibernation. In the Southland, there are three kinds of theatre: Equity, non-Equity, and A.E.A. 99-Seat. Equity refers to a professional union, Actor's Equity.

An Equity theater pays its performers a scale wage. Non-Equity is for non-union member actors who have not achieved professional status or for those for whom acting is really a hobby. It is often community theater. The third category is unique in some ways in that it is a theatre space of limited size that can use union actors, but not pay them scale wages.

Professional Repertory Theatre, San Diego

Producing legitimate theater has never been easy, but as government sponsored art grant money shrinks, the task becomes that much harder. Many large theaters are starting to use non-Equity actors.

There are five noteworthy Equity professional repertory theatres with a tradition of excellence in the Southland. Four of these have won the Tony Award for Outstanding Regional Theatre: The Old Globe (described in June), The La Jolla Playhouse, South Coast Repertory, and the Mark Taper Forum. The fifth (no Tony yet) is the:

San Diego Repertory Theatre, The Lyceum Theatre
79 Horton Plaza

San Diego, CA 92101
(619) 235-8025

San Diego Rep was founded in 1976 by Producing Director Sam Woodhouse and Artistic Director Douglas Jacobs in a former church that they called the Sixth Avenue Playhouse. They went big time 10 years later in 1986 and moved up to this two-auditorium theater in San Diego's revitalized downtown.

It is a very nice complex. The two stages are the 220-seat Space and the 550-seat Lyceum Stage. The Rep's work tends toward the daring, so occasionally it is not too popular in somewhat conservative San Diego. On the other hand, their production of *Six Women With Brain Death, or Expiring Minds Want To Know* was the longest running play in the city's history. They also have a Latin American playwright's program that produces works in both English and Spanish.

For some dinner before the show, a friend of mine who lives in San Diego swears that the soul of Downtown San Diego is to be found in:

Dobson's
956 Broadway Circle
San Diego, CA 92101
Sunday-Wednesday 11:30 a.m. to 10 p.m.
Thursday-Saturday 11:30 a.m. to 11 p.m.
(619) 231-6771

The restaurant's namesake, Paul Dobson, was one of America's first bullfighters. He is one of San Diego's most successful restaurateurs with three great places: La Gran Tapa (described earlier in the chapter), Dobson's, and Triangle's in La Jolla (described below).

Dobson's has a reputation as being a San Diego power lunch place. The plush booths even have brass plaques with the names of the most regular occupants on them. But the beveled glass and warm atmosphere also make it a romantic one. The best tables for an intimate repast are upstairs, on the balcony overlooking the bar.

In 1992, a second branch of the Museum of Contemporary Art, San Diego opened, this one actually in the city of its name:

Museum of Contemporary Art, San Diego
Downtown Annex
1001 Kettner Boulevard (at Broadway)
San Diego, CA 92101
Tuesday-Saturday 11 a.m. to 6 p.m.
Thursday 11 a.m. to 9 p.m.
(619) 234-1001

This is the second location of the Museum of Contemporary Art, San Diego, the first being the original location in La Jolla. In some ways, this location seems better for cutting-edge art because the building is a new 34-story glass tower with a view of the city outside that adds to the vibrancy of the exhibits of contemporary sculpture, paintings, and other art forms.

There is a museum store near the entrance and four galleries arranged on two levels with a total of about 10,000-square-feet of museum space. Exhibits are rotated, though a few selected pieces are on permanent display. It's fun to find Wendy Jacobs' "Breathing Wall," which expands and contracts. What shines about this museum is that it specializes in post-1950 emerging and mid-career artists.

La Jolla

The second professional theatre of note is the:

La Jolla Playhouse
2910 La Jolla Village Drive North
La Jolla, CA 92037
(619) 534-3960

There has always been a certain amount of glamour associated with the name of the La Jolla Playhouse, even though the current manifestation bears little resemblance to the original. The precursor La Jolla Playhouse was a high school auditorium, where in 1947 none other than Gregory Peck, along with Mel Ferrer and Dorothy McGuire, started an acting company called, imaginatively enough, the "Actor's Company." Peck was from La Jolla and wanted to create a venue for summer stock for film actors, much as Broadway actors have on the East Coast.

The theatre moved to this space on the University of California, San Diego campus in 1983. There are two auditoriums: the 400-seat thrust stage Mandell Weiss Forum and the 500-seat proscenium Mandell Weiss Theatre. Both feature excellent sight lines and the latest in lighting and technicals.

UCSD consists of five colleges and the Scripps Institute (see November) on a beautiful 2,000 acre backdrop. It has lots of trees and a cafe set in a eucalyptus grove. There are outdoor artworks throughout called the **Stuart Collection**. The Central University Library, designed in 1977 by William Peirera, is a dramatic inverted pyramid of glass squares on a two-story pedestal. The architect wanted "to convey the idea that powerful and permanent hands are holding aloft knowledge itself." For 90 minute tours of the campus, call (619) 534-2230.

Just outside of the university is a large mall called logically enough, **University**

Towne Center. It is a massive place with four big chain department stores, an indoor ice skating rink, plenty of fast food and stores, and a unique museum:

> **Mingei International Museum of World Folk Art**
> **4405 La Jolla Village Drive, Space I-7**
> **La Jolla, CA 92122**
> **Tuesday-Saturday 11 a.m. to 5 p.m.**
> **Sunday 2 to 5 p.m.**
> **(619) 453-5300**

What a surprise this place is! Opened in 1978 by Martha Longenecker, the name comes from two Japanese words: "Min," meaning "all of the people," and "gei," meaning "art." This pretty much describes the content and philosophy of this museum of folk art from around the world.

On the other side of La Jolla Village Drive is the third of Paul Dobson's San Diego restaurants and a great place for pre-theatre dining:

> **Triangle's**
> **4370 La Jolla Village Drive**
> **La Jolla, CA 92122**
> **Monday-Friday 11 a.m. to 10 p.m.**
> **Saturday 5:30 to 11 p.m.**
> **(619) 453-6650**

The name of this restaurant comes from the nickname of this part of La Jolla, the "Golden Triangle." The food and service are on par with the standard of excellence at the other Dobson eateries. The bar here is a 26-foot long antique work of art made of tigerwood. There is more about La Jolla in the February, July, and November chapters.

Costa Mesa

I have a lot of affection for the next of the professional repertory companies:

> **South Coast Repertory Theatre**
> **655 Towne Center Drive**
> **Costa Mesa, CA 92626**
> **(714) 957-2602**
> **(714) 957-4033**

I have taken tour groups to see so many great shows here. They are always wonderful about arranging after-theatre discussions with the actors for these groups and many of the actors are also teachers in the workshops they have here, so they can be as engaging after the show as during it.

South Coast Repertory Theatre in Costa Mesa is a remarkable artistic accomplishment. Starting in a storefront in an otherwise non-cultural area, it has grown to a two-theatre complex with 507- and 161-seat auditoriums. Winner of scores of *Drama Logue* and Drama Circle Awards, it has also been the recipient of a Special Tony Award for Outstanding Achievement. It has 23,000 subscribers and pre-sells 80 percent of its seats.

This is truly a repertory company. If you come for a few plays, you will see several of the actors in different roles. They do a mixture of classics and new work. They are considered one of the finest interpreters of the plays of George Bernard Shaw in North America. Overall, South Coast Repertory Theatre is the pinnacle of the arts in Orange County.

A short walk from the courtyard in front of the theatre is:

Scott's Seafood Grill and Bar
South Coast Plaza Towne Center
3300 Bristol Street
Costa Mesa, CA 92626
Monday-Friday 11:30 a.m. to 10 p.m.
Saturday 5:30 to 11 p.m.
Sunday 10 a.m. to 10 p.m.
(714) 979-2400

Scott's is a big inviting restaurant with a curved bar and an atrium dining room that is so pretty people get married in it. The Sunday Brunch is an orgy of food.

Around the corner is a free museum that is as surprising as its location:

Bank of America Gallery
South Coast Metro Center
555 Anton Boulevard
Costa Mesa, CA 92626
Monday-Friday 11 a.m. to 4 p.m.
(714) 433-6000

Bank of America inherited this art gallery/bank from Security Pacific in the merger. Its approximately 9,000-square-feet of gallery space is not adequate to display the enormous art collection, so exhibits are rotated. With 18,000 pieces, it is one of the largest private collections in the world. The strength of the collection is works on paper, and the permanent installation is a grouping of Post Modern deconstructed architectural forms by Judd Fine, Eric Orr, and Lita Albuquerque.

Los Angeles

The last of the Southland's professional companies has achieved remarkable critical acclaim in the '90s:

> **Mark Taper Forum**
> **Music Center of Los Angeles County**
> **135 North Grand Avenue**
> **Los Angeles, CA 90012**
> **(213) 972-7353**

I mentioned the Taper in passing when I was talking about the Music Center of Downtown Los Angeles in the February chapter. It was the second theatre to win the Tony's Outstanding Regional Theatre Award in 1977. For the 1994 Tony Awards, the Taper co-produced three of the four productions nominated for Best Play. According to Tony Award records, this is the first time this ever happened.

L.A.'s "Off Broadway"

There is plenty of small theatre throughout Southern California, but the playhouses vary greatly in quality and style. The small theatre is different in L.A., the San Fernando Valley, and the Westside for a very specific reason.

Southern California is rich in actors, writers, and directors—particularly in areas near the television and film industry. Most people who are serious about wanting to make a living as an actor naturally want to live as close as possible to where there are film or television auditions.

Talented people from all over the world want to make it in these media. This is because even a professional stage actor getting union scale makes a tiny salary compared with a film or television actor. Even what little paid theatre is out there is threatened: some of the new regional arts centers popping up in outlying areas may be multi-million dollar technical masterpieces, but they scrimp on paying the actors. They may pay one or two well-known performers for the lead parts to put their names on the advertisements, and then hire non-union actors for everything else.

What can make matters worse from an actor's point of view is that besides not paying very much (if anything) small community or large civic theatres in outlying areas tend to be extremely conservative in their play selection and style. This does not afford performers much room for artistic growth or personal satisfaction—plus there is little or no chance they will be seen by anyone from the entertainment industry.

This is why A.E.A. 99-seat theatre in the L.A. area is so different from community theater. The actors are more often professionals and the work tends to be more original and interesting, so the performers have more to sink their teeth into. Plus there is always that chance that someone from "The Industry" may come in and discover you. Even if there is little or no pay, being in a show in a tiny, not so nice theatre in the L.A. area offers an actor a much better showcase opportunity than being in million dollar art center located in a distant suburb.

People who have traveled to other countries where there is more theatre have asked me if there is a "Fringe District," a place where there is a concentration of good small theaters, in the Southland. In Southern California, this would be **Theatre Row Hollywood,** a little strip that appears suddenly along Santa Monica Boulevard between Cahuenga and Highland in an area surrounded by production companies and film studios (notably Warner Brothers).

Despite the fact that there is an amazing density of theatres in this one little zone, for a long time there was no recognition of its uniqueness. Now yellow banners proclaiming the name for all to see hang from the lampposts.

Going west, one of the first ones you will come to is the home of the:

> **Actor's Gang Theatre**
> **6209 Santa Monica Boulevard**
> **Hollywood, CA 90038**
> **(213) 465-0566**

This 99-seat space is the home of the Actor's Gang, the company co-founded by Tim Robbins. I recall meeting him when I brought a group to see the play *Carnage* being performed by the Gang at the Tiffany Theater (see August). He was so low key, I am embarrassed to say I did not recognize him, despite the fact that I had just seen the movie *Five Corners*. The Actor's Gang does some powerful work that usually has political connotations.

On the other side of the street is a remarkable theatrical complex called:

> **The Complex: Theatre 6470, the East,**
> **the Ruby, the Dorie, and the Flight Theaters**
> **6476 Santa Monica Boulevard**
> **Hollywood, CA 90038**
> **(213) 465-0383**

There are five separate theatres, all with less than 50 seats, within this historic building. It is owned by Matt Chait, who also sometimes acts, directs, or produces. Three are rentals, but the East is semi-permanently occupied by a theatre company and Theatre 6470 is rented annually by a confederation of different production groups who alternate using the space.

On the same side of the street is the:

Attic Theatre
6562 Santa Monica Boulevard
Hollywood, CA 90038
(213) 462-9720

The Attic Theatre is a true ensemble in that member actors pay dues to belong, go to classes, and appear in shows at the theater. It was founded in 1987 by Artistic Director James Carey. The second floor Attic Theatre is intimate and comfortable with a large lobby great for receptions, and its actors and director are extremely capable.

For some music and dinner, a little ways east on Santa Monica is the:

Gardenia Club
7066 Santa Monica Boulevard
Hollywood, CA 90038
(213) 467-7444

The Gardenia seats only 80 people, so it is a nice and cozy place to listen to comedy and music from some of our most talented performers. It is one of those intimate little clubs you didn't think existed in L.A. and it also serves very good Italian food.

One of the things that makes a night out on Theatre Row Hollywood such a treat is that you can have dinner right down the street at the legendary:

Formosa Cafe
7156 Santa Monica Boulevard
Hollywood, CA 90046
Monday-Saturday 11:30 a.m. to 2 a.m.
Sunday 8 p.m. to 1 a.m.
(213) 850-9050

The Formosa looks like a movie set version of a Chinese/American bar you might find in Shanghai in the late '30s. It was almost demolished in 1991 by Warner Brothers Studios, who owns the property, but it was saved through the action of the Friends of the Formosa.

You enter through a tunnel-like foyer lined with photos into a dark place with a musty smell. Inside, the walls are covered with close to 1,000 glossies of famous people. These cross several generations. A photo of a party for Hoot Gibson hangs next to a signed glossy of the "Love Boat" crew. This gives some clue to the remarkable history of the Formosa.

It started when retired prizefighter Jimmy Bernstein purchased a 1905 Red Car in 1925 to convert to a diner originally called The Red Post. He added the bar, kitchen and main dining room and decided to call it the Formosa Cafe. Boxers such as Joe Louis were regulars.

Hong Kong-born Lem Quon came to the U.S. in 1922 when he was 12. He was an Army mess hall cook and became partners with Jimmy Bernstein in 1945. He took over in 1960 upon the ex-prizefighter's death. Before his own death in 1994, he told some wonderful stories about the remarkable clientele.

Stories such as when Lana Turner danced in the aisles or that Clark Gable was bad tipper and once Howard Hughes borrowed $20. One of Quon's four stepsons from a previous marriage, Bill Jung, is now the owner. He was partners with Lem for 17 years before his death. The food is a mixture of Chinese and American and the drink list is encyclopedic.

Going north one block from Santa Monica will take you to Fountain Avenue; if you go east on Fountain (going around the junior high school at Bronson), you will come to one of Southern California's most interesting small theatres:

Fountain Theatre
5060 Fountain Avenue
Hollywood, CA 90029
(213) 663-2235

Deborah Lawlor, producing artistic director, operates this 80-seat marvel along with Artistic Director Stephen Sachs.

Sachs has a penchant for romance. His past projects have included the fairly tale like *Leonce and Lena* at Stages Theatre, and such adaptations as Italo Calvino's *The Baron In The Trees*, the Japanese fable *Winter Crane*, and *Golden Gate*, based upon the novel in verse by Calcutta-born Vikram Seth about love in modern day San Francisco.

If you continue east on Fountain, you will go past a classic small Hollywood dive/restaurant that used to be hard to miss. It formerly featured a model of a New York Skyline looming over an otherwise unremarkable street. This marked the location of:

New York George
4854 Fountain Avenue
Hollywood, CA 90029
Daily 7:30 a.m. to 8 p.m.
(213) 660-7414

Though the real "New York George" (Goodrich) is no longer the proprietor, the place still seems to have it. The $7.95 N.Y steak is the most expensive thing on the menu. They have Italian dishes such as chicken Italian and fettucini alfredo and a large selection of burgers, salads, and omelettes. But the ambiance of the place—a mixture of a Hollywood dive and an East Coast diner—makes ordering an egg cream soda almost necessary.

From here, if you continue east, you'll hit Sunset Boulevard and be in one of the creative centers of the Southland, the **Silver Lake** area, named for the reservoir. In terms of residential architecture, it is a real showplace of L.A. Modernism with several examples of work by the best architects of that school, including Rudolph Schindler, Raphael Soriano, and John Lautner (creator of the "Chemosphere House" (see June)).

Right near the intersection of Fountain and Sunset is a long time Silver Lake store:

Uncle Jer's
4459 Sunset Boulevard
Los Angeles, CA 90027
Monday-Friday 11 a.m. to 7 p.m.
Saturday 10 a.m. to 7 p.m.
Sunday 12 to 6 p.m.
(213) 662-6710

Originally opened just down the street in 1976 by owner Jerry Morley, Uncle Jer's survived the '80s and its message of environmental awareness seems more contemporary than ever. The store features clothing and all manner of gift items, including soaps and paper goods.

L.A. certainly has a large number of Mexican restaurants, but not very many Spanish ones. Going the other way on Sunset, you will find the most unusual one:

El Cid
4212 Sunset Boulevard
Los Angeles, CA 90027
Monday-Thursday 6:30 to 11 p.m.
Friday & Saturday 6:30 p.m. to 2 a.m.
Sunday 11 a.m. to 11 p.m.
(213) 668-0318

If this cabaret looks somehow different to you, it is because it was part of D.W. Griffith's movie studio built here in 1900. Fifty years later, in 1950, it was reborn as a small theatre. Now it is one of the only regular flamenco venues in the United States.

My favorite theatre in the area is a rental, but often has very interesting shows:

Olio Theatre
3709 Sunset Boulevard
Los Angeles, CA 90026
(213) 667-9556

I have always liked this 70-seat performance space. It is like a combination of a club and a theatre in that there are little round tables up near the raised stage with benches on risers behind. Right next door to the Olio is a fine Mexican restaurant:

El Conquistador
3701 Sunset Boulevard
Los Angeles, CA 90026
Monday-Thursday 5 to 11 p.m.
Friday-Sunday 11 a.m. to 11 p.m.
(213) 666-5136

In the early '70s, Jesse Pinto opened this great two-floor establishment with the festive decor and atmosphere. It has a patio downstairs and makes a perfect combination with a show at the Olio. One of the best names in small theatre in Southern California is just up Hyperion:

Company of Angels Theatre
2106 Hyperion Avenue
Los Angeles, CA 90027
(213) 666-6789

This 49-seat playhouse is the home of L.A.'s oldest repertory theatre groups, The Company of Angels.

Before you leave Silver Lake, make sure you visit a taco stand that is a shrine to connoisseurs:

Yucca's Hut
2056 North Hillhurst Avenue
Los Angeles, CA 90027
Monday-Saturday 11 a.m. to 6 p.m.
Closed Sunday
(213) 662-1214

The faithful drive across time zones for the Mexican food here.

Sunset Boulevard can take you all the way to the ocean from Silver Lake. On your way, you will pass some very interesting spots. Not too far away, going west on Sunset, is a grand building that would make a great before or after theater stop:

Hollywood Athletic Club and Drones Bar and
Grill Restaurant
6525 Sunset Boulevard
Hollywood, CA 90028
Daily 11 to 2 a.m.
dinner menu until 10 p.m., bar food until 1:30 a.m.
(213) 962-6600

The Hollywood Athletic Club building dates from 1924, but this establishment has only been here since 1990. Though it was at one time a real athletic club (with Cornel Wilde the fencing master), the name now refers to athletic endeavor of a particular (and unstrenuous) kind: billiards.

What were originally the members' dining room and gymnasium have been converted to the billiard rooms. Three antique snooker tables share the space with no less than 46 Brunswick Gold Crown billiard tables. They are incredible rooms: one of them has a high ceiling formed of white arches supported by columns.

The name of the restaurant part, Drones, refers to a London billiard club of the same name. They also have upstairs rooms where blues bands perform on Monday nights.

A little farther on is an architectural landmark that hosts an arts festival this month:

Hollywood Arts Affair
Cross Roads of The World
6671 Sunset Boulevard
Hollywood, CA 90028
usually middle of the month
Sunday 10 a.m. to 6 p.m.
(213) 462-2355

This architectural delight was the first shopping center in Southern

California. It was designed in 1936 by Robert Derrah, who also conceived the Coca Cola Building the same year (see August). He must have had Streamline Moderne ocean liners on his mind because here you have another one.

This time it is a central ship with a soaring tower and a lighted rotating globe at the top that looks like it was lifted from the opening credits to an old movie. It is flanked on two sides by English Tudor, Spanish, French Provincial, and Moorish shops to suggest foreign ports. A scene from the movie *Indecent Proposal* was filmed in one of its offices.

Though there are architects that have designed more buildings that are still standing in Los Angeles than the three remaining by Derrah, two out of his three have been named cultural-historical landmarks by the Los Angeles Cultural Heritage Board: the Coca Cola Building and this one. It is appropriate that it is the site this month of an annual event put on by the Hollywood Arts Council that celebrates art forms.

Originated in 1987 on a suggestion by Nyla Arslanian, president of the council, this one-day festival presents the artistic side of Hollywood. Approximately 100 performers are surrounded by paintings, photos, sculpture, jewelry, and crafts.

What could be the perfect theatre/restaurant combination is just a couple streets west of here on an obscure side street:

Stages Theatre Center
1540 North McCadden Place
Hollywood, CA 90028
(213) 463-5356

Located off Sunset Boulevard is this gem of a theatre with great parking and a connecting French restaurant. There are two performance spaces, 25 and 50 seats, and the work has a decidedly European flair. Artistic Director Paul Verdier has demonstrated again and again why he is the only L.A. small theater artistic director who was invited to participate in the New York Theater Festival. The quality and power of his work (*Camera Lenta/Slow Motion, Pablo, L'Amant Anglais*) hits even the most finicky theaterphile.

Next door is a truly romantic restaurant:

Cafe des Artistes
1534 North McCadden Place
Hollywood, CA 90028
Sunday-Thursday 6 to 11 p.m.
Friday & Saturday 6 p.m. ot 2 a.m.
(213) 461-6884

What a lovely spot this is! Since it is surrounded by hedges, you don't appreciate how pretty it is until you are inside. You can park across the street and enter through a garden gate and suddenly be underneath a beautiful tree, strung with little white lights, that spreads its branches like a canopy over the outdoor patio. The inside is like a country house, though the atmosphere is more like a bistro. Having dinner here is an absolutely perfect way to take the pressure off of curtain time for the Stages Theatre.

This restaurant is not only charming, but also has excellent food. Their dinners are moderately-priced fresh fish, pasta, and French entrees. They are closed Saturday nights, but if you want a wonderful way to start a Monday, Stages is one of the few theatres that has a Monday night series.

If you continue going west on Sunset and turn north on La Brea, on your left you will see the:

Open Fist Theatre Company
1625 North La Brea Avenue
Hollywood, CA 90028
(213) 882-6912

The Open Fist is another repertory company, but they focus on artistically daring shows in this excellent 99-seat space. Gifted Artistic Director Ziad Hamzeh is one of the nicest in the business.

Proceeding west on Sunset, you will come to:

Samuel French's Theatre and Film Bookstores
7623 Sunset Boulevard
Hollywood, CA 90046
Monday-Friday 10 a.m. to 6 p.m.
Saturday 11 a.m. to 5 p.m. Saturday, closed Sunday
(213) 876-0570
and:
11963 Ventura Boulevard
Studio City, CA 91604
Monday-Friday 10 a.m. to 10 p.m.
Saturday 11 a.m. to 5 p.m., Sunday 12 to 5 p.m.
(818) 762-0535

This is the place where you go to find plays. What a pleasure it was to buy copies of several shows I have enjoyed immensely in recent years—including *El Salvador* and *Savage In Limbo*. They are inexpensive too: usually $2 to $4. They also have screenplays and books on theater, TV, and film.

Of course, the Westside of Los Angeles and Santa Monica also have their share of cutting-edge small theatre. A theatre with a long established history is the:

Odyssey Theatre
2055 South Sepulveda Boulevard
Los Angeles, CA 90025
(310) 477-2055

Artistic Director Ron Sossi could truly be described as the great survivor of L.A. Theatre. I remember the old Santa Monica Odyssey on Santa Monica Boulevard, but there was one even before that—founded in Hollywood in 1969. This location is blessed with three comfortable 99-seat auditoriums, a huge lobby, and great parking.

Since the City of Santa Monica is such a progressive place, it is only fitting that the major venue for performance art would be located here:

Highways
1651 18th Street
Santa Monica, CA 90404
(310) 453-1755

The performance space at Highways is a basic black box. Co-Founder and Artistic Director Tim Miller stages over 200 performances per year.

Performance art is such an ephemeral medium. A show can be great, yet only seen by a relative handful of people. One of the very few video stores to stock tapes of well respected performance art pieces is:

Vidiots
302 Pico Boulevard
Santa Monica, CA 90405
Sunday-Thursday 11 a.m. to 11 p.m.
Friday & Saturday 11 a.m. to 12 a.m.
(310) 392-8508

Vidiots is not your average video store. It not only offers a good selection of popular videos, it features the largest selection of independent and low budget productions you will find anywhere in the Southland.

Right on the edge of Santa Monica is another major small theatre on the Southland landscape:

Burbage Theatre
2330 Sawtelle Boulevard

West Los Angeles, CA 90064

(310) 478-0897

Producers Andy Griggs and Ivan Spiegel in some ways are the only game in town in terms of putting up an astonishing number of unique shows—some of them in-house productions, some of them co-productions with outside people. The Burbage has two auditoriums: a full 99-seat theatre and a small 49-seat space in back

From either the Burbage or Highways, you are only a short hop to **Santa Monica Airport**, also known as Clover Field. It has been developed with the addition of buildings that take advantage of its scenic quality. One of these is the home of a fun and satisfying place to eat:

DC-3 Restaurant

2800 Donald Douglas Loop

Santa Monica, CA 90405

Tuesday-Thursday 11:30 a.m. to 10 p.m.

Friday-Saturday 11:30 a.m. to 11 p.m.

Sunday 11 a.m. to 2 p.m.

(310) 399-2323

Besides the stunning views of the planes taking off and landing, DC-3 has possibly the Southland's best french fries and hot fudge sundaes, along with such entrees as lamb shanks. They feature live jazz Tuesday-Saturday evening at 8 p.m.

DC-3 offers programs for parents during the week. While you eat in peace, they will trundle your dear ones off to the museum next door, which they also own:

The Museum of Flying

Santa Monica Airport

2772 Donald Douglas Loop North

Santa Monica, CA 90405

Daily 9 a.m to 5 p.m.

(310) 392-8822

Directly adjacent to the restaurant, this museum is located on the site of the first Douglas Aircraft plant. It has three levels with about 24 fully flyable planes, some on the floor, some in perpetual flight hanging from the ceiling. Next to most of the planes are video monitors showing what they looked like when they were flying.

There is a WW I Curtiss JN-4 "Jenny," a WW II Spitfire, and the first aircraft to fly all the way around the world, the 1924 Douglas World Cruiser "New Orleans." Perhaps a little less glamorous, but equally historically significant is a Douglas DC-

3 built in Long Beach in 1944. The DC-3 would become the workhorse plane of the post war period. Douglas was based in Santa Monica at the time.

There is more on small theatres in the L.A. area in the March chapter.

Dance

There are many theatre or music series that begin in September. One of the most interesting is the:

> **Art of Dance Series**
> **UCLA Center For The Performing Arts**
> **University of California, Los Angeles**
> **405 Hilgard Avenue**
> **Los Angeles, CA 90024**
> **(310) 825-2101**

Of all the fine performance series in the Southland, this one is all dance, and it usually is a variety of well-known groups that span several different styles. Performers have included the Martha Graham, Alvin Ailey, and Feld Ballet Companies. What is especially fun about this series is that it is spread out over several months, so you always have something different coming up on your calendar.

Perhaps the movie *Love Story* has forever romanticized the serene charm of the university campus in my mind. I find the picture of that earnest, naive, powerful love against the landscape of the campus to be a very compelling one. Of course, the reality of waiting in lines and feeling stressed around exam time is unromantically there, but the fantasy is still a lovely one. That is why I recommend going to the UCLA campus earlier in the day, before the show starts for a picnic. There will be no mobs of students to spoil the picture and you can enjoy the **Franklin D. Murphy Sculpture Garden.**

This imposing group of sculpture is spread over more than five acres. The collection of 72 pieces of outdoor artworks is one of the most successful examples of this medium. Blending aesthetically with the natural beauty of the UCLA campus are works by many of the most famous modern sculptors: August Rodin, Henri Matisse, and Alexander Calder, to name three. The Armand Hammer Museum described below has a free sculpture garden brochure that includes a map; or you can buy a catalog.

This is one of those places in L.A. named for someone that no one has heard of. Actually, Dr. Franklin Murphy, for whom this sculpture garden was named, is not only the former chancellor of UCLA, but also the former chairman and chief executive of the *Los Angeles Times*.

It underscores the *Times'* importance to this city that so many buildings are named for its people. Murph has several things named after him. The Dorothy Chandler Pavilion in the Music Center, which until recently was the site of the Academy Awards ceremonies, was named for the wife of *Times* founder Otis Chandler. Like Mrs. Chandler, Dr. Murphy is a great arts supporter and received the Andrew W. Mellon medal from the National Gallery of Art as part of its 50th birthday celebration in '91.

He has a hell of a sculpture garden. A nice way to "give" the day to someone would be to go to the Hammer Museum and buy the catalog, then wrap it, prepare a picnic basket, and that morning present the package to your lover with a "Let's go!"

The Hammer Museum is administered by UCLA and is located nearby at the corner of Wilshire and Westwood:

Armand Hammer Museum
10899 Wilshire Boulevard
Los Angeles, CA 90024
Tuesday-Saturday 11 a.m. to 7 p.m.
Sunday 11 a.m. to 6 p.m.
closed Monday
(310) 443-7000

A series of galleries are arranged around an open courtyard in this museum. It has rotating exhibits as well as a permanent collection.

Right near UCLA is a work of art that is a house:

The Campbell Divertimento
1150 Brooklawn Drive
Los Angeles, CA 90077

As I mentioned in the June chapter, the greatest architectural statements in the Southland are generally made by private residences most often located in the hills of the L.A. area. If you go up Beverly Glen Canyon from Sunset Boulevard and make a right on Greendale, then veer left, you will see a 75-foot-long wall of vibrant reddish stone. This is the backside of one of the largest (and certainly the most beautiful) waterfalls in a house in the world.

This is the residence of Dr. Douglas A. Campbell, economist and investment banker—as well as the publisher of this book. The waterfall and its surrounding elements were the last project of famed artist/architect Luis Barragan.

Though you cannot see it from the street, the house is fashioned in a U-shape that wraps around the waterfall, the centerpiece of the courtyard entrance way. The same stone used on the street side is carried over into the courtyard where it is fashioned into a series of steps down the inside face of the wall with a dramatic wedge form that projects out into the pond below. The water cascades down the full length of this structure like a shimmering curtain of life. The stone was imported from Mexico and when it is wet, it looks like living flesh.

The sound of rushing water adds a peaceful quality to every room in the home, with which it blends perfectly. This building in turn seems to merge into the tall greenery of the hill like some hidden treehouse.

If all this art talk has made you want to improve your mind, one of L.A.'s best bookstores is ust a short drive away on Sunset:

Dutton's Brentwood Bookstore
11975 San Vicente Boulevard
Los Angeles, CA 90049
Monday-Friday 9:30 a.m. to 9 p.m.
Saturday 9:30 a.m. to 6 p.m.
Sunday 11 a.m. to 5 p.m.
(310) 476-6263

The family name of the Dutton Brothers has been associated with books for as long as I can remember. This store stocks over 100,000 new and old titles in all genres. They also carry CD's of classical music.

If the hour gets late, the closest place to the UCLA campus for an overnight stay is an exquisite small hotel:

Westwood Marquis Hotel and Gardens
930 Hilgard Avenue
Los Angeles, CA 90024-3025
(310) 208-8765

As you walk up to the Westwood Marquis, it is impossible to believe it started life as a student dorm. The understated exterior exudes modern elegance. The interior reminds me of being inside a giant jewelry box. Chinese rugs, antique cabinets, and rich fabrics surround you.

There are 256 suites and the hotel features a beautiful pool and garden area. Sunday brunch in the Garden Terrace is a special occasion and **The Dynasty Room** is sometimes regarded as L.A.'s best restaurant.

Chamber Music

One of the most romantic and charming performance series in the Southland is:

Chamber Music In Historic Sites
De Camera Society
Mt. St. Mary's College
12001 Chalon Road
Los Angeles, CA 90049
(310) 440-1351

The title is descriptive, for that is exactly what this series is. What the title doesn't convey is that the musical performers can be a pianist, a brass ensemble, a string quartet, or several other unique small groupings of classical instruments. Sometimes a brunch or buffet is included as part of a package. The music is matched somewhat to the site, and these are a remarkable assortment of old libraries, museums, and mansions. The grandest of the latter is the:

Doheny House
Mt. Saint Mary's College
8 Chester Place
Los Angeles, CA 90007

Between 1895 and 1900, 13 mansions were built within a private 20-acre park called Chester Place. The Doheny House was originally the Posey House and was one of the last ones built. It was designed by Sumner P. Hunt and Theodore A. Eisen.

Outside it looks somewhat like a chateau, but inside it is an elaborate fantasy. A remodeling in 1933 put on the fine finishing touches, emulating the French Rococo interiors of Europe.

The concerts are held in the **Pompeiian Room**, built in 1906 from a design by Alfred F. Rosenheim.

If you are in the mood for a restaurant to match the elegance and splendor of the beautiful music and setting of the Doheny Mansion, the obvious choice is:

Rex Il Ristorante
617 South Olive
Los Angeles, CA 90014
Monday-Friday 12 to 10 p.m.
Saturday 6 to 10 p.m.
(213) 627-2300

This restaurant is one of the Southland's most successful blends of historic architecture and excellent food service. It is located in the **Oviatt Building**, which was designed in 1927 by the firm of Walker and Eisen.

The exterior has many wonderful Art Deco details—particularly the Lalique glass designed and manufactured in France. The entrance is spectacular: you pass through an elaborate iron gate into a huge, rich, 1920s interior of dark oak paneling and black Italian marble. There is a subtle Art Deco feel to everything from the lighting to the waiters' wing-collared tuxedos. Tables are spaced incredibly far apart and there are special, ornately carved triangular tables for two.

What contributes particularly to the dramatic quality of the room are the stairways that lead up to the mezzanine that overlooks the first floor dining room. The very comfortable chairs and sofas here were designed especially for this restaurant. The second floor also is where the sunken lounge and dance floor are located. The bar is very long and the dance floor is black marble surrounded by windows.

The quality of the food here matches the restaurant's peerless elegance. It is Northern Italian and is prepared by a hand-selected chef imported from Milan by the owner.

WATTS TOWERS DAY OF THE DRUM AND SIMON RODIA MUSIC AND ARTS FESTIVAL

Watts began the first part of this century as a farming community, well out of the main city. It became the junction point for several railroads due to the heavy industrial concentrations nearby, such as the automobile plants of South Gate. World War II brought even more industry to the adjacent towns, which caused many African Americans to move here because of the availability of decent paying jobs.

The African American communities of Los Angeles, basically running along Central Avenue (see February), expanded southward to connect with Watts during this period of relative prosperity. Most of the tensions and problems associated with Watts and South Central Los Angeles can be traced to the departure of these rail and industrial jobs from the area that began in the early '60s. The lack of state and federal funds for inner city development in the 1980s exacerbated the situation.

Watts has a famous tourist attraction located about two miles east of the I-110 (Harbor Freeway). If there is an artistic spirit inside you and you want to feel it stir, go and take a good long look at what could be the greatest symbol of L.A.:

The Watts Towers
1765 East 107th Street
Watts, CA 90002
Tuesday-Saturday 9 a.m. to 5 p.m.
(213) 485-2437 or (213) 569-8181

An Italian tile setter named Sabatino Rodia worked on creating these nine soaring towers, ranging in height from 13 to 100 feet, for 37 years. Without any assistance, he wired steel reinforcing rods together into a web-like structure almost like steel lace. He then coated them with cement and 70,000 individual sea shells, stones, cup handles, broken tiles, and dishes.

The gorgeous green and blue hues in the towers are from broken 7 Up and Milk of Magnesia bottles. Rodia, known occasionally as Sam, Simon, and Don Simon, was a construction laborer who brought materials he found on different jobs home with him. In the evenings and on weekends, he would work on his towers.

The people who lived near him thought he was a maniac and decried the towers as junk. Rodia was obdurate and worked on. He had the last laugh on his art critic neighbors, however. By the time he died in 1965, his towers were recognized as major works of folk art. "I had it in my mind to build something great," Rodia said, "and I did."

The site is honored now with an art center that has two great festivals back-to-back this month:

> **Watts Towers Day of the Drum Festival**
> **Simon Rodia Watts Towers Music and Arts Festival**
> **Watts Towers Art Center**
> **1727 East 107th**
> **Watts, CA 90002**
> **"Drum" normally last Saturday of September**
> **"Arts" normally last Sunday of September**
> **(213) 485-2437 or (213) 569-8181**

The art center is just a couple of doors down from the towers. It has exhibits of local artist's work. These events, sponsored by L.A. Cultural Affairs, make for an exciting weekend. The Day of the Drum Festival is just that: jazz, folk, and ethnic drummers are featured on two stages in a salute to great name drummers of the world.

The two stages for the Day of The Drum are left up for the somewhat less percussive Music and Arts Festival. This event has been taking place since 1978 and features dance and music and booths with food and arts and crafts.

ROUTE 66 RENDEZVOUS

Southern California has been the final stop of a journey for many people. For those headed West overland from the Midwest and the East Coast of the United States, it was the natural "end of the trail."

A big part of the early 20th century mythology of Southern California resulted from the fact that the most celebrated highway in America, Route 66, begins in Chicago and runs 2,400 miles across eight states and three time zones and finishes in the L.A. Officially designated as a federal highway in 1926, it has been celebrated in song and story ever since.

The building of freeways caused the death of the highway culture, but since 1989, a festival in the Inland Empire has been dedicated to bringing back those days, the **Route 66 Rendezvous.**

This three-day celebration begins inexplicably with a golf tournament, which is followed by a street dance that night. The main festivities are held in the parking lot of:

> **San Bernardino City Hall**
> **300 North "D" Street**
> **San Bernardino, CA 92401**
> **third weekend in September**
> **(909) 889-3980 or (800) 669-8336**

Though the address of City Hall is "D" Street, the parking lot is on the legendary "E" Street. There are several cruises down this street. There is an **E Street Cruise,** the **World's Best Poker Run,** and an **Open Header Cruise.** More than 1,500 street rods normally participate. Even the cops get into the act and patrol in vintage squad cars.

Entrants are limited to American-made cars and motorcycles. Lowriders and mini trucks are not allowed. The exclusion of the latter is reasonable due to the fact that they would be an anachronism. The exclusion of the former makes less sense because the lowering of customized vehicles has been occurring for a long time. On Sunday, there is a car show, many of which participated in the cruises of the previous two days.

Foothill Boulevard was (and is) Route 66. Going west on Foothill, you will come upon a survivor of the era when there was a real roadside culture:

> **Wigwam Motel**
> **2728 West Foothill Boulevard**
> **Rialto, CA 92376**
> **(909) 875-0241**

In this triumph of kishke over reason, a cluster of individual dwellings in the shape of teepees waits for the weary traveler by the road. Built in '30s, there are 19 units for rent and a carved totem pole to welcome you.

Though it is only $35 to stay here, be warned that as of the writing of this book, the grounds were not being kept up and were covered with weeds. The rooms have water beds and mirrored ceilings and feature adult movies. The establishment's motto, which is placed under the name on the sign and on their card, is "Do it in a teepee."

Continuing along Route 66, you will come to the venerable:

Sycamore Inn
8318 Foothill Boulevard
Rancho Cucamonga,
CA 91730
Monday-Friday
11:30 a.m. to 11 p.m.
Sunday 3 to 11 p.m.
(909) 982-1104

This landmark restaurant was in its heyday when Foothill Boulevard was indeed a highway. It actually started in 1848 as "Uncle Billy Rubottom's Trailside Inn." The Sycamore Inn is built around the historical monument dedicated to old Uncle Billy's hospitality.

The setting is wonderful: an enormous stone fireplace, 19th century fixtures, and red wingback chairs. Many people say it reminds them of a frontier bordello.

The food is moderate to expensive, with buffets and early bird dinner specials. This is a great restaurant to give you a feeling of old California, in the days when this area was a frontier farming community before housing tracts and freeways.

Ironically, the survivor of Route 66 dining establishments that has the truest roadhouse feel is located in the city:

Barney's Beanery
8447 Santa Monica Boulevard
West Hollywood, CA 90069
Daily 6 to 2 a.m.
(213) 654-2287

It is highly unlikely that you could ever find another place in L.A. that feels more like a truck stop—albeit a somewhat glamorous one—than Barney's Beanery. Opened in 1920, Barney's does not treat itself like a historical place. There is no printed history of the restaurant's illustrious past on the placemats. There is just a bar atmosphere par excellence and a truly huge menu.

To say the menu is gigantic is no exaggeration. It is an eight-page tabloid newspaper. L.A.'s "second best chili" is available in 18 different combinations of beans, without beans, avocado, etc. They serve close to 200 different kinds of burgers, Mexican food, potatoes, pasta, and breakfast. They even have draft root beer. There is a separate menu for beer. One of their slogans is: "When you think of beer, think of Barney's."

Barney's is a kind of shrine to drinking—beer drinking in particular. They have 35 beers on draft and 200 in bottles, along with hundreds of different mixed drinks. This is also expressed in the decor. You may have seen bar paraphernalia in other bars, but nothing will prepare you for the visual onslaught of Barney's.

The room is lit by hanging promo lamps for various brands of beer and the glow from innumerable different colored neon liquor signs. The walls and the ceiling are covered with beer company trays, old beer posters, and other accouterments of the trade. The visual jumble is enhanced by the four-color wide pleats on the booth's bench backs in pop art rainbows of pink, yellow, red, burgundy naugahyde. For entertainment they have a CD juke box, video games, pool tables, pinball, and Lotto machines.

The truck stop atmosphere hearkens back to its earlier days. For a long time, Barney's had a sign that said "No Fags," which is ironic considering it is in West Hollywood. Thankfully, that sign is gone, but the sign for the women's restroom does have "'Women' only" (in quotation marks) on the door. The men's room not only has condom dispensers, it features vending machines with sexual novelties and, of course, the ever popular "French Ticklers."

GENE AUTRY'S BIRTHDAY

The last milestone date of September that helps define the Southland's identity is the most obscure of the four. It is the birthday of the singing cowboy, Gene Autry, which is celebrated at the:

Gene Autry Western Heritage Museum, Griffith Park
4700 Western Heritage Way
Los Angeles, CA 90027
Tuesday-Sunday 10 a.m to 5 p.m.
(213) 667-2000

Gene Autry was born in Texas in 1907. He was working as a telegraph operator when none other than Will Rogers came in to send a wire. Autry got out his Sears guitar and impressed Rogers so much he suggested he go to Hollywood.

He did and made his first film in 1934. Though he was unsure of himself, the film did well enough for a contract to follow. Eventually, Gene Autry became the number one box office

The bronze sculpture by De L'Esprie, "Back in the Saddle Again," is the focal point of the courtyard at the Gene Autry Museum.

draw in the movie business for five years running. This was during the heyday of Clark Gable and Gary Cooper. He was also the first individual to be awarded a gold record.

Interestingly enough, despite his own importance in the mythology of Southern California, Autry downplays his presence in the museum. He founded the place to celebrate the West he knew growing up.

The Gene Autry Western Heritage Museum and grounds occupy 13 acres of Griffith Park in an area called Pine Meadows. By car, it is off the I-5 (Golden State Freeway) not too far from the zoo entrance.

The building itself is the largest museum in the world dedicated to the history of the American West. Costing $34 million to build, its three levels have more than 140,000-square-feet of exhibit space.

The museum's collection includes everything from a 180-piece display of frontier firearms, to Western art, to a movie exhibit. This museum is quite different than most in that the exhibits were staged by Walt Disney for theatrical effect.

One particularly poignant exhibit is the **Spirit of Community Gallery**. This program is designed to show what was going on in each community within the general frame of The Old West. In addition to the familiar image of the pioneers, there were black cowboys and Chinese people as well.

Nearby is another museum, part of which is devoted to an aspect of our Western heritage:

> **Travel Town Museum**
> **5300 Zoo Drive**
> **[Ventura and Golden State Freeways]**
> **Los Angeles, CA 90027**
> **Monday-Friday 10 a.m. to 5 p.m.**
> **Saturday & Sunday 10 a.m. to 6 p.m.**
> **(213) 662-9678**

As a boy growing up in the San Fernando Valley, this was one of my favorite places in the world. This outdoor transportation museum has a focus on Western U.S. rail history. It is the largest collection of steam locomotives west of the Mississippi. There is a miniature train ride that chugs out of a restored Southern Pacific Depot. It closes 45 minutes earlier than the rest of the park.

If you want to experience the Old West a little more, an ideal place to have lunch or go for a horseback ride is close:

> **The Equestrian Bar and Grill**
> **Los Angeles Equestrian Center**
> **480 Riverside Drive**
> **Burbank, CA 91506**
> **Daily 8 a.m. to 10 p.m. (restaurant)**
> **Horse Rental:**
> **Tuesday & Thursday 11 a.m. to 7 p.m. (summer)**
> **Tuesday & Thursday 8 a.m. to 4 p.m. (rest of year)**
> **Rest of the week 8 a.m. to 4 p.m.**
> **(818) 840-1320 (restaurant)**
> **(818) 840-9063 (equestrian center)**

The patio here overlooks the arena where world class horses are trained. This is a 75-acre complex with horse boarding and training facilities, horses to rent, and of course, the arena. They have horse shows, polo games, rodeos, and even jazz concerts concerts.

FALL HARVEST

The end of September brings the beginning of the fall harvest season, which peaks in October. Though some of them don't involve agricultural products, many fall traditions are related to thanksgiving for nature's bounty in delivering food and life.

San Diego County

The Spanish missionaries planted the first vineyard in California at the Mission San Diego. The conditions were found to be better in Escondido shortly after that. From the 1890s to the 1920s, commercial experimentation led to a peak in agricultural production in the '40s. The '50s saw the first wave of residential development, so that by the '60s, agricultural output was on the decline. The packing house closed and suburban houses took over.

Escondido, which means "hidden valley," is still one of the number one avocado producing areas in the Southland. Nearby Valley Center still has citrus groves and a few orange stands. If you want to sample some locally grown produce, on Tuesday between 3:30 and 8 p.m., they block off Grand Avenue between Broadway and Maple in downtown Escondido and farmers sell their wares directly. Call (619) 745-7506 for more information.

Every year, the agricultural traditions of the area are celebrated with the:

> **Escondido Harvest Festival, Grape Day Park**
> **Broadway between Valley Parkway and Washington**
> **Escondido, CA 92025**
> **fourth Saturday of September**
> **(619) 743-8207**

The roots of this one-day event are the "Grape Days" festivals of the 1920s that were big until '49. This festival is a pale throwback to the past. There are some certified farmers displaying vegetables and flowers, but the focus is on crafts and entertainment.

Within Grape Day Park is **Heritage Walk and Museum**. This is a group of restored buildings, many of which were moved from somewhere else, that have been lined up along a path. Each has a local history that is inscribed on a plaque mounted in front. You can pick up a self-guided tour brochure in the city's first library building, which is now the headquarters of the Escondido Historical Society.

Other buildings include a tank house, barn, windmill, and a working blacksmith's shop that provides demonstrations. A Pullman railroad car sits next to the old Santa Fe Depot. The latter building is now a gift shop.

Not far from Grape Day Park is a family-owned winery:

Ferrara Winery
1120 West 15th Avenue
Escondido, CA 92025
Weekdays 9 a.m. to 5:30 p.m.
Weekends 10 a.m. to 5:30 p.m.
(619) 745-7632

This five-acre winery was founded during the Depression in 1932. In 1971, it became a State Historical Point of Interest. Though the redwood tanks are old-fashioned, the stemmer-crusher is gleaming stainless steel. The wine selection includes both generic and varietals.

There is a deli open from 11 a.m. to 2 p.m. that makes sandwiches to order. The patio and outdoor pavilion provide a sweeping view of the 100-year-old vineyard.

If you plan on staying overnight, the premier resort in the area is a splendid getaway:

Rancho Bernardo Inn
17550 Bernardo Oaks Drive
Rancho Bernardo, CA 92128
(619) 487-1611
(800) 542-6096

This is a large property with extensive grounds and 287 rooms. You can stay in a private villa overlooking the golf course with such amenities as a fireplace and hot tub. The Rancho Bernardo Inn is a major sports, health and fitness center. The Vic Braden Tennis College is located here. The gourmet restaurant, El Bizcocho, has won numerous awards.

Rancho Bernardo was originally 17,763 acres of mission land. An English Captain named Joseph Snook took it over in the form of a grant from the Mexican government in two parcels, one in 1842, the other three years later in 1845. In 1961, it became a "planned community" of golf courses, riding trails, parks, and rolling hills all covered with red-tile roofed, white tract houses.

Fairly close to where the Battle of San Pasqual was fought, in which Mexican forces defeated the U.S. Army, is another Northern San Diego County winery:

Thomas Jaeger Winery
13455 San Pasqual Road
San Diego, CA 92025
Daily 10 a.m. to 5 p.m.
Daily 10 a.m. to 6 p.m. (summer)
(619) 738-6500

This is San Diego County's largest winery, producing about 13,000 cases of varietal wine per year. Formerly the San Pasqual Vineyards, it is was purchased in 1988 by Paul Thomas and the Jaeger family of Rutherford Hill and Freemark Abbey Wineries.

The gift shop offers some deli and picnic foods. You can picnic under grape arbors overlooking the vineyards or eat indoors. Tours are daily at 11:30 a.m.; 1:30, 3, and 4 p.m.

Near here is North San Diego County's most famous attraction:

Wild Animal Park
15500 San Pasqual Valley Road
Escondido, CA 92027
Daily 9 a.m. to 6 p.m. (June 15 to September 1)
Daily 9 a.m. to 4 p.m. (rest of year)
(619) 747-8702

Established in 1972 by the San Diego Zoo, this unique 1,800-acre facility has over 2,500 animals. They are not kept in cages, but roam in rather large habitats that recreate the landscape of the countries of their origin. There is a great 50-minute monorail ride that takes you around the entire park or you can walk over the 1-3/4 mile **Kilimanjaro Hiking Trail**, which has lookout points for each area.

The central section is called Nairobi Village. Here, you can enjoy some of the bird and animal shows and educational exhibits. There more about Northern San Diego County in the February, May, November, and December chapters.

Harvest Moon Festival

The **Harvest Moon Festival**, also referred to as the Lantern or Mid-Autumn Festival, is celebrated by over a billion people of East Asian ancestry worldwide. The Japanese call it Oban. It happens on the 15th day of the eighth lunar month, which means it can be in September or October by the Western calendar, and is often called the Thanksgiving Day of Asia.

There are family gatherings and farmers give thanks for a good harvest. Central to the observance is the positioning of the moon: it must be at its most distant point from the Earth. This is why an extra large and round full moon occurring in the fall is called a "harvest moon."

The story behind the holiday as a celebration of harvest is that one day around 2,000 B.C., 10 suns rose in the sky instead of one. Crops withered and animals died. Hou Yi, the greatest archer in Emperor Yao's Imperial Guard, shot the extra nine suns out of the sky with a magic bow and arrows. Word spread of his deed and Xi Wang Mu, the Queen Mother of the West, bestowed upon him the herb of immortality as a reward.

The herb came with instructions: 12 months of prayer and fasting must precede taking it. Yi's wife, Chang O, took the herb when her husband was away and it caused her to fly up to the moon, where she stayed and became the lunar goddess. This is why the moon is female in Asian cultures. It is also appropriate that a festival of harvest have a "yin" connotation since it is females who bring life into the world.

The festival varies in scope and location somewhat. There is usually a lantern-making demonstration, and children walk around holding a lantern as part of the festivities. Viewing the moon is a big aspect of the celebration, so sometimes portable telescopes are brought from Griffith Observatory and set up. The half-dozen boys that make up the Castelar Elementary School Lion Dance Group usually perform in their bright lion costume from Hong Kong. Sometimes events are held at this school:

> **Castelar School**
> **840 Yale Street**
> **Los Angeles, CA 90012**

Other festival sites have included Alpine Park (see February) and on Broadway. Call the Chinese Chamber of Commerce (213) 617-0396 for updated information.

Part of the celebration involves the eating of "moon cakes," rich pastries filled with sweetened lotus seeds and black beans. To try them, stop by the:

> **Phoenix Bakery**
> **969 North Broadway**
> **Los Angeles, CA 90038**
> **(213) 628-4642**

This Chinese and Western bakery has been in Chinatown since 1938. About the only really heavy sweets the Chinese eat are the moon cakes. The Phoenix Bakery has all manner of pastries—mostly Western—but if you want to try some Chinese ones for the holidays besides the moon cakes, they have several delicious tarts. I like the almond paste, the lotus seed paste, and the coconut fruit paste.

There is more about Chinatown in the February chapter.

Koreatown Festival

The Koreans call the East Asian harvest moon festival "Chusok." It is celebrated in the second largest Korean city in the world, Los Angeles, in the district known as **Koreatown.**

Koreatown officially covers the area between Pico and Beverly Boulevard from Vermont to Western, but actually extends farther west than that. It is larger than either Chinatown or Little Tokyo. More than a third of all the Koreans in the U.S. live in the vicinity.

In 1970, there were about 9,000 Koreans in the City of Los Angeles; by 1980, there were 60,000; by 1990, there were 73,000. It is estimated that about twice that many live in the county as a whole out of a total of about 350,000 Koreans in Southern California. They are one of the fastest growing immigrant populations.

Koreans have made a unique contribution to their new homeland. Unlike earlier Asian immigrant groups such as the Chinese and Japanese, who were oriented towards agriculture or fishing, the Koreans came here to do business. If there was ever a positive stereotype, it is that of the Korean work ethic and spirit of enterprise they bring to their endeavors. Around 15 percent of Koreans are self-employed, which is a far higher percentage than that of the population as a whole. In L.A., they run about five percent of the retail businesses, though they are only about one percent of the population.

The Koreatown Festival, which coincides with Chusok around the third week of the month, was begun in '73. It was started as a gesture of thankfulness by the immigrants for their new chance in a new land. The main attraction is a parade down Olympic Boulevard that runs between Western and Vermont. This includes representatives from several of the ethnic groups in the area, but obviously really showcases the Korean community. The "farmer's dance" or "nong-ak" is usually performed by a large group of about 150 young Korean Americans in traditional outfits.

The place to learn about Korean culture is the:

Korean Culture Center
5505 Wilshire Boulevard
Los Angeles, CA 90036
Monday-Saturday 9 a.m. to 5 p.m.
(213) 936-7141

The Korean Culture Center was established in 1980 and offers festivals, lectures and exhibitions. It features a library of over 10,000 books, magazines, and reference materials in both Korean and English about Korean culture.

There is a museum on the first floor. It is quite eclectic and includes such exhibits as a room furnished as it would have been during the Choson Dynasty, 8th Century woodblock prints, and the remarkable multi-media sculpture, **"Scott Joplin as the First Digital Composer"** by Nam-June Paik.

In 1988, the centerpiece of the district was built:

Koreatown Plaza
928 South Western Avenue
Los Angeles, CA 90006
(213) 382-1234

Designed by architect Ki Suh Park, Koreatown Plaza is a mauve and green, modern, somewhat fortress-like structure with urban architectural elements such as exposed steel beams, graffiti-proof tiles, and granite columns. These are combined with Korean themes expressed in the central pool with fountains and two-story tall wispy trees. It has three levels and contains 76 shops and restaurants spread over three acres of land.

It is a wonderful combination of Western-styled boutiques with traditional Korean wares. Probably the most unusual of the latter is **Chung Hwa Herbs and Acupuncture.**

On the first floor is the Koreatown Plaza Market. Distinctly Asian in focus, there is a great variety of rice in 25 pound bags, and they have nearly 50 different types and varieties of seaweed. The meat and seafood department is enormous. Pork and beef are available pre-sliced in different ways. Sashimi is also conveniently pre-cut. The overall selection of fish and shellfish is dazzling.

Though it does have a "Western Burger" stand, for the most part the **International Food Court** at the other end of the mall is more Korean than international. Most of the menus are only in their native language, but it is a great place to sample the different types of Korean cuisine.

There are certainly many different styles of Korean cooking. They are well represented in restaurants in the Koreatown area.

A lovely one to try is:

Restaurant Yi Dynasty
2500 West 8th Street
Los Angeles, CA 90057

Daily 11 a.m. to 11 p.m.
(213) 380-3346

The decor here is livened by colorful pillows and waitresses dressed in traditional outfits called "Hanboc." Here you can try "bin dae duk," ground bean pancakes cooked a pretty golden brown and filled with green onions and bean sprouts.

Korean barbecue is the most well known of Korean cuisine. Also on 8th Street is a particularly outstanding one:

Soot Bull Jeep
3136 West 8th Street
Los Angeles, CA 90057
Daily 12 to 11 p.m.
(213) 387-3865

"Soot bull jeep" is the hardwood charcoal traditionally used in Korean barbecue. Very few restaurants cook their food with it though; most use gas. Here it is used in the main pit and also in little grills on each table. There are many kinds of meat offered, including pork loin, short ribs, and chicken. They come with rice and different sauces for dipping, depending upon the meat chosen.

Most Korean meals also come with "kimchi," a hot pickled cabbage. There are actually hundreds of variations, and most of them can be found at:

Kae Sung Market
1010 South St. Andrews Place
Los Angeles, CA 90019
Monday-Saturday 8 a.m. to 7 p.m.
(213) 737-6565

This little specialty shop was opened in 1989 by Sook Jae Cho and features handmade kimchi of every description. Kimchi form a historical part of the Chusok Festival. This is because winters can be very harsh in Korea and vegetables fresh from harvest are pickled for winter storage in a big ritual called the "kimjang."

Koreatown is also the home of a unique place for a hot soak:

Beverly Hot Springs
308 North Oxford Avenue
Los Angeles, CA 90004
Daily 9 a.m. to 9 p.m.
(213) 734-7000

It surprises people to find out that there is a natural mineral hot springs under the City of Los Angeles. At the Beverly Hot Springs, you can "take the waters" of L.A.

for $30, $25 Monday-Friday before noon. There are separate floors for men and women.

Oktoberfest

Probably the least accurate name for a celebration is **Oktoberfest** because it begins in September. A traditional German affair, the first one held in Southern California was at the vineyard of John Groningen, Los Angeles' first German resident in the mid-1800s. This vineyard was located at the corner of 1st and Alameda Streets in L.A. Besides this noteworthy achievement, Mr. Groningen also made history by purchasing the original site of Yang-na (described earlier in the month under the Birthday of L.A.).

Today there are over 30,000 German Americans who call Southern California home, and there are numerous places throughout the Southland today that offer you a chance to party German style. In Munich, Oktoberfest was a nearly all-September event. In Southern California, practically all of them start around the second week in September and go until the end of October. Probably the most Bavarian setting is the:

> **Big Bear Chamber of Commerce Oktoberfest**
> **Big Bear Lake**
> **normally the middle of September-October 30**
> **(909) 866-4607**

This full-on, six-week shindig has been held in this Alpine setting every year since 1973. It really is quite elaborate and includes six or more bands, three full orchestras, and a half a dozen dancing groups. There are sing-a-longs, traditional Bavarian dances, and such stimulating activities as a beer drinking, log sawing, and yodeling contests. There is also an Oktoberfest Queen pageant. The winner of this must carry as many water-filled beer steins as she can across the dance floor.

There are booths serving such traditional German foods as sauerkraut, giant pretzels, bratwurst, pickled pigs knuckles, hot apple strudel, and of course, plenty of German beer. Other booths offer souvenirs, arts and crafts, and jewelry.

Orange County has its own place to clink beer steins that also carries on the celebration even longer—from September 8 through November 7:

> **Old World Village**
> **7561 Center Avenue #68**
> **Huntington Beach, CA 92647**
> **(714) 897-4086**

Right near the 405 freeway (off on Beach Boulevard, right on Center) is this Bavarian-styled complex that includes restaurants, specialty shops, and even a motel and chapel. The latter is a real church with regular services that are held in German and English.

Built from 1976-78, Old World Village is unique in that the 45 store owners own their spaces and also live above them, just as they do in Europe. All of them are decorated with murals—70 in total. These vary from re-creations of villages to historical scenes. Walking tours are also offered.

The centerpiece is **Old World Restaurant** owned by Joe Bischof, who not only built Old World Village, he was the original owner of the larger Alpine Village in Torrance.

The service and ambiance here are extremely friendly and the murals on the wall and German paraphernalia everywhere gives this four-room restaurant a real Bavarian feel. During the Oktoberfest, an indoor/outdoor beer hall is set up that holds 1,500.

Oktoberfest has been a custom here since the opening. It begins with a parade and the opening of the first beer keg in the festival hall. It continues with traditional music from bands that come all the way from Germany. They have a Miss Oktoberfest contest, chicken dance lessons, and traditional Bavarian dancing on Sundays.

Of course, the most established "Germanland" in Southern California has the largest Oktoberfest of all:

> **Alpine Village**
> **833 West Torrance Boulevard**
> **Torrance, CA 90502**
> **(310) 327-4384**

Alpine Village is a large complex of 24 shops, several restaurants, and huge beer garden where the Oktoberfest is held. The Alpine Market features a bakery and old-fashioned butcher/deli.

The Oktoberfest here is a particularly lively one. The beer garden overflows with revelers who dance on the tables exuberantly. On Friday and Saturday, no one under 21 is admitted. Sunday is Family Day. On Tuesday, Wednesday, and Thursday, the partying begins at lunchtime.

Besides the other German beers they sell, they also have their own microbrewery. Using the recipes of Hofbrauhous Traunstein, a nearly 400-year-old German brewery, lager, pilsner, and light are made without additives or preservatives according to the traditional German "Reinheitsebot." If the happiness of the celebration inspires you, they even have a wedding chapel.

Probably Southern California's most established German Restaurant is:

Knoll's Black Forest Inn
2454 Wilshire Boulevard
Santa Monica, CA 90403
Tuesday-Sunday 11:30 a.m. to 10:30 p.m.
closed Monday
(310) 395-2212

Owned and operated by Chef Norbert Knoll and his wife Hildegard, the Black Forest Inn has a huge menu offering traditional, regional, and contemporary German dishes.

It is a homey place with a stone fireplace and a pretty patio in a garden. The son of the owners, Ronald Knoll, took over as wine steward in 1987 and he maintains a large list of both rare and relatively inexpensive wines.

In an otherwise unremarkable part of North Hollywood is a kind of shrine to the German sausage-making art:

Atlas Sausage Kitchen
10626 Burbank Boulevard
North Hollywood, CA 91601
Monday-Friday 10 a.m. to 6 p.m.
Saturday 9 a.m. to 5 p.m.
(818) 763-2692

The outside of this bright white building is decorated with high German-style scenes of Wursthandlers (sausage-makers) at their sacred task.

The proprietor, Michael Obermayer, sausage-maker at Atlas since 1978, purchased it from its owner in 1991. He is one of the few chefs in the entire country to have served his apprenticeship at the "Erste Bayerische Fleischerschule," the most elite of the traditional Bavarian meat schools.

Though the inside is modest and simple, the main case holds some real legends of the German deli world. The Black Forest ham looks and tastes perfect. There are usually seven kinds of Bavarian-style white sausage and a large selection of German beers to go with it.

One of the most authentically German Oktoberfests is to be found in a town with a real German heritage:

Phoenix Club Restaurant
1340 South Sanderson
Anaheim, CA 92806
Monday-Thursday 11 a.m. to 10 p.m.
Friday 11 a.m. to 11 p.m.
Saturday 5 to 11 p.m.
Sunday 5 to 10 p.m.
(714) 563-4166

This is a pretty lively place even when Oktoberfest is not going on. They have big band dancing every Monday night at 8 p.m., German-style events with music and dancing, country western, Hawaiian, and Mexican themed events. The garden area is more than three acres.

The City of Anaheim was originally a colony of Germans who came down from San Francisco. It was the same group that founded The Los Angeles Vineyard Society. They had purchased a huge (1,165 acre) plot with good water from the Santa Ana River that was formerly part of a Mexican rancho. Their intent was to plant grapes.

The township officially began in 1857 as "Anaheim," which means "home by the Santa Ana River." By 1861, it was successfully producing wine.

Oak Glen Apple Picking Season

September is when harvest season begins for many crops. Southern California has two "apple countries": Julian (see May) and Oak Glen. The latter place offers orchards where you can pick your own apples right off the trees.

In order to get to Oak Glen, most people will probably be taking the Yucaipa exit off of the I-10 freeway and driving through that town to get there.

Oak Glen is so picturesque in a country way, it can be a little startling. Taking Oak Glen Road in from Yucaipa Boulevard, one thing that immediately strikes you is that the beige tract houses that spread like cancer over much of

Riverside and San Bernardino Counties seem to be in remission here.

The drive from here is like a Disneyland re-creation of some typical country road. It meanders back and forth past some neat orchards, but much of it is through oak woodland (elevation about 5,000 feet). Box elder, liquid ambers, and native sycamores give the lie to the statement that there are no seasons in the Southland with their autumn reds and golds.

Oak Glen has four seasons: the fall color and some snow in winter, lilacs in spring, and a hot summer—though it is 20 degrees cooler than the rest of Yucaipa Valley. Some say it reminds them of the Blue Ridge and Appalachian Mountains. The U-pick farms signs beckon the passerby to turn up dirt driveways.

The first apple-picking area you will come to is:

Parrish Pioneer Ranch
38651 Oak Glen Road
Oak Glen, CA 92399
Daily 10 a.m. to 5 p.m.
Daily 9 a.m. to 6 p.m. (apple season)
(909) 797-4020b

Peacocks roam free around Parrish Pioneer Ranch.

Parrish Pioneer Ranch is first geographically and was also the first apple orchard. Founded by Enoch Parrish in 1860, it was originally a potato farm. It has shrunk somewhat since its early years, but it is still a full 101-acre ranch.

It has a little village of shops, a bakery, and a restaurant called Apple Dumplins. The original home, built in 1876, is now an antique shop. Though it is somewhat commercial, the big red barn containing the gift shop and snack bar is quite a sight with the peacocks gliding around out front.

Nearby is a unique attraction of the area:

Mountain Town Wildlife Museum
39048 Oak Glen Road
Oak Glen, CA 92399
Daily 10 a.m. to 5 p.m.
Daily 9 a.m. to 6 p.m. (apple season)
(909) 797-4020

Mountain Town consists of 25 arts and crafts shops along with restaurants. If you go up path away from the main area, you will come to the Wildlife Museum. Former Disney employee Bob Bice opened this bizarre exhibit featuring about 100 taxidermied animals perched on a mountain side.

There are 11 U-pick orchards in the area. A particularly special one is off the main drag:

Wood Acres
38003 Potato Canyon Road
Oak Glen, CA 92399
Tuesday-Sunday 9 a.m. to 5 p.m.
(909) 797-8500

Though this is the smallest apple farm in Oak Glen, in some ways it is the most unusual. Owners John and Pat Woods offer over 30 different kinds of apples, including "antique apple," varieties that no one grows anymore. They also have a "pink pearl" apple that looks like its name. Flavors range from tart to sweet.

All of the trees are pruned by hand, so all of the fruit is sun dappled. They serve up apple samples almost the same way a winery offers samples of different fine vintages. The pear and apple ciders are as fine as any wine. On the property is an antique apple washer that is like a gizmo out of *Willie Wonka and the Chocolate Factory*.

If you wanted to turn a visit to Oak Glen into an overnighter, there is a charming place to stay right in the heart of apple county:

St. Anley Inn
39796 Pine Bench Road
Oak Glen, CA 92399
(909) 797-7920

This pleasant little inn opened in 1991. It has just five rooms, but all of them have private baths and balconies and cost from $125-150.

The St. Anley offers many amenities that ordinarily you would have to go to a large health resort for. Owners Kathryn and Norman Stanley are both herbolgists into holistic healing, so there are many types of facials and massages and other rejuvenating treatments you can treat yourself to here.

The property is lovely and has extensive herb gardens. It is often used for country or Victorian-style weddings. There is more about Oak Glen in the December chapter.

Valyermo Fall Festival

One of the most remarkable stories imaginable is behind one of the most improbable annual events that you can enjoy every September:

> **Valyermo Fall Festival**
> **St. Andrew's Priory**
> **Highway 138, off Highway 14**
> **Valyermo, CA 93563**
> **last weekend of September**
> **Saturday-Sunday 10 a.m. to 8 p.m.**
> **(805) 944-2178**

The St. Andrews Priory is a 650-acre ranch tended to by a small community of 26 monks of the Benedictine order. They are the oldest model of communal living in the world. This particular group was originally from Belgium, then went as missionaries to pre-Communist China.

In 1952, the Communists told them they had to leave. Their exit consisted of a (literally) 1,000-mile march under military escort. They came by ship to California and were granted some high desert land. The result is a commune whose roots are 1,500 years old.

The monks have industriously worked to convert their corner of the world into a true oasis. It is 650 acres of flatlands and hills with cinder block dormitories, a duck pond, apple orchards, and a small bucolic chapel with wooden siding and a floor of bricks.

The annual festival began as a little gathering of local ranchers in 1956. Now it is a major event that the monks and 250 volunteers prepare for all year. It has crafts, a farmer's market with just-picked produce, cooked food that runs the gamut from hot dogs to gourmet dinners, art works created here and by other monks, a petting zoo, live music, and dancers. The Society for Creative Anachronisms usually presents demonstrations of jousts and swordfighting.

OCTOBER

Fall Harvest and Festivals

Monarch Butterflies and Fall Colors

Columbus Day

Indigenous People's Day

Festival of Masks

Armenian Cultural Festival

San Marcos Renaissance Festival

Buccaneer Days Party

Halloween

Chapter Ten

OCTOBER

October is a busy, muscular month. It is the central month of a cyclical high energy time associated with the fall harvest that started in September and continues through the first few weeks of November and finally ends around Thanksgiving. The World Series provides temporary relief from the annual "football overkill" that seems to begin around the middle of summer, builds up in September, and finally climaxes in a maniacal frenzy that continues past the holidays.

There truly is a fall season in Southern California. Though people from all over the world travel to New England to see the leaves change color, we actually have quite a respectable fall right here if you know how to experience it. There are places you can find some fall colors and there are a myriad of harvest festivals all over the Southland beholden to a variety of agricultural products.

Perhaps now with the abuse of the environment so prominent in our lives, it is especially important for us to realize that we are living things that are part of a cycle that is shared with other living things. We get so caught up in the importance of our little career schemes that we have gotten too far away from looking at ourselves as just one of many life forms that inhabits the Earth.

October is always an intense month. It is traditionally associated with accomplishment and hard work. As a matter of fact, in "the old days," the harvest time was so grueling in October and early November, and the resulting store houses of food so plentiful, that most cultures developed a tradition of an early winter holiday time to follow this period as a celebration that the work was over. This tradition continues—though most of us today produce paper instead of food.

If you are in the mood for a traditional harvest festival, you have a number to choose from. Harvest festivals abound this month and depending on the particular area and its crops can feature any one of several fall-related themes.

FALL HARVEST AND FESTIVALS

Because California has such a wide variety of agricultural products, there is a literal cornucopia of festivals devoted to the various crops. Though wine is more often associated with Northern California, it actually had its start as a commercial enterprise in the Southland. Therefore many, but not all, of the harvest festivals at this time of year are associated with the grape harvest.

San Diego County

A notable fall celebration in North San Diego County that honors the tradition of the harvest is an annual event that attempts to create a mood of the old farm days with hayrides, early American crafts, folk dancing, musical entertainment, and lots of food. Overnight parking and camping are available, if you'd like to turn it into a weekend getaway. Or you can stay at the first-class local resort, the Rancho Bernardo Inn (see September). But first, find your country roots on the 40 acres of rolling farm land around here:

> **Threshing Bee and Antique Engine Show**
> **Antique Gas and Steam Engine Museum**
> **Guajome Regional Park**
> **2040 North Santa Fe**
> **Vista, CA 92083**
> **usually second Saturday of October**
> **9 a.m. to 4:30 p.m.**
> **Donation (over 15 years): $3**
> **(619) 941-1791**
> **(619) 942-5045**

The museum is a "living history" museum. It features a permanent collection of over 1,000 pieces of early farm equipment, from gas-powered, to steam-powered, to horse-powered. There is a working re-creation of a steam engine saw mill, a blacksmith and wheelwright shop, a country kitchen, and a great 1/3-scale train.

Since it is grape harvest season, you might also want to visit a nearby Northern San Diego County winery:

> **Bernardo Winery**
> **13330 Paseo del Verano Norte**
> **San Diego, CA 92128**
> **Daily 9 a.m. to 3 p.m.**
> **(619) 487-1866**

This is the oldest winery in San Diego County, having been in operation since 1889. It has its own vineyard and still uses the old-style wine presses and original wooden aging vats. The restaurant here is on the patio and there are picnic tables under shade. Both make for a fine October afternoon. There are art and gift shops in the complex that includes the winery store. Bernardo table and desert wines are only available at this store.

Temecula

From North San Diego County, it's just a hop to the wonderful little wine-producing valley of Temecula, which means "sunlight through the mist" in Shoshone. This valley is blessed with growing conditions that compare to Napa. Not only is there a good selection of small wineries, they are all very close to one another in this valley surrounded by low hills covered with vineyards.

A nice start is the lovely Victorian:

Maurice Carrie Vineyard and Winery
34225 Rancho California Road
Temecula, CA 92591
Daily 10 a.m. to 5 p.m.
(909) 676-1711

The landscaping is perfect for a picnic lunch because of the beauty of the building and grounds. I must say it is an inviting sight to drive up to, with its gingerbread exterior bordered by beautiful flowers. Likewise, the tasting room and gift shop, complete with a resident cat curled up by a window, are gorgeous.

As a picnic setting, it certainly is wonderful, but in addition, like many of the wineries here, the last few years have seen the quality of their wine quietly rise to the top. Their white zinfindel surprised a lot of people by winning the Gold Medal at the Orange County Fair in 1990.

About a minute away is the remarkable:

Mt. Palomar Winery
33820 Rancho
California Road
Temecula, CA 92591
Daily 9 a.m. to 5 p.m.
(909) 676-5047

This is the friendliest winery I have yet encountered. It

is located in a depression in between 173 acres of vine-covered hills at the top of a little road that winds up from the main one. Like Maurice Carrie, they have picnic tables on their lovely grounds.

The staff here is delightful and the tour funnier and more informative than most. The wines have won an astonishing number of awards for a broad spectrum of varieties. They produce a cream sherry that even a sherry hater like myself found exquisite.

Another Temecula winery that makes for a wonderful stop is:

Cilurzo Winery
41220 Calle Contento
Temecula, CA 92592
Daily 9:30 to 5 p.m.
(909) 676-5250

This was the first vineyard in Temecula, started in 1968 on 100 acres of land by Audrey and Vincenzo Cilurzo. When Vincenzo retired from a career as a television lighting director, he had plenty of pictures of his celebrity friends to put on the tasting room walls.

The wines here are wonderful full-bodied, unfiltered reds and fruity, well-balanced whites. They have a lovely picnic pavilion overlooking a little lake.

I would finish the day at the large and impressive:

Thornton Winery
32575 Rancho California Road
Temecula, CA 92390
Daily 9 a.m. to 5 p.m.
(909) 699-0099

The Thornton Winery was designed to not only produce champagne in the traditional manner, but as a site for concerts and large gatherings. The imposing stone building was built around the central courtyard, which in turn looks out over the hillside vista.

The property also features a gourmet restaurant, **Cafe Champagne**, with lovely indoor and outdoor dining areas. It is by far the best restaurant in the area and also offers weekend cooking classes with well known guest chefs doing the teaching.

There is a bed and breakfast nearby that celebrates the wine country:

Loma Vista Bed and Breakfast
33350 La Serena Way
Temecula, CA 92591
(909) 676-7047

The Loma Vista Bed and Breakfast is a Mission-styled structure on a hill. There are six rooms, each with private baths. Four have balconies. Full champagne breakfast is served in the dining room.

When you leave the winery area, drive to the distinctly different **Old Town** area of Temecula. The Temecula Valley was an important stop on the Butterfield Stage Line and thus Front and Main Streets are historical sites. Many of buildings have been preserved from the frontier days, and as you might expect, there are lots of antique shops. Any new buildings built in this area must conform to the motif set by the old buildings.

Small and centrally located is:

> **Butterfield Inn**
> **28718 Front Street**
> **Temecula, CA 92590**
> **(909) 676-4833**

This relatively new (but old-styled) motel/inn has a pool and spa and a friendly staff. From here it is a short walk to:

> **Texas Lil's Mesquite Grill**
> **28495 Front Street**
> **Temecula, CA 92590**
> **Monday-Thursday 11:30 a.m. to 10 p.m.**
> **Friday 11:30 a.m. to 11 p.m.**
> **Saturday 7:30 a.m. to 11 p.m.**
> **Sunday 7:30 a.m. to 10 p.m.**
> **bar open until 1:30 a.m.**
> **(909) 699-5457**

This Texas-styled restaurant has a large stage and a big following from locals. Not only is the food good and the atmosphere fun, they have a country western band that makes going here a Saturday night event. They feature the "Ya'll The Cook," cook your own steak grill where you can burn your own 24-ounce slab of protein with all-you-can-eat potatoes after 5 p.m. They also have a fine breakfast on weekends and a Sunday brunch, but the loveliest spot for breakfast in Old Town is the garden patio of:

> **The Silver Spoon**
> **28690 Front Street**
> **Temecula, CA 92590**
> **Tuesday-Wednesday 11 a.m. to 4 p.m.**
> **Thursday-Friday 11 a.m. to 9 p.m.**

Saturday-Sunday 7:30 a.m. to 9 p.m.
closed Monday
(909) 699-1015

Having breakfast in this inexpensive little restaurant, surrounded by flowers, and overlooking historic Front Street, you feel as if you were having breakfast on a movie set. There is more about Temecula in the May chapter.

Orange County

It can be hard to believe this hazy maze of shopping malls and huge tracts of homes with names like "Woodbridge" and "Turtle Rock" was once primarily an agricultural community, but it was.

James Irvine II inherited the 125,000-acre San Joaquin Ranch from his father. Irvine the Elder was the Ben Cartwright-type and raised cattle and sheep. Irvine the Younger decided he wanted to be a farmer, not a rancher, and concentrated on field crops, eventually producing huge amounts of lima beans. He also leased land to tenant farmers who grew barley.

Irvine II also deeded right of way across his domain to the Santa Fe Railroad in return for both a freight and a passenger depot. One of Orange County's first business associations was formed when the tenant farmers decided that instead of individually sacking their beans, they could build a granary together and shuttle their crop on conveyer belts into huge, tall concrete silos to await shipment.

If you want to recapture some of the feeling of early Orange County, you can sleep in one of these towering silos. Thanks to a $20,000,000 restoration project, these six-inch cement walls, built to hold 16,000,000 pounds of lima beans, have been turned into the:

La Quinta Inn
14972 Sand Canyon Avenue
Irvine, CA 92718
(714) 551-0909

Innkeepers Beverly and Lee Yagel will welcome you to this unique property, surrounded by fields planted with green peppers and tomatoes. The former granary now has 98 rooms with unpainted gray walls, decorated with quilted wall hangings and hand-colored photographs of early farm life. The furnishings are rural American. Continental breakfast, in a pretty area overlooking the pool, is included.

The train no longer stops, but it does pound past eight times per day, so you might want to request a room on the east side, farthest from the trains.

There are several other restored structures nearby. The adjacent warehouse, built in 1895 is now a landmark among Southern California bars:

Tia Juana's Long Bar and Mexican Cafe Deluxe
14988 Sand Canyon Ave
Irvine, CA 92718
Monday-Thursday 11 a.m. to 9:30 p.m.
Friday-Saturday 11 a.m. to 11 p.m.
Sunday 10 a.m. to 9 p.m.
(714) 551-2998

Where beans were once cleaned and sacked is now a delightful, bustling open-kitchen restaurant featuring the longest bar in Orange county (75 feet).

Directly opposite these former warehouses and silos are some other old buildings that were moved to the site and have been metamorphosized into modern businesses. There is a 1913 hotel for farmhands and warehouse workers (now a travel agency) and a 1912 General Store (now a "collectibles" shop). The showroom and garage of Orange County's second Ford dealership is now the site of Burrell's Barbecue. There is more about agricultural Orange County in the April and May chapters.

Rancho Cucamonga

Some of the first grapes planted in California were planted back in 1839 in Rancho Cucamonga. Every year, they have a grape festival that has become a California institution:

Rancho Cucamonga Grape Harvest Festival
Guasti Regional Park
800 Archibald Avenue
Ontario
second weekend in October
always weekend after L.A. County Fair closes
Thursday 6 p.m. to 10 p.m.
Friday 6 p.m. to 12 a.m.
Saturday 11 a.m. to 12 a.m.
Sunday 11 a.m. to 8 p.m.
(909) 987-1012
Adults: $6; Seniors: $4

This festival features various live bands on three stages. The main stage usually features oldies and the community stage features local musical groups or student dance companies.

They have a traditional grape stomp going on continuously that both adults and children are invited to participate in. This festival has some of the feel of a small town with its carnival, game stalls, pony rides, and pie-eating contest—but it is very L.A. with its 20 international food vendors. They also have wine tastings (and beer for the sacrilegious).

It is a large affair with 70 commercial booths offering a variety of goods and services and 24 arts and crafts booths. There are more than 800 volunteers. It is well organized and even has free babysitting.

This area was actually the first wine-producing region of California. Though now we think of the Napa Valley as "the wine country," prior to WW II, wine from Northern California was fairly uncommon, being primarily made for sacramental purposes.

In 1900, Secundo Guasti from Piedmont, Italy bought eight square miles of land and founded the Italian Vineyard Company where the town that bears his name is now situated. This developed into 5,000 acres of grapevines, which at one time was the world's largest contiguous vineyard. Guasti brought whole families from Italy to develop the town and its new industry.

Prohibition came and though organized crime benefitted tremendously, it was hard on family-owned wineries. Because the law permitted heads of households to make 200 gallons of wine per year for non-commercial use, many of the vintners simply became home-wineries until the dark cloud was removed in 1933, when Prohibition was repealed.

That year, the Ranch Cucamonga wineries really jumped out of the gate. For the next 25 years, it was the fastest growing wine country in the U.S. There were over 60 wineries by the 1950s that for the next decade produced about five percent of all the wine sold in America.

This was mostly sweet and dessert wines, such as Sherry and Port, which gradually was displaced in popularity by dry wines. The change in public drinking habits, plus the onslaught of the tract house monster gobbling up leafy green vineyards and spitting out row after row of beige boxes, spelled trouble for the Cucamonga Valley's wine producers. There are only 1,850 acres of grapevines left.

Today, there are three wine producers in the Rancho Cucamonga Valley. The only one to have maintained the original family grounds and buildings is the:

Galleano Winery
4231 Wineville Road
Mira Loma, CA 91752
Monday-Saturday 9 a.m. to 6 p.m.

Sunday 10:30 a.m. to 5 p.m.
(909) 685-5376

The Galleano Vineyard is third generation family-owned winery. The house was built in 1895 by Colonel Esteban Cantu and sold to Domenico Galleano in 1927. In the early days, they produced a lot of rough red wines that Italian and Yugoslavian fishermen from San Pedro (see January) would drive in for.

Today, Galleano produces 73 varieties of wine. Their white Zinfindel has won several awards. They still make the full-bodied reds, which are popular with the Basques in nearby Chino. Centro Basco restaurant, described in August, uses Galleano as a house wine.

If you can imagine the surrounding area here covered with grapevines, with crops growing in the flatlands, you can also imagine old planes crop dusting or delivering mail. One of the truly classic romantic images is the sight of a biplane soaring through blue skies with the scarves of the pilot and passenger blowing in the breeze.

You can revel in this authentic, wind-in-your-face open cockpit experience at the:

Chino Airport
7000 Merrill Avenue
Chino, CA 91710
(909) 597-3910

The Chino airport is a small airport like some of the others described in this book, such as the Santa Monica (August), Airport in the Sky (February), or Santa Paula (April). Like them, there are a lot of vintage aircraft here, but Chino is, in many ways, unique.

According to friendly airport manager Glen Porter, of the 820 planes at the airport, probably about a quarter of them are old and special. There are 19 or 20 Stearman biplanes, pre-WW II trainers in service from 1938-44. There are operating WW II airplanes galore, such as Zeros, Messerschmidts, and Spitfires.

If you would like to really savor this atmosphere, have breakfast at:

Floe's Cafe
Chino Airport
7000 Merrill Avenue
Chino, CA 91710
Daily 5:30 a.m. to 7 p.m.
(909) 597-3416

This colorful eatery is designated as a Pacific Flyer 5-Star Restaurant. The inside has lots of old aircraft and dairy farm memorabilia. It is a real original.

The Chino Airport is also distinguished by having a museum dedicated to the romance of the air:

> **The Air Museum**
> **Planes of Fame and Fighter Jets**
> **Chino Airport**
> **7000 Merrill Avenue**
> **Chino, CA 91710**
> **Daily 9 a.m. to 5 p.m.**
> **(except Thanksgiving and Christmas)**
> **Adults: $4.95; Children 5-11: $1.95**
> **(909) 597-3722**

This is the oldest non-government aviation museum in U.S., having opened in 1956. There are 100 planes in this unique museum, 26 of them fully flyable. These include American planes as well as their adversaries from Germany and Japan. The collection of WW II warbirds from the latter country is the largest in the world. They have five here; the Smithsonian Institute has only two. Both planes that saw regular service and experimental craft are featured.

One of the three museum buildings was a pilot training center during WW II called the Cal-Aero Flight Academy. They restore the vintage birds here. They are the number one restorer of antique airplanes in U.S. Besides the planes themselves, the collection includes gun turrets and a large number of wartime photos.

Not too far away from the airport and wineries is a lovely bed and breakfast:

> **Christmas House**
> **9240 Archibald Avenue**
> **Rancho Cucamonga, CA 91730**
> **(909) 980-6450**

Opened in 1983 by Jay and Janice Ilsley, this 1904 Victorian home has been lovingly restored and converted into a charming place for a weekend getaway. They have a murder mystery weekend that uses the historical background of the area as part of the plot.

There are six rooms, four with private baths. They also have a lovely tea room and a gift shop. A lot of weddings are performed in their garden gazebo. See the December chapter for what the holidays bring here.

Los Angeles

The City of Los Angeles itself has a winemaking history. The San Gabriel foothills were covered with vineyards at one time and commercial winemaking in California actually started where Union Station is today. In the 1830s, a gentleman named Louis Vignes planted a vineyard and began what would later become the:

San Antonio Winery
737 Lamar Street
Los Angeles, CA 90031
Daily 8 a.m. to 6 p.m.
Tours 9 a.m. to 3 p.m.
(213) 223-1401

This three-acre site is the oldest continuously operating winery in Los Angeles, having been founded by Santo Cambianico in 1917. They make everything from jug wine to cognac. Alas, most of the grapes come from Sonoma and Napa.

They have a self-guided tour of the original winery building that was built from boxcar sidings. Part of the winery is a museum with everything from antique cork pullers, to old bottles, to old equipment, including the mammoth aging vats.

The tasting room is quite nice. If you get hungry, they have a restaurant and deli that offers Italian food. You can either eat inside, surrounded by the musty aging barrels, or outside under the trees in the park-like patio.

Of course, the most famous manifestation of the harvest in Los Angeles is:

Los Angeles Farmer's Market
3rd and Fairfax
Los Angeles
Monday-Saturday 9 a.m. to 6:30 p.m.
Sunday 10 a.m. to 5 p.m.
(213) 933-9211

This open air market was started in 1934 by Earl Bell Gilmore. Prior to this, the 256-acre property had been used as the headquarters of an oil company, as a dairy farm, and even the field of the "Hollywood Stars" baseball team.

It was the Depression and Gilmore wanted to give farmers a place to offer their wares directly to the public. The opening was announced on the radio and people have been flocking here ever since. In addition to produce, Farmer's Market has store and restaurants, and butcher and poultry stands. My mother used to bring us here when we were little and she would buy a huge amount of meat for the family freezer.

Calabasas

In northern L.A. County, on a former ranch in the area encompassed by the
Santa Monica Mountains, is a unique fall festival:

> **Theater Arts Festival For Youth**
> **Peter Strauss Ranch**
> **30000 Mulholland Highway**
> **Agoura Hills, CA 91301**
> **normally second weekend of October**
> **Daily 8 a.m. to 5 p.m. (ranch)**
> **(818) 597-9192**

This annual festival began in 1983 and has grown ever since. There is an amphitheater where the shows take place.

The 65-acre Peter Strauss Ranch, named for the producer/actor who bought the
place in 1977, was originally a lakeside resort called Lake Enchanto. During the
'30s and '40s, it was the consummate rustic resort. The lake was formed by dam-
ming the upper reaches of Malibu Creek (called Triunfo Creek here) and it was
stocked with fish and covered with boats. Besides the lake, it had the largest swimming pool west of the Rockies, carnival-style rides, and a giant star-shaped terrazzo
dance floor that swung to big band music, which was broadcast on a radio show.

During the '60s, a scheme materialized to create a theme park called "Cornell
World Famous Places" featuring reproductions of famous places throughout the
world. These would have included the pyramids of Egypt, the Eiffel Tower, and Mt.
Fuji. But nature and finances condemned the project. First, a flood blew away the
dam, then the tax man foreclosed. Strauss bought it, improved it, and held it until
1983, when he sold it to the Santa Monica Mountains Conservancy.

Today, it doesn't look much like a resort, but it is a pretty, restful place. There
are picnic areas on the side patio of the lovely ranch house and on the tree-shaded
lawn. Just south of the house is a playground in a grove of eucalyptus trees with a
view of the ruined dam. A delightful one mile walk loop through live oaks, **The
Peter Strauss Trail**, starts here. Slow, shallow Triunfo Creek is fun to explore
because it is full of little, living creatures

Pumpkin season is celebrated in an annual two-day festival every October in a
nearby place:

> **Calabasas Days**
> **Paramount Ranch**
> **2813 Cornell Road**

Agoura, CA 91301
normally the third weekend of October
101 Freeway, Kanan Road exit, 3/4 mile to left on
Cornell Road, 2-1/2 miles south
(818) 880-4508
(818) 888-3770

There are two stories about how the City of Calabasas got its name. The more likely story is that the name comes from the indigenous people of the area, the Chumash. Calabasas Lake was a major stop for migratory wild geese. Hence "the place where the wild geese fly." Since the Chumash and wild geese have been long wiped out, this first explanation has been largely forgotten.

The popular story is that it comes from the "calabazas," a Spanish word for pumpkin. Legend has it that a wagon full of the giant orange squash crashed 100 years ago and that the resulting seed spill caused wild pumpkins to proliferate all over the area. Hence the theme of this festival.

This is a real small town-styled affair with country western music and Western style entertainment, lots of food stalls, and a seed spitting contest. There is pumpkin bowling (with both a children's and adult's division), and a pumpkin pie-eating contest.

Though there are some events held in the town proper, most of them have been moved to this site in nearby Agoura. It is perfect for this kind of event and for years was the location of the Renaissance Pleasure Faire.

The Santa Monica Mountains National Recreation Area operates this 326-acre property, which was Paramount Picture's generic Western film site up until 1980. There is a restored set of a false front Western town called, appropriately enough "Western Town."

It originally came into being because Burbank and the San Fernando Valley, popular filming locals for early Hollywood Westerns, started getting a little too populous. Paramount Ranch got its start when Valley residents began to protest the gunfights and chase scenes on horseback that went along with the filming.

Primeval filmmaker Jesse Laskey, who had made the very first feature-length film in Hollywood in 1913 with Cecil B. DeMille and Samuel Goldwyn (see March and June), picked out 4,000 acres in then very rural Agoura and Paramount Pictures bought it in 1921. Its meadows, creeks, and mountains rising in the background were seen in countless Westerns. It is said that Paramount's own logo was inspired by Sugarloaf Peak on the property (see August.)

In addition to the Westerns, in the '30s the outdoor scenes from such films as *Tom Sawyer* and *The Adventures of Marco Polo* were shot here.

In 1946, the studio sold the place, but part of it remained as an image of the Old West—this time on television. Many of the '50s and '60s TV Westerns, such as "The Cisco Kid," "Bat Masterson," and "Have Gun, Will Travel" came to life in Western Town. Though it was purchased by the National Park Service in 1979, it still sees use as a film site. The TV shows "C.H.I.P.S." and "The Fall Guy" saw action here as did the movies *Reds* and *Helter Skelter*.

It is an enjoyable, free place to visit even without a festival. Horseback riding is permitted. They have programs at the ranch that range from slide shows about the history of Paramount films to nature walks. You can explore the four miles of trails on your own or picnic at one of several sites. There are picnic tables on a grassy meadow next to Western Town.

If you like the idea of a nice walk in the outdoors, but are not Joe Hiker, this might be an ideal destination for you. There is a bulletin board at the foot of the bridge that leads into the town where all of the trails are described and illustrated. None of them are difficult.

The easy 1/2 mile **Coyote Canyon Nature Trail** starts at Western Town, follows a ravine called Medea Creek, goes through some oaks, and loops back along a low hill covered with chaparral. For a very romantic picnic, watch for a little side trail about half way. It leads to a solitary picnic table on a rise that rewards the occupants with a view of Western Town, Goat Buttes, and the rising Santa Monica Mountains that even a cameraman would be inspired by.

Another great view is at the southern end of the **5 Km. Run Trail**, which connects an abandoned car race track to several little trails. It crests near where Cornell Road meets Mulholland and provides the legendary view of Sugarloaf Peak.

Some events can be held at the most famous house in Calabasas:

> **Leonis Adobe**
> **23537 Calabasas Road**
> **Calabasas, CA 91302**
> **Wednesday-Sunday 1 to 4 p.m.**
> **(818) 222-6511**

Miguel Leonis, "The King of Calabasas," was born in 1824 in the French Pyrenees Mountains in Cambo. A wild region, Leonis grew up tough: he was an accomplished smuggler by the time he was 20.

Forced to leave his home country at this same age, he came to the little pueblo of

Los Angeles to make his fortune. A huge man for his day at 6-feet 4-inches tall, he was physically fearless and shrewd and aggressive, particularly in matters of land acquisition. Despite the fact that he couldn't speak much Spanish (or English for that matter), he was referred to by the locals as "El Basquo Grande." He built his land and empire with any means necessary.

Leonis was, in many ways, the archetype for future Valley residents. Starting with a white adobe farmhouse built around 1844, he remodeled and enlarged it in 1880 into a mansion in the Monterey style fashionable at the time.

He was also quite litigious and was quite fond of suing people, often over land he was seeking to acquire. Early Los Angeles court archives are filled with court records of his various trials and lawsuits.

"El Basquo Grande" died while returning from a celebration in Los Angeles after winning one of his many lawsuits. His wagon overturned in Cahuenga Pass in the area now occupied by the Hollywood Freeway. Because he was universally hated for his ruthlessness, it was said at the time that he was murdered. Legend has it that his ghost haunts the place now.

Within spitting distance is a classic Southern California restaurant:

Sagebrush Cantina
23527 Calabasas Road
Calabasas, CA 91302
Monday-Friday 11 a.m. to 10 p.m.
Saturday 8 a.m. to 10 p.m.
Sunday 9 a.m. to 10 p.m.
(818) 888-6020

This is the original Southern California cantina, a kind of metaphor for how we party in Southern California. Like a Valley ranch house, it has had so many additions that this mostly outdoor restaurant now resembles a small town from the Old West.

Like the premises, the menu has swelled over the years, and now it is eleven pages long. The food is excellent and includes Mexican combos, charbroiled steaks, chicken, and seafood. The $15.95 Sunday brunch (served from 9 a.m. to 2 p.m.) includes Belgian waffles made to order and champagne. They also have breakfast Saturday morning and, of course, happy hour from 3 to 6 p.m. There is live entertainment Tuesday through Saturday nights and on an occasional Sunday afternoon.

But when you say the word "romantic" in the context of the City of Calabasas, it is impossible not to mention the stunning dining experience at the:

Saddle Peak Lodge
419 Cold Canyon Road
Calabasas, CA 91302
Wednesday-Saturday 11 to 12 a.m.
Sunday 11 a.m. to 2 p.m.
(818) 340-6029

This is an elaborate, rambling, three-level restaurant that was originally a bordello. It was renovated to remove all traces of its roots, yet simulate the look of a long-established place. The decor is of a luxurious hunting lodge, with frontier saloon-style nymphs in gold frames, Wild West antiques, old books, firearms, and mounted animal heads on the wall.

Heavy log walls dominate the main dining room, lit by candles. There is library-like room on the second floor and a small private dining room with its own porch on the top floor. The bar has a floor of black flagstone. The large fireplace adds the perfect light on a cool evening.

The food could best be described as "rustic gourmet." Predictably, game is a specialty. The Sunday brunch in this rural setting is especially enjoyable.

Ojai

I can't imagine a more perfect way to celebrate fall than to head up to Ojai for the:

Bowlful of Blues
Libbey Bowl (within Libbey Park)
Ojai
normally first Saturday of October
2 p.m. to 10 p.m.
(805) 646-7230

This one-day music festival was started in 1982 and brings a Southern flavor to Ojai. It is produced by the Foundation for American Roots Music under the direction of Michael Kaufer. You will hear about seven different performances covering all regional forms of blues from Chicago blues to zydeco.

The gate opens an hour before the show starts and there are food stands selling crawfish dishes, Cajun-style vegetables, sodas, coffee, and desserts.

The Ojai Valley has many farmers. It also has a winery along the banks of the San Antonio Creek:

Oak Creek Ranch Winery
10024 Old Creek Road
Oak View, CA 93022
Daily 10 a.m. to 4 p.m.
(805) 649-4132

They have been growing the grapes and producing fine wine entirely within the Ojai Valley since 1850. This is a working ranch that also has its own organic fruit orchards, horses, and cattle. In addition to wine and orchard fruit in season, they are also noted for their boysenberries. There is a pretty picnic setting that is the perfect place to relax and enjoy the ranch's bountiful harvest.

Just where Old Creek Road turns off SR 33 (Highway 33) is the:

Arnaz Ranch
9504 North Ventura Avenue
Ventura, CA 93001
(no phone)

The Arnaz Ranch consists of an adobe from the 1800s, apple orchards, and a stand that sells apple cider which is pressed on the premises. They also sell locally grown fruit in season and a large variety of seeds and nuts.

Another Ojai institution that goes with the bounties of the harvest is the well loved:

Bill Baker's Bakery
457 East Ojai Avenue
Ojai, CA 93023
Tuesday-Saturday 5:15 a.m. to 4:30 p.m.
Sunday 7 a.m. to 11 a.m.
(805) 646-1558

The aroma of fresh baked bread here is as seductive as the Indian summer wind. Stimulate your nasal passages and sit at one of the tables in the bakery and have coffee with your donut or sweet roll. This is a regular meeting place for many of the locals.

When I take a tour to Ojai, I always bring the group to the:

Ojai Cafe Emporium
108 Montgomery Street
Ojai, CA 93023
Tuesday-Saturday 6:30 a.m. to 9 p.m.
Sunday-Monday 6:30 a.m. to 4 p.m.
(805) 646-2723

They sell over 57 varieties of whole coffee beans and bulk tea. Their signature mango ice tea served with the meals is worth a trip here in itself. It is also sold in bulk. Breakfast, lunch and dinner are served inside or alfresco in the canopy-covered patio.

If after all of this eating and drinking you feel like some exercise, go for a walk, horse, or bike ride on the:

MacDonald Bike Path & Southern Pacific

Equestrian/Hiking Trail

Foster Park (in Ventura) to Fox Street (in Ojai)

Ojai Valley

The Southern Pacific Railroad right of way that runs along SR 33 and then SR 150 has been turned into a marvelous bike and equestrian trail. The bike portion of the trail is blacktop and the equestrian trail, which is separated from the bike trail by a cedar post fence, is finished in redwood chips.

The trail is predominantly uphill from Foster Park to Oak View. Therefore, if you are going to make the round trip, I recommend parking at the park and peddling up to Ojai (about eight miles), eating lunch and relaxing, and then riding back down to your car. If you own a horse, you can park a horse trailer in Foster Park and use the trail.

Ironically, with all of its miles of pristine white sand beaches, Ventura County's restaurant most often named "most romantic" is:

Wheeler Hot Springs

16825 Maricopa Highway (Highway 33)

Ojai, CA 93023

Monday-Thursday 9 a.m. to 9 p.m. (spa)

Friday-Sunday 9 a.m. to 10 p.m. (spa)

Thursday-Sunday 5 to 9:30 p.m. (restaurant)

Saturday-Sunday 10 a.m. to 2:30 p.m. (restaurant)

(805) 646-8131

The mountain lodge here is over 100 years old. There is a big stone fireplace and the dining room has views of the creek. The natural mineral water is pumped into private redwood hot tubs. There is also a cold mineral spring that, during the summer, is also pumped into the swimming pool. They also have a renowned staff of masseurs and masseuses.

The natural ambiance and mineral baths are set off by the wonderful dining. The menu changes seasonally and the food is very contemporary in concept. They have hot tub and dinner and hot tub and brunch specials.

There is more about the Ojai Valley in the June, August, and December chapters.

Carpenteria

If there was ever a fruit other than the orange that is identified with the Southland, it is the avocado. Every year, there is a celebration of its harvest on the first weekend of this month up in Carpenteria:

California Avocado Festival
Linden Avenue
Carpenteria
first weekend of October
(805) 684-0038

If you've ever wondered what avocado pie or ice cream would taste like, here's your chance. This festival, started in 1987, really celebrates the green fruit because the area is the single largest growing region for avocados in the U.S. There are musical acts, crafts, and flowers and the whole thing is free.

Santa Ynez Valley

The Santa Barbara Vintner's Association, who hold the Santa Barbara County Vintner's Festival in April, also present a fall wine and harvest festival:

"A Celebration of Harvest"
(locations vary)
normally second Saturday of October
for information, contact:
Santa Barbara Vintner's Association
P.O. Box 1558
Santa Ynez, CA 93460
(805) 688-0881

This festival has a different focus than the spring Vintner's Festival in that, in addition to the music and wine tasting, local growers bring strawberries, broccoli, pumpkins, walnuts and even apples.

In this region, there are other celebrations around harvest time, like the annual party this charming little winery throws, where you can stomp grapes the way nature intended:

Santa Ynez Winery Harvest Party
343 North Refugio Road

Santa Ynez, CA 93460
usually first Saturday of October
12 to 5 p.m.
Admission: $25 (no tickets sold at door)
(805) 688-8381

This lovely winery offers a bucolic picnic area and a broad choice of wines. For this annual harvest festival, you get to make like the little old winemaker. You get in the huge tubs and use your bare feet. There is also wine tasting, entertainment, and a barbecue.

One of the most surprising and delightful stops in Santa Barbara County is:

Rancho Sisquoc Winery
Foxen Canyon Road
Santa Maria, CA 93455
Daily 10 a.m. to 4 p.m.
(805) 934-4332

This is a working 37,000-acre cattle ranch owned by the Flood family of San Francisco. They achieved their wealth through mining and don't live on the ranch. Though it is the second oldest vineyard in Santa Barbara County, it is comparatively small, with only 400 acres of grapes.

Because it is off the beaten track, many people miss Rancho Sisquoc—which is a shame because there is no other winery quite like it. There is a chapel called San Ramon at the entrance. There is a one lane dirt road that snakes its way to the winery. The setting in the foothills of the San Rafael Mountains in the basin of the Sisquoc River makes "The Ponderosa" look shabby.

The little ranch-style wooden winery building and tasting room has an adjacent lawn area with picnic tables. This is truly one of the better places to simply relax because there is absolutely no residual traffic noise. The view is uninterrupted; the silhouettes of cattle or farm animals munching peacefully in the distance make it even more sylvan.

The first crush came in 1972. Commercial wine production began in 1977. "Commercial" is almost too big a word because they only make about 4,000 cases of varietals a year, all of which is sold though the mail and at the winery.

There are other small, family-owned wineries in Santa Barbara County. Bill Mosby owns one such establishment that bears his name:

Mosby Winery
9496 Santa Rosa Road
right off US 101

Buellton, CA 93427
Daily 10 a.m. to 4 p.m.
(805) 688-2415

The adobe that is the main building at Mosby was built in 1853. In many ways, it exemplifies the winery as a friendly gathering place. It has a wrought iron chandelier built by the owner that hangs in an inviting living room complete with Western art and wood burning fireplace. Some may be put off by the hunting trophies. At the same time, the winery offers wonderful wine dinners here and is starting to produce some unusual Italian varietals.

A lovely place to stay while enjoying the Santa Barbara wineries and countryside is the:

Ballard Inn
2436 Baseline Avenue
Ballard, CA 93463
(805) 688-7770

This is a new building designed to look old, so what it lacks in history, it makes up for in such amenities as soundproof walls in the rooms. This is more important than it might seem—you know this if you have ever gone with a lover to a cute little Victorian B & B and listened to everyone else in their rooms while they listened to you.

Outside, it is sort of a Cape Cod Victorian Modern with a long covered porch under clapboard gables that goes all the way from end to end along the front of the building. The porch is enclosed by a white railing that matches the white picket fence that encircles the grounds. A turret forms one corner.

There are 15 guest rooms, all with private baths. Half of them have wood burning fireplaces. In each room are toiletries that celebrate the wine country: wine hand lotion, wine soap, and Champagne shampoo. Only one room has handicap access.

A Los Angeles designer, Catherine Kaufman, did the interior. There are four public rooms, including a TV room and a large living room where an afternoon cheese and pastry buffet is served. Each guest room has a motif, but the overall theme is to commemorate historical figures or events pertaining to the Santa Ynez Valley.

There is a **Wildflower Room**, decorated in pink, coral, and lavender. It has a sewing rocker and a Bloomsbury quilt. The **Equestrian Room** pays tribute to the area's proliferation of horse ranches. The former residents of the area are given representation by a **Jaradao Room**, with designs suggested by Chumash cave paintings. It uses the same colors as the cave art: red, white, and black.

The **Vineyard Room**, done with willow furniture and light hardwood floors, features a sitting area surrounded by the windows in the turret that let in morning sun. The **Western Room** approaches self-parody with its steer horns over the bed.

This motif is carried even further in the **Davy Brown Room**, named for a local fur trapper (and onetime companion to Kit Carson) who also rode with the Texas Rangers. Mercifully, there are no animal pelts, but there is a coonskin cap, some old snowshoes, and a stuffed pheasant. It is rustic all the way with a distressed oak floor, fireplace built from rocks taken from the San Ynez River, and wagon wheel quilt. Three of the room's walls are made of heavy beams and mortar in the style of a log cabin.

Probably the best room is the **Mountain Room**. Here the emphasis is on the view, which spreads out in a panorama on three sides. It also has a private balcony and a fireplace. Prices range form about $150 to about $200.

With a population of less than 300, Ballard is the smallest town in the Santa Ynez Valley. It is also the oldest, having been founded in 1880 by George Lewis. This forgotten pioneer built an adobe on a large ranch he called El Alamo Pintado, which means "The Painted Cottonwood." The town was named for his friend, William Ballard, who kept an eye on Lewis' house during his travels to Mexico.

A restaurant that has as much of a history as the town is:

> **The Ballard Store**
> **2449 Baseline Avenue**
> **Ballard, CA 93463**
> **Wednesday-Friday 5:30 to 9:30 p.m.**
> **Saturday 6 to 9:30 p.m.**
> **Sunday 10:30 a.m. to 9:30 p.m.**
> **(805) 688-5319**

This building was built in 1939 as a country store and gas station. It continued as such for the next 31 years until it was purchased and converted to a restaurant by Alice and John Elliot. The interior is a warm Country French.

And for nostalgia run amok, there is nothing quite like the:

> **Ballard School**
> **Cottonwood and School Street**
> **Ballard, CA 93463**

Yes, there really is a "little red schoolhouse" within two hours of L.A. You could not find a more picture perfect representation—right down to the steeple—of an image deeply ingrained in the American subconscious as a symbol of a more innocent age. It is flanked by two black walnut trees. Originally built in 1883, its function has continued non-stop. Kindergarten and first grade are still taught here. There is more about the wineries of Santa Barbara County in the March, April, and June chapters.

Goleta

A little later in the month, there is a fall festival in Santa Barbara County that celbrates the sourest of citrus:

Goleta Lemon Festival
usually second Saturday of October
10 a.m. to 5 p.m.
for information, contact:
Goleta Valley Chamber of Commerce
P.O. Box 781
Goleta, CA 93116
(805) 967-4618

The Goleta Lemon Festival gives you a chance to sample all of the many ways the yellow fruit is used in cooking. You can try lemonade, lemon bars, lemon cake, and lemon chicken and barbecue tri tip beef. There is also a lemon pie contest.

In addition to the lemon-related festivities, there is an arts and crafts show with over 40 artisans, continuous entertertainment, and a petting zoo and games for children. It is held at the historic:

Stow House
304 North Los Carneros Road
Goleta, CA 93117
Saturday-Sunday 2 to 4 p.m.
(805) 964-4407

The Stow House is a two-story Victorian farmhouse built in 1872. It is located on a large plot of land with several buildings and a small lake and is shaded by many different kinds of trees. The inviting broad veranda is cool under the spreading leaves of an Australian primrose tree.

The inside of the house has antique furniture, toys, and clothing—some of which belonged to the Stow family. Located on the grounds is the red barn that houses the **Horace Sexton Memorial Museum of Farm Equipment**.

Right next door to the Stow House is the:

South Coast Railroad Museum
300 North Los Carneros Road

Goleta, CA 93117
Wednesday-Sunday 1 to 4 p.m.
(805) 964-4407

Formerly the Goleta train station, this yellow building was built in 1901 by the Southern Pacific Railroad and handled passengers and freight until 1972. It was moved here near the foothills of the Santa Ynez Mountains in 1981 and is surrounded by trees, orchards, and fields. A Southern Pacific caboose is displayed on some tracks in front of the museum.

Restored outside and in, it has old photos, railroad artifacts, and exhibits you can play with. For example, there is an antique telegraph set up in the old freight office that works. The moving and subsequent restoration of the depot by Goleta Beautiful is depicted in a participant-operated slide show in the passenger waiting room.

One exhibit that always brings a smile is a 400-square-foot HO-scale model railroad exhibit with Santa Barbara as a backdrop. There is also a little bookstore that sells books about train history and the Santa Barbara area, as well as train posters and memorabilia.

On the edge of Goleta is an appropriate fall destination:

Ellwood Ranch
1300 Ellwood Ranch Road
Goleta, CA 93117
Daily 7 a.m. to 7 p.m.
(805) 968-1162

The Ellwood Ranch grows oranges that are then sold to the public in a unique way: you pick them yourself and pay 15 cents a pound. Patriarch John Doty has been at the ranch since 1920 and started the self-pick orange sales in 1969.

It is a bit of a trek to get to the place. Take the Winchester Canyon Road exit, off the US 101 freeway; the road will curve to the right, but you must actually turn right at a sign that announces, "Oranges, Poynter." You will continue between eucalyptus trees on your left and a field on your right, past the Bradley Ranch. At the fork in the road, go straight. You will continue downhill and come to the sign for the Ellwood Ranch.

The property is very impressive. It is over a mile to the U-pick orange grove. On the way, you pass acres and acres of orange groves, small canyons, and horse corrals. Right by the corrals, the elder Mr. Doty's son, Ken, has a collection of antique farm machinery. Besides oranges, Ellwood Ranch also produces and sells apples, tomatoes, and avocados.

There are signs along the way indicating "Oranges;" when you see two of them on you right, turn that way. You will pass through some trees and finally arrive at your destination.

MONARCH BUTTERFLIES AND FALL COLORS

Beginning this month and continuing through the winter, some of the world's loveliest creatures seeks warmth by migrating to some of the Southland's coastal areas: Monarch butterflies.

Their beauty is known to every child in North America. Monarch butterflies are a delicate presence fluttering by with large soft wings of yellow to brownish-red and black veins that terminate in white and colored speckled black tips.

Nineteen miles northwest of Santa Barbara is **El Capitan Creek**, which meanders down to a beach of the same name. In addition to live oaks, there are sycamores along this creek that this month will be changing color. During the migratory months, the Monarchs hang in clusters from these trees.

Though the Monarchs come from as far north as Canada, they really are a tropical insect and cannot tolerate cold. It takes a specific combination of environmental conditions for them to survive the winter. Farther up the coast, they like the coastal Monterey pine and eucalyptus groves around Pismo State Beach. The interesting thing is that the butterflies seem to return to the same wintering roosts each year, yet they have no fellows to guide them. They only live long enough for a single two-way trip.

To see them, get off from US 101 at the El Capitan State Beach exit. There are 140 campsites for both tents and motor homes up to 30 feet in length. Fireplaces and picnic tables make for a perfect fall experience. There is food service and a grocery store if you didn't pack a lunch. Walkways and stairs take you down to the somewhat rocky beach. Walk up the coast toward Gaviota.

For information, call the park at (805) 968-1033. The rangers can tell you where the butterflies are hanging out.

The monarchs go pretty far south along the coast. Another place they spend their winters is also the best place in the Southland to experience fall colors:

Big Sycamore Canyon
Point Mugu State Park
9000 West Pacific Coast Highway
Point Mugu, CA 90265
(805) 986-8591

Point Mugu State Park is named for the rocky point that juts out into the Pacific. It is quite large—16,000 acres—and extends inland for a considerable distance. There are several campgrounds and over 100 miles of trails within its boundaries.

It is also an excellent place to enjoy some fall colors in Southern California because it contains "the finest example of a sycamore savanna in the State Park system," which is easily reachable via **Big Sycamore Canyon Trail**. Here there are sycamore trees nearly 100-feet tall.

To get there, take Highway 1 to Point Magu at the south end of Ventura County. Big Sycamore Canyon Campground is 32 miles north of Santa Monica. You can park outside the entrance to the campground and just walk in. You will have a pleasant easy walk beneath the sycamores for about two miles, then you can kick back at some shaded picnic tables.

COLUMBUS DAY

Columbus Day is America's schizophrenic holiday. In 1892, the 400th anniversary of the voyage that changed the world was celebrated in the biggest party America had ever seen, the Chicago's World Columbian Exposition. By 1992, opinions were so mixed about the whole thing that most of the planned 500th year anniversary bashes ended up being cancelled or down played.

One group that usually celebrates anyway are, of course, the Italian Americans, who are justifiably proud of their most famous favorite son.

The Italian contribution to Southern California has been considerable. Southern California's lovely Mediterranean architecture of the '20s owes as much to the Italians as the Spanish and it is truly remarkable how many Italian restaurants there are in the Southland.

Italian immigrants were quite numerous during the early winemaking period. One of Los Angeles' most oddly located landmark restaurants is a throwback to these days:

> **Little Joe's Restaurant**
> **900 North Broadway**
> **Los Angeles, CA 90012**
> **Monday-Saturday 11 a.m. to 9 p.m.**
> **(213) 489-4900**

This big old building encompasses a huge lounge and six dining rooms. An Italian restaurant in the old tradition, its walls are adorned with Italian murals and various Italian objects fill every nook. Little Joe's has been here in Chinatown since

1910. It started as an impromptu kitchen on the back end of an Italian grocery.

The food is also decidedly non-trendy and portions are generous.

Though it does not have the extensive Italian immigrant communities of New York City, Southern California does have a **Little Italy** in San Diego. This collection of shops and restaurants congregates along India Street between Fir and Cedar Streets. It is here you will find San Diego's best loved pizzeria:

> **Filippi's Pizza Grotto**
> **1747 India Street**
> **San Diego, CA 92101**
> **Monday-Thursday 11 a.m. to 11 p.m.**
> **Friday-Saturday 11 a.m. to 12 a.m.**
> **Sunday 11 a.m. to 10 p.m.**
> **(619) 232-5095**

The inside of Filippi's looks like everyone's idea of a New York neighborhood restaurant: red checked tablecloths, huge salamis hanging from the ceiling, and chianti bottles and fake grape arbors. The only difference is that the pizza crust is thick, not East Coast thin.

Filippi's was started as a grocery store by Mama and Papa DePhilippis in 1949. Though they still sell Italian deli items, they expanded into selling sandwiches and pizza. There are now three generations of the family working at eleven different locations.

A few doors down is a well-known Italian bakery:

> **Solunto Baking Company**
> **1643 India Street**
> **San Diego, CA 92101**
> **Monday-Saturday 7:30 a.m. to 6 p.m.**
> **(619) 233-3506**

The bread here is legendary and is used by many of the Italian restaurants and French cafes in town. They serve food as well and a sandwich made from their fresh bread is a great experience. All manner of breakfast pastries and desserts are also offered.

INDIGENOUS PEOPLE'S DAY

Many have said that if there is a Columbus Day, there should be an "Indigenous People's Day" as well. There are two museums in the Southland that would be logical places to celebrate such a holiday. The first of these has had its share of controversy in how they handle Columbus:

The Bowers Museum
2002 North Main Street
Santa Ana, CA 92706
Tuesday-Sunday 10 a.m. to 5 p.m.
Thursday until 9 p.m.
Adults: $4.50; Students/Seniors: $3;
Children (under 12): $1.50
(714) 567-3600

This museum is dedicated to the culture of indigenous peoples. The old Bowers building was built to be a museum from its beginning in 1932. A trust was established by a rancher from Ohio named Charles W. Bowers in 1924. He died in 1929 and never saw his namesake museum.

The Bowers reopened on October 15 of 1992 after a four-year, $12,000,000 renovation. The most ironic (and controversial) exhibit is a bronze bust of Columbus. It was donated along with a quarter of a million dollars by the Orange County American Italian Renaissance Foundation. Many people saw this as contrary to the museum's entire reason for being. This would not be the first conflicting message from the Bowers: a statue of Cabrillo has been standing in a courtyard since long before the renovation.

The oldest museum to celebrate indigenous people is the venerable:

Southwest Museum
234 Museum Drive
Los Angeles, CA 90065
Tuesday-Sunday 11 a.m. to 5 p.m.
(213) 221-2164

The groundbreaking for the Southwest Museum took place on November 16 of 1911. It was performed by a woman, Elizabeth B. Fremont, who was the daughter of John C. Fremont. After the symbolic first shovelful of dirt, she gave the Fremont flag to the man who had made it possible, Charles Fletcher Lummis. The structure was finished in 1914 at a total cost of approximately $80,000.

The old Mission-style Southwest Museum building has looked pretty much the same ever since. The most obvious feature is the seven-story Caracol Tower. One of the most outstanding exhibits is the Poole Collection of Native American baskets. And the book and gift shop is a good stop just on its own, if you are looking for something a little different.

Right near the Southwest Museum is its father's house:

El Alsial
Lummis House
200 East Avenue 43
Los Angeles, CA 90065
(213) 222-0546

Harvard-educated Charles Fletcher Lummis was by all accounts a remarkable fellow. He was the first librarian of the City of Los Angeles and was friends with the great intellectuals of his day such as John Ruskin. The bell over the dining room wing was presented to him by the King of Spain.

This house was built from 1898 to 1910 out of boulders from the Arroyo Seco. The sculptor of Mt. Rushmore, Gutzon Borglum, designed the Art Nouveau fireplace.

FESTIVAL OF MASKS

Mr. Lummis would no doubt have approved of one of the world's largest multicultural festivals:

International Festival of Masks
Hancock Park
Wilshire Boulevard and Curson Avenue
Los Angeles, CA 90036
second weekend of October
Saturday-Sunday 11 a.m. to dusk
(213) 937-5544

With its stated aim of highlighting the "language" of the mask among the cultures of the world conspicuous in Los Angeles, the International Festival of Masks celebrates a myriad of traditions while promoting a synergy of unity in cultural diversity. Since its inception in 1976, the festival has enjoyed broad-based community support, spearheaded by its advisory team and a series of community planning meetings. The event's popularity has grown every year and attendance has risen to over 50,000 people.

This is a free two-day event, which culminates months of pre-festival educational programs including exhibitions, mask-making workshops in school and community centers, and demonstrations by artists. The festival grounds are structured with two stages presenting continuous dance, theater, and storytelling performances from around the world.

Sri Lankan mask dance theatre, Persian dance drama, and West African dance and storytelling are a few examples of the types of scheduled performances. In an effort to present dance pieces in their appropriate contexts, groups such as IXIM, comprised of Guatemalans living in Los Angeles, and Bakra Bata, a Caribbean/ South American music and dance company from Seattle, have performed their processional pieces on the grounds among the festival visitors.

Surrounding the stages are exhibit and vending booths showcasing the variety of masks found worldwide, including: Brazilian coconut masks, Sri Lankan animal masks, and Italian commedia dell'arte masks, to name a few. Artists demonstrate contemporary and traditional mask-making techniques and offer hands-on public workshops for all age groups.

In the international food court, visitors can revel in a global experience and enjoy a wide variety of mouth-watering foods, ranging from Louisiana Cajun cuisine to Nigerian akra and Malaysian gado gado.

The second day of the festival opens with the spectacular Parade of Masks. School groups, art centers, marching bands, families, and individuals show off their mask creations as they march down a 1/2-mile route. The parade begins at 11 a.m. on Wilshire at Cloverdale, travels west on Wilshire through the heart of the Miracle Mile and ends at the festival grounds in Hancock Park.

The Parade of Masks looks for inspiration to the carnival samba groups, Balinese processions, and other parade traditions from around the world; it is a wonderful mix of customs from the diverse communities of Los Angeles, fused with the creative imagination of contemporary artists. As in other parade traditions, groups in the Parade of Masks incorporate themes banners, movement, music, and human-powered floats in their entry.

The festival format ensures that the artists and their work are not presented as rarified objects d'art separate from day-to-day living, but as the vital expressions of a community. A wide range of artists take part in the festival, presenting both contemporary and traditional performances and representing a multiplicity of cultural communities. Participating groups have included Native Americans, Mexicans, West Africans, Koreans, Persians, Filipinos, Sri Lankans, and contemporary North American artists. Community interface and cultural exchange occur among participants prior to and during the festival.

The main producer of the festival is the nearby:

Craft and Folk Art Museum
May Company, 4th Floor
5800 Wilshire

Los Angeles, CA 90036
(213) 937-5544

For a few years, this excellent art orginization has been located in the May Company building at the intersection of Wilshire and Fairfax. That building is a 1940 Streamline Moderne classic with a gold tower that looks much like a giant confection jar on the corner.

Founded by Edith Wyle in 1972, the Craft and Folk Art Museum was originally located over the Egg and The Eye restaurant in a lovely old house across the street and down Wilshire Boulevard.

The International Festival of Masks is one of the primary vehicles for the Craft and Folk Art Museum to further its mission: to promote the quality of life by studying, preserving, and celebrating cultural expressions through the objects people use for living, their craft, design, and folk art. Edith Wyle was also the guiding light behind the festival, with her vision of uniting the cultures of Los Angeles through an object which carries meaning in nearly every culture—the mask.

One of the other sponsoring museums is right in Hancock Park:

George C. Page Museum
5801 Wilshire Boulevard
Los Angeles, CA 90036
(213) 936-2230

Next to the La Brea Tar Pits is this collection of the fossils of animals and birds that lived in the region during the ice age. All of them were excavated from the tar pits. It was first identified as a major site for prehistoric animal skeletons by a professor from USC named J.C. Merriman in 1906. Much of what was unearthed at these digs can also be found at the L.A. County Museum of Natural History (see April). Like many L.A. County museums, the Page Museum is free on the first Tuesday of the month.

Of course, the granddaddy of all museums in the Southland is right here as well:

Los Angeles County Museum of Art
5905 Wilshire Boulevard
Los Angeles, CA 90036
Tuesday-Friday 10 a.m. to 5 p.m.
Saturday-Sunday 10 a.m. to 6 p.m.
Free admission to permanent exhibits
first Tuesday of each month
Tours at 1 and 2:15 p.m.
(213) 857-6000

I always remember how overjoyed I was in elementary school when, instead of normal classes, we would go to a museum or some other municipal exhibit on a field trip. This month is a particularly wonderful time to take a day off work and go on your own field trip to this excellent museum.

There have always been good reasons to stop by the LACMA, but in recent years there have been some additions that make going much more compelling.

There is a beautiful sculpture garden called **The Iris and B. Gerald Cantor Sculpture Garden**. The Cantor's collection is said to be the finest collection of sculpture by Auguste Rodin in the world, and they have provided some noteworthy examples of the 19th century French romanticist.

The 19th century was an interesting one for sculpture. Within a very short time, it saw a period of romanticism and a reactionary rebirth of classicism. Romanticism, as far as sculpture goes, would translate visually into less attention to perfection of form and more interest in conveying a particular feeling by the way the form is depicted. Classicism would emphasize a symmetry of form and a stoicism in attitude. Most people find something in both. Generally, 19th century sculpture is large and it shows far better when well-spaced in a meandering garden. In this setting, the effect is wonderful.

The Rodin pieces are combined with some other noteworthy 19th century artist's works. You can really see the influence and counter-influence of the two styles. When you consider the intellectual uproar that was going on during the period, you can see how art really does tell the story of what is going on in society.

The most spectacular reason to go the museum is a building that is as remarkable as the art it houses, the **Pavilion For Japanese Art**.

Japanese art is displayed in homes and public places differently than we commonly do here in the U.S. While we shine spotlights on most of our paintings and sculptures, "Japanese light" is a soft, diffused light like that produced by natural light filtered through paper screens.

The structure of this pavilion is supported by cables connected to two green stone towers. The walls are of translucent plastic. The total effect is unlike any building you have ever seen or been inside of. It helps to know it was designed by the late Bruce Goff, a protege of Frank Lloyd Wright.

Inside is a collection that emphasizes the Edo period (1615-1865). The person who donated the collection is an Oklahoma oilman who displayed rare class by not demanding the building be named after him.

There were two noteworthy additions to the museum district along Wilshire

Boulevard in 1994. The first was the:

Carole and Barry Kaye Museum of Miniatures
5900 Wilshire Boulevard
Los Angeles, CA 90036
Tuesday-Saturday 10 a.m. to 5 p.m.
Sunday 11 a.m. to 5 p.m.
(213) 937-6464

This unusual museum has 14,000-square-feet of exhibit space for a very small subject. That does not mean they are not impressive. There is an antebellum mansion, a collection of miniature First Ladies, a Roman banquet hall, a 1920's Soda Shoppe, and other amazingly ornate little worlds. The Petite Elite Gift Shop sells miniature paintings, dolls, and furniture with tags from $1.50 to $100,000.

In June of 1994, a spectacular opening was held for:

The Peterson Automotive Museum
6060 Wilshire Boulevard
Los Angeles, CA 90036
Saturday-Thursday 10 a.m. to 6 p.m.
Friday 10 a.m. to 9 p.m.
(213) 930-2277

The Peterson Automotive Museum has three floors and over 200 rare vehicles, which are not just sitting on pedestals with little signs next to them. You walk past the large museum store and into a series of dioramas that start with the history of the automobile. You first see Louis Breer's blacksmith shop where he produced a car in 1901 using only basic tools.

One exhibit is about the wonderful public transportation system that used to connect the Southland, the Pacific Electric Red Car. It does not mention the widely accepted notion that oil companies worked to destroy it so they could profit from gasoline sales to automobile owners. The last train ran in 1961.

Other exhibits depict such auto-related topics as the alleys and freeways of Los Angeles. The best ones offer re-creations of some of the roadside architecture of the Route 66 era (see September). My favorite is the "Dog Cafe," which looked like a giant bulldog's head smoking a pipe.

There is a replica of a '30's adobe-styled Richfield station with a 1932 Ford awaiting service. Part of this exhibit, sponsored by Arco, is the "Evolution of the Gas Pump," starting with buckets. It is very clear something was lost when the flashing lights and elaborate details of designs from the 1930s disappeared.

The second floor has a living room where a TV plays vehicle-related shows like "Batman," "The Rat Patrol," and "My Mother the Car." The "1994 Flintmobile" from the movie *The Flintstones* is parked on this floor, along with a 1932 Bugatti Royale, Joan Crawford's 1933 Cadillac V16 Town Car, and other cars of famous people.

Also on the second floor is a gallery called "The Art of the French Motorcar," which features some really unusual, teardrop-shaped cars with covered wheel wells such as a 1939 Delahaye. Record breaking world speed vehicles are well represented by Mickey Thompson's piston-powered 406 m.p.h. car from 1960 and the one that broke his record by just three miles per hour in 1965, the Goldenrod.

My favorite car in the whole museum is the red 1959 Cadillac parked under the Coffee Shop Modern-style drive-in arch.

Not too far from the museums, just up from Wilshire on La Brea is a restaurant that is on many people's "best" list:

> **Campanile and La Brea Bakery**
> **624 South La Brea**
> **Los Angeles, CA 90036**
> **Monday-Saturday 6 a.m to 11 p.m.**
> **(213) 938-1447**

This was formerly an office building owned by Charlie Chaplin. The food served under its skylight would probably has pleased him, as would the romantic decor. Balconies planted with flowers overlook the patio. There is a tile fountain as you enter.

The name comes from the bell tower, visible through the skylight. A three-dimensional mural extends along the wall in the main dining room. Many people drive in from Orange County and as far away as Santa Barbara for their breads, which have been called the best in the Southland.

Wilshire Boulevard, in the blocks around the Museum of Modern Art, is kind of a museum of automobile art in and of itself. During the Roaring '20s, developer A.W. Ross bought 18 acres and created a new shopping district between La Brea and Fairfax. At the time, it was considered quite far away from the traditional home of top stores in Downtown L.A., but closer to the newer suburbs on the Westside.

The first notable structure to be built was the Desmond's, designed in 1928 by Gilbert Stanley Underwood. The architecture of this and other buildings here was affected by the automobile in two ways. First of all, the stores were set closer to the street with windows designed to show merchandise to passing cars. Second, the Art

Deco-style was tempered with Streamline Moderne, which was a celebration of streamlining for speed as in locomotives, airplanes, and cars. This area came to be known as the **Miracle Mile**. One of the dominant structures on the landscape here is The Wiltern Center, an incredible Art Deco masterpiece originally built in 1931. The architect was none other than Stiles O. Clements of Morgan, Walls, and Clements, designer of the Adamson House (see August).

Perhaps this is the greatest shrine to L.A. Art Deco that is still in use as a public facility today:

> **Wiltern Theatre**
> **3780 Wilshire Boulevard**
> **Los Angeles, CA 90010**
> **(213) 380-5005**

This grand theatre was originally the Warner Brothers Western Theater. The design was a collaboration between Clements and G. Albert Lansburgh, the theater architect responsible for the El Capitan and the Pacific Warner (see March), among others. It was restored by Wayne Ratkovitch of Ratkovitch, Bowers, and Perez, who also did the Oviatt Building (see September).

My brother and I used to cut school and go to the movies here. The name had been changed to the Wiltern by then. Today it has 2,288 seats and features music concerts, dance, and drama.

Also within the Wiltern Center is a great shrine to modern, imaginative restaurant interior design:

> **Atlas Bar and Grill**
> **3760 Wilshire Boulevard**
> **Los Angeles, CA 90010**
> **Monday-Friday 11:30 a.m. to 2 a.m.**
> **Saturday 5:30 p.m. to 2 a.m.**
> **closed Sunday**
> **(213) 380-8400**

This restaurant was the last project of the late Mario Tamayo, a real Southern California character who went to East L.A. High School. He opened the restaurant Cha Cha Cha on Melrose in 1986 and introduced Caribbean cuisine to Southern California's dining scene.

Atlas is like a giant piece of art. There are sun god faces gazing down at you under starburst fixtures with lighting tubes and zigzag shades. The yellow walls scatter the luminescence like candlelight.

There is a performance space and a concealed movie screen. The house drink is the Ruby, which is made with vodka and cranberry juice.

Another extraordinary building of Wilshire Boulevard is:

Bullocks Wilshire
3050 Wilshire Boulevard
Los Angeles, CA 90010

Bullock's Wilshire was constructed in the year of the Great Crash of '29 in what had been a bean field. It was a quintessential Southern California 20th century landmark right from the start: it had one of the first parking lots. Its most radical feature was that the main entrance faced this parking lot and not Wilshire Boulevard. Raymond Chandler even referred to Bullocks Wilshire in *The Big Sleep*.

This is a building of remarkable beauty inside and out. It was designed by John and Donald Parkinson, with interior by Jock Peters. You enter through the door in back through Zigzag Moderne gates. A glassed-in porte-cochere has a mural by Herman Sacks that celebrates modes of transportation in the modern age. The zeppelin is included with the automobile and the locomotive.

Bullocks Wilshire was built to be close to what at the time was Los Angeles' newest exclusive neighborhood, **Hancock Park**. This area north of Wilshire, between La Brea and Western, surprises a lot of people today that have never seen it, because the houses are exceptionally large and beautiful.

Along with the city park of the same name that encompasses the La Brea Tar Pits and the Page Museum, this area was named for Major Henry Hancock. Hancock bought the former Rancho La Brea in 1860 and it was his oil drilling that turned up the prehistoric bones that led to what would later be identified as a major scientific discovery.

There are a lot of mansions here, including one that has an official resident:

Getty House
605 South Irving Boulevard
Los Angeles, CA 90005

This is the mayor's house. It is a 1921 Tudor-style (which predominates in the area) that was purhcased by the Getty Oil Trust in the 1960s during an unsuccessful foray into the residential property market. They donated it to the City of Los Angeles in 1977. Mayor Richard Riordan has extensively renovated it.

Los Angeles Poetry Festival

The L.A. Poetry Festival happens the end of October at dozens of different venues. It is produced by poet Suzanne Lummis and the L.A. Cultural Affairs Department. For information, call (213) 660-4306.

Though there are poetry readings at coffeehouses throughout Southern California, perhaps the most special place for it is the:

>**Poetry Garden**
>**Lannan Foundation**
>**5401 McConnell Avenue**
>**Los Angeles, CA 90066**
>**Tuesday-Sunday 11 a.m. to 5 p.m.**
>**(310) 306-1004**

The Lannan Foundation is a multi-arts organization that supports visual and spoken word artists. Often they produce events at the Pacific Design Center in West Hollywood, but there are regular readings held in the garden next to the building that houses their offices, library, and art gallery.

For the Poetry Garden, artist Siah Armajani fashioned a courtyard surrounded by a wall with sea pink flowers, Japanese Maples, and hummingbirds. Part of the inspiration for it was Wallace Stevens' poem, "Anecdote of the Jar," which is engraved on the wall.

ARMENIAN CULTURAL FESTIVAL

In addition to its many other amazing ethnic statistics, Los Angeles is also a city with the second largest Armenian population in the world. There are 400,000 Armenians in Southern California. They came from Iran, Lebanon, and Russian. Every year since 1987, there has been an October:

>**Armenian Festival**
>**(locations vary)**
>**contact festival office:**
>**2224 West Olive Avenue**
>**Burbank, CA 91506**
>**usually third Sunday in October**
>**10 a.m. to 6 p.m.**
>**(818) 842-8628**

Started by a worker in former City Councilman Michael Woo's office, it was put under the direction of dancer

Young dancers in ethnic costume perform at the Armenian Festival.

Susan Ounjian. She formed a board of directors and has worked tirelessly to encourage awareness of Armenian culture. This board created a book about the event, called *Amenian Cultural Festival*.

The festival started as an Armenian-style picnic at Barnsdale Art Park (see June) with about 2,000 people and outgrew the site when the crowds increased to 7,000. There is food, music and dance, but the highpoint of the day is an enactment of an Armenian "Old Village Wedding."

East Hollywood has a large area known as **Little Armenia**, bounded roughly by Hollywood and Santa Monica Boulevards and Western and Vermont Avenues. It is the place of first entrance into the U.S. for most Armenians. You will hear more of that language than English on Santa Monica Boulevard.

One of the longest established Armenian restaurants in Hollywood is:

Carousel Restaurant
5112 Hollywood Boulevard
Hollywood, CA 90027
Daily 11 a.m. to 11 p.m.
(213) 660-8060

Krikor Greg and Rose Tcholakian will welcome you to their friendly restaurant with the long tables and the mirrored ball hanging from the ceiling. They offer a wonderful assortment of appetizers such as "sarma" (stuffed grape leaves), kebobs of all kinds, and unusual Armenian specialties.

For Armenian take-out food, the place to go is:

Uncle Jack's Meat Pies
1108 North Kenmore Avenue
Hollywood, CA 90029
Monday-Saturday 7 a.m. to 6 p.m.
(213) 664-8842

The giant red sign says "Lahmajune Hagop Danaian #1 Uncle Jack's Meat

Pies." Hagop Danian is Uncle Jack and he and his wife, Lucy, and their daughter, Maral Mangassarian, make the best Armenian pizza ("Lahmajune") and "zaatar" bread" in town.

Lahmajune is a thin crust circle covered with meat, tomato, bell peppers, garlic, and herbs. Zaatar bread is often eaten for breakfast by Armenians and is flavored with sumac and Middle Eastern thyme.

But for Armenian (and other Middle Eastern) shopping, the biggest store is:

> **Ron's Market**
> **5270 Sunset Boulevard**
> **Hollywood, CA 90027**
> **Daily 8 a.m. to 10 p.m.**
> **(213) 465-1164**

Inside this former Vons is an Armenian-run cornucopia of Central European and Middle Eastern foods. There are dozens of varieties of breads, a huge deli with every kind of smoked fish you could imagine, and piles and piles of foodstuffs from Russia, Romania, and Arab countries.

SAN MARCOS RENAISSANCE FESTIVAL

There are several Renaissance Fairs in Southern California. One of the most enjoyable is the:

> **San Marcos Renaissance Festival**
> **Walnut Grove Park**
> **corner of Olive and Sycamore, San Marcos**
> **second and third week of October**
> **usually two weekends 10 a.m. to 6 p.m.**
> **for information, contact:**
> **San Marcos Chamber of Commerce**
> **144 West Mission Boulevard**
> **San Marcos, CA 92069**
> **(619) 744-1270**

This great festival offers arts and crafts, games, entertainment and lots of food and drink. The town of San Marcos, where it is located, spreads out over rolling hills, separated by canyons and surrounded by poultry ranches and orchards.

Of course, the most romantic place to stay in the area is the wonderful:

> **Inn at Rancho Santa Fe**
> **Linea del Cielo at Paseo Elicias**

Expansive lawn and shade trees surround the Inn at Rancho Santa Fe.

P.O. Box 869
Rancho Santa Fe, CA 92067
(619) 756-1131

This luxury country inn began life in 1924 as "La Morada." In 1941, it assumed the name it has today. It was purchased in 1958 by hotelier Steve Royce, whose family continues to own and manage the property today.

There are 70 rooms, almost all of them in cottages which are arranged on a full 20 acres of beautifully landscaped grounds. They are individually decorated and have private entrances. Many have fireplaces and secluded patios.

The public rooms all exude a warmth and sense of understated country elegance. The **Garden Room**, overlooking the pool, is decorated with hand-painted murals. The **Library** has a fireplace and shelves of books. The **Vintage Room** is a replica of an old California taproom. It opens onto a patio where dining and dancing take place.

The town of Rancho Santa Fe started as a grove of eucalyptus trees on rolling hills that were planted as a source of wood for railroad ties used by the Santa Fe Railroad. This was not the greatest business venture ever conceived, so in 1928 the Santa Fe Protective Covenant was drawn up by local landowners.

This agreement greatly limited development and set aesthetic standards for building on the 6,300 acres of the ranch that homeowners must still follow. A gorgeous, exclusive community developed. Both Howard Hughes and Bing Crosby had homes here. Today Rancho Santa Fe's zip code is second only to Beverly Hills among American cities in wealth. Among its 4,500 residents are Dick Enberg, Patti Page, Robert Young, Victor Mature, and astronaut Wally Schirra.

From miles around, people drive in to get produce at:

Chino's (The Vegetable Shop) Calzada del Bosque
Rancho Santa Fe, CA 92067
(619) 756-3184

Called "The Rolls Royce of Roadsiders," Chino's offers culinary herbs, radicchio, miniature vegetables, and homegrown arugula. Every morning, chefs are queued up to select their daily choices.

BUCCANEER DAYS PARTY

One of the biggest and best parties of the year happens this month on Catalina Island:

Buccaneer Days Party
Doug's Reef Saloon
P.O. Box 5044
Two Harbors, CA 90704
usually first Saturday of October, 1 p.m. to 10 p.m.
(310) 510-0303

This is the larger of the two annual shindigs thrown in Catalina Island's secluded Two Harbors area. The other is the "South Seas Luau" in June (see that month).

This one gets a big turnout of boat owners and their guests who don pirate costumes and generally go crazy for a day. They have a huge beach tug-o-war, original games like "water jousts," and treasure hunts for kids and adults. Naturally, there is plenty of feasting and drinking.

If you don't have a boat, the most romantic way to make the trip to Buccaneer Days from the mainland would be to call:

Spanish Rake Charters
Newmark's Yacht Centre, Berth 204
Wilmington, CA 90744
(310) 830-5075

There are many fine boats you can charter in the San Pedro harbor area, but this one is not only reasonably priced, it really will give you the wonderful feeling of the lure of the sea in simpler times.

The *Spanish Rake* is an 82-foot wooden sailing yacht right out of a romance novel. It sails regularly in classic boat regattas. For $2,500, you get her and a crew of three, all insurance, docking fees, fuel, and food for 48 hours. She'll sleep six in two private and one semi-private cabins. The crew has their own quarters.

During these two days, they will take you all around the island to hidden coves and beautiful secluded spots. Except for a bloated condominium development at Hamilton Cove near Avalon, the island is nearly as lovely as it was 100 years ago.

You can take a picture of yourself with the white sails billowing and the blue water and rocky coastline in the background. Some day when you are having your gall bladder removed, you will be glad you have that picture. Call Captain Kevin P. Cassady to make a reservation. There is more about Catalina in the February and June chapters.

HALLOWEEN

In my childhood, I foolishly thought that Halloween was a holiday for children. Actually according to Hallmark Cards, one-third of all grown-ups dresses up in a costume and/or goes to a Halloween party. About $65 million is spent by adults on thus returning to childhood. This makes it the third biggest economic celebration in America—behind Christmas and the Super Bowl.

Certainly, the Southland is a melding of all the ingredients for Halloween: strange houses, graveyards, and lurid tales. Here is a sampling of places appropriate for the season:

San Diego

The City of San Diego is noteworthy for having two haunted houses, one of which has even been designated by the State of California as an "Official Haunted House:"

> **Whaley House**
> **2482 San Diego Avenue**
> **San Diego, CA 92110**
> **Wednesday-Sunday 10 a.r.. to 4 p.m.**
> **(619) 298-2482**

Besides the Whaley House, the only other domicile to be so recognized is San Jose's Winchester Mystery House. That house has a bizarre history, but for gruesome beginnings, it's hard to top the story of this landmark of the Old Town of San Diego, located in the vicinity of Conde and Arista Streets.

Before there was a building here, the lot was used for a dark purpose. A sailor who went by the name of Yankee Jim Robinson jumped ship, stole a boat, and was wounded before being caught.

While incarcerated, his wound became infected.

Despite the fact that what he did was not a capital crime, the judge (who was reputed to have been drunk at the time) sentenced Yankee Jim to hang. A makeshift gallows was built on the site of the future Whaley House where they strung him up.

As the wagon pulled away, it was apparent that something was wrong. The hangman's noose was not tied properly and it did not break Jim's neck. Instead, the sailor hung for nearly an hour as he slowly strangled in his fever delirium, screaming curses and twitching madly.

A house was built on this spot in 1857 by a New Yorker named Thomas Whaley and his bride, Anna. He was a real East Coast blue blood. Some of the earliest members of his family fought at the Battle of Hastings. Later, they avoided taxes at the Boston Tea Party.

Whaley's San Diego house would continue to be a place where justice (or miscarriages of justice) took place. The county rented a section of the house in 1869 to store records and actually serve as the County Courthouse.

Around this time, the traditional center of power in San Diego began to shift south to "New Town." The rivalry between the Old and New Towns got so fierce that the location of the courthouse became part of a real conflict: both factions wanted the nucleus of county government to be in their area. The New Town forces were able to obtain an order giving them custody of the courtroom, records, and furniture at the Whaley House.

This was not met with approval by Whaley and other Old Town property owners. They responded by fortifying the house and stationing men with rifles and pistols around the estate. Despite these precautions, the minute Whaley was out of town, the New Town property owners attacked the house at night. They held Whaley's wife and child under armed guard while they took out all of the county records and furniture.

When Whaley returned and found out what had happened, he was overcome by an anger that would consume him for 19 years—until the day he died. His widow remained until she passed on in 1913. The child who had been held at gunpoint by her father's enemies, Lillian Whaley, lived in the house alone after that. She left the house in 1953 and died in 1959, at the age of 89. The Whaley House was opened to the public in 1956.

The building today is a formidable, fully restored, two-story brick mansion with period furniture and all kinds of resident spirits. Psychics claim to have seen the ghost of Yankee Jim hanging in the very spot in the house that corresponds to where he was hanged: the arched doorway between the music room and the parlor.

The stairway is occasionally the setting for the appearance of a man with a mustache in a frock coat who is assumed to be Thomas Whaley. The aroma of his cigar sometimes mysteriously fills the air on the first floor—despite the fact that smoking has been banned in the house for many years. The small spirit of Anna Whaley walking the upstairs hallway in her nightgown has also been noted.

Other phenomena and apparitions include windows opening by themselves, burglar alarms going off for no reason, and the ghosts of a baby, a spotted dog, and a little girl who asks, "Are you my momma?"

Down closer to the harbor is another San Diego haunted house, commonly referred to as "The Spook House:"

> **Villa Montezuma**
> **1925 K Street**
> **San Diego, CA 92102**
> **Friday-Sunday 12 p.m. to 4 p.m.**
> **(619) 239-2211**

With its elaborate Victorian detailing, stained glass, and exotic turrets, the red, three-story Villa Montezuma looks like a haunted house. It was built in 1887 by a celebrated vocalist named Jesse Shepard, whose singing ability was unique to say the least. He could sing any of the roles from every full-length opera in the range called for—from soprano to bass.

He became rich and famous and performed all over the world. While appearing in St. Petersburg, he impressed even the royal family. General Jourafsky, personal medium to the Czar, gave him his first taste of the occult. He went on to study under the famous Helena Blatvatsky.

When the renowned artist announced his desire to settle in the frontier town of San Diego, two local boosters, cattle ranchers John and William High came forward and said they would build him a house. They did this not out of love of the arts, but because they bought up all the land around where the house was to be built.

The singer's presence made the property values go up and the brothers made a small fortune.

According to the *San Diego Sun* of December 17, 1887, it was "the most ornately finished and artistically furnished house in the city." Shepard called it "Villa Montezuma" and started holding performances for the local gentry. It is too bad they did not have video cameras back then, because accounts of his shows are quite fantastic. Called "musical seances," they were a bizarre combination of singing with piano accompaniment and the summoning of spirits.

The singer made sounds and threw his voice in ways that were both entertaining and terrifying. The finale was called "The Grand Egyptian March" and was perhaps the ultimate one-man-show. It was supposed to be a great battle between two mighty armies. Shepard created the sounds of the trumpets, swordfights, and even the roar of cannons.

Despite his successes at parlor performances, the cosmopolitan artist found San Diego too unsophisticated and longed to move to Europe. He sold the house to the president of California National Bank, who had the ironic name of D.D. Dare.

The eminent financier was indicted for embezzling and after his partner killed himself, he left hastily and was never seen again. This was only the first of a series of bad events to befall subsequent inhabitants of Villa Montezuma. Both of the next two owners lost the place in foreclosures.

The last owner suffered even more of a horror film fate. She was a silent film actress named Amelia Jaegger who apparently became possessed by the place. She gradually went crazier and crazier, always talking about enemies out to get her and going so far as to carry a pistol at all times. When in desperation, she sold the house for less than half of what it was worth just to be free of its curse, a judge voided the sale saying she was of "unsound mind."

Though the house is certainly creepy, the spooks here aren't as famous as those at the Whaley House. A servant who hanged himself in the tower now looks out mournfully from its windows. His sobbing or moaning is also sometimes heard. Because in life he was destroyed by the death of his wife, he is an especially unhappy ghost who roams the rooms upstairs.

The restoration by The San Diego Historical Society was very thorough. The downstairs kitchen is a working 19th century throwback. The music room has an antique doll collection. On the second floor, there is a gallery that recounts the long and strange history of the house.

Los Angeles, Hollywood, and Beverly Hills

Beverly Hills is certainly loaded with famous mansions of famous people, but the spookiest house in Beverly Hills is an import from less glamorous Culver City:

Spadena House
516 Walden Drive
[at Carmelita Avenue]
Beverly Hills, CA 90210

Designed by Henry Oliver in 1921, this was the movie set and office of Irvin V. Willst Productions. It is called the witch's house, the Hansel and Gretel house, and the fairy tale house because of its peaked thatched roof and millioned windows. It has been set in an equally original garden.

Right below Yamashiro in Hollywood (see June) is the former Lane House mansion, built in 1925. It is now the world famous:

Magic Castle
7001 Franklin Avenue
Hollywood, CA 90028
(213) 851-3313

Though it was built to look like a Gothic-inspired French chateau, now it looks more like a Transylvanian blood bank. It was a good choice by owners Bill and Milt Larson to be the clubhouse of the Academy of Magical Arts, which it opened as on January 2 of 1963.

The Larson brothers came from a magic family. Their father was a mentalist and a magician, who also happened to be Harry Houdini's lawyer. Their mother was a member of "The Magic Gals," an all woman magician's group in the 1930s.

In addition to being a magician, Milt Larson is also a splendid craftsman and the stained glass windows and woodwork that adorns the place are his handiwork.

All over the Southland, there are cemeteries with famous people buried in them, but none have the aura of:

Hollywood Memorial Park Cemetery
6000 Santa Monica Boulevard
Hollywood, CA 90038
Monday-Friday 8 a.m. to 5 p.m.
Saturday-Sunday 10 a.m. to 3 p.m.
(213) 469-1181

Cemeteries can be lovely and peaceful and this one seems all the more so because its 65 acres of enclosed lawn is in the middle of a dense urban area.

As you might imagine, there are a lot of famous people buried here. The memorial to Douglas Fairbanks, Sr. is the fanciest, Rudolph Valentino is in crypt number 1205 in a wall. Nelson Eddy, Peter Finch, and Tyrone Power all call Hollywood Cemetery home.

The most beautiful memorial in any cemetery is that of Warner Bothers' cartoon voice legend Mel Blanc. On a smooth black stone is the epitaph, "That's All Folks."

If the Hollywood Cemetery roused a curiosity about the morbid in Hollywood, one of the Southland's best and most unusual tours is the:

Grave Line Tours
Daily 12 p.m. (leaves from east side of

Mann's Chinese Theater)
P.O. Box 931694
Hollywood, CA 90093
(213) 469-4149

You won't see any grave sites in this two-hour tour inside a converted hearse, but you will go to about 100 places where some lurid or gruesome moment in Hollywood history took place. These include the cottage in the Chateau Marmont where Belushi died, the house where Bugsy Siegel was gunned down, and the site where George Reeves, TV's "Superman," shot himself.

The ride also includes interesting history and background of Hollywood not commonly known by the average person. The company is owned by Matthew and Glyneth Anderson and Matthew often leads the tours himself.

If you are really serious about knocking them dead this Halloween, try the:

Costume Shop Rental Division
Music Center/Center Theater Group
3301 East 14th Street
Los Angeles, CA 90023
Daily 10 a.m. to 5 p.m.
(213) 267-1230

No neighborhood costume rental place here. It has thousands of costumes which were created for over 20 years of Music Center productions. The Manufacturing Division has also created the costumes for other entities, such as "Star Trek," so the collection includes just about everything you could want.

After a late night of partying (or trick or treating), there is no place quite like:

The Original Pantry Cafe
877 South Figueroa Street
Los Angeles, CA 90017
Daily 24 hours
(213) 972-9279

The Pantry is like the Olympic Torch of L.A. Originally opened in 1924, The Pantry's motto is "never closed, never without a customer." There is often a line outside for a chance to sit and eat at one of the 18 counter seats and 22 tables. It has an old-fashioned cashier's cage that look like a teller's window in a turn-of-the-century bank. Waiters wear black dress shirts and bow ties.

Dinner selections are written on chalkboards so if they run out of something, they can just cross it off. The menu is dominated by steaks and hamburgers.

The clientele is "eclectic" and includes businessmen, people who get off work late, artists, street people, and club patrons getting out in the wee hours. In the early morning hours on the day after Halloween is quite a sight. It is reassuring to note that the place is owned by the Mayor of Los Angeles, Richard Riordan. In his pre-mayor days, he bought the surrounding block and was going to develop it, but he became so fond of The Pantry, he saved it instead.

NOVEMBER

El Dia De Los Muertos
(Mexican Day of The Dead)

Winter in the Desert

Minus Tide Season

Coastal Bird Watching, Wetlands

Bald Eagle Season, Los Padres National Forest

Revolution Day, Russian Southern California

Ski Season

Parade Season

Japan Expo

Holiday Shopping

Chapter Eleven

NOVEMBER

November continues the pattern set in September of being named after a number. It is the month that normally is associated with Thanksgiving, though in Southern California there are other, more noteworthy things to celebrate during this month.

There's something to be said for the second to the last month of the year. It's a real cliffhanger month, the calm before the storm. The month before finals, before the big holidays.

For some reason, beginning this month we start eating a lot of turkey. How anyone ever decided it would be a good idea to shoot one of those godawful birds and eat it is beyond me. Wild turkeys, in particular, are about as visually appealing as vultures and have the dispositions of feathered pit bulls.

In truth, the Puritans were not very good at killing the feisty birds with their clunky muskets and ate a lot more eels than turkey on that celebrated "first" Thanksgiving. Thanksgiving actually did not even become a holiday until 1863, over 240 years after the Puritans munched out.

It was Lincoln who was responsible for creating the formal legal holiday. But the tradition of a thanksgiving after the harvest and a general period of partying around the beginning of winter goes way back to pre-Christian cultures. This is refreshing news to me because not only am I not descended from the Puritans, I don't care for their traditions in general. They closed the theaters when they took over England for a while in the 17th century and are still doing their best to close everything they don't agree with today.

So, because I like the holidays, I just say I'm celebrating on a more basic level and start my season with a truly interesting event.

EL DIA DE LOS MUERTOS (Mexican Day of The Dead)

This two-day celebration begins on November 1st and peaks on All Souls Day, November 2nd, and honors the spirits of the non-living. The tradition goes back to the Aztecs and the Mayans and survived the conversion of Mexico to Catholicism by its European conquerors. Rosaries just became a new addition to the altars people built in their homes.

It is believed that on All Soul's Day, the spirits of departed ones—lovers or relatives—return for a visit. Candles are burned all night to welcome them and flower petals are laid in a path to homes where an altar and an offering of food, called an "ofrenda" is set out.

Dia de los Muertos is sort of an artistic holiday in that Day of the Dead art is a definite form in and of itself. You will see dancing skeletons and other grim but humorous figures.

There has been a lot of talk about a Hispanic museum for Southern California, and though it seems like a rather obvious thing, as of the writing of this book nothing has actually materialized. There are, however, several museums throughout the Southland that normally do some kind of Day of the Dead show at this time of year.

WINTER IN THE DESERT
Golf Cart Parade

November is the month when the cool weather really begins in the Southland. This affects our desert communities very directly as they suddenly come alive after sleeping in the blistering summer sun. There is an annual ritual to celebrate this in a most appropriate fashion:

> **Palm Desert Golf Cart Parade**
> **El Paseo to City Hall**
> **first Sunday of November at 12:30 p.m.**
> **(800) 873-2428**

Normally held on the first Sunday of the month, this is one of the most truly fitting parades in the world. Palm Desert and its surrounding communities derive a great deal of their identities from the clear, comfortable dry winter air, so perfect for retirees or vacationers with money who want to escape bad weather. Add water, and golf courses soon sprang up everywhere. At last count, there were 80 of them.

So, the choice of vehicles for this parade, though intended to be comic, is actually quite poetic in its ritual value. Unlike the floats of the contemporary Rose Parade, these are decorated vehicles, specifically the utilitarian golf cart.

They are bedecked in all kinds of ways, sometimes quite successfully, by their owners. I particularly like the fact that they are all amateurs, so this is very much a "people's parade." Without meaning to be, it is actually politically correct as well: this is possibly the only battery-powered parade in the world.

Palm Desert is also home to a unique museum:

> **Jude E. Poynter Golf Museum**
> **Victor J. LoBue Institute of Golf Management**
> **College of the Desert**

Fred Waring Drive
[between Monterey and San Pablo Avenue]
Palm Desert, CA 92260
Daily 9 a.m. to 5 p.m.
(619) 341-2491

It made me happy to find out that there really is something in the world called the "Institute of Golf Management" and it is certainly appropriate that it is located next to the driving range at the local college. This small one-room museum has clumsy-looking 19th century clubs, photos of tournaments, and antique golf scene prints, as well as such general golf stuff as golf tee molds and balls.

The Golf Museum even has the golf world equivalent of the "Old Masters:" the first Spaulding club made in America (in 1893) and one of six reproductions of Bobby Jones' classic 1926 Calamity Jane putter. The most regal part of the collection, however, is an exhibit of clubs belonging to former President Gerald Ford, which somehow I was expecting to be dented. The surrounding desert area is described in the spring chapters.

Rock Places

The Southern California deserts are all wonderful places to be once summer is really over. Many of the locations I spoke about earlier, in the spring chapters, are also quite nice during the winter—except that it is too early to see any wildflowers. Therefore the places to go in the Southland deserts during the winter are the "rock places," areas whose primary topographic interest comes from the geology of the area. This is because the slanted rays of the lower winter sun create shadows that render jagged rock shapes even more dramatic.

Vasquez Rocks

Probably the most recognizable rock formation in Southern California is:
Vasquez Rocks County Park Natural Area
10700 W. Escondido Canyon Road
Agua Dulce, CA 91350
(805) 268-0840

My dad used to take us here when I was a young boy. Rising to the height of a 15-story building and tilting at crazy-looking 50 degree angles, these contoured slabs of sandstone are among the most spectacular visible results of earthquake faults. The 745-acre park is actually only part of a 20,000-foot thick stratification of sediment that is between 8-15 million years old.

They are very easy to get to. Just take Interstate 5 to the Antelope Valley Freeway (14). Exit on Agua Dulce Canyon Road and proceed north 1-1/2 miles where the road merges with Escondido Canyon Road. Continue 1/4 mile into the park. There are two parking areas: a small one right by the park office and a larger one farther in by the biggest of the rock formations.

Because of their proximity to Hollywood, Vasquez Rocks have been used in the movies ever since the golden age of Westerns. The Cartwrights galloped around here on "Bonanza." Captain Kirk climbed up them in pursuit of the lizard-like Gorn captain in a "Star Trek" episode. Luke Skywalker met Ben Kenobe up there in *Star Wars*.

They have a long history of dramatic usage since Tataviam Indians first lived among them over 20 centuries ago. They were wiped out by the San Fernnado Mission in the 18th century and replaced with outlaws.

The name comes from the dreaded bandito Tiburcio Vasqez, who was a real Mexican Robin Hood, who hid out in the canyons and caves here during the 1850s and 1860s. He had a major shootout with the law here once and escaped, but was captured and hanged shortly thereafter in 1875. Luis Valdez wrote a play about him that premiered in 1994.

What is fun about these rocks is that they look impossible to climb, yet really aren't. It is almost as if nature wanted to build in several easy ways up each formation. The office will supply you with an interpretive brochure and a map of trails. A easy start would be to take the **Geology Trail** from near the parking lot. It will take you to a picnic area and eventually link up with the **Pacific Crest Trail**, which goes by the most remarkable of the rocks.

Joshua Tree National Monument

Joshua Tree National Monument always comes to mind when I think of rock places. The trees look even stranger in the slanted light of winter which also seems to make the area's notable rock configurations look even more prominent.

Rock formations always have great names. Since Joshua Tree has so many of them, it is fitting that there is one called **Wonderland of Rocks** within the monument's territory.

To reach it from the southern part of the East Mojave, go south from the town of Joshua Tree on Park Boulevard for four miles to the entrance to the park; you will drive 10 miles more to Hidden Valley Campground. From here, there is a two mile dirt road to the parking area of Barker Dam.

The **Barker Dam Loop Trail** is an easy 1/2 mile walk to the "lake" of the same name. It really is just a big puddle built for cows to drink out of, created by ranchers William Shay and C.O. Barker around the turn of the century when they built a dam to collect rain water. The cattlemen are long gone, but now local wildlife comes here occasionally for a sip. This includes bighorn sheep. There are interpretive signs all along the trail.

The Wonderland of Rocks you pass through on the way should last for centuries to come—unless they are flattened by an influx of overzealous rock climbers to the area. Though not spectacular in the same way as Yosemite's Half Dome, its 12 square miles of immense heaps of granite offer a great variety of challenges. Choices of rock faces number in the hundreds and there are over 1,000 "established routes" listed in climbing guides to the area.

In order to learn about the region, a pleasant and informative stop is the:

> **High Desert Nature Museum**
> **Community Center Complex**
> **57117 Twentynine Palms Highway**
> **Yucca Valley, CA 92284**
> **Wednesday-Sunday 1 to 5 p.m.**
> **(619) 228-5452**

Yucca Valley is populous (27,000 people) and fairly high in elevation (3,327 feet) and is the jumping off point for many visitors to Joshua Tree. This museum is small, but broad in scope. It could be called "Everything About The High Desert." Started in 1964, it has exhibits on history, flora and fauna, geology, and even art. They have displays of arts and crafts by local artisans and feature an "Artist of The Month."

Joshua trees certainly are unusual looking. It was the Mormons who gave the giant yucca its name because they thought its upward arching branches resembled the prophet Joshua's praying arms upraised to guide them through the desert to the promised land. Hated by some, adored by others, the trees have been torn up by the thousands by developers in other desert areas where they are not protected. Another good place to visit before entering the monument is the:

> **Oasis Visitor Center**
> **Joshua Tree National Monument**
> **74485 National Monument Drive**
> **Twentynine Palms, CA 92277**
> **Daily 8 a.m. to 4:30 p.m.**
> **(619) 367-7511**

It's a good idea to stop here first if you are planning on driving around on the dirt roads of Joshua Tree. The rangers can provide detailed maps and tell you what condition they are in, as well as the usual where-to-go and what-to-see kind of information. They also sell books and pamphlets about the history, geology, and plant and wildlife of the area. Joshua Tree covers 870 square miles and is 90 percent wilderness.

There is a pleasant walk of about 1/2 mile along a self-guided trail that loops around to finish where it started just west of the visitor's center. It takes you past the **Oasis of Mara.**

For a place to stay that has real desert charm, check in at the:

K-B Ranchotel
6048 Noels Knoll Road
Twentynine Palms, CA 92277
(619) 367-3353

This is one of two former homesteads turned bed and breakfast in the Twentynine Palms area. It is a big adobe built in 1935 with no less than six fireplaces along with the original furnishings. There are only two guest rooms, but each one has one of the fireplaces as well as its own bathroom.

The grounds cover a full five acres and feature two cactus gardens. There is a sundeck and a pretty courtyard with a fish pond surrounded by a wall. Continental breakfast and an afternoon snack is included in the low rate (approximately $55 per night for two).

There really is a landmark called "Noel's Knoll," by the way.

Another desert inn in Twentynine Palms is the:

Tower Homestead Bed and Breakfast
Amboy and Mojave Roads
P.O. Box C141
Twentynine Palms, CA 92277
(619) 367-7936

This property was originally a 160-acre homestead, hence the name. The house was built in Pasadena in 1892 and was dismantled and rebuilt on its present site in 1932.

East Mojave

The East Mojave is like a giant triangle formed by Interstates 15 on the top and 40 on the bottom and the California-Nevada border on the east.

Barstow is sometimes called the gateway to the East Mojave. It was founded in 1886 as a rail junction town that would be a hub between Central and Southern California. It is still a diesel repair station and freight classification site for the Santa Fe Railway. On the east side of town, off Highway 247, is a giant McDonald's made from old train cars.

You can get a feeling for the history of the region at the:

Mojave River Valley Museum
270 Virginia Way
[corner of Barstow Road]
Barstow, CA 92311
Thursday-Monday 11 a.m. to 4 p.m.
(619) 256-5452

This little museum has a bit of everything. Started in 1964 by the good citizens of the area, it is exactly what its name denotes. There are local rocks and minerals, including turquoise, archeological artifacts such as arrowheads, local animal taxidermy and dried and preserved wildflowers. Barstow city history is represented in the form of photographs of the city fathers, an old railroad car, and some very small looking jail cells. There is a park with picnic tables across the street.

If you want to get a taste of Barstow today, go for dinner at the:

Idle Spurs Steak House
29557 Highway 58W
Barstow, CA 92311
Monday-Thursday 11 a.m. to 9:30 p.m.
Friday 11 a.m. to 10:30 p.m.
Saturday 5 to 10:30 p.m. , Sunday 5 to 9 p.m.
(619) 256-8888

This has been an institution for a long time in Barstow. If you are nostalgic for a 1950's California-as-the-West sort of feeling, this is a real landmark.

The Idle Spurs is very large and it is that rare place favored by locals and tourists alike. The menu is what you would expect. It has two dining rooms and a dance floor, where (what a surprise) country western dancing is the norm.

A good stop before visiting the East Mojave is the:

California Desert Information Center
831 Barstow Road
Barstow, CA 92311
Daily 9 a.m. to 5 p.m.
(619) 256-8313

This small center offers some nature exhibits along with maps and information about camping, desert attractions, and road conditions.

Besides its spring wildflower display (see April), the East Mojave offers some wonderful geological formations. The first and easiest to get to is **Rainbow Basin National Natural Landmark**. It is 10 miles north of Barstow.

To get there from SR 58 in Barstow, go about 5-1/2 miles north on Fort Irwin Road until it hits Fossil Bed Road. This is an aptly named road about three miles long that takes you to the landmark. It is aptly named, because that is exactly what the landmark is.

Fifteen million years ago this was a lake and grassland that supported a large animal population. There were three-toed horses, mastodons, and even saber-toothed tigers, rhinoceros, and camels! Clearly visible to the naked eye, the fossil remains are preserved in the sedimentary rock that was once the bottom of the lake.

Like nearly every other rock or mountain place in California, the geological activity (earthquakes) that is the trademark of the state has left its mark here. The former lake bed has been lifted and folded into dramatically contoured, green, red, and brown hued hills. The coloration is primarily due to the fact that iron oxidizes at different rates depending on what else is present, thus creating a "rainbow."

There is a three mile looped dirt road at the end of Fossil Bed Road called **Rainbow Basin Loop Road** that is the official "Scenic Drive." It is quite narrow—too narrow for RVs—and the rocks tower above you like a thrill ride at Disneyland.

The mysteries of the past, as preserved in archaeological sites, has always had a certain romance to it, a romance that was heightened by the movie presence of Indiana Jones. Not too far from here is one of the few places is the United States where the average person can witness what archaeological work is really like close up:

> **Calico Early Man Archaeological Site**
> **P.O. Box 535**
> **Yermo, CA 92398**
> **(619) 256-3591**

This discovery stunned the archaeological world in 1962 because artifacts uncovered here have been dated at 200,000 years old. Previously, the first humans were thought to have existed around 20,000 years ago. The authenticity of the find has been disputed since day one by some archaeologists and anthropologists.

Regardless of the controversy, this was still the only place in North America where the most famous archaeologist of my lifetime, Dr. Louis Leakey, ever set up shop. The National Geographic supplied a big grant and Leakey worked here from 1963 until 1972, the year he died.

Studying the methods used here may debunk any notion you may have had of discovering a secret passage or key to a tomb as the principal activities of the archaeologist. Actually, it is extremely monotonous work. Once the dig sites were decided upon, the process of slowly, carefully, digging one square foot, three inches at a time with little hand tools began.

Going down 26 feet this way has produced 11,400 artifacts, but no human bones. There are lots of these man-made objects on display in the visitor's center.

The area around the East Mojave is almost like going to a unique state within the State of California. It even has its own "Grand Canyon:"

> **Afton Canyon**
> **Afton turnoff from I-15**
> **approximately 33 miles east of Baker**
> **go up three mile gravel road**
> **park in campground parking lot**

Like the Grand Canyon, the 600-foot high granite walls of Afton Canyon were cut by a river, in this case, the Mojave. Though it is considerably smaller than it once was, the river still flows year round. Because of this, the narrow, eight-mile long gorge has a lush riparian ecosystem complete with cottonwoods and willows with large areas of tall waving grasses.

There is also a considerable amount of wildlife that call the canyon home. These include stream-dwelling birds such as egrets, herons, and ibis. Creatures close to the ground include mud turtles, minnows, and frogs. Occasionally bighorn sheep come down from their mountain domain for a drink in the river.

There are numerous side canyons adjoining Afton Canyon. The largest and deepest of these is **Pyramid Canyon.** About two miles long, it has some of the most interesting rock formations in the area.

Of all of the offramps that have puzzled freeway drivers on their way to Las Vegas on the I-15, none have inspired more speculation than **Zzyzx Road,** located about 60 miles past Barstow, about six miles before you hit Baker.

The place it leads to, Soda Springs, has a fascinating history that dates back 10,000 years to the Pleistocene Period. This is probably because it is one of the few places in the East Mojave where fresh water flows above ground throughout the year.

The bed of Soda Dry Lake, which surrounds the springs area, has a sparkle to it from the mineral deposits left by the water. As early as 1871, it was being written about as a place for therapeutic baths. These stories would attract its most famous resident.

There are tales about all oases, but none more purely Southern Californian than that of the "old time medicine man" who for 30 years made Soda Springs his dream-come-true in the desert.

In 1944, Dr. Curtis Springer came here with his wife Helen and they built a resort called the "Zzyzx Mineral Springs and Health Resort." Offering a mixture of religion and folk medicine, Springer started the Zzyzx Community Church, which grew into a daily radio show broadcast from the complex's own radio station.

There were indoor baths and a giant cross-shaped swimming pool.

Never one for understatement, the good doctor called the 60 room hotel "The Castle" and the main road in the compound "The Boulevard of Dreams." He attracted lots of people and did not charge any fee for cures. Donations were, of course, welcome.

This was summarized by the sign over the contribution box by the exit: "Freely you have received, as God makes possible, Freely Give." They did—to the tune of up to three-quarters of a million dollars a year during the heyday of the place. The lucrative nature of faith brought the attention of the IRS, who charged him with income tax evasion. Springer was evicted in 1974.

The former place of spiritual and financial healing is now the Desert Studies Center of the California State University.

One of the most appropriately named roads in Southern California is **Kelbaker Road**. This is because it runs from the town of Baker on the I-15 through Kelso to the I-40 and on to **National Trails Highway**, or as it is better known, Route 66. On the way, it goes past some remarkable geological formations. It is paved most of the way and rises as high as 4,024 feet when it passes through Granite Pass.

Mojave Cinder Cones Natural Landmark is a 25,600-acre expanse, the centerpiece of which is a formation made up of 32 extinct volcanos in the shape of traffic cones. If you are wondering how so many could have gone off so close together, it is because it happened over an enormous amount of time. The first one happened 10,000,000 years ago, the most recent one around the year 900.

If you were interested in taking some time to really explore the East Mojave, you could camp, stay in Barstow, or check into the:

Hotel Nipton
HC1

P.O. Box 357
Nipton, CA 92364
(619) 856-2335

The Hotel Nipton was built in 1905 in response to the growing needs of the little railroad town as a cattle loading station for the Los Angeles and Salt Lake Line (which would later become the Union Pacific). It is only three miles from the California-Nevada border.

It has four rooms to rent, the most famous of which is the **Clara Bow**

Room. She and her husband Rex Bow were frequent guests during the 1930s. The **Harry Treherne Room** was named after the very first homesteader, the "Father of Nipton," who was a miner from England. Two other rooms have equally obscure names: one the **Senator William Clark Room**, named after a Senator from Wyoming, and the **Isaac Blake Room**, named after a local railroad entrepreneur.

Close to Nipton is **Cima Dome.** Just take I-15 (back towards Los Angeles) and turn left on Cima Road. The dome was formed by molten granite, called monzonite, into a huge pile—over 75 square miles. For thousands of years, it has been eroding until now it is an almost perfectly symmetrical, 10 mile diameter dome—the most symmetrical natural dome in the U.S. It is so big and so proportionally balanced, you can't really see what it is unless you are at a distance.

But up close, the attraction is the world's largest Joshua tree forest. You will see the sign containing directions to the forest, which is an easy two mile walk up **Teutonia Peak Trail.** You pass through the forest at an elevation of about 4,000 feet on your way to the 5,755-foot summit.

The Joshuas here are large and ancient and more densely packed together than in other places. Some of them are hundreds of years old and nearly as tall as three-story buildings.

It starts getting to be a bit of a climb once you get past the forest. After you reach the lookout point, you must pick your way up over about 1/4 mile of giant boulders to reach the pinnacle.

Cima Road continues south as Kelso-Cima Road to the town of Kelso (and the Kelso Dunes (see April). From here, you can continue going south on Kelbaker Road until you hit Interstate 40. From there, if you keep going, you will come to National Trails Highway (Route 66) just east of the town of Amboy.

The stretch of **Old Route 66** between Amboy and Essex is like an outdoor desert museum of the pre-freeway past. There are hulks of abandoned automobiles from a wide spectrum of model-years and boarded up cafes, diners, and gas stations where the ghosts of all those whose hopes and aspirations brought them through the desert to California still wait for a new generation of dreamers. For more about Route 66, see September.

An easy walk off Old Route 66 is to **Amboy Crater.** If you have ever been to the southern part of the big island of Hawaii, you will recognize the spooky volcanic terrain near the crater. The black basalt thrown out by the volcano's flare-ups coats the landscape in eerie desolation. Of course, the most spectacular cave formation in outhern California is also in the East Mojave, the **Mitchell Caverns.** They were named for prospector Jack Mitchell and his wife, Ida, who literally homesteaded them.

To get there, take Essex Road from the town of the same name. It runs northwest across I-40 to the **Providence Mountains State Recreation Area,** where the caverns are located.

If you saw Oliver Stone's film *The Doors,* the hallucination sequence in the cave with the Indian spirit was filmed here.

Once you are inside, you will understand why. Most of the formations found in the more famous caves are well represented. They all have names: cave ribbons, shields, and spaghetti, flowstone, and the more familiar stalagmites and stalactites loom out of the cool damp air. It is 65 degrees in here year round.

The caves are very old, hundreds of millions of years. They actually had their beginning when the ocean covered the area. The limestone was the bottom of that ocean. It was lifted by geological activity until it was above water.

A rainforest gradually developed until by 10-20 million years ago, it was full and lush. The thick carpet of decomposed plant life at the floor of the forest gave off carbon dioxide—which acidified the runoff. It was this primeval acid rain runoff that seeped into the cracks in the limestone and eventually made the caves.

When the weather became dryer, the water emptied from the caves. By this point, the rainwater runoff was heavy with mineral content. The slow drip, drip, drip of this water, leaving minute particles of calcite, made the cave formations.

On the way in on Essex Road, you passed a dirt road on your right called Black Canyon Road. Follow it for 8-1/2 miles and you will come to **Hole-in-the-Wall Campground**. Whether you are camping or not, you are in for a treat here.

As you move west of the campground, there is an alien landscape of volcanic rocks that have formed into winding passages and strange canyons. Follow the trail from the picnic area and you will come to Banshee Canyon, which is entered by climbing. It isn't very hard though, because set into the rocks are two sets of heavy iron rings. The Southern Calironia deserts are covered extensively in the spring chapters.

MINUS TIDE SEASON

From November through March, tides will be lower than they are at any other time of the year. This allows for explorations of a feature of the Southern California coastline unnoticed by most people: **tidepools**.

Tidepools are fascinating and beautiful little living galleries of nature. Many of the Southland's most exquisite tidepools are best seen during selected extremely low tides (called minus tides) that occur only during the winter months. It can make for a lovely little coastal expedition in the clear November air. A tide table and good shoes are all you need.

San Diego

San Diego is an amazing harbor with a weird mixture of man-made and beautiful natural topography surrounding it. Being on Point Loma is one of the best ways to appreciate this.

In the September chapter I mentioned the **Bayside Trail** and the tidepools near the lighthouse. On the harbor side of the peninsula is the mud fill that is now Shelter Island with its marinas, restaurants, and hotels. To see the natural side, drive up Point Loma from the Cabrillo Monument and make a left on Hill Street to head toward the ocean side, **Sunset Cliffs**.

This area reminds me of the Palos Verdes Peninsula in L.A. county with its rocky beauty and winding roads. With all of the hotel space in San Diego, one of the most obscure and modest of places is right here in this unique locale:

> **Ocean Manor Hotel**
> **1370 Sunset Cliffs Boulevard**
> **San Diego, CA 92107**
> **(619) 222-7901**

Though quite unpretentious, what this two-story apartment hotel has is possibly the most romantic location in San Diego. Though you might not find its white exterior and 25 nondescript rooms to be overwhelming, it is perched dramatically on the oceanfront cliffs in an otherwise residential neighborhood.

There are some great tidepools near here at Hill Street. There are two paths, both somewhat steep. The one just north of Hill Street is better than the one directly at the end of it. Don't be put off by the large boulders you must climb over at the end of both paths; just be careful. Because of the low wave action here, you will be able to see quite a variety of life in the crevasses and pools of the area.

La Jolla

Besides Sunset Cliffs, the San Diego area has other tidepool spots in La Jolla. You can learn all about tidepools at a very famous research center located here:

> **Stephen Birch Aquarium-Museum**
> **Scripps Institute of Oceanography**
> **2300 Expedition Way**
> **La Jolla, CA 92093**
> **Daily 9 a.m. to 5 p.m.**
> **(619) 534-FISH**

Scripps Institute began in 1903 with the establishment of the Marine Biological Association of San Diego. The University of California San Diego absorbed the fledgling institute in 1912. It became the first college to award doctorates in oceanography.

In 1916, Ellen Browning Scripps established an endowment fund that would be the basis for what would become the oldest and largest marine research institution in the world. The original pier where experiments were run was replaced in 1988 by a new one, which is officially called the "Ellen Browning Scripps Memorial Pier."

In 1950, they built Scripps Aquarium, which was succeeded in September of

1992 by this spectacular 49,400-square-foot center. It is divided into the museum on one side and the aquarium on the other. What makes this facility different from other marine theme parks or aquariums is that it is an interpretive center for projects that have been underway at the institute for decades.

The aquarium is simply wonderful. There is a tank that recreates a San Diego kelp bed. It is two-stories tall and holds 70,000 gallons of seawater. From a four-tiered seating structure, you can gaze upon the network of life through a 10-inch thick viewing window. The kelp forest soars 20 feet overhead as about 100 local fish swim about. These include kelp bass, yellowtail, and beautiful orange garibaldis.

There are a total of more than 3,000 animals at the aquarium and it costs about $60,000 per year just to feed them. These are divided into different areas according to region. You walk in past a tank of anchovies and sardines into the section of Northwest Coast sealife. From there, you go on to explore the warmer water of Southern California, Mexico, and even the exotic waters of Fiji.

Right next to the kelp forest is an interactive video alcove.

At the other end of the facility is the museum. The first exhibit is the Blue Planet Theater. Perhaps the most unique interactive demonstration is "Deep Diver," which simulates a dive to 3,780 feet below the surface.

In the plaza in back overlooking the pier and Pacific Ocean, there is an artificial tidepool that simulates the La Jolla coastal environment. By the main entrance, there is a bookstore with shelves full of ocean- and environmentally-oriented books and gifts.

Another wonder of La Jolla is its seven natural caves. The land entrance to the largest of them is through the:

> **La Jolla Cave and Shell Shop**
> **1325 Coast Boulevard**
> **La Jolla, CA 92038**
> **Monday-Saturday 10 a.m. to 5 p.m.**
> **Sunday 11 a.m. to 5 p.m.**
> **(619) 454-6080**

This great old store is filled to bursting with shells and other objects from the sea, as well as crystals, fossils, and nautical items.

There is an admission fee to enter the **Sunny Jim Cave** through a dark, narrow, man-made tunnel that has no fewer than 133 steps.

Across the street is the pleasant:

La Jolla Cove Motel
1155 Coast Boulevard
La Jolla, CA 92037
(619) 459-2621
(800) 248-COVE

This is the last moderately-priced, yet truly enjoyable places to stay in La Jolla. It is still owned and operated by the family that opened it 30 years ago.

The La Jolla Cove Motel has 120 rooms—almost all of them ocean view—that are spread out over four buildings. The two largest of these are the six-story annex and the original five-story main building. They are not luxurious, but they are nonetheless pretty. The terrace section is more lavish. The rooftop solarium in the main building, where continental breakfast is served, is one of the nicest spots in La Jolla. There is more about La Jolla in the February and July chapters.

Laguna Beach

A great place for a romantic getaway, that is also ideal for getting the most out of winter's extra low tides, is the:

Surf and Sand Hotel
1555 South Coast Highway
Laguna Beach, CA 92651
(714) 497-4477
(800) 524-8621

This hotel has been redecorated many times throughout its 40-year history, but never with the understated elegance achieved in the 1991 makeover by noted designer James Northcutt, who also did the Hotel Bel Air. The structure of the building, one of the largest in Laguna with its 160 rooms, is nondescript, but its location is quite unique.

This could almost be called a "tidepool hotel" because the beach it is located on isn't a people-watching or a sunning beach; it is a beach marked with rocky inlets teeming with life. All of the rooms face the ocean and have balconies. The hotel lights the beach at night so you can go for an evening stroll or sit on your balcony and listen to the surf.

The hotel has two restaurants, the casual **Splashes** and **The Towers**, Laguna Beach's most prestigious restaurant. There is more about Laguna Beach in the February and July chapters.

Palos Verdes Peninsula

Aside from the historic lighthouses and great views of the coast, the Palos Verdes Peninsula is also the home of some of the best tidepool viewing in the four coastal counties.

There are numerous tidepool areas all around the peninsula starting at Malaga Cove and Flat Rock Point at the top and finishing at Cabrillo State Beach at the bottom. What is remarkable about the Palos Verdes Peninsula is that during low tides you can walk around much of its perimeter, encountering alternating romantic coves and hidden beaches along with several distinctly different tidepool areas. There are generally fewer people by the seashore in winter.

You could begin this walk at the Point Vicente Interpretive Center (see December). There is a long gentle path from the north end of the parking lot to the cove south of Point Vicente. Be careful crossing the rocks to the tidepools here.

As you go up around the peninsula, the next tidepools you will encounter are at **Resort Point**. These are rarely visited and are rich in life, but the next area, **Lunada Bay**, named for its resemblance to a half-moon, is more popular because of its rugged beauty. **Flat Rock Point**, where you end up, is a less traveled coastal spot. This area has tidepools enclosed by slick boulders, so walk carefully. In all tidepool areas, it's important *not* to pick anything up.

If you wanted to have lunch or get some pasta salad or hot food for a picnic, Lunada Bay is the home of the excellent:

> **Viva La Pasta**
> **2325 Palos Verdes Drive West**
> **Palos Verdes Estates, CA 90274**
> **Monday-Thursday 11:30 a.m. to 9:30 p.m.**
> **Friday-Saturday 11:30 a.m. to 10 p.m.**
> **Sunday 10 a.m. to 9 p.m.**
> **(310) 541-0920**

This cheerful trattoria has over 200 combinations of delicious and inexpensive pastas and sauces. They are open seven days a week and have a Sunday brunch from 10 a.m. to 2 p.m. Portions are large, so come hungry.

Just past Point Fermin going around the Palos Verdes Peninsula is **White Point**. Just south of where Western connects with Paseo del Mar is a little street called Kay Fiorentino Drive. Take it to the pay parking lot at the end.

The little path from here takes you past the ruins of an old Japanese hotel, called The White Point Hot Springs Hotel (see January). Incidentally, the tidepools here are noted for their biological richness. Do not stay near the hot springs because marine creatures do not exist too close to them. Further out, however, are flat rocks with gaping crevices filled with beautifully colored life.

There is a second cove at White Point a bit further south that must be reached from a separate entrance. Just a short way on Paseo del Mar past where you turned down Kay Fiorentino, there is a small parking lot with its own path to this southern cove. It is worth the trip because the pools here can be simply incredible.

COASTAL BIRD WATCHING: WETLANDS

Besides minus tide season beginning this month, November is also the primary month of coastal migratory bird season.

Birds do not really "fill the skies." Just as the fishes in the oceans tend to occupy certain areas in high density, but are virtually non-existent in others, so it is with birds. A "flyway" is sort of a bird highway of the air, a route used by many different species in their migrations. Birds do not migrate south for the winter randomly, but rather move along a particular band of territory.

The **Pacific Flyway**, which crosses the Southland, extends from Canada to South America. It is one of the most important "bird freeways" in the world.

This partially accounts for one of the most surprising statistics about the Southland: San Diego is the number one county in the nation in terms of rare species sighted. L.A. is second, with about 450. This is also attributed to the fact that there are a large number of different kinds of habitats, ranging from sea level to mountain terrain.

This is one of the many reasons why coastal wetlands or estuaries are so important. Wetlands can be dry part of the year, yet be critical components of a giant web of life during the months that they are, in fact, wet. They are zones of interaction between runoff from the land to the sea and thus affect flood control. Many fish spawn in them. Mud flats that look relatively lifeless can contain life-essential worms, clams, and other marine creatures vital to the food chain. To birds in their annual pilgrimages, these are vital stops on the road—sort of like giant truck stops.

They are jewels on the overdeveloped Southern California coast, where 95 percent of the wetlands have been turned into condos, fast food restaurants, and the like. The ones that remain offer walking trails and an easy way to have a delightful interface with nature. Take some binoculars, a camera, and, if you want to get serious, a guide to wildlife or migrating birds.

San Diego

Starting at the southern end of the coast, just 1-1/2 miles from the border is the:

Tijuana River National Estuarine Research Reserve
301 Caspian Way
Imperial Beach, CA 91932
(619) 575-3613
(619) 575-2704

Imperial Beach gets lots of visitors during the summer for the United States Open Sandcastle Building Contest (see July), but it seems a lot fewer people venture a little farther south of this area. It's too bad, because not only does it have its surprises, seeing the locality first hand would help people understand some of the environmental issues raised by economic and population growth in Mexico—particularly along the border.

To get to the reserve, get off I-5 on Palm Avenue and take it west 2-1/2 miles. When you get to Third Street, turn left and go 1/2 mile and you will come to the visitor center parking lot.

The visitor's center has some interpretive exhibits about how a marshland functions biologically. They also have a nice brochure that tells you about some of the 170 species of migratory and native birds as well as the flora of the reserve. It is called *A Walker's Guide: The Natural History of the Tijuana National Estuarine Reserve*. There are guided nature walks on Saturday mornings and Thursday afternoons.

Trails begin at the visitor's center and meander through the reserve to the mouth of the Tijuana River. The mud flats are interspaced with little hills with coastal scrub growing on them. It may not be stunningly beautiful like a mountain meadow, but snowy egrets, brown pelicans, and marsh hawks like it just fine.

The danger posed by the lack of environmental controls in Mexico is painfully displayed at times here. As unbelievable as it may seem, sometimes the City of Tijuana, whose population has soared in recent years, dumps sewage right into the Tijuana River. This not only puts sewage into the Mexican vicinity, it deposits it into the estuary where it affects the migrating birds. It only makes the headlines, however, when it occasionally flows onto Imperial Beach and even up to Silver Strand State Beach.

A little farther north, in Chula Vista, is another one of the few remaining salt marsh habitats on the Pacific Coast:

Chula Vista Nature Interpretive Center
100 Gunpowder Pointe Drive
Chula Vista, CA 91910
Tuesday-Sunday 10 a.m. to 5 p.m.
Salt water tank feeding times 10:30 a.m. & 4 p.m.
(619) 422-2481

On the shore of San Diego Bay, about seven miles south of Downtown San Diego and seven miles north of the U.S./ Mexican border, are a group of salt marshes that make up the estuary of the Sweetwater River. They have been protected as the **Sweetwater Marsh National Wildlife Refuge**.

The centerpiece of the refuge, the Chula Vista Nature Center, is a large $2.5 million structure that includes exhibits that take you on an instructional tour of the various environmental zones of the area. If you have ever had the urge to feed or touch a leopard shark or bat ray, they have a 4,500 gallon salt water tank where this is encouraged. There are two observation platforms where more than 200 species of birds can be surveyed.

About four blocks away is a waterfront restaurant:

Jake's South Bay
570 Marina Parkway
Chula Vista, CA 91910
Monday-Thursday 11:15 a.m. to 9:30 p.m.
Friday-Saturday 11:15 a.m. to 10 p.m.
Sunday 10 a.m. 9:30 p.m.
(619) 476-0400

The view of the sailboats from Chula Vista Marina gliding on the blue water of the bay makes a table on the enclosed patio here a wonderful daytime dining experience even in the cooler air of November. If you like the outdoors, the bar side of the patio is open air.

The inside feels like a 19th century explorer's club. There is a kayak mounted over the bar along with old photos of various seagoing activities. Patterned after a turn-of-the-century boat-house, it has shiny brass fittings on heavy oak and mahogany panels.

Jake's is part of a small chain called T.S. Restaurants that also owns Kimo's on the island of Maui. Friendly manager Brian McCarver has been making people feel welcome since the place opened in '89. Popular for happy hour as well as for dinner, it has excellent fresh grilled fish and steaks daily. They also have an all-you-can-eat Champagne Sunday brunch from 10 a.m. to 2:30 p.m. that would round out a visit to the nature center.

Jake's South Bay at the Chula Vista Marina.

Newport Beach Back Bay

Continuing up the coast, Orange County has a large coastal reserve:

Upper Newport Bay Ecological Reserve
Back Bay
East Bluff Drive and Back Bay Drive
Newport Beach
[enter on Back Bay Drive off Jamboree Road]
contact:
Friends of Upper Newport Bay
P.O. Box 2001
Newport Beach, CA 92663
(714) 646-8009

This is the largest estuary in the Southland. The reserve was officially established in 1975 when environmentalists successfully pressured the state to buy 752 acres of marshland otherwise slated for destruction by the Irvine Company. Though this seems like a lot of territory, it is actually less than five percent of the original wetland area, which once went all the way inland to Tustin.

It was called "Bolsa de Quigara" ("the bay with high banks") by Portola's expedition in 1769. You will see why immediately, as you drive in past sandstone hills and steep limestone bluffs. It is a hidden world enclosed by steel and glass towers, suburban homes, and roaring freeways.

Back Bay Trail follows Back Bay Drive along the east shore for a little less than two miles. The other side offers numerous dirt paths and a bike trail. The latter passes over a very rustic looking wood bridge constructed of heavy timber.

From this bridge, you get a view that will help you appreciate the complexity of life in this estuary: you can clearly see three distinct tiers of different vegetation. There are a total of eight marine terrace levels in the reserve. The west shore offers some of the best views of the overall network of channels and little islands. Other views can be had from public parks outside the reserve on adjacent hills. These include Westcliff, East Bluff and Galaxy Parks.

Upper Newport Bay Ecological Reserve is a major spawning site for fish: at least 100 species visit these shallow waters on a regular basis. This includes halibut, anchovies, and California killifish. The shores are lined with cattails and reeds, occasionally livened by the sight of a mule deer, racoon, or coyote. Over 160 species of birds stop here on their migration. You will see ducks, egrets, herons, sandpipers, and endangered species such as the light footed clapper rail (which you can hear) and Belding's savannah sparrow. The latter plump little white-breasted bird is one of the few creatures on Earth able to drink sea water.

Right near here is a terrific place to grab a bite:

> **The Crab Cooker**
> **2200 Newport Boulevard**
> **Newport Beach, CA 92663**
> **10 a.m. to 10 p.m. (fish market)**
> **11 a.m. to 10 p.m. (restaurant)**
> **(714) 673-0100**

This bright red restaurant and fish market actually prides itself on the fact that there is a line everyone must wait in. The seafood is charcoal broiled, served on paper plates, and delicious. The clam chowder takes the chill off a few hours of walking around the back bay in the cool November air. There is more about Newport Beach in the July and December chapters.

Huntington Beach

A little farther up the coast in Orange County is another wetlands place to watch for migratory birds:

> **Bolsa Chica Ecological Reserve**
> **Main Entrance on Pacific Coast Highway**
> **[one mile south of Warner Avenue]**
> **Huntington Beach**

Bolsa Chica means "little pocket" and this 530-acre reserve is a pocket of life between Pacific Coast Highway and suburbia. The entrance has a secret quality to it that enhances the experience: you walk from the parking lot over a long wooden bridge that spans broad shallow stretches of tide water.

This is a wonderful place to have a great cool air walk and look for wildlife. Over 200 species of birds winter here from about the end of October through March.

Because the developers have been particularly outrageous in their disregard for this particular stretch of coast, there is a fairly organized resistance to the destruction of Bolsa Chica. The friends welcome any interest or help and also offer tours the first Saturday of each month:

> **The Amigos**
> **5811 Mc Fadden Avenue**
> **Huntington Beach, CA 92649**
> **Monday-Friday 10 a.m. to 4 p.m.**
> **(714) 897-7003**

There is more about Huntington Beach in the July and December chapters.

Santa Barbara

Though it does not have a wetlands, Santa Barbara does have a nice place to observe winter birds:

> **Andree Clark Bird Sanctuary**
> **1400 East Cabrillo Boulevard**
> **Santa Barbara, CA 93108**
> **located just west of the Cabillo Boulevard exit**
> **off the 101 freeway**
> **open during daylight hours**
> **park on the north side**

This pretty lagoon is not an estuary, but it is a refuge for freshwater birds. It is surrounded by a garden and has a bike trail and a footpath that circle the water.

It is a lovely, tranquil spot, whose desirability as a destination is heightened by the fact that it is the only bird sanctuary in Southern California that has a restaurant directly overlooking it:

Crossroads Cafe
50 Los Patos Way
Santa Barbara, CA 93108
Daily 11:30 a.m. to 2:30 p.m. (lunch)
Daily 5:30 p.m. to 10 p.m. (dinner)
(805) 969-6705

It is the bar here that has the exceptional view. Jovial bartender Troy Richardson will welcome you into a greenhouse-like setting that is as inviting as any you could find. Even the ceiling is glass and the view is delightful. The room's sunken design and chairs create a relaxed enough mood to let you stretch out. The bar top is of varnished oak and the wall opposite the reserve-fronting glass has a rock fireplace.

The restaurant seats 85 and features chops, chicken, rack of lamb, and the like. It is very cozy with dark wood chairs upholstered in forest green leather, green carpeting, mahogany trim, padded walls, and plush comfortable booths.

Very near here is the prettiest zoo you've ever seen:

Santa Barbara Zoological Gardens
500 Ninos Drive
Santa Barbara, CA 93103
Daily 10 a.m. to 5 p.m.
Daily 9 a.m. to 6 p.m. (summer)
(805) 962-6310 (recording)
(805) 962-5339

The Santa Barbara Zoological Gardens sits on property that was formerly an estate. It has a miniature train that offers an overall look at the zoo, a coastal view, and even a nice vantage

Just a short walk from the zoological garden is an unusual bed-and-breakfast:

Old Yacht Club Bed and Breakfast Inn
431 Corona del Mar
Santa Barbara, CA 93103
(805) 962-1277

Though there are plenty of Victorian-style B & Bs in the Southland, this one is all California. The Old Yacht Club consists of two houses, a Craftsman built in 1912 and a Mission Revival built in 1925. Both are furnished with antiques and oriental rugs. There are a total of nine rooms, each of which has its own private bath. A full breakfast served in the dining room is included. Because it is only a half block from the beach, towels, beach chairs, and bicycles are also provided for the use of guests.

BALD EAGLE SEASON, LOS PADRES NATIONAL FOREST

Besides the Clark Bird Sanctuary, there is another, perhaps more dramatic place to watch for migratory birds—of a particular kind—in Santa Barbara: the majestic Bald Eagle.

One of the most ironic uses of zoological nomenclature is the word "raptor," which refers to a bird of prey. It is ironic because it comes from the same root as rapist, yet in most raptor species the female is larger than the male. One of the largest raptors in the state is *Haliaeetus leucocephalus,* better known as the Southern Bald Eagle. This month begins the season to watch for them on their winter vacation in the Southland:

> **Eagle Watch Trips**
> **Lake Cachuma**
> **Santa Barbara**
> **tours run Friday-Sunday, November-May**
> contact:
> **Eagle Tours**
> **Santa Barbara Country Parks Department**
> **610 Mission Canyon Road**
> **Santa Barbara, CA 93105**
> **(805) 568-2460**

During the winter, lakes and streams are iced over in Alaska, British Columbia, and even as far south as Oregon and Northern California. Their food source being cut off, hundreds of Bald and Golden Eagles spend their winters at Central and Southern California lakes such as Lake San Antonio in Monterey County and here in Santa Barbara County at Lake Cachuma.

The eagles are not very hard to spot. They like to perch on the tops of trees around the lake to watch for fish and smaller birds to have for dinner. They are large: a wingspan of 78 to 98 inches and a length of 30 to 40 inches. Young Bald Eagles are brownish black with gray wing linings. Teenage eagles molt with patches of white body feathers showing. This eagle version of acne is called the "pinto" look. The familiar white head and tail—along with the menacing yellow hooked bill and talons—are achieved by about age four or five. The talons are one way of distinguishing a Bald from a Golden: talons look larger on the Bald Eagle because the Golden Eagle is feathered all the way to its feet.

Besides Lake Cachuma, there is another lake in this part of Santa Barbara County: **Zaca Lake**. It is a pleasant fall destination because it does not suffer so much in the dry season as rain-fed lakes since it is supplied by underground streams.

One of the few natural lakes in Southern California, it is one of the best unknown escapes in Southern California. Zaca Lake is so small, it is not on most maps. It is often overshadowed by its larger neighbor Lake Cachuma. Unlike Lake Cachuma, it is not a recreational lake. Zaca Lake is the picture of tranquility most people identify with the hidden lake retreat.

If you have ever shaken your head as a rabidly grinning jet skier roared past you, spewing noise and stink, and leaving a tidal wave-like wake in an otherwise enjoyable setting, you will particularly appreciate this area. It is very quiet: the only boats available are row and paddle boats.

There are campgrounds, but there is also an inexpensive place to stay:

> **Zaca Lake Resort**
> **P.O. Box 187**
> **Los Olivos, CA 93441**
> **(805) 688-4891**

The resort is owned by the Human Potential Foundation, which is "dedicated to the expansion of human awareness." It consists of a group of rustic log cabins with kitchens and fireplaces. The cabins are quite large and sleep up to 20. This is to accommodate groups here for swimming, fishing, and hiking. But the romantic couple will still feel at home here: they have cocktails on the terrace and candlelight dining.

There is an inspiring walk from the picnic area up **Sulphur Springs Trail** a little over two miles to a point called Cedros Saddle.

The gateway to Lake Cachuma and the Santa Ynez Valley is Highway 154 that goes from Santa Barbara through the **San Marcos Pass**. This area is a nice stop to combine with an eagle watch trip. Try lunch or dinner at:

> **Matteis Tavern**
> **Highway 154**
> **Los Olivos, CA 93441**
> **Monday-Thursday 5:30 to 10 p.m.**
> **Friday-Sunday 12 to 10 p.m.**
> **(805) 688-4820**

Mattei's Tavern was built by a Swiss-Italian immigrant named Felix Mattei and his five sons in 1886. An enterprising man, he saw that travelers on the coast railroad had to take a stagecoach to fill a gap in the route served. In those days, passengers on the Southern Pacific had to transfer to the narrow-gauge Pacific Coast Railroad from Avila Beach to the Los Olivos Station, where they would continue on by stage to Santa Barbara. He supplied food and overnight lodging at the train-to-stagecoach transfer point.

A jovial fellow and a natural innkeeper, he nonetheless was married to a high strung, neurotic woman named Lucy who was a card-carrying member of Carrie Nation's Women's Christian Temperance Union. Their conflicts over selling alcohol resulted in some of the tavern's early remodeling.

A year after opening, Lucy demanded that if liquor was to be served at all, it must be in a separate building. Poor Felix had to build a second building to house the bar. In 1891, she went completely ballistic and demanded that all liquor be banned from the premises. Mattei's Tavern remained in this dismal state until 1962, when family scion Fred Mattei passed away. It is said that considerable amounts of liquor were smuggled in during this period by thirsty patrons.

Though it no longer takes overnight guests, Mattei's Tavern is a quite a fun place to eat. Because it was family owned for so long, it is amazingly original. The structure is a pretty white Victorian with green trim covered with wisteria. It is flanked by lawns and there is a huge Port Oxford cedar in front of the building. The lettering over the front door is the same as when it was a stagecoach office.

Once inside, there is a portrait of Felix Mattei in the lobby over the fireplace that was painted by his son, Clarence. To its left is one of Lucy and to its right is a self-portrait of Clarence. There is also a charcoal sketch of Clarence's wife, Merle, and Felix's card buddy, Gus Berg. Clarence's status as the Mattei family artist has been immortalized: his palette hangs over the clock.

Each dining room has a different quality. The homespun rustic ambiance survives throughout in such details as an original fir floor in the bar. The central dining room, which was originally the family's own, has a quality of frontier elegance to it with its large chandelier and red wallpaper.

The water tower was constructed in 1886. Now it is a nesting place for owls and can be seen clearly through a glass ceiling. Its open beamed dining room is one of the most unusual in the tavern. The most popular dining room is the sun porch, built around 1910. From its white wicker chairs, you can see the former guest rooms: a collection of cottages now rented out. During the '20s and '30s, they were a popular getaway for Hollywood celebrities. John Barrymore supposedly came here to hunt doves and Ava Gardner married Mickey Roony here.

What was originally the kitchen was added on to in 1974, creating the current dining room and cooking area. The food is pleasant steak and seafood, salad and pastas.

Besides Mattei's, the area offers another venerable former stagecoach stop now a place for refreshment for the modern weary traveler on Highway 154:

> **Cold Springs Tavern**
> **5995 Stagecoach Road**
> **[below Cold Springs Arch Bridge off SR 154]**
> **Santa Barbara, CA 93105**
> **Daily 11 a.m. to 9 p.m.**
> **(805) 967-0066**

When the San Marcos Pass toll road was finished in the 1880s, this little restaurant was opened for the stagecoach passengers. Cold Springs is a collection of wooden buildings tucked into a hollow of trees. After 100 years, they look almost like they grew there. One of them was once a bottling plant for the spring water. A beer sign alerts you to the one that is the tavern.

The inside of this place is right up there with the more colorful watering holes of the Southland. It has a very low ceiling and is broken up into several box-like rooms. The walls are covered with various frontier antiques and stuffed game and there is a Wurlitzer jukebox with an appropriate selection of Americana, particularly old rock 'n' roll. When the fire is burning in the fireplace, it is as snug a winter place as can be found outside of one up in the mountains. The food is surprisingly good steak and seafood type stuff with the added feature of rustic entrees such as rabbit and venison.

About 1/4 mile above the tavern is the best view of the **Cold Springs Arch Bridge**. It was built in 1963 to circumvent the old route that wound its way up Cold Springs Canyon and is a spectacular, single, 700-foot span built of steel that towers more than 400 feet above Stagecoach Road.

Pull off onto the winding narrow road that will take you to:

> **Chumash Painted Cave State Historic Park**
> **Painted Cave Road**
> **[12 miles northwest of Santa Barbara]**

From the little parking area, go up the path and there you are.

If you are afraid of caves, don't fear this one because there is an iron grill blocking the 15-foot high entrance. It is wider than that, but not much deeper. Most of the inside walls and ceiling are decorated in designs that have been dated from between the 1500s to the 1700s.

Though you have to really peer at them, the paintings are fairly brightly colored in black, white, and reddish tones. They are clearly delineated and display an obviously developed technique. The symbols link together in geometric patterns that include images of animals, a canoe party, and fish and crops. It has been speculated that they are religious in meaning: Chumash shamans spoke to their gods in pictures.

REVOLUTION DAY,
RUSSIAN SOUTHERN CALIFORNIA

Revolution Day is the most important and symbolic holiday in Russian history. It commemorates the anniversary of the grand finale of the October Revolution in 1917: the abdication of the czar. Like Oktoberfest, which really begins in September, November 7 commemorates an event which really took place on October 25th. In this case, it is because the new socialist government immediately changed the calendar.

The October Revolution obviously brought many changes to Russia. It also brought a wave of immigrants to the U.S., many of them intellectuals of the Tolstoy school. Some of them made their way to L.A. and in 1928 built:

Holy Virgin Mary Russian Orthodox Church
658 Micheltorena Street
Los Angeles, CA 90026

Located in Silver Lake is this pretty cathedral, styled after ones found in villages throughout Russia. It is the oldest of three in L.A. As is the case in all Orthodox churches, the interior is more ornate than the exterior.

The Russian emigres to the Southland have a wide variety of ethic origins and unlike Greeks, Russian Orthodox Christians do not tend to settle in groups around their churches. Beginning in the late '70s, there was an increase in immigration from all parts of the Soviet empire and this included many Jews.

Emigrant Soviet Jews have tended to locate in West Hollywood near Fairfax, but commercial "Little Russia" is the strip along Santa Monica Boulevard in Hollywood between Fairfax and Gardner. A Georgian market here sells exceptional bread:

Tbilisy and Yerevan Market and Bakery
7856 Santa Monica Boulevard
West Hollywood, CA 90069
Daily 7 a.m. to 9 p.m.
(213) 654-7427

Georgian bread is baked in a round clay oven called a "tone." It is similar to the Persian "tannur" (described in March) and the Indian "tandoor" in that it is a wood-fired, eyball-shaped inferno in which the bread dough is slapped on the inside wall. An iron hook on a long pole is used to remove the resulting large flat loaf.

Of course, for fall revelry, there is nothing quite like:

Moscow Nights
11345 Ventura Boulevard
Studio City, CA 91604
Friday-Sunday 8 p.m. (dinner) 9 to 11 p.m. (show)
(818) 980-8854

There is nothing unrestrained about the decor in "L.A.'s Only Russian Restaurant and Cabaret." The pink tablecloths, American flags, and red carpeting are set off by gold lame curtains. The bar stools are covered in velvet. Huge chandeliers twinkle overhead and mirrors make the big room seem even larger.

The first Moscow Nights was built in 1983. The owner, Arkady Kivman, moved it to its present location in 1991. The food is heavy Russian and includes rack of lamb, caviar, and of course, chicken Kiev. Patrons drink and enjoy themselves freely. The bar is particularly well stocked in one particular category: it serves 130 varieties of vodka.

On Friday through Sunday nights at 9 p.m., there is a cabaret show described as "a Gypsy-Russian-Yiddish extravaganza." It has wonderful musicians, bizarre comedians who parody Leonid Brezhnev, and a row of chorus girls kicking up their heels. The show lasts about two hours after which dancing is offered. There is a $20 minimum for the show, so arrive for dinner at 8 p.m. Balalaika players stroll around the tables and keep everyone feeling romantic.

SKI SEASON
Los Angeles

Though Los Angeles is not known as a "ski city" by any means, the fact remains that about 1-1/2 hours from Downtown L.A., there is a surprisingly good little ski resort:

Mount Waterman
817 Lynn Haven Lane
La Canada Flintridge, CA 91011
(818) 440-1041
(818) 790-2002 (recorded snow information)

About a 3/4 hour drive past the suburb of La Canada Flintridge along the beautiful **Angeles Crest Highway** will put you here. From the highway, you can see Chair Lift 1 with the green shack at the bottom. You park right there and take the chair up the face. It disembarks at the combination snack bar, ski rental shop and restroom. There is no overnight lodging.

Though the ski area is small (23 runs on 115 acres), it has unusually long mogul runs. The mountain is almost exactly 8,000 feet, with a 1,000-foot vertical drop. The intermediate runs are up on top with the expert runs down the face. There are two other chairs that can be reached by a trail. These service the beginner runs.

This is not a very busy ski area. On weekdays, it averages 350 to 400 people and maxs out at 1,500 on the busiest holiday. It also has a friendly, unpretentious atmosphere. This may be because this is a Southern California classic. Mt. Waterman is a true non-corporate entity: a multi-generational family-owned business.

The great grandfather of Mt. Waterman's present owner, Lynn Newcomb, homesteaded Newcomb Ranch a little ways west of the present resort in the year 1888 (see May). His grandfather started the resort in 1939 with one old-fashioned rope tow. The first single chair lift was installed in 1941 and Chair 1 went into operation up the face in 1975.

The name everyone thinks of when you mention skiing close to L.A. is **Mount Baldy**. It is easily reached off Interstate 10 via Mountain Avenue, which turns into Mount Baldy Road and terminates in the:

Mount Baldy Ski Lifts
Mount Baldy Road
Upland, CA 91759
(909) 982-0800 (information)
(909) 981-3344 (snow)

Mt. Baldy boasts 400 skiable acres and a vertical drop of 2,100 feet. There are only three places in the area that offer lodging; one of them is the:

Mount Baldy Lodge
6777 Mount Baldy Road
Mount Baldy, CA 91759
(909) 982-1115

This rustic lodge offers three one-room wood cabins, one of which has a kitchenette. The mountain-style restaurant and bar is complete with a moose, deer, and elk heads and a water wheel built into foundation. A rock fireplace keeps everyone warm and on weekends, live bands perform. It is a bargain at $65 per night. There is more about the San Gabriel Mountains in the May chapter.

San Bernardino Mountains

The other ski areas of the Southland are located farther east along the east/west traverse of the San Bernardino Mountains. For as long as I can remember, the place to stop for an early morning breakfast on the way up has been:

Lloyds
32114 Hilltop Boulevard
Running Springs, CA 92382
Daily 5 a.m. to 11 p.m.
bar open until 2 a.m.
(909) 867-2311

Lloyd Soutar opened a coffee shop bearing his name in 1953. He has expanded several times and now presides over a bakery, a dining room, and a bar, along with the original business. Though the coffee shop has been remodeled Southwestern-style, the dining room and bar are still rustic. The latter features an old-fashioned copper-topped counter.

One of the largest ski areas in the Southland is:

Snow Summit
P.O. Box 77
Big Bear Lake, CA 92315
(909) 866-5766

The mountain rises 8,200 feet and is well serviced by 11 chairlifts. In 1992, they added a new 5,450-foot long quad chairlift with a 1,175-foot rise. At the top of Chair 2, they also added a lunch restaurant with a barbecue called **The Summit House**. Its glass enclosed decks offer stunning views all the way down into the San Bernardino Valley and off into the Mt. San Gorgonio Wilderness.

The other big resort in the San Bernardino Mountains is:

Bear Mountain Ski Resort
P.O. Box 6812
Big Bear Lake, CA 92315
(909) 585-2519 (information)
(909) 585-2517 (snow)

At 8,800 feet, Bear Mountain is the highest ski resort in the Southland. It is spread out over four separate peaks and has a main lift called the Bear Mountain Express, plus eight additional chairs and two pomas.

For a wonderfully snug and romantic winter place to stay in Big Bear Lake—whether you are skiing or not—it's hard to top the:

Knickerbocker Inn
869 South Knickerbocker Road
P.O Box 3661
Big Bear Lake, CA 92314
(909) 866-8221

This large four-story, vertical log mansion—with its open decks on the lake side—is quite a sight. It is on two acres of hilltop grounds, surrounded by forest. Built in 1917, it has a se-cluded air because of its heavily wooded sur-roundings, yet it is within a mile of the commercial district and lake. The view from here is of trees sloping down the hill to the lake.

It is what might be called "elegant rustic" throughout. It has a large double sided, stone fire-

A winter scene from the deck of Windy Point Inn, Big Bear.

place and a staircase made of split logs. The living room has big leather chairs and a beamed ceiling. There are 10 rooms that range from $95 to $165. Five of the rooms have private baths. There is one suite that occupies the very top floor by itself. It has a sitting room and its own private jacuzzi. All are furnished with antiques and patchwork quilts.

There is a full breakfast served either in the dining room or on the big patio deck between the main house and the converted barn in back. There is also a hot tub on this deck as well. Cheese, fruit, and drinks are served in the afternoon and coffee, tea, cookies, and cinnamon crisps are available any time.

Other choices for lodging include the **Windy Point Inn** (see May) or the **Gold Mountain Manor** (see July).

For dinner, go one street over for a truly delightful dining experience:

> **Iron Squirrel Restaurant**
> **646 Pine Knot Boulevard**
> **Big Bear Lake, CA 92315**
> **Monday-Saturday 11:30 a.m. to 10 p.m.**
> **Sunday 5:30 to 10 p.m.**
> **(909) 866-9121**

Spanish Basque Paul Ortuno opened this wonderful restaurant in 1980. They are open for lunch and dinner and for several years, it has been said to be Big Bear's finest restaurant.

Though the name would suggest English fare, the dining room is country French as is the food. It is as bright and pretty on the inside as a European cottage, with wooden beams and flowery patterns with pheasants on the wall. In recent years, they have added California cuisine with salads and pasta and lots of grilled fish, meats, and poultry. There is more about Big Bear Lake in the May and July chapters.

PARADE SEASON

Of course, if you want to get into the spirit of the holidays, there is nothing like a parade.

Mother Goose Parade

A fanciful parade for children has been taking place in San Diego County this month since 1947:

> **Mother Goose Parade**
> **starts at Chambers and Main,**
> **east on Main to Second,**
> **north on Second to Madison**
> **El Cajon**
> **Sunday prior to Thanksgiving 12:30 p.m.**
> **Bleacher seats $5**
> **(619) 444-8712**

After the Rose Parade in January, this is the most popular parade in the Southland. Some 500,000 people line the streets to see a two-hour processional over a three mile parade route.

It was started by a local businessman named Thomas Wigton. 25,000 people came to the first one and it has grown ever since. There are clowns, equestrian groups, and bands, but the overall theme is obvious in the floats: all of these portray children's books. You will see all of your favorite nursery rhymes, fairy tales, and even contemporary classics of children's literature such as Dr. Seuss represented.

If you want a choice spot for the parade, get there early. The crowds start around 8:30 a.m.. The south side of Main is best because the late morning/early afternoon sun will be behind you. Try to get a place near Main and Claydelle, across from the reviewing stand.

Hollywood Christmas Parade

One of the Southland's most famous and well-loved sights is the Christmas Tree of Stars and Lights atop the Capitol Records Building (described in March). A tradition begun in 1963, it has been created since 1968 by steeplejack Paul Gavlakover. He hauls himself and 4,000 bulbs on 36 very long strands, plus three 100 pound aluminum stars up to the very tip of the giant needle on top of the building. The sight of the all-red tree from the Hollywood Freeway, or indeed, almost anywhere in the surrounding city, is one of the signs that the holiday season is here.

Every November Southern California's most famous street has a gala Christmas parade:

> **Hollywood Christmas Parade**
> **begins at Sunset and Van Ness**
> **up Highland to Hollywood**
> **continuing east to Bronson**
> **Hollywood**
> **Sunday after Thanksgiving 6 to 8 p.m.**
> **Reserved grandstand seats: $17.75 to $24.25**
> **(213) 462-2394, (213) 469-8311 or (213) 462-2394**

This 3.2 mile procession dates back to 1931, when Santa first made his way down Hollywood Boulevard. Because of its location, it is traditionally led by a film or TV celebrity as Grand Marshal. These have ranged from Charlton Heston to Tom and Roseanne Arnold. The year prior to the completion of this book, it was Bob Hope along with his wife Delores.

There are the usual equestrian units, marching bands, and floats, but the percentage of open convertibles with celebrities in them is obviously higher than the norm. In 1993, between 750,000 and 1,000,000 people cheered Lou Rawls, Beau Bridges,

Rich Little, and Mickey Rooney among others. Grandstand seats are a little steep, but standing on the street and watching is free.

Hollywood Boulevard is always brightly decorated for the holidays and can make for a more unusual place to go Christmas shopping. For a more amorous holiday season, try stopping in:

Playmates
6438 Hollywood Boulevard
Hollywood, CA 90028
Monday-Friday 10 a.m. to 8 p.m.
Saturday 10 a.m. to 7:30 p.m.
Sunday 12 to 7 p.m.
(213) 464-7636

Playmates is owned by Michael Attie, who legend has it was in the middle of a deep meditative trance at a Japanese Buddhist shrine when he first heard that he had inherited his family's lingerie store on Hollywood Boulevard. He decided that this was a sign that he had to make the place into a "temple of lingerie."

Not only is their merchandise generally more risque and costume than that found at more vanilla, yuppie-oriented lingerie stores, but the feeling here is also quite different. As you walk in, there is a sort of shrine to female sexuality as represented by the belly dancer.

If you headed west on Hollywood Boulevard from here and happened to look down Hudson and are struck by the remarkable art work on top of an otherwise nondescript building, you have chanced upon:

Hollywood Moguls
1650 North Hudson
Hollywood, CA 90028
(213) 465-7449

The roof of this multi-use theater is adorned with a huge, shiny metal sculpture of a knight doing battle with a dragon. Inside, there is a 99-seat theater and a separate club/performance space where food is served.

On the same side of Hollywood Boulevard as Playmates a little farther up is one of the most interesting stores in the city:

Hollywood Toys and Costumes
6562 Hollywood Boulevard
Hollywood, CA 90028
Daily 9:30 a.m. to 7:30 p.m.
(213) 465-3119

This store stocks every inexpensive magic trick, costume, wig, mask, makeup kit, or doll you could imagine. If you enjoy giving bizarre or humorous little stocking-stuffers, you will be in nirvana here. This store is a real survivor too. It was originally opened in 1954 and along with the next store is one of the great classic shops of Hollywood Boulevard.

Of course, if your idea of a holiday gift involves a little camouflage, a perfect store is the:

Supply Sergeant
6664 Hollywood Boulevard
Hollywood, CA 90028
Monday-Friday 10 a.m. to 7 p.m.
Saturday 10 a.m. to 8 p.m.
Sunday 11 a.m. to 7 p.m.
(213) 463-4730

Many a low-budget Hollywood film or theatrical production has found its Army costumes or props among the aisles of khaki and drab green here. There are also machetes, fake bombs, and assorted military accouterments. If you would like to get dog tags made, they do that too. Originally opened in El Monte in 1948, the Hollywood location followed in 1955 and has been here ever since.

There are many little shops in the nooks and crannies along the boulevard. One of my favorites is:

Abyssinia Gifts from Africa
6727 Hollywood Boulevard
Hollywood, CA 90028
Monday-Thursday 11 a.m. to 7:30 p.m.
Friday-Saturday 11 a.m. to 9 p.m.
Sunday 12 to 6 p.m.
(213) 467-5453

Everywhere you look in this delightful postage stamp-sized store you will see some interesting object from continental Africa. There are little polished boxes from Egypt, beautifully patterned fabrics, and tapes of African music. I especially like their homemade incense for $1 a package.

Just strolling along Hollywood Boulevard, taking in the beautiful movie palaces, clubs, and legitimate theatres, makes for a grand holiday evening even if you didn't come for the parade. The El Capitan movie theatre (see March) often has a big new Disney release for the holidays. A delightful coffee shop that would be the absolutely perfect place for an animated meal and movie combo is:

Snow White's Cafe
6769 Hollywood Boulevard
Daily 7 a.m. to 11 p.m.
(213) 467-1220

Originally built by Disney in the late '30s to coincide with the opening of the film *Snow White and the Seven Dwarfs*, this is the second oldest restaurant in Hollywood. It is probably one of the only non-Disney properties that uses Disney characters and motifs: Snow White's Cafe is what a coffee shop in Sleeping Beauty's Castle might look like.

The ceiling in the long narrow room soars two stories above your head with heavy beams inlaid with frowning cartoon owls forming arches at what would be the first floor ceiling level. The floor in the entrance is made to look like rough hewn stone. There are seven red leatherette booths along one wall, each with its own framed dwarf. Behind the counter is a long mirror with the etched frosted image of Snow White. Beautifully colored murals depicting scenes from the movie look down from high on the walls.

The Snow White Cafe has had much restoration and will have more. It is owned by Doreet Hakman, a blue-eyed blond who was born in Transylvania. She came here in 1973 and worked for the Israeli Consulate for about a year, then bought the Bell Coffee Shop, up by the Chinese Theater. In 1981, she was able to buy the Snow White, which at that time was in a very sorry state. Now thanks to her persistence and hard work and some Community Redevelopment Agency funds, the Snow White is once again an exceptionally charming place.

They have a very good, general menu and the most expensive thing on it is $9.25. This is the kind of restaurant I loved as a child because dishes have names like "Happy's Ice Cream Sundae" and the "Prince Charming Chef Salad." There is a corned beef hash and eggs breakfast called "Walt's Favorite."

Another perfect old Hollywood place to sup on a Sunday evening in late November is:

Miceli's
1646 North Las Palmas
Hollywood, CA 90028
Monday-Thursday 3 p.m. to 12 a.m.
Friday-Saturday 3 p.m. to 1 a.m.
Sunday 3 p.m. to 12 a.m.
(213) 466-3438

Founded by the Miceli family in 1949 and still owned by them, this could be called the archetype neighborhood Italian pizzeria. Within its dark, cool interior is the forest of hanging Chianti basket bottles, the familiar red-checked tablecloths on the tables illuminated by candles in red globes, and red brick walls plastered with classic movie love scenes inside Italian restaurants. The heavy carved wood chairs upholstered in red leather are comfortable and inviting.

Do not expect the trendy "Northern Italian" food of the Southland's upscale eateries. The food at Miceli's is more like the Italian food you grew up with: cold antipasto salad, spaghetti with meatballs, and, of course, pizza not baked in a wood fired oven or topped with smoked chicken. There is more about Hollywood Boulevard in the March chapter.

Do Dah Parade, Pasadena

If there were ever anything in need of a parody, it is the tradition of the holiday parade. It is refreshing to note that Pasadena, city of the Rose Parade, is also the city of the:

Do Dah Parade
starts on Raymond at Holly
west on Colorado
Pasadena
usually Sunday of Thanksgiving weekend 12 to 2 p.m.
(818) 796-2591

Started in 1977 by Peter Apanel as a spoof of the Rose Parade, this is one of the very best holiday traditions in the Southland because it certainly is the funniest. Participants dress up in all kinds of bizarre costumes and act out some kind of mock ritual that parodies either the seriousness of traditional parade marching bands or some specific event.

One of the regular performing groups is called the "Torment of Roses." In 1993, they appeared in whiteface to represent the all-white male board of the Tournament of Roses Association. Others entrants include the Keg Banger Spill Team, the Barbecue and Hibachi Marching Grill Team, and the classic Synchronized Briefcase Drill Team in their business suits and ties. Perhaps the most comical thing I ever saw on a city street was "The Great Zsa Zsa Drill Team" in which a marching column of Zsa Zsa's (all men in drag) and a marching row of men in police uniforms periodically stop, and in one synchronized action, the Zsa Zsa's slap the cops.

Right above Pasadena, in Altadena, is a museum that seems to fall in line with the Do Dah Parade philosophy:

> **Banana Museum**
> **2524 North El Molino Avenue**
> **Altadena, CA 91001**
> **Call for appointment**
> **(818) 798-2272**

This small museum has everything you could possibly imagine in banana-themed objects. There are banana-shaped lamps, giant stuffed bananas, banana toothpaste, German banana warmers, banana incense, and banana golf putters, to name a few. The walls are covered with banana ads, photos, and posters. Admission is limited to members of the International Banana Club by appointment. It costs only $10 for a lifetime membership.

The whole thing is the product of the imagination of Ken Bannister, who started the club as a way to sell his photographic supplies. Join the club, make an appointment, and ask Ken to wear his banana tuxedo and pose with you for a picture. Someday when you are having a bad day, you can look at this snapshot and feel better.

Traditionally, there is a party after the parade at an appropriate place for it:

> **Crown City Brewery**
> **300 South Raymond Avenue**
> **Pasadena, CA 91105**
> **Sunday-Thursday 11 a.m. to 11 p.m.**
> **Friday & Saturday 11 a.m. to 10 p.m.**
> **(818) 577-5548**

Crown City Brewery has a wonderful warm and interesting atmosphere perfect for setting a holiday mood. Its enormous copper kettles, four TVs turned to sports, and wall of beer bottles from around the world create a feeling of festive fun.

In the last 10 years, a large number of "boutique breweries" have sprung up throughout the world. Crown City is of this ilk, but in addition to their own home brew, it also features a huge selection of the unusual beers from small breweries all over the U.S. There are also nine English and three American beers on tap in a total selection of over one hundred. The brewed-on-premises stuff here is sweet, frothy, and low in alcohol.

The food is quite good—particularly the barbecued. Because they are open for lunch, this is a particularly good spot to hit prior to an afternoon stroll in the nearby revitalized "Old Town."

Pasadena's renovated Old Pasadena area has brought a new nightlife to "the jewel in the valley." Covering the area roughly two blocks north and south of Colorado Boulevard between Raymond and Fair Oaks Avenues, it is a wonderful blending of beautifully preserved old architecture and an appealing mix of shops, movie theaters, and restaurants.

There is an informal cafe here that features open poetry readings every Wednesday night at 9 p.m.:

> **Espresso Bar**
> **34 South Raymond Avenue**
> **Pasadena, CA 91105**
> **Monday-Thursday 12 p.m. to 1 a.m.**
> **Friday & Saturday 12 p.m. to 2 a.m.**
> **Sunday 12 p.m. to 12 a.m.**
> **(818) 356-9095**

Located in the Renaissance Revival Block, originally designed in 1894 by Frank Hudson, the Espresso Bar was one of the first businesses to come into the slowly developing Old Town when it opened in 1978. Though there are certainly plenty of places to get coffee in the area, this is the only real coffeehouse with soul.

It is sad that success has also brought a loss of some of the latter quality from the area. Street musicians, who were welcomed when they needed foot traffic in the vicinity, are now issued tickets.

Just a couple steps away is an unusual bookstore that specializes in an exciting area of publishing:

> **Distant Lands-A Traveler's Bookstore**
> **62 South Raymond Avenue**
> **Pasadena, CA 91105**
> **Tuesday-Thursday 10:30 a.m. to 7 p.m.**
> **Friday & Saturday 10:30 a.m. to 9 p.m.**
> **Sunday & Monday 11 a.m. to 6 p.m.**
> **(818) 449-3220**

Distant Lands is what its subtitle says: "A Traveler's Bookstore." Owner Adrian Kalvinskas is a Pasadena native who was a history major specializing in turn-of-the-century California at USD. He loved the buildings of Old Town as a teenager even when it was a seedy place and it sparked an interest in historic preservation.

Kalvinskas opened Distant Lands in 1989 when he was a 21-year-old student because he wanted to contribute to the renewal of the area and felt that it had enough restaurants and boutiques. His store has 9,000 book titles, travel videos, and maps. He is expanding from 1,000 to 1,500 square and plans to stock more accessories and bags and have a travel resource center where weather and conditions throughout the world can be accessed.

One of the best restaurants in the L.A. area is here:

Xiomara
69 North Raymond Avenue
Pasadena, CA 91103
Daily 11:30 a.m. to 10:30 p.m.
(818) 796-2520

For years everyone's favorite restaurant in the Century City area was Champagne. Here, chef Patrick Healy dazzled with his food and, together with his wife, Sophie, created an informal friendly atmosphere.

Healy and his wife split up and he is now chef here. This restaurant is located in a beautiful old structure and features a fantastic interior that combines the wonderful architecture of the building with a trendy restaurant sensibility. It features a lot of textures—different woods and a bar made of Juperano granite.

The food and service were voted by the *L.A. Times* to be among the top 40 in the Southland. Specialties include crispy salmon steak, duck comfit salad, and country cassoulet. There is more about Pasadena in the January and December chapters.

Huntington Park Parade

One of the largest Christmas parades in the nation is the:

Christmas Lane Parade
runs south along Pacific from Randolph to Florence
Huntington Park
usually second Saturday of November 1 to 2:30 p.m.
(213) 585-0909 (Chamber of Commerce)

This parade was born in 1947, when Huntington Park was a suburb with a population of about 12,000. Back then, it was a march of Boy Scouts, WW II vets, and local students. Today Huntington Park is a town of about 60,000 people with a high percentage being Latino. The parade has also grown too, and has about 20 floats, marching bands, equestrian units, and about 50 waving celebrities. Grand Marshals have included boxer Julio Cesar Chavez and actor/comedian Cheech Marin.

Right near where the parade ends is a great place to get food for a holiday party:

El Gallo Giro
7136 Pacific Boulevard
Huntington Park, CA 90255
(213) 585-44336
and:
El Gallo Giro
260 South Broadway
Los Angeles, CA 90012
Sunday-Thursday 7 a.m. to 11 p.m.
Saturday-Sunday 7 a.m. to 3 p.m.
(213) 626-6926

El Gallo Giro makes you hungry the minute you walk through the door. A big, bustling place with glazed tile all around, it has separate counters for different specialties. You go to one for bakery, one for fresh-squeezed juice, one for grilled meats, and one for stews. Possibly my favorite sandwich in all the world is their "Carne Asada Torta," which is a big soft roll filled with lettuce, tomato, avocado, chiles, cheese, and thin slices of grilled meat.

In neighboring Vernon is a large work of public art that can be a catalyst for personal transformation. Diet is always high on our list of things we want to change. If you have been wanting to give up meat—whether it is because you do not want to cause suffering to animals, are ecologically minded, or because all the talk about cholesterol is getting to you—there is a shrine of sorts for you to visit in Southern California very near here:

The Great Mural of Farmer John Meats
3049 East Vernon Avenue
Vernon, CA 90058
(213) 583-4621

Words cannot describe the aesthetic impact of this cultural highlight of Southern California. Completely surrounding the Farmer John Meat Packing Plant, it is one of the largest murals in the world and depicts bucolic images of little farm boys, barns, idyllic pastures, and various farm scenes.

It is also the second greatest example of unintentional irony in architecture in L.A. The predominant feature of this mural is dozens and dozens of happy cartoon pigs. Happy pigs on the outside, while on the inside their brethren are being ground into sausage. Therefore, if your doctor's warnings have been jacking up your stress levels, drive over to the Farmer John Pig Mural and gaze at it in homage. You will feel purged forever.

JAPAN EXPO

Every November, there is a giant exposition at the Los Angeles Convention Center that showcases Japanese culture and products. It is produced by the:

Japan American Friendship Foundation
1515 West 190th, Suite 508
Gardena, CA 90248
(310) 329-7547

Located near the pub Fukuhime (see January), this non-profit organization was founded in 1980 to help foster a better relationship between Japan and the U.S. They put on culture shows, such as taiko drums and photo exhibits.

Vice Chairman John Marumoto was a former Terminal Islander (see January) who went to Manzanar and has worked with the Japanese American National Museum (see August) on exhibits of that period. Rebecca Munty, the Public Affairs director, edits the publication *Japan, Then and Now,* which discusses contemporary issues and explains traditional culture.

The City of Gardena, where the foundation is located, has had a long Japanese history that, unlike Terminal Island, was to continue on after the war was over. The adjacent City of Torrance is the location of the U.S. headquarters of Nissan, Toyota, and Honda. During the 1980s, their operations here expanded and many of their employees came over here to work. Besides the Japanese Americans who are lifetime residents of the Southland, there are about 50,000 Japanese Nationals living here that are employed by multi-national firms.

This has created a Japan-in-Southern-California community in Gardena and Torrance that is not as well known as Little Tokyo or even Sawtelle Boulevard (see August), but is a wonderful place to go shopping or eat very much like you would in Japan.

At the corner of Western and Redondo is **Tozai Plaza**. It has a Japanese motif to its architecture with its blue tile roof. There are numerous Japanese businesses here, but for one-stop sampling of Japanese cooking styles, it is hard to top. It has a several noodle joints, one with a famous name:

Tampopo
Tozai Plaza
15462 Western Avenue
Gardena, CA 90247
Monday-Saturday 11:15 to 3 a.m.
Sunday 11:15 a.m. to 10 p.m.
(310) 323-7882

If you never saw the 1987 Japanese movie *Tampopo*, you are missing one of filmdom's great comic cultural statements. It is about a Japanese girl named Tampopo (butterfly) who runs a noodle stand, but makes terrible noodles. A truck driver with a demeanor very much like John Wayne takes on the task of instructing her in much the same way Henry Higgins schooled Eliza Doolittle—except that he is coercing her to be a great noodle chef.

The interior of this restaurant is done in dark wood beams with photo murals from Japan. Whoever schooled the chef here could have helped the Tampopo of the film, because the noodles here are fantastic. For about $7, you can get a complete dinner. This would include a big bowl of ramen in your choice of broths, with pork, chicken, or vegetables. On the side is a scoop of half-fried rice with a delicious ginger taste. For dessert, smooth pink rectangles of sweet bean curd taste as good as they look.

A few doors away is a sushi bar:

Fishboy Sakanaya
Tozai Plaza
15476 South Western Avenue
Gardena, CA 90247
(310) 324-9408

Along the Redondo Beach Boulevard side of Tozai Plaza are yet two more great Japanese restaurants. One specializes in a certain kind of noodle:

Kotohira
Tozai Plaza
1747 West Redondo Beach Boulevard
Gardena, CA 90247
Daily 11:30 a.m. to 10 p.m.
(310) 323-3966

The three main types of Japanese noodles are the ramen served in big bowls of broth like at Tampopo, the buckwheat "soba" noodle, such as is featured at Mishima on Sawtelle Boulevard (see August), and the "udon" noodle, such as is featured here.

Udon noodles are like long white crayons and can be served several different ways. Warm udon with green onion, bonito, and ginger comes in a bowl. It can also come plain in just hot water. Cold udon comes on a mat. You can have it curried or put some soy sauce on it. Udon can also be dipped in soy mixed with wasabe or fish soup.

On the same side of the plaza is an American representative of a 70 restaurant chain from Japan:

FuRaiBo

Tozai Plaza

1741 West Redondo Beach Boulevard

Gardena, CA 90247

Monday-Saturday 11:30 a.m. to 11 p.m.

Sunday 5 to 10 p.m.

(310) 329-9441

The wonderful smell that wafts around the corner of the building where this restaurant is located is the first clue to what is happening inside. The second one is the small crowd of people that is usually waiting for a table or a spot at the counter. FuRaiBo serves many different dishes, but specifically they are known for "tori no karaage" or Japanese fried chicken.

It is quite unlike Southern fried. The Colonel would be shocked to discover that they marinate their chicken first, then throw it in super hot oil that sears the outside and leaves the inside soft as butter. You get your choice of spices and flavors and they are all great. The specialty is "teba sake" chicken—an order of wings only.

Across the street from Tozai Plaza is a small building with stylish neon signs:

Herzon Coffee House

1716 West Redondo Beach Boulevard

Gardena, CA 90247

Monday-Saturday 11 to 12 a.m.

Sunday 2 p.m. to 12 a.m.

(310) 327-1300

If your image of a coffeehouse is a dingy bohemian place, you will get a big surprise when you enter Herzon. The decor here is elegant and romantic enough for dinner. It is quite dark; individual Art Deco flying saucers of light suspended from the ceiling cast small pools of light over each black table—which also has its own single red silk rose. Flowers are definitely the theme: there are silk plants in containers and the wallpaper is a darkly subdued floral.

Besides a good selection of coffee (including espresso and cappuccino) there is a pretty good menu of various Japanese specialties and American sandwiches.

There are many kinds of Japanese cooking that are combinations of Japanese and Western dishes. If you continue along Redondo Beach Boulevard, you can find an example of this composite cuisine on your left just past Tozai Plaza at:

> **Spoon House Bakery and Restaurant**
> **1601 West Redondo Beach Boulevard**
> **Gardena, CA 90247**
> **11 a.m. to 9 p.m.**
> **(310) 538-0376**

This is a Japanese spaghetti restaurant, the most established one in the Southland. Suffice it to say, it is not like what you would get in your local pizzeria. They have several spaghetti dishes with toppings such as caviar from flying fish.

HOLIDAY SHOPPING

Since 1984, there has been a Thanksgiving weekend shopping tradition in Downtown L.A.:

> **Los Angeles Holiday Sale**
> **California Mart Exhibit Hall**
> **110 East 9th Street**
> **Los Angeles, CA 90015**
> **Thanksgiving weekend (Friday-Sunday 9:30 a.m. to 5 p.m.)**
> **(213) 623-5876**

The Los Angeles Garment District is a mystical place in the minds of bargain hunters. A substantial area of about 15 square blocks, there are several wholesale centers open to the public on a regular or, in this case, a very limited basis.

The California Mart is really not for the retail customers, but they offer special sales, announced on the phone recording above, where you can go in. It is a huge place. There are hundreds of manufacturers and retailers offering men's suits, leather, women's designer fashions and accessories, cosmetics, brand name perfumes, watches, costume jewelry, children's toys and dolls.

If you don't mind getting up in the middle of the night, another Downtown L.A.

institution can supply flowers to fill your house for the holidays:

Wholesale Flower Market
Wall Street [Between 7th and 8th]
Los Angeles, CA 90014
Monday-Saturday 9:30 a.m. to 5 p.m. (most outlets)
(213) 622-1966

The L.A. Flower Market is the biggest in the whole U.S.A. There are places that sell plants, others that offer gift baskets, and of course, plenty of cut flowers. After about 9 a.m. and on Saturday mornings, vendors drop their prices on these to clear out inventory.

Near here is where the old Pacific Electric Red Car Terminal was located. In its building is the oldest continually operating restaurant in the Southland:

Cole's P.E. Buffet
118 East Sixth Street
Los Angeles, CA 90014
Daily 9 to 12 a.m.
(213) 622-4090

Though the food here is not going to win any awards from the California Restaurant Writers, for nostalgia value, this place can't be touched. Cole's was founded in 1908 and is filled with memorabilia of early Southern California.

It is dark inside and the floor is covered with sawdust. On the wall across from the bar is a framed black and white photo of an earthquake ruin: San Francisco in 1906. The story told in the January chapter of the Mt. Lowe Railway that used to run above Pasadena comes alive inside Cole's: posters advertising it adorn the walls.

Cole's really is a buffet, and you stand in line with a tray. Like that other relic of early Los Angeles, Phillippe's, their specialty is French dipped sandwiches (see September). These are by far the best things to eat here, promptly made by a gentleman in a tall white hat with an air that suggests this is the most important act in the world. If you feel like some recreation after your sandwich, there are dart boards in the back rooms. There also is a full bar illuminated by Tiffany lamps.

Another early morning stop in Downtown Los Angeles that is appropriate for holiday preparation is the:

Los Angeles Wholesale Produce Market
7th and Central
Monday-Saturday 1 a.m. to 9 a.m.
contact:

1601 East Olympic Boulevard (office)
Los Angeles, CA 90021
Monday-Saturday 6:30 a.m. to 3:30 p.m.
(213) 896-4070

The L.A. Wholesale Produce Market is vast, and, as you might guess, is one of the largest in the world. The docks where the produce is laid out are 800 feet long. Each will have about 12 separate little enterprises.

Going here isn't quite like a trip to the neighborhood supermarket. Not only are the hours somewhat limited, there is a $100 minimum purchase. A lot of serious chefs do make the trek, however, because not only is everything very fresh, they have many exotic offerings, such as wild mushrooms. Produce Court, near 9th Street, and Merchants Street, by 8th, are the two primary sections of the Wholesale Produce Market.

DECEMBER

Las Posadas Procession

Boat Parades of Lights

Christmas Traditions

Hanukkah

Kwanzaa

Racing Season at Santa Anita

Whale Watching Season

Birthday of Freeways

New Year's Eve

Chapter Twelve

DECEMBER

Whether it's Christmas, Hanukkah, the winter solstice, "Kwanzaa," or just the end of another 12 month span you celebrate, there is something very special about this time of year. It's a time when spirits are high and the need to feel companionship is strong. It is a time when more than anything else, we need to love and be loved.

All of our observed traditions reflect this. The feasting, the gathering around the lit up tree, the gifts—they are all merely symbols. They are meaningless without the force of true goodwill towards others behind them.

Part of the reason Scrooge was Scrooge was that he really didn't have very much fun himself. Perhaps instead of spending all that time in shopping malls, you might invite your friends to join you at some of the places and events in this book.

Probably the most spiritually symbolic ritual of the holidays in Southern California is the beautiful:

LAS POSADAS PROCESSION

The Posadas is the Mexican pre-Christmas festivity celebrated during the nine days before Christmas Eve. Of all of the rites of Christmas, to me this is the most genuinely godly because it is about the tired and lonely search for shelter by the poor and homeless Joseph and Mary.

Though the Statue of Liberty is in New York, California in the 20th century came to epitomize the dream of people all over the world—from snowbound Midwestern Americans, to Pacific peoples looking for a new life, to runaway teenagers in Hollywood hoping to become movie stars. A search for shelter in the night after a long journey in the hopes of a better tomorrow is what the Southland is all about.

Los Angeles

On December 16, Southern California's strongest spirit of the holidays is epitomized by:

> **Las Posadas Procession**
> **Olvera Street, Los Angeles**
> **December 16-24 at 7 p.m.**
> **(213) 628-1274**

This pageant is repeated every night until Christmas Eve. In it, Mary, Joseph and company seek refuge each night in a traditional candlelight processional. They are turned away at several places until a warm hearted person takes them in. This is an occasion for a party in which a star-shaped piñata is broken.

Christmas Eve is traditionally spent in church. The heart and soul of the Hispanic community at this time of year is:

La Iglesia de Nuestra Señora la Reina de Los Angeles
Church of Our Lady the Queen of the Angels
535 North Main Street
Los Angeles, CA 90012

In 1818, Franciscan friars and Yang Na indians began work on a modest, gable-roofed adobe. It was dedicated on December 8 of 1822 in time for Christmas. In 1861, it was rebuilt and a more impressive facade was added. In 1875, a bell tower was erected.

Building continued into the 20th century. Ironically, this took the form of a renovation in 1912 designed to make it look more like a mission. The tile roof came in 1923. Though red tile roofs are identified with the first California architecture, the earliest buildings had thatch roofs, which were replaced by shingles in the 19th century.

Though the fire department banned lay people from carrying candles in the processional in 1991, seeing the clergy illuminating the street might inspire you to stop by:

Olvera Candle Shop
W-3 Olvera Street
Los Angeles, CA 90012
Daily 10 a.m. to 7 p.m.
(213) 628-7833

I have always loved the Olvera Candle Shop's old green sign with its representation of a white candle with a light bulb on top. Originally opened in the 1930s, this Olvera Street veteran carries over 250 varieties.

Christmas music and dance are offered at:

La Golondrina
W-17 Olvera Street
Los Angeles, CA 90012
Daily 10 a.m. to 9 p.m
(213) 628-4349

La Golondrina looks like Christmas with its white lights strung over its white exterior and its wagon wheels outlining the patio. Inside, a roaring fire is a welcome sight.

This restaurant was the site of the first Las Posadas in 1941. They have great food and mariachis all year round. Near the holidays, seasonal food and drink are also available. La Golondrina is housed in the historic **Pelanconi House**, which was named for its second owner, Antonio Pelanconi. It was the first brick residence in Los Angeles when it was built in 1855. The living space was on the second floor, with a winery on the first. There is more about Olvera Street in the May and September chapters.

Old Town, San Diego

There are Las Posadas Processionals in several other parts of the Southland. Probably the biggest of these is the annual:

> **Las Posadas Processional**
> **Old Town, San Diego**
> **usually Wednesday, second week of December**
> **(619) 220-5422**

This annual event got started in the late 1950s. The park tries to supplement it with other activities. These can include "pastorella" passion plays that are actually more traditional for the area.

There are many different shops in Old Town. One that might be a good choice to find a unique Christmas gift is:

> **Old Town Pottery South**
> **2470 San Diego Avenue**
> **San Diego, CA 92110**
> **Daily 10 a.m. to 4 p.m.**
> **(619) 296-0131**

I have always liked glazed and unglazed Mexican pottery. They have plenty of both, along with "chimineas" (outdoor fireplaces made of red clay), planters, fountains, and dishes. There is more on Old Town in the May chapter.

BOAT PARADES OF LIGHTS

Southern California's identity is inextricably wrapped up with the Pacific Ocean. One of our most famous holiday traditions certainly reflects that: our annual boat parades of light that manifest themselves in various places up and down the coast.

The practice actually began in the Southland as a summer event. In 1908, in celebration of the Fourth of July, an Italian gondolier who had somehow found his way to Newport Beach led a nighttime parade that was all Southern California: A Venetian gondola followed by eight Indian-style canoes. All of the boats were lit with Japanese lanterns.

By 1949, this parade had grown in scope and popularity to the point where it was causing traffic jams, so it was cancelled. When it reappeared because of public sentiment, it had become a winter event.

It is now a holiday tradition in most of the locations that have the appropriate venue: a quiet waterway which can be seen by people on shore.

San Diego

Because San Diego County has such an extensive amount of protected waterway, it is only natural that they would have more than one boat parade. The first is not a parade, but a stationary display of boats glowing with holiday lights:

South San Diego Bay Winterfest
Chula Vista
normally second Saturday of the month
starts at dusk
(619) 420-6602 (Chamber of Commerce)

The marina area here is fairly compact, so the parade was replaced by a festival centered around the decorated boats that are tied up by the dock. Because Chula Vista is now the official southern homeport for the tall ship *California*, that magnificent old ship is adorned with lights and on view for the festival. This event also features musical entertainment and children's activities. If you wanted to grab a bite to eat, you could stop by **Jake's South Bay** (see November).

The more northern portion of San Diego Bay is the site of a big boat parade:

San Diego Harbor Parade of Lights
San Diego
second to last Sunday before Christmas
starts at dusk by Naval Station
contact:
Greater Shelter Island Association
2240 Shelter Island Drive
San Diego, CA 92106

The San Diego Harbor Parade of Lights is the oldest of the San Diego boat parades, having been founded in 1971.

There is another Christmas boat parade that is a little ways north in San Diego's man-made harbor:

Mission Bay Christmas Boat Parade of Lights
San Diego
usually last Saturday before Christmas
starts at dusk
(619) 488-0501

Put on by the Mission Bay Yacht Club since 1978, this parade of about 40 boats circles the part of Mission Bay known as Sail Bay. It is accompanied by music and concludes with lighting of the tower at Sea World.

Once decorated, the 320-foot **Skytower** at Sea World is the tallest Christmas tree in the city. It is festooned with twinkling lights and can be seen for miles.

Oceanside

Up the coast a little way is the fourth of the boat parades in San Diego County:

Oceanside Harbor Parade of Lights
Oceanside
second Saturday in December at 7 p.m.
(619) 722-5751

The Oceanside Harbor Parade of lights is produced by the Oceanside Yacht Club. For this procession, about 30 boats assemble in the outer basin and do two laps around the inside harbor. Bring a blanket and watch it from the lawn around the bay.

Coastal North San Diego County is a traditional home of flower growers. None are more appropriate for the season than:

Paul Ecke Poinsettia Ranch
441 Saxony Road
P.O. 488
Encinitas, CA 92024
Monday-Friday 7 a.m. to 5 p.m.
(619) 753-1134

It is astounding how many superlatives can be applied to Southern California. Paul Ecke Poinsettia Ranch is one of them: it is the world's largest producer and breeder of poinsettia plants, growing about 10,000 seedlings per year. They supply nurseries all over the U.S.

Poinsettias became associated with this season because they appear to flower in

November and December. Actually, the colored parts are bracts, or modified leaves. Though the traditional color is red, they are now available in a rainbow of hues. These have great names to describe their colors, like "Jingle Bells" (dark red with light pink flecks), "Pink Peppermint" (peachy pink), and "Lemon Drop" (warm gold). The latter color is popular for Thanksgiving because it goes with autumn hues.

There are always new varieties and colors being developed. These are test-marketed right at the ranch. This means that by going here, you will be able to buy something you can't get anywhere else.

For 1993, these included "Curly," with pinwheeling bracts that twist in peach or white, and "Monet," which really does look like it was hand-painted pink and peach with the impressionist's eye for vibrant colors. There is more about the North San Diego coast in the May and July chapters.

Dana Point

Pretty Dana Point Harbor also has a Christmas boat parade:

Dana Point Harbor Festival of Lights
Dana Point Harbor
Normally second Friday-Saturday
(714) 496-1555 (Chamber of Commerce)

They outline the harbor here in white lights. The docks as well as the boats are decorated. At the end of Blue Lantern Street is **Blue Lantern Lookout Park**, which not only has a gazebo on the end, it offers a view of the harbor that is unmatched. Richard Nixon is said to have proposed to Pat here.

For a bite to eat, you could stop by **Watercolors Restaurant** in the Dana Point Resort or **The Old Dana Point Cafe** (see February).

But if you want to go all out on a place to spend the night during the holidays, a little ways up the coast from here is a spectacular Orange County holiday tradition:

"Once Upon A Wonderland"
Ritz-Carlton
33533 Ritz-Carlton Drive
Laguna Niguel, CA 92677
(714) 240-2000

The Ritz-Carlton Hotel is an opulent enough feast for the eyes on its own, from its exceptional cliffside location, to its extensive art collection, to its lush landscaping. With the addition of 100,000 lights and gorgeous Christmas decorations, its richness of decor becomes almost magical.

For children, they have a Children's Tea and Puppet Show and a Walk Through Gingerbread House. Sometimes the hotel also features holiday film classics on its screens and Christmas stories by its firesides. Throughout its lovely grounds carolers will stroll. If you feel like a traditional roast goose dinner, the restaurant is featuring holiday fare all month.

If you would like an elegant escape, until December 28, they usually offer a three-day/two-night "Holiday Getaway" that rivals any you could take anywhere from Southern California. For about $200 per night, single or double, you get a lovely package. They give you a deluxe courtyard room, use of the health club, free valet parking, a holiday gift basket that includes champagne, and a shopping shuttle to South Coast Plaza.

Newport Harbor

Probably the most spectacular boat parade is the:

Newport Harbor Parade of Lights
Collins Island—Balboa Island
Newport Beach
normally from December 17-23 from 6:30 to 8:45 p.m.
(714) 644-8211 (information: Chamber of Commerce)
(714) 644-6701 (bleacher seats: Jaycees)
Adults: $6; Seniors: $5; Children (under 12): $4

This is the one that started it all back in 1908. For nearly 90 years, the venerable Newport Beach boat parade has grown bigger each year. Today, over 200 boats of various sizes and degrees of electronic splendor will cruise Newport Harbor in a continuous counter-clockwise display.

If you wish to actually be on the water for the show, you can ride with:

Showboat Cruises
Newport Beach
(714) 673-0240
or:
Balboa Pavilion Cruises
Newport Beach
(714) 673-5245

Or you can take a harbor dinner cruise and even step out on the dance floor:

Hornblower's
Newport Beach
(714) 549-8866

Probably the most Christmas-y feeling place to stay for the Newport Boat Parade is the plush little:

Doryman's Inn
2102 West Oceanfront
Newport Beach, CA 92663
(714) 675-7300

Located in a restored 1921 building, the entrance to the Doryman's Inn is not that overpowering. There is no first floor: you enter by way of a small elevator and the second floor lobby is really little more than the front desk and a waiting room. But the clues to the opulence of the guest rooms are the appointments of the elevator, tiny lobby, and skylighted hallway with its hanging ferns.

The elevator is like a little magic box with an oak door, brass railings, and silk wallpaper. The front desk is heavy carved dark wood.

There are ten rooms, all with private baths with sunken tubs, canopied beds, French glass and beveled mirrors, and Italian marble fireplaces with bedside controls. Six of them have ocean views. The most expensive has a jacuzzi for two. There is a large jacuzzi on the roof and a redwood sun deck. Rates range from around $150 to about $300.

Overlooking Newport Harbor is a contemporary art museum:

Newport Harbor Art Museum
850 San Clemente Drive
Newport Beach, CA 92660
Tuesday-Sunday 10 a.m. to 5 p.m.
(714) 759-1122

This pleasant little museum, located right near "Fashion Island" in Newport Beach, offers a perfect contrast to that shopping center. Founded by thirteen Orange County art patrons in a room at the Balboa Dance Pavilion in 1962, it occupied an old printing plant on the beach for a short time, then moved here in 1977. The building has 23,000-square-feet and the collection is focused on California artists' works after WW II.

The museum has a lovely sculpture garden and though you can't quite see the ocean, you can feel its breeze. The **Sculpture Garden Cafe** has lunch and snacks. Another good reason for coming here this month is that the museum gift shop has a lot of great stuff.

Newport Beach's neighboring coastal town to the south, Corona del Mar, is the site of one of the most beloved holiday traditions in Orange County: the annual decorating of:

> **Rogers Gardens**
> **2301 San Joaquin Hills Road**
> **Corona del Mar, CA 92625**
> **Daily 9 a.m. to 9 p.m.**
> **(714) 640-5800**

Roger's Garden is a nursery located a mile north of Pacific Coast Highway at the corner of San Joaquin Hills Road and MacArthur Boulevard. It is a full seven acres of all manner of plants, but their specialty is hanging baskets.

For Christmas, they decorate over 40 trees, each with a different theme. Special gifts and decorations are available. There is more about Newport Beach in the July and November chapters.

Huntington Beach

Besides the Dana Point and Newport Harbor light parades, Orange County is also the home of the:

> **Huntington Harbor Cruise of Lights**
> **Huntington Beach**
> **Every night from second weekend in December**
> **to December 23**
> **Every hour on the half hour from 5:30 to 8:30 p.m.**
> **Cruise departures are from:**
> **Peter's Landing**
> **16400 Pacific Coast Highway**
> **Huntington Beach, CA 92649**
> **(714) 840-7542**

This is another well-established annual event, having originated in 1962. It is somewhat different in that it takes place in a residential waterfront community where homes as well as boats are decorated. For this reason, it is normally experienced from the 45-minute cruises on board boats that leave every hour on the half hour. Tickets are $8.50 for adults and $5 for children on weeknights, $9.50 for adults and $5 for children on weekends.

For a real small town Christmas feeling before or after the parade, visit Main Street in Seal Beach (see July). It is such a pretty little street to begin with, but it is absolutely adorable when decorated with lights.

Long Beach, Naples

Since 1946, a lovely community just over the border from Orange County, in Long Beach, has been serving up its boat parade in a unique setting:

Naples Boat Parade
Long Beach
starts near Marine Stadium
Appian Way and Bay Shore Drive
finishes near Long Beach Yacht Club
second Saturday of December from 6 to 8 p.m.
(310) 434-3066

This is the second oldest boat parade on the Southern California Coast. It got started during the post-WW II euphoria by two local residents: a realtor (what else?) named Sherill Muntz and an insurance man named Milard B. Hudson. The first one consisted of one boat with a portable organ and a group of carolers.

Today, it is led by the Long Beach fireboat, followed by a squadron of gondolas from Gondola Getaways (see February) in front of the decorated boats, with a floating fire breathing dragon bringing up the rear. The latter element of the show is courtesy of a local skin diving club, called the Neptune Club.

The area here is one of the nicest for an evening stroll and a chance to look at lights in the Southland. Naples Island is crisscrossed with canals with homes fronting on them that are lavishly decorated for the holidays. There is also a long tradition of putting floating trees of light in the bay between Naples and Belmont Shore.

I used to live in the adjacent community of Belmont Shore. The main commercial street that runs through both Naples and Belmont Shore is 2nd Street and for a pretty place to do a little shopping, a little strolling, and a little eating for the holidays, it is hard to beat.

A great little Naples restaurant is:
Justina's
5620 East 2nd Street
Long Beach, CA 90803
Tuesday-Thursday 5 to 9 p.m.
Friday 5 to 10 p.m.
Saturday 8 a.m. to 10 p.m.
Sunday 8 a.m. to 2 p.m.
(310) 434-5191

Owner Jerry Mashburn took over this charmer in 1990. It has Victorian flowery wallpaper and only thirteen tables. The menu includes vegetarian, seafood, game, and steak. The chef prepares five to six specials per night and also packs picnic baskets to go.

If you go over the bridge to Belmont Shore, you will notice the inlaid bricks used to widen the sidewalks. In 1993, an already pretty walking street was made more so by this project, spearheaded by Belmont Shore Business Association President Frank Colonna. During the holidays, the landscaped center island is decorated with lights and Santa is available for photos.

What makes Belmont Shore a nice place to stroll and shop for the holidays is that in addition to its inviting small town Main Street-look, it has some unusual stores. The first of these you will come to is:

> **Cargo West**
> **5280 East 2nd Street**
> **Long Beach, CA 90803**
> **Daily 10 a.m. to 9 p.m.**
> **(310) 434-2021**

This beautiful gift shop has a definite artistic quality to its merchandise.

A small shop with a catchy name is on the same side of the street:

> **Headhunters**
> **5110 East 2nd Street**
> **Long Beach, CA 90803**
> **Sunday-Thursday 10 a.m. to 10 p.m.**
> **Friday & Saturday 10 a.m. to 11 p.m.**
> **(310) 433-0677**

Headhunters sells T-shirts, art objects, underground comics, and smoking accessories.

A few doors down is a romantic store for couples:

> **The Rubber Tree**
> **5018 East 2nd Street**
> **Long Beach, CA 90803**
> **Monday 11 a.m. to 7 p.m.**
> **Tuesday-Thursday 11 a.m. to 9 p.m.**
> **Friday & Saturday 11 a.m. to 11 p.m.**
> **Sunday 11 a.m. to 7 p.m.**
> **(310) 434-0027**

Opened in October of '92 by Joy Starr, who originally hailed from Idaho. In case you are wondering, her name came from her ex-husband, Larry Starr. She had looked all up and down the Southern California coast for a location before choosing Belmont Shore. Now she and her daughter, Shana, run a store for lovers. They have sexy games, lingerie, adult toys, cards, and, yes, condoms.

For ornaments, cards and wrapping, an all-around holiday stop is:

Holly's Hallmark Shop
5012 East 2nd Street
Long Beach, CA 90803
Monday-Thursday 9 a.m. to 9 p.m.
Friday & Saturday 9 a.m. to 10 p.m.
Sunday 11 a.m. to 7 p.m.
(310) 434-5291

Holly's has been on 2nd Street since 1980. Owner Patti Allen also keeps a large inventory of gifts, such as Belmont Shore T-shirts.

Across the street is an unusual shop with great contemporary home furnishings:

Futon Design
5005 East 2nd Street
Long Beach, CA 90803
Monday-Thursday 11 a.m. to 7 p.m.
Friday 11 a.m. to 8 p.m.
Saturday 10 a.m. to 6 p.m.
Sunday 1 to 5 p.m.
(310) 433-8749

Though this store is decidedly casual, the futons and accessories they carry tend to be high-end quality. Many of them feature elegantly curved bent wood designs. The owner of this store also opened a delightful gift shop just a step away:

5001
5005 East 2nd Street
Long Beach, CA 90803
Monday-Friday 11 a.m. to 9 p.m.
Saturday 10 a.m. to 9 p.m.
Sunday 11 a.m. to 7 p.m.
(310) 439-1975

5001 has a great selection of small art objects and cards. Diagonally across the intersection is another art-oriented gift shop:

Luna
4928 East 2nd Street
Long Beach, CA 90803
Daily 10 a.m. to 9 p.m.
(310) 987-4780

This is the dream of artist Don Dame. A great deal of creativity went into its design . It is like a little jewel box of functional art. The exposed beam ceiling is often festooned with hanging objects for the season.

A great all-purpose bookstore is down the street:

Dodds Book Shop
4818 East 2nd Street
Long Beach, CA 90803
Monday-Saturday 10 a.m. to 10 p.m.
Sunday 12 to 6 p.m.
(310) 438-9948

Dodds is a good all-round bookstore. For the holidays, owner Kim Browning always carries a huge line of calendars of every theme.

There are many engaging little stores here, but a particularly charming one is on a side street, one door down from 2nd Street:

Provence Boulangerie
191 Park Avenue
Long Beach, CA 90803
Tuesday-Friday 6:30 a.m. to 7 p.m.
Saturday & Sunday 7:30 a.m. to 7 p.m.
(310) 433-8281

This tiny little espresso and bake shop has little round tables and real French charm. Owner Oliver Birkui hails from Cannes and has brought his traditional baking skills with him. They feature 14 authentic French-style breads and plain and filled croissants that are absolutely sensational.

A pleasant place for a little Italian food is a few steps away:

Papalucci
4611 East 2nd Street
Long Beach, CA 90803

Monday-Thursday 11 a.m. to 10 p.m.
Friday & Saturday 11 a.m. to 11 p.m.
Sunday 11 a.m. to 9 p.m.

This bright place has excellent pastas and Italian specialty dishes served in a very informal atmosphere.

A substantial amount of this book was written while drinking coffee made from the beans at:

> **Polly's Coffee**
> **4606 East 2nd Street**
> **Long Beach, CA 90803**
> **Monday-Friday 6:30 a.m. to 9 p.m.**
> **Saturday & Sunday 7:30 a.m. to 9 p.m.**
> **(310) 433-2996**

Opened by Mike Sheldrake in 1976, at the time it was one of the few coffee stores in the country that roasted their own beans on the premises. Now, though more do, it is still a rarity. Many coffee chain stores actually roast their beans in big factories located out of state. Polly's roaster is there for all to see and it adds a real atmosphere to the place.

Polly's has a warm and a warehouse feel at the same time. The exposed wood beams and high ceiling rise over a wood floor stained forever by innumerable coffee spills. Indeed, there have been quite few of these over the years: each month, they roast 10,000 pounds and serve 15,000 coffee drinks. The choice of beans is excellent: they even have Costa Rican "La Minita Tarrazu."

Not only do they have great on-premises roasted coffee beans here, their selection of mugs, spices, gift baskets, and other related items is superb. Polly's ships all over the U.S.

One thing to always remember in Belmont Shore is to read the signs before you park. Tickets are given with great alacrity. There is more about the area in the February and July chapters.

Long Beach, Queen Mary

The other boat parade in Long Beach is in a somewhat larger setting:

> **Parade of 1,000 Lights**
> **Channel between Queen Mary and**
> **Shoreline Village**
> **Long Beach**
> **third Saturday from Christmas at 7 p.m.**
> **Boat judging at 7 p.m. near Parker's Lighthouse**
> **(310) 435-4093**

For this parade, about 40 to 50 decorated boats proceed around the perimeter of

Shoreline Village. There are viewing areas near Parker's Lighthouse restaurant (see July).

The best store in Downtown Long Beach for holiday shopping is:

Acres of Books
240 Long Beach Boulevard
Long Beach, CA 90802
Tuesday-Saturday 9:15 a.m. to 5 p.m.
(310) 437-6980

Enclosed by a 1930's Streamline Moderne building is one of the largest collections of used books for sale on the West Coast: 750,000 volumes are divided into 500 categories and stacked in towering homemade bookshelves and fruit crates spread out over 13,000-square-feet. A favorite haunt of Ray Bradbury, it is a booklover's dream and the perfect place to find a copy of that out-of-print book you've been looking for.

Of course, Long Beach is also the home of "The Largest Bedspread Store In The United States:"

Al Greenwood's Bedspread Kingdom
2750 East Pacific Coast Highway
Long Beach, CA 90804
Monday-Saturday 10 a.m. to 5 p.m.
Sunday 12 to 5p.m.
(310) 498-9277

An entire city block is taken up by this enormous store. In his famous advertising photo, owner Al Greenwood is pictured with his crown at a rakish angle, with a scarlet cape sporting a fake fur collar, and scepter in hand in front of a frame 40-by-40 foot that supports 210 bedspreads in a spectacular tribute to cold winter nights. He has also written and produced his own highly original television advertisements since 1987.

Mr. Greenwood achieved his lofty office of Bedspread King by accident.

Al Greenwood Bedspread King.

Born in 1907, he got into the business in 1962. He was originally planning to be a sort of a Cal Worthington of bedspreads, complete with a cowboy hat, but the cartoonist he hired to design the logo gave him the crown instead, and one of the Southland's great personas was born. The Bedspread King is possibly the most perfect personification of Southern California: when you buy a bedspread, he will give you an autographed 8-by-10 photo of himself dressed in his royal attire, if you ask. He also has tracts of his personal philosophy available.

Of course, a common complaint during the Christmas shopping season is of sore feet. A proper shrine for the season is located in Long Beach:

Dr. Thomas Armberry Foot and Toe Museum

2454 Atlantic Avenue

Long Beach, CA 90806

(310) 426-3321

Long Beach podiatrist Dr. Thomas Armberry began his collection accidentally when patients kept sending him gag items related to the foot. Being a fellow with a sense of humor, he began grouping these with more serious podiatric paraphernalia such as anatomical models. Thus one of the world's most unique museums was born.

Today, there are over 9,000 pieces in the museum's collection. It is mentioned in the travel guide *Medical Landmarks U.S.A.* On display are such noteworthy objects d'art as foot-shaped lamps and unusual sized shoes. These run the gamut from famous circus midget General Tom Thumb's toddler-size dress shoes to the unreal looking size 26 monoliths of 7-foot 8-inch basketball player George Bell. There is even a spectacular "wall of license plates" that have foot and toe related messages such as CORNS, BUNION, or DR POD.

Before you leave Long Beach, be sure and check out its most noted Christmas display. The **Daisy Avenue** neighborhood in Long Beach, between Pacific Coast Highway and Willow Streets, has a long tradition of holiday decorating. Lights are strung from the giant evergreens and the individual houses display Santas, snowmen, and lighted nativity scenes. The spectacle stays up until December 26.

They have also been holding a small parade at 6 p.m. the second Saturday of the month since 1953. Call (310) 436-7703 for information. There is more about Downtown Long Beach later this month.

San Pedro

The next city north of Long Beach along the coast with a boat parade is:

Los Angeles Harbor Christmas Afloat Parade

San Pedro
Saturday & Sunday, second weekend of December at 6 p.m.
(310) 549-2245

The parade begins at the East Basin, proceeds south to Cabrillo Marina, then to the Port of L.A. The old Angel's Gate tugboat and the Los Angeles Fireboat are part of a procession of about 50 boats decorated with lights.

What makes this parade a particularly nice experience is that the best viewing areas are Ports O' Call Village (see January)—which has places to grab a bite right there—as well as Banning's Landing in Wilmington.

Marina del Rey

The most glamorous of the boat parades is the:

Marina del Rey Boat Parade
Marina del Rey, Los Angeles
usually the second Saturday of December at 5:30 p.m.
(310) 821-7614

Because of its location on the west side of Los Angeles, the Marina del Rey Boat Parade is the only one that usually has a celebrity grand marshal. It is the second largest on the coast with about 100 boats

Statue of the Mariner at Burton Chase Park.

and it's just amazing how elaborately some of them are decorated.

Public viewing is on the north and south jetties from Pacific Avenue and Vista del Mar, Burton Chase Park, (which is at the west end of Mindanao Way), and Fisherman's Village on Fiji Way. Parking is on Admiralty Way and Via Marina.

Nearby Santa Monica has a unique institution that is a delightful daytime holiday stop:

Angel's Attic
516 Colorado Avenue
Santa Monica, CA 90401
Thursday-Sunday 12:30 to 4:30 p.m.
Adults: $4; Seniors: $3; Children: $2
(310) 394-8331

This 1895 Victorian was lovingly restored and converted into a museum of vintage toys, dolls, and miniatures in 1984. Eleanor La Vove and Jackie McMahan run this amazing little institution that also functions to raise funds for the Brentwood Center For Educational Therapy. There is a gift shop and they have tea and homemade cakes on the old porch available for $5 (call first for reservations).

The displays change somewhat regularly, but beginning around the middle of November they begin a wonderful annual holiday show wherein they decorate all of the dollhouses with Christmas lights. They also bring out a special dollhouse: "Santa's Workshop" with over 120 elf dolls inside.

Santa Monica is a shopper's paradise since its stores tend to carry the more unusual merchandise. **Santa Monica Place**, the indoor mall that forms the southern end of 3rd Street Promenade (see July), is architecturally one of the most remarkable of the genre (it was designed by Frank Gehry). But for holiday gift shopping—especially for a difficult person—the place to go is:

California Map and Travel Center
3211 Pico Boulevard
Santa Monica, CA 90405
Monday-Wednesday 8:30 a.m. to 6 p.m.
Thursday-Friday 8:30 a.m. to 9 p.m.
Saturday 9 a.m. to 9 p.m.
Sunday 12 to 5 p.m.
(310) 829-MAPS

Former accountant Sheldon Mars and his wife, Barbara, bought this store (which used to be in Downtown L.A.) in 1988. Since that time, with the help of an expert staff, they have built one of the best inventories of books, maps, and travel accessories in the business.

They stock over 10,000 titles and the map selection includes about 5,000 regular maps and 15,000 to 20,000 topographic maps. There are also guide bags, toiletry kits, and all kinds of portable versions of things. Everywhere you look in this 2,500-square-foot store, you can find something interesting. The California Map and Travel Center also holds about three travel-oriented events (such as slide shows) per month.

Channel Islands Harbor, Oxnard

Ventura County has two holiday boat parades. The first of these is the:

Channel Islands Harbor Parade of Lights
Oxnard
second Saturday of December at 7 p.m.
awards ceremony 9:30 p.m. at:
Harbor Landing
2800 S. Harbor Boulevard
Oxnard, CA 93035
(805) 984-3366
contact:
Channel Island's Harbor Association
Vintage Marina
2950 South Harbor Boulevard
Oxnard, CA 93035
(805) 985-4852

This is a small (usually limited to 40 boats) parade that originated in 1965. It circles Channel Islands Harbor twice.

There is no celebrity grand marshal, just jolly old Saint Nick waving away. Viewing is good off Harbor Boulevard on the west bank or on the promenade in front of the Harbor Landing Shopping Center.

Ventura

The other boat parade in Ventura County is normally a week later:

Ventura Harbor Parade of Lights
Ventura Harbor
usually third Saturday of December
(805) 644-0169
contact:
Ventura Port District
1603 Anchor's Way Drive
Ventura, CA 93001
(805) 642-8538

After the main parade of about 40 boats, a second processional of the smaller boats go into the keys past the decorated homes. Boat rides are available on the *Bay Queen,* which carries about 20 people.

For both of the Ventura County parades, Santa Claus flies overhead by helicopter.

I recommend a restaurant near where they hold the parade:

Eric Ericsson's on the Beach
1140 South Seaward Avenue
Ventura, CA 93001
Tuesday-Sunday 11:30 a.m. to 10 p.m.
(805) 643-4783

Not quite lapping up the waves, but located where the name says, this restaurant has an extraordinary selection of fresh seafood.

Ventura County is not without its share of unusual stores for holiday gifts. Santa Paula (see April) and Downtown Ventura (see July) are even more charming with the lights of the season. Ojai (see June, August, and October) has its galleries and stores. One in particular is quite unusual:

Hardings
103 West Aliso Street
Ojai, CA 92023
Monday-Friday 10 a.m. to 5 p.m.
(805) 646-0204

Hardings specializes in mechanical, industrial, and scientific antiquities and finely engineered models. You could not find a more thoughtful gift than a piece of art that honors someone's profession

Santa Barbara

The northern-most boat parade in the Southland is the:

Yuletide Boat Parade
usually Sunday before Christmas
Santa Barbara
(805) 962-2826
contact:
Sailing Center
Breakwater
Santa Barbara, CA 93109

This parade of from 50 to 75 boats was started in '86 by Randy Schweitzer, who owns the Sailing Center. This establishment offers everything to do with sailing. They have a school and boats for hire. Dinner cruises and whale watch trips are regular features on their 50-foot sailing catamaran called the *Double Dolphin*.

What makes this parade unique is that the route was designed to allow spectators on the beach to see it. The processional goes in a three to four mile semi circular route along the beach into the harbor. The judges watch from Stearns Wharf. There is more about the City of Santa Barbara in the February, March, and August chapters.

CHRISTMAS TRADITIONS

Before all the parades of lights, San Diego had a beautiful holiday tradition:

Christmas Tree Lighting and Festivities
Hotel Del Coronado
1500 Orange Avenue
Coronado, CA 92118
December 1
(619) 522-8000
(800) 468-3533

The first Christmas tree at the Del was put up in 1904. Like the hotel itself, it was lit by the new "Edison Electric Light." In fact, Thomas Edison himself threw the switch at that inaugural celebration. This is why the annual tree lighting ceremony here is such a big event. It forms the centerpiece for a whole month of Christmas activities.

Since the Hotel Del Coronado has been in business since 1888 (see July), the old-time theme of its Christmas festivities is especially appropriate. In addition to the tree lighting ceremony on December 1, they have other delights, such as costumed characters roaming the fairytale grounds along with carolers, adding even more atmosphere to the brightly-lit historical monument. They always have special holiday dinners as well.

Coronado is a quiet place with lots of old Victorian houses. Every year, the local Kiwanis Club holds Candlelight Walking Tours, starting around December 10, to look at the vintage decorated homes. For a complete list of activities in Coronado for the holidays call the visitor's center at (800) 622-8300.

San Diego

Perhaps the best loved holiday tradition in San Diego is:

Christmas on the Prado
Balboa Park
first weekend in December
(619) 231-1640
(619) 239-0512

Balboa Park is a pleasant enough place the rest of the year (see April and June), but every Christmas since 1977, they have celebrated the holidays here in a way that makes it even better. Beginning at 5 p.m. on both Saturday and Sunday nights, more than 20 cultural organizations and museums present special free exhibits and entertainment. Gifts and ethnic foods are also offered.

Some of the highlights are Mexican folk dancing at the Spanish Village Art Center, music by the University of California, San Diego Gospel Choir at the Museum of Photographic Arts, and the Swedish Santa Lucia on both nights at the Museum of Man at 6 and 8 p.m. There is also entertainment in the Spreckles Organ Pavilion at 4 p.m. on Saturday and 5 p.m. on Sunday.

Near the Spreckles Organ Pavilion is a giant Deodar Cedar tree that is decorated for the holidays. The Cabrillo Bridge is beautifully lighted, as is nearby Mr. A's Restaurant (see February).

The most dramatic of San Diego's Christmas rituals is the annual staging of:

A Christmas Carol
San Diego Repertory Theatre
The Lyceum Theatre
79 Horton Plaza
San Diego, CA 92101
usually runs December 10-26
(619) 235-8025

San Diego Rep (described in September) renews this production of the Dicken's classic every year. It always punctuates the performance with some kind of special effects surprise that is eagerly awaited by theatregoers.

Orange County

This most famous Christmas play also has an Orange County home:

A Christmas Carol
South Coast Repertory Theater
655 Towne Center Drive
Costa Mesa, CA 92626

usually first week of December to Christmas Eve
(714) 957-2602

South Coast Rep's annual production of Charles Dicken's classic Christmas story is a major event and tickets can be hard to come by. It is truly a spectacle and not to be missed.

A tradition since 1980, the elaborate staging of *A Christmas Carol* here is different every year. The member of the company who traditionally plays Scrooge is Hal Landon, Jr., who also works in film. One of the more humorous juxtapositions in drama is to see him play Scrooge on stage here, then rent the movies *Bill and Ted's Excellent Adventure* and *Bill and Ted's Bogus Journey*. In both these movies, he plays Ted's father, a police captain who is always threatening to send him to military school in Alaska. The funniest moment comes in *Bogus Journey* when the spirit of his temporarily deceased son possesses him and he can't help but take on his son's mannerisms and speech. It is quite a display. For more about the theatre, see September.

If you are planning a holiday getaway, one of the best values in Southern California is:

Countryside Inn
325 Bristol Street
Costa Mesa, CA 92626
(714) 549-0300

The Countryside Inn is an unusual place—a sort of businessman's bed and breakfast. Looking like a countyfied Ramada Inn on the outside, its interior is charming. The lobby is an elegant marbled affair reminiscent of a small European hotel. The courtyard has a similar motif with a babbling fountain. The rooms feature nine-foot ceilings, four-poster beds and fireplaces.

Their normal weekend rates are much more like what a run of the mill motel would cost than a bed and breakfast of any charm and include buffet breakfast, fruit in the room, transportation, and evening cocktail.

In many ways, the Countryside Inn is like a giant bed and breakfast. It was built by a prominent Orange County family, the Ayers, and run by the eldest son, Don.

The most "Christmas-y" museum in Orange County is located in Santa Ana and has a special event for the season:

"Victorian Holiday"
Discovery Museum of Orange County

3101 West Harvard Street
Santa Ana, CA 92704
normally second Saturday of December
regular hours:
Saturday & Sunday 11 a.m. to 3 p.m.
Tuesday-Friday (school groups)
(714) 540-0404

This is a beautiful 11-acre complex whose purpose is to show children what life was like in the 19th century. There are four restored Victorian buildings, the main one being the gabled Kellogg mansion, built in 1898. It is filled with authentic period furnishings and objects throughout, and the landscaping incorporates a rose garden, a citrus orchard, and an herb garden. But this is not a static place to sit back and view objects.

The Discovery Museum is one of the few places where children are told "please touch." Docents coach participants in churning butter, doing laundry with a scrub board, and using a hand crank telephone. Children can also put on Victorian clothing and pick fruit. Some of the artifacts are quaint and charming, such as the antique piano, others are a little terrifying, such as the foot-powered washing machine, which is like an aerobic workout machine from hell. Where it's located in Centennial Park is also a good picnic site.

For the "Victorian Holiday," they feature local children's choirs, fresh cookies and cider, authentic decorations, and tours of the mansion every hour.

Riverside

A unique place to do a little holiday shopping, as well as have dinner and soak up some holiday spirit, is at the:

Festival of Lights
Downtown Riverside Mall
Riverside
December 1 through January 1
(909) 715-4636

The pretty, historic Downtown Riverside Mall (see April) is made even more pleasant this time of year with piped-in Christmas music, special events, and lights and decorations. The most spectacular of the latter adorn the:

Mission Inn
3649 Seventh Street

Riverside, CA 92501
(909) 784-0300

The pictures of the Mission Inn in the April chapter cannot compare to what it looks like for the season when it is elaborately lit with thousands of twinkling lights. There are also animated holiday figures on the inn and on the Orange Street side of the mall. Call for information on their special Christmas dinners and room rates.

Across from the **Universal Bookstore** (see April) is a little enclosed courtyard of antique and gift shops where musicians often play. There is a great little sandwich and pastry shop here called **The Upper Crust**. Besides here and at **Birdy's Coffeehouse** (see April), you can get sweets for the holidays at:

Simple Simon's Bakery
3639 Main Street
Riverside, CA 892501
Monday-Saturday 9 a.m. to 5 p.m.
(909) 369-6030

This mall favorite was opened by Susie Thiel in 1983. A real Idaho farm girl, she has fashioned a warm, cozy place for lunch or dessert and coffee. They have all kinds of treats, but their Christmas cookies are especially good. Good natured Cheryl Duffy, one of the bakers since 1987, is especially happy to hear it when customers are pleased.

It is a testament to the homey nature of the shops in the mall that Susie Thiel's sister, Ceann, owns two gift stores here: **Mrs. Tiggywinkles** and **The Parrot**. Other gift shops with unusual items for the holidays include **Farthings Cards and Gifts** and **Dragon Marsh** (described in April).

Oak Glen

I mentioned Oak Glen in the September chapter. One of its best farms has an annual old-fashioned Christmas program:

"Old St. Nick's Christmas Party"
Riley's Farm and Orchard
12253 South Oak Glen Road
Oak Glen, CA 92399
usually first weekend of December
Saturday & Sunday

11 a.m. to 9 p.m.
(909) 790-2364

Their motto here is, "We are 100 years behind the times." It is appropriate, because Riley's Farm is like a giant interactive museum of 19th century farm life. Besides the U-pick apple orchards that are an Oak Glen trademark, they have hay rides, blacksmith demonstrations, hootenanny hoedowns, and other U-pick crops.

For this party, "Dickens dress" is encouraged. Activities include caroling in the barn, chestnut roasting, dinner, and dancing.

Rancho Cucamonga

A bed and breakfast mentioned back in October, with the perfect name for the season, has a wonderful holiday custom:

A Christmas Carol
Christmas House
9240 Archibald Avenue
Rancho Cucamonga, CA 91730
(909) 980-6450

This Victorian bed and breakfast is heavily decorated this month and does the Dicken's classic in a most charming fashion. The action takes place in different rooms and the audience is escorted to each scene. There is a different set of actors in each room.

They have holiday gifts in the gift shop here or you could go to the local wineries such as Galleano (described in October) where they offer beautiful gift baskets.

Cerritos

One of the Southland's most spectacular neighborhood light displays is found in Cerritos:

King's Row Avenue and Castle Place
[off South Street just west of the I-605]
Cerritos

For about three blocks along these streets, a group of families decorate their homes with life-sized Christmas figures and thousands of lights. Many have individual themes, such as "Country." One even features a small hot air balloon. It has become so famous that traffic moves through this quiet suburban neighborhood in a bumper-to-bumper crawl. I would park nearby and walk for that reason, and also because it is truly an awesome spectacle and worth a prolonged look.

Little Tokyo

Of all the annual festivities for the holidays, the one that perhaps most captures the spirit of multicultural Southern California is the arrival of:

Shogun Santa
Japanese Village Plaza
2nd Street at Central Avenue
Little Tokyo, Los Angeles
first weekend in December to December 24
Daily 11 a.m. to 2 p.m.
(213) 620-8861

Shogun Santa is the familiar bearded, red-suited fellow—except for the fact that he is Japanese and also wears a Samurai warrior's helmet. Perhaps the most beau-

The yagura, or firetower, in the Japanese Village Plaza, Little Tokyo.

tiful image I never got a picture of was a little blond-haired blue-eyed girl seated on Shogun Santa's lap, beaming rapturously into his kindly old face with its improbable headgear.

Japanese Village Plaza is my favorite of the Little Tokyo shopping centers because of its lively, fun quality. It is a two-story outdoor, meandering corridor of a mall that continues to 1st Street, where it is topped by a four-story traditional fireman's lookout of natural finished wood. Wood is used throughout, and along with the cobalt blue sanchu roofs and elegant use of stone, pools, and tiny gardens, the overall effect is like a little Japanese "Main Street."

The restaurant next to the fireman's lookout tower is aptly named:

Yagura Ichiban
101 Japanese Village Plaza

350 East 1st Street
Los Angeles, CA 90012
Tuesday-Sunday 11 a.m. to 10:30 p.m.
(213) 623-4141

"Yagura" means "fire tower." This is a good all-round Japanese restaurant with a Robata-yaki bar, a sushi bar, and a tatami room.

Japanese Village Plaza has a great selection of small shops, bakeries, and restaurants. Be sure and stop in the amazing:

Plaza Gift Center
111 Japanese Village
Plaza Mall
Los Angeles, CA 90012
Daily 10:30 a.m. to 5 p.m.
(213) 680-3288

They have more merchandise piled up in here than in stores twice as big. Madonna cavorts on a row of new Sony televisions that look down upon shelves stocked with everything from plastic troll dolls to Nintendo games. They also have some very lovely Japanese gifts.

A fun and delicious dining stop is:

Shabu-Shabu House
127 Japanese Village Plaza Mall
Los Angeles, CA 90012
Tuesday-Sunday 11 a.m. to 10 p.m.
(213) 680-3890

"Shabu shabu" is a Japanese dish that is made from super thin slices of beef simmered quickly in a broth with vegetables.You cook it yourself at your own counter seat.

Right by here is a great place for treats for the holidays:

Ikeda Bakery
123 Japanese Village Plaza
Los Angeles, CA 90012
Daily 9 a.m. to 8 p.m.
(213) 624-2773

Ikeda Bakery has both Japanese and Western baked goods. Specialties include "anpan," which are cream-filled pastries, and bread made with brown rice.

Of course, for holiday browsing, it's hard to top:

> **Yaohan Plaza**
> **333 South Alameda Street**
> **Little Tokyo**
> **Los Angeles, CA 90013**
> **(213) 687-6699**

This big, bustling box of a building was built in 1985. It was designed to bring Tokyo-style shopping to Japanese residents of L.A.

The department store is a great place to buy clothes—particularly when they are marked down, because the percentage discount seems to always be greater than 50 percent. If you would like to buy someone some house slippers for a Christmas present, Yaohan Plaza has the largest selection I have ever seen. There is more about Little Tokyo in the August chapter.

Los Angeles, Downtown

The ultimate Christmas sing-along unites over 3,000 people together in the beautiful Dorothy Chandler Pavilion raising their voices to Handel's "Messiah" with the Los Angeles Master Chorale:

> **Annual "Messiah" Sing-Along**
> **Los Angeles Master Chorale**
> **Dorothy Chandler Pavilion**
> **Los Angeles Music Center**
> **135 North Grand Avenue**
> **Los Angeles, CA 90012**
> **usually about two weeks before Christmas**
> **(213) 972-7283**

The Music Center was described in the February chapter. This tradition was started in 1979 by the late Roger Wagner. It has since been copied by other musical organizations.

A truly classic place to go for a holiday meal or an overnighter is the:

> **Biltmore Hotel**
> **506 South Grand Avenue**
> **Los Angeles, CA 90013**
> **(213) 624-1011**

Christmas at the Biltmore (described in February) is a tradition going back to the 1920s. Every year they have a variety of special programs. The pastry shop always creates a number of holiday treats that can make you feel like you are back in the 19th century. The Grand Promenade is usually decorated with live fir trees. From 11:30 a.m. to 1:30 p.m., they customarily offer Chamber Music in The Rendezvous Court followed by a Holiday Tea from 2 to 5 p.m. daily. Carolers normally stroll about the hotel singing from 11:30 a.m. to 1:30 p.m.

Bernards restaurant features a special holiday menu, but it is their New Year's Eve tradition that is most unusual (see under New Year's Eve). As a rule, they also offer an excellent holiday rate on rooms.

Right near the Biltmore is one of those one-of-a-kind specialty stores:

> **The Fountain Pen Shop**
> **510 West 6th Street Suite 1032**
> **Los Angeles, CA 90014**
> **Monday-Saturday 8:30 a.m. to 5 p.m.**
> **(213) 891-1581**

Founded in 1922 by a gentleman named John Froehlich, moved in 1957, and again to its current location in 1994, this store conveys comfort through its very existence. It is a warm thought for the holidays to think that such a unique and wonderful place can survive under family ownership in L.A.: his grandson, Fred Krinke, carries on the family tradition.

And it is certainly a great one. There are both new and used pens here from Waterman, Sheaffer, Pelikan, Parker, and of course, Mont Blanc. There are even antiques for sale. Prices can range from less than $100 to over $8,000!

This store also adds to the ranks of unusual museums in the Southland with its in-house **Fountain Pen Museum**. This is a very impressive collection of over 500 antiques originally started by the store's founder, grandfather pen, as it were. There are English and Continental European, Southeast Asian, and American from the mid-1800s on. The latter are amazingly snazzy—particularly the ones from the "Roaring '20s."

If The Fountain Pen Store is the ultimate specialty store, then nine miles south of Los Angeles is the ultimate outlet mall:

> **The Citadel**
> **5675 East Telegraph Road**
> **City of Commerce, CA 90040**
> **Monday-Saturday 10 a.m. to 8 p.m.**

Sunday 10 a.m. to 6 p.m.
(213) 888-1220

This incredible structure, a landmark by the I-5, languished unused for many years until someone got the idea of turning it into an outlet mall. It is probably the only outlet mall in the world in the image of a 7th century B.C. Assyrian palace. Filmmaker William Wyler used it in *Ben Hur*. Amazingly enough, it was not built as a movie set. Originally, it was the Sampson Tire Factory, then UniRoyal.

Now it has 50 rock bottom outlet stores that range from The Gap to the United Colors of Benetton. Besides apparel outlets, such stores as Book Warehouse and Toy Liquidators make it possible to spend a full day stimulating the economy.

The Food Court includes meals from Johnny Rockets, Pachanga Mexican Grill, Sbarro—The Italian Eatery, Taipan Express, Subway Sandwich, and dessert, too, like Steve's Ice Cream, Heidi's Frozen Yogurt, and David's Cookies.

Since 1963, one of the great unusual theatre traditions in Southern California has been the:

Bob Baker Marionette Theatre
1345 West 1st Street
Los Angeles, CA 90026
(213) 250-9995

This 245-seat auditorium is the oldest ongoing theatre of its kind in the United States. Inside is a comfortable place with stars on the wall and red carpeting. Baker's handmade puppets are a sight to behold and there is always have a special program for the holidays. They have a demonstration of marionette and other puppet techniques after every show.

Earlier in the month one of Southern California's more obscure museums has an annual holiday party:

Christmas Party
Grier Musser Museum
403 South Bonnie Brae
Los Angeles, CA 90063
Wednesday-Saturday 11 a.m. to 4 p.m.
Christmas party first Saturday in December
(213) 413-1814

The Victorian Grier-Musser Museum was described in February. The Christmas party will be a traditional one and the ornate setting will make for a real feeling of being back in the 19th century. Call the museum for details.

Pasadena, Altadena, Arcadia

Perhaps the most extreme example of neighborhood decorating can be found in:

Upper Hastings Ranch
[between Foothill Boulevard and Michillinda Avenue]
Pasadena

Since 1956, homes here have been decorated for Christmas. What makes this outstanding is the sheer number: there are about 1,100 homes over a 44-block radius that are decorated.

Another longstanding holiday light tradition is very near here:

"Christmas Tree Lane"
Santa Rosa Avenue
[between Altadena Drive and Woodbury Road]
Altadena

This street is lined with 90-foot tall deodar cedar tees that are over 100 years old. Since the 1920s, in a tradition started by department store tycoon F.C. Nash, they have been beautifully lighted in one of the Southland's more surprising light shows. It is the only annual lighting display to have reached the lofty status of California Historic Landmark and is now maintained by a nonprofit corporation.

From Santa Rosa Avenue, head east on Mendocino Lane for Southern California's single prettiest decorated house:

Balian Mansion
1960 Mendocino Lane
Altadena, CA 91001

This house has the most wonderful approach to it under ordinary circumstances. The street literally ends in the greenery framed entrance of this large 1920's Mediterranean mansion that almost epitomizes the image of the Southern California dream house. For the holiday, its owner, ice cream king George Balian, festoons it with over 10,000 lights.

Nearby Pasadena has a wonderful museum with a great shop for a-typical holiday gifts:

Norton Simon Museum
411 W. Colorado Boulevard
Pasadena, CA 91105
Thursday-Sunday 12 to 6 p.m.
(818) 449-6840

The Norton Simon has a permanent collection second to none. Works by such Old Masters as Rembrandt, Raphael, and Reubens are complimented by Impressionists such as Van Gogh, Cezanne, and Renoir. Southeast Asian and Indian sculpture fill another gallery.

Besides taking in the fabulous art on display, you can also bring something special home with you: the museum store here has a fantastic selection of art cards, books, and prints.

On the second weekend of December, one of L.A.'s most famous homes is open for its once-per-year Christmas exhibition:

>**Lucky Baldwin House**
>**Los Angeles County Arboretum**
>**301 North Baldwin Avenue**
>**Arcadia, CA 91007**
>**usually open second weekend in December**
>**from 10 a.m. to 4 p.m.**
>**(818) 821-3222**

I mentioned this house in passing in the March chapter. E.J. "Lucky" Baldwin built this beautiful cottage in 1886 as a wedding present for his darling bride Lillie Bennett. He was 56, she was a mature 16. It was his fourth marriage. Lucky's luck with real estate apparently did not extend to women because she was gone before the house was even finished. It is world famous because of its role on TV's "Fantasy Island." They filmed here from '78 to '84 and then built a copy at the studio.

The Christmas open house is one of the few times the inside is made available to the public. It has old furniture and household appliances of the period.

Los Angeles, Westside

A prestigious theatre company has more than a history of holiday shows:

>*Stories of the Season*
>**Pacific Theatre Ensemble**
>**8780 Venice Boulevard**
>**Los Angeles, CA 90026**
>**Thursday-Saturday 8 p.m.**
>**Sunday 7 p.m.**
>**December 1-18**
>**(310) 306-3943**

The Pacific Theatre Ensemble, best known for their absolutely brilliant original pieces like *Slaughterhouse On Tanner Close,* has been doing holiday shows for many years. For a while, it looked as if their production of Thornton Wilder's *The Long Christmas Dinner* would be a regular Southland holiday tradition, but they changed to this program in 1993.

This show is produced by mask maker Bob Beuth. It offers holiday stories from cultures throughout the world. The staging is very unusual: the audience gets to pick from boxes wrapped like presents on stage like the TV show, "Let's Make A Deal." Each box contains a story, which is then acted out. Thus the show is different every night. Because of the fun format and the variety of cultures represented—from Eskimo to African—it is the kind of show that teaches diversity to children everywhere. Also, if you bring $2 in canned goods to donate to the Westside Food Bank, the ticket price is reduced.

Not that far from here, in a city associated with the film industry, is another unusual Southern California specialty store:

Allied Model Trains
4411 Sepulveda Boulevard
Culver City, CA 90230
Monday-Thursday & Saturday 10 a.m. to 6 p.m.
Friday 10 a.m. 9 p.m.
Sunday 12 to 5 p.m. (December only)
(310) 313-9353

This is the world's largest train store ever built as a train store (there is one in a former supermarket in Denver that has more square footage). Designed by Santa Monica architect James Mount, the building is a miniature replica of Union Station, complete with clock tower.

Allied Model Trains started life in 1946 at the corner of Pico and Westwood in a 1,200-square-foot space. It was somewhat run down and was on its third owner when in November of 1975, electronics salesman Allen Drucker gave up a good-paying job, sold his house and brought the place.

His gamble paid off, because it was right at the start of the growth in traditional Americana nostalgia. He expanded the store to 2,400-square-feet and kept building until finally he needed a bigger location. In 1989, the store moved into this 11,600-square-foot home in Culver City.

Drucker, who was brought up in the nearby hills of Westchester, could have built his train emporium plain, but took the risk and created something truly special. His fondest childhood memory was of the Christmas train layouts department stores used to put up for the holidays. He recreated that experience with six 12-foot wide show windows, each of which has a separate running train set up and a step for children to stand on when peering through the glass. There are train layouts throughout the store with one on a shelf that runs around the perimeter of whole place. Its train and cars are 30-feet long.

Allied Model Trains stocks all makes and sizes of model trains and they buy, sell, and repair. They also keep a particularly large stock of the light up miniature buildings made by Department 56, such as Dicken's Village. These are particularly wonderful at Christmastime because they go perfectly with the model trains.

For custom holiday gift giving, there is no more unique store than:

> **Kaleido**
> **8840 Beverly Boulevard**
> **Los Angeles, CA 90048**
> **Monday-Saturday 11 a.m. to 6 p.m.**
> **(310) 276-6844**

This unusual business specializes is kaleidoscopes of every manner and description. Owner Jeannine Wainrib has over 300 different kinds.

Over 90 different artists are represented. One of the most remarkable is amateur astronomer David York. He has been building kaleidoscopes full-time since 1976 and his designs are among the most spectacular.

They are meticulously hand crafted using only optical quality front-surfaced mirrors to make crisp, colorful images. They range in prices up to about $300. This will get you a triangle shaped tube a foot and a half long with stellar and lunar patterns. The wheels with the colored glass in them can be changed to produce different shows.

HANUKKAH

In 165 B.C. the Jewish revolt against the Syrians led to the dedication of the Temple. There was supposed to only be enough light to keep the flame burning for a day. Instead the lamp burned for eight days. This is the powerful symbolism of the nine-candled **menorah**, a dramatic image of faith holding up against the odds.

Hanukkah, which means "dedication" is actually a minor holiday in the Jewish tradition, but it has become a major holiday in the United States on the level of Passover Seders. It has been speculated that its rise in importance is due to the "December Dilemma" faced by American Jews when everything around them is suddenly one big Christmas party.

This has led to more public displays of the Jewish celebration, such as large outdoor menorahs. There are now over 300 such displays in Los Angeles. One of the largest is near the Christmas tree in the:

ABC Entertainment Center
2040 Avenue of The Stars
Century City, CA 90067

A kosher restaurant to make your mouth water is not too far away:

Dizengoff
8103 1/2 Beverly Boulevard
West Hollywood, CA 90048
Sunday-Thursday 11:30 a.m. to 10 p.m.
Friday 11:30 a.m. to 4:30 p.m.
(213) 651-4465

This restaurant reminds a lot of people of Tel Aviv. Its name is actually that of a fashionable main street in the Israeli city. Each table has condiments to please both Europeans and Middle Easterners. These include garlic, hot pepper Yemenite sauce, pickled turnips, and fresh coriander.

Dinner comes with a chopped vegetable salad and rice topped with white beans prepared with garlic. The menu includes several chicken dishes such as lemon/ garlic chicken and chicken schnitzel and such favorites as moussaka and goulash. The Bavarian cream is non-dairy. There is more about Jewish Southern California in the April chapter.

"KWANZAA"

On December 26, another celebration that continues through January 1, called "Kwanzaa," actually began in the U.S.A., more specifically in Southern California. "Kwanzaa" is a word coined from the Swahili expression "matunda ya kwanzaa" to mean "first fruits of harvest."

There is no festival of that name in Africa, though Africans traditionally celebrate the harvest of first crops with community get-togethers where there is feasting, singing, and dancing. This holiday actually started in Southern California: it was created in 1965 by Maulana Karenga, who is now chairman of Black Studies at California State University, Long Beach. It has grown since that time to where it is now observed by 5 to 10 million Americans.

Though it is not a religious holiday, it is quite spiritual in its message. Its purpose is to highlight a system of values and traditions that runs through African-inspired cultures throughout the world, as well as a retrospect back centuries to their origins in Africa. It is a celebration of history and family.

There are seven principles called the "nguzo saba." Each night of the celebration is devoted to a different one. These are: unity ("umoja"), self determination ("kujichagulia"), collective work and responsibility ("ujima"), purpose ("nia"), creativity ("kuumba"), and faith ("imani").

The elements of the celebration as specified by Karenga are meaningful and beautifully simple. It is almost an anti-materialism holiday. When gifts ("zawadi") are exchanged, they are supposed to be homemade or easily affordable and related to education or African and African-influenced culture.

An ear of corn ("vivunzi") is laid out on a table for each offspring in the family. These are placed on a straw place mat, called a "mkeda," that represents the reverence for tradition. Seven green, black, and red candles (called "mishumaa saba") are placed in a seven-branched candleholder called a "kinara" that symbolizes the continent of Africa and its peoples. There is a communal cup, called a "kikombe cha umoja," that is a kind of tribute to past, present, and future descendants from Africa.

On the last night, there is a big feast. Because this is a celebration of both Africa and its cultural derivatives, African food, Caribbean food, and American "soul" food can be featured.

In the Crenshaw and Leimert Park areas, there is a large "Kwanzaa" celebration:

"Kwanzaa" Parade and Festival
Crenshaw Boulevard to Leimert Park
Los Angeles
usually last weekend in December
Saturday & Sunday
(213) 292-7000

For this festival, a procession goes down Crenshaw Boulevard for about two miles and ends in Leimert Park. A king, called the "Oba," and a queen, called the "Iyaba," are selected and they preside over the parade. The parade features African dancers, school marching bands, and black cowboys spinning ropes. In the park, there are food booths and vendors, music, and performance.

Leimert Park was designed by Frederick Olmstead, who designed the gardens surrounding the La Venta Inn in Palos Verdes (see June) and Central Park in New York. Its commercial district is full of art galleries, jazz clubs, and unusual eateries.

The cultural center of Leimert Park is the:

Vision Theatre
4310 Degnan Boulevard
Los Angeles, CA 90008
(213) 295-9685

This was the former Leimert Theatre, built in 1932 by Morgan, Wall, and Clements, architects of the Mayan Theatre (now nightclub), and Adamson House (see August). It became a Jehovah's Witness Hall, then was purchased by Marla Gibb for use as a live theatre. A lot of the events for the 1993 Los Angeles Festival took place here.

One of the great cultural statements of the area is the:

Museum In Black
4331 Degnan Boulevard
Los Angeles, CA 90008
Tuesday-Saturday 12 to 6 p.m.
(213) 292-9528

Owner Brian Breye has assembled a fantastic selection of African and African American art and collectibles. The highpoint is the collection of African masks.

A few steps away is a place your nose will probably alert you to:

Phillip's Barbecue
4307 Leimert Boulevard
Los Angeles, CA 90008
Monday-Thursday 11 a.m. to 10 p.m.
Friday & Saturday 11 to 12 a.m.
(213) 292-7613
also at:
1517 Centinella
Inglewood, CA 90302
(310) 412-7135

More than one restaurant critic has proclaimed Phillip's the best barbecue in Southern California. A simple building with a green awning, it is a little like a ride at Disneyland in that the line out front leads to yet another line inside which leads to the take-out window.

This is not a place for vegetarians. Beans are about the only non-meat item on the menu. The beef ribs are huge, primitive-looking slabs of smoked meat. Other dishes include homemade hot links, chicken, and spareribs.

But if you need a cookbook, or any other African or African American book, stop by:

Dawah Book Shop
4711 Crenshaw Boulevard
Los Angeles, CA 90043
Monday-Saturday 10 a.m. to 7 p.m.
(213) 299-0335

Very near here is another wonderful restaurant:

Coley's Kitchen
4335 Crenshaw Boulevard
Los Angeles, CA 90008
Daily 7:30 a.m. to 10 p.m.
(213) 290-4010

Coley's is a Jamaican restaurant. It features jerk chicken, curried goat, and "patties": hot pastry turnovers.

Not too far from Coley's, the Baldwin Hills Crenshaw Plaza Mall looms on the skyline. It has an African American flair that is expressed in multitude of ways at a museum in the May Company:

Museum of African American Art
May Company Store
Baldwin Hills Crenshaw Plaza
4005 Crenshaw Boulevard
Los Angeles, CA 90008
Wednesday-Saturday 11 a.m. to 6 p.m.
Sunday 12 to 5 p.m.
(213) 294-7071

This small museum has masks, beautiful fabrics, and contemporary art. Delores Oduna, the gift shop manager, can show you many handmade crafts that you won't find anywhere else.

There has been a "Kwanzaa" celebration held every year since 1978 at:

California Afro American Museum
Exposition Park
600 State Drive
Los Angeles, CA 90037
Tuesday-Sunday 10 a.m. to 5 p.m.
(213) 744-7432

They have everything from African dancers to food to American jazz at this wonderful museum in Exposition Park, off the Harbor Freeway and next to the University of Southern California (see February).

Since December is gift-buying season, you might want to stop in the truly unique museum store here called **Reflections**. This store has the most eclectic assortment of interesting stuff. They have folk art and crafts from cultures as diverse as Haiti, Jamaica, and Africa. They have "American Jazz Greats" T-shirts and jars of pralines from New Orleans.

If you wanted to dine African-style, the Southern California center for several culinary treats is on Fairfax Avenue, a street more famous for a completely different culture.

Fairfax Avenue in Los Angeles is a wonder. Like Pioneer Boulevard in Artesia, you can be cruising along, surrounded by businesses from one ethnic community, then suddenly, as if you crossed a border, you are in another. North Fairfax is a traditional Jewish neighborhood. South Fairfax is **Ethiopian Restaurant Row**. This is so well established that there is even an Ethiopian Restaurant Association. Going south on Fairfax from Wilshire, you will see:

> **Nyala**
> **1076 South Fairfax Avenue**
> **Los Angeles, CA 90019**
> **Sunday-Thursday 11 a.m. to 12 a.m.**
> **Friday-Saturday 11 a.m. to 2 a.m.**
> **(213) 936-5918**

Nyala is a pleasant, African place, decorated in earth tones, that feels ethnic and Westside-fashionable at the same time. It has some of the spirit of "Kwanzaa" all year round, and the recorded music playing on the huge speakers can range from traditional Ethiopian to contemporary funk. They even have an "Abyssinian Oldies Night" where they play old Motown hits. Live music is offered on the weekends.

Ethiopian food is mostly based around a kind of a flat, soft pancake-like stuff called "injera." It is made into plate-sized sheets that the entree or appetizer is served on. Many of the dishes are stews called "wots" and the "injera" functions as a scooper: in Ethiopian restaurants, you eat with your hands.

Nearly all Ethiopian restaurants also feature Italian food because of that country's invasion in 1935.

Another great African restaurant on the same side of the street is:

> **Rosalind's**
> **1044 South Fairfax Avenue**
> **Los Angeles, CA 90019**
> **Daily 11:30 to 12 a.m.**
> **(213) 936-2486**

Rosalind's has live African music on weekends and has attracted a loyal regular clientele. They offer a wide variety of West African and Ethiopian specialties. There is more about African American Southern California in the February chapter.

RACING SEASON AT SANTA ANITA

The day after Christmas, one of the Southland's happiest traditions begins, the horse racing season at:

Santa Anita Racetrack
285 West Huntington Drive
Arcadia, CA 91007
(818) 574-7223

Every year since 1934, the San Gabriel Mountains have been the backdrop for what has grown into an 80-90 day season of racing. Originally opened on Christmas Day for a 65 day season, the Mediterranean, somewhat Art Deco-styled Santa Anita Racetrack has been called the most beautiful track in the country.

Its park-like setting offers a variety of experiences. In the Paddock Gardens, the likenesses of several jockeys are immortalized in bronze. These include Bill Shoemaker, John Longden, and Laffit Pincay—who has won more races than any other jockey in the history of Santa Anita Park. From 7:30 to 9:30 a.m. during racing season, you can come down and watch the horses being worked out.

Not too far from the track is an appropriate restaurant:

The Derby
233 East Huntington Drive
Arcadia, CA 91006
Monday-Thursday 11 a.m. to 11 p.m.
Friday 11 a.m. to 12 a.m.
Saturday 4 p.m. to 12 a.m.
Sunday 4 p.m. to 11 p.m.
(818) 447-2430

Walking into The Derby is like entering a museum of horse racing that serves food and drink. A well-settled place of brick walls, dark wood, and plush maroon booths, there are murals of race tracks, souvenirs, and photos wherever you look. The waitresses even wear the familiar tight riding silks.

Open since 1922, this home-turf is a kind of a memorial to the former boss of The Derby, a famous jockey named George Woolf who died in 1946 when his horse threw him. There are reprints of old racing columns that mention him printed on the menus and pictures of the horses he rode on the walls. The name of George's preferred mount is probably more recognizable to most people today than his: Sea Biscuit.

This is a steak restaurant that serves massive prime rib, hamburger steaks, Chateaubriand and other cuts of meat, great onion soup with melted cheese, and pungent garlic toast. There are salads, fish dishes, and chicken, but most of the patrons (who look and act like they came out of a Dick Francis novel) apparently ignore them. Also, the trend away from ordering mixed drinks made with hard liquor does not seem to have affected the bar here.

WHALE WATCHING SEASON

Whale watching season officially begins on the 26th of December, though many of the boat trips do not begin until January. From around the end of this month through March (and sometimes a little later), the California Grey whale makes a round-trip trek from the Arctic to Baja California, after having babies in the warmer southern waters. The 6,000 to 10,000 mile trip is the longest migration of any mammal in the world.

That the Southern California coastline is witness to such a remarkable natural sight as the awesome annual parade of these stately and intelligent creatures can be reassuring in a world that sometimes seems entirely man-made. Though they are not coming in as close to shore as they have in years past, you can still see them with binoculars from many places along the coast.

The land point where the first sighting of the year is officially noted is:

Point Vicente Interpretive Center
31501 Palos Verdes Drive West
Rancho Palos Verdes, CA 90274
(310) 377-5370

The museum is small, but well done, and has a touch exhibit for children and a 20-minute film on whale watching. The park connected to it offers a stunning view of the ocean, and what some think is the best spot in the Southern California to see the whale parade. It is also great for picnics.

If you look at a map of California and pinpoint this spot on the coast, you will understand why this is a such a good whale watch location: you are on the southern end of a promontory point that was once an island that now juts out into the Pacific from the coast, the Palos Verdes Peninsula (see January, June, and November).

Next to the whale watching site is the **Point Vicente Lighthouse**. This 67-foot high cement tower of a lighthouse has guided ships off the jagged peninsula since 1926. It was automated in 1971 and its 1,000 watt light focused through a five-foot lens is the most powerful in the Southland, visible for over 20 miles. There have been shipwrecks, however, and legend has it that a beautiful ghostly woman in a flowing white gown patrols the tower walkway, searching for her lost lover on the rocks.

For a bite to eat in an appropriate setting, right near here is:

The Admiral Risty
31250 Palos Verdes Drive West
Rancho Palos Verdes, CA 90274
Monday-Thursday 5 to 10 p.m.
Friday & Saturday 5 to 11 p.m.
Sunday 10 a.m. to 3 p.m. (lunch)
Sunday 4 to 9:30 p.m. (dinner)
(310) 377-0050

This restaurant is a throwback to those nautical-themed seafood restaurants by the ocean that your parents would take you to after a day at the beach. The exterior is decorated with pilings and thick ropes. The view the restaurant has is apparent from the outside.

The interior is all brass fittings and seafaring themes. The kitchen features freshly caught local fish as well as chicken dishes and steak.

San Diego

San Diego also has its share of fleets that will take you whale watching. One of the most established is:

H & M Landing Whale Watch Trips
2803 Emerson Street (Scott Street)
San Diego, CA 92106
(619) 222-1144

Next door to H & M is one of my favorite low-priced places for seafood:

Point Loma Seafoods
2805 Emerson Street (Scott Street)
San Diego, CA 92106
Monday-Saturday 9 a.m. to 6:30 p.m.
Sunday 12 p.m. to 6:30 p.m.
(619) 223-1109

What a pleasantly bustling place of fresh fish and harbor views this is! The seafood cafe is strictly a take out counter—and a very busy one. You can order fresh albacore, huge platters of fried shrimp, ceviche, a crab or even a squid sandwich on sourdough bread with cole slaw. On-premise eating is extremely casual on the enclosed patio or on the boardwalk, which fronts on the marina and the parade of dockside commerce.

The retail fish market is the place in San Diego for fresh fish, especially locally caught. They have large salt water tanks crawling with crabs and lobsters and an enormous display of different smoked fish.

The most romantic way to go whale watching from San Diego is just a bit farther down Harbor Drive:

> **Invader Cruises Whale Watch Trips**
> **1066 North Harbor Drive (at Broadway)**
> **San Diego, CA 92101**
> **(800) 262-4386**
> **(619) 234-9153**
> **(619) 234-8687**

The *Invader* is an antique, 151-foot schooner built in 1905 which was recently refitted to her original look as a racing schooner. Licensed by the Coast Guard to carry 300 passengers, it is not only San Diego's largest whale watching vessel, it is the largest passenger schooner in the United States.

Being a motorized vessel, it can maneuver easily, yet give a full tall ship experience. For the whale watch trips, they have a lecturer and an on board video show. They also have dinner cruises nightly. The snack bar is open for all cruises. For more about San Diego Harbor, see July and September.

BIRTHDAY OF FREEWAYS

Despite all of the holidays that come to a head in December, the most important date to Southern California passes without much fanfare. On December 30, the most culturally significant thing in mid-20th century Southland history occurred when the first freeway opened: the **Pasadena Freeway.**

Freeways were authorized by the legislature in 1939 to meet the growing need for some kind of super road to accommodate cars from the ever-burgeoning suburbs traveling to the city. These super roads would have no intersections and no right of access from property adjacent to them. The original name was "stopless motorway."

The Pasadena Freeway was first called the "Arroyo Parkway" when it was built in 1940. This 8.2 miles of six lane highway would turn out to be the "Mother of All Freeways." Though it is the twelfth busiest of the 26 Caltrans regional freeways, it is also the quaintest.

Its lanes are fully a foot narrower than what is now mandated, and it has no shoulders and allows no big trucks. Its curves are much more abrupt than any other in the system. Banked for 45 m.p.h., not 55 or 65, there is an exciting out-of-control feeling to a high speed drive as you careen along practically in the seat of the car next to you. Getting on the freeway is also exciting, because the onramps are as abrupt as mere side streets set off with stop signs.

An ironic sidenote to history concerns two immigrant groups from the area that used to be Yugoslavia: Croatians and Serbians. While the Croatians have a fishing tradition that goes back hundreds of years, the Serbians have a tradition of honoring military service. When they came here, the Croatians continued to fish.

For the Serbians, the urge to make war turned into an urge to make freeways: a major part of the construction of the L.A. Freeway system was accomplished by the Serbian community of San Pedro.

Today, the Southland's freeways are more famous for their traffic than for their history. According to Caltrans, the busiest day is Friday, followed by Thursday, Wednesday, Tuesday, Monday, Saturday, and finally Sunday. The greatest volume of traffic is carried by the San Diego (405) and Santa Monica (10) Freeways at 325,000 cars each daily. The latter freeway, heavily damaged in the earthquake of '94, has the dubious honor of being the most crowded in the entire U.S.

One nice thing about getting stuck in traffic in the freeways in and around L.A. is that you can get a better look at the city's freeway murals.

My favorite of these is "L.A. Freeway Kids" by Glenna Boltuch Avila. Pictured on the previous page, it is located on the south side of the Hollywood Freeway, between Main and Los Angeles Streets.

What may be the last great freeway built in the U.S. is the **Century** or **Glenn M. Anderson Freeway** opened in October of '93. It was originally called Century because it was supposed to run along Century Boulevard. Since former Congressman Anderson, head of the House Transportation Committee, worked so hard to get federal funds for the project, they changed the name in 1987 to honor him.

Glenn's freeway is 17.3 miles long and 12 lanes wide and runs between El Segundo and Norwalk and was built to carry 175,000 cars per day. With its maze of overpasses and connecting ramps to four other freeways, the San Diego (405), Harbor (110), Long Beach (705) and San Gabriel (605) Freeways, it cost $2.2 billion. It was ballyhooed as being a "highway of the future" because it has such high-tech innovations as closed circuit TV cameras to watch for accidents and sensors in the pavement to measure traffic flow.

To the average person, however it looks pretty much like any other freeway and will look that way until May of 1995 when the Green Line commuter trolley will start running up the middle, stopping at stations and connecting points along the way.

As the Southland heads into the 21st century and continuously shifts toward public transportation, its freeways will become more symbolic of its past.

NEW YEAR'S EVE

The last night of the year is also the most widely practiced night of partying of the year. Virtually every institution that serves food and drink offers some kind of New Year's Eve party.

New Year's Eve on Pine Avenue

Probably the most All-American image of New Year's Eve is that of the scene in Times Square in New York City: a city square full of people in the cold December air looking upward in anticipation of the dropping ball as a sign of a new day. The closest thing to it in the Southland is the annual:

> **New Year's Eve on Pine Avenue**
> **[intersection of 1st and Pine]**
> **Long Beach**
> **8 p.m. to 1 a.m.**
> **(310) 436-4259**

Originated in 1991 by John Morris and the Downtown Long Beach Business Association, this has grown into one of the largest New Year's Eve parties on the

West Coast. It features a laser light show, bands, beer gardens, and confetti-spraying cannons. Several downtown restaurants offer dinner packages. These include Birdland West (see May) and the restaurants named below.

The centerpiece of the celebration is the whimsical clock tower on the corner building at 115 Pine. It is an otherwise pretty somber six-story Beaux Arts office building, built in 1915. The first floor of this structure also has a magnificent restaurant:

L'Opera
115 Pine Avenue
Long Beach, CA
90802
Monday-Friday
11:30 a.m. to 11 p.m.
Saturday & Sunday
5 to 11 p.m.
(310) 491-0066

This is a gorgeous example of using an old building's architectural features to enhance a restaurant's ambiance. L'Opera was a Bank of America with a highly elaborate ceiling that spanned several rooms. To create the restaurant, the walls between the rooms were torn down and the entire ceiling was painted white. The beautiful green marble columns look right at home supporting intricately detailed beams. Large windows were added that fill the place with daylight.

The clock tower on Pine Avenue in Long Beach houses L'Opera.

The menu is large and includes numerous appetizers and special dishes.

In Long Beach, Pine Avenue is the street for a big-city feel. It has a multi-screen theater, and lots of galleries and restaurants. The first great restaurant of Pine was:

Mum's Restaurant
144 Pine Avenue
Long Beach, CA 90802
Monday 11 a.m. to 9 p.m.
Tuesday & Wednesday 11 a.m. to 10 p.m.

Thursday 11 a.m. to 11 p.m.
Friday 11 to 12 a.m.
Saturday 12 p.m. to 12 a.m.
Sunday 12 to 9 p.m.
(310) 437-7700

Mum's opened in 1987 and immediately set a standard for Downtown Long Beach with its skylights, open kitchen, and jazz band performing out front. The large menu is Califonia eclectic and includes wood fired pizza, pasta, and seafood specialties.

On weekends, Mum's opens up the second floor **Cohiba** nightclub. Every Friday and Saturday from 9 p.m., the dance floor, bar, and billiard room invite patrons to enjoy the gorgeous heavy, old wood paneled surroundings.

Biltmore Chef's Toast

The glasses clink, and the bubbly flows: this is all part of the tradition of welcoming in the new year. A unique and very intimate way to toast the coming twelve months is the:

Biltmore Chef's Toast
Biltmore Hotel
506 South Grand Avenue
Los Angeles, CA 90013
(213) 624-1011

For New Year's Eve, they have an outrageous seven-course dinner including a bottle of Dom Perignon and a traditional midnight chef's toast with the chef in the kitchen. The package also includes an open bar, party favors, and dancing to a jazz quartet. All this for about $200 per person.

World's Largest Champagne Glass

If the symbolic toast is a big part of the celebration, then Champagne is the drink of choice for the occasion. Perhaps a true understanding of New Year's Eve can be had by gazing at the World's Largest Champagne Glass, which can be found (where else?) at the:

Lawrence Welk Museum
Welk Resort Center
8845 Lawrence Welk Drive
Escondido, CA 92026
(619) 749-3448
(619) 749-3000
(800) 932-9355

The Lawrence Welk Resort was a small operation when the late band leader first opened it in 1964 as a four-room motel with a restaurant and a clubhouse, bordering a nine hole golf course. Since that time, it has mushroomed into a 1,000-acre extravaganza complete with three 18 hole golf courses as well as a plethora of tennis courts, spas, and even a legitimate theatre. A tram shuttles guests around during the day.

The museum ranks with the Lingerie Museum in Frederick's of Hollywood (see March) as a cultural statement about the Southland. It traces Welk's life from his roots on a North Dakota farm to his years on television. There were a lot of them too: at 27 years on the air, it was the longest running weekly show in television history. "The Lawrence Welk Show" started as a local program on KTLA in 1951, then in 1955 went national on ABC. It went into syndication in September of 1971 and became a PBS staple in October of 1987. The show has continued to air on public television. Welk retired in 1982.

The Champagne glass was created in the ABC Special Effects Department by Bobby Hughs and was designed by Art Director Chuck Koon. It got the bubble machine going on the 25th anniversary show in 1980.

You can get your picture taken next to a life-sized cutout of "Mr. One-ana-Two-ana." Outside, flanked by webbed poolside chairs, is a statue of him holding his conductor's baton.

New Year's Jazz Festival at Indian Wells

The most exciting and romantic thing to do for New Year's Eve is to head out to the desert for the:

Indian Wells Jazz Festival
ususally December 30-January 2
from 11 a.m. to 2 a.m.
at:
Stouffer Esmeralda Resort
44-400 Indian Wells Lane
Indian Wells, CA 92210
(619) 773-4444
and:
Hyatt Grand Champions Resort
44-600 Indian Wells Lane
Indian Wells, CA 92210
(619) 341-1000
for information, contact:
Just Jazz Productions
5011 Argosy Avenue, Suite 7
Huntington Beach, CA 92649
(310) 799-6055

Started in 1988 by Libby Huebner and her Just Jazz Productions in Palm Springs, it is now officially sponsored by the City of Indian Wells and is held in that city. It features over 20 bands and guest artists with up to six venues going simultaneously all day and into the night for three days.

You buy a three-day pass for $130 and can come and go as you please. Musically, there is something for everyone: calypso, Latin jazz, country swing, and jazz standards. Dance lessons are also offered during the duration of the festival. 92 percent of the participants come from outside the desert and 75 percent come from L.A.

The concerts are held at two resorts, and both offer a special "jazz rate" to festival revelers of $99 per night for five nights to $130 for a single night's stay.

Most of the events are held at the Stouffer Esmeralda Resort. It is a very large and grand place with 560 rooms and three pools and an artificial beach. This hotel is the festival's main headquarters and performances take over three ballrooms, the lobby lounge, and the bar at night.

The main action on New Year's Eve is in the Hall of Champions at the Hyatt Grand Champions Resort. With 335 rooms, the Hyatt is smaller and on a more intimate scale than the Stouffer. It has 20 one and two bedroom villas. Besides the concerts in the hall, performances are held in the lobby bar.

There are two separate parties at the Stouffer on New Year's Eve: a "Traditional Jazz" event that features Dixieland and swing and a "Contemporary Jazz" event that features zydeco and blues. At the festival, you must specify which events you would like reserved seating to, but you can go back and forth.

New Otani Hotel

But if your choice of things to do on New Year's Eve is affected by thoughts of where you will wake up, there is no better choice than the:

New Otani Hotel
120 South Los Angeles Street
Los Angeles, CA 90012
(213) 629-1200

January 1st is celebrated as "Oshogatsu" among Japanese and Japanese Americans living in the Southland. As described in January, the New Otani has the largest "Oshogatsu" celebration in Southern California. If you spent New Year's Eve in the hotel, you could be awakened by the festivities there in the morning on the first day of the year.

Thus, a year in the Southland comes to a close and a new one begins.

EPILOGUE

Like all things in nature, we are part of a reoccurring cycle of life. Unlike other living creatures, however, we have the power to either preserve or damage our environment to the extent that all living beings are affected—including us. Every one of us has a responsibility to ourselves and to others to control that power.

Whether you live in Southern California or are a visitor, the same end-of-the-year message applies: resolve to be informed and to participate. Things do not happen by accident. There are environmental and historic preservation groups that need your help. Be an involved person and you are romancing life itself.

Romancing the West, Inc. publishes the book *Romancing the Southland* and is the only company to offer tours to theater, film, and music festivals throughout Southern California and the West. We also produce shows and special events in unique architectural settings.

Additional copies of *Romancing the Southland* are available at a quantity discount. Please write or call for information.

If you would like to receive our free quarterly mailer of books, CD ROM's, tours schedule and special events listings call or write:

Romancing the West, Inc.
P. O. Box 349
Hollywood, CA 90078
(213) 874-6370

Bibliography

Andujar, Gloria. *La Jolla.* Andujar Communication Technologies, 1987.

Apostol, Jane. *Vroman's of Pasadena, A Century of Books 1894-1994.* Sultana Press, 1994.

Bailey, Philip. *Golden Mirages.* The Macmillan Co., 1940.

Bakalinsky, Adah and Gordon, Larry. *Stairway Walks in Los Angeles.* Wilderness Press, 1990.

Big Santa Anita Historical Society. *Angeles National Forest.* Big Santa Anita Historical Society, 1991.

Breeze, Carla. *L.A. Deco.* Rizzoli International Publications, 1991.

Burum, Linda. *A Guide To Ethnic Food In Los Angeles.* HarperCollins Books, 1992.

Chandler, Raymond. *Playback.* Mysterious Press, 1985.

Chandler, Raymond. *Farewell, My Lovely.* Vintage Crime, 1988.

Chandler, Raymond. *The Long Goodbye.* Ballentine Mystery, 1977.

Chandler, Raymond. *Killer In The Rain.* Ballentine Mystery, 1977.

Chandler, Raymond. *Trouble Is My Business.* Ballentine Mystery, 1977.

Chandler, Raymond. *The High Window.* Vintage Books, 1976.

Chandler, Raymond. *The Big Sleep.* Vintage Books, 1976.

Chandler, Raymond. *The Lady In The Lake.* Vintage Books, 1976.

Clark, Jeanne L. *California Wildlife Viewing Guide.* Falcon Press, 1992.

Collins, Adam Randolph. *Arrowhead-Big Bear, the Alps of Southern California.* Arrowhead Mountain Books, 1990.

Copage, Eric V. *Kwanzaa: An African American Celebration of Culture and Cooking.* William Morrow & Company, 1987.

Costantino, Maria. *Frank Lloyd Wright.* Crescent Books, 1991.

Culbertson, Judi and Randall, Tom. *Permanent Californians, An Illustrated Guide to the Cemeteries of California.* Chelsea Green Publishing Co., 1989.

Dana, Richard Henry. *Two Years Before the Mast.* Signet Classics, 1991.

Davis, Mike. *City of Quartz.* Vintage, 1992.

Department of Parks and Recreation. *A Visitor's Guide To California State Parks.* Sequoia Communications, 1990.

Eargle, Donald H. Jr. *The Earth Is Our Mother*. Trees Company Press, 1986.
Ellsberg, Helen. *Mines of Julian*. La Siesta Press, 1989 (revised).

Gebhard, David and Winter, Robert. *Architecture In Los Angeles*.
   Peregrine Smith Books, 1985.

Heimann, Jim and Georges, Rip. *California Crazy*. Chronicle Books, 1985.
Hensher, Alan. *Ghost Towns of the Mojave Desert*. California Classics Books,
   1991.

Karenga, Maulana. *The African American Holiday of Kwanzaa*. University of
   Sankore Press, 1987.

Lindsey, Lowell and Diana. *The Anza Borrego Desert Region*. Wilderness
   Press, 1991.

McKinney, John. *Walk Los Angeles*. Olympus Press, 1992.
McKinney, John. *Day Hiker's Guide to Southern California*. Olympus Press,
   1992.
McKinney, John and Rae, Cheri. *Walk Santa Barbara*. Olympus Press, 1990.
Miller, Bruce W. *Chumash: A Picture of Their World*. Sand River Press, 1988.
Miller, Ron and Peggy. *Mines of the Mojave*. La Siesta Press, 1986 (revised).
Munz, Philip A. *California Spring Wildflowers*. University of California Press,
   1961.

Norman, Barry. *The Story of Hollywood*. Nal Penguine, 1987.
Nunn, Kem. *Tapping The Source*. Dell, 1984.

Office of Historic Preservation, Recreation. *California Historical Landmarks*.
   Department of Parks and Recreation, 1990.

Pearlstone, Zena. *Ethnic L.A.* Hillcrest Press, 1990.
Peterson, Victor P. *Native Trees of Southern California*. University of
   California Press, 1966.

Rae, Cheri. *East Mojave Desert, A Visitor's Guide*. Olympus Press, 1992.
Rawitsch, Mark Howland. *No Other Place: Japanese American Pioneers in a
   Southern California Neighborhood*. Department of History, University of
   California, Riverside, 1983.
Roberts, Lois J. *San Miguel Island*. Cal Rim Books, 1991.
Robinson, John W. *Mines of the San Bernardinos*. La Siesta Press, 1985
   (revised).

Robinson, W.W. *Land in California*. University of California Press, 1979.

Rolfe, Lionel. *In Search of Literary L.A.* California Classics Books, 1991.

Senate, Richard L. *Ghosts of The Haunted Coast*. Pathfinder Publishing, 1986.

Schad, Jerry. *Afoot and Afield in Los Angeles County*. Wilderness Press, 1990.

Schad, Jerry. *Afoot and Afield in San Diego County*. Wilderness Press, 1991.

Schad, Jerry. *Afoot and Afield in Orange County*. Wilderness Press, 1992.

Schad, Jerry. *California Deserts*. Falcon Press, 1986.

Silver, Alain and Ward, Elizabeth. *Raymond Chandler's Los Angeles*. The Overlook Press, 1987.

Snyder, Tom. *The Route 66 Traveler's Guide*. St. Martins Press, 1990.

Stienstra, Tom. *California Camping*. Foghorn Press, 1992.

Thomas, Robert. *Golden Boy*. Berkley Books, 1984.

Tway, Dr. Linda. *Tidepools Southern California*. Capra Press, 1991.

Wallis, Michael. *Route: 66 The Mother Road*. St. Martins Press, 1990.

West, Nathanael. *The Day of the Locust*. New Directions Paperback, 1962.

There are some obscure books that cannot be purchased in regular bookstores. Some noteworthy ones are:

Jimenez, Charles Philip. *The Sleeping Mexican Phenomena*. (only available at the Little Old Bookshop, 6546 South Greenleaf Avenue, Whittier, CA 90601). *This large softcover book is a very interesting exploration of a specific example of folk art that has broader sociological implications.*

Wentworth, Alicia. *Huntington Beach Historical Data Book*. (only available at the City Clerk's Office, 2000 Main Street, Huntington Beach, CA 92648). *This 124-page book is the work of Huntington Beach's resident historian, Alicia Wentworth, who came to Huntington Beach in a trailer from New York in 1947.*

Dorr, Jean B. *A Story of Seal Beach*. Whale and Eagle Publishing Co., 1976. (only available at Bookstore on Main Street, 213 Main Street, Seal Beach, CA 90740) *This 44-page large softcover book traces the history of this little beach town in text and great old photographs.*

Board Members of A.C.F., Inc. Armenian Cultural Festival. A.C.F., 1993. (only available from Armenian Cultural Festival, Inc., 2224 West Olive Avenue, Burbank, CA 91506). *This 24-page booklet explains Armenian culture for only $2, plus tax and shipping.*

Index